New Mexico:
A Glimpse Into an Enchanted Land

By John P. McWilliams

New Mexico:
A Glimpse Into an Enchanted Land

By John P. McWilliams

INKWELL PRODUCTIONS

ISBN: 978-1-939625-27-4

Library of Congress Control Number: 2013906169

Published by Inkwell Productions
10869 N. Scottsdale Road # 103-128
Scottsdale, AZ 85254-5280

Tel. 480-315-3781
E-mail info@inkwellproductions.com
Website www.inkwellproductions.com

Printed in the United States of America

Statement of Rights & Disclaimer

Rights

Disclaimer

Table of Contents

Dedication

I dedicate this book to my loving and patient wife Ann, to our son Andrew and his wife Rebecca, and to our daughter Mara, and to our five beautiful grandchildren: Serena, Iain, Adriana, Andrés and Faith. Thank you for your continued faith and support! I dedicate this endeavor to each and every one of you!! Here's tae ye. Ta fer a' yer kindness tae me!! Tapadh leibh, mo chlann!

"Take every day of life as a gift

And live fully!

If you fear life or question it,

You'll fully never learn to live!"

Welcome!

¡¡Bievenidos todos a Nuevo México, la Tierra de Encantamiento!! (Spanish)
Welcome everyone to New Mexico, the Land of Enchantment!!

Two attributes have earned New Mexico the nickname of the Land of Enchantment: the land and the cultural traditions of its people. The rugged terrain varies from arid high desert to pine-enwrapped mountainous regions, from raw and rugged desert *mesas* to wide flat plains. It is indeed a land of great natural and pristine beauty. It is also a land immersed in several colorful cultural traditions. The sacred traditions and ways of the *Pueblo* tribes, the *Navajos*, the various *Apache* tribes, and the *Ute* flow to us from a time immemorial. Hispanic traditions have been passed down from Spanish Colonial, Mexican Provincial and New Mexican Territorial times. *Anglo*-American cultural traditions have also influenced the cultural beauty of this great land.

There is a sense of peace and tranquility in the serenity of the wide and open plains, on the desolate *mesas* or in the alpine mountaintops. The low population density allows the soul to seek its own peace, as so many other pioneers and soul searchers before us have found to be true. Artists such as Georgia O'Keefe and D. H. Lawrence found a tranquility of the spirit here that allowed them to commune with their inner selves and to release their artistic impulses. Others who seriously seek such a release of the soul, who are willing to let down the barriers and defenses that are required to survive in the civilized and developed world, can also open their hearts and their spirits to the healing that the open spaces provide. Just tune out the "busy" world and tune into the pervading sense of timelessness, and allow oneself to become anchored to the good earth that is so nourishing to the soul. The inner spirit can be released here in New Mexico by innermost contemplation and meditation, by opening to the natural beauty that surrounds us, or by opening ourselves to the native cultures, or to the Hispanic or Mexican cultures, which also are dominant here. One can go to the more rural areas where the culture of the *Norte Americanos*[1] has thrived as the cowboy culture. This is a culture of hardiness, independence, self-reliance and oneness with nature. It frees the soul. New Mexico offers so many possible worlds in a time when so many of us feel suffocated by the demands of modern life and "civilization."

So, put all that noise, hustle, bustle, traffic, overcrowding, and the demand-driven life aside for a short while! Relax, let down your guard, and open up your heart, and breathe in the soul, the spirit and the essence of *Nuevo México*. Come with us and explore some of the fundamental, beautiful aspects of this great state, and its varied cultural heritage, in the Land of Enchantment.

This land so strong, so beautiful
Of creeks, mesas, desert sand
And trees in high alpine regions
In this Enchanted Land

List of Illustrations & Maps (*)

Please note that figures which contain maps are indicated by * next to the figure number, as in Figure 1-5* for example. This notation applies to figures listed here and to the figure captions within the body text of the book. Note also that the entire caption for each figure is not given here for brevity sake. See individual figures for credits and permissions. Figures denoted with ** indicates an Archive Photograph that has been altered, cropped, etc., from the original version.

Additional note: Many Spanish noblemen possessed names that were of the form: Don ('Sir') ------ de ('from', 'of') ------, or alternately, Don ------ de ------ y ------, designating first the person's given name, followed by the father's family name, followed by (y) the mother's family name. Examples of these 2 forms are: Don Diego de Vargas, or Don Francisco Fernandez Cuervo y Valdez and Don Juan Oñate y Salazar.

Throughout this book, the lower case 'de' is used, when the full name is given, as in Don Diego de Vargas. Generally, when the full name is not written, as in Onate (vs. Don Juan de Oñate), or Peralta (vs. Don Pedro de Peralta), the last name alone is used, without the small 'de', to indicate the individual. However, in most sources, De Vargas is commonly referred to, either by his full name (Don Diego de Vargas), or its abbreviated form **with the 'De'** preceding the place name, as in De Vargas, as opposed to de Vargas, or Vargas, alone. In this case, the 'de' is capitalized, as in 'De'. That methodology is used here for De Vargas only, for consistency with other sources.

List of Tables

Acknowledgements

Every author is indebted to so many individuals in the publication of a book of this sort. I am no exception. There are so many good and talented people who have supported me in this great effort that is difficult to know where to begin. So rather than ponder, I will simply dive right in.

I owe an enormous debt of gratitude to all of the authors of the various books, booklets, pamphlets, articles and website articles, without whose efforts this book would not be possible. I have drawn from their great efforts. I especially want to thank Wikipedia®, the Free Encyclopedia, for the wealth of information obtained from their numerous sites and articles. The National Park Service (NPS) and New Mexico State Monument websites have also been very useful and informative, as has been the Indian Pueblo Cultural Center (IPCC) website.

I am of course indebted to the very fine sculptors who have supported me with their permissions to display their fine work in this book. These are Reynaldo "Sonny" Rivera (*El Adelantado* and *La Jornada*), Betty Sabo (*La Jornada*), Donna Quasthoff (De Vargas, Cathedral Basilica of St. Francis of Assisi door panels and Cathedral Park statue) and George Rivera (Buffalo Dancer, Butterfly Dancer and Deer Dancer). Thank you all! Reynaldo Rivera was very congenial and helpful. Hope Rivera was very gracious in offering one of her own photographs for inclusion in the book. I wish also to thank Fred Matteucci, who represented Ms. Betty Sabo, and Ms. Sabo's family, all of whom were very supportive. Ms. Donna Quasthoff was very helpful in drawing my attention to the central statue in Cathedral Park, and the entry door panels to the Cathedral Basilica of St. Francis of Assisi in *Santa Fe*. George Rivera is not only a fine sculptor. He is the Tribal Governor of *Pojoaque Pueblo*. Thank you Governor Rivera!

Ms. Patti Gonzales of The Albuquerque Museum was extremely helpful and responsive in seeking the museum's support for inclusion of the *La Jornada* statues and also for obtaining permission from the Moyers Estate to include the photo of "*Wind and Rain*", sculpted by William Moyers.

I am also grateful to Ms. Tracy S. Blea, Mr. Tomas Campos and Mr. David F. Trujillo and to *Rio Arriba* County for allowing me to include the *El Adelantado* statue by Reynaldo Rivera. Thanks also to the Oñate Memorial Building staff.

I wish to recognize Ms. Gail Delgado of *El Santuario de Guadalupe* for her constant assistance in contacting individuals for permissions and for her support with Father Tri of the *Santuario*. Father Tri was also supportive in spite of a busy schedule.

Ms. Delgado helped with the Archdiocese of *Santa Fe,* in obtaining photo permissions related to the *Santuario*. She was helpful too in contacting *La Reina* and De Vargas re-enactors, Samantha Talpia and Andy Lopez, respectively, to whom I am also indebted for their support. A big thank also to the Archdiocese in granting permission to use interior and exterior photographs of several mission churches, the Cathedral Basilica of St. Francis of Assisi, and especially of *El Santuario de Guadalupe*. I wish to recognize Ms. Marina Ochoa and Ms. Bernadette Lucero for their support.

Thank you Father Jim Suntum of *El Santuario de Chimayó*, who took the time and effort to answer my many questions, and to provide insight regarding the Lord of Esquipulas, the altar screen, and the Seven Stoned Crosses.

I am indebted to a number of *Fiestas de Santa Fe* performers. My gratitude extends to *Mariachi Nuevo Sonido* and their band leader Mr. Marvin R. Teitelbaum for their support. I especially wish to thank Ms. Angela Clayton of *Baile de Folklorico de Santa Fe* for her tireless efforts in obtaining parental photo permissions for each of the five young dancers and to the dancers' parents for their support.

I have had the wonderful opportunity to meet a number of very talented artists, *santeros* and *santeras* at the *Santa Fe* Traditional Spanish Market and the *Santa Fe* Indian Market. I am sincerely grateful to: Ms. Christine Montaño Carey (Tinwork), Ms. Carmelita Valdez Damron *(Retablos)*, Mr. Mark Garcia *(Bulto)*, Mr. Mel Rivera (Straw *Appliqué*) and Mr. Joe Morales (Woodwork) for allowing me to include photos of their fine work in this book. I also wish to thank Ms. Joan Morales for her assistance. A special thank you is extended to Mr. Joe Lobato for his kind understanding. Thanks to Ms. Reyes Madelena, *Jemez* potter, for granting me permission to include her beautiful pottery work. Mr. Tony Duncan is an extraordinary Hoop Dancer, winner of the 2011 Hoop Dancing World Championship. Thank you Tony for your support!

Ms. Maggie Magalnik, Director of the Traditional Spanish Market©, in *Santa Fe*, was a great help in obtaining contact information for me. Thanks to Ms. Robin Farwell Gavin, Curator of the Museum of Spanish Colonial Art, who passed along clarification information regarding reredos and *retablos*, and for her guidance and insight!

Another person who has helped me tirelessly is Ms. Dolores Martinez of *El Rancho de las Golondrinas*. Thank you Dolores. Thanks also to: Mr. Cale Chappelle (Wagon Driver), Ms. Virginia Vigil *(Carne Machucada)* and Mr. Roberto Valdez (Mexican Soldier) of *Las Golondrinas* for their support in this endeavor.

Thanks also to Mr Paul Smith, Mr. Tom Garrity and Mr. Michael Henningson of the Albuquerque International Balloon *Fiesta*. Gratitude also to Lindstrand Balloons.

Ms. Dana Ortega of Loretto Inn and Spa was very helpful in obtaining permission for the *farolitos* photograph taken of their facility. Mr. Christian Andersson of Loretto Chapel was also extremely responsive and supportive.

YTC Summit International deserves appreciation for their support regarding the Summit Collection statues, especially Mr. Francisco Gonzales.

I appreciate the help and support of Mr. Anthon Jeppesen of the Mormon Battalion Association for his help and guidance. Thanks to Ms. Irma Ruiz and Ms. Augusta Meyers of the New Mexico Rail Runner Express for their support and permission. The efforts and guidance of Ms. Anna Anaya, Mr. Dwight Capshaw and Mr. Paul Burciaga are much appreciated regarding use of the state seal photo. Ms. Mary Anne Thornton of the Daughters of the American Revolution (DAR) was helpful in providing guidance regarding the End of the *Santa Fe* Trail monument in *Santa Fe*. Special thanks also to Mr. Michael Henningson of ExpoNM for his guidance on the New Mexico State Fair.

Mr. Ray A. Valdez was of great assistance and support regarding *Zozobra*©® permissions, trademark and copyright information. Thank you, Ray. Mr. Charles Aguilar of *Los Matachines de Bernalillo* was kind enough to read and review my write-up on *Los Matachines*, for which I am very grateful. *¡Muchas gracias!*

Numerous Native American tribes were very supportive regarding the inclusion of photos taken on their lands. I wish to thank Mr. Peter Pina and Ms. Tammy Pina of *Zia Pueblo* for their assistance. *Taos Pueblo* has also been extremely helpful and supportive. Special thanks to Ms. Ilona Spruce, Mr. Antonio Mondragon, Mr. Luis Romero and the *Taos* Tribal Leaders. Likewise, I am very appreciative of the efforts and support of the *San Ildefonso Pueblo*, particularly Ms. Myra Gonzales, Mr. Stephen Martinez and the Tribal Leaders. *Pojoaque Pueblo* has been especially supportive. My appreciation is extended to Ms. Melissa Talachy and Ms. Amy Walton. A special debt of gratitude is owed to (sculptor and) Tribal Governor George Rivera for his gracious support in allowing me to include photos of his outstanding statues that can be seen on the grounds of Buffalo Thunder Resort/Casino. Thanks also to the Buffalo Thunder Resort/Casino at *Pojoaque* and to *Pojoaque Pueblo.* In addition, I wish to thank Ms. Charlene Quintana and especially Governor Mark Mitchell of the *Tesuque Pueblo* for granting me permission to use the Camel Rock photo. I also wish to extend a thank you to Mr. Mark Chino, President of the *Mescalero Apache* Tribe and Ms. Sofia Peso for their timely support. Thanks and recognition to the efforts of SWAIA.

Ms. Dora Nieto, Ms. Georgia Sanchez and Mr. Herman Nieto deserve a special thank you for their gracious hospitality shown us at the 2011 and 2012 *Santo Domingo* Feast Day celebrations.

Thanks also to Ms. Angela Hicks of the U.S. Mint for her support and assistance. Further, Ms. Margaret Kiechefer of the Library of Congress has been extraordinarily helpful in identifying and obtaining copies of archived Public Domain (PD) photos. Mr. Daniel Kosharek of the New Mexico History Museum Photo Archives has been extremely helpful in identifying and obtaining copies of archived PD photos.

Gratitude is also extended to Ms. Kristen Skopeck of the Army Corps of Engineers regarding guidance on the *Cochiti* Dam and Reservoir. Likewise Ms. Claudia Gallardo de Campbell has been helpful in providing guidance regarding New Mexico State Monuments. Ms. Christine Beckman (*Pecos* NHP), Ms. Chris Judson (Bandelier NM), Ms. Diane Souder (Petroglyphs NM), Ms. Norma Pineda (*Salinas Pueblo* Missions NM) have each been particularly helpful and supportive in providing guidance regarding their respective sites. Thanks also to Mr. Eric Valencia, also of the *Pecos* National Historical Park. The Bureau of Land Management (BLM) has been very helpful, particularly Ms. Kayci Cook Collins of *Malpais* National Monument and Mr. Danny Randall of *Kasha Katuwe* (KK) Tent Rocks National Monument, for reading and reviewing my write-up on *Kasha Katuwe* Tent Rocks National Monument, and for his helpful suggestions and comments. Thanks also to Ms. Connie Maestas (KK) of the BLM. I also wish to thank Mr. Peter Armato (*Capulin* Volcano NM) and Mr. Don Whyte (Chaco Cultural Ctr NM) for their assistance.

I wish also to recognize the support and assistance of Mr. Richard Sims, Director of New Mexico State Monuments. Appreciation is extended to Mr. Scott Smith of *Coronado* State Monument for his guidance. I wish to thank Ms. Debbie Owen of *Sandia* Tramway for her guidance and support, Mr. David Rasch of the Historical Preservation Office who provided guidance and contact information regarding the End of the *Santa Fe* Trail Monument in *Santa Fe,* and Mr. Chris Leeser of the U.S Fish and Wildlife Service for his guidance on *Bosque del Apache.*

Ms. Carlie McGinnes of the Kit Carson Home and Museum was helpful in obtaining information about the home and Kit Carson Cemetery. Thanks also to Mr. Tim Sweet of the Old Fort Sumner Museum, Mr. Juan Chavez of Fort Sumner. Also, the Sumner City Hall, for guidance regarding the museum and the nearby cemetery.

I also wish to thank Ms. Maryanne Torres of River of Lights, Albuquerque for her guidance regarding the River of Lights.

Mr. Roger Hogan of the *Cumbres-Toltec* Scenic Railroad has been very extending. He provided the railroad photo for the book and granted permission to convert his color photo to black and white for use in the book. Thank you Roger for reading and reviewing my write-up of the CTSRR, and for your prompt response!

I appreciate the efforts of the two youth organizations, 4-H and FFA, Specifically, I would like to identify Ms. Ginnie Berg of FFA and Ms. Bianca Johnson of 4-H for their untiring efforts to support this book and to obtain the required permissions.

I wish also to thank Ms. Chris Judson of Bandelier National Monument for her support and constructive comments in reviewing the text describing Bandelier National Monument.

At times the author suffered a variety of computer or printer problems. A big thank you goes to Mr. Donovan Rochester of Dotfoil in *Santa Fe* for his efforts in helping me to quickly recover and move forward with my book.

Our daughter, Mara McWilliams, is the first family member to have written and published a book: *Outta My Head and In Your Face.* Although it is currently out of print, I wish to recognize her for her great personal achievement and for "leading the way." Thank you Mara for your inspiration!

Our son, Andrew McWilliams, deserves recognition for his very worthwhile suggestions on topics for this undertaking and for his support. Thank you Andrew!

My dear wife, Ann, of forty-four years, deserves a special thank you! She has been my mainstay in this great challenge. Her patience and support have been essential and a source of encouragement throughout the writing of this book. Specifically, Ann has been my chief editor and the source of many constructive comments on content, structure, narrative flow and grammar. I could not have completed this book without my wife's kind and patient assistance and support. *Tapadh leat, mo rún!*

I wish also to thank family members and friends for their continued support and encouragement. In particular, I wish to recognize Alexis Pennachio, who generated the Population Distribution Map, and who touched up or enhanced numerous photos and maps presented in this book. Her efforts were invaluable. Thank you, Alexis!

Thanks also to Ms. Jan Marquart, a friend and fellow writer, for her constant support and guidance.

Last, but not least, I wish to thank my Publisher, Inkwell Productions LLC, and the staff for their technical and moral support throughout this undertaking. Specifically, I wish to say a special thank you to Mr. Nick Ligidakis who had confidence in me and who undertook the publication of this book. Nick has shown great patience, encouragement and faith throughout this effort. This is my first book and I greatly appreciate his confidence in me, and my project. Thank you, Nick!

In addition, Mr. Ron Birchenough, typeset and designed the book, for which I am forever grateful! Not only did he do an outstanding and highly professional job, he also demonstrated great patience with my many last minute corrections and updates. My great appreciation is extended to Ron!

I sincerely hope that I have given due credit and recognition to all the players and contributors to this enterprise. Hopefully, I have not overlooked anyone. If so, it is inadvertent and I apologize in advance and thank you all the same for your support. I could not have done this without you all!

John P. McWilliams

Preface

The reader may wonder: Why read this book when there are so many other books about New Mexico?

There are many excellent choices in the book market. I happen to possess a good number of them in my own library, and I have referred to any number of them to assist me in writing this book. The reader can see many of them listed in the Bibliography at the end of this book. But why should a reader wish to choose this particular book?

I believe this book is unique. My hope and intention is that it will fill a need among residents who wish to learn more about the state they live in and also among those who may wish to visit this beautiful and wondrous state. Today one can find any number of excellent books that probe deeply into a particular topic, such as New Mexico history, key historical players, Mexican culture, Native American *pueblo*, *Navajo* or *Apache* culture and happenings, or even tour books about places to see and things to do, including state and national monuments. However, as far as I am aware, there are no widely available books that attempt to cover all of these subjects in a single volume. This book attempts to provide a broad survey of these various New Mexican topics. If the reader is interested in seeing the "big picture", this single book can replace up to a dozen books on different topics, Further study on any given topic can be obtained by investigating other sources, written by experts in their respective fields. The depth and breadth of the subject matter presented here should satisfy most readers. It may even serve as a launching pad into further investigations and reading elsewhere.

I have written this book for the layperson. I am not a historian, an anthropologists or a travel agent. I do however have a passion and love for this great state that I hope to share with residents and travelers alike. I have attempted to communicate that passion through the text and the illustrations within this book. The target audience is the non-expert who wishes to get a single-book exposure to the great state of New Mexico.

Being cognizant of the value of limited time in today's modern and busy culture, the book is structured to accommodate this prevalent shortage of time. There are fifteen chapters and a short Afterward. Each chapter covers a specific broad topic. For example Chapter Three discusses Historical Snapshots or Chapter Eleven discusses Native American Tribes & Reservations in New Mexico. However, within each chapter there are multiple *"vignettes"* on a host of self-contained sub-topics related to the overlying theme of the chapter. (These sub-topics may occupy a third or half a page, or perhaps as many as three or four pages.) This allows the reader the convenience of reading one or more sub-topics within a chapter at a given time. Since the sub-topics are self-contained, the reader can pick the book up at a later time and continue reading with a new sub-topic. This allows the reader to jump around the book and read sections that are of interest or relevant to the reader's interest. There is very little dependency from one chapter or sub-topic to another. This gives the reader maximum flexibility in terms of reading time available or maintenance of interest.

This book contains many black and white photographs to illustrate the beauty and wonder of this state. Maps are included to facilitate an understanding of the state's history and its evolution from a Spanish colony, to a Mexican province, to an American territory and finally to a U.S. state. Hand sketches have also been included to add some variety to the illustrations. Public Domain archive photographs has also been used.

With the exception of Public Domain photographs and a few select others, all photographs, drawings and maps have been created by the author. These are noted accordingly. In addition, Public Domain archive photographs were obtained from either the New Mexico History Museum or from the Library of Congress. Most of these archive photographs have been cropped, retouched, or minimally enhanced to remove scratches or to improve the image for viewing purposes. These are denoted by a double asterisk (**) at the end of the figure caption. Key events, places or items of interest are highlighted in **bold** font in the various sections of chapters 13 and 14.

The reader can also consult Appendix A for contact information regarding New Mexico's *pueblos*, reservations, or tribal organizations.

A Glossary is also provided, consisting mainly of Spanish terms, as Spanish names and place-names are encountered frequently throughout New Mexico and throughout the book. For those readers who are not versed in the Spanish language, it may be helpful to consult this glossary, which is provided immediately following the Chapter Notes at the rear of the book. Since a great many of the Spanish names are quite colorful and interesting, the ability to decode them will add another dimension to the reading and provide some very informative insights.

A significant rear section of chapter notes is also included to provide further insight into certain topics touched upon in the text. This section also provides text and website credits as appropriate.

The Bibliography lists reference books, booklets, magazine articles and newspaper articles used in the writing of this book. A full index appears at the rear of the book for further reference.

Every attempt has been made by the author to observe and abide by copyright and trademark rules, and to recognize and denote the applicable names and other items within the text, accordingly. Additionally, a book such as this, which covers such a wide range of topics, may possibly contain a few inadvertent factual errors. Every attempt has been made to catch any such errors. The text has been crosschecked many numerous times to ensure accuracy throughout the book. However, the author apologizes in advance for any errors or oversights, which may have leaked through. Please bring any such errors to the author's or the Publisher's attention.

I have used *italics* profusely, throughout this book. Italicization of words, phrases, figure captions, titles, sentences or paragraphs, is completely my own. It was implemented primarily to facilitate in the recognition of foreign words, and terminology, but also to emphasize book, photograph or other titles. Hopefully, this has been helpful to the reader, and not a burden.

Any opinions expressed are solely those of the author, and are not those of the Publisher.

Further, the author has made every attempt to portray each of New Mexico's traditions in a respectful manner, while informing the reading public. The author appreciates all the many contributions made by so many individuals and so many cultural groups towards the making of this book.

I sincerely hope that the reader will enjoy reading and referencing this book as much as I have enjoyed writing this book. New Mexico is indeed a Land of Enchantment, and it is the author's hope that the reader will share in that view after reading this book.

Welcome to *New Mexico: A Glimpse Into an Enchanted Land*!

John P. McWilliams, March 1, 2013

Chapter One: New Mexico: The State o' Things

This land offers so much in the way of natural and stunning beauty, freedom, cultural traditions and historical heritage that it is a challenge for one to get his or her arms around it. My intent, here in this book, is to answer many of the questions that arise when one visits New Mexico. After reading this book, the reader will hopefully have a better understanding of why New Mexico is called the Land of Enchantment.

This chapter starts with a very brief summary of New Mexico's long path to statehood. It also provides a brief discussion of the state's symbols such as the state flag, nickname, seal, bird, mammal, tree, gem, vegetables and the state plant. In addition, all the state's counties are identified with typical population ranges. A brief description is given of the main tourist cities: Albuquerque, *Santa Fe* and *Taos*. A quick summary of some of the attractions in these towns is also provided. This chapter seeks to set the foundation for the chapters that follow. When places are mentioned later in the book, the reader will have some sense of the location.

Subsequent chapters discuss state historical background, three major cultural elements, cuisine terminology, interesting places to visit, Native American reservations and ceremonials, national and state monuments, state and county fairs, and the recent developments in New Mexico's future. The Land of Enchantment is here to behold! So, let's get started.

The Long Road to Statehood[1]

New Mexico was the forty-seventh state to join the union and to become part of the United States of America. It achieved this great milestone on January 6, 1912. Prior to that date it shared the area known as the New Mexico Territory, with the current state of Arizona. Before becoming a U.S Territory, New Mexico and Arizona were under Mexican control, in the area defined as the northernmost region of Mexico. These lands and others (Utah, *Nevada*, *Alta California*, western *Colorado* and the southernmost part of Wyoming) were ceded by Mexico to the U.S. upon the cessation of hostilities at the conclusion of the Mexican-American War in 1848. Later, many of these lands became U.S. Territories and then became states. However, California and Texas were admitted immediately as states in the Compromise of 1850.

This long road to statehood initially started with the invasion of this region by the Spanish *Conquistadors*. The indigenous people of this region were primarily river valley dwelling agricultural pueblo natives, some dry desert dwelling Native Americans, and some semi-nomadic or nomadic tribes of Athabascan[2] stock.

From the earliest times many Native American tribes inhabited the fertile river valleys, building entire agricultural communities around these centers. Here prosperity flourished, crops grew, animals were domesticated, and tribal religious and social traditions developed, unique to each tribe. Over time, these peoples have come to be known as the "*Pueblo*"[3] Peoples.

Just prior to the advent of the *Conquistadors*, there were also semi-nomadic tribes that came to settle in New Mexico. These tribes had migrated down from Canada. These included the *Navajo*[4] who settled in northern Arizona, but who eventually reached out eastward into northwestern New Mexico. There were various *Apache* tribes , such as the *Chiricahua*[5], who occupied southeastern Arizona and parts of southwestern New

Mexico. The *Mescalero*[6] *Apache* roamed southern central New Mexico, while the Warm Springs *Apache* occupied the southwestern region of the state and the *Jicarilla*[7] *Apache* were dominant in northeastern New Mexico. Other nomadic tribes made inroads after the arrival of the Spaniards in the centuries to follow. So at the time of the Spanish Conquest of the Southwest, both agricultural *Pueblo* Peoples and raiding semi-nomadic tribes occupied the lands of what later became the state of New Mexico.

In the mid-1500's, the Spanish *Conquistadors* set out from Mexico, which was then called New Spain. They referred to the southwestern part of the present United States, as the Imperial Spanish Viceroyalty of New Spain.

About twenty years after the *Coronado*[8] Expedition of 1540-1542, an explorer named Francisco de Ibarra, was seeking gold. He scouted out the region north of the *Rio Grande*. In the report he sent back to the central government in Mexico City, he referred informally to the explored region as *Nuevo México*, or New Mexico. In 1598, Don Juan de Oñate was appointed as Governor of this new Province of New Mexico, and with this appointment the region's name became formally established. Thereafter, the region north of the *Rio Grande* became known as *Nuevo México*, or New Mexico.

The state of New Mexico has come together over time from various bits and pieces, each controlled by different governments or factions. As mentioned above, New Mexico was initially part of Spanish-controlled New Spain (Mexico).

France ruled the extreme northeastern corner of the state until the Louisiana Purchase of 1803 under President Thomas Jefferson. Shortly after, this northeast corner of New Mexico was sold to the United States.

When the Mexican War of Independence established Mexico as an independent nation, free of Spain, in 1821, the region formerly known as New Spain was renamed Mexico. Control of the region known as New Mexico, was transferred to the newly established Mexican government.

However, in 1836 Texas declared its independence from Mexico, naming itself the Republic of Texas. The Texans then claimed the region east of the *Rio Grande* as their territory. However, the presence of the *Comanche* tribes in the eastern parts of New Mexico, known as *Comancheria* or lands of the *Comanche*s, made it difficult for the Texans to press their claims. The Texans did however make an attempt to establish their claim against the Mexican government via the failed Texan *Santa Fe* Expedition of 1841.

When the Mexican-American War of 1846 ended in 1848, Mexico ceded many southwestern lands to the United States. These included western New Mexico along with *Alta California, Nevada*, Utah, Arizona, and parts of *Colorado* and Wyoming. These lands were ceded by the Treaty of Guadalupe-*Hidalgo*. However, Mexico still maintained control over lower California, called *Baja California*.

Once independent of Mexico, most of the lands in modern day Arizona and New Mexico were formed into the New Mexico Territory by the U.S. government. The Compromise of 1850 re-ordered the new lands ceded by Mexico to the United States, and attempted to solve conflicting claims on these various lands by the opposing "slave" and "non-slave" contingents in Congress. The Compromise of 1850 resulted in the Republic of Texas being admitted into the Union as the new state of Texas. California was also carved out of the lands ceded by Mexico and it too was admitted as a state. However, from New Mexico's perspective, the Compromise was beneficial since the claim to the eastern part of New Mexico was finally relinquished by Texas.

The newly formed New Mexico Territory, however, did not include the land that was subsequently bought under the Gadsden Purchase of 1853. This purchase added the southern border area of Arizona and the "boot heel" area of southwestern New Mexico to the U.S. In 1861, *Colorado* was granted the northeastern corner of the New Mexico Territory. The outline of the New Mexico Territory included present-day Arizona. It was essentially finalized by the end of 1861. It was not until 1912, when New Mexico was admitted as the 47th state that New Mexico achieved today's boundaries.

During the American Civil War, the Confederate States of America (C.S.A.) also tried to claim the southern half of the New Mexico Territory, below the 34th Parallel as their own due to Southern sympathies expressed in that region. However, during the American Civil War, the Texans tried once again to enforce their old claim on eastern New Mexico. The Sibley Brigade was sent by the Confederacy to invade and claim New Mexico for the C.S.A. The mission failed and New Mexico remained in the Union as a U.S. Territory.

New Mexicans volunteered in large numbers as Rough Riders to fight in the Spanish-American War. They fought so valiantly that the door to statehood began to open with the turning of the century.

Finally, after many struggles and disappointments, statehood came to New Mexico on January 6, 1912 and to Arizona on February 14, 1912. The New Mexico Territory was divided into the two new states of New Mexico and Arizona. These were the last two states to be admitted within the contiguous forty-eight states. It would be more than 40 years before another state would be admitted to the U.S.

There had been countless failed attempts to achieve statehood prior to the final success in 1912. The road to statehood for New Mexico was long and difficult, but in the end triumph was achieved. On January 6, 2012, we saw one hundred proud years of statehood! Congratulations New Mexico!

New Mexico Gets Its Name

In 1598, New Mexico was formally given its name by Don Juan de Oñate, the first Governor of the region north of Mexico and north of the *Rio Grande*. He named this region the Province of New Mexico. The name has remained ever since. (Mexico, of course, is named after the *Mexica* tribe or the *Aztecs*, as they later became known. It is an *Aztec* term meaning " place of the *Mexitli.*" *[Mexitli* is also the name of a great leader and a former war god of the *Mexica.]* Oñate named the new land in the northern province in honor of the Mexican homeland in New Spain.)

An Enchanting Nickname[9]

New Mexico is reverently and lovingly referred to as the Land of Enchantment. One only needs to look around at the enchanting natural and rugged beauty in all its variety throughout New Mexico to understand how appropriate this nickname is for our beloved state. This land has a rich and colorful culture, which adds to its many charms. The Land of Enchantment appellate appears on all New Mexico auto license plates. Incidentally, New Mexico is also less well known as the Spanish State or the Colorful State.[10]

Where the (*Zia*) Sun Shines: New Mexico's State Flag[11, 12]

The New Mexico state flag is quite unique among state flags. It presents a red sun symbol centered on a field of yellow, almost gold. The red circle representing the sun is open, with the yellow background filling the center of the circle. The two colors reflect New Mexico's Spanish heritage, as yellow and red are the colors of the Spanish flag that was carried by the *Conquistadors* into New Mexico by *Coronado* and others, as early as 1540.

The red sun of New Mexico's flag has rays stretching out from the circle's circumference. There are four groups of emanating rays, with four rays in each group. This is an ancient sun symbol of a Native American *pueblo*-dwelling people called the "*T'siya*."

The Spanish adulterated the "*T'siya*" *pueblo* name into the more commonly known *Zia* (see-ah). These native people painted sun symbols on vases for ceremonial purposes, and they used the sun symbol to introduce the newborn to the warmth and nourishment of the sun. They were an agricultural people dependent on the sun's benevolence for the success of their crops and the survival of their culture. Using the "*Zia*" sun symbol, they drew images of the sun on the ground in ceremonies and possibly for protection, much as modern *Navajos* create healing sand paintings on the ground. To the *Zia*, the number four was considered sacred and holy. The number four manifests itself in all aspects of life around them. The *Zia* believed that all gifts from the gods were granted in groups of four. Some examples of these gifts are:

Four directions – proceeding clockwise, north, east, south and west.
Four seasons of the year – from the budding of new life, to the deep slumber of winter: spring, summer, fall and winter.
Four significant periods of the day – from the dawning of a new day, to its end: sunrise, noon, evening and night.
Four periods of life – from birth to death: childhood, youth, middle years and old age.

The sanctity of the number four is embedded in the *Zia* symbol centered in the New Mexico flag. At the very center of the symbol is a circle, tying all four groups of rays together in unity. To the *Zia*, the sun circle represents the circle of life and love, which has neither beginning nor end, and which holds all aspects of life together. See Figure 1-1 for a view of the *Zia* symbol used as the central motif for New Mexico's state flag.

Figure 1-1: The Zia sun symbol embedded in the New Mexico State Flag.

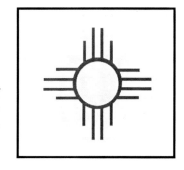

The state flag thereby embodies much of the Spanish and *pueblo* Indian heritage of New Mexico, and acts as a visual reminder of that rich and colorful heritage.

Not Just One Eagle But Two

In June 1913, a commission was appointed to develop a state seal[13, 14] for the newly admitted state of New Mexico. The New Mexico State Legislature officially defined the state seal as follows:

The coat of arms of the state shall be the Mexican eagle grasping a serpent in its beak, the cactus in its talons, shielded by the American eagle with outspread wings, and grasping arrows in its talons; the date 1912 under the eagles and, on a scroll, the motto: "Crescit Eundo." The great seal of the state shall be a disc bearing the coat of arms and having around the edge the words "Great Seal of the State of New Mexico.

The New Mexico state seal incorporates two aspects of New Mexican heritage, both its Mexican roots and its U.S. roots. This is clearly demonstrated by the embodiment of both the Mexican Eagle and the American Bald Eagle in the seal. The Mexican Eagle is shown grasping a snake in its beak and holding cactus in its talons. Nearby, a larger American Bald Eagle looks protectively and guardedly over the Mexican Eagle. See Figure 1-2. The American Bald Eagle grasps three arrows in its talons.

The source of the Mexican Eagle symbol is an ancient *Aztec* myth from Mexico. The myth is associated with the *Mexica* tribe who were seeking and who eventually found a final homeland in *Tenóchtitlán*. This later became Mexico City under the Spanish. Originally, long before the arrival of the Spaniards, the wandering *Mexica* were told of a tribal prophecy, which proclaimed that the *Mexica* would find their new homeland in the place where the tribe encountered an eagle grasping a snake atop a cactus. That place turned out to be near *Tenóchtitlán*, or present day Mexico City. The *Mexica* gave their name to Mexico, and they later became known as the *Aztecs*.

However, the Mexican Eagle on the New Mexico seal is small and is shielded by the larger American Bald Eagle, which grasps arrows in its talons, with its wings outstretched, and with it's watchful eyes guarding the Mexican Eagle. This image boldly demonstrates the change of sovereignty over New Mexico that occurred in 1848 between Mexico and the U.S. The seal also strikes a very delicate balance of dominance and protection over New Mexico, and its important cultural heritage. Therefore the state seal symbolizes and embodies New Mexico's cultural and historical heritage.

Figure 1-2: Great Seal of the State of New Mexico, on the exterior of the State Capitol Building, *Santa Fe.*

The New Mexico state motto also appears on the state seal, written on a scroll at the bottom of the seal. The motto is in Latin, *"Crescit eundo"* which means, "It grows as it grows." At first reading this statement appears rather cryptic, even awkward or confounding.

However, it should be noted that this motto was taken from a first century B.C. Latin poem written by the Roman philosopher, Lucretius, entitled, *De Rerum Natura* or the Nature of Things. It is meant as an allegory for dynamic growth and gathering strength, as in a thunderbolt moving across the sky. One might read the motto instead as "it flourishes as it grows", for this is the real meaning behind the motto.

The Ubiquitous Roadrunner

Not surprisingly, the New Mexico state bird has been designated as the common Greater Roadrunner.[15, 16] It is also known as the California Earth-Cuckoo, or scientifically as the *geococcyx californianus*. This unique bird is a species of ground foraging cuckoo. It is a common inhabitant of the deserts of the Southwest and it is non-migratory.

It is known commonly to youngsters, (and those of us who are older than we care to admit) for its appearance in the Wile E. Coyote[17] cartoons produced by Looney Tunes and Merry Melodies. In the cartoon series, the Road Runner character is often pursued by a hungry coyote, which uses extravagant ploys to capture his prey. However, Road Runner always seems to elude Wile E. Coyote until the next episode. So, one could say that Wile E. Coyote…is not nearly as "wily" as his name would imply. (Incidentally, the coyote is another common character in Native American tales, where he is known for his cunning and for his mischievous nature.)

The real roadrunner is a bird with a very distinctive look and vocalization. See Figure 1- 3. This strange bird is often referred to as the "Clown of the Desert" because of its comical appearance and its inclination to lean forward and run rather than fly. It is a large slender ground bird having a very distinctive and prominent head crest, with long legs, and an extra-large bill. It stands about 18 inches tall, and is about 24 inches long from beak to tail. It is generally speckled black, brown and white on its body with long whitish legs. It has a broad tail with white tips on the three outer tail feathers. Another distinctive feature of the roadrunner is the markings around the eyes. A bare patch of skin behind each eye is shaded blue towards the front of the eye, and is white in the middle and changes to red towards the rear of the eye. It is nature's eye makeup! And patriotic too!!

Although the roadrunner bird is flight-capable it manages to spend the majority of its time on the ground and can run at speeds up to 17 or 20 mph! This strange bird generally seems to prefer running to flying. However, if a roadrunner feels threatened or endangered it will fly to escape danger. As with other members of the cuckoo family, the roadrunner bird has two toes in front and two toes in back, which together with its long legs, makes it an agile runner, on roads or other terrain.

The bird is fast enough to catch rattlesnakes, lizards and insects for food. This unusual bird species has evolved unique capabilities that allow it to survive in the harsh desert environment. These include the ability to survive on very little water. The bird achieves this by reabsorbing water from its own feces before excretion. In addition, its nasal gland eliminates excess salt, a function usually found in the urinary tract of most other birds. It has a life span of about seven or eight years.

Another interesting fact is that the roadrunner possesses a system of thermoregulation, meaning that during the cold desert nights this unique bird lowers its body temperature to conserve energy. In so doing it puts itself into a sleepy state.

Figure 1-3: New Mexico's Roadrunner.

During the warmth of the day, it exposes dark skin patches on its back to the rays of the sun.

The roadrunner makes a slow "coo" type sound, much like a dove, that descends in pitch. It is known to make rapid clattering sounds with its beak. The roadrunner is sometimes identified as the chaparral bird or cock, ground cuckoo or quite appropriately as the snake-killer. Given its uniqueness and its preference for desert climes, it is an appropriate choice for New Mexico's state bird.

Don't Let it Bear Down on You

The American black bear was designated as New Mexico's state animal[18, 19] in 1963. It can be found in many of the national forests within the state. It was selected because it is not only common in these regions of New Mexico, but it is an animal that is very intelligent and yet it is reserved, shy and even secretive. Because of its reserved nature it is not often seen in the wild. Although it is called a black bear, it is not always black in color, but may vary from a cinnamon color to a slate gray or blue. It is a good swimmer and can run at speeds up to 30 mph. (For reference, the world record for the 100-meter sprint is 9.58 seconds, which represents an average speed of 23.35 mph or 34.25 feet per second. Hussein Bolt of Jamaica established this record during the 2012 Summer Olympics. He is the fastest sprinter on earth!) At 30 mph, the black bear can cover 44 feet in one second. No top-condition human sprinter can accomplish that feat. In other words, never think you can outrun a black bear!

The American black bear is scientifically called *ursus Americanus*, and it is the smallest and most commonly found bear on the continent. It possesses short claws that are non-retractable, making the bear an excellent tree climber. The male black bear tends to be a loner, although mother bears can often be seen foraging with their young cubs. Although quite common in forested areas, the black bear is threatened by logging, deforestation, road-kill, habitat loss, depredation, poaching and break up of bear populations.

The black bear is omnivorous, eating just about anything, including nuts, fruits, berries, grasses, roots, insects, small mammals and even carrion if it is hungry enough. The cubs are born in winter, in hibernation, and they remain with the mother until their second summer. During this time, the mother teaches the young what to eat and where to find it.

As a state symbol it is appropriate since the black bear is wild and free, yet intelligent and adaptable, as is New Mexico and as are its inhabitants.

There's No Reason to Pine (State Tree[20, 21, 22,23])

Along the roads of New Mexico, you cannot help but notice the preponderance of small *piñon*, or pine trees. This is why the official state tree of New Mexico is aptly designated as the *piñon* (pine) tree, scientifically termed the *piñon edulis*.

It is identified as a small pine tree having an irregular and rounded crown, with a scaly bark, which may even appear as small plates. The bark may range in color from a reddish brown to a gray tone. It has pine needles that are stiff and coarse in texture, curving slightly along its one or two inch length. The color of the needles varies from blue-ish green to a yellow-ish green. The needles grow together in pairs.

The tree produces one of two flowers depending upon whether the tree is male or female. Male trees produce a cluster of red, cylindrical flowers near the end of its branches. A female tree produces a purplish flower.

The *piñon* produces a small brown and gray colored cone about two inches long on a short stalk. The cone is almost oval in shape and has thick scales. Inside each scale are usually two large "pine nuts" which are edible and quite tasty. The pinecone almost looks like an opened flower in terms of its shape. These cones and pine nuts mature in late summer or early fall (September and October). Native Americans harvested these pine nuts as one source of food and nourishment. The *piñon* is quite common in and around the state of New Mexico.

Love That Color...It's so-o-o-o southwestern!

Turquoise[24] is the official gem of New Mexico. It is a blue-green gem that has been mined in the state since prehistoric times by the Native Americans. After the Spaniards came, the mining of turquoise continued and silver mining was developed. Turquoise and precious metals were mined in the old mining region of Cerrillos, along the Turquoise Trail[24] outside *Santa Fe*. The gems and precious metals were sent back to the Spain to be included in the Spanish crown jewels.

Today, turquoise and silver are used together in jewelry made by the *Navajo*, and by the *Zuni* and other *pueblo* artisans. The turquoise stones act as a beautiful and stunning contrast to the luster of the surrounding silver. The designs are exquisite and are sought after by tourists for their unique and colorful beauty, and their distinctive southwestern look. Often times, artists combine the turquoise with coral, which together with the silver makes for very attractive color combinations. The *Navajo* and the *Zuni* are particularly esteemed for their artistry and craftsmanship in producing exquisite turquoise and silver jewelry.

Muy Sabrosa![25]

What vegetables appear in most every New Mexican meal? It doesn't take much thought to identify the *chile* and the *frijole* (bean). It is therefore appropriate that these two have been designated as the official state vegetables.[26] The *frijole* is an inexpensive staple in New Mexican fare, providing protein and carbohydrates for sustenance. The red or green *chile* provides a pungency and picancy to the food, although green *chile* is the preferred form of *chile* for most New Mexicans.

Yucca, Yucca[27, 28]

The yucca flower was selected by schoolchildren in 1927 to represent New Mexico as the state flower. It is scientifically classified as the *yucca glauca*, and may also be called the soap weed yucca. There are several other aliases for the yucca: *Palmilla (small palm)*, Spanish Bayonet, *Datil* (date) and Whipple yucca. It is a member of the familiar and beautiful lily family. When it blooms in the early summer, the flowers are usually a pale ivory color extending from long stalks. It is a beautiful flower to behold. Broad leaves reside at the base of the plant, but one needs to be careful because these pointed leaves have sharp edges that may easily cut skin. These are often referred to as "bayonet" leaves. See Figure 1-4.

Yucca plants are found in many landscapes. They thrive in barren desert regions, badlands, prairies and grasslands, even in woodlands and in low mountain areas of New Mexico. The plant is pollinated by the yucca moth. It is heat and cold tolerant and drought tolerant, requiring little water or moisture. It is an attractive plant in bloom.

Given its natural beauty, the yucca is not at all "yuckey"! It also has many practical uses. The 2000 – 2001 New Mexico Blue Book and the New Mexico Legislature Handbook mention two interesting facts about this state flower:

"The yucca (pronounced "yuh' – kah") was called 'our Lord's candle' by the early settlers who saw its beautiful flowers gracing the plains and deserts of New Mexico. It is found in abundant quantities throughout the state."

"Early inhabitants found that ground yucca roots were an excellent substitute for soap. Yucca has always been popular among New Mexicans for shampoo, and it is rapidly gaining commercial favor throughout the country."

It was called "*lamparas de Dios*", by the early Spanish colonists, as in "our Lord's candle", mentioned above. Native tribes in New Mexico used it for washing hair. Apaches used the yucca leaf fiber for dental floss! The *Zuni* used a mixture of soap, derived from the yucca sap, and ground aster[29] to wash newborn babies, to stimulate hair growth. The term "*glauca*[30]" in the plant's scientific name means "bluish-green" in color, in Latin, referring to the common color of its sharp pointed leaves.

Yucca roots can be boiled to produce a "tea*. "* Drinking this "tea" is said to relieve symptoms of arthritis and rheumatism.

The fiber of the yucca bayonet leaves has been used to make sandals, belts, cloth, cording and mats. It is not well known that yucca fibers were used in World War Two to make burlap and bagging!

Figure 1-4: Yucca in bloom at *Coronado* State Monument (*Coronado* State Monument, *Bernalillo*).

During droughts, ranchers have used the yucca to serve as emergency livestock feed! Ranchers ground the whole plant into a pulp and fed it to the starving livestock. The yucca flowers are often used as forage for muledeer, pronghorn antelope, birds and other wild animals.[31]

Contrary to what many would expect, many parts of the plant are said to be tasty and useful as a food source. Southwestern Native Americans used to consume the flowers and the lowest part of the stems. (The flowers have a licorice taste.) They also ground the interior portions of the trunk into a flour. The fruit of the yucca can be roasted and it supposedly tastes like baked squash! Mmmm, that sounds good! The fruit can also be sliced thin and dried in the sun. It has a taste like figs! Sounds even better!!

No wonder it was chosen as the New Mexico state flower. It is beautiful, tasty and practical! What more could one ask?

So, where is Everyone?

New Mexico[32] is located in the colorful American Southwest. It is bordered on the east by Oklahoma and Texas, on the west by Arizona, on the north by *Colorado*, and on the south by the Mexican states of *Chihuahua* and *Sonora*. New Mexico is one of the four states identified with the Four Corners region of the Southwest. (The other three states are *Colorado*, Arizona and Utah.) Perhaps because of its name the state of New Mexico is often confused with and can even be mistakenly associated with Mexico.

New Mexico is generally rectangular in shape, almost square. It measures 342 miles across and 370 miles from the *Colorado* border to the Mexican border. Its area is approximately 122 thousand square miles. As an additional note, New Mexico resides in the Mountain Time Zone.

How Many?[33]

The population of New Mexico, per the 2009 Census indicates approximately 2.06 million residents. This produces a population density of only 16.2 people per square mile, which is very low. In fact it ranks 45th among the fifty states. Hence only five other states have lower population densities than New Mexico. This contributes to the relaxed sense of spaciousness, openness and spirituality felt by many who come to New Mexico to visit or to live. Significant traffic and higher popuation density is only experienced in and about the few major cities within the state.

If one eliminates the populations of the ten largest cities, the resulting population density is closer to about 8 or 9 people per square mile. This metric gives a clearer picture of how sparsely populated New Mexico truly is, outside the major cities.

Among all fifty states in the U.S., New Mexico shows that approximately 44% of the population is Hispanic, including descendants of early Spanish colonists and Latin American immigrants. This is the highest relative percentage of Hispanics of any state in the nation. Roughly half the state population is Hispanic.

Not surprisingly, New Mexico also claims a relatively large number of Native Americans. Only Alaska and Oklahoma have a higher percentage or relative number of Native Americans among their populations. However, *California*, Oklahoma, Arizona and Texas exceed New Mexico in the absolute number of Native American residents.

English is the dominant language or first language among 82% or the vast majority of the population. In other words, four out of five residents speak English as their first language. Significantly, 29% of the population speaks Spanish, either as a first or a second language. Some of these may of course speak English as their first language.

Up to 4% of the state's population speak *Navajo*, as a first or second language.

Today. New Mexico's culture demonstrates many traditions, festivals and celebrations reflecting these populations and New Mexico's rich past. This is due to the high percentage of Hispanic and Native Americans who reside in the state, and because of New Mexico's colorful and varied heritage.

How it's Put Together: Counties & Major Cities[34]

New Mexico is not a small state physically, but most of its area is sparsely populated, with the exception of the larger cities. More than half of the state's approximately 2 million residents live in about ten cities, with Albuquerque holding about one quarter of New Mexico's total population. The total combined population of all the remaining nine largest cities is roughly equal to the population of the city of Albuquerque!

Counties[35, 36]

There are a total of thirty-three (33) counties in the state of New Mexico. See the map of New Mexican counties and population distribution in Figure 1-5.

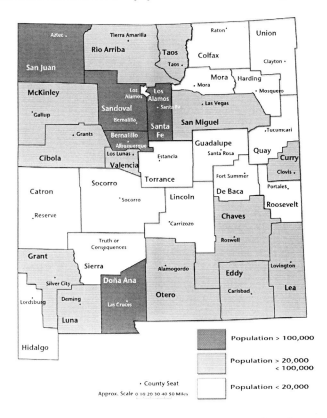

Figure 1-5*: Population Distribution across the Counties of New Mexico.
(Created by Alexis Pennachio, and used with her permission.)

Surprisingly, most of New Mexico's residents live in only five counties which have populations exceeding 100,000: *Bernalillo, Doña Ana, Santa Fe*, Sandoval and *San Juan*. These five counties account for about one half of the state's population!

Bernalillo, located just outside the city of Albuquerque, is the largest county with about 635 thousand residents. *Doña Ana* County has about 175 thousand residents and *Santa Fe* County has approximately 143 thousand residents. Sandoval and *San Juan* each have about 114 thousand residents.

Thirteen counties have populations ranging from 20,000 to 100,000. These are: Chaves, *Cibola,*[37] Curry, Eddy, Grant, Lea, *Luna*, McKinley, *Otero*, Rio Arriba, *San Miguel, Taos* and Valencia counties.

Forty-five per cent of the state's population resides in the remaining fifteen counties. These have populations less than 20,000! These counties are: Catron, Colfax, *De Baca*, Guadalupe, Harding, *Hidalgo*, Lincoln, *Los Alamos, Mora*, Quay, Roosevelt, *Sierra, Socorro*, Torrance and Union.

Harding has the smallest population, with less than 1,000 inhabitants!! *Los Alamos* is the smallest county, geographically, or in terms of area.

Another point of interest is the fact that five counties were named after U.S Presidents: Grant (Ulysses S. Grant, No. 18), Harding (Warren G. Harding, No. 29), Lincoln (Abraham Lincoln, No. 16), McKinley (William McKinley, No. 25), and Roosevelt (Theodore Roosevelt, No. 36).

Cities[38]

Albuquerque, in *Bernalillo* County, is not the capital of the state even though its population exceeds all other cities and towns in New Mexico by a very large margin. *(Santa Fe* is the state capital.)

The ten largest cities in the state, in order of descending population, are: Albuquerque, *Rio Rancho, Santa Fe, Las Cruces*, Roswell, Farmington, Clovis, Hobbs, *Alamogordo* and *Carlsbad*.

Other significant cities and towns are: South Valley, Gallup, *Las Vegas, Española,* North Valley, *Los Alamos, Los Lunes*, Silver City*, Ruidoso, Bernalillo*, Tucumcari, *Taos, Chimayó*, and *Tularosa*. This list is by no means exhaustive, but represents a sampling of the more significant or interesting cities and towns in New Mexico.

This section discusses the three towns that seem to be on every tourist's list of places to see: Albuquerque, *Santa Fe* and *Taos*. Albuquerque is the most metropolitan of the three. However, there is a great deal of cultural and historical interest in *Santa Fe* and *Taos*. There are many other towns and cities in New Mexico that have much to offer the visitor or tourist. We will restrict this brief discussion to the three cities mentioned. A brief summary review of these three towns follows. For information on other towns in New Mexico, please consult any other fine tour book on New Mexico, or consult the most current AAA New Mexico Tour Book.

Albuquerque[39]

Often referred to as ABQ, the city of Albuquerque, in *Bernalillo* County, boasts the largest population of any city in New Mexico, with 448,607 residents living in this southwestern metropolis. It is located about 60 or 70 miles south of *Santa Fe*, New Mexico's capital. Alburquerque's elevation is 4,957 feet, about 2,000 feet lower than

Santa Fe. Albuquerque is also referred to locally as the Duke City, because the city was named after the Duke of Alburquerque, in the time of the Spaniards.

Albuquerque[40] has been known by several names in its history. The city was founded in 1706. The Provincial Governor at the time named the new city *San Francisco de Alburquerque* in honor of the contemporary Viceroy of New Spain, and the viceroy's patron saint, St. Francis. The viceroy then changed the city's name to *San Felipe de Alburquerque*, to honor the King of Spain's patron saint, St. Philip.

The Viceroy of New Spain held the aristocratic title of Duke of Alburquerque, after the Spanish town of the same name. The duke's full name was Don Francisco Fernandez Cuervo y Valdez, and he served as viceroy between 1653 and 1660. At that time, Alburquerque maintained the "r" in the name. Since that time, the "r" in the original town name has been dropped to provide the current spelling of Albuquerque, New Mexico. As with other Spanish town names much of the florid style of the Spaniards has been dropped. The same fate has befallen the reference to *San Felipe* in the town name. So today, it is merely known as Albuquerque!

However, it is interesting to learn how the Spanish town of Alburquerque came to be named, as that is the basis for the name of New Mexico's largest city. The original Spanish town name, Alburquerque, may have been a corruption of the Arabic *"abu al qurk"*, meaning *"land of the cork oak."* The Spanish town was surrounded with cork trees and it was prominent in the cork industry. It had also been held under Moorish (and Arab) control prior to the Spanish *ReConquista*.[41] A different explanation claims that the town name was derived from the Latin *"alba quercus"*, meaning white oak. The cork oak tree is white once the cork bark is removed. Further, the seal of the Spanish village of Alburquerque shows a white oak, framed by a shield and topped with a crown. Regardless of the history of its name, the metropolitan New Mexico city is now just called Albuquerque.

The original town of Albuquerque, New Mexico followed a traditional Spanish layout, with a central *plaza* having a church on one side and with governmental buildings on the opposing side. During the Mexican-American War a military post or garrison was set up to protect American settlers, after the American forces invaded the region. This garrison was still active at the time of the Confederate invasion of New Mexico in March 1862. The area around the *Plaza* fell into disuse after 1880 when the Atchinson, Topeka and *Santa Fe* Railroad arrived. Today it is part of the area called Old Town. It now features many small tourist shops, art galleries, art studios and eateries. The *San Felipe de Neri* Church overlooks the *Plaza*. The *Plaza* is a quaint interesting area that still preserves some of the old Spanish "feel."

The city of Albuquerque lies in the valley below the steep and rugged *Sandia* Mountain Range. This range serves as a beautiful backdrop to the city. As the evening sun lowers in the southwestern sky, a pink glow comes over these mountainsides, giving the range its distinctive Spanish name, *Sandia*, meaning "watermelon" (color).

Fine skiing is available at the *Sandia* Peak Ski Area, on *Sandia* Mountain. *Sandia* Crest and *Sandia* Peak provide stunning views that overlook the town of Albuquerque and the surrounding area.

The *Cibola* National Forest provides opportunities to go camping, hiking, mountain biking, and even hunting during hunting season. The town also has numerous recreational parks. For the more studious or inquisitive there is the Albuquerque

Library, with multiple locations throughout the city.

Albuquerque sports many fine shops in Old Town, Nob Hill-Highland area and downtown Albuquerque. It also has some fine restaurants and hotels. Please consult the AAA New Mexico Tour Book for these locations.

Of special interest are the annual Albuquerque International Balloon *Fiesta*[R], Old Town, River of Lights, New Mexico State Fair, *Sandia* Peak Tramway, New Mexico Rail Runner Express train (to *Santa Fe*) and the Turquoise Trail (to *Santa Fe*). See Chapter Ten, Fascinating Things To Do & Places to See, for more details.

The city has many fascinating museums and cultural centers. These include: Albuquerque Museum of Art & History, American International Rattlesnake Museum, Anderson-Abruzzo Albuquerque International Balloon Museum, Holocaust & Intolerance Museum of New Mexico, Indian *Pueblo* Cultural Center, National Hispanic Cultural Center, National Museum of Nuclear Science & History, New Mexico Museum of Natural History & Science, Turquoise Museum, Maxwell Museum of Anthropology, Silver Family Geology Museum of the University of New Mexico, UNM Art Museum, UNM Meteorite Museum and Unser Racing Museum.

The University of New Mexico has its campus in the city. Albuquerque also supports a number of recreational activities that are geared towards families and children. These include: ABQ Biopark Aquarium and Botanical Gardens, ABQ Biopark Zoo and Explora.

If you like casinos, there are two within the immediate Albuquerque area. These are: Hard Rock Hotel & Casino Albuquerque and *Sandia* Resort & Casino. *Isleta Pueblo* runs and operates the Hard Rock Hotel and Casino. *Sandia* Resort & Casino offers something special. It is located on *Sandia Pueblo* lands with the *Sandia* Mountains as a majestic backdrop. The views of the *Sandia* Mountains are spectacular. The casino features well over a thousand slot machines and many card game tables, and even a non-smoking poker table. The resort hosts big name performers in the outdoor amphitheater during the summer months. Beautiful rooms and suites are available for overnight stays. The resort has several small eateries and a few fine dining restaurants including *Bien Shur* on the top floor of the resort. Not only is the food superb, the view of nighttime Albuquerque is stunning. The resort also has a spa on site. A statue of a male *pueblo* Deer Dancer stands outside the hotel entry, while statues of *pueblo* women greet the visitor in the main lobby lounge area. A beautiful golf course is available for golfers. *Sandia* Peak Tramway is outside the resort but is very close by.

A number of interesting activities and sights to see in Albuquerque are highlighted in Chapter Ten, Fascinating Things To Do & Places To See.

For more detailed information about Albuquerque, its sights, recreation, lodging or dining, please consult a current version of the AAA New Mexico Tour Book, or contact the Albuquerque Convention and Visitors Bureau at: 20 First *Plaza* N.W., Suite 601, P.O. Box 26866, Albuquerque, NM 87125, or call at (505) 842-9918 or toll free at (800) 284-2282.

Santa Fe[42, 43]

Santa Fe, the capital of the state of New Mexico, is located in *Santa Fe* County. It is the fourth largest city in the state with a population of approximately 62,000 and an elevation of 6,989 feet. It is the oldest capital city in the United States, and it just completed its 400th Anniversary celebration in 2010.

Although Don Juan de Oñate, the first Spanish Colonial Governor, claimed the region for the Spanish Crown and named it the province of *Santa Fe de Nuevo México*,[44] there is some controversy as to who actually founded the town of *Santa Fe*. Notwithstanding, Governor Don Pedro de Peralta did indeed establish the town as the administrative and governmental center of the imperial province in 1610.

Santa Fe was founded where a small *Tewa* village had once existed. This site was near the current *Santa Fe Plaza*, and near the *Santa Fe* River, which provided needed water. The *Tewa* called it *"Ogha Po'oge"*, meaning "down at the white shell bead water."[45]

The full name given the Spanish town reflects the verbose, cumbersome and florid style of the Spaniards. It is *La Villa Real de la Santa Fe de San Francisco de Asís*: the Royal Town of the Holy Faith of Saint Francis of Assisi. The *Santa Fe* portion of the city's name honored a walled military town of that same name founded by Ferdinand and Isabella of Spain. *Santa Fe ("Holy Faith")*, Spain was the last Moorish stronghold in Granada, southern Spain, before it fell in the Spanish *ReConquista* (Reconquest).

As with Albuquerque, the cumbersome Spanish name has been reduced to a simpler and more manageable form, in this case, *Santa Fe*. Who could have remembered its full Spanish name anyway!? Imagine calling for aid: "Help! *La Villa Real de la Santa Fe de San Francisco de Asís* is on fire!" By the time anyone spat it out the town would have burned down, no doubt!

High desert and mountains surround the city. The area features stunning sunsets and awe-inspiring natural beauty. In the northwest lie the imposing *Sangre de Cristo* Mountains. To the southeast, in the distance, one can see the *Jemez* Mountains. High desert lies between *Santa Fe* and the *Jemez* Mountains. With its *pueblo* style architecture, *Santa Fe* is uniquely beautiful, reflecting its Native American and Spanish heritage. *Santa Fe* is widely known as a cultural center, with a multitude of first-class art galleries and museums (art, historic and cultural), and for its fine restaurants and hotels. It is also known for its unique historic and religious buildings.

The *Plaza Mercado*, in the center of the downtown or Old Town area, is the one region that all visitors are attracted to, with its many interesting tourist shops, featuring exquisite turquoise and silver jewelry, beautiful *pueblo* pottery and *Hopi kachinas*, Spanish-style crafts and art, first class clothing stores, and restaurants. In the center of the *Plaza* there is a small simple obelisk dedicated to the fallen of the Indian Wars, and the Union troops who fought in New Mexico during the American Civil War at *Glorieta*, *Valverde* and Peralta. The Palace of the Governors is situated along one side of the *Plaza*, which is usually occupied in the daytime with dozens of *pueblo* natives and *Navajos*. They sit on the sidewalk against one of the palace walls eager to sell their goods and crafts. During the summer months, the *Plaza* is the site for many weekend and special activities that may include cultural music and dance, modern music, singing, arts and craft shows, etc. It is the focal point of this colorful town. Museums and galleries surround the *Plaza* area, and side streets. Some of the finest art in the world is presented here, whether it is sculpture, oil or acrylic paintings, or mixed media art. The Georgia O'Keefe Museum[46] is also near the *Plaza* area. Various interesting sites within a block or two of the *Plaza* are the Cathedral Basilica of Saint Francis of Assisi, Loretto Chapel and *El Santuario de Guadalupe*. Another area that features many fine galleries is along Canyon Road, about a mile from the *Plaza*. It features paintings, sculpture, fine jewelry, rugs, carpets, and crafted furniture.

Santa Fe also has symphonic orchestral and chamber music, and international dance troupes featured at the nearby Lensic Theater.

Major museums in and around *Santa Fe* include: Bataan Memorial Military Museum & Library, Center for Contemporary Arts and CCA Cinematique, Georgia O'Keefe Museum, Museum of Contemporary Native Arts, Museum of Indian Arts and Culture, Museum of International Folk Art, Museum of Spanish Colonial Art, New Mexico History Museum, New Mexico Museum of Art, Randall Davis Audubon Center, *Santa Fe* Childrens' Museum and Wheelwright Museum of the American Indian.

Day trips are also available for white water rafting, on the *Rio Grande* further north. Fine skiing is available at the Ski *Santa Fe* Resort, on the *Sangre de Cristo* Mountains, with stunning views overlooking *Santa Fe*.

The *Santa Fe* Forest provides opportunities to go camping, hiking, mountain biking, and even hunting during hunting season. The town also has numerous recreational parks. For the more studious or inquisitive there is the *Santa Fe* Library, with multiple locations throughout the city.

There are so many sites to see in *Santa Fe* that it would take multiple busy and lengthy visits to see the biggest part of it.

The Capitol Building, the state government center, is also located along with many other state government buildings in *Santa Fe*. The architectural layout of the Capitol is designed to represent the *Zia*[47] sun symbol of the New Mexico state flag. There are two interesting statues at the rear of the state Capitol grounds. One is a modernistic interpretation of a Hoop Dancer, to the left of the stairway leading up to the building. The other is an abstract statue of a Buffalo Dancer, on the corner with *Paseo de Peralta*. In the front of the Capitol Building, near the Old *Santa Fe* Trail, there is a beautiful modern style statue of a *Mescalero Apache*. There are also other fine statues around the Capitol area.

Santa Fe also features the annual *RODEO! de Santa Fe* each summer. It is located on Rodeo Drive on the other side of town. This same site hosts the *Santa Fe* County Fair and other attractions throughout the year. This exciting town also features[48] the annual *Fiestas de Santa Fe (Santa Fe Fiesta)*, *Santa Fe* Traditional Spanish Market©, *Santa Fe* Indian Market® and the Burning of the *Zozobra*©®.

The fascinating and interesting *El Rancho de las Golondrinas*[49] lies nearby. Outside *Santa Fe* within short drives are the *Chimayó* Sanctuary, the *Santa Fe* Opera and the *Tesuque* Flea Market. The last two sites are located alongside Highway 84 in *Tesuque*, in the north just outside of the town. Highway 84 leads to additional roadways, which can take the visitor to the *Chimayó* Sanctuary.

The Turquoise Trail can provide a full and fun-filled scenic drive from *Santa Fe* through various old mining towns, shops and restaurants towards *Sandia* Crest and finally to Albuquerque. Alternately, the New Mexico Rail Runner Express train operates between *Santa Fe* and Albuquerque. It travels through the high desert landscape and has stops near several *pueblos*. Cultural events are sometimes offered on the train ride during tourist season.

Many of the native *pueblos* surrounding or near *Santa Fe* have casinos on their grounds. Some are within a short drive of the town. One of the newest resort/casinos is the Buffalo Thunder Resort/Casino. This recreational resort provides many slot machines and card tables, top line entertainers, a spa, fine dining restaurants, craft and tourist shops, clothing shops, a sports bar, and fine rooms and suites for lodging. Spread throughout the resort, indoor and outdoor, are many fine sculptures and statues of Native Americans posed in traditional dress involved in dance stances or other traditional activities. The visitor is greeted outside the lobby entrance with a fine statue of a *pueblo* Buffalo Dancer.

Chapter Ten, Fascinating Things To Do & Places To See, highlights a number of interesting activities and sights to see in and around *Santa Fe.*

For detailed information on these and other features of *Santa Fe* please consult the most current version of the A A A New Mexico Tour Book, or contact the *Santa Fe* Convention and Visitors Bureau at 201 Marcy St., *Santa Fe*, New Mexico 87504, or call at (505) 955-6200 or (800) 777-2489.

Taos [50, 51]

Located about 65 miles further north than *Santa Fe*, the elevation of *Taos* is almost the same as *Santa Fe's*, at 6,952 feet. *Taos* is a small town with a population of only about 4,700 people. This town lies within the shadows of the *Sangre de Cristo* Mountains. The setting still has a frontier feel and look. It is also known for its art shops and galleries. The official name of this quaint town is *Don Fernando de Taos.* It was first established in 1615 and was called *Fernandez de Taos.* The nearby *adobe* dwellings of *Taos Pueblo* were built in 1350 AD. This *pueblo* is recognized as one of the oldest continuously inhabited communities in the United States.

Taos was the home of Charles Bent, the first Territorial Governor of New Mexico and of Kit Carson, the famous trader, trapper, scout, Army officer, Indian fighter and rancher. Visitors can see their homes, which have been converted into museums. Kit Carson Park is located in the center of the Old Town. This park contains the Kit Carson Cemetery where Kit Carson and other famous historical persons are buried.

As in *Santa Fe*, the *Plaza* is the heart of the Old Town and is the place where visitors head. There is a large cottonwood tree in the *Plaza*, providing ample shade in the hot summer months. This area also sports a small but quaint gazebo. Small shops and eating-places surround the *Plaza.*

The *Taos Plaza* is located just off *Paseo del Pueblo Norte* (North *Pueblo* Drive) between Kit Carson Road and *Camino de la Placita* (Little *Plaza* Road). The site dates back to the 18th century as a place where local meetings and key events took place.

Near *Taos* is the *San Francisco de Asís* Mission Church. This can be found in *Ranchos de Taos* on the way to *Taos.* This is a fine example of Spanish Colonial architecture. Also, ten miles west of *Taos* on US 64, there is the *Rio Grande* Gorge Bridge. The bridge is about 20 minutes outside of *Taos.* This bridge spans the *Rio Grande* and is 650 feet above it. The span is 1,272 feet across. A walk path across the bridge is easily accessible. This is reserved for the brave of heart who have no fear of heights.

The *Taos Pueblo*, two miles north of the *Taos Plaza*, is a "must-see" site. Proceed via *Paseo del Pueblo Norte*, then drive half a mile north on the entrance road to the parking and registration area. There is an admission fee to enter the *pueblo* grounds.

Taos Pueblo is a living community that has a fresh-water creek running through it, named Red Willow Creek. The site is distinctive for its well-preserved *adobe pueblo* buildings, many of which still house native families and tourist shops. The *San Geronimo* Church lies nearby, with its simple architectural style and interior. Visiting *Taos Pueblo* is like taking a step back in time, to another era and another place. It is worth the visit!

The road to *Taos* is also a convenient place to seek out white-water rafting outfitters to raft the nearby *Rio Grande*. The surrounding mountains and forest provide opportunities for hiking, camping, mountain bike riding, winter skiing at *Taos* Ski Valley and other activities. Unlike *Santa Fe* and Albuquerque, *Taos* has little in the way of nightlife, although there are a few spots in town. The locals are called *Taoseños.*

There are a few museums of interest in *Taos*. These are: Charles Bent Home & Museum, Ernest L. Blumenschein House & Museum, Kit Carson Home & Museum, Harwood Museum of Art, Mabel Dodge Luhan House, Martinez *Hacienda,* Millicent Rogers Museum, and *Taos* Art Museum.

Twenty miles northwest of *Taos* is the D. H. Lawrence Ranch, the 1920's home of the famous English writer.

For detailed information on these and other features of *Taos* please consult the most current version of the AAA New Mexico Tour Book.

Chapter Two: The Lay of the Land

What Did You Say 'Bout Geography?

The landscape of New Mexico is more varied than most people might expect. The deserts range from white to sandy to reddish in color, and from totally barren to scrubby. The terrain varies from flat-topped *mesa*s to snow-capped mountain peaks. But what is less known is that large areas of the state are heavily forested! These forests belie its more common image as an arid state. Although in fact the state is relatively dry, with a mere 250 square miles of surface water in the entire state.

This chapter gives a brief overview of the basic geography of New Mexico or what may be called the "Lay of the Land." It mentions the major river systems, mountain ranges and *mesas*, and outlines the basic geography of the land. It defines the Continental Divide and the three major watersheds into which the state's rivers eventually flow. Although this chapter may be drier than those that follow, the author considers it necessary to understanding elements of other chapters in the book. For example, it gives context to the subsequent historical chapters. When mountain ranges or rivers are mentioned in the text, the reader will already have some sense of what that means and will recognize the relevant region of the state.

(Note: Geography isn't everyone's favorite subject! In spite of what is said above, please feel free to skip this chapter if this sentiment applies to you! Also, be sure to consult the Spanish Glossary of Terms at the rear of the book for assistance with Spanish words and place-names.)

Overview

New Mexico[1] can be divided into roughly four geographical regions: Great Plains or High Plains region in eastern New Mexico, Rocky Mountain region in the north central part of the state, Basin and Range region in the southern and southwestern part of the state, and finally, the *Colorado* Plateau region in northwestern and central western New Mexico.

The easternmost region is a southern extension of the Great Plains, which runs southerly from the high plateaus in the north down to the Mexico border. The flowing rivers have etched the deep canyons found in this high plateau region. It is common to find large cattle and sheep herds here. Further south of the high plateau and south of the Canadian River, is the area referred to as the High Plains or Staked Plains. It too is part of the Great Plains region of New Mexico. This is called *Llano Estacado*[2] in Spanish. In this area, dry farming or farming using extensive irrigation is possible. The Canadian River flows across this easternmost region towards Texas and the Mississippi River Watershed. The Pecos River flows south through the *Llano Estacado,* and then flows eastward into southern Texas. It eventually joins the *Rio Grande* on its way to the *Rio Grande* Watershed.

The second significant region, in northern central New Mexico, contains the extension of the Rocky Mountains down from *Colorado*. The *Rio Grande* cuts a long valley into these mountains from north to south. The *Sangre de Cristo* Mountains are part of the Rocky Mountain Range. They occur to the east of the *Rio Grande* and contain Wheeler Peak, near *Taos*. At an altitude of 13,161 feet, Wheeler Peak is the highest peak in New Mexico. The *Nacimiento* and *Jemez* Mountain Ranges lie in the north central region and on the western side of the *Rio Grande*.

Further south, beyond the *Sangre de Cristo* Mountains, there are mountain ranges separated by large flat areas called basins. This area is known as the Basin and Range region. The region extends south from *Santa Fe* to the Mexican border and west to the Arizona border. It is bordered on the east by the *Llano Estacado*. Contained within the Basin and Range Region are the *Sandia* and *Manzano* Mountains, near Albuquerque. Still east of the *Rio Grande* and further south, are the *Oscura, Capitán, Sacramento* and Guadalupe Mountains. A little further west but still east of the *Rio Grande* are the *San Andrés, Fra Cristóbal, Caballo* and Organ Mountains.

The *Tularosa* Basin ("Reeded" Basin) lies within the Basin and Range Region and also lies east of the *Rio Grande*. It serves as a great example of this type of geological region. It is a broad valley in central southern New Mexico and it lies between the *Sacramento* Mountains in the east and the San *Andrés* and *Oscura* Mountains in the west. It lies in the *Chihuahuan* Desert. The *Tularosa* Basin is bounded in the south by the Franklin and Hueco Mountains, and in the north by the *Chupadera Mesa*. Because no water can flow out of it, it is termed a "endorheic basin'. This basin extends north and south 150 miles and east/west by 60 miles at its widest point. It includes *La Jornada del Muerto*[3] Desert, the Carrizozo *Malpais* volcanic fields, White Sands Missile Range and the White Sands National Monument.

The Basin and Range region occupies about one-third of the land area of the state. It includes the southwestern part of the state, such as *Luna*, Grant, *Hidalgo*, Catron, *Socorro, Doña Ana* and *Sierra* counties. In this area, the Basin and Range region extends westward to the Arizona border and up to the area touching the southern borders of Valencia and *Cibola* counties. Mountain ranges in this southwestern part of the Basin and Range region include the *Mogollón, Magdalena, Mimbres, San Francisco, San Mateo*, Pyramid*, and Florida Mountains as well as the Black Range,* and numerous others. The western region is quite arid and rugged. Desert basins separate many of these mountain ranges. Significant basins in the Basin and Range region include *Tularosa* Valley*, La Jornada del Muerto* and *Estancia* Valley.

The fourth geographical region and the remaining one-third of New Mexico lies in the northwesternmost parts of the state. This area lies south of the Rocky Mountain Range and is known as the *Colorado* Plateau. It contains rugged mountain ranges such as the *Chuska* Mountain Range in the north, and the *Zuni* Mountains, a little further south of that range.

Four great river systems are found in the north and southwestern regions. These are the *San Juan, Zuni, Gila* and the *Puerco* River systems.

Continental Divide

The Continental Divide separates the direction of flow of all rivers in the northern half of the Western Hemisphere. The flow direction and the watershed they finally flow into, are determined by which side of the Continental Divide (CD) a river is physically located upon. On a map the Continental Divide is generally indicated by a ragged dashed or dotted line, that meanders roughly north and south through the entire northern Western Hemisphere. In so doing, it traces a path through New Mexico from its northern border with *Colorado* to its southern border with Mexico.

It extends from *Rio Arriba* County, just a few miles northeast of *Chama* in northern

New Mexico to the southern border of *Hidalgo* County in southern New Mexico. As the CD meanders through the western part of the state it extends across the following counties: *Rio Arriba,* Sandoval, McKinley, *Cibola,* Catron, *Sierra,* Grant, *Luna* and *Hidalgo.*

Major River Systems:[4]

Without rivers and mountains, New Mexico would indeed be a very barren and arid place: a land consisting only of xeric plants, insects, reptiles, and some few species of birds and mammals that over eons had adapted to dry, water-scarce environments. Rivers are more than just a geological feature of the land. They are a series of lifelines that provide life and sustenance, not only to the people, but to many species of life in New Mexico. Figure 2-1 shows the main rivers and mountain ranges of New Mexico.

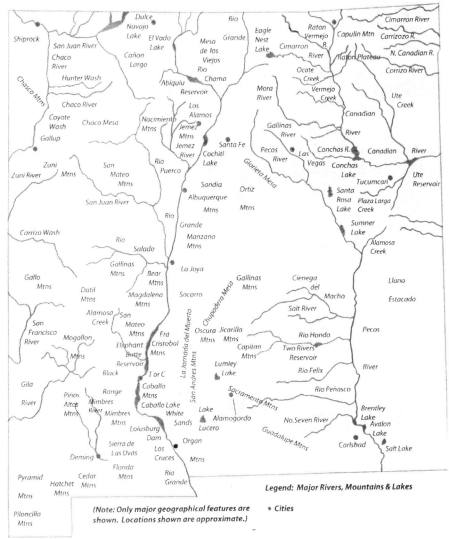

Figure 2-1*: Major Rivers, Mountain Ranges & Lakes of New Mexico.

However, rivers not only sustain life. They also produce much of the state's natural beauty. They provide us with lush and verdant valleys, and water for irrigation of crop fields. Their fertile valleys have enabled cultural development, adding to the charm and attraction of New Mexico.

Today these rivers provide recreational activities too, such as boating, river rafting, swimming, windsailing, fishing, etc.

The major river systems of this state flow towards one of three great watersheds: the Mississippi River Watershed (MW) or the *Rio Grande* Watershed (RGW), both east of the Continental Divide, or the *Colorado* River Watershed (CW), west of the Continental Divide. The three major rivers and their tributaries east of the Continental Divide are the *Rio Grande*, *Pecos* and Canadian Rivers. The *Rio Grande* is the eighth longest river in the U.S. The *Pecos* River becomes a tributary of the *Rio Grande* once it has reached Texas. However, even though the *Pecos* River is considered a river system of its own in New Mexico, it is considered part of the *Rio Grande* Watershed, which finds its own separate path to the Gulf of Mexico.

The Canadian River and its tributaries form part of the Mississippi River Watershed, in the northeastern region of the state.

The *Colorado* River Watershed lies to the west of the Continental Divide, in the western part of the state. Four rivers and their tributaries flow westerly to the *Colorado* River Watershed. These are the *Gila*, *Puerco*, *Zuni* and *San Juan* Rivers. The *Puerco* and *Zuni* Rivers form part of the Little *Colorado* River System (in Arizona), which joins up with the *Colorado* River in Arizona.

The *San Juan* River lies in northwestern New Mexico. The other three rivers are located further south in the western part of the state. See Figure 2-1.

River Systems of the Mississippi River Watershed

The main river system that flows eastward to form part of the Mississippi River Watershed is the Canadian River System.

...Canadian River System

The Canadian River System starts in *Colorado* and flows down into northeastern New Mexico, near *Raton* close to the *Colorado* border. Eagle Nest Lake is sourced from the Canadian River as it flows down from the *Sangre de Cristo* Mountains. It proceeds southerly until it reaches *Conchas* Lake, just northwest of Tucumcari. It then changes direction and proceeds easterly until it crosses into western Texas. This great river feeds *Conchas* Lake and *Ute* Reservoir.

As it proceeds from the *Colorado* border to the Texan border numerous tributaries connect with the river. Between the northern state border and *Conchas* Lake the main tributaries are *Vermejo* River, *Cimarron* River, Ocate Creek, *Vermejo* Creek, *Mora* River, *Cañon Largo* and *La Cinta* Creek. The *Conchas* River joins at *Conchas* Lake, and it picks up *Ute* Creek as it reaches *Ute* Lake. The Canadian River then proceeds eastward into western Texas, where other tributaries join the river.

Major River Systems of the *Rio Grande* Watershed

The *Rio Grande* Watershed consists of two great River Systems: The *Rio Grande* and the *Pecos* River, which joins it in Texas on its long journey to the Gulf of Mexico.

...Rio Grande River System

The great *Rio Grande* finds its source in the mountains of *Colorado*. It is the Granddaddy of New Mexican rivers. As it winds down into northern New Mexico, tributaries add to it. The *Rio Grande* traverses the entire length of New Mexico from its northern border with *Colorado* southward to the state's border with Texas and Mexico at *El Paso*. It roughly bisects the state into its eastern and western halves. The *Rio Grande* actually flows into the Gulf of Mexico, once it crosses the state of Texas.

The *Rio Grande* has cut a deep gorge into the surrounding terrain near *Taos* and

Figure 2-2: River rafting in the *Rio Grande* Gorge, near *Taos*.

just south of it. This area is called the *Rio Grande* Gorge. A spectacular road bridge crosses it just outside *Taos* and it is called the *Rio Grande* Gorge Bridge. The deep gorge and the bridge are frequently photographed. Further south, river rafting is a popularly enjoyed activity. See Figure 2-2.

Cochiti Dam was built in the mid-twentieth century to store excess floodwaters and to control flooding in regions further south, such as Albuquerque. See Figure 11-10 for a view of *Cochiti* Dam & Lake.

In the southern part of the state, the *Rio Grande* feeds the *Bosque del Apache* Wildlife Reserve in *Socorro* County. This reserve also acts as a floodplain for regional flood control. Just a few miles further south the river becomes wide enough to allow the establishment of two major reservoirs. These are Elephant *Butte*[5] Reservoir and *Caballo*[6] Reservoir, both in *Sierra* County. These reservoirs store water for dry periods and they provide regional flood control. They contain and store the excess waters produced by the spring and summer melting of the *Colorado* snow packs, far to the north. As a fringe benefit, they provide man-made lakes that allow recreational activities for the local populations.

Eventually, the *Rio Grande* turns southeasterly as it approaches the junction of *El*

Paso, Texas, the New Mexico border, and the Mexican border town of *El Ciudad de Juarez*. As the *Rio Grande* leaves New Mexico, it forms the border between the U. S. and Mexico. It continues its southeasterly flow along the southern Texas border until it reaches the Gulf of Mexico.

Pueblo life attached itself to the *Rio Grande* river valleys and their tributary valleys, where irrigation was established and agriculture flourished, causing the extensive cultural development along these same valleys, which adds so much to the diversity and beauty of this land.

The *Rio Grande* Watershed has numerous major tributaries. As the *Rio Grande* flows southward, its tributaries add to its flow. These are: Red River, *Rio Hondo* (of northern New Mexico), *Rio Pueblo de Taos, Embudo Creek, Rio Chama,*[7] *Pojoaque* River, *Santa Fe* River, *Jemez* River, *Rio Puerco, Rio Salado,* and *Alamosa* Creek. The *Pecos* River System never joins the *Rio Grande* River in New Mexico, but in Texas instead. Nonetheless it is considered part of the *Rio Grande* Watershed.

...*Pecos* River System

The *Pecos* River maintains its separate and distinct identity within New Mexico. The *Pecos* River starts in the *Pecos* Wilderness Area of the *Santa Fe* National Forest

Figure 2-3: *Pecos* River near *Bosque Redondo.*

area in southeastern *Mora* County. It meanders southeasterly until it reaches the *Santa Rosa* area, in Guadalupe County. The *Pecos* River then turns southward, and eventually proceeds across the southern border into Texas. See Figure 2-3.

As the *Pecos* River proceeds southward from *Pecos* through New Mexico towards the border with Texas, numerous tributaries join the river. These New Mexican tributaries begin with the *Gallinas* River, then *Pintada Arroyo* in Guadalupe County, and Taiban Creek in *De Baca* County. The next group of tributaries continues with *Arroyo* or *Cienega del Macho, Gallo Arroyo, Rio Hondo, Rio Felix, Rio Peñasco* and Black River near Carlsbad. *Rio Hondo* has three sub-tributaries of its own: *Rio Bonito, Rio Ruidoso* and the *Berrendo* River. The southern *Rio Hondo* fills the Two Rivers Reservoir.

On its long southern path to Red Bluff Lake across the border into Texas, the *Pecos* River sources several major lakes along its route, including *Santa Rosa* Lake,

Sumner Lake, Brantley Lake and Avalon Reservoir.

The *Pecos* River joins the *Rio Grande* in southwestern Texas. It too is a legendary river, like the *Rio Grande*. The legend of *Pecos* Bill is associated with this major tributary river of the *Rio Grande*.

River Systems of the *Colorado* River Watershed

Four main New Mexican rivers and their various tributaries eventually flow westward into the *Colorado* River Watershed. These main rivers are: *Gila*,[8] *Puerco*, *Zuni* and *San Juan* Rivers. The *San Juan* River has five tributaries of its own: the Chaco River, *La Plata* River, *Animas* River, *Los Piños* River and *Navajo* River. The *Gila* River's main tributary is the *San Francisco* River, which, in turn, has its own Tularosa tributary. Both the *Zuni* River and the *Puerco* River become tributaries of the Little *Colorado* River of Arizona.

...*Gila* River System

The *Gila* River is sourced in southwestern New Mexico, from the western slopes of the Black Range in *Sierra* County. It flows down southwesterly through the *Gila* National Forest and the *Gila* Cliff Dwellings National Monument, and into southern Arizona. Eventually, it joins the *Colorado* River near Yuma, Arizona.

The *San Francisco* River is the main tributary of the upper *Gila* River. This tributary originates in Arizona but sweeps an eastern arc into southwestern New Mexico before it turns back into Arizona again where it joins the *Gila* near Clifton, Arizona. The Tularosa River is a tributary of the *San Francisco* River.

...*Puerco* River System

Sourced in McKinley County, on the western slopes of the Continental Divide, the *Puerco* River is a significant tributary of the Little *Colorado* River. It extends from northwestern New Mexico into northeastern Arizona and across the Painted Desert and the Petrified Forest regions of Arizona. It eventually becomes a tributary of the Little *Colorado* River, in Arizona.

...*Zuni* River System

The *Zuni* River is also a tributary of the Little *Colorado* River in Arizona. The *Zuni* River is approximately 90 miles long, and it originates from the western slopes of the Continental Divide in *Cibola* County. It traverses southwesterly through the *Zuni* Indian Reservation.

...*San Juan* River System

This river lies in the extreme northwestern corner of New Mexico, just southeast of the Four Corners area. It flows into southeastern Utah where it eventually finds the *Colorado* River, as a tributary to that great river. It sources the *Navajo* Reservoir in *Rio Arriba* and *San Juan* counties. The *San Juan* River has numerous tributaries including Chaco River, *La Plata* River, *Animas* River, *Los Piños* and the *Navajo* River.

Internal River System (Interior Basin with no watershed)

There is one river in New Mexico that flows towards no watershed, but instead ends up in an interior land-locked water basin, within New Mexico. That river is the *Mimbres* River. The *Mimbres* River is 91 miles long and is located in southwestern New Mexico. It is sourced from the southwestern slopes of the Black Range Mountains. It flows into a small basin east of the town of Deming, New Mexico.

Major Mountain Ranges[9, 10, 11]

A large number of visitors to New Mexico are often surprised to learn that the state has many mountain ranges, a good number of which are forested. Claims by authorities run from a low count of 26 to as many as 110 mountain ranges. Regardless of how one counts there are clearly many ranges in the state. Some of the most significant or notable mountain ranges are:

Animas Mountains – *Hidalgo* County
Brazos Mountains – *Rio Arriba* County
Black Range Mountains – *Sierra*, Grant County
Caballo Mountains – *Sierra* County
Capitán Mountains – Lincoln County
Cebolleta Mountains – *Cibola*, McKinley, Sandoval Counties
Chuska Mountains – *San Juan*, McKinley Counties
Datil Mountains – Catron County
Fra Cristóbal[12] Mountains – *Sierra* County
Gallinas Mountains – Socorro County
Guadalupe Mountains – *Otero*, Eddy Counties
Jemez Mountains – Sandoval County
Jicarilla Mountains – Lincoln County
Ladrón Mountains – *Socorro* County
Magdalena Mountains – *Socorro* County
Mangas Mountains – Catron County
Manzano Mountains – Torrance, Valencia Counties
Mogollón Mountains – Catron County
Nacimiento Mountains – *Rio Arriba*, Sandoval Counties
Organ Mountains – *Doña Ana* County
Oscura Mountains – Lincoln, *Socorro* Counties
San Andrés Mountains – *Sierra*, *Doña Ana* Counties
San Francisco Mountains – Catron County
San Mateo Mountains - *Socorro* County
San Juan and *San Pedro* Mountains – *Rio Arriba* County
Sacramento Mountains – Catron County
Sandia Mountains – *Bernalillo*, Sandoval Counties
Sangre de Cristo Mountains – *Santa Fe*, *Taos*, *San Miguel* Counties
Tularosa Mountains – Catron County
Zuni Mountains – *Cibola*, McKinley Counties

These mountain ranges add to the natural beauty and stunning scenery found throughout the enchanting state of New Mexico. Many occur within the five national forests located in the state. Many also include some of the state and national monuments discussed later in the book.

Mesas[13]

Around New Mexico you can't help but notice the unique geological formations known as *mesa*s scattered throughout the state. A *mesa* is a flat-topped mountain. The term *mesa* comes from the Spanish, meaning "table" because of the flat top shape. These formations are caused by erosion. The geological theory is that at one time these *mesas* were flat surfaces on a plateau, having no valleys. It is thought that over time, rivers eroded the plateau, cutting valleys into it. Over time, the valleys eroded further. *Mesas* result from the area of the original plateau that escaped the erosion around it.

Although there are many *mesas* in New Mexico, one of the most famous is the Enchanted *Mesa*. This is a sandstone *butte* located in *Cibola* County, about 2.5 miles northeast of the *Acoma Pueblo*. In Spanish it is called *Mesa Encantada* and in *Keresan* it is called *Katzimo* or *Kadzima*. Long ago, the people of *Acoma* lived atop the Enchanted *Mesa* with their fields and water sources down in the valley below. A natural stone ladder or ramp formed by natural forces provided access to the *mesa* top. Inhabitants fled the *mesa* after a severe thunderstorm washed away the natural access to the top. Only un-scalable steep faces remained around the *mesa*. The inhabitants found their new home atop the nearby White Rock *Mesa* or *Acoma Mesa*.

There are a countless number of *mesas* in New Mexico. Two other *mesas* worth mentioning are White *Mesa* on the *Zia Pueblo* lands and Black *Mesa* near *San Ildefonso Pueblo*. See Chapter Eleven.

Lakes, Dams and Reservoirs [14, 15, 16, 17, 18]

Lakes in semi-arid New Mexico? Really!! Well, surprisingly there are said to be 4,502 lakes, ponds, reservoirs and fishing bodies within the State of New Mexico! It is impossible to review or even list all of them. However, the largest lake in New Mexico is Elephant *Butte* Lake, south of *Socorro*, alongside the town of Truth or Consequences. Another large body of water is *Caballo* Reservoir in *Sierra* County.

Many of these lakes and reservoirs are sourced from the numerous rivers that flow through New Mexico towards their watersheds. Not all these fresh water bodies allow fishing, swimming, boating, or even camping. Please check before visiting. Here is a partial list:

Catron County: *Quemado* Lake, Snow Lake.
Chaves County: Skull Lake, Two Rivers Reservoir.
De Baca County: Lake Summer or Summer Lake
Doña Ana County: Burn Lake, Isaak Lake, *Las Cruces* Reservoir, *La Mesa* Lake, *Lucero* Lake
Eddy County: Brantley Lake, Avalon Lake, Salt Lake
Grant County: Blue Evans Lake
Guadalupe County: *Santa Rosa* Lake
Lincoln County: *Bonito* Lake
Los Alamos County: *Los Alamos* Reservoir

McKinley County: Black Rock Reservoir, Eustace Lake, McGaffey Lake, Whiskey Lake.
Quay County: *Ute* Reservoir.
Rio Arriba County: *Abiquiu*[19] Reservoir, Heron Reservoir, *San Juan* Reservoir.
San Juan County: City Reservoir,
San Miguel County: *Conchas* Lake, Storie Lake
Sandoval County: *Cochiti* Lake (Reservoir and Dam), Deer Lake.
Santa Fe County: Nichols Reservoir, Talaya Hill Reservoir.
Sierra County: *Caballo* Reservoir, Elephant *Butte* Lake.
Socorro County: *Sedillo* Hill Reservoir.
Taos County: Baldy Blue Lake, Eagle Nest Lake, *Latir* Lakes, Talpa Reservoir
Otero County: Silver Lake.
Union County: Stone Lake

To find out which of the lakes and reservoirs above allow recreational activities, please consult the following sites:

www.goingoutside.com/lakestates/nm.html

www.fishingworks.com/lakes/new-mexico/

www.wildernet.com/pages/area.cfm?areaID=NMLR&CU_ID=1

www.emnrd.state.nm.us/PRD/BOATINGWeb/boatingmainpagewaters.htm

Many of these water bodies are beautiful and scenic in their own right, and are often near other natural sights or monuments mentioned in this book.

Other smaller lakes exist throughout the entire state. Most, but not all, Native American reservations within New Mexico have some small lakes or ponds on their lands.

Some Reservation lakes and ponds are mentioned in Chapter Eleven, Native American Tribes & Reservations in NM.

National Forests in New Mexico
Many visitors to this land are amazed to discover that millions of acres of New Mexico are included within the national forest system and are under the protection of the U.S. government. Most expect nothing but desert and dry landscapes, and are completely taken aback to see so many Alpine forests within the state. These forested regions allow one to explore the natural beauty of the wilderness areas of New Mexico. Most of these national forests allow fishing, hunting during hunting season with permits, backpacking, hiking, horse-back riding and informal camping. There are usually no formal improved campsites. Fishing may or may not be permitted depending upon the local Ranger Station and conditions. Please consult the local Ranger Station for the most current information and status on allowed activities.

Travelers should dress properly and appropriately for hiking and camping activities, and must be mindful of the season. Tourists should also be alert to the fact that there are various active hunting seasons for these forests. Consult the nearest Ranger's Office for further information. Caution also needs to be exercised because wild and dangerous species do make these forests their homes. Some of these animals include bear, wild hog, wolf, bobcat, coyote packs and mountain lion, among others. Even deer and elk can be dangerous in the rutting season. So plan your forest adventure with safety and security in mind. Further, always remain aware of your surroundings, using all your senses. Remember: a national forest or wilderness area is not the local park, and caution need always be exercised. A list of the New Mexico forests under U.S. government protection follows and includes (in alphabetical order) the following:

...**Carson National Forest**[20] (*Taos*) – There are six Ranger Stations in this forest: *Camino Real, Canjilo, El Rito, Jicarilla, Questa* and the *Tres Piedras* Ranger Districts. Local Ranger District offices are located in *Peñasco, Canjilon, El Rito,* Bloomfield, *Questa* and *Tres Piedras*, respectively.

...**Cibola National Forest (& National Grasslands)**[21] - There are four major noncontiguous Ranger Districts within this forest: the *Sandia*, Mountainair, Mount Taylor and *Magdalena* Ranger Districts. In addition, the *Rita Blanca* Grasslands and the *Kiowa* National Grasslands are also contained within the jurisdiction of the *Cibola* National Forest in New Mexico, under the *Kiowa* and *Rita Blanca* Ranger District.

...**Gila National Forest**[22] - There are six Ranger Districts in the *Gila* National Forest: Black Range, *Quemado*, Glenwood, Reserve, Silver City and Wilderness Ranger Districts. Black Range Ranger District is located in Truth or Consequences. The Wilderness Ranger District is located in *Mimbres*.

...**Lincoln National Forest**[23] - There are three Ranger Districts: Smokey Bear Ranger District in Lincoln County, *Sacramento* Ranger District covering *Otero* and Chaves Counties and the Guadalupe Ranger District covering *Otero*, Chaves and Eddy Counties.

...**Santa Fe National Forest**[24] – The forest headquarters are located in the city of *Santa Fe*. Ranger Districts include Coyote, Cuba, *Española, Jemez* and *Pecos/Las Vegas* districts.

Chapter Three: Historical Snapshots

To truly appreciate New Mexico, it is important to understand the key historical events that shaped the destiny and character of the Land of Enchantment. The Spanish Conquest of the Southwest, the Mexican period, the American annexation of these lands, and the native cultural and historical responses to these intrusions have helped to form the unique traditions, history and cultural character of this region. In many respects, the feeling of the Old West has not quite died away, especially in the more rural areas of the state. The frontier may be more subdued now, but if one opens up one's senses to the surroundings, the frontier spirit is still present and alive!

In addition, New Mexico ushered in the Atomic Age for the entire world, with a giant leap from the frontier world into the current age. The Afterward briefly addresses a new frontier: commercial space travel that is currently being ushered in by the foresight of state government leaders and courageous entrepreneurs. This current chapter touches on historical highlights that helped to shape this land and to mold its people.

In this chapter, a brief overview is given of selected key events in New Mexico's history. The topics address the Ancient Peoples of the American Southwest, *Coronado*'s 1540 Expedition, *Pueblo* Revolt of 1680, Spanish *Santa Fe ReConquista* of 1692-93, *Penitentes*, Texan *Santa Fe* Expedition of 1841, Mormon Battalion, Mexican Cession of the Southwest to the U.S., Compromise of 1850, Gadsden Purchase of 1853, *Santa Fe* Trail, American Civil War in New Mexico, the "Long Walk" and Fort Sumner/*Bosque Redondo*, *Victorio* Wars, Buffalo Soldiers in New Mexico, Lincoln County War, Warm Spring *Apache* & *Geronimo* Wars, Rough Riders, Becoming a State, Pancho Villa's Crossing the Border, *Navajo* Code Talkers and the Trinity Atomic Test. This group of topics represents a sampling of the significant historical events in the history of New Mexico.

The Ancient Peoples: *Anasazi,*[1,2,3,4] *Mogollón,*[5] *Hohokam*[6]

Up through the Ice Age, hunters were the primary people to inhabit the land we now call New Mexico. Once the Ice Age ended, the climate in the New Mexico region grew drier and warmer, causing much of the game to disappear towards more hospitable areas, and so the hunters followed them. Once the big game hunters vacated, the region eventually became filled with the people of the Desert Culture. They developed in two stages. The First Stage occurred between 6000 BC and 2000 BC. They hunted small game, fished and gathered edible plant foods. They were hunter-gatherers. The Second Stage occurred between 2000 BC and 500 BC. This stage of the Desert Culture saw the development of agriculture, the building of shelters, and the making of baskets for food storage. They also milled grains. The people began to adopt a more stationary lifestyle and a more sedentary culture. As time passed, three main Desert Cultures developed and flourished in the American Southwest. These were the pre-Columbian *Mogollón*, the *Anasazi* and the *Hohokam* cultures. The *Mogollón* and *Anasazi* cultures developed in the region now identified as New Mexico. As an additional note it is thought that the *Anasazi* were possibly ancestral to the modern *Pueblo* Peoples of New Mexico and the *Mogollón* may have been ancestral to the *Hopi* of Arizona and the *Zuni* of New Mexico. The *Hohokam* were possibly ancestral to the *Pima* Indians of

Arizona.[7] Since the *Hohokam* developed in what is now Arizona it will be mentioned no further here.

The *Mogollón* Culture, named after the mountain region in which the culture developed, were the first of the two great ancient New Mexican cultures to develop advanced ways of living. They learned many of these techniques from the people of Mexico. From the Mexicans, the *Mogollón* Culture learned how to cultivate corn, squash and red beans, and how to make pottery. They became a truly agrarian society by 300 BC. They began to construct permanent homes called pit homes. These homes were half underground, with the bottom half made from the pit that was dug, while the upper half was covered using some natural material. Pit houses were also built for food storage to alleviate suffering during droughts. The houses were usually built closely together to form villages. Religious buildings were also constructed. The *Mogollón* Culture most likely peaked around 1050 AD. Eventually the culture subsided, but it may have lasted until about 1500 AD.

Further north, emanating from the Four Corners[8] region, the *Anasazi* Culture began to take hold starting around 1 AD. The name *Anasazi*, is a *Navajo* word meaning "the ancient ones" or possibly "ancient enemy."[9] There are four periods of development associated with the more slowly developing *Anasazi* Culture.

The first period is called the Basketmaker Culture or the Modified Basketmaker Culture[9] because of their great skill in making baskets to serve their needs, including baskets that are so tightly woven that they were used to carry or store water. They borrowed the use of *atlatl*[10] from the Mexican Aztecs to facilitate hunting. They also bred two different domestic dog breeds. From 500 AD to 700 AD, the *Anasazi* Culture progressed further to develop more permanent houses and settlements. They learned from the southern *Mogollón* Culture how to cultivate corn, squash and beans, and to grind grains using the *metate*[11] and the *mano.*[12] In addition, they learned how to store food, to make pottery and to make other useful items such as sandals, rope, etc. The bow and arrow were also being used as effective hunting tools and weapons. Their villages were built up with pit houses and even included a religious center. This development is still included within the Basketmaker Culture, which transitioned about 700 AD to the next *Anasazi* period.

The second period from 700 AD to 1050 AD is termed the Developmental *Pueblo* Culture. The *Anasazi* people began to build *pueblo*-style homes with small groups of houses having a central pit house that became their *kiva*, or religious gathering place. Only the men were allowed to use the *kiva*. The *Anasazi* of the Developmental *Pueblo* Culture also produced finer pottery and they learned to cultivate cotton and to domesticate the turkey. They developed the "cradle boards" used by so many Native American mothers to carry their infants so that they were free to use their hands to do other work. Some archeologists divide this Developmental Period further into *Pueblo* Period I and II,[13] but the development over this 350-year timeframe is more of a continuum than such a division implies.

The Great *Pueblo* Period lasted from 1050 AD to 1300 AD, and disappeared just two hundred years prior to the arrival of the Europeans. Some archeologists refer to this period instead as the Classic Period.[14] It is considered the third period of this culture. During the Great *Pueblo* Period, dwellers learned to use stone masonry to build multi-story homes and apartment buildings. They also learned to build cliff dwellings. Irrigation systems, reservoirs, dams and ditches were used to control the water supply and to water the crops. Roads began to appear for travel and trade. Their culture became so dominant that it began to spread southward into the American Southwest of today. Fine examples of their magnificent achievements can be found today in the ruins at *Pueblo Bonito* in Chaco Canyon, New Mexico and at *Mesa Verde, Colorado.*

In 1276, a twenty-three year drought brought devastation and abandonment of the *Anasazi* dwellings. These peoples apparently moved south to settle in areas that were already inhabited. These areas were around *Zuni*, the *Rio Grande* River valleys and the mountainous regions of western New Mexico. The resultant crowding caused tensions and a decline in architecture, the arts and crafts.

The fourth and final development phase of the *Anasazi* is called the *Rio Grande* Classic Period that occurred between 1300 AD and 1450 AD. Although it is viewed as a period of general decline, some achievements are noteworthy. This is the period in which the Bandelier Cliff Dwellings and the *Puyé* Cliff Dwellings were developed. The *Rio Grande* Classic sites around *Los Alamos* were developed in this period, as was the *Pecos Pueblo.* Also, large multi-storied dwellings were commonplace.

After this period these sites were abandoned, and the peoples moved into the *Rio Grande* Valley and to the *Acoma-Zuni* areas, where they are primarily located today. These peoples were therefore the ancestors of today's *pueblo* dwellers. When the Spaniards arrived they saw up to 70, 80 or more different *pueblo* villages. Today there are only 19 *pueblos* remaining! Because many villages had multi-storied buildings, the Spaniards were reminded of towns in their native Spain. They called these villages *"pueblos",* meaning village or town.

Chasing Golden Windmills:[15] The *Coronado*[16] Expedition

The initial motivation for *Coronado*'s 1540 Expedition into the American Southwest was to seek riches in the fabled Seven Cities of *Cibola*, also known as the Seven Cities of Gold. The location of this site was reputed to be deep in the desert, many hundreds of miles north of Mexico City. Four shipwrecked survivors of the ill-fated Narvaez Expedition gave reports of a place called *Cibola* with its vaulted wealth. Among the survived adventurers was Álvar Núñez *Cabeza de Vaca* (Cow's Head) and an African slave or Moor named Estéban Dorantes.

The target of these rumors, the *Zuni-Cibola* Complex, lay near *Zuni*, New Mexico. Upon learning of these fabled cities, the Spaniards organized an expedition under the Franciscan Friar Marcos de Niza, with Estéban as his guide. Before long, Estéban was ordered to scout ahead of the friar and his entourage. Hearing confirmation of the fabled cities from another monk that he encountered on his way, Estéban proceeded onto *Cibola*. He reached *Hawikku*, one of the fabled seven cities, located in what is now central western New Mexico. *Zuni* tribesmen here killed Estéban and his companions were forced to flee. Upon returning to Mexico City in New Spain, Friar de Niza claimed that the expedition continued even after Estéban's death. He said that they were close enough to *Cibola* to see the fabled region from afar. He made exaggerated claims about the houses being decorated with turquoise, pearls and precious jewels. Some historians believe that the mica flakes embedded in the clay of the *adobe* buildings may have scintillated in the desert sun, causing the grand illusion from afar.

The gold lust of the Spaniards was further enflamed with these reported findings. A military expedition was organized with Francisco Vásquez de *Coronado* as the commander, taking Friar de Niza as his guide. See Figure 3-1. He departed New Spain on April 22, 1540 with his retinue of 335 Spaniards, 1,500 Mexican natives, some monks and some slaves. When *Coronado* finally reached *Cibola* he found that there were no treasures there and that the tales from de Niza were in fact lies. He found too that he had been misled on another matter. The site was not close to the sea as was previously claimed. To the great disappointment of the expedition, the entire region of *Cibola* merely consisted of six or seven modest *adobe pueblos* or villages, nothing more! Subsequently, *Coronado* occupied the region with military force and set up a camp as a base for future explorations. De Niza was sent back to New Spain in disgrace.

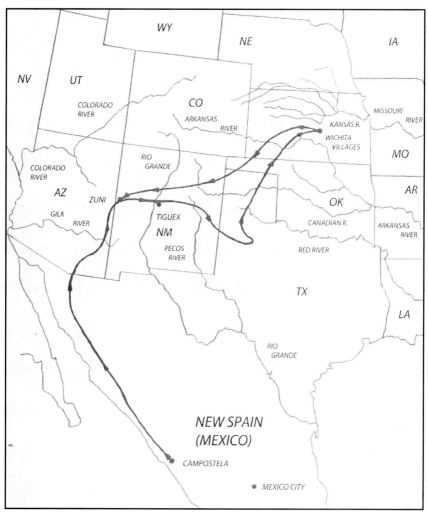

Figure 3-1*: *Coronado*'s Expedition in search of *Cibola* and *Quivira*.

Later, *Coronado* sent out small parties that ultimately learned of and obtained forced entry into several *Hopi* villages. They were the first Europeans to view the Grand Canyon and the *Colorado* River. Another small party found a collection of *Pueblos* along the *Rio Grande* to the east. *Coronado* then decided to set up his winter quarters in one of these small villages. The village was named *Tiguex*, which lay across the river from present-day *Bernalillo*, near Albuquerque, New Mexico. In a short time, conflict erupted between the Spaniards and the natives of the region. This resulted in the brutal *Tiguex* War, which resulted in the destruction of the *Tiguex Pueblo* and the deaths of many natives.

While in this region, *Coronado* heard of another fabled city called *Quivira*, far to the east. So, in the spring of 1541, he led another expedition east in search of *Quivira*. See the map of *Coronado*'s expedition in Figure 3-1. He crossed the width of what is now the state of New Mexico. He traversed the *Llano Estacado* of eastern New Mexico and the Texas Panhandle. From there he moved on to the Great Plains where he saw herds of bison beyond number. The Spaniards were awed by the vastness of the Plains they encountered.

Eventually *Coronado* found a camp of Native Americans that he called *Querechos*. The Spaniards apparently expected the native tribesmen to be impressed or intimidated by their weapons and armor, or their "big dogs" (horses). However, the *Querechos* were unimpressed. They were nomads whom most historians generally agree were probably *Apache*. *Coronado* then left the *Querechos* and proceeded southeast in his continuing search for *Quivira*. Eventually he and his retinue left the Plains and dropped down into canyon country, where he came across a people he called the *Teyas*. Most historians believe that the *Teyas* may have been a *Caddoan* people related to the *Wichitas*. The *Teyas* told *Coronado* that he was headed in the wrong direction. They probably wanted to remove the threat of the Spanish forces by sending them away from their own location. He was told that he should head north instead. After this news, *Coronado* began to lose faith in his mission. He then sent most of his entourage back to New Mexico, while he continued forward with a much smaller reconnaissance group.

After a month's more journeying, he reached a very wide river, which is thought to be the Arkansas River, near Dodge City, Kansas. He did encounter the lands and the people of *Quivira* in what is now central Kansas. However, once again he was diappointed. There was nothing around but mostly-naked natives and straw-thatched villages. There was no wealth of precious metals or stones. The *Quivira*ns were probably ancestors of the *Wichitas*. He decided to return to New Mexico once again. Before doing so he ordered the Indian guide who had misled him concerning the "wealth" of the *Quivira*ns, to be garroted.

Finally, *Coronado* returned to New Mexico but after a short time he returned to New Spain disappointed and disillusioned. His expedition had been a failure. He was forced into bankruptcy, and hundreds of Native Americans had been killed during his failed mission. *Coronado* had chased his golden windmills, only to find they were a delusion. He died on July 21, 1554. Because of *Coronado*'s explorations the Spaniards settled into the northern parts of New Spain, which became the Province of *Nuevo México*.

Coronado's legacy was the exploration of the southwestern U.S. and even parts of the mid-western U.S. His futile efforts to find riches led to increased European knowledge and understanding of the regions he explored. He opened the door to this region that eventually became settled by thousands and then millions of Europeans. And it all started with the legend of the Seven Cities of *Cibola*.

America's First Revolution: *Pueblo* Revolt of 1680[17]

When the Spaniards subdued the *Pueblo* Peoples of the *Rio Grande* after the *Coronado* Expedition, they set up towns, such as *Santa Fe*. They maintained a military presence to crush any uprisings from the natives, and introduced Christianity while they denigrated the native religions. *Pueblo* Peoples were enslaved under the Spanish system of *encomiendas*.[18] The traditional economies suffered and disease spread among the unprotected native populations, decimating their numbers. Religious persecution of the practitioners and symbols of the native beliefs was led by the Franciscans. It was severe and brutal. The most significant positive of the new "world order" was the relative calm and peace that was enforced by the Spanish military intervention against the marauding *Apaches* and *Navajos*. Nonetheless, a deep smoldering resentment against their Spanish masters brewed over time. With the increase in *Apache* and *Navajo* raids and the rise in deaths from disease, the *Pueblo* Peoples lost confidence in the Spanish military and the civil authorities. They also became disillusioned with the new faith and gradually reverted to their traditional beliefs and religious practices.

Spanish persecution renewed at a feverish pace as the missionaries seized every prayer stick, *kachina* doll, mask or religious symbol they could obtain. They forbade native religious dances. In 1675, Governor Juan Francisco Treviño, commanded the arrest and seizure of 47 *Pueblo* religious leaders. These religious leaders were accused of witchcraft. Of the forty-seven leaders arrested, four were sentenced to hang. Of these, three were hanged as ordered. However, to avoid the disgrace and dishonor of being publicly hanged, the fourth leader committed suicide. Public humiliation and punishment faced the remaining 43 medicine men. They were publicly whipped and were then held as prisoners of their Spanish overlords. This incident only fired the already simmering resentment and hostility towards the Spaniards. Subsequently, *Pueblo* leaders organized their people and marched on *Santa Fe* to demand the release of the imprisoned religious leaders. Most of the Spanish soldiers were engaged elsewhere fighting the *Apache*. Without any significant military backing in force, the Governor had no choice but to release the prisoners. Unknown to the Spaniards at the time, they released a *Pueblo* medicine man from the *Ohkay Owingeh*[19] *Pueblo*, who would soon lead a major native *pueblo* revolt against Spanish rule. His name was Popé or Popay, pronounced Po-Pay'.

Upon his release, Popay began to plan an uprising, along with the other *pueblo* leaders. This was a difficult and challenging undertaking as the *pueblo* inhabitants spoke eight different languages and were separated by hundreds of miles. To facilitate communication about the timing of the planned revolt, messengers were sent to each *pueblo* with a knotted cord. The number of knots represented the number of days until the uprising. Each day one cord would be untied, decreasing the number of remaining knots by a count of one. When no knots remained, that signaled the beginning of the planned revolt. The revolt was originally planned for August 11, 1680. However, the Spaniards learned of the plan. So, Popay advanced the revolt timing by one day to August 10. This allowed the revolt to occur before the Spaniards could stop it. *Isleta Pueblo*[20] was the only *pueblo* not to participate in the coming revolt. The *Isleta Pueblo* later served as a welcome haven from the political storm for the Spanish survivors of the revolt.

The *Pueblo* Revolt started on August 10, 1680 with the initial uprisings occurring at the *Taos* and *Picurís Pueblos*, and also at other *Tewa pueblos*. Almost two score Franciscans, and 380 Spaniards were killed, including men, women and children. Surviving settlers fled to the Spanish town of *Santa Fe* or to *Isleta Pueblo*, which was the only *pueblo* not to participate in the revolt. Later, on September 15, 1680, the survivors at *Isleta Pueblo* fled further south to *El Paso del Norte*[21]. Soon after, Popay and his followers approached *Santa Fe*. Being surrounded and besieged by the native rebels, with the water supply shut off, the barricaded Governor Antonio de Otermin called for a general retreat. As a result, three thousand Spanish settlers were compelled to flee the town. They fled the entire province and headed for *El Paso del Norte*, hundreds of miles south of *Santa Fe*.

Neither the *Isleta Pueblo* nor the *Piru* or *Piro Pueblo* of *Socorro* participated in the *Pueblo* Revolt. However, the *Keres*-speaking tribes, the *Zuni* and other tribes south of *Santa Fe* soon joined the widespread *pueblo* rebellion. The apparent unity against the Spaniards was not entirely true, as a number of *pueblos* unwillingly agreed to the rebellion under fear of Popay.[22]

To reduce encumbrances, the fleeing Spanish Colonials left many of their horses behind. The *Puebloans* gathered these abandoned horses. This event helped the further spread of horses to the Plains tribes. The Spaniards had been successfully driven out of the native lands. However, the following years saw only native disunity, drought and increased depredations by the nomadic *Navajo* and *Apache* tribes. Nonetheless, the *Pueblo* natives had thrown off the shackles of Spanish over-lordship. They were free of the overbearing Spaniards…for now.

Although it is not widely recognized, the 1680 *Pueblo* Revolt and fight for freedom was actually the first American Revolution.

Spanish *ReConquista* of *Santa Fe:*[23] 1692-93

The Spanish had been expelled from the city during the *Pueblo* Revolt of 1680. The following twelve years were spent in exile much further south in *El Paso del Norte*, which is now located in *El Ciudad de Juarez,*[24] Mexico. During the Spanish exile, raids by the nomadic tribes increased, a seven-year drought ensued, and political divisions occurred among the tribes as to who should occupy *Santa Fe* and how it should be ruled. In this period, the Spanish were also able to mount a raid against the *Zia Pueblo*. This raid destroyed the *pueblo* and resulted in the killing of 600 inhabitants.

These various events weakened the *pueblos* and made them vulnerable to a Spanish resurgence. Don Diego de Vargas[25] was appointed General by the Spanish King to lead an expedition of the exiled colonists to re-conquer *Santa Fe*. The Spaniards surrounded the city with cannons and threatened the natives in the town with certain death if they refused to surrender. With that threat, De Vargas was able to victoriously re-enter the town on September 14, 1692. He achieved a bloodless re-conquest of *Santa Fe*. Figure 3-2 shows a statue of Don Diego de Vargas, which stands in the small park adjacent to the Basillica Cathedral of St. Francis of Assisi in *Santa Fe*.

However, the re-conquest was still incomplete. In the next few years two other uprisings were attempted but they were brutally suppressed. Unlike the reconquest of *Santa Fe* in 1692, these suppressions were not "bloodless." It took until the early 1700's before complete Spanish control over the *pueblos* and the region was re-obtained.

Although the independence of the *pueblos* was short-lived, they did eventually gain some concessions from the Spaniards. They were left free to practice their own religions and to preserve their culture, without persecution. The *Pueblo* Peoples were also granted more legal rights in the Spanish courts. The Spaniards now allowed Governors to be elected by the *pueblos* to represent the *Pueblo* Peoples in the governing of the colony. Another great benefit resulting from the revolt was the elimination of the despicable *encomienda* system that enslaved so many native peoples. So ended the *Pueblo* Revolt of 1680.

Figure 3-2: Don Diego de Vargas, Reconqueror of *Santa Fe*, 1692 -93. Donna Quastoff, sculptress. (Cathedral Park, *Santa Fe*. Statue dedicated by *Caballeros de Vargas*. With permission of Donna Quasthoff.)

Without these guarantees from the Spaniards after the *Santa Fe ReConquista*,[26] it is doubtful that so much of the color and the beauty of the *pueblo* traditions would have survived to this day! Although their battlefield victory was short-lived, the uprising of 1680 saved the *pueblos* from cultural and religious extinction.

See *Santa Fe* Recovered: *Fiestas de Santa Fe*, in Chapter Ten: Fascinating Things To Do & Places To See. The referenced section discusses the *Fiestas de Santa Fe* (*Santa Fe Fiesta*), the current-day Spanish celebration of the Reconquest of *Santa Fe*.

An Opening of Doors: Liberation From the Spaniards

The Mexican War of Independence lasted 11 years, starting in 1810 and finally ending with Mexico's independence from Spain in 1821. The long-term effects of this war were significant to New Mexico. For one thing, New Mexico transferred from being a territory or province of Spain to that of the new nation of Mexico.

It caused the withdrawal of many Catholic priests from parishes all over New Mexico, giving impetus to the rise of *Los Penitentes* discussed in the next subsection of this chapter. It also brought about increased trade with the *Anglo*-American traders, trappers and merchants coming from the east. The more relaxed trade rules of the Mexican government allowed trade with foreigners, whereas such trade was forbidden under Spanish rule. It had one other indirect effect.

It brought about the development of the *Santa Fe* Trail as a wagon road, because of the increased trade opportunities under the new Mexican government seated in New Mexico. In so doing, it opened up New Mexico to settlement by easterners. *Anglo-Americans* began to settle in the region. Hitherto, foreigners of any kind were treated with suspicion and were either turned back or imprisoned, according to the whims of the Spanish provincial governor. All that changed with Mexican Independence on September 27, 1821. New Mexico became more of an open society.

The Brotherhood – *Los Penitentes*[27]

The Penitents are a lay fraternity of Roman Catholic men active in northern New Mexico and southern *Colorado*. In Spanish, their full name is *Los Hermanos de la Fraternidad Piadosa de Nuestro Padre Jesus Nazareno*, or The Brothers of the Pious Fraternity of Our Father Jesus the Nazarene. More briefly, they have been referred to as *Los Penitentes, Los Hermanos* or the *Penitente* Brotherhood.

The roots of *Los Penitentes* date back a full millennium to the days of the Medieval flagellant monastic orders of Spain and Italy. However, Penitents arose in the nineteenth century in New Mexico as a result of Mexico's liberation from Spain in 1821. Because of financial hardships, the Mexican church leadership decided that the Franciscan, Dominican and Jesuit missionaries had to be withdrawn from the regions within New Mexico. The missionaries were replaced by secular priests, but in much smaller numbers. Many isolated communities found themselves without a resident clergyman. Instead, they could only look forward to an annual visit by a parish priest.

Responding to this serious shortage of resident priests throughout New Mexico, community leaders in secluded areas gathered together to pray, to offer spiritual support and social assistance to members of the community, in the absence of a priest. *Los Penitentes* sought to provide continuity to their worship practices and to their Catholic faith. Their meeting houses were called *moradas* and their sacred songs of worship were called *alabados*. *Los Penitentes* were recognized for their ascetic practices, including self-flagellation with whips of cactus or yucca. Flagellation occurred in private ceremonies during Lent, and in public processions during Holy Week, ending with the reenactment of Christ's Crucifixion on Good Friday. The Penitents believed that forgiveness of their sins came only from spiritual and physical pain and suffering. They also sought forgiveness for man's crucifixion of Jesus Christ on the Cross. Flagellation was also thought to cleanse and prepare the soul for spiritual illumination.[28]

Los Penitentes became disassociated from the Church and their rituals developed independently, outside ecclesiastical control. Over time, they began to develop their own rituals. The formal Roman Catholic Church saw these as outside their system and therefore an ecclesiastical threat. In their worship houses or *moradas*, the worshippers faced one another, rather than the altar or a priest, as in the formal Church. This demonstrated their egalitarian philosophy and practices. Over time, they became leaders of the isolated communities.

Los Penitentes saw a large part of their duty and mission to provide comfort to the poor and suffering, and to solace to the bereaved. In essence they performed what we today would think of as welfare or social services.

There is a reproduction of a *morada* that stands on a hill at *El Rancho de los Golondrinas*. It is a replica of the South *Morada* at *Abiquiu*. The hill is designated symbolically as *El Calvario* (Cavalry). See Figure 3-3, which shows a reconstructed *morada*. The noun *morada* is derived from the Spanish verb, *morar*, meaning "to dwell", as to dwell in a house of worship. A typical *morada* contained three rooms. The main worship area was termed *la capilla,* or "the chapel." Here sacred rites were performed. It is the area housing the altar, the chapel and the *crucificio* (crucifix). It also had religious *bultos* (carved statues of saints) and *banderas* (religious banners) on display behind the altar. Here the emphasis of the religious ceremonies was focused on *La Sagrada Pasión y Muerte del Señor Jesucristo Redentor* (the Sacred Passion

Figure 3-3: A Reconstructed *Morada* at *El Rancho de las Golondrinas.*

and Death of Jesus Christ, the Redeemer).

The second room in the *morada* was called *el comedor*, or the dining room. This area also had ritual objects within it.

The third and final room was named *la enfermeria*, or infirmary (hospital), and it was used for cleansing after the ritual flagellation.

If modern *Penitentes* (Penitents) are asked whether flagellation is still performed, the requestor will receive no answer.

If one gets the chance to visit either *Abiquiu* or *El Rancho de las Golondrinas*, be sure to take a look at the *moradas* in these places. It is extremely interesting and enlightening.

The "Americanization" of the Church in New Mexico in the early 1800's by Bishop (later Archbishop) Lamy[29] and his successor, sought to suppress the brotherhood, and drove it underground. The Church apparently did not want this unorthodox form of worship to thrive and to eventually crowd out the orthodox Church and its teachings.

The practice of self-flagellation, a carryover from the old monastic orders of Medieval Europe did not conform to Lamy's vision of Americanizing the Church in New Mexico. The forced suppression of *Los Penitentes* gradually drove the brotherhood underground giving rise to its identification as a "secret" society. In 1947, reconciliation between the Catholic Church and the Penitents occurred when the Church formally recognized *Los Penitentes*. This brotherhood continues to be active in northern New Mexico and southern *Colorado*.

Got Grit 'n Goin' Southwest - Take the *Santa Fe* Trail[30, 31]

Prior to the era of the "iron horses" or the railroad, frontiersmen, traders and settlers followed the *Santa Fe* Trail. This transportation route extended from Missouri to *Santa Fe*, New Mexico. It was also a vital commercial and military highway in the early west. The route directly crossed through *Comancheria*, the Land of the *Comanches*. The *Comanches* often demanded compensation for the right of way. Many traders found it more profitable to trade with the *Comanches* than with the merchants and settlers in *Santa Fe*. The trail crossed the hunting grounds of numerous tribes such as the *Comanche, Kiowa, Arapaho,* Plains *Apache,* and southern *Cheyenne*. It also crossed the homelands of the *Osage, Kaw* or *Kansa, Jicarilla Apache, Ute* and various *pueblo* tribes, as the trail meandered from Missouri, across Kansas and *Colorado*, to the final destination in *Santa Fe*, New Mexico. See the map in Figure 3-4, showing the path of the *Santa Fe* Trail.

A trader named William Becknell in September 1821 used this trail (Mountain Route) to bring trade to *Santa Fe* from Missouri. He actually followed an old trail used by Indians, and others before him. He was nicknamed the "Father of the *Santa Fe* Trail." Becknell's trading expedition, was the act of a desperate man, as he was bankrupt and facing jail for non-payment of debts. He took to the trail in an attempt to escape his lenders and to perhaps change his fortune. He returned one year later with mules laden with silver and goods from *Santa Fe*. His venture had succeeded and the *Santa Fe* Trail was established as a trade route to the markets of the Southwest. It is no coincidence that Becknell chose September 1821 to proceed with his bold undertaking. This was the same year that Mexico won its independence from Spain, and with it came a more open and liberal policy towards trade with the neighboring Americans. Becknell was at the right place at the right time!

In 1825, Senator Thomas Hart Benton got the U.S. Government to survey and document the trail. In 1833 -1834, three enterprising traders Charles and William Bent, together with Ceran St. Vrain, built Bent's Fort in *Colorado*, a trading post just ahead of the Arkansas River crossing taken by the more northerly Mountain Route of the *Santa Fe* Trail. It eventually crossed the *Raton* Pass into New Mexico. Later, the same trail was used by American troops to attack the Mexicans in *Nuevo México*, leading to the Mexican-American War of 1846 - 1848. Eventually the *Santa Fe* Trail became an economic lifeline supporting the military and the local economies of the American Southwest. In the 1860's, up to 5,000 wagons a year traversed the 800 to 1,000 mile-long trail. Wagons were capable of hauling two to three tons each. These wagons were initially made in Pittsburg, but eventually were constructed in Missouri.

The second trail to *Santa Fe* was opened up later in time. See the discussion of the two routes later in this discussion.

Santa Fe grew as a trade nexus, with goods arriving from Missouri via the trail, traders shipping goods south via the *Camino Real* or *Chihuahua* Trail and other traders loading up stock cattle for the move northwards again. The freight wagons used to haul trade items in the Southwest were usually hauled by either mule or oxen, and were driven by muleskinners and ox drivers. The most popular and most capable muleteers were called *arrieros*.

The advent of the railroads in the 1860's started to reduce the use of the trail. The real impact came in 1878 when the railroad reached the *Raton* Pass, New Mexico, along the Mountain Route of the *Santa Fe* Trail. In 1880, the railroad reached *Santa Fe*, and the use of the overland trail declined sharply. However, in its heyday, the trail helped to open up the west to settlement and to commercial enterprise.

The *Santa Fe* Trail was about 800 to 1,000 miles long and it crossed dry, arid plains, deserts and mountains. It was often subject to violent attack from *Apaches* or *Comanches*. Later, caravan sizes were increased and mules were used to replace the oxen. This was done to discourage these warriors from further raids and depredations. The trail lacked much in the way of food or water access. Weather conditions were not always favorable. Heavy rainstorms and lightning storms were frightening to travelers and to the stock animals they often brought along. The open plains offered practically no protection or shelter from the vagaries of the weather. Rattlesnakes were another risk and danger. Death from rattlesnakes was not uncommon. For those brave enough, or foolish enough, to venture onto the trail late in the year, severe and deadly snowstorms could be encountered. The lack of trees and shelter in some areas allowed the storms and winds to rage relentlessly. If new settlers were foolish enough to embark on the trail too late in the year, snowstorms could be mercilessly cruel and cause death from exposure. Such conditions led to loss of human life and exacted an especially vicious toll on the oxen and mules, which often died from severe exposure. The *Santa Fe* Trail was not for the timid or the weak of body or spirit, but it served as one more pathway to the Southwest, both before and after the Mexican Cession.

The *Santa Fe* Trail took one of two possible paths between Independence, Missouri and *Santa Fe*, New Mexico. As noted earlier the Mountain Route was the earliest route used to reach New Mexico. Regardless of the route, the *Santa Fe* Trail brought thousands of new settlers westward. It started in Independence, Missouri on the Missouri River. Near the beginning, it passed just south of Fort Leavenworth and then proceeded diagonally across the width of Kansas. Midway across, it passed by Fort Larned and then Fort Dodge. At Fort Dodge, the trail split into two separate branches. The more northerly route took the traders or settlers further west, following the north bank of the Arkansas River, until it reached Bent's Fort in *Colorado*. This was called the Mountain Branch. Once at the fort, the trail crossed to the southern bank of the Arkansas River and then proceeded in a southwestern direction towards *Raton* Pass that leads through the mountain border between modern *Colorado* and New Mexico. It then continued almost directly south to Fort Union. From there it turned southwesterly again to *Las Vegas*, and then onto the final destination at *Santa Fe*, New Mexico.

The other branch was called the *Cimarron* Cutoff, the *Cimarron* Crossing or the Middle Crossing. It crossed the Arkansas River just passed Fort Dodge, and then took an almost direct southwesterly tack to Fort Union and then to *Las Vegas*, New Mexico. Soon after it reached *Santa Fe*, New Mexico. In summary, the entire *Cimarron* Route

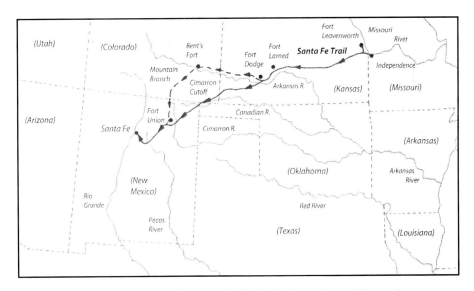

Figure 3-4*: Map of the *Santa Fe* Trail - Independence, Missouri to *Santa Fe*, New Mexico Territory, mid 1800's.

Missouri, into and across Kansas, and after Dodge City and Fort Dodge it separated from the Mountain Route and headed towards the southwest, crossing the western corners of Kansas and Oklahoma, and the southeastern corner of *Colorado*, as it entered the northeastern corner of New Mexico, en route to *Santa Fe*.

So, the two different routes of the *Santa Fe* Trail diverged shortly after reaching Dodge City or Fort Dodge, Kansas, from Missouri. The more northern Mountain Route was also called *Raton* or Bent's Fort Route. It was considered the longer and more difficult of the two possible routes to *Santa Fe*, but it was also seen as the safer route. The more southerly alternate route was called the *Cimarron* Route. Some called this pathway the Desert Route. It passed across the *Cimarron* Desert. The easternmost part of the *Cimarron* Route was without reliable water sources, making this route more dangerous to travel, even though it was more direct and shorter than the Mountain Route. This dry segment was termed *La Jornada*, the Journey. It was located between the Arkansas River and the *Cimarron* River, roughly between Fort Dodge, Kansas and the area just south of Ulysses, Kansas. This parched region was also called the Waterscape. Once the *Cimarron* River was reached, to the relief of many travelers, the river was followed through the rest of Kansas.

After reaching Watrous, New Mexico, the two routes converged again and continued through *Las Vegas* and *Glorieta* to *Santa Fe*. Fort Union was built just north of *Las Vegas*, New Mexico, to protect both routes of the *Santa Fe* Trail and their travelers. It was actually built on the path of the Mountain Route. The juncture point of the two routes lay a few miles south of the fort position, close enough for any required military intervention. The journey from Missouri to *Santa Fe* often took about a month to complete.

Segments of the *Santa Fe* Trail and their wagon trail ruts can still be seen today. See the Old *Santa Fe* Trail section in Chapter Thirteen. Wagon ruts can also be seen at the Fort Union National Monument, just north of *Las Vegas*. In addition, there is a small stone monument that marks the end of the *Santa Fe* Trail. It is located on the *Santa Fe Plaza*, unnoticed by most passersby. It stands on the edge of the *Plaza* on East *San Francisco* Street, near the corner with Old *Santa Fe* Trail. The end of the *Santa Fe* Trail is marked at that spot. It was erected in 1910, and it indicates the trail was used between 1822 and 1879. See Figure 3-5.

Figure 3-5: End of the *Santa Fe* Trail Monument, at the *Santa Fe Plaza*. (Erected in 1910 by the Daughters of the American Revolution and the Territory of New Mexico.)

Ambitious Endeavor: Texan *Santa Fe* Expedition[32, 33]

After 1836, the newly formed Republic of Texas[34] claimed the territory equal to the eastern half of the modern state of New Mexico. Expecting that New Mexicans would welcome a merger with the Republic, Texas launched a commercial and military expedition to secure the claimed lands in 1841. Texas, of course, was also interested in gaining control over the lucrative *Santa Fe* trade route that crossed through the northeastern part of the disputed territory, as well as the *Santa Fe* area itself. Of course, the region was still a province of Mexico at that time, which led to subsequent complications and the eventual failure of the ambitious enterprise.

The idea of the venture was hatched by the President of the Texas Republic, Mirabeau B. Lamar, without the consent of the Republic's Congress. The expedition started out on June 19, 1841 and arrived in New Mexico in mid-September of the same year. The effort was a disaster from the beginning. It included 21 ox-drawn wagons loaded with $200,000 in trade goods and the merchants to trade them. There was also a military escort of about 320 soldiers with a company of artillery. The military escort was meant to ease the safety concerns of the accompanying merchants for their personal well-being and for the security of their trade goods.

Disorganization and poor preparation hounded the entourage from the start. They suffered Indian attacks, and a lack of sufficient food and water for their summer crossing. They lost their Mexican guide and then struggled to find their way towards *Santa Fe*. Upon finally arriving at *Santa Fe*, they expected to receive a warm welcome. Instead, a detachment of about 1,500 men from the Mexican Army met them. It was agreed between the two parties that the Texans would be escorted out of Mexican territory, and conducted safely to the border. Realizing that they were vastly outnumbered and exhausted from their journey, the Texans agreed to the terms. The Mexicans gave the Texans some supplies.

However, the following day, the Mexican Army returned with the Mexican Governor, Manuel Armijo. The Texans were bound and mistreated. Then the Mexican leader demanded that the Texans be killed, but he put the matter to a vote by his officers. That very night, the Mexicans held a council to discuss the issue. In the end, the Military Council voted to spare the lives of the Texans – by a single vote. The Texans were then marched 2,000 miles to Mexico City, where they were held for a year until American diplomats were able to secure their release. The holding of the Texans for a year only increased tensions between Mexico and the United States, up until the Mexican-American War broke out in 1846.

Long Trekkers: The Mormon Battalion[35, 36]

Few may know about the Mormon Battalion. It was the only religion-based battalion ever in the U.S. military. They served between July 1846 and July 1847, at the beginning of the Mexican-American War. It was an all-volunteer unit of about 550 Church of Latter Day Saints (Mormon) men with some accompanying (33) women and (51) children. The men of the Mormon Battalion were mustered into service with the U.S. Army of the West, under the command of General Kearny on July 16, 1846. Kearny also commanded other non-Mormon volunteer units from Missouri and New York, as well as regular artillery and infantry battalions, and Kearny's own 1st U.S. Dragoons.

The Mormon's had struck a deal with the U.S. Government. To escape further persecution for their beliefs, they intended to migrate across the Rocky Mountains to the Salt Lake Valley, to settle there. They sought federal assistance and aid for their migration. Just at this same time, war broke out between the U.S. and Mexico. Seeing the possibility of a win-win deal they approached President James K. Polk. The deal struck provided federal assistance on condition that the Mormons join the Army on a one-year enlistment, and that they march to protect the lands of the Southwest and southern California from Mexican forces. Brigham Young saw this as the financial help he needed, while it could also be a huge public relations win. As an added benefit, their march across the Southwest would take them close to their proposed new homeland in Utah. Many Mormons had escaped the persecution in Nauvoo, Illinois when they fled the city, crossed the Mississippi, and settled with the *Pottowatomi* Indians along the banks of the Missouri, near present-day Omaha, Nebraska.

So you ask, what has any of this got to do with New Mexico? The Mormon Battalion helped to protect the Southwest from the Mexican Army. In addition, the march to *San Diego*, California occurred in two stages. The first stage took the Mormon Battalion from Nebraska and Council Bluffs, Iowa to *Santa Fe*, New Mexico via the *Santa Fe* Trail. They marched down the Missouri and entered the northeastern corner of Kansas, made a rough diagonal across the state, and entered New Mexico's northeastern corner using the *Cimarron* Cutoff of the *Santa Fe* Trail as they proceeded to *Santa Fe*. Once they reached *Santa Fe*, command of the Mormon Battalion was given to Lt. Colonel

George Cooke. There, most of the women and children and the sick men were sent to *Pueblo, Colorado.*

The second stage started at *Santa Fe,* New Mexico. Within four months Cooke earned the respect of the men in his volunteer battalion, as he led them an additional 1,100 miles across some of the most defying and challenging terrain in North America, through the American Southwest to *San Diego,* California. Cooke's orders were not only to complete this march but also to build a wagon road along the way. This road later served to transport thousand of new settlers to the Southwest and to California.

The route[37] taken to *San Diego* required the troops to proceed south along the *Rio Grande* to the *Pima* villages along the *Gila* River, where they picked up the *Gila* Trail to the *Colorado* River. They then forded the *Colorado* River and proceeded along the southern edge of the Imperial Sand Dunes and across the Imperial Valley. They followed the valley to the *Vallecito* Wash (Little Valley Wash) and then onto the notorious Box Canyon. The walls of the wash were so narrow that wagons could not cross. The Battalion men had to hewe the sidewalls to allow the wagons to pass. Eventually they made it through into California and onto *San Diego.*

Figure 3-6: Mormon Battalion Monument near *Santa Fe,* New Mexico. (The original monument was erected in 1940 by the Committee for the Erection of the Mormon Battalion Monument in New Mexico and the Utah Pioneer Trails and Landmarks Association.)

There was one rather humorous incident along the way, called the Battle of the Bulls.[38] In this "battle", which occurred on December 11, 1846, a number of Battalion hunters fired on some wild cattle that had stampeded towards some of the soldiers in the rear of the Battalion. This firing only caused more chaos, and eventually a dozen or so bulls were killed, three men were wounded and a couple of mules were gored to death by the errant cattle.

Later that same month, the Battalion captured and secured Tucson, Arizona from a small Mexican detachment, without a single shot being fired. The Mormon

Battalion never engaged in any battle confrontation with enemy forces but their mission helped to open up the American Southwest to new settlers. From their start in Iowa, the total march to *San Diego* was 1,900 miles - no small accomplishment!! It is thought that the longest segment of the Mormon Battalion march through the various southwestern states occurred across the state of New Mexico.

Today, there are numerous monuments to the Mormon Battalion throughout the American Southwest. In New Mexico, there is a pyramid stone monument dedicated to the honor of those brave men of the Battalion and their families. See the photo in Figure 3-6. It is located along Interstate 25, between *Santa Fe* and Albuquerque. Take Exit 257 and proceed about one and a half miles down the frontage road that parallels the southbound side of I-25. The memorial stands on the right side of the frontage road. The monument contains a metal plaque showing the route of their long march. It also has a text summary of their march and their contribution to the westward expansion of the U.S. The monument is a stone pyramid with the plaque on one face, and with an encircled six-pointed star at the apex of the pyramid. It stands out distinctively against the open barren fields surrounding it and against the open New Mexico sky.

Cession of the Southwest to the U.S.: Mexican-American War[39, 40]

(This discussion is not meant as an exhaustive or complete discussion of the Mexican-American War. The goal is not to describe the entire campaign, or its effects on neighboring states, except as that might have affected New Mexico. Instead, this summary will emphasize the role of New Mexico in the Mexican-American War, and the benefits derived to New Mexico after the war.)

It is interesting to note a name given to this war, by Mexico. It sheds light on their view of the war. In Mexico it is often called *La Intervención Norteamericana* or the North American Intervention. To Mexico and Mexicans it was seen as U.S. intervention in Mexican national matters regarding a rebellious region, namely Texas. Mexico never recognized the breakaway of Texas, or its establishment of the Republic of Texas in 1836. The U.S. annexation of Texas in 1845 was seen in this light, as an aggressive land grab of Mexican lands by the United .States.

The war between Mexico and the U.S. occurred between 1846 and 1848. The major event that ignited the conflict was the 1845 annexation of the Republic of Texas by the U.S. Although the Texans had declared their independence in 1836, Mexico turned a blind eye to the event, but swore that formal annexation of these northern territories of Mexico by the United States would be viewed by Mexico as an act of war. President Polk had ambitions to extend the U.S. landmass towards the Pacific Ocean. The annexation helped to fulfill his purpose, even at the risk of war.

At that time New Mexico was still Mexican territory. However, after 1836 the Republic of Texas claimed the eastern part of what is today the state of New Mexico. The Texans claimed the *Rio Grande* as the western boundary of the Republic of Texas. Texas tried to enforce their territorial claims in the failed Texan *Santa Fe* Expedition of 1841. After the Republic of Texas was formally annexed to the U.S. as the 28th state in 1845, the disputed region was once again claimed as part of the newly formed state of Texas. With the Compromise of 1850, the disputed region eventually became the eastern part of a new U.S. territory: the New Mexico Territory.

President Polk ordered General Taylor into the region between the *Nueces*[41] River and the *Rio Grande*, known as the *Nueces* Strip, located between eastern New Mexico and western Texas. A U.S. fort was built in this area on the banks of the *Rio Grande*. Mexican forces encountered and killed about 16 of about 70 U.S. soldiers on a patrol in this area. It became known as the Thornton Affair, after the U.S. commander Captain Thornton. This became a pretext for the U.S. to be the first to declare war on May 13, 1846. So began the Mexican-American War.

The subsequent events of the war, including the invasion of Mexico and the capture and surrender of Mexico City, can be found detailed in many fine history books.[42]

The outcome of the war was very consequential for New Mexico and for the entire Southwest. With the war concluded, all future conflict between Texas and Mexico ended. Furthermore, under the ensuing 1848 Treaty of Guadalupe-*Hidalgo*, Mexico agreed to cede the territories of *Alta California*, *Nevada*, Utah, Arizona and New Mexico,[43] a good part of *Colorado*, and the southwestern corner of Wyoming, to the United States. In return the United States paid Mexico a sum of $15 million that was actually credited against prior debts owed the U.S. by Mexico. Please refer to the map shown in Figure 3-7, showing the lands ceded by Mexico to the U.S. by the Guadalupe-*Hidalgo* Treaty of 1848.

Figure 3-7*: Western U.S. following the Treaty of Guadalupe-*Hidalgo* (1848).

Let's Deal! – The Compromise of 1850[44]

The famous Compromise of 1850 was very beneficial to New Mexico, even though the state was part of the New Mexico Territory at the time. Further, the New

Mexico Territory included what is now the state of Arizona. The lands ceded by Mexico following the Mexican-American War included the New Mexican lands west of the *Rio Grande*. The lands east of this great river had been claimed by Texas since Texan Independence in 1836. Figure 3-7 shows the U.S. lands after 1848 but just prior to the Compromise of 1850.

The Compromise of 1850 released those eastern New Mexican lands from Texan claims and granted them to the newly formed New Mexico Territory, which as a result extended the territorial lands from the current western border of Texas to the eastern border of California. Figure 3-8 shows the map of the Southwest following the Compromise of 1850. Later, in the early twentieth century, the territory would be split again to form the current states of New Mexico and Arizona.

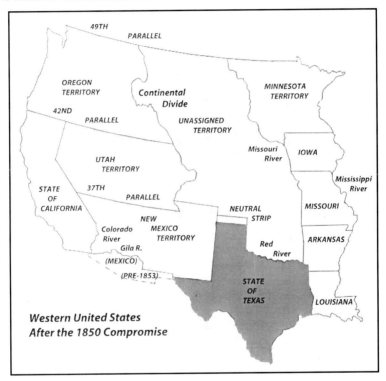

Figure 3-8*: Western U.S. following the Compromise of 1850.

This great Congressional action came about as a solution to the slavery issue as it applied to new states joining the United States of America. It was an attempt to maintain balance in the distribution of slave and non-slave states within the Union. Henry Clay, the famous Whig legislator, drafted the Compromise, but it was pushed forward with the help of Democrat Stephen Douglas. The Compromise helped to temporarily postpone a civil war and to reduce sectional tensions.

The crucial compromise action by the Congress actually consisted of five separate bills that were passed in September 1850. Conflict and tension arose when the disposition of the new lands ceded by Mexico were being considered by Congress.

California applied for statehood shortly after the Gold Rush. It wanted to be a free state. Texas claimed the lands in New Mexico east of the *Rio Grande*. The South wanted the southern part of California as slave territory. Mormon pioneers claimed Utah, then called Deseret, and wanted admission as a state. New Mexico rejected Texan claims and applied to become a state of its own. In 1850, Texas invaded *El Paso* and took possession of the town. Finally, after several years of wrangling, a compromise was worked out to defuse these issues and to create some balance in the various conflicting claims.

In the end, Texas relinquished its New Mexican claim in return for debt relief ($10 Million to repay Mexico) and for keeping the Texas Panhandle. The federal government assumed the Texas debt. *El Paso* was maintained in Texan hands. California was admitted as a free state. The Utah and New Mexico Territories were denied statehood at that time and they remained territories. However, as a concession to the South, these two territories would vote on whether to allow slavery or not. These regions were populated mostly by non-Southerners and the lands were unsuited to plantation agriculture, so the prospect of them voting to become "slave" states was slim at best. The South also got the unpopular Fugitive Act that forced non-slave states to return runaway slaves to their former masters. Further, the region of Washington DC that rejoined Virginia was allowed to maintain slavery, whereas the part of Washington DC that did not rejoin Virginia maintained slavery but banned the slave trade.

All in all, there was something for everybody in this deal. Like any compromise there was also much to dislike about the solution. However, New Mexico was perhaps the biggest winner, since the deal terminated all future claims by Texas on the lands east of the *Rio Grande*. It essentially doubled the size of the current state of New Mexico!! Only three transactions needed to be completed to obtain the state's current borders: the Gadsden Purchase of 1853, the granting of the northeastern strip of the territory to *Colorado* in 1861, and the splitting up of the New Mexico Territory into the current states of Arizona and New Mexico in early 1912. Without the Compromise of 1850, the eastern half of the current state could very well have remained part of the state of Texas!

"Boot Heel" of New Mexico - Gadsden Purchase of 1853[45, 46]

As described earlier in this chapter, the Mexican-American War ended in 1848, and the subsequent Treaty of Guadalupe-*Hidalgo* ceded large areas of land in the southwest to the United States. These areas included all of the territory corresponding to the current states of California, *Nevada*, and Utah, as well as most of the northern and central part of the current state of Arizona, and the western parts of the current states of New Mexico and *Colorado*. In addition, the southwestern corner of Wyoming was ceded by the terms of the treaty. The Louisiana Purchase and the Texas Annexation of 1845 established the eastern parts of the current states of *Colorado* and New Mexico as part of Texas. (In 1845, the Republic of Texas was voluntarily annexed to the United States as the 28th state. At that time the new state of Texas claimed the region east of the Rio Grande. This claim was denied in the Compromise of 1850.)

However, there was a stretch of land along the U.S. border with Mexico that was sought after, by the U.S. This was the region that covers the southernmost areas of modern day Arizona and the "boot heel" of southwestern New Mexico. See Figure 3-9.

These areas included the present day cities of Tucson, *Sierra Vista* and Yuma, Arizona and the southern part of *Hidalgo* County in New Mexico. In the mid 1800's the railroad was expanding into the newly acquired areas of the U.S. Southern entrepreneurs wanted to see a railroad connecting the southern states with the Pacific Ocean. A route through the southern regions of Arizona and New Mexico ceded as a result of the Mexican-American War was much too rugged and mountainous to be practical. An alternate route running somewhat further south, into what was then Mexican land was much flatter and much more suitable for building an east-west southern railroad. This became the motivation for the subsequent Gadsden Purchase of 1853, in which the desired region was purchased from Mexico for the sum of $10 million. This amount purchased about 300 million acres for about 33 cents per acre!!

The U.S. Ambassador to Mexico at the time, who facilitated this treaty, was James Gadsden. In Mexico, this purchase is called *La Venta*[47] *de la Mesilla*, the Sale of *Mesilla*. This purchase occurred during the administration of President Franklin Pierce, with the strong influence and support of Jefferson Davis, the Secretary of State, and later President of the Confederate States. The lands purchased included the territory south of the *Gila* River and west of the *Rio Grande*.

What is less well known is that James Gadsden[48] was elected President of the South Carolina Railroad Company in 1839. He had a vision in which all the southern railroads would join together into a single integrated rail system that would extend all the way west to the lucrative ports of the California coast. Such a rail system would allow the South to become economically independent of the industrial North. Railroad engineers subsequently advised him that the best route lay south of the current U.S. border. This was the driving force behind Gadsden's effort to secure the lands of the Gadsden Purchase from our southern neighbor, Mexico.

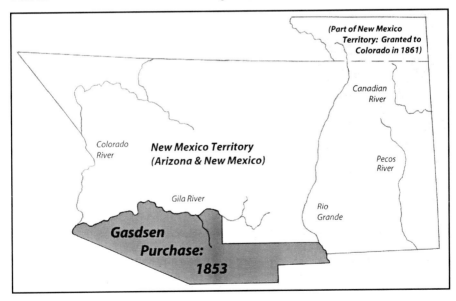

Figure 3-9*: Gadsden Purchase of 1853 added to New Mexico Territory.

In 1854, the people of Arizona requested that the region be made a separate territory. The suggested name for the proposed U.S. Territory was Gadsonia,[49] in honor of James Gadsden.

The Gadsden Purchase proved to be the last major territorial expansion in the contiguous U.S. Figure 3-9 shows the territory acquired by the U.S. via the Gadsden Purchase of 1853. Without the Gadsden Purchase of 1853, the outline of the southern border of New Mexico would be absent the well known "boot heel." At the time of the Gadsden Purchase the New Mexico Territory still encompassed the northeastern lands that eventually became part of southern *Colorado*, in 1861.

Civil War in New Mexico: Prelude to *Glorieta*[50, 51]

The New Mexico Territory of the United States comprised the current states of New Mexico and Arizona. Texas had always cast lustful eyes on the New Mexican territory east of the *Rio Grande*. They had claimed that region since the establishment of the Republic of Texas in 1836. They sought to enforce their claims with the failed Texan *Santa Fe* Expedition of 1841. Their desires certainly did not dissipate after the Mexican-American War and the cession of much of the current American Southwest to the United States in 1848. When the American Civil War broke out in 1861, yet another opportunity presented itself to the Texans and to the Confederacy itself.

Prior to this bloody war and at its very beginning, settlers in the southern part of the New Mexico Territory, in the areas surrounding *Mesilla* (later part of New Mexico state) and Tucson (later part of Arizona state), were feeling that the territorial government in *Santa Fe* was too far removed to adequately consider their needs or concerns. This situation worsened, and the sense of abandonment only increased as the war drew Union troops away from the territory. Secession conventions were held in the disaffected areas. In 1861, *Mesilla* and Tucson made a decisive vote to secede from the Union territorial government and to join the Confederacy. Subsequently, they formed militia companies to defend themselves. In July 1861, Lt. Colonel John Baylor, commander of a battalion of Texas mounted rifles, invaded the southern half of the New Mexico Territory. He defeated Union troops at the Battle of *Mesilla*. He then declared the territorial region south of the 34th parallel as the Confederate Territory of Arizona. See Figure 3-10.

In the meantime, as they viewed the map the Confederates saw new opportunities. *Colorado* was in the midst of a gold rush or boom. California and its Pacific ports lay across the western border of the newly declared Confederate Territory of Arizona. The mining riches of *Nevada* lay to the north and were ripe for the taking. Territorial ambitions grew as the Confederates also considered the purchase or seizure of the northern Mexican states of *Sonora* (meaning "loud") *Chihuahua* and even *Baja California*.[52]

Not only would capturing these assets support the Confederate expansion, increase trade and provide wealth to finance the war, it would deny and weaken the Union in the same measure. To achieve these goals, General Henry Hopkins Sibley offered his ambitious plan to the Confederate President Jefferson Davis who quickly approved the scheme. The initial thrust of the plan was to invade the Union-held New Mexico Territory through *El Paso* and to then proceed north up the *Rio Grande*, securing the eastern portion of the current State of New Mexico. Following the subjugation of New Mexico, he would proceed north along the eastern side of the Rocky Mountains to attack and seize *Colorado,* and its gold riches. He would then proceed to subdue Fort Laramie, Wyoming, the strong western military outpost along the Oregon Trail. Accomplishing these goals, he would then turn west towards *Nevada* and California.

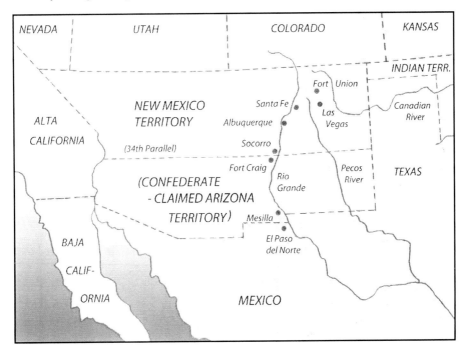

Figure 3-10*: The (Failed) Confederate Territory of Arizona.

In February 1862, Sibley acted upon his plan. His immediate goal was to invade New Mexico near *El Paso* and Fort Bliss, proceed up the west bank of the *Rio Grande* towards the territorial capital at *Santa Fe,* and then head northeasterly towards the storehouses at Fort Union,[53] New Mexico. Figure 3-11 shows the actual path of the Sibley Expedition. However, Sibley knew that he could not leave sizable Union forces in his rear. He knew he had to somehow deal with the 3,800 man Union force stationed at Fort Craig,[54] just south of today's *San Antonio,* New Mexico. Sibley tried to lure the Union force out into the open for a pitched battle. An initial surge of Union troops from the fort ended in a hasty Union retreat.

Sibley then ordered his Confederate troops 6 miles further north to *Valverde*[55] Ford, hoping to outflank his Union adversaries. Canby's forces attacked the Confederates at *Valverde,* but they were driven back in retreat towards Fort Craig. Here, in the relative safety of the fort, Canby refused to surrender. The famous Kit Carson fought with distinction, as a Lieutenant Colonel, at the Battle of *Valverde.* Sibley's problem was his limited three days of rations and supplies for his forces. This disabled him from continuing his siege at Fort Craig or from retreating back to *Mesilla.* Considering these restraints, he decided to proceed towards *Santa Fe,* in an attempt to sever Canby's communication and supply lines, and to hopefully capture much needed supplies for his forces in *Santa Fe*. Because of Sibley's loss of the horses, the weakened state of the surviving horses and the need to transport the wounded, Sibley's column proceeded north much more slowly than expected. Meanwhile, Canby disbanded many of his forces and sent them north to perform *guerrilla* warfare against Sibley's forces. He hoped to trap the Confederates between his own forces and those at Fort Union.

The Confederate forces eventually reached Albuquerque on March 2, 1862, taking the town without a fight. Sibley then took *Santa Fe* on March 13, 1862.

The Union troops had evacuated the two towns and had gone onto Fort Union

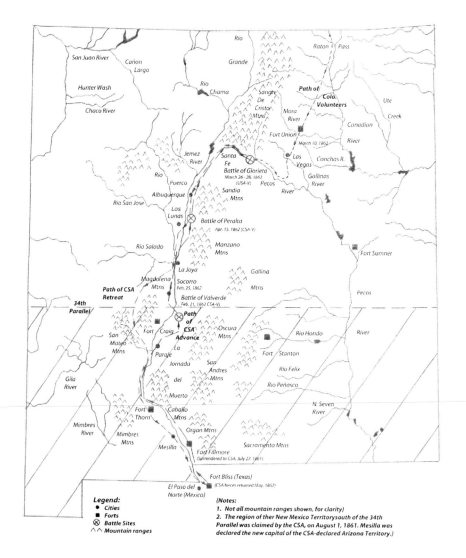

Figure 3-11*: American Civil War in New Mexico Territory, 1862.

in northern New Mexico.

The delay in the Confederate march north allowed the Union forces to remove the targeted supplies from the two towns and to retreat to stronger quarters. Just as significant and fateful for the Confederate enterprise, Union reinforcements in the form of *Colorado* volunteers, also known as "Pike's Peakers", had managed to reach Fort Union. Here the *Colorado* Volunteers met up with the New Mexico Volunteers and regular troops of the U.S. Army. A mix up in orders and leadership between the two Union commanders, General Canby at Fort Craig and Colonel Slough at Fort Union, resulted in a decision to advance the 1,342 men from Fort Union towards *Santa Fe.* In so doing, the weary Confederate forces unknowingly were on a collision path with fresh Union forces from the east. They met at *Glorieta*, New Mexico.

Even Best Laid Plans: *Glorieta Pass,* [56-59] The Gettysburg of the West

General Selby knew that he had to reach and take Fort Union, and to obtain their supplies in order to attain his larger goal of securing *Colorado* for the Confederacy. Colonel Slough of the Union forces also knew that Sibley and his forces had to be stopped before reaching Fort Union. A large contingent of the 1st *Colorado* Volunteers, some of the New Mexico Volunteers and several companies of regular troops now comprised the 1,500 man Union force approaching Sibley. The Confederate forces reached the *Cañoncita*[60] area and camped at Johnson's Ranch in *Apache* Canyon, near *Glorieta* Pass.

Meanwhile, Chivington's[61] advance party of Coloradans arrived at Kozlowski's Ranch on March 25, 1862. Here they learned of the nearby presence of Sibley's forces. Next morning, March 26, Chivington encountered a Confederate scouting party under Major Charles Pyron.

A heated battle took place that drove the Confederates back to Johnson's Ranch. Chivington took light losses (5 killed) while the Confederates took much heavier losses (about 50 killed and 70 captured). Chivington did not press his attack, as he feared much greater enemy forces would be encamped at the ranch. So, he withdrew. The next day saw no action, but the Confederates were busy burying their dead. So passed March 27, 1862. The final fateful day of this clash between these two opposing forces occurred on March 28, 1862.

In spite of the March 26 setback, Sibley's forces made a serious attempt to break through in the direction of Fort Union. They proceeded eastward towards *Glorieta* with their 1,300 man retinue. Marching again to oppose them was the Union Army. Chivington took one third of the Union troops with him in an attempt to outflank the enemy. He took a trail up the side of the *Glorieta Mesa.*[62] He hoped to attack the Confederates in the rear. In the meantime, the Confederate forces advanced down the valley below towards the main Union forces. Although Chivington caught sight of the Confederate advance from above, and he sent back word to warn the Union troops, the bloody engagement still took place. The Union command expected Chivington to break through the enemy rear at any moment. This, of course, never happened. The thick brush on top of the *mesa* caused Chivington to completely bypass the Confederate rear. However, they found instead the lightly protected Johnson's Ranch and the entire Confederate supply train of food, clothing and ammunition. After a short skirmish, the supply train was overtaken and burned. Nearly 80 filled wagons were destroyed and hundreds of horses and mules were lost to the Texans. Texan hopes of successfully reaching the gold fields of *Colorado* were now completely destroyed, regardless of the outcome of the battle underway up the valley at *Glorieta* Pass. The Union forces were soundly defeated at *Glorieta*, and they were forced to retreat back to Koslowski's Ranch. Unknown to the Texans, they had won the battle but they had lost the war!

With this fateful setback, Sibley saw no choice but to abandoned his *Colorado* plans. His troops were outnumbered and now they had very limited supplies and ammunition, He saw retreat as his only option. So, he retreated with his forces towards Albuquerque. After a few skirmishes, he left the town on April 12, 1862 to start his retreat back to Texas. Canby met Sibley's forces at Peralta, where a skirmish ensued. A sandstorm allowed the Confederate forces to escape and to continue southward. They continued their retreat through *Mesilla* and eventually on to Texas. Some small forces were left behind at Fort Thorn, but they were insufficient to effectively counter any Union troops, and these troops too retreated in early July. The Texan force returned to Texas, beaten, decimated and exhausted, carrying their wounded.

The Battle of *Glorieta* Pass is often referred to as the "Gettysburg of the West". This is a rather grandiose assertion. The magnitude of the two battles is totally incomparable, as are the losses in men killed and wounded. The two battles did each endure for a three-day period, but the intensity at *Glorieta* pales compared with the onslaught and the slaughter at Gettysburg. However, the appellation is most appropriate in one important sense. The Battle of *Glorieta* Pass stopped any further expansion into the west by the Confederacy, just as Gettysburg was the high point of the Confederate armed effort in the east. In both cases, the Confederacy recoiled and drew inwardly, like a wounded animal.

The Confederacy had lost their ambitious attempt to capture New Mexico, Arizona, *Nevada, Colorado* and even California. They had lost their chance at turning the tide in their favor in the American Civil War, and in reshaping the future destiny of the American Southwest. Destiny and fortune changed forever in the Battle of *Glorieta* Pass, far off in the New Mexico Territory.

Failed Policy – The "Long Walk" and Ft Sumner/*Bosque Redondo*[63 - 66]

The historic Fort Sumner was named after the New Mexico Military Governor Edwin Vose Sumner. Congress authorized the establishment of the fort on October 31, 1862. General James H. Carlton justified the need for the fort as necessary to stop reputed depredations of settlers in the *Pecos* River Valley by *Mescalero, Kiowa* and *Comanche* bands. The nearby 40 square mile *Bosque Redondo* was set up next to the fort as an encampment area, to contain up to 9,000 *Navajo* and *Mescalero Apache* natives.

The forced march of thousands of *Navajo* from their homelands in Arizona and western New Mexico to the *Bosque* was such a hardship to the old, the infirmed and the very young, that the memory is ingrained in the *Navajo* tribal consciousness. In January 1864, Kit Carson and the U.S. Army, rounded them up, after the successful Canyon de Chelly Campaign against the *Navajo*. Following this success, Carson left exhausted to return to his home. During the next couple of winter months, the subdued *Navajo* were forced by the U.S. Army to walk from their homeland, between 300 and 450 miles east, across the width of New Mexico to the *Bosque Redondo* encampment at Fort Sumner, in the *Pecos* River Valley.

The *Navajo* had their own name for *Bosque Redondo*. They called this place *H'wééldi*, meaning "Place of Suffering." This long forced march at gunpoint, of men, women and children, elderly and young, with the few possessions they could carry, was seared into the tribal memory as the "Long Walk." The trek took about 18 days. It resulted in about 200 *Navajo* deaths. The stated purpose for their internment at Fort Sumner was to re-educate these nomadic tribes in modern farming techniques, and to eventually allow them to become self-sufficient, so they could abandon their raiding lifestyles.

The *Navajo* were filled with foreboding. They had long been warned against crossing the three rivers.[67] It was a sort of taboo. In their infamous "Long Walk" the *Navajo* had to cross three major rivers: *Rio Puerco*, *Rio Grande* and the *Pecos* River. As it turned out their forebodings became realized in the misery experienced during the forced march and in their subsequent occupation of *Bosque Redondo*! The *Navajo* were also uneasy about leaving the Four Sacred Mountains of the *Navajo* homelands.

The U.S. authorities apparently lacked the foresight to realize that placing two tribes who were mutual enemies within the same perimeter might be a formula for disaster! Instead, they forced about 8,500 *Navajo* and about 500 *Mescalero Apache*, sworn enemies, to settle together at *Bosque Redondo*. The result seemed obvious and perfectly predictable: failure!!

Once settled, the tribal peoples faced numerous challenges to survival. In 1865 and 1866, corn production was adequate, but in 1867 corn production was a complete failure. These attempts at farming failed, *Comanche* raids ensued and many suffered in this grand failed experiment. The woods were too small to provide ample shelter or firewood. It soon became apparent that the whole *Bosque* scheme was a disaster. Not surprisingly, the two tribes disagreed and fought over most things. The land offered little water and there was insufficient firewood for the large populations forced to resettle there.

The land could not support the inhabitants with food, warmth or water. Soon disease too began to spread. The alkaline water from the nearby *Pecos* River caused many to develop intestinal problems. There was great suffering. Many of the imprisoned natives died of disease and starvation. The *Mescalero Apache* soon took it upon themselves to leave the hellhole. The *Navajo* stayed somewhat longer but eventually they were released back to their homelands in June 1868. A portion of their former homeland had been turned into a reservation for the newly recognized *Navajo* Nation. They trekked back to the *Navajo* homeland in a line that was ten miles long.

The U.S. policy towards the *Mescalero Apache* and the *Navajo* was an abject failure. It was misguided, misdirected and harsh. It is perhaps a sad irony that the hardship and suffering of these two native peoples at *Bosque Redondo*, created the impetus for the U.S. to set up two large reservations for the survival of these peoples. The *Mescalero Apache* Reservation was set up around the *Sierra Blanca* near *Ruidoso*, New Mexico. The *Navajo* Nation was also formally recognized. A large tract of the *Navajo* original homelands was set aside as a *Navajo* Reservation. These reservations saved their respective peoples from extinction. Approximately one third of the *Navajo* Nation Reservation is located within New Mexico!

After Fort Sumner was abandoned in 1869, a rancher and cattle baron named

Lucien Maxwell purchased the site. Upon purchase of the property, Maxwell converted one of the officers' quarters into a twenty-room house. When Lucien died in 1875, the property passed to his son, Peter Maxwell. Referred to as the Maxwell House, Sheriff Pat Garrett shot Billy the Kid dead in this house on July 14, 1881. In later years, flooding of the nearby *Pecos* River washed away any remains of the house.

Bosque Redondo/Fort Sumner was a deadly place for the *Navajo,* the *Mescalero Apache* and for Billy the Kid! Fort Sumner/*Bosque Redondo* is discussed briefly as a state monument in Chapter 14.

Victorio **Wars** – See Relentless Pursuit: Buffalo Soldiers in New Mexico, and Warm Springs *Apache* and *Geronimo* Wars, elsewhere in this chapter.

Relentless Pursuit: Buffalo Soldiers in New Mexico[68, 69, 70]

Remember the reggae song of the eighties by Bob Marley entitled "Buffalo Soldier", in which he sings in praise of the "Buffalo Soldier" heroics and bravery, and their fight for survival? Well, the 9th and 10th U.S. Cavalry Regiments, called the "Buffalo Soldiers", served dutifully and bravely in New Mexico, in the late 1870's in the Lincoln County War, and during the *Apache* Wars in the 1870's and 1880's, particularly against *Victorio* and his Warm Springs *Apache* band, and *Geronimo*.

It is thought that the "Buffalo Soldiers" appellation was first assigned by the plains tribes, such as the Cheyenne, who likened them to the buffalo, because of their black curly kinky hair and dark features, as well as for their tenacity in battle, even after receiving multiple wounds, fighting like cornered buffalo. The nickname stuck over time.

After the traumatic and bloody American Civil War, the U.S. military experienced a severe shortage of manpower for their missions in protecting settlers in the West, maintaining the expansion westward, quelling Indian uprisings, mediating feuds between rugged entrenched cattle barons, or between mining developers, and the like. This manpower shortage had to be solved and so Congress called for the formation of "Black Cavalry" regiments, the first ever to be employed in peacetime. President Ulysses S. Grant called for the formation of the first two regiments (9th and 10th) in 1866. Two other regiments (24th and 25th) were formed later.

Blacks saw these formations as an opportunity to become educated and to play a role in the new liberated society. Each regimental chaplain was required to educate the recruits. Many black veterans from the American Civil War enlisted. Employment opportunities for freed blacks with little education were scarce. The government saw this large available and unutilized manpower pool as an opportunity to fill their military ranks. The regiments were maintained under the leadership of white officers who, because of their literacy and education, could do the necessary paperwork, and were considered more qualified to lead. The nation was not yet ready, at that time, to accept the concept of black officers in command positions. Colonel Edward Hatch of Iowa and Colonel Benjamin H. Grierson, of Illinois, commanded the 9th and 10th U. S. Cavalry Regiments, respectively. They each had excellent American Civil War records.

The 9th and 10th Regiments of Buffalo Soldiers saw action in the American Plains and in Texas before their assignment to New Mexico. In the winter and spring of 1875 – 76, they were assigned to Fort Stanton, in Lincoln County, New Mexico. Fort

Stanton is located in *Mescalero* country and their duties included watching over the actions of the *Mescalero Apache* in the region. These troops were involved in actions to contain the *Chiricahua Apache* and the Warm Springs *Apache*, and in relocation efforts to resettle the Warm Springs *Apache* from their New Mexico homeland to the inhospitable reserve at *San Carlos*, in Arizona. They were also called out to mediate in hot disputes between local power brokers in the Lincoln County War. Eventually however, they sought to restrict future activities of this sort so as to avoid getting in the middle of local political and civil disputes.

While stationed in New Mexico, the Buffalo Soldiers built housing for laundresses and a post hospital at Fort Stanton. They fought fires at Fort Wingate, Fort Union, *Ojo Caliente*[71] (Warm Springs) and at Fort Stanton. They extended and made improvements on the North Star Road in the Territory. They also escorted U.S. Mail safely through hostile Indian territories. These regiments also suppressed *Ute* uprisings in northern New Mexico (near *Chama*) and in southern *Colorado*.

Victorio ("Conqueror") was the chief of the Warm Springs *Apache*, around *Ojo Caliente* ("Hot Eye" or "Warm Springs") in this time period. Washington had decided that his band should be relocated to the *San Carlos* Reservation, in eastern Arizona. This hellhole ensured their ultimate demise and death. This barren area was unsuitable for agriculture and hunting, and it was torrid in the summer with temperatures near 130 degrees Fahrenheit, with little or no shade. It was infested with flies and other biting, flying insects. And it was not their homeland. It was an inhospitable place of impending death. Some of *Victorio's* band succumbed to the pressure and they were resettled there because they wanted the violence to cease. Others, like *Victorio*, saw this as dishonorable, and a slow undignified death to boot. They swore to die in battle rather than be sentenced to a slow, tortuous and undignified death. So began the so-called *Victorio* Wars.

Victorio sought revenge against innocent settlers and any unfortunates who crossed his path. The Buffalo Soldiers were sent to stop him and to capture him and his band. The 9th and 10th Regiments of the Buffalo Soldiers pursued *Victorio* and his Warm Springs *Apache* band relentlessly in the *San Andrés* and *Mogollón* Mountains, and in the White Sands area and further west, basically anywhere his trail led them. He had about 300 or 400 men, women and children with him. Eventually the Buffalo Soldiers were able to deny *Victorio* easy access to water sources, which led him and his band into Mexico.

Once there, the military of Mexico and the U.S. coordinated their efforts to trap *Victorio*. The Buffalo Soldiers blocked his return access to the *Rio Grande* and his homeland, while Mexican troops surrounded him at *Tres Castillos*,[72] in *Chihuahua*,[73] Mexico. There his band was defeated and decimated. *Victorio* was killed, some say by his own hand. The *Victorio* Wars were now over. *Victorio* was now dead but in an ironic sense, he was perhaps ultimately victorious, in that he died a "free man" as he would have wished, in 1880. *Victorio's* demise would never have come about without the tenacious pursuit of the Buffalo Soldiers through some of the harshest and most difficult campaign conditions anywhere, and without their denial of supplies and watering holes to *Victorio* and his band. This eventually forced them into the trap set by the Mexicans at *Tres Castillos*.

The Buffalo Soldiers, in helping to destroy *Victorio* and his band, hastened the pacification of the southwestern region of New Mexico, and allowed westward expansion and settlement to continue. However, the *Apache* Wars would continue for five more years against *Nana* and other residual Warm Springs *Apache*, and against the *Chiricahua Apache*, until the eventual surrender of *Geronimo* and his band in 1886.

The 10th Regiment had the lowest desertion rate in the army, even though many of their assignments were in the worst regions of the country and in New Mexico, with its harsh and rugged terrain. A total of nineteen Medals of Honor were awarded to Buffalo Soldiers in all the Indians Wars.

From the four Buffalo Soldier regiments involved in the Indian Wars, thirteen enlisted men and six officers were awarded the Medal of Honor, a record of distinction and bravery. Nine Buffalo Soldiers received the Medal of Honor while serving in the New Mexico Territory.

Buffalo Soldier regiments also served in the Spanish American War where they earned five Medals of Honor. They participated in the Philippine-American War of 1899 -1903, and with General Pershing in the Mexican Expedition of 1916. There is a statue at Fort Seldon that honors the brave service of the Buffalo Soldiers.

Feuding Unabated: Lincoln County War[74, 75, 76]

See Relentless Pursuit: Buffalo Soldiers in New Mexico in this chapter, and Lincoln County Courthouse in Chapter Fourteen, State Monuments of New Mexico. See also *Santa Fe* Ring and the Kid's Elusive Pardon in Chapter Four, Key Historical Characters.

The Lincoln County War was a violent struggle between two factions, who sought economic control of the cattle industry and the retail mercantile businesses in which they were involved and invested. A total of about 19 people were killed in the ensuing war. Lucrative government contracts and local assets and investments were at stake in this vicious war between major local cattle-barons and businessmen. An escalating series of murderous battles ensued between the two factions, the Murphy-Dolan-Riley[77] faction and the Tunstall-McSween[78] faction. Events turned so violent and murderous that at one point the 10th U.S. Cavalry, stationed at Fort Stanton, was ordered by Washington, DC, to intervene. The intervention was brief and was never repeated because of the complicated local politics of the situation. The jaded and one-sided actions of the corrupt commanding officer, Colonel Nathan Dudley, who stood idly by while the McSween home was set ablaze by the Dolan-Murphy-Riley faction, also caused the government to avoid further interference in civil matters. Dudley was not a neutral actor as shown by his inactions and his leanings towards the Murphy-Dolan-Riley faction because he owed Murphy money on an outstanding loan.

In the Lincoln County War, both John Tunstall and Alexander McSween were killed. The Murphy-Dolan-Riley faction burned McSween's residence down to the ground. The corrupt and vicious Murphy-Dolan-Riley faction had the Sheriff and the "Law" on their side. They were powerful enough to buy influence, via the *Santa Fe* Ring. The story began in Lincoln County, New Mexico.

In the 1860's, a businessman and former soldier, Lawrence Murphy joined in a partnership with Emil Fritz to further business opportunities in Lincoln County. They and later partners became wealthy in a short time due to their fleecing of new settlers with fraudulent land deals and by defrauding the government on their cattle contracts. Soon, their business became the sole supplier to local farmers and ranchers, developing a monopoly in the region. They had no competition, and so they charged exorbitant prices for their goods. In so doing, they generally enraged the locals. Their political and legal cover for all these outrages was provided by inside connections with the politically corrupt center of gravity in *Santa Fe*, i.e. the Ring.

Figure 3-12: Lawrence Murphy, businessman, soldier, mercantilist. Primary leader of the Murphy-Dolan-Riley faction, in the Lincoln County War. (Sketch based on Public Domain photo.)

Oftentimes, they sold land to new settlers that they did not own, using false land deeds. Further, when the new settlers failed to make payments they foreclosed on the properties, making a fortune through these devious and corrupt practices. They also obtained large lucrative contracts with the U.S. Army to provide beef to the army posts and to the newly formed Indian Reservations. They found ways to deceive the recipients, and instead either provided low quality beef or less beef than expected. Another tactic was to sell cattle that they had rustled from others. The culprits were able to receive political cover from their political allies in *Santa Fe*. See Figures 3-12, 3-13 and 3-14.

In 1863, Emil Fritz was diagnosed with kidney disease. He then sold his share of the business and returned to his homeland in Germany. Although the trip was only a visit, Fritz died there. In 1869, James Dolan joined the business as a clerk. Soon, their business began to thrive because of their corrupt dealings and monopolistic control of the goods sold. Dolan became Murphy's partner in 1874. Murphy sold his business

Figure 3-13: James Dolan (left). Leader of the Murphy-Dolan-Riley faction, in the Lincoln County War, following Murphy's relocation to Santa Fe.

Figure 3-14: John Riley (right). Member of the Murphy-Dolan-Riley faction.

(Sketches based on Public Domain photos.)

share to Dolan in 1875, and moved north to *Santa Fe*. Later, in November1876, John Riley joined as a partner in the business. However, Murphy continued to use his influence with the *Santa Fe* Ring to protect and provide legal license to his former partners in Lincoln well into 1878. Murphy was diagnosed with bowel cancer in March 1877 and died in October 1878.

The climate was ripe for some new competition in the mercantile and banking businesses. This came along in the form of a new business enterprise set up by rancher John Tunstall, and attorney/businessman Alexander McSween in April 1877, together with the financial backing of the wealthy rancher, John Chisum.[79] See Figures 3-15 and 3-16. This rival business was seen as a direct threat to the Murphy-Dolan-Riley faction, and they sought the new enterprise's demise, by vicious and violent means. What galled the Murphy-Dolan-Riley faction was that they were losing business to the Tunstall-McSween faction, who were dealing in fair and above-board business practices! They supported a law and order approach, contrary to the established corrupt approach of the old faction.

Figure 3-15: John Tunstall (right). Businessman, mercantilist, rancher. Leader of the Tunstall-McSween faction. Murdered in February 1878, setting off the Lincoln County War.

Figure 3-16: Alexander McSween (left). Partnered with John Tunstall, in mercantile and banking businesses, in Lincoln Town. Leading member of the Tunstall-McSween faction.

(Sketches based on Public Domain photos.)

Murphy hired two gangs to goad the Tunstall-McSween faction into a fight. These were the Jesse Evans Gang and the John Kinney Gang, two outlawed gangs. They began rustling Tunstall's cattle. Murphy summoned his hireling, Sheriff William Brady. Then Murphy manufactured a false claim that Tunstall owed him money, which was patently untrue. A Writ of Attachment was created to detach a herd of horses from Tunstall in payment of the false claim. The Writ was to be served to Tunstall on his ranch by Sheriff Brady and the twenty rustlers whom he had deputized for the purpose.

Tunstall hired some ranchers and cowboys as bodyguards to protect himself and his assets. Dick Brewer, a former Murphy employee, was hired as Turnstall's foreman, along with ranchers, Frank and George Coe. Two gunmen, Doc Scurlock and Charlie Bowdre were also hired. Later, two others joined the group along with Billy the Kid.

Sheriff Brady, to protect himself, didn't join the posse sent to serve the writ to Tunstall. The "posse" included members of the Jesse Evans Gang. The drunken posse didn't find Turnstall at his ranch. They encountered him leading a herd of his horses towards *Ruidoso*. On February 18, 1878, they shot and killed him on sight without serving the false writ and without any hesitation or pretext.

This started the Lincoln County War. The injured faction then formed the Lincoln County Regulators, under the initial leadership of Dick Brewer, to bring Tunstall's killers to justice. This was in essence a vigilante group. Billy the Kid was a close and loyal friend of the murdered John Tunstall and he sought revenge for the killing of his good friend. This was the start of Billy the Kid's murderous decline to his eventual fatal demise at Fort Stanton.

Several of the Tunstall killers were tracked down and killed. Sheriff Brady, with the powerful backing of the *Santa Fe* Ring was able to have Billy the Kid branded as "Wanted Dead or Alive." Other members of the McSween faction were likewise branded. It was rumored that Dolan offered a $1000 reward to have Alexander McSween killed too. The corrupt *Santa Fe* Ring gave the Murphy-Dolan-Riley faction the semblance of legality to their illegal and corrupt activities.

However, Sheriff Brady and three others were gunned down soon after as they were walking, heavily armed past the Tunstall-McSween store on their way towards the Court House. The killers were Billy the Kid's group of Regulators. Sheriff Brady was killed, although there is no convincing evidence that Billy the Kid was the actual killer of the sheriff. Nonetheless, he was charged with the killing. Warrants were issued for the Kid's arrest for the murder of Sheriff Brady.

Later, a gunfight ensued at Blazer's Mill in which Buckshot Roberts, who was on the Regulators' kill list as one of Tunstall's murderers, was shot and killed. However, before he died he managed to kill Dick Brewer, the Regulators' leader. For a short while after, Frank McNab became the new leader, but he too was killed in a shootout at the Fritz Ranch.

Billy the Kid then assumed the leadership of the "Regulator" gang. Following the Brady incident, the "Regulator" gang fled Lincoln. Eventually, after events seemed to have quietened down, Billy the Kid and his "gang" quietly made there way back to McSween's house. They were discovered staying at the McSween residence, although McSween himself was not there initially. Since the killing of Sheriff Brady, a new hireling had been appointed sheriff by the Murphy-Dolan-Riley faction. He was Dad Peppin. Learning of the other faction's presence at the McSween residence, Sheriff Peppin placed gunman around the residence. This was the beginning of the five-day gun battle that became known as the Battle of Lincoln. It was July 15, 1878.

Eventually gunfire was exchanged between the two groups. The *Torreón* Tower, used in prior times to protect residents from *Apache* attacks, was occupied by men of the Murphy-Dolan-Riley faction to fire at members of the opposing faction. (See Chapter 14 to view a photograph of the *Torreón* Tower.) With the ensuing stalemate, the Murphy-Dolan-Riley faction decided to send to Fort Stanton for troops to dislodge the McSween group.

Through political connections in *Santa Fe* and in Washington, D.C., the Murphy-Dolan-Riley faction was able to get the U.S. Army from Fort Stanton to intervene, rather ineffectively and rather one-sidedly. The Murphy-Dolan-Riley faction burned down the McSween residence with impunity and with no restraining action from the troops. Alexander McSween had finally returned to his home to find it burning down.

With the residence burning, Billy the Kid and others made a run for it, and succeeded in escaping the firestorm. However, McSween was shot and killed near a doorway. Sheriff Peppin had already posted a reward for McSween, but his killer never collected because Billy the Kid killed him during the fray. A warrant was still outstanding against Billy the Kid and others for the earlier killing of Sheriff Brady.

Eventually, Billy the Kid was captured at Fort Sumner by Sheriff Pat Garrett and then brought to trial in the town of *La Mesilla* ("Little Mesa"), otherwise known simply as *Mesilla*, for the killing of Sheriff Brady. Although it is not clear whether the Kid was actually the one who shot Brady, he was still held responsible since he was the leader of the gang that did shoot and kill Brady. He was found guilty and sentenced to be hanged by the neck until dead. He was then removed to Lincoln. Being held prisoner in the makeshift jail on the second floor of the Old Lincoln County Courthouse, Billy the Kid knew that he had to attempt an escape or surely die. Somehow, he managed to get a six-shooter away from one of his guards and killed Sheriff Bell. Later, he obtained a shotgun, and he shot and killed Sheriff Olinger. (Refer to Chapter 14 to see a photo of the Old Lincoln County Courthouse/Jail and another of the courthouse window and site where Olinger was shot.) Stealing a horse he rode rapidly out of Lincoln town. The stolen horse was later returned to the owner. Two months later, Billy the Kid was tracked down in Fort Sumner where Sheriff Pat Garrett shot him dead by controversial means.

Billy the Kid was certainly the most notorious character during this time period. However, he was only a small-part player in a much bigger drama, the Lincoln County War, as described above. With the cancer death of Murphy in October 1878, the bankruptcy of Dolan's mercantile business in 1878, the murder of Tunstall, the death of McSween followed by the destruction of the McSween residence, and the eventual murder of Billy the Kid, by Sheriff Pat Garrett in 1882, the Lincoln Wars finally came to an end. Most of the key participants were now dead or ruined. The violent end of the Lincoln County War closed an era of lawlessness, and marked the real beginning of a calmer, more peaceful time in which real law and order could finally prevail. The only threat that remained to the settlers was the murderous depredations of the indigenous *Apaches* fighting to preserve their own homeland and way of life. It was to be a murderous clash of cultures, and a fight for survival.

Warm Springs *Apache* and *Geronimo* Wars[80]

The conflicts to pacify the southwestern *Apache* consumed much of the late 1800's, beginning in earnest following the end of the American Civil War. There were two basic components of these southwestern *Apache* Wars. One was the conflict with the Warm Springs *Apache*, first under *Victorio* until his death at *Tres Castillos* in Mexico. This was followed by the continued encounters with the same band under the new leadership of *Nana*.[81] The other conflict was with Geronimo's[82] *Chiricahua* band.

Separately, there was a relatively brief war with the more northerly *Jicarilla Apache* between 1849 and 1854, but this will not be discussed here. Also, there were numerous skirmishes with the *Mescalero Apache* of south central New Mexico. However, the significant wars in New Mexico were waged against the Warm Springs *Apache* and the *Chiricahua Apache*.

The *Chihene* Band of the *Chiricahua Apache* in southwestern New Mexico was commonly called the Warm Springs *Apache*. The U.S. Army recognized *Victorio* as their chief in 1873. Several futile attempts, starting in 1870 through 1877, failed to completely resettle this band in the *San Carlos* Reservation in Arizona. Some of the band permanently left the reservation in August 1879. This started the so-called *Victorio* Wars. *Victorio* was successful in raiding local and Mexican communities, and in eluding capture by his pursuers. He succeeded in an engagement at *Las Animas* Canyon in September 1879. He was held responsible for the raid on settlers around *Alma*, New Mexico, and for the massacre that ensued in April 1880. He was also held responsible for the subsequent attack on Fort *Tularosa*. His good fortune ended in October 1880, at *Tres Castillos*, Mexico, where he died and many of his band were killed by Mexican soldiers, ending the *Victorio* Wars.

Nana and his warriors had been able to avoid the Mexican ambush at *Tres Castillos*, and they were able to escape into the *Sierra Madre*. *Nana* renewed the conflicts, leading raids against vulnerable settlers and U.S. Army supply trains. *Nana* was about 80 years old at this time! Eventually, he was captured but subsequently escaped to join *Geronimo* and his renegade band.

Meanwhile, the *Apache* Wars had been ongoing with *Geronimo* and his *Chiricahua* Band. *Geronimo* fought U.S. and Mexican intrusion into *Chiricahua Apache* lands, in modern-day Arizona, for several decades. *Geronimo's* depredations extended into *Sonoro* and *Chihuahua*, Mexico, as well as southwestern New Mexico in the American Southwest. *Geronimo* and his band became famous for their daring and for their ability to escape capture. In later years, *Nana* and Lozen[83] of the Warm Spring *Apache* joined *Geronimo's* band. However, in 1886, General Nelson A. Miles was given the assignment to corner and capture *Geronimo* and his warriors. The band was hounded relentlessly until they finally surrendered to Miles on September 4, 1886 at Skeleton Canyon, Arizona.

Geronimo, his band, and other *Apache* who acted as scouts to help the U.S. Army track him down, were all sent as prisoners to Florida. So ended the *Apache* Wars. With these wars finally at an end, the complete pacification and settlement of New Mexico was able to proceed unimpeded.

New Mexican Rough: The Rough Riders[84]

Although many have heard of Teddy Roosevelt's Rough Riders and their famous charge up *San Juan* Hill to help free Cuba from Spanish rule in the Spanish-American War of 1898, few are aware of the role played by New Mexicans, nor of the subsequent outcome for the New Mexico Territory, nearly fourteen years later.

Teddy Roosevelt sought out cowboys, ranch workers, Buffalo Soldiers, ex-Indian fighters and other "hard" men of the American Southwest for the recruits he needed for the newly formed First U. S. Volunteer Cavalry. The U.S. had declared war against Spain, after the sinking of the Maine, and so began the Spanish-American War to free Cuba of Spanish domination. Roosevelt, who was actually second in command, believed that these men from the West would make the best soldiers for this campaign. It was also thought that men from these areas would be best acclimated to the climate of Cuba. Lieutenant Colonel Roosevelt sought out volunteers from Arizona, New Mexico, Oklahoma, Texas and the Indian Territory.

The War Department formally requested that New Mexico provide 340 volunteers for combat service. The Governor of New Mexico also provided cavalry and a battalion of riflemen. The New Mexico Territory provided 30%, or nearly one third of the Rough Rider troops. Before heading off to Florida to prepare for their assignment to Cuba, the New Mexican volunteers gathered in 1898, at the Palace of the Governors building in *Santa Fe*, New Mexico, where they took the Oath of Allegiance. These volunteers executed themselves with bravery and they participated in the successful taking of *San Juan* Hill. Eventually, the Spanish were defeated in Cuba. The territories of *Puerto Rico*, Guam and the Philippines were ceded to the U.S.

In recognition of their fine soldiering, Teddy Roosevelt, who had just recently been elected (1898 – 1900) the new Governor of New York State, attended the Rough Riders first reunion, which was held in *Las Vegas*, New Mexico, in 1899. *Las Vegas* had provided a significant number of the volunteers from the territory. It also became the annual host for subsequent re-unions. One significant event took place during a speech given by Teddy Roosevelt. He promised to do whatever he could to assist in New Mexico Territory's quest for statehood.

For many, the Spanish-American War was seen as a test of loyalty and allegiance for the largely Hispanic soldiers from New Mexico Territory. After all, they had an historic connection with Spain in their past, and the enemy in this new war was Spain. However, the bravery and loyalty of the New Mexican volunteers was clearly demonstrated, and Americans began to believe that the New Mexicans had now earned their right to statehood. Since 1848 and prior to the Spanish-American War, the New Mexico Territory had been bypassed for statehood fifteen times.

Roosevelt was elected Vice President in 1900 on the McKinley-Roosevelt ticket. Vice President Teddy Roosevelt became the 26th President of the United States, on September 6, 1901, upon the assassination of President William McKinley. Even after he won the Presidency in his own right in the election of 1904, he did keep his promise to work towards that goal of New Mexico statehood. However, he did not run for another term, and was unable to achieve that outcome. It was not until January 6, 1912 that New Mexico finally became the 47th state of the United States.

The contribution of the Rough Rider volunteers from the New Mexico Territory to the success of the Spanish-American War, helped bring about the acceptance of the idea of statehood for the territory, where previously there had been many decades of opposition. Without the Rough Riders, statehood for New Mexico might have taken many more years or decades to achieve.

Becoming a State[85]...finally

New Mexico took over six decades to become the forty-seventh state in the United States. It was a lengthy and difficult struggle. In the end, persistence paid off when on January 6, 1912 the eastern half of the New Mexico Territory finally became the state of New Mexico. Numerous, separate attempts had been made in the preceding half-century or more to achieve this goal.

The first attempt occurred in 1850, just a couple of years after the cession of these lands by the Mexican government to the United States. Local officials had drafted a state constitution that was put before the electorate, who voted overwhelmingly in favor of it. The people also elected a legislature and executive officials. There seemed to be great promise in the air. However, Congress burst the bubble when it passed the Compromise of 1850, later in the same year. That Congressional Bill denied the statehood request and assigned territorial status instead to the region.

Other attempts were later made to draft a new constitution. These efforts failed at the polls in 1872 and 1889. In desperation, an attempt was made to establish a single joint state in concert with Arizona, but the voters likewise rejected this option.

There was national prejudice against the region and its heavily Hispanic and Catholic population. The New Mexican culture and history was too different and foreign to the predominantly white *Anglo*-Protestant nation. The American people were suspicious of the region's historical links with Spain and Mexico. All these sentiments probably postponed the entry of this region as a state into the U.S. Some thought that changing the region's name to something less Hispanic might help the cause. Names like *Navajo* and Lincoln were proposed and ultimately rejected.

Another factor in slowing New Mexico's march towards statehood may very well have been its sparse population. A minimum population[86] of 60,000 was required to qualify for statehood. Even today New Mexico is sparsely populated relative to other states, especially when one discounts the populations in the five or six most populous counties of the state. The development of the railroad in New Mexico was a great factor in bringing settlers and commerce into the territory, causing large surges in local populations. This all occurred in the late 1800's, qualifying the territory on a population basis before eventual statehood in 1912.

The question of allegiance and loyalty seemed to be lurking beneath the surface. Teddy Roosevelt's Rough Riders' successful participation in the Spanish-American War went a long way towards removing such doubts, as a large number of the volunteers were New Mexicans. Still, in spite of continued efforts to gain statehood status, it took until June 20, 1910 for President William H. Taft to sign an Enabling Act, which authorized a constitutional convention within the territory, to prepare for admission as a state into the U.S. This was a significant breakthrough! Following this authorization, over one hundred delegates from every county in the territory convened on October 3, 1910 to draft a state constitution, which was subsequently approved by the voters on January 21, 1911. At this point, the prize of statehood was within reach.

On January 6, 1912 President William H. Taft signed the long awaited document proclaiming New Mexico as the nation's forty-seventh state. It was a territory no longer....finally!!

Pancho Villa Crosses the Border[87]

Columbus, New Mexico in the spring of 1916 was a small town of little note, except that it did host a neighboring military post, Camp Furlough. The army post had about 350 soldiers from the 13th Cavalry. This provided the sleepy town with a false sense of security that seemed to isolate it from the Mexican Revolution flaring wildly across the southern border.

That false sense of security was quickly dispelled when Mexican revolutionaries under General Francisco "Pancho" Villa crossed the southern border from the southwest, to attack the small town of Columbus.

It seems that the *Villistas*[88] were more intent on raiding than killing. Surprisingly, the army camp was not seriously attacked. The camp and horse stables received minor damage. Instead, most of the destruction was directed towards the business district of the town. However, the noise and activity in the town drew the attention of the American army commanders. Machine guns were set up in front of the Hoover hotel and at another street intersection. The *Villistas* were caught in a lethal crossfire. By the time the raid was winding down in the wee hours of the morning, 70 to 75 *Villistas* were killed, while 18 Americans were killed, mostly civilians.

There are several theories that attempt to explain the motivation behind the failed attack. One theory supposes an arms deal with a local supplier that went sour, resulting in non-delivery of paid-for arms and ammunition. Another theory claims that the *Villistas* were short on arms, ammunition, food, clothing and other supplies. These supplies were needed to keep their mission alive. Columbus, being so close to the border provided a convenient target of opportunity. The third theory assumes that the attack was an act of revenge for President Woodrow Wilson's support of Pancho Villa's adversary, Venustiano Carranza, the new President of Mexico. Regardless of which theory is correct, the outcome was the same, namely the U.S. Government responded in force to the attack across its southern border.

A punitive expedition was initiated under the leadership of General John J. "Black Jack" Pershing. His mission was to cross the border into Mexico, find and capture Pancho Villa, and bring him back to the U.S. for retribution. The number of troops in and around Columbus swelled to such a great number that Columbus held the distinction of having the largest population of any city in New Mexico, at the end of 1916.

The Punitive Expedition of 1916 -1917 lasted eleven months and utilized trucks and airplanes, used for the first time in American warfare. This mission marked the end of nineteennth century warfare. The expedition also marshaled several thousand troops. The mission to capture Pancho Villa ultimately failed, even though U.S. forces extended as far as 300 miles into Mexico. The expedition was called to a halt in early 1917. Pancho Villa was assassinated in Parrall, Mexico in 1923.

The Punitive Mexican Action of 1916 -1917, firmly established the sanctity and inviolability of New Mexico's southern border, as a national border.

What's That You Say? *Navajo* Code Talkers[89]

Recently, there has grown a greater awareness of the role that *Navajo* Code Talkers played in the Pacific theater during World War Two. One reason for this was the release of the 2002 film, entitled *Windtalkers*, a fictional story about *Navajo* Code Talkers who enlisted in the U.S. Marines during World War Two. Although the film received controversial reviews, it increased awareness of the heroic roles played by these brave Native Americans during that war. Code Talkers or wind-talkers, communicated secret tactical messages using coded language. Messages were transmitted over telephone or radio communication nets using informally or formally developed code words utilizing their native *Navajo* language. This methodology greatly increased the security of American military communications in the Pacific theater, especially in the frontlines where secure tactical communications were especially productive and saved lives.

What is less known is that other Native American tribes acted as Code Talkers during World War II. These included *Cherokee, Choctaw, Comanche, Lakota* and *Miskwaki* bilingual soldiers. Even less known is that soldiers of *Basque* descent were utilized for the same purpose, in areas where *Basque* was less likely to be known.

However, the number of *Basque* speakers was limited, and there was the minute but real risk of possible Asian exposure to the *Basque* language due to the early Portuguese exploration and trade ventures in Asia several centuries ago. So, it was decided that it would be better to exploit *Navajo* bilingual speakers instead.

It is also interesting that Code Talkers were first used in World War I. Choctaw Indians served in the U.S. Army as Code Talkers. Because of Germany's awareness of the successful use of Code Talkers in the First War, an attempt was made to have some thirty German anthropologists sent to the U.S. to learn several native languages, before the Second World War broke out. However, these anthropologists had a nearly impossible time learning the unfamiliar Native American languages and their dialects. Eventually, they gave up trying. However, knowing of these attempts by the Germans to learn native languages, the U.S. military was extra cautious and therefore reluctant to use Native American Code Talkers in the European Theater.

The use of *Navajo* in the Pacific Theater was no accident. The *Navajo* language is particularly difficult to learn and to master, especially, if it is not one's native language. *Navajo* has a complex grammar and it is an unwritten language. It has always been spoken only in *Navajo* lands, in Arizona, Utah and New Mexico, and so it could be used essentially as an undecipherable coded language. The language has an unusual syntax and it has tonal qualities, unlike European languages.

Chester Nez, the last surviving *Navajo* Code Talker, gave the following explanation of the *Navajo* language: "Pronunciation…is complex. *Navajo* is a tonal language with four tones: high, low, rising and falling. The tone used can completely change the meaning of the word…Glottal and aspirated stops are also employed…speakers of any other language are generally unable to properly pronounce most *Navajo* words…The conjugation of verbs in the *Navajo* language is also complex…English can be spoken sloppily and still be understood. Not so with the *Navajo* language."[90]

Its dialectal variations also add another level of complexity that make it essentially unintelligible to anyone without extensive exposure to the language. It would be very difficult for a non-speaker to distinguish unfamiliar sounds used in *Navajo*. There is another unique feature of *Navajo*, in that a speaker who acquires the language later in life sounds quite different from someone who was born and raised with the language. This diminishes the chance of an imposter being able to successfully transmit a false message. It has been estimated that there were fewer than thirty non-*Navajos* who could comprehend the language at the beginning of the war. That certainly made the *Navajo* language desirable for secure communication purposes.

It was found that the *Navajo* Code Talkers were more efficient than the machines of that era. Code Talkers could transmit a coded message about 90 times faster than a contemporary coding machine. What would take a machine tens of minutes to process and transmit, took the Code Talkers tens of seconds. Agreed-upon English words were used to represent letters of the English alphabet. The *Navajo* equivalent of these English words were transmitted. The English word usually started with the same letter as the alphabet letter it was encoding. For example the code for the letter "z" was the English word zinc that was then translated into the *Navajo* word *"besh-do-tlitz."* Hence "z" became encoded as *"besh-do-tlitz."*[91] Some selected commonly used combat-associated words were given unique nomenclatures in *Navajo*. Some examples would be the *Navajo* word for "potato" to indicate a hand grenade, or the *Navajo* word for "tortoise" to indicate a tank. Even a *Navajo* speaker listening could make no sense of the grammatically incorrect sequence of *Navajo* code words. It just sounded like mumbo-jumbo, and that was the very intent!!

Since the *Navajo* do not divide the year into twelve months, they used descriptive concepts[92] to describe a month, such as January. It was described in English as "crusted snow" to relate the concept of a "cold month." This descriptive concept was then translated into its equivalent *Navajo, "yas-nil-tes."* Eventually, to avoid the possibility that encryption experts could use "letter frequency" to decrypt a message, the Code Talkers added two more words to represent any given letter in the alphabet. Hence,[93] "…when a Code Talker transmitted the *Navajo* letter A, he could then use the *Navajo* word for "ant", or "apple' or "axe." The Code Talkers might spell a word containing three "A's" using each of the three words for "A." This broke the pattern of one-letter-one-word, a pattern in which a code cracker might discover the symbol for E, the most common letter in English, and other letters based upon how frequently they were used." With these different variations, the code grew to about seven hundred words in total!

The *Navajo* Code Talkers helped maintain secure communications in the Korean War and early into the Vietnam War. The operation was terminated and declassified in 1968. Fourteen years later, in 1982, President Reagan finally recognized the Code Talkers for their heroic contributions. He designated August 14, 1982 as "*Navajo* Code Talkers Day." In the year 2000, President Clinton awarded the Congressional Gold Medal to twenty-nine (29) World War Two *Navajo* Code Talkers. President George W. Bush, in July 2001, awarded the Congressional Gold Medal[94] to four surviving *Navajo* Code Talkers, while twenty-four (24) additional medals were awarded to the families of deceased Code Talkers. Eighteen *Choctaw* Code Talkers were later given posthumous Texas Medals of Valor in recognition of their World War One service, by the state of Texas in 2007. Finally, on December 13, 2007, the Code Talker Recognition Act honored every Code Talker who served in the U.S. Military granting each participating tribe with a Congressional Gold Medal and a silver duplicate medal for each individual Code Talker. The recipients included eight *Miskwakis.*

The recognition given finally to these brave and heroic Native Americans from various tribes took a long time in coming. Of special interest to New Mexicans is the 2000 Congressional Medal of Honor awarded to the brave heroic *Navajo*-American Marines who contributed greatly to the Allied success in the Pacific Theater. The obverse side of this distinguished medal shows a pair of Code Talkers communicating over a radiotelephone, in a jungle. The text around the rim says "*Navajo* Code Talkers, by Act of Congress 2000." The reverse side of the medal shows the U.S. Marine symbol in the center. Around the top of the rim it states USMC WWII. Around the lower part of the rim there is text written in *Navajo*, which according to the U.S. Mint website[95] translates as "The *Navajo* language was used to defeat the enemy."

There is a handsome monument dedicated to *Navajo* Code Talkers in Window Rock, Arizona. It is dedicated to all Code Talkers of the *Navajo* Nation, whether they hail from Arizona or New Mexico. The monument is a sculpture showing a *Navajo* American in combat outfit and gear, crouched down on one knee, talking into a radio held in his right hand, with a radio transmitter and an antenna, both mounted on his back. It is an impressive monument to these heroic Native American soldiers from the Southwest.

There is one more interesting but complementary aside here. During World War Two, in the European Theater, the British military utilized bilingual Scottish Highlanders as Code Talkers. They spoke *Scottish Gaelic*, to the utter dismay and confusion of the Germans, who couldn't recognize the language.

Unholy Trinity[96]

On July 16, 1945, the world saw the dawning of a new and frightening era, the Atomic Age. The three-year efforts of the Manhattan Project team resulted in the detonation of the first atomic bomb in the *La Jornada del Muerto*[97] desert about 35 miles southeast of the small New Mexican town of *Socorro*. This unholy event was called the Trinity (Nuclear) Test.

Trinity tested the design and development of a risky and challenging nuclear weapons concept that implemented an implosion-type plutonium device. Prior efforts had utilized a simpler and less risky gun-type design using Uranium-235 that resulted in the "Little Boy" bomb that was dropped over Hiroshima, Japan on August 6, 1945. The new plutonium device was successfully tested at the Trinity site and was referred to as the "Gadget" for security reasons. The "Gadget" was detonated 100 feet above ground on top of a specially built tower. The Trinity explosion produced an explosive power equivalent to 20 kilotons of TNT. This riskier but successful "implosion-type" device proved the design concept that was implemented in the "Fat Man" bomb dropped over Nagasaki, Japan on August 9, 1945

At the time, there were fears held by some scientists that the earth's atmosphere might be ignited by the Trinity Test, threatening all life on earth. A classified report produced several years later demonstrated that this fear was unfounded. Others feared that perhaps the entire state of New Mexico would be incinerated. This too proved unfounded. Nonetheless, this gives one the sense of foreboding and uncertainty that preceded the world's first nuclear detonation.

Most observers, such as military officers, high ranking government officials and scientists, observed the Trinity Test from 10 miles distance. The detonation took place at 5:29:45 Mountain Time in the morning. The detonation created a blinding flash, for one or two seconds. It generated intense heat. A variety of colors were produced covering the range from purple to green and lastly white. The load noise of the shockwave took 45 seconds to reach the observers. This shockwave was felt over 100 miles away. The now-infamous mushroom cloud reached 7.5 miles into the atmosphere. The blast left a small crater at the detonation site that was 10 feet deep and 1,100 feet wide. The silica of the sand in the crater had been melted into radioactive glass, which was named trinitite.

Seven years later, in 1952, the detonation crater was bulldozed and the remaining trinitite removed. The 51,500-acre site was designated a National Historic Landmark[98] on December 26, 1965. The landmark includes the base camp where the scientists and support staff lived, ground zero (the detonation site) and the Schmidt/McDonald ranch house where the plutonium core was assembled. The base camp is not available for public viewing.

A 12-foot tall lava rock obelisk marks the detonation site. It is called the Trinity Monument. The site is opened to the public twice yearly, on the first Saturday in April and in October. Although residual radiation does still exist at the Trinity site, a one-hour visit exposes the visitor to about what one receives on an average day from natural radiation and from medical sources. The site is still popular with those interested in "atomic tourism."

There are a few ironies associated with the Trinity Test. It was conducted in the *La Jornada del Muerto*, named centuries before by the Spaniards, meaning "a day's journey of death" or even more starkly "the route of the Dead Man." It was conducted near the town of *Socorro*, named by the Spaniards who were relieved at their survival of the trial of passage through *La Jornada del Muerto*. *Socorro* means "succour" or "aid", in Spanish. Does this represent a cry for "help" at the dawning of the new Atomic Age, or does it signify that the bomb might "help" to end the long deadly and brutal Second World War? The name of this unholy and frightening test was Trinity, the name also given to the triple form of God in the Christian belief system.

J. Robert Oppenheimer,[99] the director of the Manhattan bomb development program, said he was inspired by one of John Donne's[100] poems, written just before his death, that makes some subtle references to the multiform of God. It is also said that upon witnessing the Trinity Test detonation, Oppenheimer, who was versed in *Sanskrit*, quoted a verse from the *Bhagavad Gita*.[101] "Now I am become Death, the destroyer of worlds." How very fitting...and frightening! With the bombings of Hiroshima and Nagasaki, Japan, 148,000 people were killed immediately, and many thousands died later from radiation sickness or cancer induced by the radiation.

The state of New Mexico, through the scientific efforts at *Los Alamos*, and through providing the site of the Trinity Test, ushered in the infant Atomic Age. It is also very interesting and ironic to note that New Mexico is once again ushering in a new and more inspiring age, the infant Second Space Age. New Mexico is working in partnership with private industry in the construction of the world's first commercial space port. Again, it is located in "*El Jornada del Muerto*" desert. The first unholy but significant quest is identified with horror, fear and death, while the second quest is a positive and hope-filled development that brings out the very best in us, as human beings. It is almost as if this new quest is a second more hopeful chance for us all.

Chapter Four: Key Historical Characters

Certain historical personages stand out as one learns of New Mexico's past. It is always arguable whether history makes the person or the person makes the history! However, one thing is clear. There is definitely an interaction between the events of a given age, and a bold individual's response to those historical events. How one responds to these events often determines and shapes future happenings, and may even remold both the destiny and the character of the individual. There are many individuals who could be included here. However, the scope of this chapter and this book is limited. The historical individuals identified and discussed here represent a short survey of central characters that were key to the development of this great state of New Mexico. A wide variety of fascinating and bold individuals, and even influential groups of people, helped create the cultural and historical mix that makes this state so unique and wonderful today: the land we call the Land of Enchantment.

This chapter will give short overviews of *Coronado*, Don Juan de Oñate, the *Pueblo* leader Popay, the *Comancheros*, the *Ciboleros*, Charles Bent, Kit Carson, the *Mescalero Apache* Santana, *Victorio & Nana* (Warm Springs *Apache*), *Santa Fe* Ring, Territorial Governor Lew Wallace, Billy the Kid, the Female *Apache* Warrior Lozen, Geronimo and J. Robert Oppenheimer. There is a mix of Spanish, Native American and *Anglo*-American historical characters highlighted in this chapter. Each has made his or her own contribution to New Mexico's unique heritage.

Francisco Vásquez de *Coronado*

See Chasing Golden Windmills: The *Coronado* Expedition, in Chapter Three: Historical Snapshots.

El Explorador Y El Gobernador:[1] Don Juan de Oñate y Salazar[2]

Both respected and reviled, Don Juan de Oñate y Salazar, was a Spanish explorer and the first colonial Governor[3] of New Spain's[4] province of New Mexico. See Figure 4-1. Oñate was born in 1550, in the New Spain (Mexican) city of Zacatecas, to wealthy Spanish colonists and owners of silver mines. In 1595, King Philip II of Spain wanted to have the northern frontier of New Spain defined more clearly, in what is now New Mexico and its neighboring states. The king wanted to spread the Roman Catholic faith and to set up new missions in the region. In 1598, Oñate initiated an expedition that crossed over the *Rio Grande,* near modern day *El Paso*. Within days he claimed all the territory beyond the *Rio Grande* for Spain. During the summer of that same year, he progressed up the *Rio Grande* towards the northern part of New Mexico. Eventually he camped among the *Pueblo* Indians he found in the valleys of the great river, at the *Ohkay Owingeh Pueblo*, which he renamed *San Juan de los Caballeros*. Soon after he founded the province of *Santa Fe de Nuevo México*. He also appointed himself the first Spanish Governor of the region. A few years later he moved his small colony across to the western side of the *Rio Grande* and there founded *San Gabriel Pueblo*, as the new Capital of *Nuevo Mexico*. Oñate's subsequent conquest of the indigenous peoples has been chronicled in the *Historia de la Nuevo México*, written by Gaspar Pérez de Villagrá, who captained Oñate's expedition.

Figure 4-1 shows Oñate as a fearless, determined leader of men, courageously spurring forth his soldiers, as *El Adelantado[5]*, the Governor of a new unconquered land. The inscription on the brass plate on the base of this statue, sculpted by Reynaldo "Sonny" Rivera, reads, "Captain General and First Governor of New Mexico, 1598 – 1610."

It soon became apparent that Oñate ruled both the colonists and the natives with a stern and sometimes cruel hand. As an example of the extreme measures he is said to have taken, consider what is said to have happened to the people of the *Acoma[6] Pueblo* when a small skirmish arose in October 1598. At that time, the Spanish military,

Figure 4-1: Close-up of the Don Juan de Oñate Statue, entitled *El Adelantado,* by sculptor Reynaldo Rivera. It stands in front of the Oñate Monument Center, just north of *Española*. It is a *Rio Arriba* County-owned facility. (With permission of Reynaldo Rivera and *Rio Arriba* County.)

which occupied the region, demanded some tribute items from *Acoma*, food or goods that would have jeopardized the ability of the *Acoma* people to survive the coming winter. The *Acoma* leadership refused and resisted, causing 13 Spaniards to be killed. Among those killed was Don Juan de Oñate's nephew. Oñate retaliated in 1599 with a cruel vengeance. Legend has it that some eight hundred *Acoma* villagers were killed. The remaining 500 women and children were enslaved by Oñate's decree. It is said that...he then ordered the soldiers to amputate the left foot of every *Acoma* man over the age of 25! This additional punishment was meted out to eighty men of the *pueblo*. The *Acoma* people consider this to be part of their history. To the present day, the Acoma people have never forgotten this alleged punishment.

However, it is also important to review some of Oñate's major accomplishments. In 1601, Oñate set out on an expedition that led him onto the Great Plains, as far as the *Wichita* area of Kansas. There the expedition encountered the wide Arkansas River and met tribes that appear to have been of *Caddoan Wichita* stock. The natives lived in round homesteads that were dispersed throughout the village. These dwellings were thatched with grass and were big enough to accommodate up to ten inhabitants. These peoples were organized enough to provide granaries for the storage of corn, beans and squash that they grew in nearby fields. The Spaniards met various tribes, had a few minor skirmishes and then eventually returned to New Mexico in November

1601. Oñate appears to have come close to the area *Coronado* had found near *Quivira*, although *Quivira* is thought to have been further north than the area Oñate found.

In 1604 -1605, Oñate launched yet another expedition, only this time it was to the west. The expedition explored the lower valley of the *Colorado* River. They followed this to the river mouth at the Gulf of Mexico in January 1605. The expedition's purpose was to find a port that would allow direct shipment of supplies from New Spain to the new northern province. This would allow traders to circumvent the difficult, lengthy and costly overland route.

In these two great endeavors, Oñate explored the geography of the eastern and western parts of the Southwest, giving it definition and thereby increasing European knowledge of this region. Ultimately this increased the flow of colonists and travelers through this newly documented area.

However, rumors of Oñate's conduct towards colonists and natives reached the ears of the powerful elite in Mexico City. In 1606, Oñate was recalled to Mexico City. He finished his plans for the founding of the new town of *Santa Fe*, and then resigned his post in 1607. It would take his successor, Peralta (1610-1612), to actually follow through and implement Oñate's plans for the new town. Oñate was tried and convicted of cruelty during his administration. He was initially banished from New Mexico, but an appeal was initiated that later cleared him of all charges. After some time, Oñate returned to Spain where he died in 1626. He has been referred to as "the Last *Conquistador*."

While Oñate has been honored and recognized for his explorations and for his early administration of the new colonial province of *Nuevo México*, he has also been criticized and reviled for his alleged cruel treatment of the *Acoma Pueblo* natives. In 1991, a bronze statue dedicated to Oñate was established at the Oñate Monument Center in northeast *Española*. This center is located between mile markers eight and nine on NM 68 northbound. Initially, the statue was located behind the pale pink center building, obstructed from easy view, by the building itself. Today, the statue stands out in front of the center facing the highway (NM 68). The movement of the statue to its current position greatly facilitates a clear and unobstructed view of the monument from NM 68.

The *Acoma Pueblo* people of modern times still remember Oñate's alleged actions towards their people centuries ago. The tour guide at *Acoma*, a native, recently mentioned it to a small visiting group of tourists. The tribal memory of Oñate and his alleged cruelty towards their people in the past is still alive today. This may have been revealed in the response to the 1998 New Mexico celebration of the 400th anniversary of Oñate's arrival in New Mexico. Some who were opposed to the Oñate statue protested the anniversary by cutting off the left foot of the statue. A note was left that stated "Fair is fair", in apparent retribution for Oñate's alleged action against the people of *Acoma*, over 400 years ago. The sculptor, Reynaldo Rivera, recast the foot on the statue within two weeks of the incident.

The vandals described themselves as the "brothers of *Acoma*." The director of the Oñate Monument and Visitors' Center, Estevan Arellano stated, in a local newspaper article, that he believed the vandalism was not perpetrated by a Native American or by an *Hispano*, but perhaps by someone looking to stir up conflict between the two groups[7]. If such a group existed, it was not officially recognized by the *Acoma Pueblo* according to Petuuche Gilbert, realty officer for the *Pueblo Acoma*.[8] So the issue remains controversial. Was the destructive act committed by Acomites or by a small group of anarchists? No one knows for sure!

According to a newspaper article[9] published shortly after the incident: "Asked what spirit he intended to convey in his sculpture of Oñate, (Reynaldo) Rivera responded that he wanted to capture the undeniable bravery of the man who walked away from great family wealth in Mexico to explore unknown terrain in what became New Mexico." Continuing, Rivera is quoted as saying, "So, for me to make this man honorable, I wanted to have him with the strong sense of force and a big sense of pride that he had a precious cargo (Spanish Colonials and their belongings) with him...He was certainly a man of action." More significantly, Rivera responded to the claim that someone associated with the *Acoma Pueblo* may have damaged his work in protest against Oñate, by saying, "You've got to think that it was the nature of discipline of 400 years ago. I don't think that *Acoma* had anything to do with it...." In other words, one has to judge one's actions by the standards of the time. Also, Rivera felt the destructive action was a sort of prank. (Note: In the quotes above, the parenthetical comments have been added, by the author, for clarification only.)

On April 21, 2007, another much larger equestrian statue portraying Oñate mounted atop his Andalusian horse was unveiled in the city of *El Paso*.[10] At 34 feet in height it is the largest bronze equestrian statue in the world. The local population and the Spanish Ambassador to the U.S., Carlos Westendrop, welcomed the statue's unveiling. However, *Acoma* tribal members were present to protest the statue.

No matter what event one talks about in history, there are always two perspectives. In the case of Don Juan de Oñate, he is lauded and highly respected among Hispanic communities for his strength, his courage, his daring and most of all for his exploration and leadership qualities. Those same qualities are often looked upon differently by those who see themselves as the oppressed or conquered peoples. So, it is not unusual to see Oñate as a figure that is both revered and reviled. It depends upon which culture one vews him from. In the end, the historians need to sort out who the real Oñate is, and what he did or did not do!

In spite of these reactions to the various depictions of Oñate, he contributed greatly to the exploration and understanding of the American Southwest. In the end, Don Juan de Oñate's legacy is a mixed and controversial one. It should be recognized that his explorations helped open up the Southwest to European settlement. And among other things, that is his legacy as well as the legacy of New Mexico.

The First Revolutionary: Popé or Popay[11]

Popé or Popay, pronounced Po-pay', was a great man who organized the *Pueblo* Revolt of 1680 against the Spaniards. See Figure 4-2. He was a religious leader of the *Ohkay Owingeh Pueblo*, aka *San Juan Pueblo*. He was a resourceful man, who was able to drive the Spanish settlers and their military out of *Santa Fe* and the upper *Rio Grande* Valley for about a decade. In this sense, he was America's first documented revolutionary! The *Santa Fe ReConquista* of 1692-93 reversed the results of the *Pueblo* Revolt. See the discussion in Chapter Three regarding the *Pueblo* Revolt of 1680.

Popay remains a mysterious historical figure. Not much is known about his fate after the *ReConquista*. There are several differing tales about him that have survived. One tale says that he became so overbearing after the Revolt that he ordered, under pain of death, the burning of all vestiges of Spanish culture and the Catholic faith. This order supposedly included the killing of cattle and other livestock, and the burning of fruit trees. In this same tale, he supposedly ordered the disunion of any marital unions performed by the Spanish priests, and ordered the natives to seek new wives under the old traditional practices. Another tale says that he returned to the *Taos* area after the revolt and lived there *"incognito"* to avoid future persecution by the returning Spaniards and by other *Puebloans* who disagreed with his policies, or who did not support him. Others say that he simply disappeared. To this day no one really knows the truth. His impact on *Pueblo* history and culture cannot be denied. If Popay had not acted to organize the *Pueblo* Revolt of 1680, the Spaniards would probably have eradicated *Pueblo* culture.

Figure 4-2: Popé or Popay, Leader of the 1680 *Pueblo* Revolt, and the first American Revolutionary. (Sketch based on the statue sculpted by Cliff Fragua, which can be seen in Washington, DC.)

In 1995, the bilingual play *Casi Hermanos*,[12, 13] written by Ramon Flores and James Lujan was produced and presented in Albuquerque, New Mexico. It depicts the events prior to the revolt, from the viewpoint of two half-brothers who meet on the battlefield.

Taos playwright James Lujan, also wrote another play,[14] *Kino and Teresa*, an adaptation of *Romeo and Juliet*. It was produced and presented in Los Angeles in 2005. It draws together historical figures and their literary counterparts, to show how disparate cultures mix and thrive in New Mexico.

A fine statue of Popay was unveiled on March 21, 2005 in the National Statuary Hall in the rotunda of the U.S. Congress building in Washington, DC.[15] Cliff Fragua, a Native American artist created this fine statue. It is slightly larger than life size, with Popay holding a knotted cord in his left hand (the signal to time the revolt) and a bear fetish in his right hand. A pottery bowl stands behind him representing the *Pueblo* world and belief system. His right shoulder and upper back are exposed to show the many scars received from the Spanish whipping he and so many other native religious leaders endured just prior to the 1680 *Pueblo* Revolt. He stands wearing the *Pueblo* kilt or kirtle with a garment draping over his left shoulder and arm. He wears wrapped moccasins, and a knotted band across his head and over his hair. To the *Pueblo* people, Popay is a hero who helped to preserve the *Pueblo* culture, religious beliefs and traditions that have survived through time. One hundred years before the American Revolution, he organized and led the very first American Revolution.

Los Comancheros[16, 17]

The *Comancheros* were mostly Hispanic and mixed blood traders from central and northern New Mexico, who traded with the *Comanche*. The term *Comanchero* is Spanish for "one who deals with the *Comanche*." There is often confusion between the two. However, they were two different peoples who traded with one another for mutual benefit. Initially, the *Comancheros* brought a variety of both manufactured and agricultural goods to trade with their *Comanche* trading partners. These included items such as cloth, flour, tobacco, sugar, whiskey, beads, tools, knives, steel arrow points, coffee, pumpkin, onions, and also, muskets, pistols and ammunition. In exchange, the *Comanche* traded buffalo and deer hides, beef jerky, tallow,[18] mules, livestock such as Texas longhorns, and female and child captives obtained from their raids into the Texas frontier and northern Mexico. These captives were of course sold as slaves.

Trade with the *Comanche* started after an intense period of raids and hostilities on Spanish Colonial settlements. In 1779, the new Spanish Colonial Governor, Juan Bautista de Anza, undertook a punitive expedition against the *Comanche*. A number of years later, in February 1786, a treaty was signed, with the *Comanche* ending hostilities and opening a period of trade that gave rise to the *Comanchero* traders.

The *Comancheros* came from the indigent classes of New Mexico. They were considered poor, shabby, uneducated and rude. The *Comancheros* dressed with jackets patterned with horizontal stripes and baggy pants reaching to the knees, wearing long stockings and moccasins. To protect their heads and faces from the sun, they wore a large conical-crowned, wide-brimmed *sombrero*. They were hardly a threatening image… in the early period of the *Comanchero* trade!

Over time, as the *Anglos* began to settle in New Mexico, the "booty" of the *Comancheros* was often high-jacked by *Anglos* to further their own material wellbeing, taking full advantage of the *Comanche* trade, without the risk exposure. This is exactly opposite the image presented of them in Hollywood movies. They were more often victimized and stolen from, than the perpetrators of such crimes, at least initially! Nonetheless, the *Comancheros* had to have been courageous to brave the environmental hazards and the personal hazards of trading with one of the most feared nomadic tribes on the western plains.

The *Comancheros* used several means to transport their goods. These varied from burro pack trains to the old Mexican-style *carretas* (carts), to hand-hewn wooden carts drawn by a few oxen. The *carretas* were quite pathetic in appearance. The wheels were eccentric and not quite circular, usually formed by cutting off the ends of large logs. Sometimes, the wheel diameter was increased by attaching additional pieces of timber to the perimeters of the cut off log portion. A cottonwood log served as the axle, which penetrated a whole cut into the center of each "wheel." A small square wicker wood box and a pole completed the *carreta*. It was not uncommon to see abandoned broken axletrees along the "old Mexican cart trails" of the *Comancheros*. Over time, the *Comancheros* obtained larger, more sturdy carts and wagons to transport their trade goods.

The *Comanchero* used one of two trails, the southernmost and the northernmost. They both led into *Comancheria* country and the western Texas plains. The southernmost trail began at *Santa Fe* and headed southeasterly towards the *Pecos* River, then down towards the *Bosque Redondo* area, near Fort Sumner, in east central New Mexico. From there, two sub-branches headed eastward into Texas, across the Texas High Plains to either *Cañon del Rescate*[19], near Lubbock, Texas or to trading sites near Quitaque, Texas.

The second, or northerly route started at *Las Vegas*, New Mexico. It headed in a generally easterly direction towards the Canadian River. One sub-branch headed southeasterly across the Texas High Plains towards Quitaque, while the other sub-branch lead down the Canadian River towards a trading ground at *Las Tecovas*, just west of *Amarillo*, Texas.

When the U.S. stepped up its campaign against the *Comanche*, after the conclusion of the American Civil War, the *Comancheros* did their best to support their trading partners and allies. Firearms and ammunition were supplied to the besieged *Comanche*. Over time, the *Comancheros* seem to have become involved with the slave trade, at first involving other native victims, and later captives from Mexico, Texas and other locations. They also got more seriously involved in trading arms with the *Comanche*, to the detriment of settlers. Eventually the *Comancheros* developed a bad reputation among settlers and U.S. troops. In the 1870's the *Comancheros* even participated in cattle raids alongside the *Comanche* raiders! This latter period in their development seems to be what Hollywood has latched onto. Western movies often portray *Comancheros* as ruthless and violent *banditos*. The degree to which these traders were able to supply the *Comanche* with contraband and to participate in *Comanche* raids is still controversial today.

Nonetheless, *Comancheros* were colorful and interesting characters produced by the rugged frontier living conditions in New Mexico.

New Mexican Buffalo Hunters: The *Ciboleros*[20, 21]

Another group of Hispanic New Mexicans that became legendary and part of the local folklore, were the *Ciboleros* or Buffalo Hunters. These are less well known. These Hispanic villagers banded together after the fall harvest to go on expeditions to the eastern plains. They sought meat to supplement their mostly vegetable diet. They also sought the hides and the sheer thrill of the hunt. They hunted on the Great Plains and in the Texas Panhandle. Eventually they formed a frequent presence on the eastern plains of New Mexico, on the *Llano Estacado*. Many of the *Ciboleros* went east from *Santa Fe*, *Taos* or even from *El Paso*. In the fall and winter, the buffalo herds moved from summer grazing on the Great Plains into the area around the Canadian River, making the herds very accessible to the *Ciboleros*.

The *Ciboleros* sought out the buffalo herds and hunted them using long lances. Less often, bows and arrows were used. More often, the *Ciboleros* rode bareback alongside the buffalo, thrusting their lances into the heart of the animal. By riding bareback, they avoided getting their saddle and gear caught up with the buffalo horns during the hunt.

Once the buffalo (bison) were killed, helpers came behind the hunters to butcher the slain animals and to cut the meat into strips in Indian fashion. The meat was then pounded and dried to make beef jerky to facilitate storage and transport. Every part of the slain buffalo was used.

Hides were scraped and kneaded using buffalo brains. They were also tanned. These hides were formed into rugs and robes. The robes were very useful during wild winter storms, keeping the wearer warm and providing protection from the real prospect of freezing to death. Buffalo fat was cut and cooked to reduce it to tallow, which was used for cooking or for making candles. The tongue was dried and later traded or sold as a delicacy. Horns were used as spoons or for decorative purposes. Even the long neck and shoulder hair was used to make coarse clothing. At the end of the hunt, *carretas* were loaded up with beef, hides, tallow, and buffalo tongues.

The *Ciboleros* then headed home laden with their catch, to the adulation and gratitude of the villagers. The weeks spent hunting allowed the *Ciboleros* to return home with meat to supplement their diet, especially through the harsh winter ahead. They also brought other buffalo goods. The returning *Ciboleros* were often greeted with a *fandango*[22] dance, in celebration of their success.

Cibolero hunting parties often consisted of about 150 hunters. These hunters often brought items such as homemade bread, beads, sugar, flour, coffee and trinkets to trade with Indian hunting parties. These goods were used to appease the Indian hunters they encountered. Over time, the buffalo herds became decimated because of the killing efficiency of the *Ciboleros*. The various tribes even grew concerned about the level of decimation. The effect of these hunts together with the large-scale hunts of the *Anglo-Americans* quickly reduced the size of the buffalo herds and started to threaten the life mode of the Plains Indians.

The *Ciboleros* and the *Comancheros* thrived until the 1870's when the buffalo herds and the nomadic Indian bands began to disappear.

Bent on Success - Charles Bent[23]

The first U. S. Military Governor of the newly acquired New Mexico Territory in 1846 was Charles Bent. See Figure 4-3. As enterprising young men, Charles and his younger brother William started out from St. Louis in 1828 with a wagon full of goods to trade. Their destination: *Santa Fe*, New Mexico. They established trading contacts during their numerous travels. Eventually, they set up a number of fortified trading posts along the Arkansas and Canadian Rivers.[24] Among others, they established Bent's Fort on the Arkansas River in *Colorado* and Fort *Adobe* on the Canadian River.

Due to his trading successes, Charles Bent rose to power and eminence. In 1846, he was appointed Military Governor of the new territory that had been seized by American armed forces. Though his office was in *Santa Fe*, he maintained his residence and store in the town of *Taos*. However, he met an early and vicious death. He was scalped and murdered on January 19, 1847 during the *Taos* Revolt.[25] The women and children escaped through a hole in the wall.

Charles Bent's wife, Maria, and frontier hero Kit Carson's wife, Josefa, were sisters, making Bent and Carson brothers-in-law! Charles Bent is buried at the *Santa Fe* National Cemetery in *Santa Fe*. The Governor Charles Bent House can be viewed today as a museum in *Taos*.

Figure 4-3: Charles Bent, First Military Governor of New Mexico. He was killed in 1847, during the *Taos* Revolt. (Sketch based on Public Domain photo)

The "Real" Kit Carson:[26, 27] More Heroic than "Pulp" Fiction

"Kit" Carson was born Christopher Houston Carson on Christmas Eve 1809 in rural Missouri. He played many significant roles in the exploration and settling of the west. He certainly led a challenging and exciting, full life in every sense. During his life, he was a fur trapper, a scout and a guide for John C. Fremont's two exploratory expeditions into the American West. Carson was a frontiersman and a hunter. During the Mexican-American War, he was a lieutenant in Fremont's California Battalion. Kit Carson was also a cross-country courier and a seasoned Indian fighter and campaigner. Later in life he became a rancher and even drove cattle in that lucrative trade.

He helped open up trails and passes through the western mountain regions of the new west. He helped to tame the Native American tribes, paving the way for western expansion and settlement.

Carson first became famous because of the reports sent back by Fremont to Washington, DC about his explorations and expeditions. One expedition was to California and the other was to the Oregon Coast. Fremont fully credited Kit Carson for his competency as a scout and guide. This elevated Carson to national fame.

He married twice before he met Josefa Jaramillo, the daughter of a prominent *Taos* family. They married in 1843. Carson's two previous wives were Native Americans from the *Arapaho* tribe and the *Cheyenne* tribe, respectively. However, Josefa was the love of his life. They had eight children together.

Over time, Carson became fluent in Spanish, *Navajo, Apache, Cheyenne, Arapaho, Paiute, Shoshone* and *Ute*. Figure 4-4 shows a mature Kit Carson.

Carson gained further recognition for his controversial but successful "scorched earth" campaign against the intransigent *Navajo* buttressed in the "impenetrable" Canyon de Chelly area of Arizona. His success led to the gathering of the survivors of the *Navajo* tribes people, and the forced march of about 8,500 *Navajo* men, women and children across Arizona and most of New Mexico to their final incarceration camp at the *Bosque Redondo* next to Fort Sumner.

Figure 4-4: Kit Carson, scout, trapper, Indian fighter, cross-country courier, Brigadier General, rancher and Indian Agent.** (Photo is part of Brady-Handy Collection, c.1860 – 1868. Courtesy of the Library of Congress, Prints and Photographs Division)

This traumatic event was scorched into the memories of the *Navajo*. It has been called the "Long Walk." See the discussion in Chapter Three regarding the "Long Walk." After much loss of life at *Bosque Redondo* due to disease and starvation, the *Navajo* were finally released to go back to a portion of their lands that were set up as a reservation of the new *Navajo* Nation. Carson carried out his orders as he was charged. He believed that with the relentless encroachment of new *Anglo*-American settlers on their homelands and hunting grounds, the only chance for the survival of the natives was through the reservation system where they could be shielded and separated from white hostility and culture. Later in life he became an Indian Agent and did his best to truly represent the needs of the *Ute* and the *Jicarilla Apache* in northern New Mexico

During the American Civil War, Carson had served as Colonel of Volunteers in New Mexico, and fought bravely at *Valverde*. In 1865, General Carleton recommended him to be brevetted as Brigidier General for his military service at the Battle of *Valverde* and for his services in quelling the *Comanche*, *Mescalero Apache* and *Navajo* tribes. In later years, he became a rancher in *Taos*.

During his lifetime, all kinds of "pulp fiction" books came out supposedly recounting his many adventures as a trapper, frontiersman and Indian fighter. He ignored these false fictional stories and never let them turn his head from his duty. Although some may disagree with his creed and his actions, he was a man of his times, and a very courageous, loyal and dutiful servant to the U.S. during a difficult and hostile period in our history. He died on May 23, 1868 at the relatively young age of 59, from an aortic rupture. He remained very well respected by military leaders, common men, trappers and scouts, Native Americans and politicians.

He was said to be an honorable, humble person and simple-hearted; beloved and respected by many in his time. Some recent authors have a different view of him that is more sympathetic to the Native Americans that he helped to subdue. There is no doubt that *Navajo* and others suffered greatly as a consequence of his actions in performing "his duty", and that is indeed tragic! Since he left no written record of his own feelings in these difficult times, it is impossible to know exactly how he viewed them. Their enemies, the *Ute* and other tribes actively participated in the action against the Navajo at Canyon de Chelly.

This paragraph gives a possible glimpse into Carson's thinking. The key is to examine his actions at the time. It is interesting to note[28] that, when General Carlton first suggested his campaign against the marauding *Navajo*, Kit Carson offered his resignation, which was dated February 3, 1863. Carlton wanted the *Navajo* raids eliminated. He had also heard rumors of gold found on the *Navajo* lands! Carlton used the force of his personality to keep Carson engaged and to follow his orders, which he eventually did in subduing the *Navajo*. Carson employed *Ute* warriors, enemies of the *Navajo*, in his campaign. Although the *Ute* served him well, they wanted to gather *Navajo* booty. When Carson refused, they abandoned the campaign and returned home to the north. Although Carson subdued the *Navajo* at Canyon de Chelly in Arizona with his scorched earth campaign, he took a much-needed rest or leave from the U.S. Army shortly afterwards and returned home. He was exhausted and feeling unwell. The greatest part of the notorious "Long Walk" march occurred after Carson's temporary departure. However, he was held responsible for the tribal hardships that ensued.

Later in 1864, he requested and obtained the position of Superintendent of *Bosque Redondo*. He undertook this position in an attempt to facilitate the retraining of the *Navajo*, and to oversee their needs and well being during the transition. Ultimately, he became disillusioned as he saw that Carlton's plans were ill-conceived and ill-fated, causing suffering among the *Navajo*. He felt frustrated with the bureaucratic corruption and lack of positive action. Finally, by mid-Septemmber 1864, Carlton had re-assigned Carson to a mission in Texas against the *Comanche*.

History is often tragic because of misunderstandings, different perspectives and the inevitable clash of different cultures. Oftentimes individuals are caught up in the whirlwind of history, in the historical and cultural changes that dwarf the individual, his actions and his sentiments. As a result, people are slaves to their own culture's perspective and are often blind to the opposing viewpoint. Or if they are not blind, they are often powerless to stop the march of history. Unfortunately, in a clash of cultures, all perspectives suffer, cultures suffer and individuals suffer. A sense of fairness also falls victim to the need for survival. One can always try to re-write history from the distance of more than one hundred years, in the comfort of a warm, secure home. However, those conditions did not exist in Carson's time. Bold and firm action was required to survive. No one can truly know what it was like to live in those times, because one cannot rid oneself of modern moral values and biases, which are irrelevant and out-of-place for that time period.

With each side trying desperately to "survive" on their own terms, the result is inevitable injustice and tragedy. Events and circumstance are much greater than the individual. Each side sees the need to survive on its own terms, which can only be incompatible with the opposing culture's terms of survival. Usually, there is only one perspective that wins brutally in the end! That is the persective of the strongest, the victor. Different time, different lens!!

Kit Carson was just one of many individuals caught up in such a brutal whirlwind. He and others from that time period cannot be judged using modern values or moral codes. Was *Victorio* a bad man because he killed so many white settlers? Inevitably and unjustly, many innocents died! He too was fighting for his own peoples' survival by whatever means he could. And he too was caught in a tumultuous violent storm, not of his own making!

Today, Kit Carson's Home and Museum can be seen and visited in downtown "Old Town" *Taos*. Kit Carson's gravesite can also be seen at the Kit Carson Cemetery in *Taos*.

An interesting read on Carson's exploits in the mid 1800's can be found in the non-fiction bestseller, *Blood and Thunder*[29] by Hampton Sides. The book places Carson and his deeds in the context of the times, with proper attention to Native American views.

Mescalero Peacemaker: Santana[30]

Often in history we learn of the warriors, the empire builders and the "shakers and makers." Less is known of the patient and trying work of the true peacemakers, but the work of the peacemakers deserve our attention, recognition and gratitude for they are the ones who save lives and cultures, the ones who build where others, more famous, destroy.

Santana, War Chief of the *Mescalero Apache*, was one such New Mexican peacemaker. Santana's name is not well recognized, although he needs to be! Most people today think of the famous and well-known guitarist and rock bandleader Santana, famous for his Latino rock beat, rhythms and melodies that have enraptured millions. The *Mescalero* Santana is hardly known by those same millions! Figure 4-5 shows a sketch of Santana, based on a rare photograph of the *Mescalero* War Chief.

It seems strange that a "war chief" should be acknowledged as a "peacemaker", but the truth is that Santana, after years of warfare, had an epiphany. In his early years, Santana was known among the *Anglo*-American and Hispanic settlers for his ferocity and cunning in war. He was a very credible and feared war chief of the *Mescalero Apache* tribe in the mid 1800's in New Mexico. He ultimately came to realize that the *Anglo*-American onslaught was relentless and that his people were ultimately doomed to extinction, unless another path to survival was found.

Realizing also that he would become a target for his warlike actions, he retired into the safety and security of the *Sacramento* Mountains until matters settled down. When he reappeared eight years later, he was ready to lead the *Mescalero*s towards peace. Through negotiation, he secured a reservation for his people on their homeland in the sacred *Sacramento* Mountains and the *Sierra Blanca* near *Ruidoso*, in south-central New Mexico.

A local man, J. H. Blazer, owner and operator of Blazer's Mill on the *Rio Tularosa*, was cautiously approached and over time a strong and lasting friendship developed. Through this friendship, Santana found a trusted and abiding ally who helped him to understand the foreign *Anglo*-American culture and to settle differences between the two cultures, in the interest of saving the future of the *Mescalero* people.

In the winter of 1877, Santana caught pneumonia and died. He had successfully saved his people from annihilation by the relentless expansion westward of the *Anglo*-Americans. He died knowing that it was possible for people from two entirely different worlds and cultures to become steadfast and true friends. Perhaps there was hope after all!

Today the *Mescalero Apache* Reservation is one of the most beautiful in the nation. This fine casino/hotel resort overlooks a man-made lake and onto the *Sierra Blanca*. Hunting in the mountains of the reservation is also popular. None of this would have been possible if not for the peaceful, pragmatic and timely vision of Santana, War Chief of the *Mescalero.*

Figure 4-5: *Mescalero* War Chief, Santana, who secured peace and reservation lands for his people. (Sketch based on a Public Domain photo.)

Freedom Fighters: *Victorio*[31,32] & *Nana*[33]

Victorio has been introduced in discussions in the previous chapter. He was called *Bidu-ya or Beduiat* by his people. *Victorio* was born in Mexico but he grew up among the *Chihene* band of the *Chiricahua Apache*, and eventually became their chief. It is also thought that he may have had kin among the *Navajo*, who called him "he who

checks his horse." *Victorio*'s sister (or perhaps his cousin) was Lozen, the "Woman Warrior", also described briefly in this chapter. *Victorio* was the prime actor in the *Victorio* Wars of the late 1800's. As described elsewhere, he died in Mexico in 1880. He fought and died for his people, their freedom and way of life. See Figure 4-6.

Figure 4-6: *Victorio*, stalwart and fierce leader of the Warm Springs *Apache*, or *Chihene Apache*. (Sketch based on a Public Domain photo.)

Nana, known by his people as *Kas-tziden*, meaning "broken foot" in *Apache*, became chief of the Warm Springs *Apache* upon the death of *Victorio* in 1880. He was more often known among *Anglos* as "*Nana*", his Mexican name, which means "grandma." He was the nephew of *Delgadito* ('Skinny'), another famous *Apache*. *Geronimo* was also known to *Nana,* since he married one of *Geronimo*'s sisters. *Nana* fought alongside the famous *Apache* warriors *Mangas Coloradas* ("Colored Sleeves") and *Victorio* while they lived. This great old warrior was eventually captured by U.S. troops but then escaped to join *Geronimo* and his band. Although in his eighties, *Nana* fought alongside *Geronimo* through the final days of the *Apache* resistance.

He surrendered with *Geronimo* in 1886. He was sent to Fort Marion as a prisoner but he was released to go to Fort Sill, Oklahoma in 1894. He died there in May 1896, at the very advanced age of 96. Of all the fierce *Apache* warriors, *Nana* had the longest fighting career. He fought into his mid eighties! He too was a true freedom fighter. See Figure 4-7, showing the tough but effective old warrior.

Figure 4-7: *Nana*, Leader of the Warm Springs *Apache*, after *Victorio*'s death.** ((Photo by Ben Whittock, c. 1880-1890, Courtesy Palace of the Governors Photo Archives (NMHM.DCA) neg. # 16321.)

The "Notorious" *Santa Fe* Ring[34, 35]

The *Santa Fe* Ring was prominent in New Mexico politics around the end of the 19th and the beginning of the 20th Century. Their power extended throughout the territory. It was a group of connected corrupt lawyers and land speculators who accumulated great wealth through fraudulent land deals, political corruption and influence. Many of the key political figures in this era in New Mexico were involved or associated with the corrupt *Santa Fe* Ring. As a result, the Ring held almost complete political control over New Mexico during this period. Most state politicians in *Santa Fe* were either part of the *Santa Fe* Ring or were in collusion with it. Many were involved directly with corruption for their own political or material gain. In other cases, they ignored instances of corruption, to the detriment of many fair and honest people in the state. They were most active during the 1870's. They formed fraudulent deals to obtain money and huge tracts of old Spanish land grants. The *Santa Fe* Ring was involved in both the Lincoln County War and the early phases of the Maxwell and Grant dispute. The Lincoln County War is described in Chapter Three. The Colfax County War centered around the eviction of squatters on the controversial Maxwell Land Grant[36, 37]. Roughly ten times as many folks died in the Colfax County War than in the notorious Lincoln County War. Perhaps, Billy the Kid's involvement has brought more attention to the latter.

Among those connected with and protected by the *Santa Fe* Ring, were individuals such as Lawrence Murphy, Emil Fritz, James Dolan and John Riley, the corrupt, violent and ruthless mercantilists and ranchers who dominated life and politics in Lincoln County from the late 1860's until the deadly Lincoln County War that peaked in mid-summer 1878.

During the period of the *Santa Fe* Ring, millions of acres of New Mexico territorial lands were transferred to private ownership through complex and fraudulent methods implemented by the attorneys of the Ring. They facilitated the corrupt or quasi-legal transfer of communal lands from thousands of Hispanic and Native American natives to the newly arrived *Anglo*-Americans. They failed to recognize Spanish titles or land claims when the documentation of those titles had become lost over time. To those they enriched with millions of acres of land, they sought compensation for their legal services in land in lieu of cash, and so became huge landholders themselves. It is estimated that 80% of the land was transferred from the original holders to the *Anglo*-Americans by these fraudulent methods!

Thomas B. Catron, a well-known attorney and later a notable territorial politician, who helped bring fruition to the quest for statehood, acquired several million acres of land, for his work in dealing with 75 land grant claims over time. Catron County in southwestern New Mexico is named after him.

Lucien Maxwell's original Mexican grant was for 97,000 acres, but he was finally granted 2 million acres, some say by the efforts of the *Santa Fe* Ring! However, in 1876, Lucien Maxwell had already been deceased two years and the new owners of the Maxwell Land Grant aggressively pursued the forced removal of the land's squatters. When these settlers and squatters in Colfax County refused to be driven off the land, the Colfax County War broke out. About 200 people were killed in that county war. The corrupt *Santa Fe* Ring continued in power into the early years of the 20th Century.

Lew Wallace[38] - New Mexico has Something in Common with *Ben Hur*! Huh?

Most folks are familiar with the 1959 epic color film *Ben Hur*, starring Charleton Heston. It was based on the novel *Ben Hur: A Tale of the Christ* written by Lew Wallace in 1880. What is less known is that the author, Lew Wallace, wrote his famous novel while Governor of the New Mexico Territory, a post he held between 1879 and 1882. Lew Wallace wrote the final Crucifixion scenes of his novel within the confines of the Palace of the Governors. It is said that he wrote the scenes after returning from a stressful and tense meeting with Billy the Kid in Lincoln County, in the spring of 1879. It was during a severe and heavy thunderstorm that he wrote by the light of a shaded lamp, huddled in the shuttered Governor's study within the Palace of the Governors, fearing an assassin's bullet from outside, over the tensions of the Lincoln County War.

See Figure 4-8. Wallace served as Territorial Governor, during the Lincoln County War. In 1879, he solicited Billy the Kid's help, as an informant, in rounding up some of the miscreants in exchange for a Governor's pardon from Wallace. The politics of the time however did not allow the Territorial Governor to fulfill his end of the deal.

Figure 4-8: Lew Wallace, Territorial Governor of New Mexico, during the Lincoln County War. (Sketch based upon a Public Domain Photo.)

Prior to his term as Territorial Governor, Lew Wallace served in the Union Army during the American Civil War. He participated in the actions at Fort Henry and Fort Donelson in 1862, and at the Battle of Shiloh in April 1862. His role in Shiloh was clouded in controversy, damaging his reputation. This was due to his seemingly tardy arrival with his troops at the Shiloh battlefront. He later fought and delayed Confederate General Early's advance on Washington, D.C., at the Battle of Monocacy in July 1864. He also served on the military commission trial of the conspirators in the Lincoln assassination of 1865. He served as the Territorial Governor of New Mexico from 1878 to 1881. Lew Wallace died of cancer on February 15, 1905.

Billy the Kid's Elusive Pardon

The story of Billy the Kid[39] is both fascinating and controversial. As recently as 2010, former Governor Bill Richardson sought a pardon for Billy the Kid. Perhaps this was an attempt to draw attention to this notorious character to encourage increased tourism to the Land of Enchantment. However, there must have been some basis for this apparently strange request.

The fact is that a deal was made in the late 1870's, in the midst of the Lincoln County War, between then Territorial Governor Lew Wallace and the "outlaw" Billy the Kid. The deal was for the Kid to serve as an informer against the corrupt and notoriously violent Murphy-Dolan-Riley faction, situated in the "cow town" of Lincoln, New Mexico. This was to be in exchange for a pardon from the governor, for his past deeds. However, circumstances never allowed either party to complete his end of the bargain. And so, Governor Richardson attempted to complete the state government's end of the deal, more than 130 years later! He was unsuccessful!

After the Kid went on a killing spree, following the murder of his friend John

Tunstall, the same Territorial Governor Lew Wallace apparently changed his view of the Kid. A few months before the Kid's death, he put a price on his head. So, even the Governor at the time had changing views of the now infamous Billy the Kid. See Figure 4-9 for his famous portrait.

Just outside the entrance to the *Bosque Redondo* Monument in Fort Sumner, there is a small gift shop and museum, called the Old Fort Sumner Museum & Gift Shop. Here, there are copies of letters sent by Billy the Kid to Territorial Governor Lew Wallace that show Billy the Kid repeatedly requesting that the Territorial Governor answer his previous requests for him to respond to his letters. Apparently, his attempts were in vain. The handwriting is very neat, attractive and legible, not what one would expect! These letters give a sympathetic insight into the personality of Billy the Kid.

There is much confusion and controversy over Billy the Kid's beginnings. The notorious Billy the Kid was born in New York in 1859, of Irish descent. It is thought that his biological father may have been a William McCarty. However, he apparently died early in the marriage. In this version, Billy was named William Henry McCarty, but was called Henry by his mother. Others claim that Catherine McCarty was his mother's maiden name, and that she married a William H. Bonney. In this case, Billy's birth name would have been William H. Bonney, Jr. Some time in Billy's toddler years, the family moved out to Indianapolis, Indiana and then west to Kansas. During this time period, his "father" died. Billy's widowed mother met another gentleman named William Antrim, either in Indiana or later when she moved to *Pueblo, Colorado.* It is likely that the mother moved to *Colorado* for health reasons, because she was already suffering from tuberculosis. She subsequently married William Antrim, either in Indiana or in *Colorado.* So, Billy the Kid's later aliases (William Bonney, Henry McCarty, William Antrim) were actually tied up with his birth name, his mother's maiden name or his name by one or more of his stepfathers.

The Antrims' soon moved to *Santa Fe*, New Mexico, and then five years later moved southwest to Silver City, a flourishing silver mining town at the time. While in *Santa Fe*, at the tender age of eight years, Billy learned the habit of dealing three-card Monte. Over the years he became very proficient and adept at it. It was in Silver City, as a young boy, that Billy met and came to know Jesse Davis, aka Jesse Evans of Lincoln County War notoriety. Some versions state that the Kid left Silver City suddenly, at the age of twelve, after an ugly incident following an insult hurled at his mother. It is said that, at the right moment, Billy killed the insulter and started on his life of crime. However, there is much uncertainty about Billy's younger life. Other versions about his early start on a life of crime also exist, but it is difficult to know which are true and which are not. After the Silver City incident, Billy was always known to possess an impulsive and uncontrollable temper. After his mother had passed away, Billy the Kid was arrested in Grant County for stealing cheese. It was April 1875. Later that same year in September, Billy the Kid was arrested once again, this time for possession of clothing and firearms, that belonged to a Chinese laundry owner. Some say he had possession but they were actually stolen by a fellow boarder at the boarding house where he was staying. However, he escaped the local jail within two days and became a fugitive thereafter. Nonetheless, his loyalty to family and friends was also unquestioned.

Some time after the jail escape, Billy the Kid ended up in Arizona. Here he supposedly engaged in horse rustling with John R. Mackie. Because of these daring deeds he became known as "Kid Antrim." In 1877, he became involved in an incident at Fort Grant with a local bully named Frank "Windy" Cahill, a blacksmith and Irish immigrant. On August 17, an encounter broke out between Windy Cahill and Billy the Kid. After some taunting verbal remarks from Cahill, Windy threw Billy the Kid to the ground. Somehow the Kid reached for a gun and shot Cahill to death. Some witnesses to the incident claimed that Billy McCarty shot Cahill in self-defense. The killing of Cahill caused Billy to flee Arizona and to return New Mexico.

It is indisputable that the Kid was a force to be reckoned with! After many years, he became an accomplished cattle and horse rustler, and gun handler. Eventually he settled in around Lincoln and the Fort Sumner area. Soon after, John Tunstall an English rancher and entrepreneur hired him. He then became involved in the subsequent vicious and deadly Lincoln County War. It is true that Billy the Kid did kill men! However, in almost every case, he fought in self-defense or in revenge against members of the Murphy-Dolan-Riley faction who had killed his friends. In other cases,

he shot down men who sought him out to murder him, for gain or fame.

In many ways, he had become a survivor. Billy the Kid was generally liked by most of the locals who knew him. He was popular among the women for his courteous and mild manner, his kindliness to elders and for his bravery.

Figure 4-9: Billy the Kid (1860 – 1881), aka Billy Antrim, Billy Bonney or Billy McCarty: a Winchester Model 1873 lever-action rifle at his side.** (Photographer unknown c. 1880. Courtesy of the Library of Congress, Prints and Photographs Division.)

He was considered a good dancer, and often was seen at local dances. He was fluent in Spanish and had many friends among the Hispanic community. He often wore a *sombrero*!

He was no innocent and he was a young man with whom you did not want to be on the other side of an argument. He was quick-witted and decisive, but he was a deadly man to cross, in spite of his young years. He lived in deadly violent times, and encountered deadly violent men who sought to do him in.

When Billy killed the two deputies, Bell and Olinger, upon his escape from the old Lincoln County Courthouse and Jail, he was acting in self-preservation. Even the mother of Bob Olinger, one of the two deputies that were killed, basically said that her son (Bob Olinger) had been murderous from a young age and deserved what he got in the end. It is said that few in Lincoln regretted Olinger's demise. (The site where Olinger was shot outside the Lincoln County Jail is shown in Chapter Fourteen.) Some saw Olinger as a killer behind a badge!

"The Kid" was considered to be fiercely loyal to his friends. So when his friend John Tunstall was killed in cold blood he naturally sought revenge. He joined Sheriff Brewer and the Regulators, a group of deputized vigilantes formed to seek revenge for the cold-blooded murder of John Tunstall by the "authorities", who were on the payroll of the Murphy-Dolan-Riley faction.

When the Murphy-Dolan-Riley faction killed Brewer, the Regulator leadership briefly went to Frank McNab. After he too was killed, Billy the Kid quickly assumed leadership of the Regulator gang. Later, many crimes committed by others were attributed to Billy the Kid because of his notoriety and name recognition. According to Mrs. Barber,[40] the former Mrs. McSween, "Billy was a whole-hearted boy – kind and loyal to all those deserving such a return from him. The best citizens of Lincoln County were his friends and admirers. He was universally liked. The native citizens, in particular, loved him because he was always kind and considerate to them and took much pleasure in helping them and providing for their wants... Billy was a graceful and beautiful dancer..." This is hardly a condemning portrait from McSween's widow, a woman who knew Billy reasonably well. Billy the Kid was a product of the violent times he lived in and he was a survivor. Does that excuse all his misdeeds? Certainly not, but it does give us insight into the person of Billy the Kid.

The former Mrs. McSween also condemned the killing of Sheriff Brady: "The murder of Sheriff Brady was Billy the Kid's own doing and was without excuse or palliation...The murder was bad diplomacy. It was worse than a crime. It was a blunder. It flouted public opinion and gave the McSween cause a blow from which it never recovered."[41]

On the other hand she also said: "The Kid was not half as bad as some of those who were after him and determined to kill him...despite the fact he had killed his two guards, Bell and Olinger, in making his escape, he had the community completely on his side...Hardly anyone believed he had received a fair and just trial..."[42]

To shed further light on Billy the Kid, it is important to look at his nemesis and eventual killer, Sheriff Pat Garrett. Some claim that before becoming sheriff, Pat Garrett and Billy the Kid were friends, hanging out in saloons drinking, gambling and rustling cattle together. Former New Mexico Governor Antonio Miguel Otero claimed that the two were so well known around their favorite hangout at Old Fort Sumner, that they were known as "Big Casino" and "Little Casino"[43]. However, if this is true, such friendship did not stand in Garrett's way to get his man.

Garrett accepted the sheriff's position offered by the Murphy-Dolan-Riley faction on their condition that he hunt down and kill Billy the Kid. In contrast, Billy the Kid was fiercely loyal to those he deemed his friends. Even the method by which Sheriff

Pat Garrett got "his man" was considered controversial, and haunted Garrett for many years of his life. He awaited "the Kid's" arrival in Pete Maxwell's unlit room in Old Fort Sumner ready to get "the Kid" when he entered Maxwell's room. Supposedly Maxwell's daughter or sister, had been romantically involved with the Kid, and Maxwell was not too happy about this prospect. It is said that in the past, Maxwell had employed Garrett. So, Garrett knew of the Kid's hangout in Old Fort Sumner.

On July 14, 1881, Sheriff Garrett waited in the dark for Billy the Kid's arrival at Maxwell's house. He was sitting alongside Maxwell on his bed, armed with a loaded and cocked pistol. It was said that Billy the Kid eventually arrived in stocking feet, with no boots on, carrying a knife to cut some beef off a hanging carcass on the patio. He called into the unlit room, asking in Spanish, "who's there?" He was answered with a deadly shot from Garrett's gun. So ended the notorious Billy the Kid. (Please see the play *Billy the Kid*, by Chicano playwright and novelist, Rudolf Anaya, for a sympathetic and Hispanic presentation of Billy the Kid's last days.)

The controversy behind Garrett's method of killing Billy the Kid, hounded Garrett for the rest of his life. After the incident, Garrett wrote a book to defend his actions. He claimed that Billy the Kid carried a gun that fateful day. However, many historians tend to believe that "the Kid" was only carrying a knife to carve the beef. Garrett did represent "law and order", but that law was tainted by the corruption of those who hired him, namely the Murphy-Dolan-Riley faction in Lincoln County. Many years later, Garrett claimed regret at having killed Billy the Kid. Perhaps he really regretted killing him. Maybe, he simply wanted to undo the attention and notoriety he received for his past action, as the killer of the notorious "Kid." One author[44] claims, "that the two were neither chums nor enemies." This contradicts former New Mexico Governor Miguel Antonio Otero's claim about them being good friends!

The very same author quotes Garrett as saying, about Billy the Kid,[45] "He minds his business, and I attend to mine." He quotes Garrett as saying, "He visits my wife's folks sometimes, but he never comes around me. I just simply don't want anything to do with him, and he knows it, and knows that he has nothing to fear from me as long as he does not interfere with me or my affairs." Obviously, Garrett knew Billy the Kid and had met him. Beyond that, only the deceased actors in this drama know the truth. Later, Garrett went on to become a well-known and respected law-enforcer.[46, 47] So, we must wonder: what is the truth about Billy the Kid? No one knows for sure!

Aware of this mixed image of Billy the Kid, New Mexico Governor Richardson once again brought him up for pardon in 2010. The bid however was unsuccessful, as the evidence for and against Billy the Kid is still so controversial. One thing is sure. In the Lincoln County War, Billy the Kid appears to have been on the side of the honest folk and fair-minded businessmen of Lincoln. No, he wasn't on the side of the "law", but then again the corrupt and violent Murphy-Dolan-Riley gang and the *Santa Fe* Ring represented the "law." The "law" in Lincoln at that time was not necessarily the side of "justice" or "right." The "law" was "bought and paid for" by corrupt, fraudulent and vicious businessmen and politicians, who wanted no one to stand in the way of their greed or power grabbing. They "owned" the "law" and utilized it for their own purposes. Damned be anyone who crossed them or who violated "their law." That speaks for itself!

Billy the Kid's impetuosity, his need for revenge, his murderous rage, his youthful recklessness and his belief in his own ability to get out of any bad situation, eventually led him to his death at the hands of the corrupt power-brokers and the "law" of his day, whom he had opposed. In the end ruthlessness abounded on both sides of the Lincoln County War, and took many of the significant actors to the grave. Billy the Kid met a deadly end…without the promised, elusive pardon he so craved!

Lozen:[48] Women's Liberation, *Apache* Style

In modern times, we celebrate and practice women's liberation each and every day. However, Lozen, the sister (or possibly cousin) of *Victorio*, of the *Ojo Caliente* or Warm Springs *Apache*, was as liberated as any woman today. She rode with the men, engaged in combat, and was held in very high regard for her strength, endurance and prowess, by her fellow *Apache* warriors. After *Victorio*'s death, Lozen rode and fought with Geronimo and his *Chiricahua* band. The *Chiricahua* called Lozen "the Woman Warrior."[49] Her people called her "the shield of her people."[50]

It was not unusual among *Apache* tribes for wives to accompany their warrior husbands when they went on raids. They performed domestic chores. However, they were prepared and often fought alongside their men when the camp was endangered. It was also common for new widows[51] to seek personal physical revenge against their husbands' killers. In these cases, they would go out on murderous raids against the perpetrators, and the widow played an active and personal role in seeking revenge for her loss. However, once vengeance had been obtained these women usually returned to their more domestic roles. It was unusual for a woman to choose the warrior path as a full time role. Lozen was different in this regard. Some of her motivation for choosing this life style may have come from an emotionally wrenching love experience as a young maiden.

It is said that when she was very young she fell in love with a visiting Seneca Chief, named Gray Wolf. He was passing through the Southwest seeking a new homeland for his people, under pressure from the U.S. Government. Apparently, he moved on and Lozen was left broken-hearted. She swore that no man would ever cause her such pain again. So, she adopted the warrior life style. It appears her motivation arose from having been jilted at a tender age. In addition, she apparently enjoyed the warrior role.

It is said that she was an excellent horsewoman and a sharpshooter with a rifle. She was held to be extremely brave and knowledgeable on battle tactics. There was one other attribute[52] she possessed. She appeared to have the ability to sense the direction from which an enemy would approach. She would stand in a position of supplication, with her arms upstretched and palms upward. She'd rotate slowly until she sensed a tingling in her palms. This told her the direction of the enemy, while the intensity of the tingling told her the relative distance. This unique ability was utilized and manifested often in her fighting career.

It is also said that before one battle engagement, Lozen,[53] fearing for her brother's life, had the other warriors pledge to eat *Victorio*'s body rather than let it fall into enemy hands! It turned out that he survived the encounter. It is thought that *Victorio* died at *Tres Castillos* because Lozen was not with him to tell him where the enemy was located. She was absent[54] from the fray because she was escorting a native woman and her baby across the *Chihuahua*n Desert towards the *Mescalero Apache* Reservation. Once she arrived she learned that her brother, *Victorio*, had died at his own hands rather than be captured by his enemies.

Lozen participated in all the usual warrior ceremonies, and even helped to plan tactics and strategies for battle. Years ago, little was known of Lozen because few *Apache* wanted to talk about Lozen and her exploits. They felt that outsiders would not understand her and so they kept the knowledge to themselves, until recently.

Victorio, leader of the Warm Springs *Apache* and brother or cousin to Lozen, said of Lozen: "I depend on her as I do *Nana*."[55] When a group of the Warm Springs *Apache* left the deplorable *San Carlos* Reservation in Arizona in 1880, Lozen escorted the women and children to safety. After completing this mission, she returned to the male warriors. She always carried a rifle, a cartridge belt and a knife. It is reputed that she once killed a longhorn steer single-handedly armed with only a knife.

Once while riding and fighting with Geronimo and his *Chiricahua* Band against the Mexicans, they found themselves under attack and a warrior dropped a much-needed ammunition pouch. The pouch contained 500 cartridges. Lozen went back, crawled into the line of fire and safely retrieved the much-prized ammunition pouch!

When Geronimo and his band surrendered in 1886, Lozen was among the *Apache* band. She and others were sent to the Mount Vernon Barracks in Alabama. She died there of tuberculosis at the relatively young age of about 50 years. Fellow *Apache* prisoners buried Lozen secretly. She lived her life as a truly liberated woman, choosing her own "warrior" path.

Life-long Vengeance: *Geronimo*[56]

Just about everyone has heard of the great *Chiricahua Apache* War leader, *Geronimo*. This was not his real name. His people called him *Goyaale*, meaning "one who yawns." It is often spelled *Goyahkla* in English. He was born into the *Bedonkohe* band of the *Chiricahua Apache*, near Turkey Creek, a tributary of the *Gila* River in New Mexico. Prior to 1848, this area had been part of Mexico. In the past, *Goyahkla's* grandfather had been a chief of the *Bedonkohe* band. After his father died, his mother took him to live with the *Chihene* (Red Paint people) *Apache* band. By the time he was 17 years of age, he was married and had three children. Then a tragedy struck which changed the entire course of his life.

In March 1858, 400 Mexican soldiers from *Sonora* attacked *Geronimo's* camp. The men were away trading at the time. *Geronimo* returned to find his wife, his children and his mother killed by the Mexicans. That event compelled him towards intense hatred for the Mexicans!

Goyahlka received his more familiar name from the Mexicans. During a battle against Mexicans, *Goyahkla* continued to repeatedly attack the Mexican soldiers with knife in hand, seemingly impervious to a hail of bullets. In terror, the Mexicans made feverish appeals to Saint Jerome or *San Jeronimo (San Geronimo)*, in Spanish. The new name stuck over time. See Figure 4-10.

Geronimo was not a chief but a war leader. His hatred for the Mexicans was always greatest, because of the Mexicans' murder of his family. *Geronimo* and his band continued their raids and their marauding streak until their surrender in 1886 to General Miles. However, the U.S. promise that the warriors would be reunited with their families in exile, was not kept until about a year later. The warriors were sent as prisoners to Fort Pickens, in Pensacola, Florida, while their families were sent to Fort

Mason.

They were only reunited in May 1887 when they all were sent to Mount Vernon Barricks, Alabama. This is the place where Lozen eventually died of tuberculosis.

Figure 4-10: *Geronimo* or *Goyahkla* as he appreared during the *Apache* Wars. (Sketch based on a Public Domain photo by Camillus S. Fly, 1886.)

They were held here for seven years until they were again transferred to Fort Sill, Oklahoma in 1894.

In February 1909, *Geronimo*, at the age of about eighty, was thrown from a horse on his way home. He lay in the cold through the night until a friend found him in poor condition. He died on February 17, 1909 of pneumonia. He died a prisoner of the United States in Fort Sill and he was buried in the *Apache* Indian Prisoner of War Cemetery at the fort. On his deathbed, he confessed that he regretted his surrender in 1886. A tragic end to a brave and courageous fighter!

"Father of the Atomic Bomb" – Oppenheimer[57]

Being a father is considered by most human beings to be a "blessing", but can that have been the case for the "father of the atomic bomb"? As the director of the Trinity Test,[58] Kenneth Bainbridge, said to Oppenheimer after witnessing the first atomic blast, "Now, we are all sons of bitches." Oppenheimer was proud of their scientific achievement but afterwards became concerned about the genie he had worked to release, as the scientific director of the intense monumental World War II program to develop the first nuclear weapons, called the Manhattan Project.

As a young physicist, Oppenheimer made significant contributions to the field of theoretical physics, with work on molecular wave functions, the theory of electrons and positrons, nuclear fusion processes, and his prediction of quantum tunneling. He also made contributions, together with his students, in the modern theory of neutron stars and black holes. In addition, he made contributions in quantum mechanics, quantum field theory and cosmic rays. He is considered the founder of the American school of theoretical physics.

When still a young man of 18, Oppenheimer visited New Mexico to recover from an illness. It was here that he came to love horseback riding and the Land of Enchantment. He bought a ranch in New Mexico not far from *Los Alamos*. This love for New Mexico along with practical considerations caused him to later select the secluded *Los Alamos* site as the headquarters for the famous Manhattan Project and perhaps also the Trinity site near *Socorro*, New Mexico. These locations were both sparsely populated, a factor that was essential for security reasons. He and other scientists worked for the University of California, which was under contract with the War Department. This way no one had to join the military directly during their work on the Manhattan bomb development project.

Oppenheimer worked diligently to ensure the success of the Manhattan Project, with a staff of 6,000. The result was the development of two different bomb designs. One was called the "Little Boy" using Uranium 235 and a gun-type detonator. The second design used plutonium, which produced a much higher explosive yield, but required an implosion-type detonation scheme. The first bomb design, "Little Boy", did not need to be tested as the design was much more conservative, safer, and predictable. On the other hand, "Fat Man', required a much more advanced and riskier approach that could not be verified by any means but by a nuclear test (Trinity).

Not only was Oppenheimer a brilliant scientist and project leader, he was also a very literate man who could read *Sanskrit* in the original language. He was knowledgeable in the classics. After the war, the FBI investigated him for his personal associations. He was put under constant surveillance. In 1949, the House Un-American Committee interrogated him. He disagreed with William Teller, the father of the hydrogen bomb, on the efficacy of the hydrogen approach but afterwards recanted once the approach was proven. Eventually, Oppenheimer's security clearance was revoked because of his socialist views and friendships with known Communists! However, he was never found to have ever been disloyal to the U.S. in spite of his questionable associations! He spent the final years of his life, after the war, cautioning against a nuclear arms race, and the need for international nuclear controls to stop the proliferation of the very kinds of weapons he had helped to create.

After World War II, he took the position of director of the Institute for Advanced Study at Princeton. He also served on the U.S. Atomic Energy Commission as a chief technical advisor. He was awarded the Enrico Fermi Award in 1964 for his contributions to the nation. The award was an olive branch of reconciliation extended towards him by the U.S. Government to compensate for post-war suspicions and government actions taken against him, and for the earlier revocation of his security clearance. He worked post-war to try to put the genie back in the bottle, working to prevent proliferation of the deadly technology. Shortly after, in 1965, Oppenheimer was diagnosed with throat cancer. He died on February 18, 1967, at the age of 62.

Oppenheimer was no doubt a brilliant and sophisticated scientist who was always surrounded by controversy. Nonetheless, his efforts ushered in the Atomic Age that helped to bring a rapid conclusion to World War II. His achievement as technical director of the Manhattan and Trinity Projects must still be recognized as monumental. Regrettably, though countless Japanese civilians died, countless numbers of Allied soldiers were spared because of the war's quick and decisive conclusion. New Mexico played a central role in those developments.

Chapter Five:
Native American Customs, Traditions and Selected Crafts

The Land of Enchantment is rich in its cultural heritage, with its unique and colorful history. Among the most colorful and intriguing elements of this cultural heritage are the Native American traditions that have survived through adversity and numerous challenges from a time immemorial to the present day. These traditions enrich all our lives, bringing us not only an appreciation of something ancient and sacred, but of a connectedness with Mother Earth, the source of all life. They hearken us back to a simpler, more primal age, one in which nature touches us and we touch nature. This identification with the natural world has almost been broken in the modern technological world. However, a glimpse of it can be regained by understanding some of the Native American customs and ceremonials.

This chapter discusses some of the more common traditions and beliefs. It also touches on a few of the better-known natives crafts. A deeper view can be obtained by reading chapters eleven and twelve, which review the many reservations within New Mexico, and some of the many ceremonials that are opened to the public throughout the year. Perhaps the best way to open up the spiritual self is to attend some of these very same ceremonials on the reservations, in their ancient and natural settings.

The following topics are discussed briefly: Corn Maidens, Coyote Tales, Holy People (*Yei bei chi*) of the *Navajo*, *Kachinas*, *Kokopelli*, *Koshare & Kossa*, *Mescalero* Medicine Basket, Mudheads, *Navajo* Sand Painting, Pottery, Prayer Sticks, Spider Grandmother, Storyteller, Three Sisters and Turquoise & Jewelry.

Corn Maidens

Corn was essential to life and sustenance for the *Pueblo* Peoples, in the same way that the buffalo was essential to the lives of the Plains Indians. Corn became the very symbol of life itself. In *Zuni* mythology and indeed among many tribes, the Corn Maidens were the bringers of life. Corn Maidens are often reproduced in representative form using various media. Sometimes they are carved out of wood, or fine stone. Others are formed from small painted pear-shaped gourds, which are decorated and shrouded in corn husks. Corn Maidens may also be carved out of antler horn and decorated with turquoise, beads and other stones. Sometimes the corn kernels are represented by crosshatch markings on the body of the figure. The Corn Maiden image may also be represented in rugs or on paintings.

There is a beautiful and colorful painting of a Blue Corn Maiden shown on page 17 of the fascinating book entitled *Southwestern Indian Ceremonials* by Mark Bahti. It is painted by Gilbert Atencio. It shows a Corn Maiden holding six ears of blue corn in her left hand, and a bowl of blue corn kernels in her right hand. At her left foot stands a piece of pottery holding five ears of blue corn. She is wearing a turquoise necklace and a blue *manta*, which hangs over her right shoulder. She also wears the traditional embroidered red belt of the *pueblos*. A tassled sash suspends down her right side from her waist. This painting demonstrates the native *pueblo* reverence held for the Corn Maidens.

The *Hopi* may represent the Corn Maiden as a *kachina*. The Corn Maiden *kachina* is the most common female *kachina* form, and it is thought to purify the women who grind the corn for ceremonial or other purposes. The Corn Maiden theme and mythology is common to most Native American tribes: *Pueblo* tribes, *Apachean* tribes, Plains tribes and eastern woodland tribes.

Among the *Apache*, the young maidens of the puberty rite often have corn pollen or cattail pollen applied to their face as preparation for the puberty ceremony. The Corn Maidens are believed to flee the fields after the harvest with the approach of the cold winter months, but they return as the spring and the planting season approaches once again. The *Zunis* celebrate the return of the Corn Maidens each year at the beginning of May, with their annual Green Corn Dance ceremony.

Coyote Tales[1]

To the average American urbanite, the coyote is an unfamiliar animal, seldom seen or encountered. Perhaps, the only coyote ever seen is on a TV nature show. To others who live in the rural west, the coyote is a familiar beast sometimes seen alone in the daytime, but most often recognized traveling in small packs foraging for food, and making their distinctive howls in the dark of night. They look somewhat like a fox, but with mangy coats. One can feel, sense and hear their presence as they punctuate the silence of night with their howls. The coyote is intelligent and has learned to survive in spite of traps, paucity of food, poison, and the danger of being hunted down. He is a clever and savvy survivor.

However, to Native Americans throughout this country, the coyote is a familiar animal that has always been the subject of countless entertaining and (often) humorous tales of trickery, cunning, thievery, cheating, cowardice and bravery, strength and weakness, lechery and gluttony! The coyote was often seen as half animal and half human. H can change shape. He can be generous or petty in nature.

The coyote is a cultural hero, and as Old Man Coyote he creates animals, humans and the earth. Like the Greek Prometheus, Old Man Coyote is the bringer of fire, the sustainer of life and warmth, and the means to survive the winter. He brings daylight to the native peoples. In this role he instructs humans on the proper way to live. As the Trickster, he can be gluttonous, greedy and a thief. Numberless exploits show him competing with other animals, such as the Badger, Rabbit or Fox for food or for women. At times, he wins. At other times he loses in his amorous gambles. He often features in tales wherein he outwits his opponents, and sometimes he may even outwit the "high and mighty." For all of his wit and his scheming ways, he is never remorseful. So he brings delight and humor to the listener or even the reader of these tales. Sometimes one can recognize the human condition in some of his endeavors. In others, one just has to laugh at the ridiculousness of his situation. He is the comic relief in a life of hardship and pain. If you get the chance, read some of these coyote tales. They are very enjoyable!

Holy People (*Yei bei chi*)[2,3] of the *Navajo*

The *yei* or *yeii* are akin to spirits, gods, demons or monsters among the *Navajo* people. Selected beings among the *yei* are known as *Diyin Dine'e*, or Holy People. They are associated with natural forces and they are looked upon as benevolent supernatural beings. They help communicate between the *Navajo* and their gods. They intercede on behalf of the *Navajo* people.

The first four Holy People the *Navajo* encountered included Talking God (*Hastseyalti*), Growling God, Black God and Water Sprinkler, the brother of Talking God. *Yei bei chi* is an alternate name for Talking God, who usually speaks for the other Holy People. Strictly speaking however, the term *Yei bei chi* means "maternal grandmother of the *yei*." During the annual *Yei bei chi* Nightway or Night Chant, the *Navajo yei bei chi* dancers call forth the four *yei*'s mentioned above together with eight other male *yei*.

The Night Chant ceremony is actually a curing or healing ceremony, particularly for nervousness or insanity.

This ceremony extends over the last two nights of the nine-day Night Chant ceremony and the dancers are masked representing the various *yei* gods, spirits or supernatural beings. The ceremony is usually held once in the winter when the snakes are asleep, and there is little liklihood of lightning. An initiation rite is usually conducted to orient and inform youths, male and female, to the secret of the masked gods. In preparation, these youths are purified, by having their hair washed and their bodies smeared with white clay. Further, the boys are given sacred meal and then they are ceremonially whipped with yucca leaves. However, the young girls are marked with corn meal on various parts of their bodies: feet, head, shoulders and hands. In addition, they are touched with white and yellow corn enwrapped in twigs of spruce. Soon after this initiation ceremony, the masked performers reveal their true identities to the young initiates, showing them that they are merely humans, impersonating the *yei*. Each *Navajo* adult is expected to participate in the initiation ceremony four times during his life. See Chapter Twelve for a brief discussion of the *Navajo* Night Chant and *Yei bei chi* dancers.

The *Navajo* Nation occupies a large part of northern Arizona, and extends into northwestern New Mexico. However, there are a group of rock formations in Monument Valley in the state of Arizona, within the lands of the *Navajo* Nation, that are thought to represent the *Yei bei chi*. These rock formations are recognized as a *Navajo* sacred site.

Kachinas[4]

Contrary to what most may think, a *kachina* is not a doll. Instead it is a religious being or spirit, who is sacred to the religious and cosmological beliefs of *Pueblo* Peoples throughout the Southwest. This concept originated with the western *Pueblo* Peoples (*Acoma, Hopi* and *Zuni*), but has also been adopted by more eastern *Pueblo* Peoples (*Laguna* and *Isleta*). The *kachinas* are also called *katsinas*. *Kachina* spirits may represent anything in the natural, spiritual world or the cosmological universe. It can be an honored ancestor, a spiritual site or a natural phenomenon. The *Hopi* have over 400 different *kachinas* in their pantheon of gods and spirits. Each *Hopi* village or non-*Hopi Pueblo* has its own individual and favorite *kachinas*. There are *kachinas* identified with the sun, stars, thunderstorms, corn, wind, insects, etc. The *kachinas* are thought to share human-like family relationships, with sisters, brothers, uncles, grandparents, etc.

Although the *kachinas* are revered and respected, even honored, they are not worshipped. Instead, they are venerated and shown respect in the hope that each spirit will utilize its particular power to protect humans, bring rainfall, protect crops, heal the sick, and generally improve the humans' lot in a treacherous unpredictable world. The underlying concept is the belief that all phenomena, all physical entities and all objects in the world are animate and exhibit a life force or essence that is unique to that entity.

The term *kachina* has also been applied to the *Kachina* Dancers, who wear uniquely carved and decorated masks, and dress in traditional garb meant to represent the image of the spirit. They perform dances in their religious ceremonies, to show reverence to the *kachina* spirit and to beseech their protective support.

Kachina dolls or figurines, are carved from wood, usually cottonwood, and are decorated in the recognized costumes and headdresses of the particular *kachina*. These figurines are given as gifts to children to help them recognize the forms of the numerous *kachina* spirits. Among the Arizona *Hopi* the carvings are usually produced by the children's uncles. They are given as gifts to uninitiated young girls at two different times of the year: the Bean Dance (Bean Planting Ceremony) performed in the spring, and the Home Dance Ceremony performed in the summer.

Many *Kachina* Dancers and their figurine counterparts, wear a foxtail hanging down from their belt, at the rear. This does not indicate that the *kachina* is a fox. It is primarily the costuming and mask of the upper body that determines the identity of the *kachina*. The figurine shown in Figure 5-1 is a White Bear *Kachina*,[5] but he too wears a foxtail! His name is *Qötsahònkatsina*. He is thought to have powers of healing.

Figure 5-1: White Bear *Kachina, Qötsahònkatsina*.

That Happy Flute Playing Rascal: *Kokopelli*[6, 7, 8]

It is difficult to travel anywhere in New Mexico, or elsewhere in the American Southwest, without encountering images of the *kokopelli*. The images may be cast in metal or wood, or they may be portrayed on canvas or in other painted media. Most people have no trouble recognizing the *kokopelli* image. This appears to be true whether they are from the American Southwest, or from some distant part of the world.

The *kokopelli* is normally presented as a humped-back figure bent over playing a flute as he steps forward, wearing a *Hopi*-type native skirt. He usually shows three or five locks of hair extending upward from the top of his head, although these may represent feathers instead of hair. In either case, the hair locks or feathers almost appear like antennae extending from the head. Figure 5-2 shows the *kokopelli* motif on a gate in a *Santa Fe* home.

The *kokopelli* has been revered for millennia by the tribes of the American Southwest. He is primarily a fertility deity. One could think of him as the Don Juan or the Casanova of the Southwest. However, this concept would trivialize his important role as a deity, who helps to ensure the fertility of the fields, of the animals they hunt and of the people themselves, so that they may procreate and continue as a people. He is a god of the harvest. In this role, he is associated with childbirth, agriculture, and the fertility of the crop fields. Some tribes claim that the *kokopelli* carries grain seeds and even babies on his back.

Figure 5-2: *Kokopelli* motif on a gate in a *Santa Fe* home.

Further, he is known as a trickster and is generally associated with music, hence, the flute. The flute has a second more subtle meaning. In his association and protection of agriculture, the playing of the flute by the *kokopelli* chases away the bleak and cold winter, and hastens the return of the warm, verdant, life-nourishing spring.

At *San Ildefonso Pueblo*, the *kokopelli* was recognized as a wandering minstrel, carrying a sack of new songs on his back, which he traded for old songs. These people also saw the *kokopelli* as the bringer of fertility, or as a god of the harvest.

It is thought by some that the *kokopelli* may be playing a "nostril" flute such as was done in many primitive societies. The player holds the flute to one of his nostrils to play the instrument. This practice is based on the ancient belief that a person's soul or spirit enters and leaves the body through the nostrils. The flute is generally forbidden to women. This ancient primitive belief may be the root for the common expression, "God Bless You" when someone sneezes. In Christian times, it was thought that internal demons were departing from the body through the nose, hence the call for God's blessing as the evil spirits departed.

Kokopelli petroglyphs are found throughout New Mexico, and the American Southwest. The early Spanish explorers first learned of the humpbacked flute-playing fertility figure from the *Hopi* and adopted the *Hopi* name for this strange god. The name, *kokopelli*, is thought to derive from the *Zuni* or *Hopi* term for a god, *"koko"*, and from a unique desert fly, called a *"pelli."* The *"pelli"* is a predatory "robber fly" that has a hump on its back and which steals the larvae of other insects. In another interpretation, the name *kokopelli* is a different compound word formed from *"koko"* meaning "rain people" and *"pelli"* or *"polo"* meaning "hemisphere" or "hump."

The *kokopelli's* "flute" has also been interpreted as the prominent proboscis of this fly. Petroglyphs among the *Mimbres*[9] and *Hohokam*[10] Peoples show the *kokopelli* as a figure that more closely represents an insect than a human being or a deity. This humpbacked deity is also known by other names. These include: *Kokopele, Kokopeltiyo, Kokopilau, La Kokopel*. The *Zuni* name given to the *kokopelli* is *Ololowishkya*. Regardless of his assigned name, he is widely recognized by his physical image.

Among the *Hopi*, the male *kokopelli* is sometimes shown with his own consort, called *Kokopelli Mana*. However, his function as a real figure of fertility and fecundity should not be forgotten or overlooked. The *Pueblo* Peoples needed fertile fields to sustain life through agriculture, just as they needed fertile females to ensure the continuation of their own populations. They turned to the *kokopelli* to ensure fecundity in each realm of their lives.

Lastly, there is yet another interpretation of the *kokopelli* as a trader, perhaps from Mexico, who frequented the *pueblos*. As an *Aztec* or *Toltec* trader, or *puchteca*, he wears a parrot or macaw feather headpiece, bearing a sack of trading goods on his back, and carrying a cane or walking stick to help support the weight on his back. He can be shown with a flute, which he plays to announce his arrival at the *pueblo* as a friendly trader, instead of an enemy. In this sense, he is presented as a bringer of gifts.

The *Hopi-Tewa* of Arizona's First *Mesa*, came from the *Rio Grande* area of New Mexico. They have a legend of a large black trader, whom they call *Nepokwai-i*. He carries a large sack of buckskins, with which he makes moccasins for the young women. This legend may have taken its source from the real life figure, Estéban, a Moor who served as a scout during Friar Marcos de Niza's Expedition of 1539. This expedition set out to explore the Southwest at that time. Estéban was a large man who was followed by a group of women granted to him by other tribes. He wore colorful feathers and bells on his wrists. He also wore a plumed crown. The legend says that he entered the *Zuni* village of *Hawikku* and was murdered by the natives because he demanded women and gifts, angering the elders. One has to wonder whether Estéban the Moor initiated the legend of a gift-bearing traveler, or whether he merely fit the archetypal model, and thereby helped to perpetuate it in the minds of some tribal peoples.

Among the *Navajo*, the "Water Sprinkler" deity is sometimes associated with the *kokopelli*, as a minor deity who brings rain and food.

Whatever the origin of the *kokopelli*, and whatever interpretation we accept, we must keep in mind that native cultures don't always put things into neat little boxes, as we tend to do in the Western cultures. Instead, it is perfectly acceptable in the native spiritual world to allow all the interpretations to overlap and to remain equally relevant without contradiction. We perhaps need to become equally as open, and accepting of the many facets of the *kokopelli*, and to embrace them all with open welcoming hearts and without contradiction.

The *kokopelli* remains an ancient figure, yet he has found new relevance in modern times among non-tribal tourists. In this sense, he is eternal and satisfies some underlying mysterious need in each of us, whether we are ancient or modern!

Koshare & Kossa[11, 12, 13]

The *koshare* are one of two ritualistic societies among the *Pueblo* Indians, that perform both sacred and comic acts. The other group is the Mudheads,[14] which are discussed later in this chapter. The *koshare* are a secret society among the southern

Keres Pueblo Indians. They are also known as *"Koshairi", "Kwerana"* or *"Quiranina."* A similar secret society is known among the *Tewa Pueblo* Indians north of *Santa Fe.* They are known as the *"Kossa"* or *"Kwirana."* In both cases, these secret societies are associated with fertility, weather control and ceremonial supervision. They are involved and present in each *pueblo*'s annual Feast Day celebration. The *koshare* hold their initiation and occasional dance in the month of February. The *kossa* hold a similar event in September. It is said that up to four years of training are required before final initiation into these secret societies.

The *koshare* costume is quite different from that of the Mudheads. Some *koshare* have their bodies painted with alternating horizontal black-and-white stripes. Their faces may be painted white, with black semi-circles around the eyes and mouth. Sometimes the body is painted with black dots on a white body instead. They often wear black-and-white skullcaps with tall horns extending out from each side on top of the head. These horns are usually capped with corn husks. Alternately, they may wear a single corn husk projecting vertically from the crown of the head. They may wear a small medicine pouch attached around the neck by a thong. They usually wear black breechclouts and a woven sash. In addition, they often wear hide ties on their arms and legs, and high-topped moccasins. However, the *koshare* may instead wear bunches of pine on his arms to represent life everlasting.

The *koshare* coordinate the movements of ceremonial dancers and help to maintain the required decorum of the dance. They also participate in the dance as they weave through the dancers almost transparently, and without diminishing the flow or rhythm of the dance. When they are not dancing, they act more as comic actors. However, this stops once the dances begin and the solemnity of the dance overtakes the *koshare.*

As comic actors, the *koshare* reinforce socially acceptable behavior and ridicule unacceptable behavior. They also provide comic relief in contrast to the solemn sacred rituals. They may perform activities in a reverse or backwards fashion. They may perform an act incorrectly. Conversing backwards is also performed. They fight over food, or mock the animal movements of the animal dancers. The northern *kossa* act similarly.

At *Taos,* on *San Geronimo* Day (September 30), the *Taos "chiffonete"* perform similar misdeeds. The term *chiffonete* seems to be of border Spanish origin. The *chiffonete* are similar to the *koshare* or *kossa,* acting at times in a comical manner. However, both *Taos* and *Picuris* celebrate their annual Feast Days with a unique event. The *chiffonetes* try to climb a thirty-foot or forty-foot pole, to bring down a sacrificed sheep or other food at the top. They first try to shoot it down with tiny arrows. Each *chiffonete* then tries to climb to the pole top to retrieve the goods.

Picuris holds its pole-climb each year in early August during the *San Lorenzo* Feast Day celebration.

Medicine Basket (*Mescalero Apache*)[15]

The "Medicine Basket", or *"Ts' aa' "* in the native *Mescalero* language, is a symbolic basket used in puberty rite ceremonies for young *Mescalero Apache* maidens. A Medicine Basket is made from willow or sumac branches. Its contents are usually herbs, roots, sacred colored paints, a pollen bag, a tobacco bag, fire sticks, an eagle feather and a medicine man's deer hoof rattle. These items are considered to be part of the *Apache* universe and symbolize the elements used to guide the young maiden through the puberty ceremony, and into womanhood. Henceforth, she will be accepted by all the tribal people, as a fully mature woman. The contents of the Medicine Basket are meant to guide her through the rest of her life.

An over-sized example of what a Medicine Basket looks like can be seen at the Inn of the Mountain Gods Resort/Casino in *Mescalero*, near *Ruidoso*, New Mexico. It is a huge water fountain crafted in the likeness of a Medicine Basket. It can be seen as one descends from the main hotel lobby down towards the lower lounge area. A plaque describes the meaning behind the basket used in the *Mescalero Apache* Puberty Rite, or Maiden Ceremony.

Muddled Thinking: Mudheads or *Koyemsi* [16, 17, 18, 19]

Mudheads are the second ritualistic group among some *Pueblo* Peoples, and they too perform both sacred and comic functions. They are known as *koyemsi* or *koyemshi*. The Mudheads are best known among the *Hopi* and *Zuni*. Clear thinking is not one of their attributes! They lack even the most rudimentary natural intelligence and they are easily confused.

They drum, dance and play games with the audience before sacred ceremonials begin. These clownish figures act as comic relief in counterpoint to the sacred ceremonies. They often award prizes to the winners of races or simple games. However, they too are *kachina*s, so they may even participate in some of the sacred ceremonies, along with other *kachina*s.

These characters are easy to recognize. They wear unusual and distinctive masks. The head mask is soaked in red mud, giving rise to the name "Mudheads." They wear masks made of brown cloth, hide or sack, which give their heads a rounded appearance. The material is gathered at four key points to form a small ball, which is then filled with cotton, dirt or seeds, and then tied. These form round wart-like protrusions on the top of the head, on the left and right sides of the head, where ears would normally be, and in the middle of the back of the head. They have no ears and no nose. Their two eyes and their mouths, appear like short hollow cylinders extending out from the facial surface. Holes are made in these protrusions to allow the Mudhead impersonator to see and breathe. A simple pattern is painted onto the area between the eyes and the two knobs in the ear positions. A band is drawn around the neck area to maintain the round shape and to allow the wearer to pull it over his head as a mask. Often a small bag containing seeds from native crops hangs by string around the impersonator's neck. The band and the small bag are covered with a black neckpiece. Often, the Mudheads wear little more than a breechclout or a kilt, and moccasins. Their upper bodies are bare and mud-splotched. They cannot speak. Instead, they utter unintelligible sounds. See Figure 5-3 for an image of a *koyemsi* or Mudhead.

However, besides acting in a clownish fashion, Mudheads also represent the deformed, incomplete offspring of illicit incestuous unions. They serve as a warning to the people to obey the taboo laws forbidding such social activity. Mudheads are a caution demonstrating the tragic results of disobedience of the laws of social and tribal behavior, and a warning against evil and forbidden deeds. This aspect is seen in the *Zuni* legend concerning the origin of the Mudheads.

In the distant past, a Rain Priest sent his son & daughter to seek new lands for his people to settle in. The maiden rested on a mountaintop while the son explored the country. When he returned he found his sister sleeping. He desired her and then he forced her to sleep with him. The sister was naturally upset, angry and distraught about the incident, but that same night gave birth to ten children. The first child was born normal. However, the other nine were incomplete and infertile in the sense that their "seeds of generation" were not internal to their bodies. Instead, these seeds were contained within large wart-like knobs that began to grow on their heads. Their mouths were also misshapen and puckered, so that normal speech was impossible. They garbled their speech to the point of being

Figure 5-3:
Mudhead or *Koyemsi*

unintelligible, and they appeared silly. The Rain Priest's wayward son and the nine deformed offspring became known as the *"koyemshi"*, *"koyemsi"* or Mudheads. The father decided they should not appear in public without wearing masks to hide their shame and their deformities. *Hopi* masks show the four knobs, the puckered mouth and the bulging inverted eyes. *Zuni* masks may show several additional smaller knobs on their heads.

Another *Zuni* legend highlights the *koyemsis'*, or the Mudheads', extreme stupidity and lack of basic intelligence. They do not know how to do the simplest of things. Once, a human took pity on them and tried to instruct them how to do basic things, but they failed in each endeavor and seemed un-teachable! They failed at climbing a simple ladder. They didn't know how to build a simple house, or how to sit on a chair. They attempted all these activities in an upside down, reverse manner...and failed miserably! Finally, the *Zuni* instructor tried to teach them how to procreate. An old woman volunteered to help teach them. Even in this endeavor, they failed miserably. The old woman could only laugh at their unsuccessful attempts. Finally, the instructor gave up on them. They were simply too dimwitted and hopeless!!

Yet, we respond to them with laughter and even with pity for the fate decreed on them by the foolish and devastating actions of others, in violation of social taboos. They are pitiful but lovable simpletons!! But they also caution us on the dire consequences of passionate disregard for societal laws.

Painting in the Sand: *Navajo* Sand Paintings[20, 21]

It is nearly impossible to travel through the American Southwest, New Mexico and Arizona particularly, without encountering examples of *Navajo* Sand Paintings.

These are also called dry paintings. Although very beautiful, colorful and artistic in the presentation of the primal images, these are commercial items intended for trade or sale to curious and appreciative visitors and tourists. They are not "true" sand paintings, which are transient, ephemeral and are meant for healing ceremonies only. Today's commercial sand paintings are made by slowly allowing the various colored sands to trickle through the hand onto an epoxy-covered particleboard. The sand is made from different kinds of crushed rock, stone and minerals. Some colors occur in natural form. Various colored materials are mixed together to produce other colors that do not occur naturally. The resulting "sand painting" image is then placed in a picture frame and hung on the wall for display. The 1940's saw the advent of these permanent commercial sand paintings.

However, true impermanent sand paintings are sacred and have been used by *Navajo* medicine men throughout their history for healing ceremonies and religious rituals. The healing ceremony is usually performed on the floor of the sick patient's *hogan*.[22] These impromptu sand paintings are meant to be transient and each is made for the purpose of healing the sick patient. The healing ceremony may last for some number of days. A new painting incorporating new images is painted each day and destroyed at the end of each day. The ritual is sacred to the *Navajo*. The paintings are considered spiritual living entities that must be treated with appropriate respect and reverence. Many of the genuine paintings show images of the *Yei bei chi*, the *Navajo* Holy People. While the medicine man creates the sand painting, he chants, soliciting the Holy People to come into the painting to help heal the sick patient. A rainbow *yei* is usually drawn around most *Navajo* Sand Paintings, with his body curving around the south, west and north sides of the sand painting. The rainbow *yei* image, often considered to be associated with the rain god Water Sprinkler, is placed in these directions to protect the sand painting from hostile influences and also to protect the user from the overwhelming power of the god shown in the sand painting. Since the *Navajos* believe that no evil can come from the east, the direction of the rising sun, there is no need for protection in that cardinal direction.

After the sand painting is completed, the medicine man checks his work for accuracy, symmetry and order. If the sand image is ritualistically inaccurate or flawed in some manner, it will reduce the effectiveness of the painting as a healing tool. Lack of harmony with the universe and within the patient's life is considered to be the root cause of disease. Therefore, the healer seeks to restore the missing desired harmony,[23] by means of the sand design's internal symmetry and order. It is essential to ensure this balance and order is reflected in the sand painting. Once the medicine man has confirmed that he has produced an effective healing tool through his sand design, the sick person will be asked to sit on the sand painting.[24] The medicine man then chants to the spirits and continues with the sacred ceremony.

Sitting on the sand painting is the means by which the patient can absorb the spiritual power from the Holy People, who come to take away the illness. At that point, the sacred sand painting has served its spiritual purpose, absorbing the illness. It is then considered dangerous and toxic, and so it must be destroyed. And so the ritual ends. This sacred process usually takes about one half of a full day and night cycle. The healing process begins with the creation of the sand painting, continues through its ritualistic and spiritual use, and ends with its destruction. For exceptional healing, which may require several days, the healing ceremony is repeated each day using a different set of images and a new sand painting.

To preserve the sanctity of the ritual, and the spiritual potency of the images and the sand paintings, certain taboos and rules have been established. These taboos are meant to preserve the appropriate respect for the healing ceremony and for the medicine man performing them.

Images of the *yei*, and of the *Yei bei chi* dancers are also patterned into *Navajo* rugs. There is some controversy around these permanent images of spiritual beings or religious ceremonies being sold commercially, because they are considered sacred to the beliefs of the *Navajo* peoples.

To protect the sanctity of the ritualistic sand painting, commercial sand paintings contain purposeful errors and inaccuracies. They are commercially produced, and use reverse colors and other variations. It would be considered an act of profanity to create an authentic sand painting for display or commercial purposes. Even so, these altered images on boards are very attractive and very popular with tourists, for their imagery, colors and symbolism.

Pottery-

Native American pottery is known worldwide for its high quality, fine and unusual design, various color forms, and its generally appealing aesthetic value. Variations in technique, color and design among the various *pueblos* serve to maintain the high level of interest in these beautiful works of art. Pottery, of course, was first developed to serve very pragmatic functional needs, such as food preparation and storage. Over time pottery makers sought to distinguish their pottery through innovative techniques and designs.

Sometimes the clay itself provides distinction. For example, micaceous clay

Figure 5-4: Beautiful *Jemez* Pottery by Native American potter Reyes Madalena (By permission of Reyes Madalena.[25])

contains small particles of mica that give the finished pottery a shiny, scintillating look that does not occur with other clays.

Black pottery is often produced by firing the pottery under a smoking stack of manure or of cow chips. The slow burning manure produces the needed smoke. The porous clay absorbs the carbon in the smoke. This turns the pottery black as it hardens.

Some pottery is produced preserving the natural color of the clay. Differentiation is achieved by using different methods of scribing on the pottery surface, or by using different line widths, patterns or stylistic animals. Some designers use white clay slips[26] to produce contrast with the basic red clay or even with blackened pottery. There is a large variation in techniques, clays, geometric patterns and animal motifs among the *pueblos*. See Figure 5-4 for examples of *Jemez* pottery. Some artists use variations in the shape of the pottery, molding two mouths instead of one, or by molding climbing animals (lizards, reptiles, etc) onto the pottery itself. Horsehair is sometimes applied to the off-white outer surface after the pottery is heated. It produces fine swirling black lines on the pottery surface. Other artists produce polychrome designs, by using different clays or by applying different color slips to a base clay color. Yet others produce square vessels instead of the conventional rounded pottery. *Cochiti* is famous for producing Storyteller pottery discussed later in this chapter. There are enough different pottery types and styles to appeal to everyone.

Prayer Sticks[27]

Pueblos have various prayers for health, fertility, sustenance and rain. They perform dance prayers in solicitation to the divine spirits to help in these needs and requests. A prayer stick is sometimes used to facilitate these prayers. The *Zuni*, for example, place prayer sticks in crop fields around the time of the June Corn Dance. These prayer sticks are intended to bring the tribe's requests for fertility and rain to the divine spirits, so that maize (corn), bean and squash crops grow, bringing a bountiful harvest.

These sticks are usually about seven inches long and are made of cottonwood. They may vary in color and shape, according to the particular petition and the requestor. However, they usually have a feather attached. The stick itself is meant to represent the divine spirit to whom the plea or petition is being made. The feather, which enables birds to fly, and carries them through the skies near to the divine spirits, is seen as a kind of messenger to the spirits. The prayer is breathed into the "spirit" of the feathers or plumes. In this way, the prayer may be carried to the spirits above to be heard by them. It is hoped that the prayer will be received, heard and acted upon for the benefit and the well being of the people.

It's Spider Grandmother![28, 29]

There is a well-known comic book character who has spider-like qualities, who may be able to save the threatened, prevent crimes, catch the "bad guys" and save the world from near catastrophe, but, he cannot create! Spider Grandmother, on the other hand, can create by thought alone!

She is one of the three most important deities in the *Pueblo* mythological system that includes Spider Grandmother or Thought Woman, Sun Father and Corn Mother. Spider Grandmother is the Creatrix, although sometimes the creative process is shared or performed in partnership with Sun God, depending upon whether the source of the tale is *Navajo, Zuni* or some other *Pueblo* tribal tradition. Spider Grandmother or Thought Woman merely needs to imagine "something" and through the thought process that "something" manifests itself. Now that's a powerfully magic woman!!

She weaves reality and the future, just as a spider spins her web. The spider creates an ever-changing silken web, while Spider Grandmother weaves and creates the web of life. The *Hopi* believe that Spider Grandmother together with Sun God fashioned the first humans from the red clay of the earth. To the *Navajo*, Spider Grandmother is deeply respected and revered for it is she who taught the *Navajo* to weave so skillfully and beautifully. It was Spider Grandmother who taught *Navajo* women how to build the first loom from exotic materials including sky, earth, sunrays, rock crystal and sheet lightning. She then taught them how to weave on the newly created loom.

The lowly spider may appear as merely an insect to many, but to the initiated and the spiritually aware, this seemingly lowly being can pass on tremendous wisdom to the receptive. Spider Grandmother is a symbol of the creative process, and its unending continuous nature. Its ancient nature also represents wisdom and knowledge, or long life experience. The stories of Spider Grandmother are passed down orally from generation to generation, although some *Navajo* elders say they only tell these tales during the winter months, while the spider sleeps, so as not to offend her!

Once Upon a Long Time Ago: The Storyteller[30]

The image of the old Native American storyteller surrounded by eagerly listening children is seen throughout the American Southwest and in the state of New Mexico, in particular. These clay pottery images are very popular. The Storyteller is portrayed either as an elderly male or female, and is usually shown with the mouth open, in the act of telling a tale to an audience, which consists of a number of young but enthralled children, climbing lovingly all over the storyteller. These Storyteller dolls are associated with the native *Pueblo* Peoples of New Mexico.

Helen Codero made the first Storyteller doll of contemporary times in 1964. It originated from the *Cochiti Pueblo*, just outside *Santa Fe*. The inspiration for the Storyteller doll was Ms. Cordero's grandfather, who was a tribal storyteller. The clay pottery Storytellers are usually painted in earth tones: black, beige, white, light and dark brown, reddish brown, and gray. Other colors are sometimes used but less frequently. The adult telling the story is usually a seated female with a warm rounded maternal shape. However, the Storyteller may also be an elderly, grandfather figure.

The wide appeal of the Storyteller dolls is due to the image of nurturing love, caring and devotion that it portrays. It demonstrates the strong loving family values of the *Pueblo* Peoples and many other non-*pueblo* people resonate with these positive values. It also shows the respect and reverence with which the elders are held. Another aspect associated with the Storyteller figure is the value of maintaining the continuity of family or tribal tradition through the transmission of stories to the young. Children rarely learn through lecture or even through direct instruction. Instead they most often learn best by example, and better yet through stories. Children process and maintain the lesson or moral that is embedded within the story, without intellectualizing the experience. It becomes part of who they are and what they believe, without any memorization, coercion or lecturing. It is probably the most effective way to communicate cultural, traditional and spiritual values to children. And it is all done in a loving, endearing, enjoyable and personal way. It is a method of entertaining and teaching, from the wisdom of the elders to the innocence of the young. It is no small wonder that the Storyteller image remains so very popular with peoples from every corner of the world.

The Three Sisters (Maize, Beans, Squash)[31]

Agriculture was of the utmost importance to many Native American peoples for their survival. The Three Sisters refer to the three main agricultural crops of these peoples. These crops are maize (corn), climbing beans and squash. When planted together, the three crops benefit from each other! The *Pueblo* Peoples of New Mexico instituted the planting of the Three Sisters, in a planting technique known as companion planting, in which the three crops are planted close to each other. Each cluster of the three crops is planted in the soil in flat mounds that are about one foot high and a foot and a half wide. Several maize seeds are planted in the center of the mound. Bean and squash seeds are planted around them. As each crop grows it benefits from the presence of the others.

The climbing beans need a pole to climb and to wrap around. Maize stalks substitute for the poles and the bean stalks wrap around them. Squash, being a ground crawling vine, spreads along the soil and blocks the sunlight, preventing weeds from flourishing. Beans provide nitrogen to the soil that is needed by the other crops. Mulch is provided by the squash leaves, which help to retain moisture in the soil. The prickly vines of the squash deter pests. Beans contain the amino acids lysine and tryptophan, needed for the human body's production of protein and niacin. Maize, on the other hand, lacks these very same amino acids. Consumption of both beans and maize together provides a balanced diet. The Native Americans certainly knew what they were doing!

Of course, maize was a multi-colored corn, unlike our yellow corn of today. There was blue, red and multi-colored maize. The maize was usually ground down into meal form using a stone *metate* and *mano*. The *Taino* word for the crop was *maiz*. The Spaniards adopted this word, as *maiz*, to describe what we call corn.

The ancient *Anasazi* successfully practiced companion planting with the Three Sisters in the arid desert environment of New Mexico and Arizona. Other tribes of the Southwest, including the *Tewa*, added a fourth sister in the form of a plant known as the "Rocky Mountain bee plant", which attracts bees to help with the pollination of the beans and the squash.

Interestingly, the reverse side of the 2009 U.S. Sacagawea one-dollar coin[32] shows the Three Sisters planting method, with the field attended to by a female dropping some additional seeds into the apparently productive field.

Turquoise and Silver Jewelry

The southwest region of the U.S. is famous for its exquisitely beautiful turquoise and silver jewelry. Turquoise has been mined for ages in the *Cerrillos* area, along the "Turquoise Trail" of New Mexico. Here Native Americans mined turquoise for years prior to the advent of the Spanish *Conquistadors*. The Spaniards later mined silver in the region and shipped their findings back to Spain. Mining continued into the 19th century with the coming of the *Anglo*-Americans. This region is still mined today. Other areas of New Mexico were also mined. Silver City is named after the silver mining that took place there in the 19th century. Whatever the native peoples could not mine themselves they obtained through trade and barter. Silver smithing was learned from the Spaniards. Today the quality of work done by various tribes in designing and fabricating silver jewelry with embedded stones such as turquoise, coral, mother of pearl, and other stones, is outstanding. Such jewelry is sought by visitors from all over the world.

It is not unusual to see Native American women regally adorned with stunning turquoise and silver necklaces, wrist bracelets, belts and rings at Feast Day events and other happenings such as the *Santa Fe* Indian Market[®]. They often wear traditional Squash Blossom necklaces. Females may also wear turquoise necklaces without the silver. Exquisite silver bracelets inlaid with coral or turquoise are also very popular with tourists.

Rings and earrings may also be worn with turquoise laid into a silver setting. The contrast between the turquoise stones and the luster of the silver can be quite breathtaking. At the Indian *Pueblo* Cultural Center in Albuquerque, it is not uncommon to see young maidens who have come to perform traditional dances, wearing stunning turquoise and silver jewelry. Set against their *mantas*, their long jet black hair, and feathered headdresses the visual image is quite remarkable and dramatically appealing. Men may wear turquoise and silver belt buckles, rings and earrings. The *Zuni* and the *Navajo* are world famous for their fine craftsmanship in turquoise and silver jewelry.

Chapter Six:
Hispanic Customs, Traditions and Selected Crafts

A colorful and rich Spanish Colonial and Mexican cultural inheritance has also been bequeathed to us from the days prior to the American invasion and annexation of New Mexico in the mid and late 1840's. This inheritance has come to us annealed in the crucible that was the New Mexican frontier, to form a uniquely New Mexican heritage and culture. These Hispanic customs and traditions are still alive today and they permeate the cultural experience that draws so many visitors each year to this Land of Enchantment.

This chapter briefly discusses a small number of the most significant and most interesting customs, beliefs and traditions. These include: *Chimayó, Cinco de Mayo*, Crosses, *Farolitos* and *Luminarias, Los Matachines, La Pastorela and Las Posadas Plays, Retablos, Ex Votos* & Reredos, *Ristras*, Roadside Memorials, *Santa Fe Fiesta, Santos* & *Bultos*, Straw Appliqué, Tinwork, *Virgen de Guadalupe*, Weeping Woman (Lady) and Traditional Woodworking.

Oh, It's a Long, Long Walk to *Chimayó[1]*

Although *Chimayó* is known for its Spanish weaving with its own unique patterns, there is another attraction to *Chimayó* that causes pilgrims to walk there each year from *Santa Fe* and surrounding areas. *El Santuario de Chimayó* is believed to be a miraculous healing site! See Figure 6-1.

Chimayó can be reached from *Santa Fe* by taking I-84/285 north towards *Española*. At the traffic light just beyond Cities of Gold Casino, take US 503 towards *Nambé*, Continue on US 503 for about 7.3 miles past the *Nambé* Falls turnoff. Drive until a small sign on the left points to *El Santuario de Chimayó*. This is Juan Medina Road. Take this road for about 3 miles to the parking lot at the rear of the *Santuario*.

On the walk from the parking lot towards the front of the mission church on the *Santuario* grounds, there is a short walkway with a lawn on the right side and a chain link fence on the left side. Along this chain link fence, visitors have left ribbons and twig crosses enmeshed within the structure of the fence, either in reverence or in solicitation for divine or saintly intervention. On the right side of this walk, on the far side of the lawn are seven arched stone crosses. These represent the seven days of creation. See Figure 6-2. Behind these crosses the narrow but swift-moving *Rio Santa Cruz* feeds the neighboring irrigation ditches or *acequias*, providing much needed water to the surrounding crops and fields.

However, the main attraction here is the small chapel called the *Santuario*. The high ground upon which the chapel is built is revered and is associated with miraculous healing powers. Pilgrims journey here to this healing site to receive relief from their afflictions through the power of prayer. The mission church is very simple in style. Reredos and *retablos[2]* surround the interior of the mission church and the altar. At the left of the altar, there is a small entry into two rooms. Within this area, in the small room to the right, there is a hole in the floor filled with dirt blessed by the resident priests. Pilgrims often kneel over this hole and scoop up small handfuls of the healing dirt and rub it on their arms and faces to receive its holy gift. In an adjacent room there are abandoned crutches and leg braces of those who purportedly were healed at this site.

Figure 6-1: *El Santuario de Chimayó*. (Archdiocese of *Santa Fe.*)

Figure 6-2: Seven Stone Crosses at *Chimayó*. (Archdiocese of *Santa Fe.*)

The hole containing the healing dirt (*El pocito de la tierra*) is said to be the spot where Don Bernardo Abeyta unearthed the cross of the Lord of Esquipulas[3] in 1810. The story behind this find is that Don Bernardo *de la Encarnación* Abeyta, a *Penitente*,[4] was praying with other *Penitentes* among the hills of *El Portrero*.[5] It was Good Friday night and there was a new moon, making the night darker than usual. He saw a light shining from one of the hills near the *Santa Cruz* River Valley. He and others went down to the spot to investigate. The light seemed to shine from below the earth. Don Bernando dug out the earth with his bare hands, to find a large cross. The cross was not crafted in the area. It portrayed *El Señor de Esquipulas*, the *Mayan* name for Jesus Christ. At *Chimayó* a mission church was built between 1814 and 1816 around the miraculous site. The crucifix[6] that Don Bernando found is the centerpiece in a tabernacle built within the reredo that stands behind the altar in the *Chimayó Santuario* Church. Molleno, also known as the *Chili* or *Chile* Painter, is said to have painted this reredo.

There is yet another tradition associated with the Cross of Esquipulas. In this tradition, documents from Durango, Mexico state that the first settlers in the *Chimayó* area included a priest who originally came from Esquipulas, Guatemala. He took with him a large wooden cross and preached to the local Chimayan natives. Eventually, the natives killed him. His body was subsequently buried in the hills of *El Portrero*. Years later, the nearby *Santa Cruz* River flooded, uncovering the body of the deceased priest and the large wooden cross. Some older folks recognized the body and the cross, which was associated with his hometown of Esquipulas, Guatemala. So, the cross came to be known as the crucifix of Our Lord of Esquipulas. The body and the cross both were uncovered at a location that was long held sacred by the local *Tewa* natives, long before any foreigners came to Chimayó.

Within the *Santuario*, in the small room adjacent to the "*El pocito*" (the well) room, there is a small enclosure that contains a statue of *Santo Niño*, the Christ child. He is portrayed as a small Spanish pilgrim boy. Many visitors pray here and pay reverence. (Less than two hundred yards from the front entry to the *Chimayó* Sanctuary is another church dedicated to *Santo Niño*, the Child of Atocha.[7] This chapel is a short walk from the *Santuario*.)

Within the central part of *El Santuario de Chimayó*, there are a total of five reredos. The central reredo is located behind the altar and it contains the small tabernacle with the statue of Christ on the Cross, as *El Señor de Esquipulas*. There are four other reredos located within the *Santuario*, two on each side of the nave. The two reredos on the left side are thought to have been painted by José Rafael Aragón of Cordova or Cordoba. The reredo on the right side, nearest the entrance to the *santuario* was painted by Molleno, and the other right side reredo is thought to have been painted by Miguel Aragón.

The entry to the nave of the *Santuario* also presents two large *bultos*.[8] On the right there is a huge *bulto* of Jesus Christ, standing with his hands tied with rope. His body is bloodied and he wears the crown of thorns on his head. His face shows his torment. On the opposite side there is another *bulto* showing Christ on the cross.

Some pilgrims walk to *Chimayó* from as far away as Albuquerque (~ 90 miles). About 30,000 pilgrims visit the site on Holy Thursday and Good Friday, during Holy Week. Throughout the year about 300,000 visitors come to *El Santuario*. In former times, the pilgrims would eat the dirt to absorb its power and its holiness. Today, pilgrims merely rub the dirt upon themselves. Some may simply take it with them and keep it. The dirt is replenished daily from the nearby hillsides. Over 25 to 30 tons are replaced each year. The dirt is blessed daily by one of the mission priests. *Chimayó* is often called "the Lourdes of America" because of its similar reputed healing powers.

It is said that the local *Tewa* peoples revered the site, long ago, for its healing powers, and that a hot spring flowed near the sacred site.

No one can dispute the healing power of faith and prayer. Healing miracles can happen as long as the faith is real and very strong. Medical practitioners are very much aware of this. Perhaps it is the belief in something greater than oneself. Perhaps it is just a mystery. Or, perhaps it is simply the need to believe. In any case, *Chimayó* is a sanctuary that draws the faithful every year. It is an interesting place to see and visit.

Cinco de Mayo:[9] **Mexican-American Celebration**

This holiday is celebrated in parts of Mexico, but in recent decades it has also been adopted by Mexican Americans in the U.S. In particular, it is celebrated in the states of the American Southwest, including New Mexico, where large Mexican American populations reside.

Cinco de Mayo, means the Fifth of May. This holiday commemorates the victory by Mexican forces over French forces at the Battle of Puebla, on May 5, 1862. The Mexicans were outnumbered two to one by the French. In the U.S., the holiday has come to represent Mexican American culture and heritage. It has become a symbol and a celebration of unity and pride.

The *Cinco de Mayo* celebration has its foundation in the French invasion of Mexico in 1861. The incident that triggered the invasion was a declaration on July 17, 1861 by the Mexican President, Benito Juarez, that payment of all foreign debts would be suspended for two years. This drastic measure resulted because of the ruinous state of the Mexican Treasury following the Mexican-American War. France, Spain and Britain sent naval forces to Mexico. They appeared off the coast of Veracruz ("True Cross") , demanding payment. Negotiations with Spain and Britain resulted in withdrawal of their forces. France however, saw this as an opportunity to set up a new empire, and so the French invaded Veracruz and drove on towards Mexico City.

The French were stopped temporarily at Puebla, before they reached Mexico City. However, the Battle of Puebla, in 1862, was only a temporary victory for the Mexican forces. After several more years of fighting between the French invaders and the Mexicans, the French finally captured Mexico City, and installed Maximilian I as Emperor of Mexico. The French occupation of Mexico lasted only three years, between 1864 and 1867, when Maximilian was finally overthrown and executed by the Mexicans.

It is no coincidence that the French invaded Mexico during the American Civil War. Perhaps France intended to come to the aid of the Confederacy via Mexico. An invasion of Mexico might facilitate that. It would also undermine the Union. Had the French succeeded in their imperial endeavors, the outcome of the American Civil War may have been quite different, and the shape and destiny of New Mexico might also have been very different.

Crosses (*Las cruces*)

Crosses, crosses everywhere…in churches, in homes, etc. Their prevalence is a reflection of the strong religious heritage that has been handed down from Spanish Colonial times and from the days of Mexican rule. In those times, Catholicism was being spread throughout the Southwest, seeking the conversion of the natives. The cross was symbolic of the fervent religious faith of the new settlers and of the newly converted indigenous peoples.

The cross is called "*la cruz*" in Spanish, with the plural being "*las cruces.*" Throughout New Mexico, one can find crosses of all types and styles, and made of almost every conceivable kind of material. The most common are carved in wood, or are rendered in wrought iron. Wrought iron crosses come in many exotic and creative designs with scrolls, loops and curved motifs in the Baroque Spanish Colonial style.

Some crosses may be symbolic in style, and yet be very artistic and creative in design, or they may be more realistic and simple, with representations of Jesus Christ on the Cross. Modern wooden crosses are often inlaid with stones, or with other types and colors of wood, to give more depth and artistry to the design. Older Spanish Colonial crosses often reflected a disquieting realism and simplicity, carved by priests themselves or by local craftsmen. These commonly displayed an agonizing Christ on the Cross, either left unpainted or alternatively, painted in near natural colors.

More recently, a style imported from Mexico has become popular. These are made on a wooden frame, which is overlaid with beaten tin. Holes and scrolling type patterns are punched into the tin. Inlaid within sections of the tin frame are small *Talavera* tiles with multi-colored designs on them. These crosses too, are extremely attractive. However, these represent an imported Mexican style rather than the native Spanish Colonial style.

Yet other remarkably beautiful crosses are made using straw *appliqué* following the old Spanish Colonial tradition, as described later in this chapter.

Crosses can be also carved in wood, following the traditional woodworking tradition passed down from generation to generation of New Mexicans, from the time of the Spaniards. See also the brief discussion on woodworking at the end of this chapter.

As an interesting aside, there is a city in New Mexico named *Las Cruces*, or The Crosses. One has to wonder how this unique name came about. The story is that the area retains the name given by Spanish explorers. At some time in the Spanish period, a Spanish caravan was unfortunate enough to become victimized by a group of *Apaches* who killed many in the Spanish party. Some time later a different group of explorers passed by the same site and seeing the unburied corpses, they went ahead and buried the bodies using crosses to mark the burial sites. These crosses came to be a stark reminder of those massacred here. In 1848, a town was founded near this site and it was named *Las Cruces* in honor of the unfortunate victims killed nearby and of their memorial crosses.

And Let There Be Light: *Farolitos* and *Luminarias*

Best-known in areas with a strong Spanish or Mexican heritage, such as *Santa Fe*, the Christmas tradition of *farolitos* ("little lanterns") and *luminarias* ("luminaries") still burns strong. At this holy and festive time of year, the outlines of homes and buildings are accented with *farolitos*. They illuminate the buildings and provide a warm surrounding glow. *Farolitos* are traditionally made by filling the bottom of a small brown paper bag with sand to anchor a small candle within. The candle is then lit carefully to provide a gentle warm glow emanating from the *farolito*. In more recent times, there has been some migration towards commercial electric *farolitos*, which utilize plastic bags with electric light bulbs. Artificial *farolitos*[10] decorate the exterior outline of state government buildings, shops, and hotels, etc., during the winter holiday season. See Figure 6-3. They add their own unique and warm ambiance.

Farolitos are often complemented by the blaze and warmth of *luminarias*, or small

Figure 6-3: *Farolitos* illuminate the buildings of The Spa and Inn at Loretto. (With permission of The Spa and Inn at Loretto, *Santa Fe*.)

log bonfires. The *luminarias* are said to represent the fires attending the Bethlehem shepherds on the first Christmas Eve. They are traditionally lit on Christmas Eve. *Luminarias* burn brightly along the Canyon Road of *Santa Fe* at Christmas time.

Although *farolitos* and *luminarias* are two distinctly different things in northern New Mexico, the terms *farolitos* and *luminarias* are used interchangeably in some of the more southerly parts of the state.

Dance of *Los Matachines*[11, 12, 13]

Los Matachines is an ancient morality play or ritual drama that demonstrates the triumph of good over evil through dance. Its roots are in both Europe and Africa, and the Spaniards reportedly first introduced it to the Americas. *Los Matachines* was derived from a type of European folk drama that reflected the conflict between the Christians and the North African Moors. The Spaniards brought the morality play to

America as a means of Christianizing the Native Americans. It was first performed in New Mexico in 1598, when the region was a northern province of New Spain.

The morality dance mutated once it reached the New World. The symbolism evolved to be either a simple representation of good verses evil, as mentioned above, or in some traditions it even incorporates elements of the clash of culture between the conquering Spaniards and the indigent natives. In this second version, *El Monarca (The Monarch)* represents Moctezuma. *La Malinche* represents innocence and purity. It is even suggested that *La Malinche* may represents the Virgin Mary bringing *El Monarca* to the Christian faith. Another character, *El Toro*, represents evil or sin.

The origin of the dance name, *Los Matachines*, is masked in mystery. Some claim that the obscure term may have originated in Spain, which was occupied by the Moors or *Los Moros* for 900 years. The ritualistic dance then represented the conflict between the "good" Spanish Christians and the "evil" conquering Moors, in the persons of *La Malinche* (Good) and *El Toro* (Evil).

Because of this near-millennium of Arabic influence, it is thought that the term *Matachine,* applied to this ritualistic dance drama, may have derived from the Arabic *mutawajjihin*, meaning "a mask wearer." This is in agreement with the general interpretation expressed by some members of the dance group *Los Matachines de Bernalillo*. In *Bernalillo*, the *Matachines* tradition is associated with *San Lorenzo*. The Dance of *Los Matachines* has been performed in *Bernalillo* since 1692, when De Vargas recovered *Santa Fe* from the revolting *Pueblo* natives.

Among New Mexicans and southern Coloradans,[14] *Los Matachines may* also mean ..."a person who dances in the ritual dance." Some may say it means "masked ones" instead, in agreement with the potential Moorish or Arabic origin of the term described above.

Today, this dance is the only dance that is performed by both Hispanic and Native American communities during *fiestas*. Of course, each *pueblo* or community puts their own twist on the drama, with variations in the costumes and the drama, but the result is still memorable and colorful, and should not be missed if you have the opportunity to view this celebration. Hispanic communities seem to prefer to perform this dance in the summer and warm months, and around the time of the *San Lorenzo* Feast Day, on August 10th of each year. On the other hand, *Pueblo* Indian groups seem to prefer to perform the ritual dance in the Christmas season.

The two cultures may view the ritual dance differently, as they each represent the opposite sides of the cultural and historical experience. One side represents the conqueror, while the native side represents the subjected culture. This is bound to color their perspective on the dance's meaning!

The following description is based on the *Matachines* dances as performed by a group from *Bernallillo*, called *Los Matachines de Bernalillo*, who have danced at *El Rancho de las Golondrinas*. Variations may occur between dance groups and between Hispanic dance versions and Native American dance versions. There are apparently several different versions of the dances, and dance traditions.

In the *Bernalillo* group dance version, there are certain key characters in the dances. *El Monarca* (The Monarch) is the leader and director of the dances. He wears a distinctive headpiece that looks like a crown, and the other dancers follow his lead.

El Toro is dressed with a mask that has bull horns projected from the top, and he represents Evil. This figure usually leans his weight forward on two canes that represent the bull's forelegs. In various parts of the dance, *El Toro* taunts or attempts to intimidate *El Monarca* and *La Malinche*.

El Abuelo, the Grandfather, is unmasked and uncostumed. *El Abuelo* represents Conscience. He carries a whip, which he uses to constrain the actions of *El Toro* (Evil) throughout the dances. In some traditions, *El Abuelo* is sometimes portrayed as one of two possible "clowns."

La Malinche is a young pre-pubescent girl, no older than eight or nine years of age, dressed in a white Confirmation dress. In some traditions, she wears a pastel colored dress instead, such as pink or light green or light blue. *La Malinche* represents Innocence and Purity.

One thing that is quite confusing is that *La Malinche* is the same name given to Malinali, Cortés' translator and lover. This ambiguity between the "good" "*La Malinche*" of *Los Matachines* and the "detested" "*La Malinche*" seems to be irreconcilable and unresolvable. This is true of many folk traditions, and it seems to be equally so in this case. Who knows?

Danzantes is the term given to the *Los Matachines* dancers. The dancers wear multi-colored costumes of varying materials, and their faces, heads and bodies are covered. Their faces are covered with black cloth and a black fringe to keep their identity hidden from the audience. They wear miter-like headpieces that show a religious figure or symbol. A light colorful silk type of shawl hangs down the back. In addition, colorful ribbons run down their backs. They usually carry a religious symbol or a small colored, flowered trident, fan or rattle in their hands as they dance. At many times during the dance, two parallel lines are formed. At other times, they dance towards each other or dance in a circle. They dance to the music provided by a single violin player with a guitarists and/or a sole drummer. The dance of *Los Matachines* is certainly colorful and fascinating.

In the *Bernalillo* version, there are nine movements in total, although sometimes one or two movements are deleted in performances because of time constraints. The nine movements are:

La Marcha: The Processional to the dance area.
La Cruz: The Cross (dance)
La Mudanza: The Movement (dance)
La Malinche: The Innocent (dance)
El Toro: The Bull (Evil) (dance)
La Cruz: The Cross (dance)
La Tendida: Obeisance or bowing to the four cardinal directions. (dance)
La Promesa: The Promise, by the individual to God (final dance)
La Corrida: The Run or Recessional

Some versions, especially *pueblo* versions, include a motif that involves Moctezuma, the *Aztecs,* the conflict between the Spaniards and the *Aztecs*, and eventual conversion and reconciliation. In these versions, *El Monarca* represents Moctezuma, and the dance play is about Moctezuma becoming a bird, which then flies northward to warn the northern tribes about the impending appearance of the Spaniards. Moctezuma teaches these tribes the dance, to protect them from the approaching aggressive white, bearded strangers. In this case, Moctezuma represents the native element. The dance performance reflects the reconciliation and the joining of faith between the two cultures, the native and the Spanish.

(In yet other related versions, Moctezuma as *El Monarca*, is seen as fleeing his people, with *La Malinche* or Malintzín, portraying Cortès' mistress. *La Malinche* then lures Moctezuma back from the desertion of his people. The people are then reunited with their leader and king, and *El Toro* is killed, as the initiator of all this chaos and evil. This version is more prevalent in Mexico.)

The *Matachines* dances are held throughout New Mexico at various times of the year. The dance is often held at *El Rancho de las Golondrinas* (Ranch of the Swallows), while a number of native *pueblos* perform the dances around Christmas time, with inevitable differences and variations.

La Pastorela[15] & *Las Posadas* Plays[16]

Christmas time in the Land of Enchantment is a uniquely beautiful experience. Colorful cultural traditions from the past come alive again. Visitors and locals alike partake of *posole* and *empañadas*, or of other New Mexican foods smothered in *chile verde*. *Farolitos* outline buildings with their warm comforting light. *Las Posadas*[17] processions are seen and heard as *Los Peregrinos*[18] sing their requests for shelter for Mary and Joseph. *La Pastorela*[19] or *Los Pastores*[20] liturgical plays are performed in towns throughout New Mexico. These traditions have been handed down from the time of the Spaniards.

There are two main Christmas traditions: *La Pastorela* or *Los Pastores,* and *Las Posadas. La Pastorela* will be discussed first. It is also called *Los Pastores*, meaning "the shepherds." It is a theatrical performance centered on the shepherds as they traveled to Bethlehem to see the Christ-child. It dates back to the Middle Ages in Europe, when the Roman Catholic Church used these short liturgical plays to instruct the masses. Although they were often entertaining, they were not meant for entertainment but for instruction in the Bible stories and in church doctrine. As the Spanish Conquest of the Americas got underway, the Spaniards brought these traditions with them to the New World. The religious orders, especially the Franciscans, found these musical plays to be a useful and effective tool in converting the native populations to the ways of Christianity.

The story behind *La Pastorela* involves the travails of a group of shepherds on their way to greet the baby Jesus in Bethlehem (*Belen* in Spanish). Some of the main characters are Bato the shepherd, Bartolo the lazy shepherd and *Gila* the beautiful young shepherdess. Of course, there is also the archangel Gabriel, Joseph, Mary and the baby Jesus, too. *Demonio*, representing Lucifer, adds tension and drama to the play. The story starts when the archangel Gabriel announces the birth of the Christ child and he invites the shepherds to see the *Santo Niño*[21] in *Belen*. *Demonio*, of course, provides temptations along the way. Bartolo demonstrates the lazy side of his own personality and *Gila* becomes an object of lust via the prompting of *Demonio*. *La Pastorela* is a morality play that shows the eternal struggle between good and evil, and the final salvation through the recognition of God and goodness in the person of the Christ child.

Las Posadas represents the other popular New Mexican Christmas tradition. *Las Posadas* means "inns" or "lodging places" in Spanish. It is a musical celebration that also dates back to the Spanish Colonial period. This tradition commemorates the journey of Mary and Joseph to Bethlehem, and the difficulties they encountered in trying to find a place of shelter in the town of Bethlehem. This is an annual procession of the pilgrims led by Joseph and Mary seeking shelter. Sometimes the archangel Gabriel is included in the entourage. They arrive at various inns singing their song requesting shelter, only to hear a song of rejection from the hosts or owners. This cycle is repeated until their request is accepted and they finally find a place of lodging. They are invited within where the *Santo Niño* is born to great rejoicing. A feast usually follows this glorious event. Oftentimes, children play the roles of Joseph, Mary and the pilgrims. In the times of the Spanish Conquest of the Americas, this play was used to instruct the natives that a Christian life requires sacrifice. Choosing to be Christian may mean facing rejection by non-believers. In this way, the Christmas story, as well as Christian principals, were taught in a visually colorful and instructive way.

Las Posadas is usually sung on Christmas Eve. The *peregrinos* (pilgrims) end their quest when they arrive at the local church, where the Joseph and the Virgin Mary find the lodging they sought. A priest then offers Mass, in keeping with the tradition of Christmas Midnight Mass.

These celebrations are found throughout the state during the Christmas season. *La Pastorela* and *Las Posadas* bring a sense of beauty, color, joy and wonder to the Christmas celebration that is unique to New Mexico.

Retablos,[22] *Ex Votos*[23] & Reredos[24]

Another aspect of Mexican and Spanish Colonial culture that has been transmitted over time to New Mexico is the *"retablo"* tradition. *Retablos* can be found and seen in the more northern parts of New Mexico, such as *Santa Fe* and *Taos*, as these areas have strong Spanish Colonial roots. These unique articles are referred to as *"Laminas"* in Mexico. In Mexico, they are devotional oil paintings venerating various Catholic saints or *santos*. In addition, some *retablos* may portray Jesus Christ or the Virgin Mary, sometimes holding or nursing the infant Jesus. The *retablos* can be painted on a variety of materials such as canvas, sheets of tin, zinc, wood or copper.

In New Mexico, perhaps because of the shortage of some of these materials, or because of the high cost associated with importing them from Mexico or Spain, the *retablo* was instead created on rectangular pieces of wood. These wooden *retablos* are typically found in many of the mission churches set up by the Franciscans monks throughout New Mexico. As with Mexican *retablos*, they portray images of saints, of Jesus Christ or of the Virgin Mary or perhaps of the Virgin of Guadalupe. In the past, these *retablos* were painted by priests or local folk artists. Those who created these and other images of the saints or santos (see *bulto* discussion later in this chapter) were termed *santeros*. Examples of *retablos* can be found at *Chimayó, San Francisco de Asís* Mission Church, and other mission churches in New Mexico.

The term, *"retablo"*, means "behind the altar." These examples of votive folk art were placed or hung behind a church altar. This particular form of folk art is rooted in Spanish history. The Franciscan monks brought the practice of *retablos* from New Spain, now Mexico, to the northern province of *Nuevo México* (New Mexico). The *retablo* is also deeply embedded in the traditional religious beliefs of Mexican culture from the 17th through the 19th century. Local craftsmen and artists of both Old and New Mexico created the art of the *retablos*. They inspire a deep sense of religious fervor and devotion that is quite apparent to the viewer. *Retablos* possess a unique and beautiful charm of their very own, and are collected for their color, symbolism, spirituality and historicity.

Modern *retablos* are often found in religious gift shops associated with mission churches, or at the Traditional Spanish Market© in *Santa Fe*. Some are more commercial in appearance, while others are clearly hand-painted and of higher quality. Examples of these are shown in Chapter 10.

In any case, *retablos* typically show a particular saint who can be recognized by associated dress and religious symbols. These modern *retablos* are usually painted on a wood board, about 6 inches by 10 inches in size. A coating of white *gesso*[25] is applied to the surface to seal it and to provide a smooth painting surface. The surface is then painted. The paints are often derived by the *santeros* or *santeras,* using natural materials. Finally, it is often sealed with a *piñon* sap varnish sealer. The images are often quite beautiful. They are made for home altars and for decoration. Larger *retablos* are found in mission churches, on large reredos or as part of altar screens.

Figure 6-4: Spanish Colonial reredo, or *retablo mayor*. (*Coronado* State Monument.)

A second religious tradition is the "*Ex voto*" painting. It is a special form of small devotional painting that is intended to give thanks to God, Jesus Christ, the Virgin Mary, the Virgin of Guadalupe or a saint for protection already received by someone who has experienced a personal but threatening or dangerous episode, such as a natural disaster or severe illness. The term "*ex voto*" comes from Latin meaning "from a vow", probably referring to a protected person's vow to give thanks for the protection received. An "*Ex voto*" is usually smaller than a *retablo,* and it should display the protected person in the dangerous event, the sacred protector and some inscription explaining the events, date and location of the event. These devotional paintings can be made as a votive offering at a shrine or kept at home for private contemplation and prayer. An *Ex voto* is usually no more than a few inches wide and tall.

Another religious item of interest is called a reredo, or altar screen. The word reredo has its roots in Middle English and French. It is commonly used by *Anglo-Americans* and by scholars to describe altar screens. Hispanic New Mexicans don't seem to recognize the word. Instead they refer to altar screens and even smaller painted boards as "*retablos.*" A reredo or altar screen was usually carved from wood in shallow relief. These depicted religious themes or figures. They could also have been made from materials other than wood, such as stone, ivory, metal or a combination of materials. A reredo is associated with a church altar. In modern terms, the reredo may often be thought of as the composition, while the elements within it often are called *retablos*. However, this definition is not absolute, as the term reredo and *retablo* are used interchangeably when referring to altar screens and their contents. One has to keep in mind the cultural ethnicity of the speaker.

Among Hispanics, the reredo or main altar screen is usually referred to as a "*retablo mayor,*"[26] while a reredo in a side altar is referred to as a "*retablo colateral.*"[27] Among non-Hispanics, the term reredo is often used instead to describe an altar screen, all of it or the component elements of it.

See Figure 6-4 for an example of a reredo, or a *retablo mayor,* imported from New Spain to New Mexico in Spanish Colonial times.

Whatever the correct terminology is, these works of folk art are fascinating historically and culturally!

What's a *Ristra?*[28, 29]

Have you noticed those charming, decorative, usually deep red-colored cascades hanging from doorways, home and hotel entrances, and in lobbies? Also used as Christmas season ornaments, these very attractive, beautifully colored hanging clusters of red *chiles*, belong to a long-standing Southwestern tradition.

Called a "*ristra*" by the locals, the term is a noun meaning "string" in Spanish. Numerous red *chiles* are strung together in cascading clusters. These decorative clusters are very appealing to the viewer. However, *ristras* are produced for more than their beauty or visual appeal. The original purpose was to complete the ripening process for *chiles* of all types.

Starting in mid-September and extending through the first frost, green *chiles* experience a maturing process. As they remain on the vine and continue to mature, they turn a deep red color, characteristic of the *ristra*'s rich coloration. They are then picked. The red *chiles* are usually set aside for two or three days after picking and before stringing, allowing the stems to dry and harden. This facilitates the eventual stringing together of the *chiles*. Otherwise, the stems may be too weak and break during the stringing process. Good ventilation is essential in the final drying process. Red *chiles* are then traditionally strung together to allow further drying in the Southwestern sun.

Once fully dried on the *ristra*, the red *chiles* are stored for eventual use in traditional New Mexican, Mexican and Southwestern dishes. Oftentimes, the dried *chiles* are sold as pods or they are ground into a powder for purposes. Alternately, the red *chile ristra* might be sold as a decorative item. Green *chiles* are not used for making *ristras*. Green *chiles* are immature. If strung, as in a *ristra*, they will shrivel and dry to a dull orange color.

Chile peppers vary in size, color, and texture, giving rise to a wide variety of possible *ristra* creations. Often used are the New Mexico #6 *chile* or the Nu-Mex Big Jim. The New Mexico #6 is a mild type of green *chile*. Even the popular California or Anaheim *chile* pepper is used, with its six to eight inch long pods. Smaller *ristras* and wreaths can be created from the smaller Pequin *chile* pepper.

Locals often keep *ristras* hanging around their domiciles or *tiendas* (shops) throughout the year, as a good luck talisman. By the end of the old season, the old *ristra* is removed and replaced with a new, brightly colored, freshly strung *ristra* for the upcoming year and the new season.

Because of their uniqueness and color, *ristras* are often used for decoration during the Christmas Season. Decorative *ristras* come in a variety of lengths and shapes, including wreaths and the more traditional cascades. Natural *ristras* are usually lacquered or sprayed with a preservative making them inedible. These shiny, bright red lacquered *chile* pepper *ristras* then present a beautiful, creative and Southwestern alternative to the more conventional poinsettas and holly, used for Holiday Season decoration.

Commercial suppliers also make artificial *ristras* of plastic, metal or ceramic. They often include green- and red-colored *chiles* consonant with Christmas colors.

Want more variety? *Ristras* can also be strung together with garlic bulbs, corn husks and/or Indian corn itself. So if you fear vampires, who knows? Such a garlic-enlaced *ristra* offers interesting but unverifiable potential.

Ristras have entered the mainstream as popular designs on T-shirts, and as decorative motifs on cookie and storage jars, napkins, dinnerware, linens, etc. This is due to their attractive colors and their association with good-luck, domesticity, earthiness, and the sense of welcome that they project. After all, it is that feeling of welcome or *bienvenidos* that greets the eye and warms the heart, as one passes within the traditional Southwestern home entry (*la entrada*) or doorway regaled in traditional *ristras*. It hails "*mi casa es su casa*", or "my house is your house", without a single audible utterance.

The humble *ristra* represents something both basic and fundamental. It symbolizes continuance of tradition, the welcoming arms of a loving family or dear friends, the gratefulness for a successful autumn harvest, the peace and security of the *hogar* (home), and the deep satisfaction of the nearness of nature. It is this and much more that simply cannot be adequately put into mere words. The *ristra* is something we respond to without really knowing why. It appeals to our primal, nonverbal intelligence for which only a visceral response is appropriate. And so we are drawn to it, satisfied that beyond its simple colorful beauty, there is something deeper and more profound that stirs within us, while we remain enraptured by it's own unique mystery.

From humble practical applications, the lowly Southwestern *chile* pepper "*ristra*" has arrived on the scene. From its start as a simple and traditional curing methodology, it has evolved as a decorative motif and as an artistic inspiration. It will always remain a quiet but profound symbol of all that is good, warm, loving, welcoming, and earth-connected. They've sure come a long way!!

Roadside Memorials: Forever Remembered[30]

The placing of memorials along the roadside is a tradition in the American

Southwest that reaches back to the early Hispanic settlers. Roadside shrines commemorate the last place a loved one was either fatally injured or killed after an auto accident, as opposed to a gravesite where the deceased is actually buried. The shrine usually contains a small crucifix and some memorial flowers, with a sign indicating the victim's name and often the memorial date. Oftentimes, there are several crosses in cases of multiple deaths associated with the site.

These crosses are usually called "*descanso*" crosses. This name comes from an old custom, in former times, when a funerary procession would proceed from the local church, mission or cathedral to the burial site, carrying the coffin or coffins of the departed. The coffin bearers would take periodic rests or "*descansos*" from their travails before proceeding again on their way to the cemetery. A small cross was placed at each "*descanso*" location to commemorate the processional stop.

This practice has carried over into modern times, to commemorate the last location a loved one suddenly met death, usually alongside a highway, near where the fatal accident occurred. What is really remarkable is the enduring love and devotion shown in the care of these memorials throughout the year. They are often attended to by family members and close friends, with fresh or plastic flowers on the anniversary date, Valentine's Day, birthdays of the deceased, Easter, Christmas, etc, with the appropriate floral arrangements or other momentos. It is very heartwarming to observe the loving attention given to these roadside memorials.

The New Mexico Dept. of Transportation is generally respectful of these roadside memorials, even though they are not required or expected to protect them. These memorials have not only a personal significance for the victims' survivors, but they also serve as a caution to all drivers of potential dangers and serve as a reminder to drive safely.

This quaint and heartwarming custom is seen on roadways throughout the state. Hopefully this warm and comforting tradition will never pass away!

Santa Fe Recovered: *Fiestas de Santa Fe (Santa Fe Fiesta*[31, 32]*)*

The commonly termed *Santa Fe Fiesta* occurs one weekend after Labor Day, in September, at the end of the tourist season. It is officially called *Fiestas de Santa Fe*. The *Fiestas* were first established in 1712 to celebrate the Spanish re-conquest of *Santa Fe* from the rebellious *pueblo* Indians. It took twelve or thirteen years to recover *Santa Fe*, after the Spaniards were driven out by the rebelling natives. The *Pueblo* Revolt started in 1680, but *Santa Fe* was only retaken in 1692–1693.

When De Vargas re-entered *Santa Fe*, he brought with him a statue called Our Lady of the Rosary or Our Lady of the Assumption. This was a religious icon of the Virgin Mary that had first arrived in northern New Mexico from before the time of the *Pueblo* Revolt of 1680. On his expedition to reconquer *Santa Fe*, De Vargas promised to carry the icon in a yearly procession if he succeeded in recapturing *Santa Fe*. He also vowed to build a special chapel for the icon to abide within during the remainder of the year. Our Lady of the Rosary or Our Lady of the Assumption has over time come to be identified as *La Conquistadora.*[33] See *La Conquistadora* in Figure 6-5.

A prequel to the *Fiestas de Santa Fe* begins with the *Novena* Masses held twice daily in the Cathedral Basilica of Saint Francis of Assisi in *Santa Fe*. This normally occurs early in July, about two months prior to the actual *Fiestas de Santa Fe* celebration in September. The Knighting and Coronation of Don Diego de Vargas and of *La Reina de Santa Fe*[34] are each re-enacted. A procession then takes the statue of *La Conquistadora*, from *La Conquistadora* Chapel in the Cathedral Basilica of Saint Francis of Assisi, to the *Rosario* (Rosary) Chapel, a few miles distant. This chapel is located at the *Rosario* Cemetery adjacent to the National Cemetery in *Santa Fe*. This site is believed to be the location where De Vargas made his campsite during his reoccupation of *Santa Fe*.

Throughout the week, nine different Masses are held here. On the weekend ending this pre-*Fiesta* celebration week, *La Conquistadora* is returned again, from the *Rosario* Chapel to the Cathedral Basillica.

Figure 6-5: *La Conquistadora*, or Our Lady of the Assumption, in the (Old *Parroquia*) Cathedral Basilica of St. Francis of Assisi, *Santa Fe*. (Archdiocese of *Santa Fe*.)

Masses are made as a tribute honoring the promise made by Don Diego de Vargas to *La Conquistadora* to pay annual tribute to her for his mission of reconquest. The *Fiestas de Santa Fe* celebration occurs in early September, the weekend after Labor Day. See Figure 6-6. The secular celebration is usually kicked off unofficially on a Thursday evening, with the Burning of the *Zozobra*©® ("Old Man Gloom®") at Marcy Field Park.

Figure 6-6: *Fiestas de Santa Fe* Re-enactors: De Vargas with *La Reina*, as they appeared at Marcy Field Park, on the evening before the beginning of the 2011 *Fiestas de Santa Fe* (With permission of the re-enactors)

(See the Burning of the *Zozobra*©® in Chapter Ten.) After this dramatic cathartic event, participants usually march to the *Plaza*, shouting "*Viva la Fiesta*."

The following few days at the *Plaza* are filled with music, entertainment, parades, food and a general good time. On early Friday morning (6 AM) of the *Fiestas de Santa Fe* celebration weekend, the religious observation of the *fiesta* starts with a Mass held at the *Rosario* Chapel. It is called *El Pregon*[35] *de la Fiesta*, marking the start of the first full official *fiesta* celebration day. The *Plaza* hosts an Arts & Crafts Show, and live entertainment throughout the entire weekend celebration. At about noon on Friday, the official opening of the *Fiestas de Santa Fe* is declared.

Early on Saturday there is usually the Pet Parade or *El Desfile de los Niños* (Children's Parade). Another highlight occurs that same Saturday afternoon. It is called *La Entrada*, a play that portrays Don Diego de Vargas' victorious entrance into the *Santa Fe Plaza*, along with his *cuadrilla*.[36] Specially selected citizens appear on horseback wearing seventeenth century dress. They re-enact the victorious re-entry of Don Diego de Vargas and his colonials into *Santa Fe* in 1692. It is considered a high honor to be selected to play the role of De Vargas in the celebration.

Figure 6-6 shows re-enactors as De Vargas and *La Reina*. After *La Entrada* the entertainment begins. The *La Merienda*[37] Fashion Show is usually presented at a local theater shortly after *La Entrada*. Other entertainment also follows. Figure 6-7 shows the *Mariachi Nuevo Sonido* band playing as it proceeds to the *Santa Fe Plaza* at the commencement of the secular events. Traditional Mexican and New Mexican dancing is also featured at the *Fiestas de Santa Fe*. See Figure 6-8.

The activities continue into Sunday, the following day, with a solemn procession

Figure 6-7: The *Mariachi Nuevo Sonido* (New *Mariachi* Sound)
Band playing en route to the *Plaza* during the 2011 *Fiestas de Santa Fe*.
(With permission of the *Mariachi Nuevo Sonido* Band.[38])

Figure 6-8: Traditional Dancers of *Baile Folklorico de Santa Fe*
performing on the *Plaza* at the 2011 *Fiestas de Santa Fe*.
(With permission of *Baile Folkorico de Santa Fe*.[39])

from the Palace of the Governors to the Cathedral Basilica and then by a Pontifical Mass. The festivities resume in the early afternoon with the aptly named Hysterical/ Historical Parade. Some locals call it *El Desfile de la Gente* or the People's Parade. Various neighborhood groups build competing floats for the parade. The ceremonies are concluded on Sunday evening with the Closing Ceremony at the *Plaza*. This is followed by a Mass of thanksgiving held in the Cathedral Basilica of Saint Francis of Assisi. The final event is a candlelight procession from the Cathedral Basilica to the Cross of the Martyrs, located in Old Fort Marcy Park. This last site commemorates the martyrdom of some twenty-three Franciscan priests who were killed during the 1680 *Pueblo* Revolt. See Figure 6-9.

Figure 6-9: Cross of the Martyrs, in Old Fort Marcy Park, *Santa Fe*.

The *Fiestas de Santa Fe* is a much-anticipated colorful multi-day event in *Santa Fe*, and with good reason. It is a celebratory *fiesta*, with religious and historical overtones, but it is also a time for letting go of fears from the past year, and it is a time of music, dance and merriment. What's not to like!?

Holy *Santos* (*Bultos*)[40]

Santos, derived from the Spanish meaning saints, are a traditional New Mexican religious art form. They can take one of two forms: *bultos* or *retablos*. *Retablos* have already been discussed earlier in this chapter. *Bultos* are three-dimensional sculptures carved in wood or ivory, depicting a religious figure, such as an angel or saint.

As part of the Spanish colonization, the Spanish introduced icons to assist in converting native peoples to Roman Catholicism. At first, many of these icons were imported from Spain, but over time this distribution method became costly, unreliable and untimely. To circumvent these issues, priests and craftsmen made imitation copies of the more genuine Spanish Baroque statues. Gradually, native styles and themes produced a style of *santos* that was unique and different from the original Spanish Baroque style. These native *santos* became very popular throughout northern New Mexico and they became devotional icons. Some *santos* attracted pilgrims who came to see them and to pray by them in the church which housed them.

Eventually, local craftsmen took over the production of *santos* from the priests. These local craftsmen became known as *santeros* or carvers of *santos*. They were often self-taught with no formal training. Alternatively, they may have served apprenticeships under masters.

A particular type of *santo* is called a *bulto*. It is a carving "in the round"[41] made from a single piece of cottonwood root, pine or aspen. A *santero* usually carved it with a knife. It was then covered with a mixture of native gypsum and glue, called *gesso*, to prepare the sculpture for painting. Yucca fibers, human and horse-hair were used to make brushes. Homemade pigments were then used for the paint. Vegetation, clay, ochres and minerals were used. These were then ground down in the final stages to create the paint pigments. Contemporary *santeros* (male) or *santeras* (female) may or may not use homemade pigments. Chapter Ten presents an example of a modern *bulto* from the summer 2011 *Santa Fe* Traditional Spanish Market©.

Not all genuine *bultos* from the Spanish Colonial period were completely painted. Some were unpainted, some were minimally painted and others fully painted. See the reference to *bultos* in *El Santuario de Chimayó* discussed earlier in this same chapter in the section entitled, *Oh, It's a Long Walk to Chimayó.*

Bultos are a unique and fascinating heritage of northern New Mexico.

Straw *Appliqué* [42, 43]

Another art form that is still very popular and is still thriving today among descendants of Spanish Colonialists is called straw *appliqué*. This art form is applied to different articles to produce stunningly beautiful and delicate designs. European marquetry is a similar art form and straw *appliqué* is a variant of this popular technique. However, marquetry uses small, thin pieces of colored and contrasting materials of various kinds to decorate a surface. These materials may vary from different woods and metals, to other materials such as ivory or bone. Mother of pearl or tortoise shell may also be used. Some of these materials are expensive and were difficult to obtain in New Mexico, so other more common materials were found and used instead. Straw was readily available and inexpensive. In New Mexico, the straw *appliqué* art form uses straw instead of the more expensive materials used in marquetry to decorate a surface.

There are two variations in the techniques used in marquetry, which have affected the methods used in straw *appliqué*. One technique is called veneer marquetry, which is the application of a thin decorative veneer to a surface. The second technique is called inlay, wherein the surface is carved out slightly to allow the decorative material to lie within the resulting shallow cavity. In New Mexico, straw *appliqué* artists sometimes apply both techniques, veneer or onlay, and inlay, to achieve gorgeously beautiful effects in their designs. Other artists apply only the veneer or onlay technique. Either way, the results are very beautiful!

The straw *appliqué* art form was practiced over a thousand years ago in North Africa. The Moors eventually transferred it to Spain. Some centuries later, Spanish artisans spread the art form throughout the newly conquered lands of New Spain in the Americas. Because of its innate beauty, straw *appliqué* was often substituted for mother-of-pearl inlay in the region of the upper *Rio Grande* Valley, where many Spanish Colonialists had settled.

In these regions of New Mexico, the wood was often stained black and a delicate beautiful straw design was deftly placed onto the wooden surface using a mixture of pine pitch and soot, as an adhesive. The straw design was composed of finely cut dried wheat straw or corn husks.

Some historians believe that straw *appliqué* died out as an art form in the late nineteenth century, but was revived in the early twentieth century by Eliseo Rodriguez.

The veneer or onlay method is probably the most prevalent technique used in New Mexico. A subject piece is often carved or made of wood. The piece could be a crucifix, a jewelry box, picture frames, candleholders or some other item. It is usually painted or stained to seal the surface and to present a better color to the product. Then the process of adding the straw *appliqué* begins. Thin pieces of straw are cut down the middle and then cut into shorter lengths. These pieces are then carefully and delicately glued to the surface in conformance with the desired design. Although the straw design may appear like it is inlaid, it is not. Instead, it is applied on top of the subject piece's surface in thin strips. Sometimes the artist may apply a coat of varnish over the entire piece to present a smooth even surface that may give the illusion of inlay. This is done to seal the surface and the straw onlay.

Figure 6-10: A Straw *Appliqué* Crucifix, by artist and *santero* Mel Rivera, shown at the 2011 *Santa Fe* Traditional Spanish Market©. (By permission of Mel Rivera.[44])

Straw *appliqué* is often used to enhance crucifixes, and the design in this case is usually of a religious nature. Designs on jewelry boxes and other items are generally non-religious in nature. Whatever the subject piece and whatever the design theme, articles with straw *appliqué* are usually very beautiful, delicate, and artfully done when created by a true artisan! See Figure 6-10 for an exquisite example of a straw onlaid crucifix.

Tinwork

The occupation of New Mexico by U.S. troops in 1846 brought many changes to

New Mexico. Among these was the growth in the development of tinwork. This art form continued to flourish after Bishop Lamy's appointment to New Mexico in 1850. Lamy attempted to bring *Santa Fe* to a higher level of sophistication and culture. So he discouraged the production of native religious works such as *retablos*. However, tin cans began to be imported from Europe in large numbers, in this same time period. Also in vogue in this period were European prints framed in tin. These various elements combined to cause a surge in tinwork within New Mexico. This art form also saw a revival in the 1930's that has continued to this day.

The art of creating exquisitely beautiful tinwork has been passed down to contemporary times. The artisans use pliable tin, which is silver in color. It is often called "the poor man's silver" because of its natural luster. The working tin is usually cut from much larger thin sheets of tin. Special cutting tools are used to produce scalloped edges. Punches are used to make designs on the metal. The metal is hammered to make borders, designs and to create various forms. Items of tinwork may include empty frames, framed mirrors, ornaments and crosses. The craft is often passed on, from generation to generation, in northern New Mexico, among descendants of the early Spanish Colonialists. See Chapter Ten in the section describing the *Santa Fe Traditional Spanish Market*©.

The Much Revered Virgin of Guadalupe[45]

The Mexican influence on New Mexican culture is evident in the deep reverence shown by many Hispanics in this state and elsewhere towards the Virgin of Guadalupe, called *Nuestra Virgen de Guadalupe*.[46] The image of the Virgin of Guadalupe is easily recognized. It shows a holy woman with her head tilting slightly downward, and with her hands clasped in a prayerful pose. She is enshrouded within an array of emanating rays of beatification, signifying her sanctity and spirituality.

The Virgin of Guadalupe stands atop a crescent moon wrapped in folded cloth. At the base of the image there is an angel, presenting the Lady or perhaps supporting the weight of all above it. It stands as a celebrated Catholic icon among Hispanics.

According to the legend,[47] a converted Mexican peasant, Juan Diego,[48] was walking from his home to Mexico City, to attend Mass on the morning of the Feast of the Immaculate Conception, December 9, 1531. On his way, he saw a young woman, surrounded in light, on the Hill of *Tepeyac*. The young woman spoke to him in *Nahuatl*, his native language, asking him to have a church built on that site dedicated in her name. The legend indicates that Juan Diego recognized the young woman as the Virgin Mary. When he related the story of his experience to the Spanish Archbishop, Juan Diego was told to return to the site of his vision and to request some miraculous sign to prove what he had seen. The peasant was told by the Holy Lady to climb to the top of *Tepeyac* Hill (*El Cerro de Tepeyac*) to gather some flowers. It was winter, with no expectation of finding any flowers growing on the hill's summit. However, to his surprise, Juan Diego found many flowers growing there. He gathered the flowers. Then the Virgin Mary assisted him in arranging the flowers within his *tilma* (pleasant cloak). Juan Diego returned to the archbishop to show him his find. When he opened his cloak, all the flowers fell to the floor, leaving an image of the *Virgen de Guadalupe* imprinted on the cloak that had previously held only flowers.

Tepeyac, the site of Juan Diego's vision, was the very site where a decade or so before, a local temple dedicated to the mother-goddess, *Tonantzín*, had been destroyed, and a chapel was built in its place. This chapel was dedicated to the Virgin Mary.

The begging question is why is the Virgin of Guadalupe not called the Virgin of *Tepeyac*? The name of the Lady or Virgin of Guadalupe may have derived from the Extremadura area of Spain, which was the homeland of many of the *Conquistadors*, including Hernán Cortés. Our Lady of Guadalupe is the name given to one of three Black *Madonnas* in Spain.[49] The associated shrine was one of the most important shrines dedicated to the Virgin Mary in the medieval kingdom of Castile, Spain. The shrine resides in the monastery of *Santa Maria de Guadalupe*, located in the Caceres Province within the Extramadura region of Spain.

Scholars[50] have also indicated that the *Nahuatl* name used by the Virgin to refer to herself was *Coatlaxopueh*, pronounced as quatlasupe, meaning, "the one who crushes the serpent" (the feathered serpent, *Quetzalcoatl*). Notice that this *Nahuatl* pronunciation is very close to the Spanish "Guadalupe." In 1675, Luis Becerra Tanco proposed another thesis.[51] He proposed that her name in *Nahuatl* was *Tequatlanopeuh*, meaning " she whose origins were in the rocky summit." Again, this is similar in pronunciation to the Spanish "Guadalupe." The suggestion being that her *Nahuatl* name was mispronounced by the Spaniards and thought to have been Guadalupe, the nearest Spanish equivalent in sound.[52] So, the mystery continues about the true origins of the name Virgin of Guadalupe.

The *Virgen de Guadalupe* legend was rapidly adopted by the Spaniards and the native peoples, because it contained elements from both cultures. Further, the exploration and colonization of the Royal *Province de Nuevo México* by the Spaniards, and the later colonization by the Mexicans brought this significant and spiritual religious tradition to New Mexico.

The image of the Virgin of Guadalupe left as an impression on Juan Diego's *tilma* is full of Christian and pagan symbolism[53] that would have been meaningful and significant to the *Nahuatl*-speaking native population around *Tepeyac* and Mexico City, as well as to the Spaniards. This imagery will now be described, based largely on information gathered from Catholic sources. (See note 53.)

Some of the imagery associated with Our Lady of Guadalupe is contained in several verses found in the *Book of Revelations*, Chapter 12.[54] The first verse contains two references, as follows: "A great portent appeared in heaven: a woman clothed with the sun, with the moon under her feet, and on her head a crown of twelve stars." Verse 2 continues with: "She was pregnant…" Finally Verse 5 says: "And she gave birth to a son, a male child, who is to rule all the nations…"

The light surrounding the image of the Virgin of Guadalupe brings to mind the image of a "woman clothed with the sun" from *Revelations*. One could also interpret the emanating rays as a sign of God's blessing, or even of the Lady's sanctification and beatification. However, to the natives of Mexico the rays could also be seen as a symbol of their highest god named *Huitzilopochtli*,[55] the *Aztec* war god and sun god. By standing in front of the rays, the Lady could be interpreted as eclipsing the sun's power as well as that of this most powerful native god.

The Virgin is usually portrayed standing atop a crescent moon, consistent with the image in *Revelations* of a woman who has "the moon under her feet." Among Christians, the crescent moon under her feet may represent her eternal virginity and purity. It may allude to her Immaculate Conception. For the Meso-American natives, the moon symbolizes their god of darkness. *Tezcatlipoca*[56] was known as the unseen night god. In standing on the crescent moon, the Virgin of Guadalupe shows her power over the forces of darkness and the pagan god (s) of the natives.

The Virgin of Guadalupe's eyes look downward in humility and compassion. This humble posture conveys a message to the natives that she is not God, but rather God's servant. In contrast, the native gods are often portrayed as looking forward directly and boldly, with wide-opened eyes, in a posture of power, defiance and strength. Her humble and compassionate posture was sure to make her appear much more approachable and receptive than many of their native gods. She is usually, but not always, portrayed with dark skin and hair, identifying her with the natives of Mexico.

It is also suggested that her humble posture may denote a gesture of offering, in this case, her unborn child Jesus.

Other symbols appear to be encoded into the image. The angel below the Lady appears to embody both innocence and wisdom. Some suggest that the angel below her image may be presenting the Holy Lady as the harbinger of a new Christian era. Still others say that the Lady is being supported or transported on the shoulders of the angel, which again may symbolize the dawning of a new age. However, the pagan native experience only knew of emperors, kings, queens and royal dignitaries, or the powerful elite being carried upon the shoulders of subjects or servants. This portrayal would again indicate to the natives, the Lady's high and noble standing. The gold border of her mantle would also indicate the same to the indigenous peoples. Our Lady is usually shown wearing a mantle that is a blue-green or turquoise color. To the pagan natives, this color is associated with gods and royalty, or with life and fertility. In Christian imagery, this color usually represents eternity and ever-lasting life.

The Lady comes as the Mother of Heaven, as symbolized by the stars on her mantle. To the natives, the stars symbolized that she is supernatural in nature, although she is not God. In this image, Our Lady of Guadalupe differs slightly from the *Revelations* image wherein she wears "...on her head a crown of twelve stars." However, the two images, though different, are similar, in that heavenly stars are used to represent her heavenly nature. It is said that the stars on her mantle represent the constellations as they appeared in that region on the night of Juan Diego's vision.

The color of The Lady's dress is usually shown as a pale-red or rose color, representing the early dawn, or the coming of a new Christian age.

Her sanctitity is symbolized by Her wearing a gold-encircled cross brooch under the neck of her robe. She wears a girdle or bow around her waist. Perhaps this was symbolic to both Christians and pagan natives alike, but in different ways. To Christians, this may be another sign of her virginity. To natives, the bow may have appeared to be a four-petaled flower, called the *"nahui ollin"*, the flower of the sun, plentitude and new life.

Another interesting observation is that the bow rests high on the Lady's slightly swelling abdomen. This may indicate she is not only a virgin, but that "She was pregnant..." according to *Revelations* 12:2, as mentioned earlier. So the identification of Our Lady of Guadalupe with various aspects of the woman described in *Revelations* is quite dramatic and astounding.

There is one more allusion that needs to be highlighted, namely *Revelations*

12:5, wherein "...she gave birth to a son, a male child, who is to rule all the nations..." For Christians, this male child would be recognized as Jesus, the Christ-child. The image suggests that the new Christ-child is to be born "again" among the peoples of the New World.

Therefore, the image of the Virgin of Guadalupe that is familiar to most Hispanics is full of rich Christian and pagan symbolism, that was embraced by the native Indians and the Spaniards, and was eventually transmitted to New Mexico. After the image was revealed the conversion of native Indians to Christianity increased rapidly and dramatically. It also spread northwards into the northern province of *Nuevo México*.

Today, millions of Roman Catholics, from old Mexico, New Mexico or other parts of the American Southwest find great solace and comfort in the Virgin of Guadalupe. Apart from any historical or intellectual analysis, Our Lady of Guadalupe has been worshipped and revered for her humility, grace and sanctity, for hundreds of years, and indeed still is to this very day!

In *Santa Fe*, New Mexico, there is an old *adobe* church, called *El Santuario de Guadalupe*. It is the oldest extant shrine in the United States dedicated to the *Virgen de Guadalupe*, the patron saint of Mexico. See the section in Chapter 10, which discusses *El Santuario* in more detail.

The Weeping Lady (*La Llorona*)[57, 58, 59]

La Llorona is Spanish for "Weeping Woman" and it is pronounced "la yohr-rohn'-ah." It is a popular legend and folktale that appears to have originated in Mexico but has become transmitted and adopted among Spanish-speaking peoples throughout the American Southwest and even in other parts of the U.S. Stories centering on *La Llorona* are part of the Hispanic culture of New Mexico.

The basic story is that *La Llorona* was originally a beautiful but proud young woman named Maria. She longed to fall in love and marry a handsome dashing young man. For Maria, that would be the ultimate in happiness. One day she encountered such a man and they both fell in love, and married. However, the husband had certain faults, one of which was vanity and a roaming eye. Maria was happy at first and even had two children. One day he left her for another woman. This rejection was too much for her to bear. Resenting her children as the cause for her rejection, she led them to a nearby stream. In her distraught state, she drowned her two children. She then either fell dead or she killed herself, in remorse for her recent foul deeds.

It was said she was denied entry into Heaven because of her sins, at least until she could find her slain children. So she wanders the earth endlessly seeking her children in vain crying out, "ah-h-h-h mis hijos" or "oh my children." As she searches, she weeps incessantly and so she is called *La Llorona*, the Weeping Lady.

It is also said that she may kidnap children for her own if they wander or disobey their parents. Although her crimes are unforgivable and heinous, she still evokes compassion because of her remorse and her eternal suffering.

Another version strikes close to home in New Mexico. In this tale, Maria is not at home, when her children are kidnapped and drowned in the *Santa Fe* River. Overcome with understandable grief, she kills herself. Again, she is rejected at the gates of Heaven, and she must roam seeking her unfortunate dead children. Here, *La Llorona* is said to claim wandering children that go near the *Santa Fe* River.

Some say the story of *La Llorona* may have been influenced by a Mexican *Aztec* legend about a goddess, *Cihuacoatl* or *Coatlicue*. The goddess supposedly appeared shortly before the Spanish *Conquista* (Conquest) of Mexico by Cortés. She was found weeping for her lost children, foretelling the fall of the *Aztec* Empire.

Still others claim that *La Llorona* was identified with *La Malinche*,[60] the Native American woman who acted as Cortés' interpreter and guide. Some hold nothing but disdain for her because they believe she betrayed Mexico by helping Cortés. In the folktale, *La Malinche* falls in love with Cortés and has his child. However, as Cortés is a Spanish nobleman and *La Malinche* is an indigenous woman, he looks elsewhere to find and marry a Spanish woman of noble birth. *La Malinche* seeks revenge and so kills her child. (Playwright and novelist Rudolfo Anaya wrote an excellent play using the theme of *La Malinche* as *La Llorona*. The play is entitled *The Season of La Llorona*. It is collected in *Billy the Kid and Other Plays, Rudolfo Anaya, Published by University of Oklahoma Press,* 2011.) However, there is no evidence to show that *La Malinche* ever killed any of her children. In 1933, a Mexican film appeared called *La Malinche*, and starred Adriana Lamar.

Nonetheless, tales of the Weeping Lady continue in New Mexico. They serve as cautionary tales to Hispanic youngsters. Some parents advise and warn their children that bad behavior may cause *La Llorona to* kidnap them. These tales advise against staying out late at night after dark, for fear of being visited by the Weeping Lady. The tales also serve to caution young girls not to be seduced by fame, wealth, status, materiality, or vanity, or to believe in declarations or promises that may be too good to be true. *La Llorona* is held up as an example of bad motherhood, of casting away her responsibilities, while shirking real love for her children to obtain an ephemeral, vain and unquenchable physical love. Because she acts in desperation, the Weeping Woman is seen to be weak, an undesirable personality trait. Instead she should be strong, accept her bad choice of a husband or lover, learn from the mistake and move on to a better life, stronger for the experience. It is clear that many levels of moral instruction are present in this tale that continues to thrive and to morph in the Hispanic regions of New Mexico. With each new telling, the Hispanic ideal of motherhood is reinforced by the contrast provided by *La Llorona*.

The Weeping Woman is just one more example of the rich cultural inheritance that helps to make the New Mexican traditional heritage so colorful and meaningful.

Traditional Woodworking

Another Spanish Colonial tradition that continues to this day in New Mexico, is woodworking. In this tradition, artisans and craftsmen create masterpieces carved in wood, representing *santos*, angels, religious images and scenes from the Bible, crucifixes, wooden rosaries and the like. They may even carve *santos* without treating the unfinished wood, keeping the wooden image in its natural unfinished state.

Many crucifixes and other carved wooden objects are intricate and beautiful, highlighting the natural raw beauty of the wood itself, enhanced by the artist's vision, skill and creativity. These fine works stand on their merits. Figure 6-11 shows a crucifix carved by an artist and craftsman, who has been a woodcarver from childhood. Note the intricate floral motif decorating the wooden cross. This crucifix contains 240 wooden petals, each individually handcrafted. A beautiful, wonderful living tradition!

Figure 6-11: Woodworking tradition: A petalled crucifix by artist and *santero* Joe Morales. (By permission of Joe Morales.[61])

Chapter Seven:
Anglo-American Culture and Curiosities

Anglo-American culture is recognizably more secular than the Native American or Hispanic cultures. Perhaps we are drawn to these cultures to fill the spiritual void that is endemic in many modern societies. One cannot deny the technological marvels produced by the *Anglo*-American culture. Over time, the American Culture has advanced through a sequence of technological advances including the Pony Express, the railroad, the telegraph, electricity, the telephone, the automobile, and of course the more modern technologies, such as the computer, cell phones, the Internet, social-networking , etc. However, the intent of this chapter is not to laud or even explain these and other technologies or their cultural impact. That exercise can be left to others.

Still, *Anglo*-American culture has introduced some interesting and fascinating elements into the cultural *pot-pouri* that is New Mexico. It is worth explaining a few of these curiosities. The great and robust cowboy culture has shaped much of the frontier here in New Mexico. It is still alive and survives in the rural regions of this state and this country. Much of American and New Mexican character has been formed from the ideals of the cowboy. So that is where we will begin our survey. Other topics will follow.

Figure 7-1: *Wind and Rain,* sculpted William Moyers, at The Albuquerque Museum of Art and History. (By permission of The Albuquerque Museum of Art and History.)

This chapter will touch on: Cowboy Culture, Decorated Steer Skulls, Jackalope, Painted Horses, *Pecos* Bill, Roswell UFO Incident, Smokey the Bear and Truth or Consequences.

Cowboy Culture

Just about everyone has seen photographs or watched movies about the American cowboy. He is thought of as independent, self-sufficient, handy, skilled, diligent, brave, honest and fair, except of course for the "bad guys." These ideals reflect *Americana* and qualities that built this great nation. See Figure 7-1. In this fine statue, named *"Wind and Rain"*, a cowboy is buttoning up his rain overcoat in preparation for foul weather. His horse stands by. This captures the tenacity and strength of the American cowboy!

In local rural communities throughout New Mexico, today's youth are living and learning the cowboy and farming ways everyday on small *ranchitos* and homesteads.

Perhaps you have wondered about some of the exterior features of the cowboy, such as their gear. Here are some simple questions and answers related to cowboy gear:

Question: Why are his boots pointed, and not squared off at the toe?
Answer: It is to allow the rider to easily put his boots into the stirrups.

Question: Why does a western saddle have a horn at the front?
Answer: The horn allows the cowboy to hold his rope to pull against when holding a steer or other animal on the other end of the rope.

Question: What is beef jerky?
Answer: It is an old way of processing fast food, and it was learned from Native Americans. It is beef that has been seasoned and dried, allowing it to be packed and carried on long trips. It is an easy food to handle and to eat. It is western "fast food."

Question: Why does a cowboy hat turn up on the sides and have a deep crease on top from front to back?
Answer: The upturned sides keep the rain from running off sideways. This channels the rain towards the rear of the hat where it can run off. The deep top crease is to allow rain on the top of the hat to again run down to the rear and then run off.

Question: Why does a cowboy wear chaps?
Answer: Chaps protect his legs from the wear and tear of hard riding, from brush and from rough contact with cattle and with bulls' horns.

Question: Why did he wear a kerchief?
Answer: Kerchiefs keep the ubiquitous dust from getting into his nostrils, mouth and lungs. You haven't lived til you've experienced a biting sandstorm! Imagine the dust kicked up while driving cattle!

Question: Spurs?
Answer: Horses respond more quickly to spurs in a given situation.

Question: Why is a lasso stiffened?
Answer: Ever tried throwing a regular un-stiffened rope, especially to corral an animal? It doesn't work very well! The stiffening allows the cowboy to form his loop and to better control the lasso.

Figure 7-2: The next generation:
"You gotta start 'em young!"

Figure 7-3: "Let's get goin'."

Without strong personal characteristics, the American Southwest and the American West could never have been explored and settled in any great numbers. The taming of this region was accomplished by the pioneer or frontier spirit, which later gave rise to the cowboy culture! Fortunately the cowboy culture still lives on through yet another generation of young Americans. See Figures 7-2 and 7-3.

Decorated Steer Skulls

Georgia O'Keefe made famous the image of steer skulls in various paintings, including *Cow Skulls: Red, White and Blue*. Some paintings include a flower attached to the skull, perhaps to soften the hard image. The steer skull has become an icon of the Southwest. It evokes a sense of timelessness, and of the cycle of life and death. Yet we connect to these images because they possess their own primitive beauty. A decorated steer skull is usually bleached and then decorated with all manner of materials such as beads, leather, rope, feathers, acrylic paint or colorful stones, such as turquoise, etc. Often the horns are varnished, or they may even be covered or tipped with silver or other material. These skulls, in their various artistic forms, are sought out both by tourists and locals. It is not unusual to see one or more of these mounted on a living room wall in a Southwestern home. See Figure 7-4.

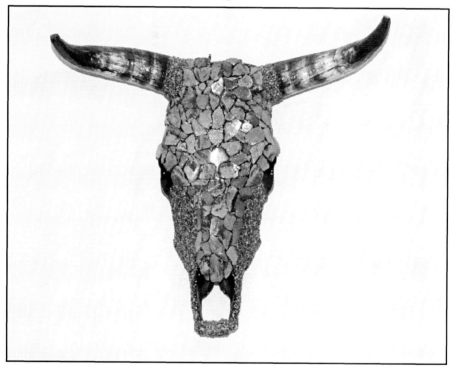

Figure 7-4: Decorated Steer Skull

Clearly, there are many other curiosities associated with cowboy gear. The items above are meant only to tickle your curiosity. However, the most important legacy of the cowboy culture is the self-sufficient, solid work ethic and the "can do" attitude.

The Horny Jackalope

The jackalope[1,2,3] is an antlered form of rabbit. It represents a cross between the rabbit and the antelope. It is even said that it may be a cross between a pigmy deer and a species of the "killer rabbit." It may also be called an antelabbit or a stagbunny. Some believe it is now extinct. See Figure 7-5. This creature is rarely seen, yet it is also suggested that small groups of jackalopes may still be thriving in the American West! When called upon, it will use its antlers aggressively to defend itself, and so it is sometimes referred to as the "warrior rabbit." It has also been suggested that the jackalope has a unique ability to mimic the human voice in songs and the like! There are also claims that this creature mates only when lightening bolts cross the sky and so he becomes unusually vocal during thunderstorms.

The best way reputedly to capture this cagey rabbit is to lure it with whiskey as it appears to have a particular liking for the alcoholic spirit. Of course, the jackalope is easier to hunt when it has been slowed down after consuming some whiskey!

According to legend, the female jackalope can be easily milked while sleeping, as it lies on its back with its belly exposed when it sleeps. However, any attempts to milk the jackalope are fraught with all kinds of danger should the jackalope awake during this

process! Therefore, it is not advised! Some say that jackalope milk can be used for medicinal purposes. If one is successful in milking the jackalope, one will discover that the milk is fully homogenized due to the active and powerful leaping of the creature.

Interestingly, jackalope milk is said to be a powerful aphrodisiac, giving rise to its appellation as the "horny rabbit." Of course, it's antlers help with that nickname too.

Well, as you've probably surmised the jackalope is clearly a hoax! It is part of the folklore of the West. The 1939 written origin of this fabled creature has been attributed to Douglas Herrick, a native of Douglas, Wyoming.

However, let's not be dismissive of the horned rabbit[4,5,6] quite yet! Horned jackrabbits and cottontails were known throughout the West by pioneers in the 1900's. Hornlike growths on rabbits and hares do occur in nature. The growths may project from the head, or even around the mouth. The cause of the unusual growths is apparently an infection from the *Shope papillomavirus*.

Figure 7-5: Jackalope - the fabled antlered jackrabbit.

So, it appears that the legend of a horned rabbit or hare has some real basis in fact. The more fanciful image, of course, is more entertaining and more curious. It has become part of the folklore of the American Southwest.

Oh What Pretty Painted Horses!

A novel tradition has developed in New Mexico, and the rest of the American Southwest. It started in the 1990's when some innovative artists decided to paint some life-size horse manikins, with colorful abstract and traditional Southwestern themes. These painted horses became popular overnight, and were seen throughout the American Southwest in shopping malls, standing free, life-size and beautiful on the shopping mall floors.

Over time these painted life-size horse manikins faded away from view. However, the idea transformed itself. Commercial companies took up the theme, producing much smaller hand-held ceramic, porcelain or plastic replicas of these painted horses, now ranging in size from about four to eight inches in height. They are available in various colorful designs: Native American war ponies, horses with an American flag motif, with a Southwestern design, or even with mechanical engine parts illustrated upon them, etc. These commercial painted horses are found most easily in airport terminal shops, and tourist shops, and they generally cost under $100. However, some specialized designs may cost considerably more. Items can also be purchased at various sites online. Just do an on-line search for "painted horses."

One of the first and the most common painted horse series is the *Trail of the Painted Ponies Collectibles* series. However, lately different manufacturers are introducing other series. For example, Western Giftware produces two different painted horse series: *Horse of a Different Color*, and the *Marcia Baldwin* series. All these painted horses are not only beautiful, but they have become "collectibles" in their own right.

Wild, Wild *Pecos* Bill

The *Pecos* River is sourced in the *Sangre de Cristo* Mountains of New Mexico. It extends southeasterly into Texas and then passes through southwestern Texas, where it joins the great *Rio Grande*. *Pecos* Bill[7] is rumored to have been an American character that developed from 19th century pioneers as they crossed western Texas, into New Mexico and Arizona. However, rather than "folklore" the tales of *Pecos* Bill have been identified as "fakelore", invented by the author Edward O'Reilly in the early 20th century. The tales were first published in 1916 for the Century Magazine. The tales were subsequently collected and re-published in 1923 in a book entitled *Saga of Pecos Bill*. The author claimed the tales were derived from oral tradition, but contemporary folklorists rejected this claim. *Pecos* Bill tales follow the tall tales genre of Paul Bunyan and John Henry.

Subsequent authors such as James Cloyd Bowman added to these invented tales. In 1937 he published a book entitled, *Pecos Bill: The Greatest Cowboy of All Time.* It was considered a children's book, and it was awarded the Newbery Honor in 1938. Various cartoon strip versions of the character were produced in the 1930's. The name was changed to *Pecos Pete.* In 1948, Disney came out with an animated version under the Melody Time Label.

Pecos Bill tales involve stories of superhuman feats of bravery and prowess. These include the ability to ride a tornado, or to use a rattlesnake as a lasso. *Pecos* Bill was reputedly born in Texas in the 1830's. As an infant he fell out of a covered wagon somewhere near the *Pecos* River. His hasty and sudden departure went unnoticed by his family. The infant was subsequently found and raised by a coyote pack! Later, his brother found him but he had to convince the youngster that he was not really a coyote!

Later, according to the story, he grew up to become a cowboy. His horse was named Widow-Maker because only *Pecos* Bill had the courage and skill to ride him, and still survive. Widow-Maker liked to eat Dynamite, so he was no ordinary horse! *Pecos* Bill had many extraordinary adventures, and he is now part of the heritage of the West.

Even though he was supposedly born in Texas, the biggest course of the river that identifies *Pecos* Bill runs through most of eastern New Mexico.

Calling All Aliens: The Roswell UFO Incident

Controversial as this topic is, most everyone has heard of the supposed 1947 UFO Incident,[8, 9] that occurred on a ranch outside of Roswell, New Mexico. The alleged crash of a "UFO" vehicle, or whatever it was, actually occurred closer to the town of *Corona*. However, the Roswell Army Air Field (RAAF) stationed in the town of Roswell was called in to investigate the situation. Personnel from the field's 509th Bomb Group were assigned to reconnoiter the mysterious crash site and to recover the crash debris. The crash purportedly occurred sometime in June or July of 1947.

Since that time there have been countless conspiracy theories presented via book or article publications, video, TV and radio shows. The controversy still continues today, especially among UFO proponents.

UFO advocates claim that alien bodies, some alive, were transported from the site, and were never again seen or acknowledged by the military. They also insist that the recovered material was from a "flying saucer or disk." Never mind that scientists and engineers have come to the tentative conclusion that rotating disks are aerodynamically problematic (with current technology).

The U.S. military insists that the crash debris was that of a high altitude surveillance balloon belonging to a classified program called "*Mogul*." The balloon had an antenna dish attached to allow it to monitor Soviet ballistic missile tests and atomic bomb tests, via the detection of sound waves. This was the conclusion of the GAO and U.S. Air Force Report of 1995. A second report, from the same sources, released in 1997, concluded that reports of alien bodies recovered from the crash, were likely transformed memories of similar past accidents. Through the decades since the 1947 event, more and more conspiracy theories have been proposed, more sightings have been attached to the original event, and more complex scenarios have been declared. The Roswell UFO Incident has become a pop culture phenomenon. Whatever side one takes in this controversy, the topic is nonetheless fascinating. As a result, Roswell has become the UFO capital of the world. For more additional intriging information on the Roswell UFO Incident visit this site:

www.roswellfiles.com

UFO proponents can visit the International UFO Museum and Research Center in Roswell. It is open daily from 9 am to 5 pm. Exhibits focus on the Roswell UFO Incident of 1947. They also have exhibits and information about other "UFO" sightings. Roswell also holds a yearly UFO Festival in early July. The festival usually lasts several days.

Some may see the Roswell UFO Incident as an Occam's Razor[10] event. A visit to the Robert H. Goddard Planetarium might then be more interesting and informative. It is open only on weekdays from 9 am to 5 pm.

For further exploration of the U.S. Space Program and its achievements a visit to the New Mexico Museum of Space History in *Alamogordo,* is well worth the drive and the visit. It features outdoor exhibits of early rocket and missiles, an indoor IMAX theatre, and exhibits of artifacts from the space program throughout the decades. There is even a shuttle simulator, with a display screen, that allows the visitor to attempt a simulated landing of the Shuttle. It's great fun for all family members.

Smokey the Bear: **Really!**

Many of us are familiar with *Smokey the Bear*[11] from his TV and billboard cautions against smoking in the forest and leaving campfires improperly extinguished. We have seen his animated image, wearing a Ranger's hat, wearing blue jeans, often holding a shovel, ready to fight forest fires. But how many know the real story?

Prior to the inception of *Smokey the Bear*, the U.S. Forest Service started a campaign to alert Americans to the dangers of wildfires. This started in 1942, World War Two, as a result of attempts by the Japanese to use forest fires as a weapon against the U.S. Several unsuccessful attempts were made between 1942 and 1945 to intentionally set forests ablaze off the west coast of the U.S. This was attempted by means of the Japanese Lookout Air Raids of 1942, the launching of floatplanes (with incendiary bombs) from surfaced Japanese submarines, and by the launching of some nine thousand (9,000) fire balloons into the jet stream. Some 10% made it to the continental U.S.

These war efforts intensified the campaign by the U.S. Forest Service to make Americans aware of wild fires and to take precautions to prevent their accidental occurrence. Thus, a bear was adopted as the mascot to convey the conservation message on August 9, 1944. The name Smokey was the nickname of a New York City Firefighter, "Smokey" Joe Martin, who had courageously suffered burns and blindness during a 1922 fire rescue mission. In 1947, *Smokey the Bear's* famous slogan was adopted: "Remember…only YOU can prevent forest fires."[12]

So, you might ask, what has any of this to do with New Mexico? Well, in the spring of 1950, there was a great wildfire in the *Capitán* Gap region of Lincoln National Forest in Lincoln County, New Mexico. The fire destroyed a total of 17,000 acres. A black bear cub was caught in that blaze. The poor terrified animal had managed to climb a tree in an attempt to escape the conflagration, but he suffered from burned paws and hind legs. Thankfully, the small bear cub was rescued safely. Because of the burns to his paws, he was originally named "*Hotfoot Teddy*". Eventually that name was changed to the familiar *Smokey the Bear*. After his recovery, he was flown to the National Zoo, in Washington, D.C., where he lived for the next 26 years of his life. He died on November 6, 1976.

His remains were flown back to *Capitán*, New Mexico. He was buried at the Smokey Bear Historical Park in *Capitán*.[13] The plaque by his gravesite reads, "This is the resting place of the first living Smokey Bear...the living symbol of wildfire prevention and wildlife conservation."

Smokey Bear Historical Park (Museum) is located in *Capitán*, Lincoln County, New Mexico. Kids love this place. It's geared for children. For current schedules and information access the following web site:

www.smokeybearpark.com
or call (575)-354-2748.

The Truth About Truth or Consequences

Most folks have heard of the *Truth or Consequences* TV Game & Quiz Show. In 1950, Ralph Edwards, the game show host, proposed a contest to help promote his NBC Radio show of the same name. He promised to transmit his program from the first town or city willing to rename itself after the quiz show. The town of Hot Springs won the contest. Shortly thereafter, Hot Springs renamed itself Truth or Consequences.[14]

Over the next fifty years, the host of the show visited the town during the first weekend of May! Each year, in May, the townsfolk celebrate this event with a *fiesta* that includes a beauty contest, a parade and a stage show. A dance in Ralph Edwards Park is also part of the *Fiesta* celebration. The parade includes celebrities such as the Hatch *Chile* Queen.

New Mexico locals refer to the town as T or C. The hot springs are still a feature and attraction of the area, drawing many tourists and visitors each year. Nearby Elephant *Butte* Lake is another attraction. The *Geronimo* Springs Museum and the Hamilton Military Museum can be found in T or C.

Chapter Eight: Bits and Pieces

There are a number of subjects that are difficult to pigeonhole into one particular category. These topics may be more multicultural in nature than some. They may not be cultural at all but are still of interest because they are relevant to some aspect of New Mexican life. A few of these topics are discussed briefly in this chapter and they include *Adobe & Pueblos*, Gourd Art, *Hornos*, *Kivas & Kiva* Fireplaces, Next Generation (4-H and FFA), Tumbleweeds, and Western Windmills.

Adobe & Pueblos

One distinctive feature of architecture in New Mexico, especially in areas like *Santa Fe*, *Taos*, and Native American communities throughout the *Rio Grande* Valley, is the ubiquitous presence of authentic *pueblo* and modern *pueblo* style homes and buildings. The term *pueblo* comes from the Spanish meaning "town." The invading *Conquistadors* were reminded of the Spanish *pueblos* or towns of their homeland when they saw the Native American villages along the *Rio Grande*.

So the question that comes to mind is, what exactly is a *pueblo*? Or *adobe*? Let's start with the last question first. *Adobe* is the name applied to mud "bricks"[1] that were made by the indigenous peoples. The people of *Kuaua Pueblo* did not have lime to make true mortar. However, they improvised by using a mixture of ashes, coal and dirt. According to Pedro de Casteñeda,[2] who was a member of *Coronado*'s 1540-1541 Expedition, "...they gather a large pile of grasses and twigs and set it afire. And when it is half coals and ashes they throw a quantity of dirt and water on it and mix it all together. They make round balls of this, which they use instead of stones after they are dry, fixing them with the same mixture which comes to be like stiff clay." These "mud balls" were a manageable size and weight. They did not fashion bricks in our sense of the word.

Later methods of *adobe* construction in New Mexico used a different technique[3] that resulted in much larger and heavier *adobe* "bricks." These mud bricks were comprised of clay mud, straw, sand and water. *Adobe* was made by repeatedly stepping on the mixture until a thorough mix was achieved. The bricks were then formed, by placing the mixture into a rectangular wooden mold, measuring ten (10) inches wide, eighteen (18) inches long and five (5) inches thick. The molds were then removed and the molded mixture was then left to dry in the sun. The resulting bricks each weighed about fifty pounds. A hefty lift!!

An authentic *pueblo* building[4] is made using *adobe* bricks, *adobe* mud, and timbers and it may be a single level or several stories high. The genuine *pueblo* structure is characterized by flat, mud-coated exterior walls, few windows (if any), a flat roof, *vigas* or timbers (to support the roof) that are either visible or invisible to the exterior, and wooden ladders to reach the upper or lower levels. The *pueblo* is usually earth-toned in color.

In colonial and territorial days, *pueblo*-structure walls were built using a stone foundation, provided stone could be found. *Adobe* bricks were then placed upon the stones and built up to the desired height for the wall. At corners, the bricks were alternated in direction to form a strong corner support. *Adobe* mud was filled between bricks and between layers of bricks. Once the walls were finished, large timbers called *vigas* were placed across the width of the house, supported by the tops of the front and back walls. Sometimes the *vigas* protruded out from the front and back exterior walls. Flat boards were then laid across the *vigas* from one *viga* to another. A layer of *adobe*, brush or about eight inches of dirt was then applied on top of the planks to complete the roof. Usually the exterior walls were then plastered with clay, giving the *pueblo* its distinctive earth-tone color. The interior of the *pueblo* was usually dim. The doors were usually made of pine. Sometimes animal hides or rugs were thrown on the earthen floors to add character or color to the interior.

Modern *pueblo*-style homes are made using modern home construction methods that comply with county and city building codes. The exterior of these *pueblo*-style homes simulates the authentic *pueblo* house, with a flat roof and a design layout that is generally rectangular. The exterior may be made of real *adobe*, or it may be stucco over a wooden frame interior or a cinder block interior. It may even be made of straw bale interior with a stucco-finished exterior. Water drainage or rain run-off from the flat roofs is usually accomplished using wooden and metal "*canales*[5]" at the roofline on one or more exterior walls. The stucco color usually is an earth tone, similar in color to an authentic *pueblo* house. See photos of the northern and southern parts of the *Taos Pueblo* shown in the *Taos Pueblo* section of Chapter Eleven. These two figures show typical authentic Native American *pueblo* homes.

Many homes in *pueblo* villages have an external bee-hived shaped oven called an *horno*.[6] Modern *pueblo* houses may have exposed *vigas,* tiled floors and interior "*kiva*"[7] fireplaces in one or more corners of the house.

Hey, That Art is Really "Gourd"!!

The "Gourd art form" involves creating works of art by painting various images, symbols and motifs on dried gourd shells. The surface of the gourd is usually carved, sanded, burned, dyed and polished. The practice of processing and painting the gourds is an ancient tradition among the *Navajo*, *Hopi* and *Pueblo* nations of the American Southwest. The finished gourds may also be lacquered to protect the painted images. Many modern artists, from all walks of life, create wondrously beautiful pieces of art using gourds as their canvas.

Many painted gourds are truly beautiful works of art, and easily catch the eye of the beholder. Some more adventurous artists incorporate other media, such as cornhusks and beads, to create unique Southwestern-themed figures. Many such gourds have become collector's items.

Hornos, kivas, & kiva fireplaces

Look around any *pueblo*, or even in the backyards of homes throughout New Mexico and you will see a small beehive shaped structure, no more than about four or five feet tall, with a hole in the top of it, and with an open front. The front entry to the oven is usually raised above the ground, by about one foot, to minimize fatigue from bending.

The structure is usually coated on the outside with *adobe* mud, in a tan or reddish tan color. This is an *horno,*[8] an outdoor oven. It takes its name from the Spanish *horno*, meaning "oven" or "furnace", simply enough. Native Americans and early settlers of the American Southwest used the *horno* for cooking. However, what is less widely known is that, the Moors were the first to introduce the "*horno*" into Spain. From Spain it was exported to New Spain (Mexico) where it was introduced into the Southwest, and into New Mexico, in particular. See Figure 8-1.

Using an *horno* to bake bread generally requires setting a fire within the oven, waiting until the fire dies down to embers and ashes, removing the ashes and then placing the bread to be cooked within. The cooking relies upon internal heat radiating from the heated bricks and *adobe* within the *horno*. The cooked bread is removed after the proper amount of cooking time.

Corn can be steamed by a modification of this method. The corn is steamed without removing the husks. Instead of removing the embers, they are doused with water to create steam. In another variation, the embers are moved to the sides of the *horno*, and the water is applied to the hot brick floor of the *horno* to produce steam. However, to do this effectively requires that the *horno*'s two openings (top and side) be sealed closed.

Cooking meat requires a different approach. It requires that the oven be fired to a very high temperature. The coals are then moved to the rear of the *horno*. This allows the meat to become sufficiently well cooked. Again, both the entry and the smoke hole at the top of the *horno* need to be covered with mud, a wooden board or some other material to help keep the interior hot enough to cook the meat. The *adobe* walls naturally retain moisture in the cooking process. All this with no electricity bill! What's not to like?

Kivas are another traditional feature of the *pueblos* in the American Southwest. They are associated with the religious and spiritual beliefs, and the cultural traditions of the *pueblo* natives. A *kiva* is generally an underground ceremonial room, within the *pueblo* community, used for the observance of religious rituals and ceremonies.

Figure 8-1: *Horno*- outdoor oven. (Courtesy of *Coronado* State Monument Park.)

These rituals and ceremonies are often associated with the *kachina* belief system. There is a continuity of belief between the modern *puebloans,* and the ancient *Anasazi, Mogollón* and *Hohokam puebloan* peoples. Among the ancient *puebloans,* the *kiva*s were usually round, although there are four-walled exceptions too. Some *kiva*s today are square-walled, as at *Santa Clara Pueblo.* Since the *kiva* is generally underground it requires a wooden ladder to descend into the *kiva.* However, some *kiva*s were built above ground. The roof is usually timbered with a hatchway for access to the lower chamber from above.

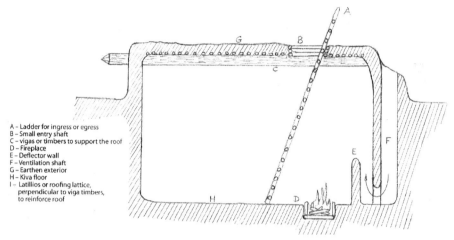

A – Ladder for ingress or egress
B – Small entry shaft
C – *vigas* or timbers to support the roof
D – Fireplace
E – Deflector wall
F – Ventilation shaft
G – Earthen exterior
H – Kiva floor
I – Latillios or roofing lattice,
   perpendicular to viga timbers,
   to reinforce roof

Figure 8-2: Cross-section of a *pueblo* underground *kiva.* (Concept courtesy of *Coronado* State Monument Park.)

Women were usually not permitted within the *kiva*, except to bring food. Tribal men use the *kiva* for secret ceremonies and meetings. See Figure 8-2.

The ancient walls were usually composed of fine masonry enlivened with colorful and dramatic images of their *kachinas*, and other traditional, mythological or spiritual symbols. Examples of these beautiful and lively *kiva* murals can be seen at the Visitor Center Museum at the *Coronado* State Monument near *Bernalillo.* Figure 8-2 shows a cross-section of an underground *kiva.* The *kiva* usually has a fire pit in the center or off to one side of the *kiva* floor. The belief in an underground emergence is held by a number of southern *pueblos* but not all. (Some northern *pueblos* believe that their ancestors emerged from a body of water.)

*Kiva*s also have an air intake shaft and pathway, which brings ventilation into the *kiva* from above. Right in front of the ventilation hole is a short wall that acts as a diverter to minimize air blasts or drafts, and to prevent heat from quickly escaping the *kiva.* Behind the wall, near its inner side, a small hole in the floor is used to allow a small fire for warmth in the winter months. Aside from preventing any air blasts from extinguishing the warmth-giving fire, the deflector wall also reflects the fire's heat back into the center of the *kiva.* Large *vigas* or timbers support the roof. A set of smaller diameter cross poles, called *latillas,* are laid across the *vigas* and are laid perpendicular to them, forming a lattice to support the dirt, mud or *adobe* placed on the exterior top of the *kiva.*

The *Coronado* State Monument *kiva* also has reconstructed murals painted on the interior walls so that the *kiva* interior looks much as it did in pre-Columbian times. One can enter this *kiva* via the ladder that is in place. The *kiva* has four walls, with half of the *kiva* above ground and the other half underground. This *kiva* is really worth visiting and examining, as it really gives one a feel for the inside of a *kiva*, which can rarely be found elsewhere.

You can also see a real subterranean *kiva*, in *Pecos* National Historical Park in *Pecos*. At this location, one also enters the underground *kiva* by descending a wooden ladder. So please be careful!!

Unfortunately, no wall murals are present at the *Pecos kiva*. See Chapters 13 and 14 for pictures of the exteriors of *kivas* at *Pecos* National Historical Park and at *Jemez* State Monument.

Kiva fireplaces are well known throughout the American Southwest, and particularly in *Santa Fe*, New Mexico. Figure 8-3 shows an indoor *kiva* fireplace. These fireplaces are an innovative, creative and attractive addition in many new *pueblo*-style homes. *Kiva* fireplaces are usually built into the corner of a room, without any sharp or rectangular edges, rounded and beehive in shape with an inverse u-shaped opening, and they are often built of *adobe*. They are considered to be very efficient fireplaces. *Kiva* fireplaces convey the charm and enchantment of the American Southwest. A *kiva* fireplace has one thing only in common with a real *pueblo kiva*: its name.

Figure 8-3: Indoor *kiva* fireplace at a
Santa Fe home.
(With the permission of the owners.)

The Next Generation of Young Americans: 4-H and FFA

Two key organizations are working to develop the next generation of young Americans. These wonderful and constructive organizations are 4-H and the Future Farmers of America or FFA. They both seek to keep America's youth strong in heart and body. The 4-H and FFA organizations teach youngsters to develop "hands-on" technical skills and personal growth through programs that teach them responsibility, character building, physical development, health, and confidence building.

The 4-H Organization:

The 4-H organization has approximately 6.5 million young members in the U.S. between the ages of 5 and 19 years. The organization's name represents the four areas of personal development that they emphasize: head, heart, hands and health. The 4-H motto is "To make the best better", while its slogan is "Learn by doing."

As stated on the 4-H website:

(http://www.4-h.org/about/youth-development-organization)

"With an expansive network reaching every corner of the country, 4-H is the nation's largest youth development organization. More than 6 million 4-H youth in urban neighborhoods, suburban schoolyards and rural farming communities stand out among their peers: building revolutionary opportunities and implementing community-wide change at an early age.

As the youth development program of the nation's 109 land-grant universities and the Cooperative Extension System, 4-H fosters an innovative, "learn by doing" approach with proven results. The 4-H Study of Positive Youth Development, a longitudinal study conducted by the Institute for Applied Research in Youth Development at Tufts University, shows youth engaged with 4-H are:

* Nearly two times more likely to get better grades in school;
* Nearly two times more likely to plan to go to college;
* 41 percent less likely to engage in risky behaviors;
* 25 percent more likely to positively contribute to their families and communities.

...Unparalleled Reach and Scope

With 540,000 volunteers, 3,500 professionals, and more than 60 million alumni, the 4-H movement supports young people from elementary school through high school with programs designed to shape future leaders and innovators. Fueled by research-driven programming,

4-H'ers engage in hands-on learning activities in the areas of science, citizenship and healthy living.

...Leading by Example

The caring support of adult volunteers and mentors inspires young people in 4-H to work collaboratively, take the lead on their own projects and set and achieve goals with confidence. 4-H'ers chart their own course, explore important issues and define their place in the world. 4-H'ers stand up for themselves and their communities." (By permission of the 4H organization.)

In some of the more rural communities, youth are introduced to agricultural and ranching tools, technologies, animal husbandry, and the farmer or rancher way of life. In this way, they learn independence and self-sufficiency, through local 4-H sponsorship of youth rodeos and farm competitions.

The 4-H Emblem is shown in Figure 8-4.

The 4-H Pledge reads as follows:
"I pledge my **head** to clearer thinking.
My **heart** to greater loyalty,
My **hands** to larger service,
And my **health** to better living,
For my club, my community,
My country and my world."
(Permission of the 4H organization)

What better character qualities can young people be imbued with?

18 U.S.C. 707

Figure 8-4: The 4-H Emblem (a Federal Mark.) (By permission of the 4-H organization)

The National Future Farmers of America (FFA) Organization:

The FFA, or Future Farmers of America, is a smaller organization with more than 540,000 members. According to the National FFA website (at www.ffa.org), "The National FFA Organization (also known as Future Farmers of America) envisions a future in which all agricultural education students will discover their passion in life and build on that insight to chart the course for their educations, career and personal future.

FFA makes a positive difference in the lives of students by developing their potential for premier leadership, personal growth and career success through agricultural education.

Agricultural Education prepares students for successful careers and a lifetime of informed choices in the global agriculture, food, fiber and natural resources systems."

Figure 8-5: The Future Farmers of America (FFA) logo. (Courtesy of the FFA)

The FFA is not just about production agriculture. Members have more than 300 career opportunities to explore. They regularly hold youth competitions in related areas. The

FFA logo is shown in Figure 8-5.

New Mexico has numerous chapters of these two important organizations throughout the state. Through their efforts the farming and ranching way of life is alive and kept sustainable. And the cowboy culture and ethos, which is more visible in the rural areas of New Mexico, is likely to continue to be part not only of our heritage but also of our future. Some of its young members may one day become future ranchers, farmers or even professional rodeo competitors! Or they may choose some other profession due to the training they receive in these two worthy youth organizations. In Figure 8-6, a large-horned Big Horn Sheep exhibited by the FFA is shown.

Figure 8-6: Big Horn Sheep (FFA),
at the 2011 New Mexico State Fair

Those Terrible Tumbleweeds

Throughout the American West and the Southwest you will certainly encounter the ubiquitous, noxious tumbleweed. Even though the tumbleweed may have gotten into the U.S. accidentally with the import of flaxseeds into South Dakota from Russia in the 1870's, it has both adapted and thrived in the open plains and desert areas of the West and Southwest. It has become so common and prevalent in these areas that it is a well-recognized symbol of desolation and loneliness, associated with the open and sometimes barren frontier regions of the West. It is not uncommon in Western films to see a character enter a particularly desolate area or town, and then to see a tumbleweed or two roll along the terrain, accompanied by the eerie whistling sound of the wind. The sense of bleakness and isolation is palpable.

Tumbleweeds are most often seen in the fall or early winter, when the winds pick up, dislodging the mature and dried plant from its weak and shallow roots. Because the tumbleweed plant is shaped roughly like a large ball, the wind causes it to tumble easily and rapidly across the open plains and desert areas. It often lodges itself near the base of juniper or *piñon* trees, in brush, against fences, or any other impediment in its path. Usually the tumbleweed consists of the entire dried out plant, with the exception of its roots, which remain in the ground.

This plant or weed[9] is particularly noxious for at least three reasons. First, it is embedded with many thorns, making it difficult and painful to handle, especially once it dries out late in the season. Second, each weed consumes a copious amount of water, which is then denied to adjacent desirable plants and grasses. Third, its tumbling action damages the protective topsoil, leading to further soil degradation and wind erosion.

The tumbleweed[10] is classified as a diaspora, which uses its wind-driven mobility to spread its "propagules" (seeds or spores). These propagules are spread as it tumbles, or once it comes to rest in moist soil. The plant is embedded with many thorns that may also fall to the ground. Whether they are present on the immature plant, on the dried tumbleweed or on the ground, these thorns are particularly vicious, and painful if stepped upon. Animals often pick them up on their unguarded paws, and they will gnaw away at them to remove the pernicious and painful thorns.

Bob Nolan,[11] one of the founding members of the Sons of the Pioneers, composed the song *Tumbling Tumbleweeds* in the 1930's, while working as a caddy in metropolitan Los Angeles, California, of all places! The song became famous with the Gene Autry film of the same name. The song likens the "tumbling tumbleweeds" to his rootless life as a drifter, "drifting along with the tumbling tumbleweeds." The lowly tumbleweed has risen to the level of a metaphor!

Round and Round They Go – Western Windmills/Pumps

A common feature in many rural parts of New Mexico, and in rural parts of the U.S. is the windmill,[12] wind turbine[13] or wind pump.[14] Although these terms are often used interchangeably, the windmill is generally used to turn a mill, or to grind grains, as a food production machine. The wind pump is more often seen in the west to pump up water for drinking, or as a means to pump away water from a waterlogged location. The term wind turbine is most often used to describe a machine that uses the wind to generate electricity.

Once a very common feature of the landscape in semi-arid areas, wind pumps were used for either pumping water up from wells below, or for draining low-lying areas of land where water collected. Wind pumps allow excess water to be drained for agricultural planting or for building purposes. Wind pumps have been used to collect drinking water for cattle, in remote areas with ranches and farms. Windmills used as wind turbines are still found in rural areas, where electric power is either unavailable or is too costly.

Daniel Halladay[15] invented the self-regulating windmill, wind pump or wind turbine in 1854. Often constructed from wood, these structures can also be made of steel. See Figure 8-7. This structure can easily be recognized by its multi-bladed circular wheel, which sits atop a lattice tower made of wood or steel. The circular wheel features a large number of blades in order to turn in low winds, and still produce reasonable torque to enable the pumping action. They tend to be self-regulating in high winds, by means of the rudder on top. Usually, a gearbox or a crankshaft resides within the top of the tower, to convert the rotational energy of the wind machine into reciprocating strokes, which are carried downward by means of a rod to the pump cylinder below.

Figure 8-7: Wooden-frame Wind Pump

Even though it appears to be pure *Americana*, the wind pump is an ancient mechanism that has been used in various forms throughout Africa, Asia and Europe. The wind pumps seen in the U.S. and in rural areas of New Mexico are just adaptations of earlier windmill technologies. It requires very little maintenance beyond periodically changing the oil in the gearbox. The older wooden windmills or wind pumps are, and probably always will be, associated with the West. They are associated with a sense of rugged independence, self-reliance and self- sufficiency, and with "being off the grid." Look around New Mexico today. You can see them still.

Chapter Nine:
So, What's So Hot About New Mexican Cuisine?

New Mexican cuisine reflects the region's climate, and its long and varied cultural heritage. This unique cuisine contains mixed elements from the Native American, Spanish, Mexican and *Anglo*-American cultures. In pre-Columbian times, New Mexico's current borders encompassed some of the areas occupied by the *Navajo*, various *Apache* tribes, and also the *Pueblo* Peoples. The Spanish Conquest of the Southwest brought the Spaniards and their own style of cuisine. Later, when Mexico gained its independence, the Mexican culture continued to influence the evolving cuisine. When the Mexican-American War ended, there was a new influence from the incoming U.S. tastes of the new *Anglo*-American settlers.

This uniquely rich and distinctive history has combined, over the centuries, with the unique local agricultural conditions and the hot dry summer climate, to produce a New Mexican cuisine that is similar to, yet quite different from the cuisine styles of neighboring states, such as California, *Colorado*, Arizona and Texas.

This short chapter touches upon what makes New Mexican cuisine distinctive. It also describes briefly the meaning behind the Spanish or New Mexican terminology for various dishes, desserts and pastries. *Tamales, burritos, chorizo, flan, empañadas,* etc., are briefly described. The intention is not to be exhaustive, but rather to arm non-Hispanic visitors to this great state with a working knowledge of the food terminology. This in turn should allow for informed dining choices and a more enjoyable dining experience here in the Land of Enchantment.

Chile: The Magic Ingredient in New Mexican Food
Distinct from the Tex-Mex cuisine, popular in Arizona and Texas, New Mexican cuisine[1] makes extensive use of the New Mexican *chile*. Although both red and green *chiles* are used in dishes, the milder green *chile* is more common and more popular. The color of the *chile* depends upon the stage of maturity and ripeness reached by the *chile* at harvest time.

Chile is the state's largest agricultural crop. Green *chile,* or *chile verde,* is the popular and distinctive ingredient in most every New Mexican dish from *enchiladas* to *burritos*. It is even found in common American fare such as cheeseburgers and French fries. Green *chile salsa* adds a gentle tanginess and spiciness to the food, giving it a distinctive flavor.

However, green *chile* can be quite spicy! If you don't like spicy food or you cannot eat it, then New Mexican food laced with the milder green *salsa* or the generally more biting red *salsa*, may not be the thing for you. For those who enjoy and relish such tastes, one can only say *"Muy sabrosa!"*[2]

Other distinctive elements of New Mexican cuisine include blue corn, the stacked vs rolled *enchiladas*, and the donut-like *sopaipillas*. Hmmm. *Sopaipillas* filled with honey!! Mmmmm good!!

Food Terminology in New Mexican *Comida* (Food)[3]
This short section should provide non-Hispanic visitors with a decent working knowledge of the commonly-used food terminology in New Mexico *comida*.

Buen provecho!! (Good eating!!) The following is a short list of some of the more common culinary terms:

Arroz con leche: A desert dish made of rice, sugar and milk. It is sweet, light and delicious. It is like a very light rice pudding with milk.

Atole: The central ingredient is corn that is made into a thick, warm gruel.

Birria: A spicy meat stew that is most often made with lamb or goat, although it can be made with pork. It is made with dried roasted peppers to produce its spicy taste. It is often eaten with corn *tortillas*, onion, *cilantro* and lime. It is a tasty winter meal.

Bizcochito: A cookie with an anise or licorice flavor.

Bollo: A bun or roll.

Burrito: This well-known and popular item is a medium-sized white flour *tortilla* filled with shredded meat (beef, chicken or pork), beans, sour cream and green *chile*, and then rolled. It may also be served with a covering of melted cheese and smothered with green or red *chile* sauce (*salsa*).

Breakfast *Burrito*: Another popular item, it is a smaller version of the *burrito* above modified to contain breakfast foods such as fried meat, sausage or *chorrizo*, ham or perhaps bacon, fried chopped onions, scrambled eggs, cheese, fried diced potatoes and the ubiquitous green *chile*.

Caldillo: This is a thin stew, or soup made with beef or pork, potatoes, and of course, green *chiles*.

Caldo: A thin soup or broth.

Carne adovada: This dish is comprised of marinated and cooked cubes of pork. The marinate sauce is made of red *chile*, garlic and *oregano*.

Carne machucada: Crushed or pounded dried beef jerky (*cecina*) cooked with red *chile salsa*.

Cecina: Dried or jerked (cured) beef.

Chalupa: This *tortilla* dish is made from a corn *tortilla*, which is fried into a bowl shape. It is then filled with shredded meat (beef, pork or chicken) and beans. It may be topped with *guacamole* and/or *salsa*.

Chicharrones: These are small tasty pieces of deep fried pork rind with little meat.

Chicharrones de cuero: These are deep-fried strips of pork skin.

Chile Sauce & *Chile* Stew: The sauce is made from cooked red or green *chiles* using a variety of recipes. It is often served hot over many New Mexican dishes or even over hamburgers or cheeseburgers. Chopped roasted green *chiles* are used to make green *chile*. However, dried and ground red *chiles* in powder form are used to make red *chile*. Flour may be added as a thickener. Spices such as coriander, cumin and *oregano* may be added for additional flavor. New Mexican *chile* is distinct from Mexican *chile*. New Mexican green *chile* is made using *chiles*. However, in Mexico the green *chile* is made using *tomatillos* instead.

A fine green *chile* stew can be made using pieces of pork, larger pieces of the *chile* plant, and by adding onions, carrots and potatoes. Other ingredients and spices may be added to enhance the flavor. This thicker version of green *chile* is popular in Albuquerque-style New Mexican food.

Chiles: *Chiles* are often referred to as *chile* peppers. These peppers are members of the capsicum species. Capsaicin is the active ingredient that gives the *chile* its spicy flavor. The New Mexico *chile* is a subspecies of the Anaheim pepper. It is commonly and simply referred to as *chile*. Green *chiles* are picked before the crop fully ripens. These green *chiles* are fire-roasted and then peeled. New Mexico green *chiles* can be mild in spiciness or they can be hotter than *jalapeños*. The capsaicin levels in the New Mexican *chile* tend to be higher than those found in other regions due to the unique climate of New Mexico. When the same *chile* plant fully matures and ripens it turns a red color.

Red *chiles* are generally more piquant or spicy than the green *chiles*. They can be roasted but they are more often ground into powder or flakes. Freshly dried red *chiles* are string-bound into hanging decorative bundles called *ristras*.

Most of the best New Mexico *chiles* are grown near the town of Hatch, in southern New Mexico. In the north, *Chimayó* is well known for its *chile* pepper.

Chile con queso: Literally, "*chile* with cheese", this is a dip made from *chile* and melted cheese.

Chiles rellenos: Literally, "stuffed *chiles*", these are stuffed whole green *chiles*, dipped in an egg batter, and then deep-fried. This dish uses the New Mexican pepper, rather than a Poblano pepper, used in the Mexican version of the dish. Cheese is usually used as the stuffing.

Chimichanga: This is a meat-and-bean *burrito* that is deep-fried to form a crispy outer shell. It may also contain *chile* sauce and cheese. *Chimichangas* are a fast-food form of traditional dishes. They can be frozen and stored, and then quickly fried as needed. Because they are rigid and can be held easily, this fast food is preferred by people who are mobile and "on the go."

Chorrizo: This popular sausage is usually seasoned with garlic and red *chile*. It is spicy and it is usually ground or finely chopped to serve as a breakfast side dish. It can also be eaten as a spicy sausage. It is often a favorite ingredient in breakfast burritos.

Cilantro: This green herb is also called Mexican parsley, and it is very healthy to eat. It has a pungent taste that is often used as a fresh topping for all types of *salsa*s, dishes and soups (*caldas*). The seeds of *cilantro* are known as coriander. Less common in traditional New Mexican cuisine, it is used more frequently in the *Santa Fe* cuisine style.

Empañada: Often seen as a desert, it is a small turnover filled with fruit or meat.

Enchiladas: These are corn or flour *tortillas* filled with meat (usually chicken), and/or cheese. The *enchilada* can also be stuffed with cheese only. They are either rolled, or stacked, and covered with red or green *chile* sauce and cheese. A flat *enchilada* is the stacked version, referred to in New Mexico as a *Santa Fe* style *enchilada*. Another New Mexican variation includes flat *enchiladas* made with blue-corn *tortillas*.

Flan: This favorite and delicious desert item is a rich egg custard covered with caramel. One of my personal favorite deserts!!

Flauta: Made by filling a flour *tortilla*, rolling it tightly and deep-frying it.

Frijoles: Literally, "beans." This usually refers to pinto beans, although *frijoles negros* or "black beans" can be requested instead. *Frijoles refritos* are "refried beans."

Gorditas: Cooked small pieces of pork.

Guacamole: Love avocado? You'll probably love *guacamole,* which is mashed avocado, with spices, chopped onion, tomatoes, garlic, *cilantro*, lime and *chile* added for additional spicy flavor.

Huevos rancheros: This modern dish, literally, "ranch eggs", consists of fried eggs covered with a red or green *chile* sauce. More traditionally, it is eggs poached in *chile*.

Huevos estrellados: Eggs fried "sunny side up."

Huevos fritos: Fried eggs or eggs "over easy."

Huevos revueltos: "Scrambled eggs."

Jalapeño: This is a small, fat *chile* pepper, which is known for its extreme spiciness. It can be freshly chopped for *salsa*, sliced and pickled for *nachos*, or split and stuffed with cheese. New Mexicans generally favor green *chiles* over *Jalapeños.*

Menudo: This is a traditional spicy soup made with sheep's stomach (tripe) and a red *chile* pepper base. It is also called *menudo colorado*, or "colored *menudo*." Chopped onions and *cilantro*, cooked hominy, crushed *oregano* and crushed red peppers are often added to the base. It is usually served with *tortillas*. Boiled tripe may be chewy, with a texture similar to *calamari*, but if properly prepared it can become quite tender. It has a unique smell and flavor. It is an acquired taste and it is not for everyone.

Natillas: This is another soft custard dessert favorite.

Oregano: This is a flavorful and tangy herb, which is often associated with Italian food. Mexican *oregano* spice is most often used instead in New Mexican cuisine.

Pico de Gallo: Literally, "rooster's beak", *Pico de Gallo* is a cold *salsa* made with chopped fresh *chiles*, tomatoes, onions and *cilantro*.

Pasole/pazole: Both green and red *chile* versions of this thick stew exist. It is made with hominy[4] corn, pork, *chile*, onions and garlic and left to simmer for several hours.

Quesadilla: Derived from the Mexican word *queso*, meaning "cheese", it is a corn or flour *tortilla* filled with cheeses and flavorful spices. It may even contain onions or *cilantro*, red pepper, etc. It is heated on a stovetop or grill until the cheese melts. It may be served folded over in a half-moon shape or unfolded with the ingredients contained between two *tortillas*.

Salsa: Literally, "sauce." It usually contains a mixture of fresh uncooked red *chiles*/peppers, tomatoes, onions, which may be blended or mixed with tomato paste. This produces a texture that is more like a sauce than the popular *pico de gallo*. It may also contain a noticeable amount of vinegar and even *cilantro*. There is a green *chile* variant, as opposed to the red *chile* style just described. It may use cooked *tomatillos*, instead of tomatoes, and may even include avocado.

Salsa picante or *picante* sauce: Literally, "hot or spicy sauce." This thin, vinegary, spicy sauce is made from puréed red peppers, tomatoes and added spices. In New Mexican cuisine it has generally been replaced by the red *chile salsa*.

Sopaipilla: Like donuts? Then you'll love *sopaipillas*! This is puffed fried bread. It is often filled with honey or honey-butter as a dessert. It is a great favorite of locals and tourists alike! A corner of the *sopaipilla* may be bitten off to add the honey just before eating it. Although it is mostly considered a dessert, the *sopaipilla* can be stuffed with meat, beans, cheese and *chile* sauce to provide a nourishing meal. In northern New Mexico, *sopaipillas* may be served with *sopas* (soups*), posole* or *menudo.*

Taco: Since the presence of *Taco* Bell throughout the country, most everyone knows what a *taco* is and has tasted at least one *taco*. It is a corn *tortilla*, fried and folded into a u-shaped trough. *Tacos* are filled with cooked meats and beans, together with fresh chopped or shredded lettuce, onions, tomatoes and cheese.

Tamale⁵ (taken from *tamal* in Spanish; plural *tamales*): Shrouded in a cornhusk, the *tamale* contains meat rolled in corn meal dough called *masa*. It is then steamed, and may be served with red *chile* sauce. New Mexican *tamales* may blend red *chile* powder into the *masa*.

Taquito: This is a deep-fried variant of the *taco* that is tightly rolled. It is usually longer than a *flauta* and it is made from a corn *tortilla*.

Tortilla: A *tortilla* is a flatbread made from white wheat flour or from corn. New Mexican *tortillas* are typically thicker than their California equivalents.

Tostada: A *tostada* is merely an open-faced *taco*. *Tostada* in Spanish means "toasted".

Tres leches: Literally, "Three milks." A cake desert. A kind of spongy cake made using three kinds of milk, namely by soaking the sponge in evaporated milk, condensed milk and heavy cream. It is a sweet and delicious. Butter can be added to the three milks to make it heavier and richer or the cake can be made without the butter, resulting in a lighter taste and texture. A favored birthday cake special!!

Other Popular New Mexican Fast Foods
Certain fast foods are unique to this area. These items are identified next.

Chilindrinas: Pork with flour, vegetables, sour cream and *guacamole*.

Elotes: This is nothing more than boiled or roasted corn on the cob. The husk is often pulled back around the base of the cob.

Frito pie: This is like a *taco* only with *frito* ("fried") chips instead of a fried *tortilla*. It consists of fried chopped meat, lettuce, tomato, onions, beans, cheese, and of course, green or red sauce.

Navajo Taco: Again, the ingredients are the same as a *taco* or *frito* pie, except that a *sopaipilla* is used to contain the food.

Sopaipillas: Usually served with honey, as described in the previous section. It can also be used like a *taco*. See *Navajo taco* above.

Torta: Sandwich.

Turkey legs: This is a popular item too. It is just a cooked turkey thigh on the bone.

Papillas: Small fried pieces of potato.

Note: Many of the foods described in the previous section can be made as fast foods. See above.

Common New Mexican Refreshments
Many names of refreshments derive from Spanish. These are described briefly below.

Agua: Water
Agua fresca: Cooled bottled water
Coca: Coca-Cola
Café: Coffee
Cerveza: Beer
Champurado: Hot chocolate with cinnamon and *maseca* (corn flour)
Chocolate: Chocolate
Helado: Ice cream

Hielo: Ice
Horchata: Rice milk drink
Leche: Milk
Refrescos: Soda, soft drinks
Té: Tea
Vino: Wine

¡¡*Buen Provecho*!!

Chapter Ten: Fascinating Things To Do & Places to See

There are countless things to do and places to see in the Land of Enchantment. Where does one begin? This chapter highlights some selected sights that are either just plain fun, exhilarating or educational. A number of these happenings or attractions occur in or around Albuquerque, *Santa Fe*, and *Taos*, New Mexico. Other worthy sights have been selected from various parts of the state to show the state's diversity. This chapter identifies sights and activities that are not necessarily reviewed in prior or following chapters.

The topics discussed in this lengthy chapter are: Albuquerque International Balloon *Fiesta*®, Old Town Albuquerque, River of Lights, *Sandia* Peak Tramway; (Georgia O'Keefe) Art Museum, *(Santa Fe)* Indian Market®, Loretto Chapel, Palace of the Governors, (Cathedral Basilica of) St. Francis of Assisi, *(El) Santuario de Guadalupe*, *(Santa Fe* Traditional) Spanish Market©, (Burning of the) *Zozobra*©®. *(El Rancho de las) Golondrinas*, Outdoor *(Santa Fe)* Opera, *Puyé* Cliff Dwellings, (New Mexico) Rail Runner Express, Turquoise Trail; Charles Bent Home & Museum, Kit Carson Home & Museum, *Taos Plaza, Taos Pueblo*; *Rio Grande* Gorge Bridge, *San Francisco de Asís* Mission Church (in *Ranchos de Taos)*; *Bosque del Apache, Cumbres & Toltec* Scenic Railroad, Fort Sumner/*Bosque Redondo*, Hubbard Museum of the American West, *La Jornada del Muerto*, Rodeos and the Very Large Array. The topics proceed from those sights in and around Albuquerque, sights in and around *Santa Fe*, others in and around *Taos*, and finally some selected few outside those three areas.

Up, Up and Away- Albuquerque International Balloon *Fiesta*®[1]

This event is an annual festival of hot air balloons held at the Balloon *Fiesta*® Park, in Albuquerque. It is a nine-day event that occurs in early October, featuring hundreds of multi-colored hot air balloons. It is the largest such event in the world. This event attracts tourists from all over the world.

There are several key general attractions within the festival, including Dawn Patrol, Mass Ascension™, Special Shape Rodeo™ and Balloon Glow.

The Dawn Patrol uses positioned lighting systems to allow the balloons to fly in the dark hours before sunrise. They take off before sunrise and return when the daylight allows the landing sites to be seen. The Dawn Patrol, with their illuminated balloons, detects wind patterns (speed, direction) at various altitudes prior to the mass ballooning to follow.

The Mass Ascension™ has been photographed by many thousands of people. It is a favorite subject for calendars, magazine photos, advertising and the like. In this popular event, hundreds of colorful hot air balloons are released simultaneously in one of two waves. Their launchings are scheduled and controlled by handlers called zebras, because of their black and white striped uniforms. The sight of hundreds of multi-colored hot air balloons ascending together, rising up from the green fields below to the azure skies above is exhilarating, beautiful and unforgettable.

The Mass Ascension™ is like no other experience you have ever encountered. It starts at 7 am. Trucks hauling small trailers are pulled onto the huge field. The huge deflated balloons are rolled out onto the field from the trailers. Some balloons are already inflated and ready to go. Others can be seen getting ready. Carrier baskets are laid sideways on the ground and attached. Fans blow into the balloons to inflate them. Once each balloon has sufficient air within it, the burners are ignited and the heat is directed into the opening of the balloon. See Figure 10-1. One can see the heat waves causing the nearby air to shimmer, as the heated air enters the balloon. The sound of the heated blast can be heard roaring as it is ignited. It all adds to the thrill of this unique experience. The balloon begins to rise sideways from the ground. A handler holds onto a long rope that is attached to top of the balloon to control its motion and to keep it tethered. As the balloon rises, the basket is gently moved from its horizontal resting position on the ground to its desired upright position. The balloon then stabilizes in its vertical pre-launch position. It is near ready to go, as the balloonists enter the basket for lift-off.

Figure 10-1: Heating up Hot Air Balloons at the 2011 Albuquerque International Balloon *Fiesta*®.

Other balloons lift off the ground. As they lift off the crowd cheers each launch. The atmosphere is electric. Cameras click away. The excitement is energizing! Folks mill around, waiting with anticipation the next lift-off, and hurrahing excitedly with each success. The crowd is filled with families who have brought along their young children to share in the thrill and the exhilaration of this exciting event! Before long there are hundreds of multi-colored, multi-shaped balloons filling the skies above. Balloons from all over the world and from various commercial enterprises are present. There are stagecoach balloons, flying pink elephants, bumblebees, ladybugs, butterflies, milching cows, shark balloons, as well as the more conventional round or conical balloons. See Figure 10-2. The balloons drift in one direction as they ascend. Once aloft at higher altitudes the Albuquerque Box Effect takes over, and you can see the balloons drift back towards their starting locations. See Figure 10-3. Eventually all the balloons are launched, and the crowd moves towards the eating and carnival-type recreation areas. The sight and the experience of the Mass Ascension™ is awe-inspiring! It is an unforgettable experience. It is the thrill of a lifetime!!

Figure 10-2: Novelty Balloons: Here's Lookin' at Ya! (A Lindstrand Balloon, at the 2011 Albuquerque International Balloon *Fiesta*®.)

The Special Shape™ Rodeo is another very popular event with families with young children. Balloons of all shapes and sizes are released representing cartoon characters, animals, weird objects and other themes that appeal to youngsters of all ages.

In the Balloon Glow evening event, a selected number of balloons remain stationary while their propane burners remain illuminated to provide a warm nightglow. The Balloon Glow applied to the Special Shape™ Balloons is called the "Glowdeo™."

There are other special balloon events that are scheduled specifically for balloon specialists and experts.

The Albuquerque International Balloon *Fiesta*® is possible because of a unique phenomenon that occurs in the Albuquerque area: the Albuquerque Box Effect. The cool Albuquerque mornings in October and the "box effect" ensure that the *fiesta* can be conducted in a safe and fairly predictable manner. The winds usually come from the south (southerly) at lower altitudes. At higher altitudes, the wind blows northerly. The approach to navigating the balloon is to first ascend from the field in a southerly direction. As the balloon ascends higher, the northerly winds prevail, carrying the balloon back to its origination point. These wind patterns result in safe navigation of the balloons each year, to the welcome relief of thousands of visitors and joy riders.

Figure 10-3: Up, Up They Go! (At the 2011
Albuquerque International Balloon *Fiesta*®.)

The Balloon *Fiesta*® is a wonderful colorful event for both participants and non-participants. One can be bold and participate in a hot air balloon ride, or one can just sit back and enjoy the colorful view. However, the balloon rides are expensive (~$300/person). You don't have to ride a balloon however, to partake in the sheer thrill of the Balloon *Fiesta*®. There is adventure, excitement, color, fun and food. There's no way to lose!

Back in Time - Old Town, Albuquerque
Dating back to the Spanish founding of the city in 1706, Old Town Albuquerque remains an historic link to its Spanish past. It comprises about ten blocks of historic *adobe* buildings, which enclose a central *plaza*, a common feature of old Spanish towns. A gazebo occupies the center of the *Plaza*. There are also two brass cannons on the *Plaza* grounds that were captured at the time of the Confederate invasion of New Mexico. Many of the *adobe* buildings have been converted or modernized as restaurants, small tourist shops, art galleries or art shops. As a result, it is a popular shopping and tourist destination for many. Walking tours of the district are provided by the nearby Albuquerque Museum. In the Christmas season, the streets and walkways are lined with *farolitos*, adding a beautiful ambiance to the district.

Old Town is a well-established tourist attraction. There are several attractive *placitas*² located behind the main streets. See Figure 10-4. Here one can find interesting and novel shops that are very appealing to visitors and tourists alike. Southwestern jewelry vendors are located along the *Hacienda* walls, much like the vendors on the

Figure 10-4: A *placita* in Old Town Albuquerque.

Figure 10-5: *San Felipe de Neri* Church in Old Town Albuquerque.
(Archdiocese of *Santa Fe.*)

sidewalk of the Palace of the Governors in *Santa Fe*. Here visitors can find beautiful turquoise/silver and other Southwestern jewelry for reasonable prices.

The *San Felipe de Neri* Church,[3] built in 1793, lies on the north side of the *Plaza*. It is the oldest building in the city.

The original church was established in 1706 and it was located on the northwest side of the *Plaza*. The Governor at the time, Don Francisco Fernando Cuervo y Valdez originally named the church *San Francisco Xavier*, after the Viceroy of New Spain. It was later renamed *San Felipe de Neri*, by the Duke of Alburquerque, honoring the patron saint of King Philip II of Spain. The original building was completed in 1719.

Seventy-three years later, in 1792, the original building collapsed under heavy rains. The current church was built the following year to replace the destroyed original mission church. In 1861, the two towers were added. A parish school and a convent were added in subsequent years. The church is simple, attractive, and historic. The church is shown in Figure 10-5.

Just east of the Old Town, lie several interesting museums: The Albuquerque Museum of Art and History, the New Mexico Museum of Natural History & Science, and the Explora Science Center and Childrens' Museum. All of these museums are worth seeing! Outside, in the front of The Albuquerque Museum of Art and History are more than 60 impressive statues. Perhaps the most impressive is the collection of

Figure 10-6a: *La Jornada* at The Albuquerque Museum of Art and History, sculpted by Reynaldo Rivera and Betty Sabo - showing Don Juan Oñate leading the Spanish Colonists into *Nuevo México*. (With permission of the artists or their representatives, and The Albuquerque Museum.)

Figure 10-6b: *La Jornada* at The Albuquerque Museum of Art and History, sculpted by Reynaldo Rivera and Betty Sabo – showing Spanish Colonists pushing a ox-drawn *carreta* up an incline. (With permission of the artists or their representatives and The Albuquerque Museum.)

Figure 10-6c: *La Jornada* at The Albuquerque Museum of Art and History, sculpted by Reynaldo Rivera and Betty Sabo – showing a female Spanish Colonist carrying a baby, and riding on a donkey. (With permission of the artists or their representatives and The Albuquerque Museum.) statues that are part of *"La Jornada"* exhibition. See the three photos in Figure 10-6 (a through c). *La Jornada* in Spanish means "day's journey."

The statue set shows the *Conquistador* and future Governor Don Juan de Oñate leading a small group of Spanish colonists into a brave new land, *Nuevo México*. A native scout stands just behind his right shoulder, while a missionary priest, with a crucifix on a standard, follows close behind hisleft shoulder. This dynamic scene also shows a mother carrying a young child, together on a donkey. Nearby, an ox team struggles to pull a heavily laden cart while men use poles to try to dislodge the wheels from the mud. Other men on horseback are pulling the front of the cart with ropes. A wolf is even seen threatening the small hardy group. The scope of the statue set is massive and realistic. In viewing these statues one can sense the courage, stamina and optimism of the small party in overcoming daunting physical challenges to colonize the new lands of *Nuevo México* in the late 1500's, led by a courageous and strong leader, Don Juan de Oñate. The collection is truly outstanding in scope and execution It is a fine work of historical art! Please be sure not to miss this stunning and inspiring statue set!

Dazzling Lightshow - River of Lights,[4] Albuquerque

The Christmas Holiday season starts each year in Albuquerque with the River of Lights exhibition. It is located within the Albuquerque Botanical Gardens and is featured between Thanksgiving and the end of December, although it is usually closed on Christmas Eve and Christmas Day. It is a sight to behold and a perfect attraction to visit in the holiday season. In 2010, the gardens were illuminated with all kinds of artificial light displays of jungle animals such as giraffes, elephants, rhinos, tigers, monkeys, hippos, etc. Displays featured illuminated insects such as bumblebees, dragonflies, scorpions and butterflies. There were illuminated birds flying and nesting, as well as fantastical creatures and figures. Representations of flowers could be seen and trees were beautifully decorated and illuminated with colorful lights. Visitors followed multiple walk paths through the gardens in the evening and after dusk to see the beautiful colorful light works that were a wonder to all, young and old, who came to see this magical display. Some of the light displays simulated the motion of the creatures, while others were static.

All the light sculptures are designed and built by the Albuquerque BioPark's staff of artists and craftspeople, who are clearly very talented and creative. Local choir groups gather to sing Christmas carols, while vendors sell fast food and beverages, or cotton candy. Other vendors sell colorful light sticks and other items for children. Unique gift items for purchase are also available on the garden grounds. The River of Lights draws thousands of visitors each season because of its beauty and popularity. Children of all ages love the place and the experience. It has become an annual tradition in the Albuquerque area, although visitors come from all over the state and beyond to participate in this beautiful tradition. The decorations and the ornamentation change from year to year, depending upon the theme chosen for that year. Some of the display items may be different from what was displayed during the 2010 season, as described above. An "underwater creatures" theme was added for the 2011 Holiday Season.

What a View! - *Sandia* Peak Tramway,[5] Albuquerque

Want to see Albuquerque from the *Sandia* Peak? Then venture onto Tramway

Blvd and follow it to the *Sandia* Peak Tramway. See Figure 10-7. It will carry you from the northeast side of the city of Albuquerque up by cable car to *Sandia* Mountain peak. The panoramic view of the city below is spectacular. The tramway can carry 50 passengers at one time. Two tramway cars can ascend and descend at the same time. Local billboards advertise *Sandia* Tramway as "the world's longest tramway." If you suffer from acrophobia or feel wobbly at great heights this adventure may not be for you!

Worried about safety? No need. New tramcars were installed in 1986 and new rails were installed as recently as 2009. Furthermore, the system has numerous safety and backup features, such as multiple braking systems and a grounding system in the event of a thunder/lightning storm. Still concerned?

There is an alternate route to the *Sandia* crest-line via a roadway that runs up the back side of *Sandia* Mountain. *Sandia* Crest lies about a mile or so north of *Sandia* Peak, where the tramway stops on the summit. However, it is best to take the road to the Crest during good weather months (spring or summer).

The tramway ride to the top takes about 15 minutes. It proceeds at a speed of about 12 mph. "Flights" to the top leave about every 15 minutes. From the peak, viewers can see not only all of Albuquerque, but also large areas of New Mexico

Figure 10-7: *Sandia* Tramway to *Sandia* Peak, Albuquerque.

that surround the city. There is a restaurant on top called the High Finance Restaurant. Hiking, backpacking and nature hikes are made available from the top by the Forest Service.

Mountain biking is available in the summer months. Skiing is available on the far side of the mountain during the ski season. Many other activities are available if you wish to be physically active.

However you decide to get there, by tramway or car, the view from the top of *Sandia* Mountain is worth the trip.

Georgia O'Keefe Art Museum – *Santa Fe*

This museum perpetuates the artistic legacy of Georgia O'Keefe, renowned for her abstract images of New Mexico or images inspired by the culture and landscape of the Land of Enchantment. She is recognized for her abstract paintings of flowers, steer skulls, rocks, shells and landscapes using a style that has become recognized as American modernism. Her art is indeed unique and recognizable.

One can experience examples of Georgia O'Keefe's beautiful art at the Georgia O'Keefe Museum in *Santa Fe*, New Mexico. The museum is located about three blocks from the *Santa Fe Plaza*.

Santa Fe Indian Market®, ...Just Love That Southwestern Art

On the third weekend of August, at the height of the tourist season, *Santa Fe* holds its *Santa Fe* Indian Market® celebration. The Southwestern Association of Indian Affairs (SWAIA) sponsors the event each year, for the preservation and development of Native American cultural arts and crafts. Huge crowds gather over the weekend to peruse and to buy the many beautiful works of art, pottery, jewelry and other crafted items that are displayed in the hundreds of display booths, surrounding the *Santa Fe Plaza* area. The high standards and superior quality of the exhibits are always maintained from year to year. The beauty and creativity of these exhibits are truly stunning. Hundreds of artists use ancient and modern tribal motifs for gourd art, jewelry, pottery, oil or acrylic paintings, native craft items, statues, blankets, sand paintings and native instruments (flutes, drums), etc.

Figure 10-8: Browsing at the 2011 *Santa Fe* Indian Market®

It is a lively, enjoyable and colorful cultural experience.

See Figure 10-8. If you love silver jewelry with coral, turquoise or mother of pearl you'll find many beautiful examples here. You'll find beaded necklaces and bracelets of all kinds. Beautifully handcrafted pottery from many of the *pueblos* and other tribes are on display and for sale here. In addition to the many items mentioned above, one can also find embroidered shirts, dresses, women's tops, vases, wooden sculptures, Indian *tacos*, *sopaipillas,* etc. It's all here. And the quality of the goods is high too.

On street corners one can often see musicians playing Native American flutes, or perhaps a Hoop Dancer performing to a thrilling primal native beat. See Figure 10-9, which shows Tony Duncan, 2011 World Hoop Dance Champion, dancing at the 2011 *Santa Fe* Indian Market®.

Figure 10-9: Tony Duncan, 2011 Hoop Dancing World Champion, performs his magic at the 2011 *Santa Fe* Indian Market® (With permission of Tony Duncan.[6])

This market event is an opportunity to maintain and encourage the Native American heritage of New Mexico. You are sure to pick up something by which to remember the event. It is an experience not to be missed!

The "Miraculous Staircase"- Loretto Chapel,[7,8] *Santa Fe*

The Sisters of Loretto Chapel believe that the well-known spiral wooden staircase within is a miracle sent in answer to prayer. The Loretto Chapel was completed in 1878. See Figure 10-10, for an exterior view of the famous chapel. The exterior architecture is quite beautiful and often overlooked. Upon completion of the chapel, it was noted that there was no access to the choir loft, 22 feet above the chapel ground floor. When carpenters were asked to provide a solution, the only alternative offered was to use a ladder. However, a ladder or a conventional staircase would have consumed too much of the small chapel's interior space.

The sisters made a *novena*[9] to St. Joseph, the husband of Mary, the earthly father of Jesus Christ, and the patron saint of carpenters. On the ninth and final day of prayer, a man mysteriously appeared at the chapel. Legend says that he appeared on a donkey and carried his tools seeking work. After several months the beautiful and stylish spiral staircase was completed and the carpenter disappeared, without being paid. After seeking the carpenter without avail, they concluded that the craftsman must have been St. Joseph, to whom they had been praying. Their prayers had been answered in miraculous fashion!

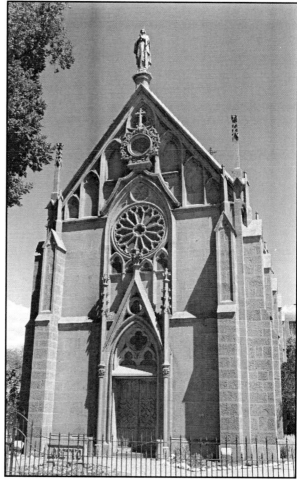

Figure 10-10:
Loretto Chapel, *Santa Fe*.
(With permission of the
Loretto Chapel.)

The staircase is indeed magnificent in structure and design. It appears to have no visible support and indeed this is one of the two mysteries associated with the staircase. The other is the identity of the carpenter.

The staircase was built with wooden pegs, and without any nails. It spirals around 360 degrees twice, and appears to be suspended in air. No one other than the nuns saw the carpenter or any delivery of lumber to the chapel.

In the late 1990s, Mary Jean Straw Cook, author of *Loretto: The Sisters and Their Santa Fe Chapel* (2002: Museum of New Mexico Press), appears to have solved the mystery.[10] The author claims that the carpenter was an expert woodworker named Francois-Jean "Frenchy" Rochas. He had left France and had come to *Santa Fe* around the time of the mysterious building of the "miraculous staircase." The author found evidence that linked Rochas to another French contractor who had worked on the chapel at that time. Further, Cook's investigations led the author to an 1895 death notice in The New Mexican, which unequivocally named Francois-Jean Rochas as the master builder of the famous "miraculous staircase" in the Loretto Chapel.

Regarding the unconventional construction of the staircase,[11] the need for a central pole support or newel is often cited as a necessary structural component. This supposed need however is disputed. All spiral staircases do not need a central pole support or newel. Lateral or outer supports can serve the same purpose. The secret of the Loretto Chapel staircase construction lies in the carpenter's use of an inner wood stringer of relatively small radius. This tight radial stringer acts as a concealed central support. This technique is not unique and is quite well known to most fine carpenters. Further, there is an outer support to one of the columns supporting the loft. It is believed that the staircase is made of spruce.

Whether one believes in the miraculous nature of the staircase or in the technical explanation, or whether one believes the carpenter was St. Joseph or the French master wood-worker, Francis-Jean Rochas, the Loretto Chapel staircase is a beautiful and graceful wonder to behold. It is well worth seeing!

Palace of the Governors[12]

Located on the *Plaza* in *Santa Fe*, New Mexico, the Palace of the Governors is an *adobe* structure, which served as the seat of government for New Mexico for centuries. It is the oldest continuously occupied public building in the U.S. See Figure 10-11.

The construction was initiated by Don Pedro de Peralta in 1610, the newly appointed Spanish Governor of the region known as the colony of New Mexico, which then comprised much of the present day Southwest, including the current states of New Mexico, Arizona, *Nevada*, Utah, *Colorado* and California. This region experienced many historical upheavals over the centuries, including the *Pueblo* Revolt of 1680, the Spanish *ReConquista* of 1692/93, Mexican Independence in 1821, and finally the American Invasion and Occupation of 1846. Over this long period, Palace ownership passed from one government to another. With Mexican Independence in 1821, the Mexican province of *Santa Fe de Nuevo México* was administered from the Palace of the Governors. In 1848, when Mexico officially ceded New Mexico to the United States, the Palace of the Governors became the first territorial capitol of the New Mexico Territory.

Figure 10-11: Palace of the Governors, *Santa Fe*.

Lew Wallace served as Territorial Governor during the Lincoln County War and wrote his famous novel: *Ben Hur: Tale of the Christ* in the offices of the Palace of the Governors.

In 1909, the New Mexico State Legislature established the Palace as the Museum of New Mexico, even though the region was still a U.S. territory at the time. The Palace served as the site of the state history museum. In 2009, a new state history museum was established and opened next to the Palace. The Palace of the Governors building was declared a Registered National Historic Landmark in 1960, and an American Treasure in 1999.[13]

Today, many native peoples gather daily to sit in the front of the Palace, displaying and selling native jewelry and other crafts to the passing tourists. It is a very popular attraction that benefits both the native vendors and curious tourists. It is one more element that adds to *Santa Fe's charm.*

Archbishop's Legacy - Cathedral Basilica of St. Francis of Assisi, *Santa Fe*

Fine examples of the Spanish Colonial style mission churches exist throughout New Mexico. Examples can be found at *El Sanctuario de Chimayó*, at the *San Francisco de Asís* Mission Church in *Ranchos de Taos*, or in *Santa Fe* at *El Santuario de Guadalupe*. What they all have in common is a simple construction of *adobe* and timber. The Franciscans and the native builders used materials that were readily available to them from the surrounding land. Roofs were supported by giant *vigas* and the walls were constructed of *adobe* bricks and mud. The altar area usually exhibited reredos or paintings that were imported from Mexico or Spain, or that were

Figure 10-12: Cathedral Basilica of St. Francis of Assisi in *Santa Fe.*
(Archdiocese of *Santa Fe.*)

handcrafted by local artisans. Many have hand-painted *retablos* (on wood panels).

They have their own unique but simple beauty.

However, the Cathedral Basilica of St. Francis of Assisi in *Santa Fe* is very different in many ways. It is a cathedral, not a mission church. Its structure reflects that elevated status! It is built using stone and it has two large towers. No *vigas* are visible. It has a pitched roof instead of the *pueblo* style flat roof. *Adobe* was not used. See Figure 10-12. The inside of the Cathedral Basilica is magnificent in scope in comparison to the Spanish Colonial mission churches. It has beautiful stained glass windows. Most mission churches have only simple glass windows or none at all. Beautiful, graceful arches run from supporting columns to the high roof. The style is Romanesque. It is unique and very different from the mission churches in New Mexico! The Cathedral Basilica of St. Francis of Assisi is a "must see" for anyone who visits *Santa Fe*.

Jean Baptiste Lamy conceived the cathedral[14] design while still a bishop. It was started in 1869 but it was not completed until 1886. (Bishop Lamy was elevated to the position of archbishop on February 12, 1875.) The original cathedral concept required tall spires or steeples rising about 160 feet above the towers. However, the final building never included these spires. The cathedral was built around the original Old *Parroquia*,[15] or the Chapel of Our Lady of the Assumption, located in the left transept of the cathedral. Lamy built the cathedral to give recognition of God's grace. Lamy was a Frenchman from Auvergne, France. He wanted this cathedral to reflect the type of magnificence he had seen in his native land, as a tribute to God's greatness. The Old *Parroquia* (Mission Church) was a simple *adobe* structure that was built in 1725 around the original chapel built by De Vargas, which he had dedicated to the *Madonna*. Archbishop Lamy built his cathedral around portions of the Old *Parroquia* that included the chapel.

Figure 10-13: Statue of Archbishop Lamy, which stands in front of the Cathedral Basilica of St. Francis of Assisi in *Santa Fe*. (Statue sculpted by J. Jusco.)

The Cathedral Basilica as it stands today has a full-sized statue of Archbishop Lamy out front, before the entry into the cathedral. It is to the right of a small set of steps that leads from the street up onto the church grounds. The statue was sculpted by J. Jusco and donated to the cathedral by Miguel Chavez in 1915. See Figure 10-13, which shows a sketch of the statue of Archbishop Lamy. Here the

Archbishop stands proudly in front of his creation, a man of vision and purpose.

To the left of the same set of steps there is a statue of St. Francis of Assisi, with a tame wolf by his side. It shows a smiling and benevolent saintly man, Saint Francis of Assisi, to whom the cathedral is dedicated.

Figure 10-14: Statue of Saint Francis of Assisi, which stands in front of the Cathedral Basilica of St. Francis of Assisi, *Santa Fe.* (Statue sculpted by Betty Sabo.)

Saint Francis of Assisi is clothed in a simple burlap robe that is tied at the waist. One can almost feel the texture of the burlap. He seems extremely approachable and humble as he extends his left hand forward in a benevolent greeting or solicitation. Refer to Figure 10-14, which shows a sketch of the statue of Saint Francis. Betty Sabo sculpted this fine statue.

Yet another statue in colored bronze is of a saintly Native American named *Kateri Tekakwitha*[16, 17] who lived between 1656 and 1680. She is the first Native American, north of Mexico, to be sainted in the Roman Catholic Church. Estella Loretto sculpted this statue. The Knights and Ladies of the Holy Sepulchre donated the statue as a gift to the church.

Tekakwitha was a Mohawk-Algonquin native from New York who was an early convert to Christianity. She was known as the "Lily of the Mohawks." On June 22, 1980, Pope John Paul II beatified *Kateri Tekakwitha.* Until her recent canonization, she was referred to as Blessed *Kateri.* Pope Benedict XVI canonized her as Saint *Kateri Tekakwitha,* on October 21, 2012.

Two large doors lead into the Cathedral Basilica. Each door has ten inset bronze panels showing various images in bas-relief. Donna Quastoff sculpted these fine panels. They depict events in the region's Spanish American history and the cathedral's construction and history.[18] Inside the Cathedral Basilica, one is immediately impressed with the paintings in the vestibule, as well as by the stained glass works within the cathedral itself. The roof reaches to great heights in beautiful graceful arches. Attractive stained glass windows adorn the sidewalls. The Stations of the Cross appear on either side of the main area of the church. The area around and behind the altar shows huge spiritual paintings.

To the left of the altar, in the left transept, is a segment of the old chapel area with the statue of Our Lady of the Assumption. See Figure 6-5 in Chapter Six. This wall is all that remains of the original *parroquia*. Here a small wooden statue, representing the *Madonna*, overlooks the faithful below. It was carved in Mexico and originally brought to *Santa Fe* in 1625, as Our Lady of the Assumption.

Later, after the exile of the Spanish from *Santa Fe* during the *Pueblo* Revolt of 1680, and after the re-conquest of *Santa Fe* in 1692-93, her name was changed to *La Conquistadora*, or Our Lady of the Conquest. She is thought of as the conqueror of the heart. The Old *Parroquia* chapel was rebuilt and dedicated to her on the site of the original parish, which had been burnt down by the natives during the *Pueblo* Revolt. The *parroquia* reconstruction effort was in partial fulfillment of a promise made by De Vargas in return for his successful mission to re-conquer *Santa Fe* and the rebellious natives. Today, the *Madonna* is known by multiple names: Our Lady of the Rosary, Our Lady of the Assumption, or *La Conquistadora*. The *Madonna* is housed within the old chapel area of the Cathedral Basilica to the left of the central altar.

The Cathedral Basilica has a rear upstairs balcony, above the main entry. It is opened only during services. Here one has a panoramic view of the interior of the Cathedral Basilica from the rear towards the front altar. The cathedral is an inspiring and beautiful sight, full of grace and subtle dignity.

As one exits through the front doors of the Cathedral Basilica, outside and to the right there is a small adjacent city park, called Cathedral Park, which can be reached by passing by an arched wrought-iron gateway, which reads *"Dios da y Dios quita"*[19] at the top. Behind this closed cemetery there is a small memorial to the early settlers of *Santa Fe*. This gateway is usually locked. The Cathedral Basilica owns this small cemetery behind the gateway.

In the small adjacent Cathedral Park, there are two statues of note. One is a much-overlooked fine bronze statue of Don Diego de Vargas, the re-conqueror of *Santa Fe*. A small plaque describes his historical role. See Figure 3-2 in Chapter Three. This statue, sculpted by Donna Quastoff, stands just behind the railing separating the park from the front street.

Also, in the center of this little park there is another larger three-tiered statue. It celebrates over 400 years of settlement by Europeans and their contributions, together with the contributions of the Franciscans who accompanied them and who advanced the Catholic faith in this region of New Mexico. It commemorates the Spanish settlers of 1598. It shows a priest, a Spanish soldier and a small colonial family standing on the top tier of the bronze statue. The middle tier shows daily artifacts, tools, a guitar and harvest items. There is also an opened book of the *Historia de la Nuevo México.*[20] The top two tiers are supported on the backs of several livestock animals: an ox, a sheep, a pig or sow, and a mule or donkey. A goat and a rooster also stand near the other livestock at the base of the monument. The statue is quite impressive. As with the statue of De Vargas, it is often missed or bypassed by tourists and visitors. Bernabé or Bernie Romero developed the design concept and Donna Quasthoff sculpted the statue. It is worth the time to seek out these nearby statues that relate so much to New Mexico's history.

On the opposite side of the Cathedral Basilica, at the right rear of the Cathedral Basilica grounds there is another sight that is often passed by, without notice. It is the Stations of the Cross Prayer Garden. It is a small garden in a peaceful and serene setting. A short concrete walkway takes one around the Stations of the Cross that are captured in various roughly hewn bronze statues. The emotional impact of this meditation garden and its 14 or 15 statues, sculpted by Gib Singleton, is quite palpable. The statues were dedicated in the garden on October 4, 2010. The statues are currently on a long-term loan from the Private Collection of Tia. Again, this small garden is very quiet and excellent for meditation. Following the path around to each of the Stations of the Cross is a moving experience and highly recommended!

The architect of the beautiful vision that is now the Cathedral Basilica of Saint Francis was Bishop (and later Archbishop) Lamy. He instituted church reforms, built schools and a hospital. He tried to develop a sense of refinement in the colonial town and in the church. He sought to reduce the influence of the thriving *"Penitentes"* movement, in his efforts to "Americanize" the Church. His life in New Mexico, and the challenges faced are described in Willa Cather's fictional novel, *Death Comes for the Archbishop.*

Archbishop Lamy was successful in realizing his dream of bringing refinement to *Santa Fe.* It is demonstrated within and immediately around this beautiful Cathedral Basilica. Over the years, the addition of new statues and other dedications has only increased the appeal of this remarkable landmark. Please be sure not to miss it!

El Santuario de Guadalupe[21]

In *Santa Fe,* New Mexico, there is an old *adobe* church that is considered the oldest extant shrine in the United States dedicated to the *Virgen de Guadalupe,* the

Figure 10-15: *El Santuario de Guadalupe, Santa Fe.*
(Courtesy of *El Santuario de Guadalupe* and the Archdiocese of *Santa Fe.*)

Figure 10-16: José de Alzibar's magnificent huge painting of the *Virgen de Guadalupe* and Juan Diego's vision at *El Santuario de Guadalupe, Santa Fe.* (Courtesy of *El Santuario de Guadalupe* and the Archdiocese of *Santa Fe.*)

patron saint of Mexico. El Santuario de Guadalupe was built between 1776 and 1796, following the old colonial style, using *adobe* bricks and timber. See Figure 10-15.

The *adobe* walls are three feet thick. The mission church is laid out in the shape of the cross, with a nave, altar and two transepts (left and right), like other mission churches. Large timbers or *vigas* support the lofty roof. These *vigas* are supported by corbels that protrude from the inside tops of the supporting sidewalls. The inside walls are whitewashed *adobe*. The sidewalls of the nave each have five small paintings of the Stations of the Cross. The adjoining walls of the two transepts each show two other stations, making a total of fourteen stations. There is a small balcony, above the entry to the church. It is accessed by a small spiral-type wooden staircase on the right side.

Straight ahead, behind the small altar, there is a very large and magnificent painting. This old painting occupies almost the entire wall behind the altar, and dwarfs the altar! This is the famous painting of the Virgin of Guadalupe, by Mexican artist José de Alzibar. It was painted in 1783. Various sections were painted separately, rolled up and transported to *Santa Fe.* A mule caravan brought this painting the long distance from Mexico City to *Santa Fe.* Upon arrival the various segments were stitched together to form this massive magnificent painting. It was then hung in its entirety for all parishioners to see and to marvel. See Figure 10-16.

This majestic painting shows six major panels, with the Trinity portrayed in the top central panel, and the Virgin of Guadalupe in the panel below it. The four remaining panels illustrate the story of Juan Diego and his vision of the Virgin of Guadalupe. A faded picture of the Virgin of Guadalupe also hangs on one of the walls of the right transept, where the musicians and choir usually are seated during services. In the left transept, there is a statue of (Saint or *San*) Juan Diego in a position of prayer. The statue is situated against one of the left transept walls, facing another large (but smaller) painting of the Virgin of Guadalupe that hangs high on the opposite wall. This second painting of the Virgin of Guadalupe is done in an old style. This large beautiful and significant painting is much smaller than the painting behind the altar!!

Figure 10-17: Statue of Virgin of Guadalupe, on the grounds *of El Santuario de Guadalupe, Santa Fe.* Sculpted by Georgina "Gogy" Farias. (Courtesy of *El Santuario de Guadalupe* and the Archdiocese of Santa Fe.)

Exiting this left transept there is a small history room that describes the church's history and notable events. A small gift shop adjoins this room.

A wonderful bronze statue of the Virgin of Guadalupe stands outside in the small yard behind the sanctuary. Georgina Gogy[22] sculpted this statue in August 2008. It is easily accessed from Guadalupe Street in *Santa Fe.* Flowers usually surround and adorn the base of the statue. See Figure 10-17.

The statue is remarkable and it is easily recognizable as the Virgin of Guadalupe. If one walks down the stairs behind the concrete space and proceeds to the parking spaces below, one will see six large dedication stone plaques with tiled faces, four on the right side of the stairway and two others on the left side, as one descends the stairway. These large dedication markers show tiled images of Juan Diego, and events associated with his vision.

One other interesting point of note is the medium-sized stone monument on the same slopes separating the upper *Santuario* and the lower parking lot. It lies to the left as one descends the stairs from above. There is a paved and sloped driveway that joins the parking lot below and the upper level of the *Santuario*. As one returns to the upper level by walking up this driveway, the stone can be seen to the left. It is very simple and it was dedicated just recently, on August 17, 2011. The inscription is simple. It says *"Cerro de Tepeyac"*, suggesting the metaphor that *El Santuario de Guadalupe* in *Santa Fe* symbolically sits on top of *El Cerro de Tepeyac*, the Hill of *Tepeyac*, where *San Juan Diego* had his remarkable vision. That vision changed the face and development of Roman Catholic Christianity in *Nueva España,* or New Spain, and later in *Nuevo México* or New Mexico.

Figure 10-18: A skillfully crafted Painted *Bulto,* representing *San Mateo,* by s*antero* Mark Garcia, shown at the 2011 *Santa Fe* Traditional Spanish Market©.
(By permission of Mark Garcia.[23])

Olé Olé! Santa Fe **Traditional Spanish Market**©

Want to view or buy traditional Spanish Colonial arts or crafts, or their contemporary equivalents? Be sure to visit the popular Traditional Spanish Market© in *Santa Fe.* Held on the *Plaza,* during the last full weekend of July, about one month prior to the *Santa Fe* Indian Market®, it is sponsored by the Spanish Colonial Arts Society to cultivate and to recognize the artistic achievements of the participating artists and craftsmen (and women) in local Spanish arts. The items on display and for sale include woodwork, carvings, jewelry, weaving, ironwork, furniture and many other items in various media. One can find three-dimensional carvings of *santos* (*bultos*), *retablos* of the various *santos*, exquisite tinwork pieces, crosses and other articles crafted with straw *appliqué*, wood carvings, weavings and other Spanish Colonial style crafted items. Food purveyors sell *burritos, tacos, carnitas*, etc. with *chile,* of course! It is another colorful event in *Santa Fe* that expands upon the cultural heritage of northern New Mexico. See Figures 10-18 thru 10-20. A second smaller Traditional Spanish Market© occurs indoors in early December.

Figure 10-19: Beautiful modern *retablos* displayed at the 2011 *Santa Fe* Traditional Spanish Market©. Created by *santera* Carmelita Laura Valdez Damron. (By permission of Carmelita Laura Valdez Damron.[24])

Figure 10-20: *Santera* Christine Montaño Carey proudly displays her beautiful Tinwork, at the 2011 *Santa Fe* Traditional Spanish Market©. (By permission of Christine Montaño Carey.[25])

Burning of the *zzzzzZozobra*^{©®},[26] *Santa Fe*

The *Zozobra*^{©®} is a giant marionette, representing "Old Man Gloom®". It is burned in effigy, in the autumn of each year, the evening before the start of the *Fiestas de Santa Fe* (*Santa Fe Fiesta*) celebration. It is officially called Will Shuster's *Zozobra*^{©®}. Each year, the Kiwanis Club of *Santa Fe*, builds a new *Zozobra*^{©®}, to raise funds to help the children of the *Santa Fe* area.

The Will Shuster's *Zozobra*^{©®} official tagline says: "Will Shuster's *Zozobra*^{©®} is a *Santa Fe* tradition presented by The Kiwanis Club of *Santa Fe* the first Thursday after Labor Day. Funds raised provide college scholarships to *Santa Feans*, grants to non-profits who focus on the children and youth of *Santa Fe*, and an endowment whose goal is to fund the college scholarships allowing even more funds to be given to the community." It is an event well worth experiencing, and it serves a very worthy community cause!!

The name *Zozobra*^{©®}, applied to the marionette, actually comes from the Spanish word *zozobra,* meaning *"anxiety"* or *"worry."* Hence, the symbolism is very clear!

The burning marks the secular beginning of a three-day long celebration. Many locals think of it as the unofficial start of the *Fiestas de Santa Fe*, also known as *Santa Fe Fiesta*. The marionette built for the 2011 celebration was exactly 49 feet 11 inches tall, and merited a place in the Guinness Book of Records. The burning usually occurs at Marcy Field Park.

The Burning of the *Zozobra*^{©®} is an event that is eagerly anticipated each autumn in *Santa Fe*. It has been enthusiastically adopted and embraced for over eighty-eight years and it has become part of the popular culture of *Santa Fe*. See Figures 10-21 and 10-22.

What better way to cast away the doom and gloom of the year past, with all its worries and cares, than to burn the *Zozobra*^{©®}, the very symbol of that gloom!? By burning this representation of the dark recent past, participants cast off past troubles, and let the flames consume their worries and concerns. They may then look forward with a fresh new perspective towards the coming year, unburdened by the negativity of the recent past.

To actively participate in this annual cleansing, one need only contact the offices of the *Santa Fe* Reporter in advance of the celebration, and drop off written declarations of the personal gloom one wishes to dispel. Some folks will even put legal papers into the gloom box, to be burned, along with the other submitted written items, at the foot of the giant *Zozobra*^{©®} during the celebration. If this first opportunity is missed, there is still a chance to enter your own wishes into the gloom box on the celebration day, but before the burning starts, after dusk. A tent is set up to accept the written inputs. Each year, tens of thousands observe this unique event in *Santa Fe*. The *Zozobra's*^{©®} hair color changes from year to year. The *Zozobra*^{©®} Festival was used as a setting for the 1947 film entitled *Ride the Pink Horse.*[27] There is a patent on the marionette.

This famous celebration is not of ancient origins, although it does hearken back in some ways to ancient pagan Celtic celebrations, such as the burning of the Wicker Man.[28] Julius Caesar recorded this Celtic or Gaulish custom long ago. There are several main differences however, between this brutal ancient custom and the modern Burning of the *Zozobra*^{©®}.

First, the Wicker Man, of Celtic times, was usually meant as a living sacrifice to the Celtic gods.

Second, the Wicker Man often had imprisoned within it, live animals and war captives or criminals, as sacrifices. The sacrifices were engulfed in the flames, as the Wicker Man was set ablaze.

Figure 10-21: Old Man Gloom® at Marcy Field Park, *Santa Fe*. (With permission of the Kiwanis Club of *Santa Fe*.)

Third and most importantly, William Howard Shuster, Jr. presumably developed the idea of the effigy and the ritual Burning of the *Zozobra*©® in 1924,[29] for therapeutic and cathartic purposes. It had nothing to do with the ancient Celtic rites. Further, the Burning of the *Zozobra*©® is a charitable event, to benefit the youngsters of the *Santa Fe* area!

Nonetheless, it is interesting to discuss the pagan rites as well as the *Burning Man*, of Nevada. The ancient Celtic practice associated with The Wicker Man burning was immortalized in the 1973 film *The Wicker Man*.[30] Subsequently, a fictional book of the same title was published in 1978, by authors Robin Hardy and Anthony Shaffer.[31] It was based on the 1973 film. An updated version of the film was released in 2006, starring Nicholas Cage.[32] However, the original setting, the outer isles of Scotland, was changed to an island off the coast of Washington state, in order to appeal to American audiences. The ending in both movies is chilling.

A similar but unrelated celebration, which involves the burning of a large wooden effigy, occurs each year in Black Rock Desert, *Nevada*. It is called the *Burning Man*.[33] It started as a bonfire ritual in celebration of the Summer Solstice in *San Francisco*, 1986. In this much smaller initial celebration, a nine-foot wooden man effigy was burned. Over the years, the effigy has grown to about forty feet in height. The event later moved out into the *Nevada* Desert, as the effigy grew in size and the event grew in popularity. According to the *Burning Man* website,[34] the emphasis is on "…community, art, self-expression and self-reliance…"

The initial Burning of the *Zozobra*©® preceded the first *Burning Man* event by more than six decades. The inspiration in each case is also different. The *Burning Man* may, at one time, have been a mutated celebration of the Summer Solstice (late June). However, the timing of the event has tended to move towards the end of August, in

recent times. As pointed out above, it is about self-expression.

The Burning of the Zozobra©® represents a psychologically therapeutic purging of negative feelings. For participants, it allows a new, fresh start to the coming year and it has a charitable objective!

Figure 10-22: The Burning of the *Zozobra*©®, at Marcy Field Park, *Santa Fe*. (With permission of the Kiwanis Club of *Santa Fe*.)

Interestingly, the Zozobra©® celebration occurs just prior to the Autumnal Equinox (late September), after which the winter soon approaches. The ancient Celtic New Year began on the evening of October 31/November 1, when Halloween is celebrated. So, the Burning of the Zozobra©® and the purging of the old year's negativity and gloom occur about six weeks before the start of the Celtic New Year. Coincidence? Could William Howard Shuster have intended this to be, or is this just pure chance at work? I'll let the reader be the final judge of that!

In spite of all this, the Burning of the Zozobra©® is still its own unique event. In most every respect, except for the actual burning of an effigy and the coincidental timing, the Burning of the Zozobra©® has really nothing to do with either the ancient Wicker Man burnings or the modern *Burning Man*.

The famous marionette called Old Man Gloom® is stuffed with shredded paper, by local children. Marcy Field Park opens around 2:30 pm and the band entertainment starts at 3 pm. Local access roads are usually closed around 4:30 pm, so getting a parking spot early and getting in early is important, to beat the rush. Crowds really start to gather around 5 pm and certainly by 6 pm. Different bands play all kinds of music, as the crowds gather. Before dusk, the Spanish Colonial re-enactors, who are part of the upcoming *Fiestas de Santa Fe* celebration, appear to invite the crowd to the weekend's festivities. *Mariachi* bands also play. Re-enactors file through the crowds. The entire atmosphere is magical and like a gigantic party. Nearby vendors sell turkey legs, *elotes, chimichangas, frito* pies, etc.

Eventually dusk comes and the marionette becomes illluminated with various colored stage lights. Its head turns and its arms move. Its neon eyes glow in the approaching dark. The three large buttons down the front of his long flowing tunic glow. A stage show with dancers begins. Eventually fire-dancers appear swirling open-flame torches. Meanwhile, Old Man Gloom® turns its head and points to segments of the audience, in a mocking gesture. Its mouth opens as it emits a low groaning sound. It almost seems real, as the crowd starts to chant repeatedly, "Burn it! Burn it! Burn it!" The excitement is palpable as the music and drumbeat hastens towards a climax. Soon, the marionette is set afire and the paper relics of the everyone's gloom from last year are burned. Fireworks race to the heavens and explode in multiple beautiful colors.

Meanwhile the marionette burns. You almost feel sorry for its demise, as its internal framework collapses to the ground in flames. Even more fireworks are ignited, rising high into the dark night sky and bursting in colorful showers. The spectacular show is now at its end, and 25,000 excited locals and tourists race to the exits. The throngs descend down the road to the *Santa Fe Plaza,* exclaiming aloud, *"Viva La Fiesta! Que Viva!!"* And so the *Santa Fe Fiesta* weekend begins!

El Rancho de las Golondrinas: A Step into the Past

Ever wonder what Spanish Colonial or New Mexico Territorial frontier life was really like? How would you like to experience just a small taste of it? Well, you can! Just south of *Santa Fe* proper there is a 200-acre ranch in a rural farming community that serves as a living history museum! It is called *El Rancho de las Golondrinas* or "the Ranch of the Swallows." This *rancho* dates from 1710. Situated along the Old Spanish *El Camino Real*, or the "Royal Road" from Mexico City to *Santa Fe*, the *rancho* became an important and popular *paraje* or "stopping place." It is located in *La Cienega ("the Marsh"),* just outside *Santa Fe* proper. Now established as a living history museum, it is set up to demonstrate the history, culture and the heritage of the 18th and 19th centuries in New Mexico. There are some original colonial buildings on

Figure 10-23: Wagon Rides at *El Rancho de las Golondrinas, La Cienega.*
(By permission of Cale Chappelle, wagon driver.)

the ranch that date from the 1700's, while other historic buildings from other parts of northern New Mexico have been reconstructed at *Las Golondrinas*. The village comes alive with villagers dressed in period costumes to show what frontier life was like in New Mexico in its early days. There are 69 different local building or activity sites to check out on this ranch.[35]

These include a winery, a fruit orchard, rootcellar, old molasses mill, country store, shepherd's cabin, leatherworking shop, goat barn, wheelright shop, weaving workrooms, defensive tower, corrals, barns, threshing ground, a blacksmith shop, etc. This gives a visitor some idea of the variety and scope of the *rancho*. See Figures 10-23, 10-24 and 10-25.

Special events, festivals and weekend events are staged to convey the costumes, the music, the dances and other aspects of life during the Spanish Colonial, Mexican Provincial and New Mexican Territorial eras.

Figure 10-24: A living history presenter, in the aftermath of a re-enacted skirmish, portraying a Mexican soldier, at the time of the U.S.-Mexican War (c. 1846), also known as the Mexican-American War, at *El Rancho de las Golondrinas, La Cienega*. (By permission of Roberto Valdez, re-enactor.)

For example, the Fall Harvest Festival which occurred on the weekend of October 1 and 2, 2011, included some of the following activities: crushing grapes by foot for wine making, making *ristras* by stringing red *chile*s, tin stamping, corn husk doll making, wagon rides, making bread using *hornos*, carding, spinning and weaving wool, blacksmithing, milling, making *tortillas* and *tamale*s, pressing apples to make cider, a beading workshop, *retablo* making and painting workshop, and exhibits of farm animals and *burros*.

Various forms of scheduled events included old-time music, *Los Matachines de Bernalillo* Dancers, *Ballet Folklorico de Santa Fe* (traditional Hispanic dancing) and a U.S.-Mexican War skirmish re-enactment.

There is so much activity and entertainment one can't help but be amazed. It's a fun-filled day for all! Grandparents, families, couples, singles and kids love it. There is no way to be bored. It's just impossible!

There is a fine giftshop and bookshop at the *rancho*, if one wishes to pick up a

Figure 10-25: Virginia Vigil cooking *carne machucada* at *El Rancho de las Golondrinas, La Cienega.* (With permission of Virginia Vigil, re-enactor.)

novel gift or learn more about New Mexico history or culture. A food vendor is available to fill the belly when the need arises. There is also a gristmill and a reconstructed *morada* on the *rancho*, as well as other notable buildings, farm buildings or cabins of historic and cultural interest. The atmosphere is informative, exciting and fun-filled.

A schedule of the many enjoyable, entertaining and educational activities held throughout the year is available at the following website:

www.golondrinas.org

The *rancho* is usually closed during the winter months, reopening again in the spring. If you have a chance and your schedule permits, spend a day at *El Rancho de las Golondrinas*, on the outskirts of *Santa Fe*. It is a memorable experience. Guaranteed!

Santa Fe Outdoor Opera:[36, 37] Singing to the Stars Above
Take St. Francis Drive (Highway 84) northward out of *Santa Fe* towards *Tesuque* and eventually you'll come upon a large open-roofed bowl structure on a hill towards your left, in the *Tesuque* area. This is the *Santa Fe* Opera building. It was first constructed in 1957, but it had to be rebuilt after its eleventh season due to a serious fire that caused significant damage to the structure. The current structure can hold 1,400 people. The theater is open on its sides and is partially open to the evening stars above. It looks out onto the natural high desert and mountain landscape of beautiful *Tesuque*. This site was selected because it is far from any urban noise, traffic or hustle bustle.

The opera season opens in early July and runs through the end of August.

Many have been attracted by the quality of its productions and its lavish style. It usually hosts one premiere each summer season, more than most opera houses in the country. The season usually presents the standard repertory as well as newer and lesser-known works. The productions hosted here require up to 500 support staff. The Opera House employs an Opera Titles[38] display system at each seat and in the standing room area that allows viewers to choose either an English or Spanish translation of the opera script.

There is also an Apprentice Program[39], that allows aspiring opera singers and technicians to serve in the chorus, as understudies or to gain stage management experience. It supports the transition from academic experience to professional experience, for young artists and stage technicians.

Visitors travel from all corners of the earth to attend the famous *Santa Fe* Opera. If you are visiting *Santa Fe* or are near the city, be sure to attend this world famous opera house. You won't be sorry!

Puyé Cliff Dwellings[40, 41]

This fascinating site allows the visitor to see cliff dwellings, early *pueblo* architecture, ancient *kiva*s and grand panoramic views of the surrounding valley. The *Puyé* Cliffs Welcome Center is located at the Valero Gas Station, located about a mile down the road from the sacred Black *Mesa*, and it is located on Highway 30 and *Puyé* Cliffs Road. A short scenic drive into the park takes the visitor along the *Puyé* Cliffs Scenic Byway to the interior Visitor Center and parking lot. A former Harvey House is located here near the base of the *Puyé* Cliffs. It was formerly a Bed & Breakfast in the early 20th century, but it is now used as an interpretive center and gift shop. Personal photography is allowed.

This site was declared a National Historic Landmark in 1966. The *Puyé* Cliff Dwellings are *pueblo* remains, located in the lands of the *Santa Clara Pueblo*, in the *Santa Clara* Canyon. These remains, near *Española,* were occupied from about 1250 AD until about 1577 AD, when drought forced the inhabitants to abandon the site, for a location closer to the *Rio Grande*. Individual homes may have set up in the area around 900 AD, but these did not form into villages until two or three centuries later. The name "*Puyé*", in *Tewa*, means "where the rabbits assemble or meet."

Oral traditions seem to suggest that the current occupants of *Santa Clara Pueblo* are the descendants of the former inhabitants of the abandoned *Puyé* Cliff Dwellings. When the site was actively occupied, up to 1,500 residents lived here. See Edward S. Curtis' photo, as he saw the *Puyé* Cliffs in 1925, shown in Figure 10-26. They haven't changed!

There are two levels of *pueblo* remains at this site. The lower level comprises cliff and cave dwellings carved into the cliff face. This level runs a little more than one mile long around the *mesa* base. Dwelling remains are also present on the *mesa* top. This second level is less than half a mile long. Stone paths with hewn handholds, or wooden ladders connected the two levels that were cut into the cliff face.

Dwellings are carved into the 200 feet high cliff faces. The cliff ridge is formed from volcanic tuff, making the cliff faces relatively soft enough to carve into, using wooden tools. Some 740 rooms have been carved out of the cliff faces. It is believed that these cave rooms were in fact back rooms to other structures that were built in front of these cave rooms. Foundations have been found that suggest that buildings were built in front of the cave rooms and against the cliff base. It has been suggested that these structures were built with talus[42] blocks to a height of several stories.

Lines of post-holes have also been found along the cliff faces, suggesting that these may have supported roof beams for the larger frontal structures. They may also have served as anchor points for wooden ladders or for walkways to reach the cliff rooms. Cliff ladders or rough stairways with hand and footholds allow access to the cliff tops. A large "Community House" lies at the top of the cliffs. It has been partially reconstructed.

Figure 10-26: *Puyé Cliff Dwellings.*** (Photo by Edward S. Curtis, c. 1925. Courtesy Palace of the Governors Photo Archives. (NMHM.DCA) neg. # 144662)

The free-of-charge *Puyé* Cliffs Scenic Byway is a seven-mile byway leading to the cliff dwellings. It allows the visitor to see expansive views of the surrounding *Santa Clara Pueblo* region, as well as much farther views of the natural wonders of Northern New Mexico. However, entrance to the cliff-dwellings site itself requires payment of an entrance fee. It is educational and it is situated in a location that affords fantastic views of the surrounding landscape! Don't miss the *Puyé* Cliff Dwellings!

Please consult the following website:

www.puyecliffs.com/history.htm

New Mexico Rail Runner Express[43, 44] (*Santa Fe*/Albuquerque)

The New Mexico Rail Runner Express is a commuter rail service that runs between *Santa Fe* and Albuquerque. See Figure 10-27. It joins the metropolitan communities of these two cities. It runs from *Belen* on the western side of Albuquerque, through *Las Lunes, Isleta Pueblo*, downtown Albuquerque, *Los Ranchos, Sandia Pueblo*, downtown *Bernalillo, Kewa* (*Santo Domingo*) *Pueblo* and into *Santa Fe*. Much of the route shadows Interstate 25, but it does deviate where necessary to reach its various stations. The New Mexico Rail Runner Express services the central New Mexico corridor. Many commuters live in Albuquerque but commute to work in government offices or private industry in *Santa Fe*. The express rail service was built to address this commuting need. The ticket prices are reasonable when one considers the cost of automobile travel, including gasoline costs and vehicle wear and tear. Day, monthly and annual passes are available for purchase too. Children under ten years of age are free. Besides the standard commuter service provided during normal commute hours, service is also provided for special events such as *Lobos* games, Albuquerque international Balloon *Fiesta*[®], holiday season, etc.

The train consists of a locomotive and three or four carriages. The train is an attractive off-white color with the red head of a roadrunner bird emblazoned on the locomotive's sides. The sides of the rail carriages show an image of a bird's body, with streaming red and yellow feathers. The New Mexico Rail Runner Express name is a play on New Mexico's state bird, the roadrunner. A single track supports travel in only one direction at a time, since traffic flow is determined primarily by commuter needs.

The New Mexico Rail Runner Express has also become a tourist attraction with its colorful roadrunner-like logo and its traverse through beautiful desert landscapes. To make the express railway more attractive and feasible to riders, the New Mexico Rail Runner Express connects with Amtrak and Greyhound in downtown Albuquerque.

Figure 10-27: The New Mexico Rail Runner Express train, that runs between *Santa Fe* & Albuquerque. (With permission of the New Mexico Rail Runner Express.)

There are also shuttle service connections to Moriarty, *Los Alamos*, *Española* and *Las Vegas* (NM) and connections to ABQRide routes at *Los Ranchos*/Journal Center and *Bernalillo* County/International Sunport (ABQ Airport) stations. Smaller shuttle services connect *Socorro, Belen, Los Lunas* and *Taos*. Several *pueblo* communities provide shuttle service connections to the *Santa Ana, Isleta* and *Pojoaque Pueblos*, connecting their casinos to the nearest rail station.

In 2012, the University of New Mexico Department of Theatre and Dance provided a weekly performance of Shakespeare on board the train each Saturday in June, July and August. Please consult the following website: www.nmrailrunner.com

The monthly New Mexico Rail Runner Xpress Magazine also offers great trip ideas using the train.

Riding the New Mexico Rail Runner Express has become an event for visitors to experience. So take a ride through some stunning desert landscapes under big skies and tour *Santa Fe* or Albuquerque to cap off the experience!

Turquoise Trail[45, 46] (*Santa Fe*/Albuquerque)

This scenic and historic trail extends from *Santa Fe* to Albuquerque. It travels along State Highway 14 and is part of the National Scenic Highway. It includes *Sandia* Crest Scenic Byway or State Highway 536, the high point near the end of the trail. The route is approximately 54 miles long and runs nearly parallel to I-25 between *Santa Fe* and Albuquerque. The trail not only provides historic sights, but it also leads past gift shops, galleries, small restaurants and other interesting points. The Turquoise Trail is probably so-named because of the mining of turquoise that was so prominent in this area.

The *Navajo* once marched along its path on their "Long Walk" towards their incarceration at Fort Sumner and *Bosque Redondo*.

On this scenic drive, one can check out the old historic mining towns of *Cerrillos* ("Little Hill"), Madrid and Golden. *Cerrillos* and Madrid are designated as Historic Villages.

Cerrillos was a prominent mining town in the 1800's. Here turquoise, gold, silver, lead and zinc were extracted from the surrounding hills. Pre-Columbian Native Americans and the Spaniards were the first to mine the area. Turquoise and later silver was mined here and then shipped to Spain to become part of the crown jewels of Spain. The town had 22 saloons and 4 hotels in its heyday in the 1880's. Even today the town has a frontier feel to it, with a number of old buildings still standing in the town. The western film *Young Guns* was shot along Main Street and First Street in the middle of this small mining town.

Cerrillos has a small mining museum and shop at the *Casa Grande* Trading Post. Visitors can purchase small stones mined from the surrounding hills. Various old antique mining machines used in the mining heydays stand outside the mining museum. The town also has a small antique shop.

The nearby *Cerrillos* Hills Historic Park is 1,100 acres suitable for hiking, mountain biking and horseback riding. A dozen of the pre-1900 mines have been developed within the park for educational purposes and as historical attractions. For more information, check the following web site: www.cerrilloshills.com

Madrid also lies along the Turquoise Trail. Madrid was once a prominent coal-mining town, supplying coal for the *Santa Fe* Railroad, locals and the U.S. Government. However, those days ended long ago. Present day Madrid has been transformed from a former dying mining town into a quaint little tourist town. Many of the old mining buildings have been recovered and converted by enterprising merchants and retailers. The town thrives during the tourist season because of its history, its novel shops and it's setting. The town hosts quality shops and galleries. If you long for the old soda fountain shop days, you can get a delicious ice-cream cone, soda, or sundae at Jezebel's Soda Fountain. It's like a trip back to "the good ole days"!

Of course, there are also many galleries, boutiques, Bed and Breakfasts, and even a tavern and a saloon. There's the popular Mine Shaft Tavern and the Old West Saloon. The entry to the Old Coal Mine Museum is via the Old West Saloon. This museum features a 1901 Richmond Steam Engine, mining relics and old cars. It is well worth seeing. A day's outing at Madrid is both relaxing and enjoyable!

The town of *Dolores* ("Sorrows") lies south of Madrid, in the Ortiz Mountains. In 1825, it was the site of the first gold rush west of the Mississippi, long before the California and *Colorado* gold rushes.

As one proceeds yet further south, one can see the *Sandia* ("Watermelon") Mountains on the right, in the west. These mountains lie within the *Cibola ("Buffalo")* National Forest, which can also be seen. To the left, towards the east one can see the Ortiz Mountains. At *Sandia* Park, State Highway 536 extends westward to the right. This is the *Sandia* Crest Scenic Byway that takes the traveler to the crest of the *Sandia* Mountains. The road to the crest-line is asphalt and is well maintained. The drive to the top is gradual and manageable, but tends to have many turns as the summit is approached. The summit is at an elevation of 10,678 feet. The view from the Observation Deck at the summit is awe-inspiring and worth the road trip. However, the winds can be quite gusty at the crest-line. So be careful and dress appropriately. The surrounding *Sandia* Mountain Wilderness is available for hiking, bird watching and other outdoor activities. The *Sandia* Peak and the tramway summit stop lie about a mile or two further south of the crest-line reached by Highway 536. Please note that *Sandia* Peak and *Sandia* Crest refer to two different and separate locations near the summit.

Returning back to *Sandia* Park and then to the Turquoise Trail, turn right towards the south. Here, one soon encounters Cedar Crest. This town is home to the Museum of Archeology & Material Culture. This outstanding museum allows exploration of the region's pre-historic Native American past.

Finally, the Turquoise Trail loops through *Tijeras* ("Scissors") and around Interstate 40, and then shortly afterwards, rejoins I-40 from the south at Exit 175 just east of Albuquerque. *Tijeras* is considered the entry to the Turquoise Trail from the Albuquerque side. Here, one will find the *Cibola* National Forest office where one can obtain more information and brochures about the Trail and the various sights along the way. *Tijeras* also hosts the *Tijeras Pueblo* Archeological Site.

Tijeras is the best point of entry for a return trip on the Turquoise Trail, from Albuquerque north towards *Santa Fe*.

For more information on the Turquoise Trail, consult the website:

www.turquoisetrail.com

Charles Bent Home & Museum: *Taos*

Another interesting place to visit is the Charles Bent Home & Museum. It is located in *Taos*. As you may recall from Chapter Four, Key Historical Characters, Charles Bent was appointed as the first American Military Governor of the New Mexico Territory. His term in office was prematurely terminated when he was scalped and murdered during the *Taos* Revolt of 1847. He was killed in his home,[47, 48, 49] although his wife and other family members did manage to escape to safety through a hole that was dug in a wall. An Indian slave saved Mrs. Bent's life, allowing her to escape. However, the slave was killed. Charles Bent, although loved by Americans, Mexicans, and *Pueblo* Indians alike, held his office for only three months before he was killed in the revolt. He represented the resented new American authority and that sealed his fate!

The Bent House & Museum is located a few hundred yards north of Kit Carson Avenue just west of *Paseo del Pueblo Norte*. It can be found at 117 Bent Street, one block north of the *Taos Plaza*. The museum also has a small art gallery of western art. There is a small admission fee to enter the museum. The store and museum staff are very amenable and knowledgeable about the circumstances of the Bent family and their ordeal. The staff is friendly and more than happy to share their knowledge.

Kit Carson Home & Museum: *Taos*

The home of the famous frontiersman, Kit Carson and his third wife Josefa Jaramilla, is also located in *Taos*. It has been converted into a museum. The home is a simple single-story *adobe* Spanish Colonial style dwelling. It is located on 228 Kit Carson Avenue, less than one block (or approximately one tenth of a mile) to the east of the main road through *Taos*, namely *Paseo de Pueblo Norte*. See Figure 10-28.

The entry to the home/museum takes the visitor into a gift shop and small museum. This area may at once have served as a barn. Here books, DVD's and frontier-related gifts can be purchased. For a small fee the visitor can enter the museum and watch a short video portraying Carson's full and rich life, in the first room of the house. This room adjoins the three other furnished rooms on display. It was once used as the children's room.

The role of Kit Carson in the video is played by one of Carson's direct descendants! The video is very informative and enjoyable to view. Various period artifacts are presented in wall hangings and casements within this same room. After viewing the video, the visitor can walk through a small doorway, leading into the main living area of the Carson home. This room and the two other display rooms in the home are set up much as they would have been in the mid-to-late 1800's.

Carson bought the home in 1843 for his new bride, Josefa Jaramillo. As one walks

Figure 10-28: Kit Carson Home & Museum, *Taos*.

Figure 10-29: Gravesites of Kit and Josefa Carson, in Kit Carson Park, *Taos*.

through the home, one encounters simple furnishings and framed photographs of Carson's beloved wife and of a mature Kit Carson, on the walls. This four-room adobe home, with 21 vigas, was considered very comfortable for the period.

Josefa Carson died giving birth to their eighth child. Kit Carson grieved for her and he too died within a month. His last words were supposedly, "*Adios compadres*", or "Goodbye friends"

Kit Carson is buried in the cemetery in Kit Carson Park, less than half a mile northeast on the *Paseo del Pueblo Norte*. See Figure 10-29. The cemetery is located in the right rear of the park near the volleyball, basketball courts and baseball field. A black iron fence surrounds the gravesite and makes it easy to find. Kit Carson's wife, Josefa, is buried here, and Kit Carson is buried next to her. Other Carson members are also buried here. Many *Taos* notables and historic persons, including a number of victims murdered during the *Taos* Revolt of 1847 are buried elsewhere in this cemetery. Padre Martinez and Mabel Dodge Luhan are also interred in this small cemetery.

Taos Plaza

The heart of *Taos* is the *Taos Plaza*. It is in the center of the small town. It is a fine place to just sit and relax. There is a large cottonwood in the *Plaza*, which provides a shady umbrella over the center lawned area. Oftentimes, small arts and crafts shows, and other trade shows are set up in this setting. Small retail and tourist shops, and eateries wrap around the outer perimeter of the *Plaza*. The *Plaza*'s central location makes it a short walk to some of *Taos*' key sights, small restaurants, and Kit Carson Park.

Taos Pueblo

This world famous *pueblo* is located just a few miles north of *Taos* Town. It can be reached by proceeding north on *Paseo del Pueblo Norte* out of *Taos* Town. For more details on directions and what the visitor can expect to see at the *pueblo*, please refer to the discussion of *Taos Pueblo* in Chapter Eleven: Native American Tribes & Reservations in NM.

Rio Grande Gorge Bridge: *Taos*

This bridge spans the *Rio Grande* Gorge. It is 12 miles west of *Taos* on US-64, and it is part of US-64. The drive from *Taos* is quite scenic, taking the visitor through a flat beautiful valley that is bordered by the *Sangre de Cristo* Mountains on the east and by the *San Juan* Mountains on the northwest. See Figure 10-30.

The continuous steel deck truss bridge is 1,280 feet long and stands 650 feet above the *Rio Grande* Gorge below. It is defined as a cantilever truss bridge. It is classified as the fifth highest bridge in the U.S.[50] There is a parking lot in both directions on the east side of the span. A walkway allows pedestrians, hikers or the courageously curious to walk out to the mid-span Observation Deck. At first, one wonders what all the fuss is about because the bridge has no overhead towers or cables. It looks just like the road used to approach the bridge. But the wonder of the bridge becomes apparent as one walks out to the center and looks at the gorge, and the river far, far below! The vertical view to the gorge below can be dizzying, with steep cliffs falling to the distant river waters, at the bottom of the gorge. See Figure 10-31. It is certainly not for everyone. If you suffer from acrophobia, this might not be the best adventure to attempt. The parking lot view may be sufficient!

The *Rio Grande* Gorge Bridge has featured in several films: *Born Killers, Wild Hogs, Twins, She's Having a Baby* and *Terminator Solution.*[51]

To get a powerful image of the bridge's understructure and the *Rio Grande* Gorge below, one can be more adventurous and take a short hike on the left far side of the bridge (if you are coming from the *Taos* area). This location provides some unique photo opportunities. Merely cross the bridge to the western side, or the far side of the bridge if you have come from the direction of *Taos*. There is small parking lot on this side. There is also an entry to a hiking trail that extends along the southern topside, adjacent to the gorge. Signs are posted to caution about the dangers of going off these trails towards the cliff edge. Please heed the signs and be careful! A hike as short as one quarter or one half mile can provide a vantage point that yields excellent photo opportunities. Children should not venture into this area! Pets are not allowed, unless they are leashed. Do not wear sandals or smooth-soled shoes or sneakers. Hiking boots are the most appropriate footwear. Enjoy the spectacular view!!

San Francisco de Asís Mission Church – *Ranchos de Taos*

This Spanish Colonial mission church can be found on the way to *Taos* at the *Ranchos de Taos Plaza* on Hwy 68. This church is not the oldest in New Mexico. However, it represents one of the finest examples of Spanish Colonial and Franciscan architecture in the state. It is dedicated to Saint Francis of Assisi, the founder of the Franciscan Order. See Figure 10-32.

The church was built sometime between 1710 and 1815. No one knows for sure! It was built with tens of thousands of *adobe* bricks and secured with *adobe*, acting as mortar. Twenty-eight large timbers, called *vigas*, support the roof. Inside the church, on each side, carved wooden corbels support each *viga*.

Figure 10-30: *Rio Grande* Gorge Bridge, outside *Taos*.

Figure 10-31: *Rio Grande* Gorge, outside *Taos*.

These corbels are embedded deeply into the walls. The *vigas* are visible both within and outside the church building.

The church was built sometime between 1710 and 1815. No one knows for sure! It was built with tens of thousands of *adobe* bricks and secured with *adobe*, acting as mortar. Twenty-eight large timbers, called *vigas*, support the roof. Inside the church, on each side carved wooden corbels support each *viga*. These corbels are embedded deeply into the side walls. The *vigas* are visible both within and outside the church building. The supporting corbels are visible inside the church at the juncture of the sidewalls and the ceiling. The church's architectural design is simple, yet elegant.

As with many Spanish mission churches, the building is laid out in the form of the cross. The nave runs down most of the length of the church with pews on either side. Before one reaches the altar there is an area to the right and to the left, representing the two arms of the cross. These two areas are called transepts. The altar lies directly ahead like the head or top of the cross.

A small choir loft lies above the entry to the church. Access to this balcony is by means of a small staircase to the left rear of the church as one enters the church. The wooden pews in the nave are simple in design. On either side of the nave are small paintings showing the fourteen Stations of the Cross. Behind the altar, there is a giant altar screen or reredo. The reredo is a wooden frame that is decorated in a traditional folk-art style. The altar screen has nine panels within it, that contain religious paintings or *retablos*, on canvas, in the Mexican style. The center panel shows the Crucifixion scene, and just below it is a statue of Saint Francis of Assisi. To the right of the altar is

Figure 10-32: *San Francisco de Asís* Mission Church, *Ranchos de Taos.* (Archdiocese of *Santa Fe.*)

a recess that contains another reredo with nine panels. This is a *retablo colateral* or side *retablo,* with multiple smaller *retablos* within it. The lowest center panel shows a carving of Christ on the Cross, with a female saint on either side of Him. The eight remaining panels contain *retablos* painted on wood, instead of canvas. The recess area opposite this reredo does not show anything of interest, except for a large painting of the Virgin of Guadalupe that hangs high on the recess wall.

In the early 1800's, a Mexican *santero* named Molleno[52] painted the reredos and the wooden *retablos.* However, the natural colors used by Molleno started to fade with age. Hence, two modern New Mexican artists, Luis Tapia and Fred Vigil, later restored the work.

A nearby parish building contains one other item of interest and even of mystery: the Shadow of the Cross. This painting shows a life-size figure of Jesus Christ standing barefoot by the shore of the Sea of Galilee. He wears a brown robe with a light blue garment over his shoulders. The French-Canadian artist Henri Ault painted the work in 1896. Mrs. Herbert Sydney Griffin gifted the painting to the mission many years later.

The mystery arises from the apparent shadow of a cross, which appears over the left shoulder of Christ, but only in the dark!! In total darkness, the image of Christ turns into a shadow, while the sky seems to glow. The image is not constant. It appears to become dimensional. Even the shadow of the cross over Christ's left shoulder seems to come and go, or vacillate. It is unknown what causes the sky to become luminous. The painting was completed before radium was discovered. Testing for radioactivity has been negative. All known luminous paints oxidize over time, and lose their luminosity. Yet, this mysterious painting remains luminous at night, and it is more than 100 years old! Scientists have tested the soil, air and water around the artist's home, and have found no evidence of radioactivity. The painting remains a mystery. It was once housed in the mission church. However, tourists and devotees picked away portions of the painting, in the lower left corner of the piece. To protect the painting, it was transferred into the nearby parish building.

Visitors to the mission can view a 20-minute video, in the parish building. It explains the background and history of the mission church. The video also discusses the Shadow of the Cross Mystery. The painting is housed in the same room so that viewers can view the painting both in normal lighting conditions and in total darkness. The visitor can then ponder on this great "mystery."

"Apache Woods": *Bosque del Apache*[53, 54]

This wildlife refuge receives its name from Spanish meaning "forest of the *Apache*" or *"Apache* Wood", referring to a time when *Apaches* frequented the riverside forest and marshes here. Its official name is *Bosque del Apache* National Wildlife Refuge. It is located on either side of the *Rio Grande* at the intersection of Highway 380, Highway 1 and Interstate 25, near *San Antonio,* in *Socorro* County. Within the county, the entire refuge comprises a total of 57,333 acres. However, the core of the refuge is composed of 3,800 acres of the *Rio Grande* flood plain and an additional 9,100 acres of farmland and wetlands. Being a major flood plain for the *Rio Grande,* the refuge reduces the effect of heavy rains on the surrounding areas and towns. Driving loops and hiking trails are made available to visitors. Some 377 different species of bird have been observed at the refuge. See Figure 10-33.

The wetlands are a refuge for cranes and geese during the winter months. Other species include waterfowl, shorebirds and birds of prey. Both the wetlands and the wildlife attract great visitor interest throughout the year. The diversity of birds reaches peaks in spring and fall. However, the best time of year to observe the greatest number of birds is between November and February. During this time up to 10,000 Sandhill cranes and over 20,000 Ross and Snow geese can be seen *en masse*. The sight is truly incredible and awe-inspiring, as sights of this many free birds is no longer a customary nor frequent sight in our over-developed civilization.

Figure 10-33: *Bosque del Apache, Socorro.*

"High" Adventure on the *Cumbres & Toltec* Scenic Railroad

Seeking "high" adventure? Check out the *Cumbres & Toltec* Scenic Railroad in northern New Mexico. This attraction advertises itself on their website[55] as "America's Highest and Longest Coal-fired Steam-operated Narrow-Gauge Railroad."

Further, the same website home page[56] states: "The *Cumbres & Toltec* Scenic Railroad is hidden away in a little-known corner of the southern Rocky Mountains, and is a precious historic artifact of the American West. Built in 1880 and essentially unchanged since, the C&TSRR is the most outstanding and best known example of steam era mountain railroading in North America. The *Cumbres & Toltec* Scenic Railroad is known around the world for its spectacular scenery, unique machinery, and historic structures."

From *Chama*, New Mexico, this narrow gauge railroad[57] crosses the *Rio Chama* and then climbs towards the *Cumbres* ("Crests or summits") Pass at a height of 10,015 feet, the highest point of any U.S. railway. After crossing the pass, the train then proceeds to the halfway point at Osier, *Colorado*. Here it meets up with a train coming in the opposing direction from *Antonito* ("Little Anthony"), *Colorado*. From Osier the two trains each continue forward to their termination points, exchanging returning passengers. The trains run daily between late May and mid-to-late October. The trip is made by steam locomotive and takes about six hours. Visitors may take the round trip

Figure 10-34: High Adventure on the *Cumbres & Toltec* Scenic Railroad.
(With permission of the *Cumbres & Toltec* Scenic Railroad and Roger Hogan,
Photo taken by Roger Hogan.[58])

between *Chama* and Osier, or they may take the full trip from *Chama* to *Antonito*, with return via charter bus to *Chama*. See Figure 10-34.

Besides providing six different travel options, which cover starting or returning from *Chama*, *Antonito* or Osier, by bus or train, there are three different train travel classes available to choose from.[59] These include coach class, tourist class and parlor class, with coach class being the least expensive and the most common. Parlor class is chosen for a highest level of comfort, but with a correspondingly higher fare price. Children (ages 2 through 12) are allowed at reduced fares. Children under 2 years of age are admitted for free. Snacks, films and gifts are available for all classes. The train also has an Open-Air *Gondola* or Observation Platform to allow travelers to view the spectacular scenery and breathe the air while making the trip.

This high adventure allows one to experience travel on the old narrow gauge rail system via steam locomotive, as in a bygone era. It also allows one to experience the crossing of the *Rio Chama*, and the climb to *Cumbres* Pass, while enjoying the natural beauty of the surrounding dramatic scenery. For more information, visit their website at: www.cumbrestoltec.com
or, one can reach the *Cumbres & Toltec* Scenic Railroad at the following phone number: 1-888-286-2737.

Hubbard Museum of the American West: *Ruidoso* Downs, NM

This unique museum is dedicated to capturing the essence and artifacts of the Old West. Located in *Ruidoso* Downs, this site has displays of various types of carriages, wagons, stagecoaches and horse-drawn vehicles spanning hundreds of years. It also displays some of the riding and ranching gear of the settlers and ranchers, including spurs, bits, bridles and saddles.

Outside, in front of the museum are beautiful life size statues of various horse breeds: standard, Morgan, Arabian, American paint, Appaloosa, American Quarter and Thoroughbred. These statues comprise the "Free Spirits at Noisy Water" display created by David McGary.[60]

The museum also has displays on various aspects of Native American culture, Hispanic culture and American Pioneer culture. It is an educational resource, not only for visitors and tourists, but also for schoolchildren. Kids love the place and it is often frequented by local schoolchildren as a field trip. There is an interactive learning center for kids called "Friends, *Amigos* and *Chuune.*" They often present special events, performances and demonstrations of cultural and historical interest. It is an enjoyable experience for anyone interested in New Mexico's multicultural past.

The museum is open daily from 9 am to 5 pm. More information can be obtained by calling: (575) 378-4142 or visit their website at: www.hubbardmuseum.org A few hundred feet away from the museum is the Billy the Kid Scenic Byway, another interesting place to visit and view.

New Mexico's Death Valley: *La Jornada del Muerto*[61]

This is the Spanish name given to a 110-mile barren stretch of desert that runs north from Fort Seldon, (just northeast of *Las Cruces*) to the area just southeast of *Socorro.* This strip lies at the northern end of the White Sands Missile Range. This inhospitable and barren valley lies between two sets of mountains in the east and two mountain ranges in the west. In the south, the *San Andrés* Mountains form the eastern edge, and the *Caballo* ("Horse") Mountains form the western edge of the valley. However, further north, the *Oscura* (" Dark") Mountains bound the valley in the east, while the *Fra Cristóbal* ("Brother Christopher") Range bound it in the west. The *Rio Grande*, the river of life, flows just beyond the western slopes of the two western mountain ranges.

In contrast, *La Jornada del Muerto* is essentially uninhabited. It is a land of death separated from life by a few arduous miles over the blocking *Caballo* and *Fra Cristóbal* Mountains. This empty void is given its gloomy and dreaded name because it truly is a valley of death. There is no water for sustenance, no grazing for livestock, no firewood for warming in the cold desert evenings and no shelter from the burning sun. The blazing heat in the summer months is intense. Water is tantalizingly close… yet so very, very far!! The name *La Jornada del Muerto* means "the day's journey of the dead man" or "trail of the deadman", in Spanish. It might also be interpreted less literally as "the journey of death." The Spanish *Conquistadors* named the region. To the early *Conquistadors* and Spanish Colonial settlers crossing this barren hostile region to head northward, the region was fraught with all kinds of terrors, and difficulties, especially when they were on horseback or had oxen driven wagons full of belongings and foodstuffs. It usually took several days to a week to cross, in spite of its relative flatness. See *La Jornada* statue set, Figures 10-6a through 10-6c in Chapter Ten, which portrays both the courage and the struggles of the early Spanish Colonial settlers.

The first northward crossing of this hostile landscape brought the early *Conquistadors* to a small thriving agricultural *pueblo* village. It was not one of the Seven Cities of *Cibola* that they expected, but their relief was so great that they named the *pueblo, Socorro*, which is Spanish for "help" or "relief."

To give a sense of the deadliness of this desert area, it is useful to note that just after the *Pueblo* Revolt of 1680, the Spanish Colonials, as well as members of the *Socorro, Estancia Basin* and the northern *Isleta pueblos*, evacuated their *pueblos* and fled south to *El Paso del Norte*[62] (modern day *El Paso*, Texas). The path they took was through *La Jornada del Muerto*. Of the 2,000 people who started the journey, only 1,200 survived the crossing of the dreaded valley. Even today, one needs only to see the flat, dry and barren landscape to sense the dread and deadly fear associated with the region. Nonetheless, the rugged beauty of the area and its surroundings is stunning! *La Jornada del Muerto* Volcano and the Carrizozo *Malpais*[63] Lava fields lie in the northern-most part of the region.

Because the White Sands Missile Range occupies most of this desert region, tourist access is generally unavailable, except for two specified days during the year, one in early spring, the other in early autumn. Hernce, the hostile, barren beauty of *La Jornada del Muerto* usually must be observed and admired from afar.

On an equally somber note, it is worth mentioning that the Trinity Site, the site of the first nuclear test explosion took place in the northern end of *La Jornada del Muerto*, between the towns of Carrizozo and *Socorro*. The test was conducted on July 16, 1945 within the White Sands Missile Range. It is uncanny and ironic that the world's first nuclear explosion took place in a desolate, barren but deadly place that was aptly named *La Jornada del Muerto*. One has to wonder. Was this a subconscious decision?

Ride 'em Cowboy: Rodeos

What better symbol of the American West and of the cowboy culture is there than the All-American Rodeo? New Mexico hosts many rodeos throughout the year. They can be found in rural areas, as well as in major cities such as *Santa Fe*, Albuquerque, *Taos*, etc. They are also hosted at several large Native American gatherings. Rodeos are also sometimes presented at state fairs. See Figures 10-35 and 10-36.

The name rodeo[64] is derived from the Spanish verb *rodear*, meaning "to surround" or "to go around." It is equivalent to the English term "roundup." American rodeo[65] grew out of the practice of cowboys herding cattle and other livestock. The rodeo events are based on the skills required of these cowboys in the performance of their daily tasks. Today, rodeos include competitive sports involving horses, steer and other livestock. These events have been developed to test the skills and speed of the competitors, male and female. Rodeos usually include steer wrestling, saddle bronco riding, bareback bronco riding, bull riding, barrel racing, tie-down roping and team roping. These events are usually divided into two basic groups: rough stock events and timed events. Rodeo clowns provide comic relief. They also help to steer unruly beasts away to protect fallen competitors.

Today, rodeo professionals travel throughout the country competing for large cash prizes, and of course, for fame and recognition. Some rodeos include or are even specifically set up with events and activities for young people. Rodeos are among the many events hosted at the New Mexico State Fair and the *Navajo* Nation gathering at Shiprock.

Figure 10-35: An American Tradition: Ride 'em cowboy! (Photo taken at the 2011 New Mexico State Fair Rodeo.)

Figure 10-36: Team Steer Roping at the 2011 New Mexico State Fair Rodeo.

To find a schedule of rodeo events in New Mexico throughout the year consult the following website:

www.nmrodeo.org/UPCOMING_RODEOS.htm

or go to the lower part of the page at the following website:

www.coyotesgame.com/Rodeo.html

Now THAT's a Very Large Array- *Socorro* County

Situated between the towns of *Magdalena ("Magdalene")* and *Datil ("Palm date")*, and about 50 miles west of *Socorro*, in *Socorro* County, New Mexico, the Very Large Array[66] (VLA) is a radio astronomy observatory. It is part of the National Radio Astronomy Observatory and lies on the Plains of *San Augustin*, at an altitude of 6,970 feet.

It is an array of 27 individual parabolic dish antennas that are aligned along the arms of a Y. Each of the three arms of the Y-shaped configuration is 13 miles long. The multiple antennas act in concert to behave like one giant antenna with a given aperture size. The antennas can be relocated to fixed locations, within the field, to change the array configuration. There are four common configurations that are deployed on a continual rotational basis throughout a sixteen-month cycle. For each configuration the antennas are relocated to allow the effective antenna diameter of the array to vary from its maximum to its minimum size.

Contrary to popular belief the VLA is NOT used for extraterrestrial search, but for astronomical investigations of known astronomical objects and phenomena including quasars, pulsars, gamma ray bursts, radio emitting stars, astrophysical masers, black holes, the sun and the planets, and radio galaxies, etc.

The VLA is in a remote location in the desert and accommodations are sparse. However, the VLA is open to the public throughout the year during daylight hours. There is a self-guided walking tour available. There is also a Visitor Center, which is infrequently staffed. Several films and numerous placards describe the technical aspects of the processing of the 27 antenna signals and the purpose of the Observatory. An explanation of the Enhanced VLA or EVLA is also provided. The EVLA uses advanced digital processing techniques and fiberoptics to greatly expand the Observatory's capabilities. The weather in the region is quite variable. So come prepared for possible hardship. U.S. 60 goes right through the VLA site. It's quite awesome!!

Chapter Eleven:
Native Tribes & Reservations in New Mexico

Many tourists are drawn to the fascinating and colorful traditions and ceremonies of the many Native Americans still living in modern day New Mexico, and other parts of the American Southwest. Our state is blessed with numerous Native American Reservations. Their cultures have survived even though obvious accommodation has occurred. Many of these reservations are opened to the public at various times of the year, and under certain restrictions they allow tourists to visit, and enjoy selected native ceremonies.

In New Mexico, there are nineteen Indian Reservations occupied by *pueblo*-dwelling Native Americans. In addition, there are three major *Apachean* Reservation systems, namely the *Navajo* Nation (with four non-contiguous reservations), the *Jicarilla Apache* Reservation and the *Mescalero Apache* Reservation. The Northern *Ute* stand alone as neither *Puebloan* nor *Apachean*. Instead, they are *Uto-Axtecan*, like the *Hopi* of Arizona. While the *pueblo*-dwellers were a sedentary, peaceful people who emphasized agriculture and fixed living quarters in settled villages (Sp. *pueblos*), the non-*pueblo* tribes were predominantly mobile, active, and semi-nomadic with minimal agriculture. They often frequented in raiding to supply many of their needs.

This chapter will discuss briefly each of the eight Northern Group *Pueblos*, the eleven Southern Group *Pueblos*, the four *Navajo* Reservations, the *Jicarilla Apache* Reservation and the *Mescalero Apache* Reservation. Brief discussions are also included on other tribes that have influenced the history of New Mexico but do not have reservations here.

The discussions within this chapter are organized into the following four sections:

PART A: The 19 *Pueblo*-Dwelling Tribes

PART B: *Apachean Tribes* & Reservations (*Navajo* Nation including *Ramah, Alamo* and *Tojahiilee Navajo, Jicarilla Apache, Mescalero Apache*) and *Apache* Tribes of the Past

PART C: *Uto-Aztecan* (Mountain *Ute*) Tribe & Reservation

PART D: Eastern Raiders & Traders of the Past (*Comanche, Kiowa* and *Lipan Apache*)

(Caution: Most *pueblos* and other reservations have restrictions on photographing, video or audio recording, sketching or even writing. Some *pueblos* allow these activities, with special paid fees obtained at the *pueblo* Governor's Office during non-religious events. All forbid these activities during Feast Day or religious celebrations. Violation of these rules may result in confiscation of the offending equipment. Visitors need to remain aware that we are all invited guests to these religious native celebrations and that this courtesy extended towards us should be returned with respect for the native rules and customs. The Native Americans are very gracious and their ceremonies are colorful, enjoyable and significant. It is also advisable to bring bottled water, as dehydration is quite possible while watching these ceremonies under the beating sun. Be sure to also bring some loose light covering and/or umbrella to provide shade from the sun. You also may wish to bring folding chairs for sitting.)

PART A: The 19 *Pueblo*-Dwelling Tribes

At the time of *Coronado's* Expedition, in 1540, there were approximately 70 to 90 *pueblo* villages in New Mexico. Today there are only nineteen (19)! This decrease over the centuries is due to various factors, including losses from war, drought, and decimation from exposure to European diseases. Some loss may also have been due to attrition and acculturation. Figure 11-1 shows the distribution of the nineteen *pueblos* along the various river valleys through central northern and central western New Mexico. It also shows the other tribal reservations located in the state.

Most present day reservations associated with the *pueblo*-dwelling Native Americans are clustered along or close to the east or west banks of the *Rio Grande* and its tributaries. The great river and its tributaries provide life and sustenance to the neighboring peoples and to the crops they grow, in their basically agricultural villages. All but three of the present day *pueblos* are located along the *Rio Grande* in the region spreading from Albuquerque north to *Taos*. Several other *pueblos* are located outside this region however, such as *Acoma, Laguna,* and *Zuni.* Again, please refer to Figure 11-1.

The *pueblos* are collected into two groups: the Southern *Pueblos* and the Northern *Pueblos.* The city of *Santa Fe* separates these two *pueblo* groups. The eleven Southern *Pueblos* include *Cochiti, Santo Domingo (Kewa), San Felipe, Jemez, Zia, Santa Ana, Sandia, Isleta, Laguna, Acoma* and *Zuni.* The eight Northern *Pueblos* include *Taos, Picurís, San Juan* or *Ohkay Owingeh, San Ildefonso, Santa Clara, Nambé, Pojoaque* and *Tesuque.*

Pueblo Name	Spoken Language	P	M	E	N	*Pueblo* Name	Spoken Language	P	M	E	N
Cochiti	Keres		x	x		Taos	Tiwa	x			x
Santo Domingo (Kewa)	Keres		x	x		Picurís	Tiwa	x			x
San Felipe	Keres		x	x		San Juan (Ohkay Owingeh)	Tewa	x			x
Santa Ana	Keres		x	x		San Ildefonso	Tewa	x			x
Zia	Keres		x	x		Santa Clara	Tewa	x			x
Jemez	Towa		x	x		Nambé	Tewa	x			x
Sandia	Tiwa	x			x	Pojoaque	Tewa	x			x
Isleta	Tiwa	x			x	Tesuque	Tewa	x			x
Laguna	Keres		x	x							
Acoma	Keres		x	x							
Zuni	Zuni		x	x							

Table 11-1[1]: *Pueblo* Spoken Languages and the Groups To Which They Belong.
(P = patrilineal, M = matrilineal, E = exogamous and N = non-exogamous)

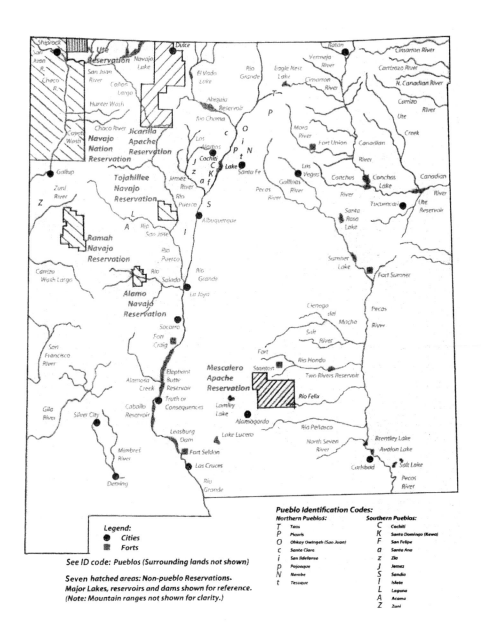

Pueblo Identification Codes:

Northern Pueblos:		Southern Pueblos:	
T	Taos	C	Cochiti
P	Picuris	K	Santo Domingo (Kewa)
O	Ohkay Owingeh (San Juan)	F	San Felipe
c	Santa Clara	a	Santa Ana
i	San Ildefonse	z	Zia
p	Pojoaque	J	Jemez
N	Nambe	S	Sandia
t	Tesuque	I	Isleta
		L	Laguna
		A	Acama
		Z	Zuni

Legend:
- ● Cities
- ▦ Forts

See ID code: Pueblos (Surrounding lands not shown)

Seven hatched areas: Non-pueblo Reservations.
Major Lakes, reservoirs and dams shown for reference.
(Note: Mountain ranges not shown for clarity.)

Figure 11-1*: Native American Reservations and *Pueblos* of New Mexico.

Most *pueblos* are named after a Spanish patron saint, which was assigned by the early Spanish monk orders. Although most *pueblos* have retained these Spanish names, others have reverted back to rename their *pueblos* in their native tongue such as *Ohkay Owingeh (San Juan)* and *Kewa (Santo Domingo)*.

Each year every *pueblo* celebrates a Feast Day in recognition of their patron saint. Surprisingly, a number of *pueblos* also celebrate the patron saints of other *pueblos*.

There are three basic language groups[2] among the nineteen *pueblos*. These three groups are: *Keres, Kiowa-Tonoan* and *Zuni*.

Keres is the most prevalent language among the southern *pueblos*. There are seven *Keres*-speaking tribes: *Cochiti, Santo Domingo (Kewa), San Felipe, Santa Ana, Zia, Laguna* and *Acoma*. In addition, one southern *pueblo* speaks *Zuni*, a language unrelated to any other *pueblo* language. The two southern *pueblos*, *Sandia* and *Isleta*, speak *Tiwa*, and the remaining *pueblo (Jemez)* speaks *Towa*. These last two languages, *Tiwa* and *Towa*, comprise two of the three branches of the *Kiowa-Tonoan* language.

The third branch of the *Kiowa-Tonoan* language is *Tewa*, the dominant language of the northern *pueblos*. Therefore, the three branches of the *Kiowa-Tonoan* language are branches are:

Towa Branch (1): *Jemez.*
Tewa Branch (6): *Ohkay Owingeh* or *San Juan, San Ildefonso, Santa Clara, Pojoaque, Nambé* and *Tesuque.*
Tiwa Branch (4): *Taos, Picurís, Sandia* and *Isleta.*

All the *pueblo*s of the Northern *Pueblo* Group speak *Tewa*, except for *Taos* and *Picurís*, which speak *Tiwa*. Table 11-1 summarizes which *pueblo* languages are associated with each *pueblo* and each *pueblo* group.

The seven *Keres*-speaking *pueblos*, the *Towa*-speaking *Jemez Pueblo* and the *Zuni*-speaking *Zuni Pueblo* are historically exogamous[3] and matrilineal[4]. These Peoples also believed that the People originally emerged from underground. The two southern *pueblos* that do not share these beliefs are the two *Tiwa*-speaking *pueblos*, *Sandia* and *Isleta*.

In contrast, all eight *Tewa*, the two *Tiwa*-speaking *pueblos* of the Northern *Pueblo* Group, and the two distinct *Tiwa*-speaking southern *pueblos* (*Sandia* and *Isleta*) tended historically to be non-exogamous[5] and patrilineal.[6] They believed that the People emerged from underwater. For example, the *Taos Pueblo* people believed that they originally emerged from the waters of the sacred Blue Lake in the *Sangre de Cristo* Mountains.

Discussions to follow of the nineteen *pueblos,* proceed first with the eight *pueblos* of the Northern *Pueblo* Group, and then with the eleven *pueblos* of the Southern *Pueblo* Group. In so doing, the order of discussion is *Taos* through *Tesuque*, and then *Cochiti* through *Zuni*. This takes us from the northernmost *pueblo* (*Taos*) in a southerly direction, and finally in a westward direction towards *Zuni*, through the extant *pueblos* of New Mexico. See Tables 11-2a and 11-2b for a summary of the facilities and recreational options available at each of the 19 *pueblos* and at each of the various non-*pueblo* reservations.

Reservation	Grp	Visitor Center	Accommodations	Fishing**	Camping	Swimming	Golf	Casino	Notes
									** with purchased day permit
1. Northern Pueblos: (NP)	NP								
Taos	NP	No	No	No	No	No	No	Taos Mountain Casino	*Taos* Indian Horse Ranch. (See *Taos* Ski Valley.)
Picuris	NP	Yes	No	Tutah L., Paan-na Pond	Yes	No	No	No	Campsites unimproved. Fishing at lake and pond w/permit.
Ohkay Owingeh	NP	No	Ohkay Resort, Ohkay RV Park	San Juan Lakes	Yes	No	No	Ohkay Casino	Nearby *San Gabriel Pueblo* remains. Fishing w/purchased permit.
Santa Clara	NP	No	*Santa Clara* Casino & Hotel.	No	No	No	No	*Santa Clara* Casino & Hotel.	Ancient Storytelling Learning Ctr. See *Puye* Cliff Dwellings.
San Ildefonso	NP	Yes	No	Small fishing	No	No	No	No	No hiking at Black Mesa. *San Ildefonso* Tribal Museum.
Pojoaque	NP	Yes	Buffalo Thunder Resort, Cities of Gold Hotel	No	No	In BTR pool only.	*Towa* Golf Resort	Buffalo Thunder Casino, Cities of Gold Casino	*Poeh* Cultural Center.
Nambé	NP	No	No	Yes	Yes	No in lake.	No	No	*Nambé* Falls & Lake. See buffalo herd.
Tesuque	NP	No	Camel Rock Suites	Tribal pond.	No	Yes only in cascade pools (3)	No	Camel Rock Casino	Tesuque Flea Market, Camel Rock. Fishing w/permit only.
2. Navajo & Apache Reservations:									
Navajo Nation (Nav) Reservation	Nav	No	No	Yes @ *Navajo* L. State Pk.	Yes @ *Navajo* L. State Pk.	Yes @ *Navajo* L. State Pk.	Yes @ *Navajo* L. State Pk.	Fire Rock Casino, Flowing Waters Casino, Northern Edge *Navajo* Casino.	*Navajo* Lake State Park. Shiprock Pinnacle.
Mescalero Apache (Ap) Reservation	Ap	No	Inn of the Mountain Gods Hotel & Casino.	Yes. See notes.	Yes.		Inn of the Mountain Gods Championship Golf Course.	Inn of the Mountain Gods Hotel & Casino. Casino *Apache*.	Ski *Apache* Resort. The Cultural Museum. *Sierra Blanca*. *Mescalero* Lake & others. Big game hunts. St. Joseph's Mission Church.
Jicarilla Apache (Ap) Reservation	Ap	No	Best Western Jicarilla Inn & Casino.	Yes See notes.	Yes			Best Western Jicarilla Inn & Casino (*Dulce*) Apache Nugget Casino.	*Jicarilla* Lake System. Enbom, Horse, Stone, *Mundo*, *Dulce*, Hayden and *La Jara* Lakes. Big game hunts.

Table 11-2a: : Facilities & Recreational Options at the 8 Northern *Pueblos*, and at the *Navajo*, *Jicarilla Apache* and *Mescalero Apache* Reservations.

Reservation	Grp	Visitor Center	Accommodations	Fishing**	Camping	Swimming	Golf	Casino	Notes
1. Southern Pueblos: (NP)	SP								** with purchased day permit
Cochiti	SP	See notes.	No	Cochiti Lake.	Tetilla Peak Rec. area only.	Cochiti Lake.	Pueblo de Cochiti Golf Course	No	See *Cochiti* Lake Visitor Center at neighboring *Cochiti* Lake. *Kasha Katuwe* Tent Rocks.
Santo Domingo (Kewa)	SP	No	No	No	No	No	No	No	*Santo Domingo* Mission Church. Annual Corn Dance.
San Felipe	SP	No	No	No	No	No	No	Casino Hollywood.	
Jemez	SP	*Walatowa* Vis. Ctr.	No	Yes. See notes.	No	No	No	No	Fishing at Holy Ghost & Dragonfly Lakes.
Zia	SP	No	No	Yes	No	No	No	No	*Nuestra Señora de la Asunción* Mission Church. (*Zia*) Cultural Center.
Santa Ana	SP	*Tamaya* Cultural Center	Hyatt Regency *Tamaya* Resort & Spa. *Santa Ana* Star Hotel.	No	No	No	Twin Warriors Golf Course. *Santa Ana* Golf Course.	Hyatt Regency *Tamaya* Resort. *Santa Ana* Star Casino.	
Sandia	SP	No	*Sandia* Resort & Casino	Yes. See notes.	No	No	*Sandia* Resort & Casino	*Sandia* Resort & Casino	*Sandia* Lakes Recreation Area. *Bien Mur* Market Ctr. *Sandia* Buffalo Preserve.
Isleta	SP	No	Hard Rock Hotel & Casino	Yes. See notes.	Yes. See notes.	No	*Isleta* Eagle Golf Course	Hard Rock Hotel & Casino / *Isleta* Gaming Palace	*Isleta* Lakes Campground. *Isleta* Lakes Recreation Area.
Laguna	SP	No	*Apache* Canyon Ranch B&B	No	No	No	No	Dancing Eagle Casino	*San Jose* Mission Church in Old *Laguna*. Guided bow & rifle hunts.
Acoma	SP	Yes	Sky City Casino & Hotel	*Acomita* Lake.	No	No	No	Sky City Casino & Hotel	*Haak'u* Museum. Elk hunts.
Zuni	SP	Yes	Inn at *Halona*	*Nutria* L., *Estacac* L., *Pescado* L., and *Ojo Caliente* L.	*Zuni* Mtn area only.	No	No	No	*Nuestra Señora de Guadalupe* Mission Church; a "must see." *A:shiwi A:wan* Tribal Museum. Big & small game hunting by permit only.

Table 11-2b: Facilities and Recreational Options at the 11 Southern *Pueblos*.

Northern *Pueblo* Group (8)

The Northern *Pueblo* Group contains eight *pueblos:*[7] *Taos, Picurís, Ohkay Owingeh (San Juan), San Ildefonso, Santa Clara, Pojoaque, Nambé,* and *Tesuque.* They all lie along or near the valleys of the *Rio Grande* or its tributaries, between *Taos* and *Santa Fe.*

Taos – Located 65 miles north of *Santa Fe, Taos Pueblo* is on the northern edge of *Taos* town. It is designated a National Historic Landmark and a World Heritage Site. From the center of *Taos* town, take the road named *Paseo del Pueblo Norte* out of town and along Hwy 64. Proceed past the *Katchina* Lodge and bear to the right at the Y in the road. This road is *Camino del Pueblo,* headed northeast. The road passes the *Taos* Mountain Casino on the left. Continue for about two miles until you enter the *Taos Pueblo* parking lot, just outside the *pueblo* village. The *pueblo* village is opened every day, Monday through Sunday. There is a small entry fee.

Figure 11-2: *Hlauóma* or North *Taos Pueblo.* (Note the multi-stored homes, the *horno* and the drying racks in the foreground.) (With permission of the *Taos Pueblo.*)

No commercial photography is allowed without special written permission and fees. Personal photographs, videographing and sketching are allowed for a nominal fee. No pictures are allowed of the nearby church interior, ceremonies or *kivas.*

Photographing individuals is not allowed without their consent. (However, photography is allowed at the *Taos Pueblo* Pow-Wow, which is not held within *pueblo* village grounds.) Tours can be set up via *Taos Pueblo* Tourism Department from April through early November.

Taos Pueblo is well known and easily recognized for its *pueblo* buildings, with inclining wooden ladders, and for the stream that runs through the center of the *pueblo* village. Of all the *pueblos, Taos* is the most photographed. See Figure 11-2. The *pueblo* village has no electricity and no indoor plumbing, in keeping with its attempts to preserve the *pueblo* as close to its ancient state as possible. The *Taos Pueblo* people speak *Tiwa,* the third branch of the *Kiowa-Tonoan* group of languages.

Taos Pueblo and town take their names from the *Tiwa* word meaning the "place of the red willow", referring to the red willows that line the banks of the central creek that runs through the pueblo. The *Tiwa* name is pronounced "*Tuah-tah*." It may alternately mean "Our Village" or "At Red Willow Canyon Mouth"[7].

The *Sangre de Cristo* Mountains dominate the skyline in the east and a small river runs through the center of the village, to supply fresh running water to the inhabitants and to irrigate the crop fields. This river or creek is called the Red Willow Creek by the *Taoseños*. Among Hispanics it is known as the *Rio Pueblo de Taos*. This small creek

Figure 11-3: *Hlauqíma* or South *Taos Pueblo*. Please note the roof access ladders and the *horno*. (With permission of the *Taos Pueblo*.)

Figure 11-4: The Bell Tower Remains of the Old *San Geronimo* Mission Church at *Taos Pueblo* (With permission of the *Taos Pueblo*.)

separates the *pueblo* into two small regions.[8] The region north[9] of the stream is called "*Hlauóma*" or "*Hlaauma*" meaning "cold elevated", while the region south of the creek is called "*Hlauqíma*" or "*Hlaukkwima*" meaning "cold diminished." The adjective "elevated" (north) or "diminished" (south) refers to the region's location. See Figures 11-2 and 11-3. The small river or creek is sourced from the sacred Blue Lake, high up in the *Sangre de Cristo* Mountains.

Only about 50 to 150 people live in the village year round. Most live in or around *Taos* town in modern homes but maintain a property within the *pueblo* for ceremonial purposes. The big Feast Day in *Taos* is *San Geronimo's* (St. Jerome's) Day, celebrated each year on September 30.

The much-photographed *San Geronimo* Church lies near the entrance to the *Taos Pueblo*. It was built in 1850. A statue of the Virgin Mary is centrally located near the altar. The *Taoseños* parishioners equate the Virgin Mary with Mother Earth. Parishioners seasonally change the colored clothing that drapes over the Virgin Mary and the surrounding saints. The church is attractive but simple in its ornamentation.

The homes in the *pueblo* have distinctive *adobe* walls, flat roofs, *vigas* and ladders. Drinking water is obtained from the *pueblo's* central creek.

In olden days and during the time of the Spaniards, the ground floors of the *pueblo* buildings did not have any doors and the exterior walls did not have any windows. Ladders were required to gain access to the roof and upper floors, and to access the ground floor rooms, which were used primarily for storage. In addition a protective wall surrounded the entire town. Today, that wall is still visible around the *pueblo* perimeter. This made the village very defensible in the event of attack.

An old cemetery can be seen to the left of the entrance, near the outside wall, but within the *pueblo*. The ruins of an old bell tower can be seen within the cemetery walls. These are the only remains of the original *San Geronimo* Church. See Figure 11-4.

During the planning for the *Pueblo* Revolt, Popay hid within the *Taos Pueblo* walls. *Taos* warriors also participated in the 1680 revolt.

Because of *Taos'* location near the mountain passes that lead to the Great Plains, *Taos Pueblo* was a trade nexus, first with the Plains Indians, then with the *Comanche* and *Apache*, and also with the Spaniards. Over time, they traded with the Mexicans and finally with the *Anglo*-American trappers, mountain men, traders and settlers.

In 1847, the local Hispanic settlers and many natives feared the recent invasion by American forces and the potential loss of their lands and rights, and so they revolted. This resulted in the *Taos* Revolt and the murder of the newly appointed American Territorial Governor of New Mexico, Charles Bent. His home can be seen as a museum in *Taos* Town.

As a consequence of this uprising, Colonel Stirling Price was sent north with troops from *Santa Fe*. The original *San Geronimo* mission church was assaulted, as it had been fortified by rebelling local *Taos Pueblo* natives. The church was eventually overwhelmed by the U.S. troops. *Taos* tribal leaders were taken to *Taos* Town *Plaza* and hanged for their part in the insurrection. The original *San Geronimo* Church was also burned, leaving only the bell tower that still stands today. Spanish priests had built this original *San Geronimo* mission building around 1619, using Indian labor. The remains of that bell tower and the adjoining cemetery can still be seen in the northwestern corner of the *pueblo* grounds.

Today, the *Taos* tribe owns and operates the *Taos* Mountain Casino, which is the only totally non-smoking *pueblo* casino in New Mexico. The casino hosts the Lucky 7 Café for light informal eating. It is located on the local road leading into the village.

Camping is not allowed in the village or at the Blue Lake Wilderness area. However, camping is permitted within nearby Carson National Forest. Since there are no accommodations these must be obtained in or around *Taos* Town. Horseback riding within the *Taos* Indian Horse Ranch allows more of the natural lands of the reservation to be seen, since otherwise such activities are not permitted. There is a small *pueblo*-style restaurant located on the *Pueblo* Road just outside the village, called the *Tiwa* Kitchen. It serves modestly priced homemade food in a *pueblo* traditional style. It has a corner fireplace and music to bring warmth to the dining experience.

There are numerous artists, art galleries and fine traditional crafts shops in the village itself or on *Pueblo* Road leading to the village. One can find fine art, micaceous and non-micaceous pottery from various *pueblos*, Storyteller pottery, silver and stone jewelry, moccasins, knives set in antler, oil paintings, wooden carvings, beadwork, wooden flutes, fine photographs and more. Be sure to check out the Tony Reyna Indian Shop located on *Taos Pueblo* Road and *Wahleah's Taos Pueblo* Gallery within the historic village.

Picurís – The *Picurís* (Pee-kuhr-ees') *Pueblo* reservation is located near *Peñasco*,[10] NM. It lies just southwest of *Taos* and east of the *Rio Grande*. It is about 60 miles north of *Santa Fe*. From *Santa Fe*, take I-84/285 north to *Española,* and then follow NM 68 up the *Rio Grande* Gorge to *Embudo*. Turn right (east) onto NM 75 and follow for about 13 miles. Finally, turn left (north) onto either of two paved village access roads.

Other than *Taos, Picurís Pueblo* is the only other *pueblo* in the Northern *Pueblo* Group in which *Tiwa* is the native language. The *pueblo* name, *Picurís*, is derived from the *Tiwa* term *Pikuri*, meaning "Those Who Paint." The Spanish explorer, colonizer and Governor, Oñate, named the *pueblo*, *Pikuria*, a name derived from the *Tiwa*.

The village is tucked away in a high valley alongside the beautiful *Rio Pueblo*. Because of its secluded location and its small size, it is less well known to visitors and tourists than many other *pueblos*. It is often referred to as the Mountain *Pueblo* or the *pueblo* in the Hidden Valley. Prehistoric ancestors once occupied this region and at one time built an impressive seven or eight story *pueblo*. The *Picurís* tribe flourished in the past because their *pueblo* is situated near two major passes through the *Sangre de Cristo* Mountains that lead onto the Great Plains. As a result, the *Picurís Pueblo* became a central trading area, where Plains tribes came to barter their goods.

After the *Pueblo* Revolt, the *Picurís* abandoned their *pueblo* site and headed onto the Plains in Kansas where they lived with their *Apache* allies. A decade later the Spaniards coaxed some of the tribal members back to the *pueblo*. Over time, disease, *Comanche* raids and other factors diminished the *Picurís*, but they are now making a comeback.

Picurís has a Visitor Center and adjoining museum. The museum features artifacts from the 1961 archeological work done on the old local *Picurís* remains. Some of the *pueblo* facilities are closed, as of this writing. Please consult with the *pueblo* (See Appendix A) before making any firm plans. Self-guided or guided tours are available.

At *Picurís Pueblo*, one can see the only multi-storied round tower *kiva* among all the *pueblos*. It was built around 1500 AD.

Photo and sketching permits can be obtained for a fee. A limited number of unimproved campsites are also available. The Visitor Center hosts the Hidden Valley Restaurant for casual meals. Accommodations however are not available. Fishing for rainbow trout is made available with a purchased day permit at *Tutah* Lake by the Visitor Center, or at *Puun-na* Pond by the entry road. Fishing is normally open between March and October. The Visitor Center has a small gift shop that displays works by local *Picurís* artists. Other artists sell arts and crafts out of their homes.

Picurís is a small *pueblo*, but it famous for its pole-climb by the *chiffonete* (northern ritualistic society) on the Feast Day of *San Lorenzo*, August 8th. In the morning, foot races are held. These are followed by various native dances, until the late afternoon when the pole-climb begins.

The *chiffonetes* clown around until it comes time to climb the 40 or 50-foot pole, which has a sheep carcass and other foodstuffs at the top of the pole. It is lots of fun to watch their antics as they try the formidable climb to the top of the massive pole. Not at all for the weak or the weak of heart!!

The *pueblo* has its own mission-style church dedicated to Saint Lawrence on the edge of the *plaza*. The architecture is typical of Spanish Colonial mission churches, with its *adobe/viga* construction and its crucifix-shaped layout. Interestingly, outside the church, on the left side wall, a *kiva* ladder reclines against the church wall and leads to the mission church roof. *San Lorenzo* Mission Church is similar in style to the mission church at the *Santo Domingo Pueblo*. Both have a small bell above the entrance and a small walled courtyard that leads to the church entry, with several cross-marked gravesites within the courtyard. A large cross stands in the front courtyard. The front top outline of the *San Lorenzo* Mission Church roof area, above the entry, was designed by a *Picurís* native. The design reminds the visitor of the shape of some *tablitas* worn by female dancers in some of the native *pueblo* dances. This same stair-step design is meant to represent cloud formations.

The walls inside the mission church are whitewashed, with the perquisite 14 Stations of the Cross portrayed in small, framed pictures along the walls, on either side of the nave. The altar is simple. A reredo lies behind the altar. It has five panels on the top half of the reredo. In the top middle there is an image of the Virgin of Guadalupe. She is flanked on either side with two *retablos* of Catholic saints. In the center of the bottom half of the reredo, there are three panels with a painting of Saint Lawrence featured in the center. He is flanked, on either side, by a *retablo* of a saint. Exposed large beams or *vigas* support the roof. These *vigas* are supported, at the top of the sidewalls, by turquoise-color painted corbels. Several wide turquoise painted beams also support the roof at other critical points.

Picurís is known for its unique micaceous[11] pottery. This pottery is made from a mica-flaked clay. Once the object is formed with the clay, it is fired without any glaze. This allows the natural beauty of the clay to present itself in an attractive golden brown pottery that scintillates in the sun.

Ohkay Owingeh (San Juan) – This *pueblo* was known as *San Juan* until recently. That was the name assigned to the *pueblo* by the Spaniards. Its name has recently been changed back to its pre-Spanish *Tewa* name *Ohkay Owingeh*, which means "place or village of the strong people." The Spanish Conquistador Don Juan de Oñate assigned the name *San Juan* (Sahn Huahn) to the *pueblo* in 1598, in honor of his patron saint, John the Baptist. The full name was *San Juan de los Caballeros.*[12] Don Juan de Oñate first settled here.

San Juan Pueblo was the home of the native leader of the 1680 *Pueblo* Revolt, Popé or Popay. He drove the Spanish Colonialists out of New Mexico, until their return in 1692 under Don Diego de Vargas. A modern statue representing this *Pueblo* leader is on display at the Capitol Rotunda in Washington, DC. Figure 4-2 presents a sketch of this large statue of Popay. A small representation of this statue can be found in the lobby of the *Ohkay* Casino, in a small casement. It stands about one foot tall. See Chapter Four, Key Historical Characters, under the section entitled *The First Revolutionary: Popay.*

The *pueblo* is located on the southern edge of *Rio Arriba*[13] County in northwestern New Mexico. It lies about 5 miles north of the town of *Española*. It can be found near the confluence of the *Rio Chama* and the *Rio Grande.* Head one mile north from *Española* on NM 68. Then turn left (west) onto NM 74. Continue one mile to the village center.

Ohkay Owingeh is the largest of the six *Tewa*-speaking *pueblos*. It hosts the Bureau of Indian Affairs Northern *Pueblos* Agency and the Eight Northern Indian *Pueblos* Council.

Game playing can be found at *Ohkay* Casino. Accommodations are available in the adjoining *Ohkay* Resort. RV's will find accommodations at the 84-site *Ohkay* RV Park. There are various tent sites for camping. Fishing is allowed at *San Juan* Lakes with purchased permits. Fish include bluegill, catfish and bass. However, there is no Visitor Center. Art galleries can be seen in the village such as the *Oke Oweenge* Crafts Cooperative, Aquino's Art Gallery and Norman Pacheco's Native American Fine Arts. Crafts. Other items such as moccasins, gourd art, jewelry and wooden flutes are for sale at Sunrise Crafts or *Pueblo* Harvest Foods. Dining is available at the inexpensive Harvest Café in the casino or at the more exclusive *El Paragua*[14] in *Española*. The site of old *San Gabriel Pueblo*, the second Spanish settlement in New Mexico, can be visited nearby and across the river. The location is indicated by a small memorial marker.

Ohkay Owingeh Pueblo celebrates its Feast Day for their patron saint, *San Juan Bautista,* on June 24th. Various dances are performed at the *pueblo*.

Santa Clara – Another popular *pueblo*, the *Santa Clara* Indian Reservation is located in *Española* near Highway 84. From I-84/285 cross to the west bank of the *Rio Grande*, then take a left southward on NM 30 south for about one mile, which leads you to the village entrance. A more scenic route is to take I-84/285 north from Santa Fe to NM 502 past the *San Ildefonso Pueblo* to the west bank of the *Rio Grande*. Continue onto NM 30 north to the village entrance. *Tewa* is the native language here.

The native name for the pueblo is *Kha-P'o*, meaning "Valley of the Wild Roses." These peoples originally inhabited the prehistoric *Puyé* Cliff Dwellings[15] in *Santa Clara* (Sahn-ta Clah'-ra) Canyon. The site was abandoned after a drought in the 16th century. The cliff dwellings are located above the present village, in a canyon of the *Pajarito* ("little bird") Plateau. Several hiking trails are available that lead from the canyon floor up several ladders to the *mesa* top, where the remains of a four-story *pueblo* can be seen. Guided tours are available April through September, and self-guided tours are open daily, year round. Take NM 30 south to Mile Marker 5 and then onto Forest Service Road 602. The ancient *pueblo* site is seven miles further on a gravel road. See Chapter 10 for a discussion of the *Puyé* Cliff Dwellings.

The Ancient Storytelling Learning Center makes available various select tours and custom outings to the *Puyé* Cliff Dwellings, the village, artists studios, pottery making demonstrations, or even traditional feasts at a tribal member's home. The price varies with the nature of the tour. Singing Water Gallery also provides tours. The numerous shops and galleries located in the village, cater to native *pueblo* art, pottery, jewelry, and various crafts.

At *Santa Clara Pueblo*, *pueblo*-style homes are loosely scattered around the central dirt floor *plaza* where tribal dances are held. There is an above-ground square *kiva* on the edge of the *plaza*. During tribal dance celebrations dancers emerge from and return to the *kiva*. A Roman Catholic mission church lies nearby.

The annual *Santa Clara* Feast Day (Saint Claire) celebration held each August 10th is conducted within the central *plaza* of the *pueblo*. Usually several different dances are performed. The scale is smaller than *Santo Domingo's* but there may be several dance groups performing different dances at the same time in the several pockets of the *plaza*. The dancers are very colorful, with the women wearing beautiful *tablitas* and various different costumes, and the men also wearing different costumes throughout the event. During this celebration, the visitor may see several different dances performed, such as an abbreviated Corn Dance, a Rainbow Dance, a Summer Dance, a Winter Dance, *Comanche* Dance, etc. The program varies from year to year. However, the color and beauty is spectacular. Listen carefully, and one can sense the subtle changes in the dance rhythms. The dancers adjust their foot movements to the changes and hesitations in the primal rhythms. If you get the chance, be sure to see the Feast Day celebration at *Santa Clara* on August 10th. You won't be disappointed!

Many *pueblo* residents work in nearby *Los Alamos* National Laboratory, but a significant number of artists and craftsmen reside and work in the *pueblo*. These artists developed the original black-on-black pottery that has since been promoted in *San Ildefonso*.

Several distinctive pottery styles are attributed to the *Santa Clara Pueblo*, including redware and black pottery styles, the widespread use of deep carving in the pottery and the shallower *sgraffiti*[16] etching style. Redware and blackware use the same clay. Blackware is fired using manure to create a deep smoke. The porous pottery absorbs the carbon smoke.

The tribe operates the *Santa Clara* Casino & Hotel, on the north side of *Española*. Please keep in mind that photographs and sketching on the *pueblo* grounds is allowed only with a purchased fee, on non-Feast Days. However, neither is allowed on Feast Days!

San Ildefonso – The *San Ildefonso* (Sahn eel-deh-fohn'-so) Indian Reservation is located between *Pojoaque* and *Los Alamos*, just 25 miles northwest of *Santa Fe*. From *Santa Fe*, take 84/285 north for about 19 miles, then turn west onto NM 502. Continue

Figure 11-5: *San Ildefonso* Mission Church at *San Ildefonso Pueblo.*
(By permission of *San Ildefonso Pueblo.*)

another 6 miles and turn north (right) onto BIA 401, the village access road. Take this to the Visitor Center in the village. *San Ildefonso* is a popular sight for many tourists, especially those near *Santa Fe*. The village is set in a beautiful and scenic setting. The *pueblo's* central *plaza* is large and very suitable for the numerous ceremonials that are open to the public throughout the year. Figure 11-5 shows the Mission Church at *San Ildefonso Pueblo.*

The native name for the *pueblo* is *Po-who-ge,* meaning "Where the Water Cuts Through." The natives are *Tewa* speakers who were originally settled around *Mesa Verde*, CO and later Bandelier, NM. Some time in the past they moved south to several villages that have since been abandoned. The present village dates from the 1300's.

The tribal government does not support development of gaming or tourist-oriented facilities on the reservation. As a result, many of the *pueblo* residents work off the reservation, or they work in the *pueblo* as artists, artisans and craftsmen, making pottery, jewelry and other items. *San Ildefonso* is renowned for its distinctive black-on-black pottery that can fetch prices in the six figures! However, the *San Ildefonso* artists also make other forms of pottery. These include beautiful redware and polychrome vessels that are smoothed and carved into varying forms, figurines or pottery. A common theme in their pottery is the *Avanyu* water serpent. Its rippling spine represents the summer rain clouds and its forked tongue signifies lightning.

San Ildefonso celebrates its Feast Day on January 23 usually with Buffalo, *Comanche* and Deer Dances. Tourists find the *San Ildefonso Pueblo* irresistible. Perhaps it is because of their unique world famous black-on-black pottery or maybe it is because of their ceremonial dances. Either way it is a *pueblo* worth visiting.

San Ildefonso's Tewa Visitor Center is available on the reservation but it is quite

Figure 11-6: Black *Mesa* at *San Ildefonso Pueblo.*
(By permission of *San Ildefonso Pueblo.*)

small. There is also the *San Ildefonso* Tribal Museum, which displays old photos of tribal activities, artifacts and examples of local arts and crafts. Informative displays show the process of making pottery. Several high quality shops and galleries can be found on the village *plaza*, displaying fine examples of pottery, jewelry, animal figurines, belt buckles, etc.

On the north side of the huge *plaza* there is a massive and extremely impressive cottonwood tree. It must be about 8 feet in diameter. You can't miss it! There is also a round above-ground *kiva* in the middle of the *plaza*.

There are a number of restrictions at *San Ildefonso Pueblo*. The central *plaza*, *kiva* and church are off-limits even with the paid fee. The *pueblo* provides no dining or other accommodations. These can be found in nearby *Española* or *Santa Fe*. Picnicking at the fishing ponds is permitted but camping is not. The *pueblo* does however allow fishing in the small fishing ponds, with a purchased permit. Swimming is prohibited, as is hiking to the Black *Mesa*, the *Rio Grande* or other reservation sites. Sketching is prohibited at this *pueblo*, although for a small dollar amount a permit will allow photography. Again, no recording of any kind is permitted on their Feast Day celebration.

The Black *Mesa* is considered sacred ground. This volcanic outcropping lies very close to *San Ildefonso*. Figure 11-6 shows a view of Black *Mesa*, from near the *San Ildefonso Pueblo*. This side of the *mesa* is less steep and more scalable than other sides of the *mesa*. Black *Mesa* was used as a bulwark against the Spaniards in the *Pueblo* Revolt of 1680. The people retired to the top of the Black Mesa, seeking safety on its heights above the valley below. In this way, they were able to resist the Spaniards. To this very day, Black *Mesa* is beautiful, majestic and quite impressive.

Figure 11-7: *Prayer at Nambé Falls, Nambé.***
(Photo by Edward S. Curtis, c. 1925, Courtesy Palace of the Governors
Photo Archives (NMHM.DCA) neg. # 144709.)

Nambé – This reservation lies just north of *Tesuque*, off 1-84/285, and just south of *Española.* It is 20 miles northwest of *Santa Fe* off 1-84/285. From 1-84/285, turn east (right) onto NM 503. Continue for 3 miles to the *pueblo* entry road towards *Nambé* Falls. This road is NP 101 and is named *Poechunu Poe.* To proceed to the *pueblo,* you must shortly afterwards turn right onto an unpaved road that takes you to the village *plaza.* Here, on the left side of the small *pueblo plaza,* there stands a circular *kiva.* Less than 100 yards away, to the right of the *kiva* there is the Catholic church of St. Francis of Assisi. A small cemetery lies perpendicular to the church on its left side.

To proceed instead to the scenic *Nambé* Falls or the *Nambé* Lake, stay on NP 101 for about 5 miles. This brings you to a small entrance hut called the *Nambé* Falls Ranger Station. Here a small fee is charged for entry. The road straight ahead leads higher up to *Nambé* Lake. The dirt road to the right leads to the parking area for the falls. The *Nambé* are also *Tewa* speakers.

"*Nambé*" in *Tewa* means "People of the Round (or bowl-shaped) Earth." It was once an important trading center for many northern *Pueblo* Peoples. They celebrate the Feast Day of St. Francis of Assisi on October 4. Buffalo and Deer Dances are usually performed during this annual event.

During the Spanish Conquest of the Southwest, *Nambé* was the main cultural and religious center for the *Pueblo* Peoples. Hence, the Spaniards tried unsuccessfully to destroy *Nambé.* Today, about 1,800 people call *Nambé* home. The patron saint of *Nambé* is St. Francis of Assisi.

Although *Nambé* is quite close to *Santa Fe*, it is off the beaten track for most tourists. However, it is located in a beautiful setting among the foothills of the *Sangre de Cristo* Mountains. The location has a stream running through it and a triple cascade waterfall.

In 1974, the U.S. Bureau of Reclamation built a dam on the *Rio Nambé*. This caused the tribal prehistoric lands and ruins to be flooded but it also created *Nambé* Lake. The lake area is reached via the left entry road at the Ranger Station. The lake is usually open daily in the warm weather months. The view from the lake area is spectacular, especially looking westward towards the *Rio Grande* river valley and surrounding areas. Fishing for rainbow trout in the lake is permitted with purchased permits. Swimming however is not allowed. Stream fishing is also forbidden. Hiking and picnicking are popular. Camping facilities with 12 RV sites and tent sites are available at the foot of *Nambé* Falls Canyon.

The lower entry road on the right at the Ranger Station leads to a parking lot and to several trails that go alongside the *Nambé* Falls and Creek, or go slightly above it. Several hiking trails are indicated. A small sign greets the visitor in *Tewa* with "*Bepuwaveh Nanbé Owìngeh!*" or "Welcome to *Nanbé Owìngeh!*" There is a hiking trail that takes one along the small creek on the left. If one is willing to wade in the shallow creek waters, one can reach the small pool at the bottom of the lowest and smallest cascade of the falls. Figure 11-7 shows a photograph taken by Edward S. Curtis, showing a prayerful offering by a *Nambé* native at the pool just below the lowest cascade of *Nambé* Falls. The photograph was taken over 100 years ago, but the natural beauty and serenity of the site has not changed. Wading and swimming is allowed in each of the pools at the bottom of each cascade, even though swimming is forbidden in *Nambé* Lake!

One may instead cross the creek via a footbridge near the parking lot, and choose one of two hiking trails to view the higher cascades of the falls. There are a total of three cascades. The lowest is also the smallest, only four or five feet high. The lowest cascade is reached by taking the lower trail through the creek, mentioned earlier. The two higher cascades are much more dramatic, falling much farther. To see them best it is necessary to take one of the hiking trails higher. The climb is manageable but can be somewhat arduous and steep near the top of the trail. The trails do not however go all the way to the summit or even to the lake. They terminate at a point just high enough to view the higher cascades of Nambé Falls. However, the view is spectacular and well worth the hike!

Nambé provides no Visitor Center and no dining facilities or accommodations. The tribe does however maintain a small buffalo herd for spiritual reasons. Tours can be arranged to see the herd through the Governor's Office. Photography or sketching of ceremonies is prohibited, although these activities are permitted of non-ceremonial subjects for personal purposes with the purchase of a photo permit. *Nambé* has no formal art galleries although some artists do sell out of their homes. There is no casino associated with *Nambé Pueblo*. This reservation is quiet and less well known, but its natural beauty and setting is a sight to behold!.

Nambé Falls and *Nambé* Lake are beautifully preserved. The region is serene and peaceful, in a naturally beautiful setting!! Most years, a colorful Native American ceremonial is held at *Nambé* Falls on the Fourth of July weekend. It is open to the public. However, schedules can change without notice, so please check on-line before planning to attend this ceremonial.

Pojoaque – This small *pueblo* is located on the outskirts of *Santa Fe*, off I-84/285 North, slightly east of the *Rio Grande*, and south of *Nambé*. To get there, take I-84/285 northwest from *Santa Fe* for about 15 miles. Exit the highway at the stoplights that appear at Gutierrez or Viarrial Streets. The village center lies on the ridge above the highway. The village access road, County Road 109, is at the end of the Cities of Gold Casino grounds.

Tewa is spoken here by a limited number of natives, but attempts to revive the language are underway. The native name for the *pueblo* is "*Po-suwae-geh*", meaning "Water Drinking Place." It is the smallest of the *pueblos*, both in land and population. Much of its land has been lost to Hispanic and *Anglo*-American settlers. It almost

Figure 11-8: *Pojoaque Poeh* Cultural Center.
(With permission of *Pojoaque Pueblo*)

ceased to exist until the *pueblo* was re-established in 1933. Photography and sketching are not allowed. Also, there are no tours available, nor is camping permitted. The patron saint is Our Lady of Guadalupe (*Nuestra Señora de Guadalupe*). The patron saint Feast Day is celebrated on December 12th.

The *Pojoaque* Visitor Center has a large collection of pottery from many different *pueblos*, traditional and contemporary jewelry, stone and bronze sculptures, *Hopi kachina* dolls, Storyteller clay figurines and other native items. The Visitor Center also holds native dances occasionally on weekends, so please call the center in advance. The *Poeh* ("pathway") Cultural Center and Museum provides educational programs in traditional arts and crafts...but to natives only. The museum is open to the general public and exhibits the work of *Pojoaque* and other northern *pueblo* artists and artisans.

The *Poeh* Cultural Center has a walk-thru exhibition, featuring numerous dioramas, in various rooms that portray the developmental journey of the *Pueblo* Peoples from ancient pre-historic times, through pre-Columbian times, the Spanish Conquest of the Southwest and colonization, into more modern times. It gives the native perspective on this development. See Figure 11-8.

The *Pojoaque* (Poh-hwa-kay) tribe owns and operates the Cities of Gold Casino as well as the newer and more modern Buffalo Thunder Resort/Casino. The Cities of Gold Hotel has 125 guest rooms, the Gold Dust Restaurant, conference rooms and a gift shop. The Golden Buffet located within the casino provides modestly priced meals. The Cities of Gold grounds include a 36-hole golf course. The name of the casino and hotel is a play on the legend, the Seven Cities of Gold, and the modern quest for riches at the slot machines and gaming tables within.

The newer Buffalo Thunder Resort/Casino features 395 luxury rooms decorated in a Southwestern *pueblo* style. Outside the front entrance to the hotel stands an impressive bronze statue of a Buffalo Dancer, sculpted by George Rivera, while in the main lobby there are other native exhibits. The resort features the *Wo'P'in* Spa, an outdoor pool lounge and the 36-hole *Towa* Golf Resort. The casino provides 1,200 slot machines, 18 gaming tables, and a poker room. Fine dining is available at the Red Sage Restaurant, with more casual dining at the *Pueblo* Deli, Turquoise Trail Bar & Grill, or at the Lobby Bar. Buffet meals are available at the Painted Parrot Buffet.

On the second floor above the casino one can find some extraordinary sculptures, by George Rivera. These include a female Butterfly Dancer with a tapestry of feathers down her back, and a male Deer Dancer, leaning forward on two sticks that represent the deer's forelegs. These are in the wide walkways where some fine shopping and restaurants are available. The resort also hosts regular entertainment from first class national headliners.

George Rivera is not only a very fine sculptor. He is the current Governor of the *Pojoaque Pueblo*!

Tesuque – Called *Te-tsugeh* by the native Tewa speakers, it means "Narrow Place of Cottonwood Trees." The reservation is located just 5 or 10 minutes north of *Santa Fe*, via I-84/285 North. Take I-84/285 North from *Santa Fe* for about 6 or 7 miles. Take Exit 172 off the highway (on the right). Cross under the I-84/285 overpass to the frontage road, that runs alongside I-84/285 South. After 1.9 or 2.0 miles, take a left onto Tribal Road 806. Half a mile down the road, cross the *Tesuque* Creek. *Tesuque Pueblo* lies straight ahead. A right turn leads towards the village *plaza* and church. The reservation is set along the *Tesuque* Creek. Two and three story *adobe* buildings enclose the central *plaza* with its Catholic Church. The *Tewa Tioux* Gallery displays and sells native jewelry, pottery, embroidery, drums and *pueblo*-style weavings. Most tribal residents work off the reservation, in *Santa Fe*.

Photography and sketching are prohibited, as is camping. Purchased-permit fishing at a tribal pond is allowed for trout: rainbow, brook, cutbow and German brown. Aspen Ranch, permits fishing and picnicking within the *Sangre de Cristo* Mountains.

Tesuque celebrates its annual *San Diego* Feast Day on November 12th. Various dances are performed at the *pueblo*.

Tesuque is known for its drum makers and for the production of small brightly

Figure 11-9: Camel Rock, *Tesuque*. (With permission of the *Tesuque Pueblo*.)

painted clay figurines called Rain Gods. Other artisans create jewelry, weaved handcrafts, painting and beadwork. *Tesuque* also operates the *Tesuque* Flea Market, also known as the *Santa Fe* Flea Market. This is an outdoor bazaar, just off I-25, near the outdoor *Santa Fe* Opera House.

The *Tesuque Pueblo* runs the Camel Rock Casino and the Camel Rock Suites. Access to the natural landmark, Camel Rock, after which the casino and suites are named, is open to the public on the other side of I-84/285. See Figure 11-9 for a photograph of this natural formation, Camel Rock.

Southern *Pueblo* Group (11)

Eleven *pueblo* tribes are included in the Southern *Pueblo* group.[17] These are *Cochiti, Santo Domingo (Kewa), San Felipe, Jemez, Zia, Santa Ana, Sandia, Isleta, Laguna, Acoma* and *Zuni*. *Cochiti* is the northernmost *pueblo* in this Southern *Pueblo* Group. *Zuni* is the furthest west and the furthest from the *Rio Grande* Valley

Cochiti – The *Cochiti Pueblo* is located around the *Cochiti* Lake area, just northeast of the *Santo Domingo Pueblo*. It is south of the Bandelier National Monument and just north of I-25. It lies just southwest of *Santa Fe*. To get there, take I-25 Exit 264, followed by NM 16 to NM 22, and then to BIA 84. The village is 3 miles further south. It is located within Sandoval County and northeast of *Santo Domingo* on the western side of the *Rio Grande* just below White Rock Canyon.

The *Cochiti* (Koh'-chee-tee) are the northernmost speakers of the *Keres* language. Their native name is *Katyete* or *Ko-chits,* meaning "stone people." In past times, these people built an extensive irrigation system of ditches or *acequias* to bring life-bringing water from the *Rio Grande* to their crop fields of corn, alfalfa, beans, squash and fruit trees.

In the early 1970's an earthen dam was built across the *Rio Grande* just upriver from *Cochiti*. This 5.3 mile long dam is one of the ten longest earthen dams in the world. When the dam was built *Cochiti* homesites had to be relocated. Sacred sites were also flooded and permanently covered with the waters of the newly created *Cochiti* Lake. The lake is actually a large reservoir created by the dam.

The *Cochiti* Dam backs up the water from the river, far up into the White Rock Canyon. The dam prevents flooding in the Albuquerque area. In the flooding season, two overflow dams hold the excess floodwaters. These dry dams are located in *Jemez* and *Galisteo*. During the dry season, these two rivers are normally dry, but they receive overflows from the *Cochiti* Lake/Dam, when excessively heavy rains or excessive snowpack melts come down from the *Colorado* mountains. In April 2005, excessively hot weather in *Colorado* caused huge amounts of snowpack to melt. The *Rio Grande* is sourced in *Colorado*. These waters eventually reached the lake, formed by the *Cochiti* Dam. *Cochiti* Lake rose 26 feet over a four-day period. Water was released gradually over the next few weeks, avoiding a possible flood in the Albuquerque area.

Cochiti Lake is now a popular recreational site for restricted swimming, fishing, sailing and windsailing. See Figure 11-10 for a view of *Cochiti* Dam and Lake from the *Cochiti* Dam Visitors Center.

The *Cochiti Pueblo* itself has no Visitor Center. Neither tours nor accommodations are available. However, there is a small Visitor Center, operated by th BLM, overlooking the *Cochiti* Dam. Camping is available at the *Tetilla* Peak Recreation Area on the east side of the *Rio Grande*. Simple fare is available at the restaurant in the clubhouse of the *Pueblo de Cochiti* Golf Course.

There is also a modest mission church on the *pueblo* grounds.

In 2001, *Kasha Katuwe* Tent Rock National Monument was created and located on federal grounds west of the *pueblo* lands. The monument protects a formation of

Figure 11-10: *Cochiti* Dam and Lake, *Cochiti.*

tipi-shaped rocks carved into a mountain of volcanic tuff.[18] The foothills along the cliff face are dotted with Ponderosa pine, juniper and *piñon*. *Cochiti Pueblo* and the Bureau of Land Management co-manage this site. This monument is discussed in Chapter 13.

The Storyteller[19] pottery motif was initiated at *Cochiti*. To this day the *pueblo* is world famous for its attractive, heartwarming Storyteller pottery. On July 14 *Cochiti* celebrates its Feast Day of Saint Bonaventure (*San Buenaventura*). A Corn Dance is usually performed in celebration.

Santo Domingo (Kewa) – The *Santo Domingo* (Sp. Saint Dominic) *Pueblo* is known for its turquoise jewelry and for the annual Corn Dance performed on August 4th. More recently, they have renamed themselves the *Kewa Pueblo*. This *pueblo* is located immediately northeast of *San Felipe Pueblo* on the eastern bank of the *Rio Grande*, and southwest of *Cochiti,* southwest of *Santa Fe*. Take I-25 to Exit 259, and head west on NM-22 into the *Rio Grande* Valley. Cross the small bridge and circle under it, and then proceed about one mile to the village center.

Keres is the spoken language of the *Santo Domingo* (Sahn'-toh Doh-meen'-go) *Pueblo* residents. The *Keres* name *Kewa* means "*pueblo*" or "village." This *pueblo* is reluctant to promote tourism or visitation. It is more closed than some other *pueblo* communities. As a result, there are no tours, no accommodations, no camping and no recreational facilities.

Of interest is the mission style *adobe Santo Domingo* church. As mentioned in the discussion of the *San Lorenzo* Mission Church in *Picurís*, the *Santo Domingo* Mission Church is similar in structure. It too has a small courtyard enclosing the entry area to the church. A small bell tower stands above the entry. There are a few crosses in the sides of the courtyard marking gravesites. The mission church is laid out in the shape of the crucifix with whitewashed *adobe* walls and exposed *vigas* supporting the roof. The Stations of the Cross also appear on the sidewalls of the nave. The front altar is again simple in design and structure.

The *pueblo* has a long central *plaza* that runs approximately on an east-west axis. There are two above ground circular *kivas*. One lies on the eastern end of the *plaza,* the other lies more than halfway down the *plaza*, in a westerly direction from the first *kiva*. During the annual *Santo Domingo* Feast Day celebration on August 4th, when the famous Corn Dance is performed, thousands of visitors come to view the dance celebration, which consists of hundreds and sometimes more than a thousand dancers. Visitors and viewing villagers gather on either side of the long *plaza,* and on the balconies and roofs of the *pueblo* houses lining the *plaza*. They also gather around the base of the easternmost *kiva*. Vendors are set up on the dirt streets leading to the plaza. Here, vendors sell pottery, moccasins, *pueblo* kilts, native-crafted jewelry, native pottery from various *pueblos,* paintings, and other items of interest. Other vendors sell food and refreshment.

During the Feast Day, native residents graciously open their homes to the incoming visitors, offering meals and refreshment. No writing, sketching, photography or recording of any kind is tolerated. Violation may result in confiscation. Asking too many probing questions is not well tolerated. It could result in being asked to leave. This is done in the interest of maintaining and conserving their traditional culture. So please respect the wishes of the *pueblo*, as visitors are merely guests, and have an obligation to be respectful of the hosts' wishes. See the discussion in Chapter 12 of the Corn Dance for more information on the famous *Santo Domingo* Corn Dance.

In 1598, Spanish Governor Don Juan de Oñate called on the 38 *pueblo* governors at the time to pledge allegiance to the Spanish Crown. This first gathering occurred at *Santo Domingo Pueblo*, and it continues today with the All Indian *Pueblo* Council holding its initial meetings of the year here.

A famous *Santo Domingan*, Alonzo Catiti, led the *Santa Domingo Pueblo* and other *Keres*-speaking *pueblos* in the 1680 *Pueblo* Revolt. However, Catiti died in a battle fighting De Vargas, in 1692.

Historically, the *Santo Domingans* have been known as traders and as exemplary beadmakers. Today, they are still known as excellent "*heishi*" bead makers. This term comes from a *Keres* word meaning "shell", because shells were a common material used in the past for the fabrication of beads. *Heishi* beads are recognized by their tubular-style or pill-shaped beads.

San Felipe – The *San Felipe* (Sp. Saint Philip) Indian Reservation lies just northeast of *Santa Ana,* and on the western bank of the *Rio Grande*. The *pueblo* lies off I-25 Exit 252, 3 miles west on the *pueblo* access road and on the west bank of the *Rio Grande*. It is located just south of the *Santo Domingo Pueblo*. The *Keres* name for the *San Felipe Pueblo* is *Katishtya*, meaning "sticky earth place." *San Felipe Pueblo* lies near the *Rio Grande.*

The *pueblo* is famous for its annual Green Corn Dances. *Keres* is the native language of the people of *San Felipe* (Sahn-Fay-lee'-pay). It is one of the least frequently visited *pueblo* villages. There is no Visitor Center, no accommodations, no camping and no recreation. The *pueblo* celebrates its *San Felipe* Feast Day on May 1st each year. On this day they celebrate with the Green Corn Dance. As with so many of the previously mentioned *pueblos*, photography and sketching is strictly prohibited on the reservation.

The *San Felipe Pueblo* owns and operates Casino Hollywood located immediately off I-25 Exit 252. At the same location there is a Travel Center that includes the *San Felipe* Restaurant, the R & T 4-Way Shopper and Grill and the Travel Center Gift Shop.

Jemez - *Jemez* (Hey'-mez) is the only *pueblo* where *Towa* is spoken. It is located in Sandoval County, a few miles northeast of the town of *San Ysidro,* on the southwestern corner of the *Santa Fe* National Forest. To get there, one takes I-25 to *Bernalillo,* and then takes the exit for US 550 North & West. This road is followed for about 23 miles, until one passes the turn off for the *Zia Pueblo*. Continue a few miles beyond the *Zia Pueblo* turnoff, until the White *Mesa* appears on the left. At *San Ysidro,* near the 23-mile marker, take a right turn onto NM 4 heading north. The village is set in the deep and dramatic *Cañon de San Diego*, alongside the *Jemez* River. Some residents of *Jemez* are ancestors of the occupants of the old abandoned *Pecos Pueblo*. See the discussion of the *Pecos* National Historical Park in Chapter 13.

The native name for the *pueblo* is "*He-mish*" meaning "the people." The historic main village of *Jemez* is generally closed to the public, except on special celebration days, such as the annual Feast Day celebration of *San Diego* on November 12th, when various native dances are performed.

There are no accommodations within *Jemez Pueblo*. These can be found a little further north in the very attractive nearby town of *Jemez* Springs. This beautiful resort town is located north of the *Jemez* Reservation. The *Jemez Pueblo* allows fishing for trout, channel catfish and largemouth bass at Holy Ghost and Dragonfly Lakes, with purchased day permits. Guided tours are available to various art galleries or to nearby natural wonders such as *Jemez* State Monument, Soda Dam, *Valle Grande* and Bandelier National Monument. Photography and sketching is strictly prohibited on the reservation, but is permitted at the *Jemez* Red Rocks area.

The *Walatowa* Visitor Center is located a few miles north of *Jemez* village on NM 4 at Red Rocks, an area of great natural beauty, with its red rock formations. The center has a small museum, gift shop, conference rooms and restrooms. Fine examples of art, jewelry, pottery and other native crafts are available here. *Jemez* village is called *Walatowa*, meaning "the place", in *Towa*. *San Diego de Jemez* Mission, built in 1880, resides in the village.

Jemez pottery is known for its black-on-red and black/red-on-tan coloration. Artisans create Storytellers, clay Corn Maidens emerging from ears of corn, jewelry, beadwork, embroidery, belt weaving and sculpture.

Zia – This *pueblo* is located about 35 miles northwest of Albuquerque. It lies within Sandoval County in two non-contiguous areas, one northwest of *San Ysidro* and the other southeast of the town. Access to the *pueblo* village is obtained by heading north on I-25 to *Bernalillo*, where one takes the exit to US 550 North and West. *Zia Pueblo* lies 17 miles west on US 550, on the village access road. The turnoff occurs just before the White *Mesa* appears on the left on US 550 North. Figure 11-11 shows the White *Mesa, Zia*. The *Zia* community lies at the foot of the *Jemez* and *Nacimiento* Mountains.

The *Zia Pueblo* people have decided not to develop any gaming or tourist-oriented facilities on their land, probably to help preserve their culture and to reduce the inevitable acculturation. *Zia Pueblo* is set upon a rocky ledge overlooking the *Jemez* River valley below.

The *Zia* also speak *Keres*. The *Keres* name for *Zia* is *T'siya*. The people believe that they originally came south from the Four Corners area of the American Southwest. New Mexico's state flag uses the distinctive *Zia* sun symbol. The film *All the Pretty Horses* was filmed on *Zia* lands.

This *pueblo* is known for its distinctive pottery, which often implements a motif that includes a large "open-eyed bird with split tail", outlined in black but filled with a tan brown or orange brown color.

There are no accommodations provided at *Zia Pueblo* and camping is forbidden. Tours are not available. A small 30-acre lake is nearby that allows angling year round for catfish in the warm months and trout in the cold months, with purchased permits. Row boating is available. There is a small Cultural Center that displays *Zia* artifacts and describes *Zia* history. The *pueblo's* church named *Nuestra Señora de la Asunción*[20] is also worthy of note. Our Lady of the Assumption Feast Day celebration,

Figure 11-11: White *Mesa,* alongside U.S. 550, on *Zia Pueblo* lands.
(With permission of *Zia Pueblo*)

associated with *Nuestra Señora de la Asunción,* is observed on August 15th. A Corn Dance is usually performed. There are no gaming facilities at the *Zia Pueblo.*

The nearby White *Mesa,* off U.S. 550 is located on *Zia* Lands. It can be seen as far away as Mile Marker 8 on Hwy 550. The white appearance of the *mesa* is due to the high concentration of gypsum in the soil (similar to White Sands). Dirt biking is allowed on White *Mesa.*

Santa Ana – The *Santa Ana* (Sp. "Saint Ann") *Pueblo* lies north of I-25, and north of *Bernalillo,* in Sandoval County. Take Exit 242 on I-25 to get on to US 550 North and West. Take this road about 2.5 miles north to *Tamaya* Boulevard, opposite NM 528, to reach the tourist facilities. To reach the *pueblo,* continue northwest on US 550 for an additional 8 miles. Signs on the right point to the *pueblo* access road. The *Santa Ana puebloans* probably originated from the Four Corners area of the American Southwest.

Spaniards named this *pueblo Santa Ana* (Sahn'ta Ah'na). However, the native *Keres* name for the *pueblo* is *Tamaya,* meaning "in the center." As with the previously mentioned *pueblos,* photography and sketching is strictly prohibited at the *pueblo.* The *Santa Ana* Feast Day celebration takes place annually on July 26th, with various dances performances.

The *Santa Ana Pueblo* owns and operates the *Santa Ana* Star Casino with gambling tables and slot machines. The *Santa Ana* Star Hotel provides 288 guest rooms. The *Santa Ana* Golf Course is a 27-hole golf course that overlooks the *Rio Grande* Valley.

Accommodations are provided at the beautiful Hyatt Regency *Tamaya* Resort & Spa, featuring 350 guest rooms and suites, five restaurants, business meeting facilities, a beautiful 18-hole golf course, a huge 16,000 square foot spa and fitness center, three outdoor pools, a gift shop, deli, salon, culture center and tennis courts. Outside the entry to the hotel area, one is greeted by an outstanding set of bronze statues of *pueblo* natives in various stances, with two small streams of running water.

According to the art brochure[21] available from the Hyatt Regency *Tamaya* Resort, the statue set honors "both past and present generations." Sharon Fullingim sculpted this beautiful statue set. The various figures in the statue set are also described. The "grandmother dipping water out of the fountain is known as "Water Woman" and represents the *Santa Ana Pueblo's* relationship with the life-giving force of the *Rio Grande*." To the right of the grandmother stands a young farmer in a cornfield holding a hoe. He represents "the tribe's agrarian past." In the forefront of the group an old man is shown with two children. He represents the "Storyteller"…"the customary way the tribal members pass their history on to each generation." Finally, the foremost figure is "Welcoming Woman" who "with hand extended, (is) welcoming guests to the resort in much the same way her ancestors welcomed many colonists and travelers to the *pueblo*." The statue set is beautiful and truly welcoming! The Hyatt Regency *Tamaya* Resort is stunning with fine facilities and awesome scenic views. Drop by. But be warned, you may not want to leave!!

This beautiful resort offers children's programs and horseback riding. It also provides a nature trail along the *Rio Grande*. The *Tamaya* Cultural Center in the Hyatt Regency makes available the art, cultural legacy and history of the *Santa Ana* people. The surrounding view is exceptionally beautiful with the *Sandia* Mountains as a spectacular backdrop.

Santa Ana artists and craftspeople work in embroidery, weaving, turquoise jewelry, pottery, and in creating ceremonial dress. Their pottery is usually red clay covered with a cream-colored slip painted with geometrical designs, flowers, turkey eyes, etc.

Sandia[22]- This *pueblo* is one of the two southern *Tiwa*-speaking *pueblos* and it is located directly east of *Rio Rancho*, and butts up to the *Sandia* Mountains, and the *Cibola* National Forest. It lies on the east side of the *Rio Grande*, between the river and the forest further east, in the region between *Bernalillo* in the north and Albuquerque to the south. It can be reached by taking I-25 Exit 234 onto NM 556, and then proceeding west for 2 miles. Then take NM 313 north for 3 miles to the entrance. It is located west of I-25. A brown signpost on the right side of the road, near the adjacent railroad tracks, indicates that the *Sandia Pueblo* turnoff is very near, just down the highway. The signpost refers to the *pueblo* by its native name, *Tuf Shur Tia*, meaning "green reed place." The entrance is one-quarter mile further down the road. It requires crossing the railroad tracks on the right.

The Spaniards named the *Sandia* Mountains, and hence the *pueblo*, after the watermelon-colored hue given to the mountains by the setting sun. The *Sandia* Casino is located at a different site on the *pueblo* grounds, with a spectacular view of the *Sandia* Mountains as a majestic, natural backdrop. It is located on the eastern side of Interstate 25.

The *Sandia* people are among the very few *Pueblo* Peoples who still weave willow and yucca baskets. *Sandia* artisans also create traditional redware pottery and new ceramic-style pottery. The *San Antonio de Padua* Church stands at the north end of the village. There is no Visitor Center and no tours. Camping is not allowed. Photography is prohibited in the *pueblo*.

The *Sandia* Lakes Recreation Area on the *Sandia* Reservation allows fishing.

There are three small lakes that allow fishing for trout, catfish and smallmouth bass. A small convenience shop sells bait and tackle. A fee is charged for fishing on the lakes. It has hiking trails that meander through the surrounding cottonwood trees that line the east bank of the *Rio Grande*. It is a "must see" attraction. The area teems with wildlife birds in particular, such as geese, ducks, blue herons, songbirds and bald eagles. The lakes are located just off NM 313, one mile north of NM 556.

Wonderful accommodations can be found at the beautiful *Sandia* Resort and Casino. This resort is located off Tramway Boulevard, Exit 234, on I-25. This resort/casino lies east of I-25. The building architecture of the resort/casino is crescent-shaped and in *pueblo* style. Outside the hotel entrance there is a beautiful statue of a *pueblo* Deer Dancer, sculpted by Estella Loretto. In front of the hotel entrance on the right of the casino is a magnificent golf course and a spectacular frontal view of the *Sandia* Mountain Range. The resort/casino houses many slot games and gaming tables, informal eateries, a spa, a sports bar, a lounge and several restaurants. The lounge has two beautiful statues of *pueblo* women in traditional garb. The resort also has a huge amphitheater that showcases entertainment headliners. The hotel portion has hundreds of guest rooms and suites. *Bien Shur*, (meaning "Blue Mountain," in *Tiwa*), features a first class restaurant with a stunning view of Albuquerque and the surrounding area. It is especially spectacular at night when the city lights up.

The *Bien Mur* ("Big Mountain", *Tiwa*) Market Center is a "must see" tribally-owned arts-and-crafts shop. High quality native-crafted items can be purchased here. The facility is round and *kiva*-shaped. It is located next to the 107-acre *Sandia* Buffalo Preserve, across Tramway Boulevard from the casino/resort. More than 20 bison are on the preserve. Each year *Sandia Pueblo* celebrates its *San Antonio* Feast Day on June 13th in honor of its patron saint, Saint Anthony. A Corn Dance is usually performed.

Isleta[23] - The other *Tiwa*-speaking southern *pueblo* is *Isleta*. The *pueblo* name *Isleta* (Iz-let'-tah) was assigned by the Spaniards, which means "little island." The *Tiwa* name for the *pueblo* is *Tuei*, meaning "little island", as in Spanish. This refers to the *pueblo's* proximity to the *Rio Grande*. Although the river is more controlled today, at one time the river would create wide floodplains that isolated the *pueblo* village in a sea of water.

The *Isleta* inhabitants were originally of *Shoshone*an stock, and called themselves *Shiewhibak*, which means "knife laid on the ground to play with." The *Isleta* Reservation lies southwest of Albuquerque, but primarily in *Bernalillo* County, although parts do extend into Valencia County. It is located on either side of *Bosque* Farms and south of I-40. It can be reached off I-25 Exit 215, and then south on NM 47 to NM 147. It extends across both banks of the *Rio Grande*, from the northern part of Valencia County in the western part of the reservation to the *Manzana* ("Apple") Mountains and the *Cibola* National Forest in the east.

Isleta has no Visitor Center, no museum, no tours and no accommodations. *Isleta* grounds do support a three-story gaming casino, the *Isleta* Gaming Palace, near the village. The *Isleta* Lakes Campground is located one mile off I-25 Exit 215 on NM 47. This site provides 40 RV spaces and 100 tent sites around three lakes situated near the *Rio Grande*. The *Isleta* Lakes Recreation Area is located along the *Rio Grande*.

Cottonwood trees lace this area. The lakes are stocked with trout, bluegill and channel catfish. Fishing is available with purchased day permits. However, wading and swimming are prohibited. For those who enjoy golfing, the *Isleta* Eagle Golf Course provides a 27-hole course that overlooks the *Rio Grande*. The *Shirpoyo* Art Gallery and Katie's Trading Post allow visitors to view or purchase quality *pueblo* art and craft items, respectively.

The beautiful new Hard Rock Hotel and Casino is also located on *Isleta Pueblo* grounds. It hosts the *Isleta* Eagle Golf Course. In addition, the resort makes available to visitors many modern accommodations, gaming facilities and headliner entertainment.

Isleta celebrates its *San Augustín* Feast Day on August 28th in honor of Saint Augustine. Various native dances are performed.

Laguna – The *Laguna* (Sp. "Lagoon") *Pueblo* spans across I-40, both north and south of the highway. It is immediately east of the *Acoma* reservation, but still west of Albuquerque. It is just west of *Isleta Pueblo* and southwest of the *Tojahiilee* (formerly *Cañoncita*) *Navajo* Reservation. *Laguna Pueblo* is located primarily within *Cibola* County. The *pueblo* reservation lands include several small villages: Old *Laguna*, Paguate, *Mesita* ("Little *Mesa*"), *Paraje* ("Rest stop"), *Encinal* ("Oak grove") and Seama. Old *Laguna* is the main village and it can be seen from I-40, on a hilltop crowned by the white *San José* Mission Church.

The *San José* Mission Church is most easily reached by taking I-40 to Exit 114. Then turn left onto *San José* Road. Take this to Friar Road and then right onto the road. This leads directly to the hilltop mission church, which overlooks the town of Old *Laguna* and nearby I-40. Although photography and sketching the *San José* Mission Church are allowed with a permit received from the Governor's Office, it is strictly forbidden elsewhere within the *pueblo*. However, it is forbidden here too on Feast Days.

The *San José* Mission Church at Old *Laguna* is a "must see" attraction. Little changed since it was first built in 1699, it stands out against a mountain backdrop, overlooking the village below. The church interior features a beautiful altar screen made by a local *santero*, carved and painted *kachinas*, pottery candleholders, a unique colorful ceiling showing the moon, sun and rainbow, and a beautiful altar floor decorated with *pueblo* designs.

Laguna (Lah-goo'-nah) *Pueblo* is named *Ka-waikah* in the native *Keres* tongue, meaning "lake people."

Local legend says that an ancient tribal leader, Broken Prayer Stick, led their people from a place called *Shipop* to a place where a beaver had dammed a small river creating a lake or *laguna*. Here the people settled and formed a small village. They named the village *Ka-waikah*. This original village most probably lies beneath Old *Laguna*.

Tribal guides conduct guided bow hunts and rifle hunts on the *pueblo* territory. *Laguna Pueblo* celebrates its *San José* Feast Day on September 19th, honoring Saint Joseph. Usually, Buffalo, Eagle and native social dances are celebrated at Old *Laguna* during this celebration.

The *pueblo* owns and operates the Dancing Eagle Casino and nearby *Apache* Canyon Ranch Bed & Breakfast which has four luxury rooms. The Dancing Eagle Supermarket features native *pueblo* arts, crafts and jewelry. The Indian Art Center also showcases art from *Laguna Pueblo* and nearby *pueblos*.

Acoma – Exit 108 for *Acoma Pueblo* lies off I-40, just a few miles west of Old *Laguna*. This exit takes you to the Dancing Eagle Casino. It also takes you to Route 22, which leads directly to the *Acoma* Reservation. It is primarily contained within *Cibola* County, although some portions of the tribal territory extend into northwestern *Socorro* County and into the northeastern corner of neighboring Catron County.

Figure 11-12: *Cliff Perched Acoma. Acoma Pueblo* atop White Rock *Mesa*
with the Enchanted *Mesa* in the right background.** (The dominant structure
on the White Rock *Mesa* top is *San Estéban* Mission Church.)
(Photo by Edward S. Curtis, c. 1904, Courtesy Palace of the Governors Photo
Archives (NMHM.DCA) neg. # 144527.)

Acoma Pueblo lies atop White Rock *Mesa*. It is one of the oldest continuously inhabited villages in the entire U.S. *Acoma* is also called Sky City. *Acoma* has no running water or electricity, so most residents live in nearby villages at *Acomita* ("Little *Acoma*"), McCarty and Anzac, along the *Rio San José*. Only about a dozen families live atop the *mesa* year round. See Figure 11-12. *Acoma* (Ah'-koh-ma) is called *Haak'u* in the native *Keres* language, meaning "to prepare or plan" or "a place already prepared."

Mesa Encantada (Enchanted *Mesa*), in *Cibola* County, was once occupied by the ancestors of the *Acoma Puebloans*. However, they were forced to abandon the site after a severe storm made the steep walls of the *mesa* unscalable. They then adopted the White Rock *Mesa*, or *Acoma*, as their new home. There is an *Acoma* legend that states that the People were to settle where the land echoed four times, in response to a call. The *Haa'ku* site answered that prophecy and so was settled by the *Acoma* People. Occupation started around 1150 AD. The original home, known in

Keres as *Kadzima* or *Katsimo*, can easily be seen from *Haa'ku* or White Rock *Mesa*, also known as Sky City.

The view from the top of the *Acoma Mesa* is stunning and well worth the trip. One can see the active volcano Mount Taylor in the north, which is currently quiet, and their former native home, known as the beautiful Enchanted *Mesa* in the south. Spectacular landscapes and geological features surround the *Acoma Mesa*. For visitors, access to the *mesa* top is only by means of a tour bus. Cars are parked at the parking lot behind the Sky City Cultural Center and the *Haak'u* Museum. This is also called the Visitors Center (VC) and it is located at the corner of *Haak'u* Road and *Kaatsiima* Drive. The tour fee includes a photo permit, the bus ride to the *mesa* top and a guided tour. It is well worth the $20 per adult or $17 per senior. The tour guide is well informed, congenial and helpful. The tour takes about one and a half hours. It includes the *mesa* top, the museum, and the mission church. Native vendors will be seen on the tour selling their wares. Tours are not available on the *San Estéban* Feast Day, September 2.

Photography is strictly limited and/or prohibited without a paid permit. Video recording or sketching are strictly prohibited, as is the use of binoculars or audio recording equipment. Video devices may be publicly destroyed, if used. Respect for the rules is absolutely essential. If in doubt, ask first! Also, be sure not to take photographs of the Enchanted *Mesa* or other features encountered on the inward trip, before first obtaining a photo permit. Violation may cause confiscation of your camera or memory card!

Visitors to *Acoma* must also observe a strict dress decency code. Out of respect for the *Acoma* residents, visitors are NOT permitted to wear "revealing" clothing such as halter or tank tops, strapless tops, high-cut shorts or high-cut skirts. VC staff will advise violators to alter attire prior to any tour to the top of the *mesa*, or, the visitor will be provided with a cover up.

Anthropologists theorize that *mesa* tops were desirable to farming peoples because they provided protection from roaming and raiding nomadic tribes such as the *Navajo* and the *Apache*, and they provided early warning because of the wide field of view from the *mesa* tops. In addition, placing religious centers atop these *mesas* was akin to building them on top of pyramids, closer to the heavens, as in the case of other Meso-American civilizations such as the *Aztecs, Mayas* or *Incas*.

Access to the *mesa* top today is by means of a paved road, but this was once a dirt road, built in the 1940's to allow a film crew and its equipment to get to the *mesa* top. For residents, the standard access to the top was and still is via a rough-hewn series of steps and stones that form a very steep pathway on the western face of the *mesa*. Handgrips have been carved into the sandstone to facilitate the steep climb or descent. This pathway is very steep and hazardous. It is not for the timid or those suffering from acrophobia! The Spaniards once built an alternate pathway on the south side of the *mesa*, but it is unused. Friar Juan Ramirez built this alternate road. He was the same monk who built the *San Estéban del Rey* Mission Church on the *mesa* top. It was built to allow horses to access the *mesa* heights. Edward S. Curtis took several photographs of this horse trail that can still be viewed today.

There is some limited drinking water from natural cisterns around the top edge of the *mesa*. Other cisterns occur towards the inhabited area of the *mesa* top, but they are not used for drinking. They are used instead for laundry, and other non-potable uses. It is interesting to note that *hornos* or outdoor ovens, at *Acoma,* are not made of *adobe,* as in most other *pueblo* villages. Instead, they are made of lava rock and sandstone with a small amount of *adobe* used as mortar. This is because *adobe* cracks with heat.

The homes on top of the *mesa* were built over many time periods and some have been reinforced over time. Centuries ago, the *pueblo* homes had no windows or doors on the ground level. Instead, a wooden ladder was used to access the building. Other ladders allowed descent into the lower rooms or to the upper levels. When enemies appeared, the ladders were withdrawn and hatches were closed. Inhabitants remained within the lower levels or fought from above, with spears or bows and arrows. Within the lower level, a fire with a vent provided warmth and some light. A small square opening, about 6 inches square, allowed outsiders to speak with the insiders.

Kivas were the native religious centers. Usually they were round in shape, in deference to Mother Earth. When the Spaniards came, the *Acomites* instead built rectangular *kivas* to mislead the Spaniards into thinking the people were entering the similarly shaped homes, and that they were not practicing their native religion. As with many other southern *Pueblo* Peoples, the *Acomites* believed that the People originally emerged from underground, at the beginning of time. Entering a *kiva* is meant to represent a return to the earth, and leaving the *kiva* represents a re-enactment of this emergence. That is one reason why the *kivas* are considered sacred.

Near the southern side of the *mesa* top, there is a natural cistern that was once used for laundry work. In addition, one can also see small natural round depressions in the surrounding rock, that enabled the women to use these depressions as *metates* to grind corn. There is only a single tree on the *mesa* top. It is a cottonwood tree and it is located right next to one of the natural cisterns. The native guide jokingly referred to this tree as the "*Acoma* forest"!

In the past, there were twenty-one (21) *Acoma* clans. Now there are only thirteen (13). The Antelope Clan was the most populous clan at the advent of the Spaniards. Since then the Antelope Clan elders have traditionally chosen the tribal leaders and officials.

The final stop on the tour is the *San Estéban del Rey* Mission Church on top of the *mesa*. Photographs of the church exterior are allowed but photography of the adjacent cemetery or of the church interior is prohibited.

It is said that initially there was great resistance to the Spaniards and to the new foreign Catholic religion. Legend has it that one time a young girl fell over the cliffside. All thought the fall was fatal. However, the young girl survived, having fallen into the arms of one of the Franciscan friars. From that day forward, converts to the new religion increased dramatically.

The building of the church was started in 1629 under the direction of the Franciscan friar, Juan Ramirez, and it took until 1640 to complete. This construction required moving 20,000 "tons" (40 million pounds) of earth and water from the valley below up the steep stone pathway to the *mesa* top! As many as 168 men and women may have died, as a result of this arduous construction process. The walls near the base of the mission church are 10 feet thick! It was built to serve as a fortress, as well as a church. The church has two tall belfry towers and very heavy entry doors.

This church is unlike many of the mission churches discussed in this book. It does not appear to be laid out in the shape of the cross, as with the *San Francisco de Asís*

Mission Church in *Ranchos de Taos*, or *El Santurio de Guadalupe* Mission Church in *Santa Fe*. There are no transepts. However, immediately above the entry, inside the church, there is a railed balcony. The interior of the church is massive, with very high (70 feet) ceilings, supported by huge round timbers or *vigas*. These timbers support the roof, resting on huge carved corbels at each end. The church interior is a large open space, with whitewashed walls and pictures of seven Stations of the Cross on either sidewall. The church nave is an open area with only three rows of pews near the front altar and several benches lined up along the sidewalls. Parishioners must stand, lean against the sidewalls, or sit on the packed dirt floor during services. Perhaps they bring foldup sitting chairs. The altar is also unique.

The altar shows a huge reredo with seven panels. Four large thick timbers are mounted vertically and they form the outer edges of the reredo. The reredo is divided into three sections, from left to right. The leftmost and rightmost sections each have two vertical panels. The center section is different. It has three vertical panels. An image of Jesus Christ occupies the single top center panel of the reredo. Below this panel, there is a painting of the Virgin Mary. *San Estéban* or St. Stephen is shown below the Virgin Mary. Images of other saints appear in the four remaining outer panels. On either side of the altar, near the front, are two very stylish and attractive parrot motifs, native symbols for beauty and essential moisture. Parrots live in the tropical rain forests of the Amazon. Hence, they are identified with rain.

The altar timbers are painted red and white, like a barber pole. Red represents the native religion. The timbers were hued from the forests on Mount Taylor. They were carried roughly thirty miles to the church, and the timbers were not allowed to ever touch the ground during transit. Upon arrival, they were then built into the huge panel set behind the altar. The altar timbers are suspended above the ground and embedded into the reredo structure. What is beyond incredible to imagine is how the natives transported these timbers, as well as the roof timbers, from their point of origin, across the many miles to the *mesa's* base, and then up the cliff faces to the *mesa* top!! There was no access road at that time! There was no use of a wheeled vehicle, either!

Each year, *Acoma* celebrates its *San Estéban del Rey* Feast Day on 2 September, with a Harvest Dance. The church is opened for this occasion. *Acoma* also celebrates the Christmas season, with various dances, from the 24th through the 26th of December.

Sadly, *Acoma* is the site of Don Juan de Oñate's alleged harsh punishment against its native inhabitants when they rebelled against the Spaniards' tribute requests, that resulted in the death of Oñate's nephew. See Chapter 5 for a discussion of Don Juan de Oñate and his alleged harsh reprisal against the people of *Acoma*. If the charges against Oñate are indeed true, he earned the eternal hatred of the *Acoma* people.

The *pueblo* operates the Sky City Casino & Hotel along I-40. Catfish and rainbow trout fishing are available at nearby *Acomita* ("Little Acoma") Lake. Elk hunts are also available in September and October.

La Ventana ("The Window") Natural Arch on Route 117 is a nearby attraction, near the northwestern border of the *Acoma Pueblo* reservation. It can be found near the eastern edge of *El Malpais* National Monument. It is actually located within the *El Malpais* National Conservation Area, which is managed separately by the Bureau of Land Management (BLM).

Acoma Mesa is unique. Even though it is located in a relatively remote location, it is well worth the visit. The surrounding landscape is simply stunning and beautiful. The view of the Enchanted *Mesa* is incredible. The people are friendly. The tour is very informative and helpful.

Zuni – The *Zuni Pueblo* may be approached from the north via NM 62 or from the east via NM 53. This second approach is the Grants-through-*Ramah* route that passes *El Morro* National Monument and other natural sights. Chapter 14 briefly discusses *El Morro* (Inscription Rock) National Monument.

The *Zuni* (Zoo'-nee) speak their own unique language, unspoken by all other *pueblo* tribes in New Mexico. *Zuni Pueblo* is the largest in both area and population, located west of the Continental Divide, and south of Gallup, near the Arizona border. The *Zuni* are known for their carved stone animal fetishes, of bear, badger, wolf and other beasts. *Zuni* silver and turquoise jewelry is distinctive.

The patron saint of *Zuni* is Our Lady of Guadalupe (*Nuestra Señora de Guadalupe*[24]). Unlike all the other 19 *pueblos*, it is the only *pueblo* that does not publicly celebrate its Feast Day. The resident Catholic population is also quite small, as native traditions still abound. In addition, the *pueblo* is not open to the public for many other traditional religious ceremonies. *She-we-na*, meaning the

Figure 11-13: *Zuni Pueblo.*** (Photo by Edward S. Curtis, c. 1925, Courtesy Palace of the Governors Photo Archives (NMHM.DCA) neg. # 144730.)

"middle place" is how the *Zuni* refer to their homeland. The *Zuni* people refer to themselves as *A'shiwi*, meaning "the flesh." The familiar name, *Zuni,* is a Spanish adaptation of the *Keres* word "*Sü/nyitsa*", whose meaning today is unknown. *Keres* is spoken by many of *Zuni's* eastern *pueblo* neighbors.

Zuni may be the oldest *pueblo* in New Mexico. Figure 11-13 shows *Zuni Pueblo,* as it appeared to Edward S. Curtis in 1925, Pit house remains, and others, dot the area and attest to the *Zuni's* long presence in the region. The current village, occupied since 1690, is called *Halonna Idi:wanna.*

Hawikku, ten miles southwest of *Zuni,* is the first *pueblo* that *Fray* Marcos de Niza and Estéban Dorantes saw in 1539, during their expedition from New Spain. The *Zuni* later killed Estéban Dorantes at *Hawikku,* after he continued forward without *Fray* Marcos de Niza. It was the first *pueblo* to be conquered during *Coronado's* 1540 Expedition. The remains of *Hawikku* ("gum leaves" in *Zuni*) *Pueblo,* have been designated a National Historic Landmark.

A small Visitor Center is located along State Highway 53, in the village of *Zuni.* Here, visitors can obtain a map of *Zuni* or photo permits. Some interesting exhibits can also be viewed here. Tours can be arranged at the Visitor Center. The *A:shiwi A:wan* (pronounced similar to Aa'-shee-wee Aa'-wan) Tribal Museum is located nearby, in the old *Zuni* village of *Halonna Idi:wanna,* (diagonally across from the *Halonna* Market). It contains displays about the *Zunis,* their history, and cultural artifacts. Many exhibits by local artists are inspired by the nearby ancestral home of the historical *Hawikku Pueblo,* encountered by *Coronado* in 1540.

The local mission church, *Nuestra Señora de Guadalupe,* was built in 1629. The mission interior is a "must see." The *Zuni* celebrate both ancient and adopted faith traditions. This is highlighted within the walls of the mission church. The inside walls of this traditional *adobe* church are so beautifully decorated, with inspired murals by *Zuni* artist, Alex Seowtewa, that some have called the mission "the Sistine Chapel of the Americas." The murals depict natural landmarks, the four seasons and life-sized *Zuni katsinam (kachinas).* The church no longer holds services but it is open weekdays 9 am to 4 pm, for tourists. It is located in the old village. To reach this mission, turn onto *Pia Mesa* ("Pious *Mesa*") Road, which is at the four-way stop on NM 53. Turn left (east) onto Sunset. Follow the river, and then turn left (north) onto Mission Street.

Four small eateries are provided within the *pueblo* grounds. The *pueblo*-style Inn at *Halona* provides the only accommodations within the village. It is a small, friendly and very accommodating eight-bedroom Bed-and-Breakfast. Gallup also provides accommodations. Camping is available in the *Zuni* Mountain corner of the reservation. Fishing is allowed at *Nutria* ("Otter"), *Ojo Caliente* ("Hot Spring"), *Estace* and *Pescado* ("Fish") Lakes, with a purchased permit. Hunting for small game, as well as deer and elk, is permitted with a hunting permit. Numerous arts and crafts shops, trading posts and galleries lie along the main street, NM 53. Here visitors can find exquisite jewelry, pottery, *kachina* dolls, hand carved fetishes, paintings and prints.

Zuni silver jewelry artists and craftsmen are among the best in the world. They are renowned for their settings of shell and stone in sterling silver. Their pieces may include turquoise, mother-of-pearl or coral. *Zuni* designs are exquisite and beautiful. Artists also engage in weaving, fetish jewelry and pottery. They are not as well known as the *Santa Clara* or *San Ildefonso Pueblos* for their pottery, but still there are some exceptional *Zuni* pottery makers. Their design motifs often include tadpoles (representing spring), dragonflies and butterflies (summer), or frogs (winter).

PART B: *Apachean* **Tribes & Reservations (***Navajo* **Nation including** *Ramah, Alamo* **and** *Tojahiilee Navajo, Jicarilla Apache, Mescalero Apache***) and** *Apache* **Tribes of the Past**

Although the *pueblo* tribes and their reservations seem to dominate New Mexico they are not the only Native American tribes or reservations in the state. Four tribes in New Mexico are non-*puebloan*. These tribes were nomadic or semi-nomadic in nature. These are the *Navajo* Nation, *Jicarilla Apache*, *Mescalero Apache* and the Mountain *Ute* tribes. The *Navajo*, *Jicarilla Apache* and *Mescalero Apache* languages are all Southern *Athabascan*, while Mountain *Ute* is *Uto-Aztec*an, as is *Hopi* of Arizona.

***Navajo* Nation**[25] - The main *Navajo* Nation Reservation is north of I-40 and Gallup, in northwestern New Mexico. It spreads across McKinley and *San Juan* Counties, and continues into western Arizona and southeastern Utah. It is the largest reservation in New Mexico. The *Navajo* often call themselves the *Dineh* or *Diné*,

Figure 11-14: *Navajos near Shiprock Monument,* NW New Mexico.**
(Photo by William Marion Pennington, c. 1909. Courtesy Palace of
the Governors Photo Archives (NMHM.DCA) neg. # 89512.)

meaning "the People." The more commonly recognized name, *Navajo*, comes from the 18th century Spaniards, who referred to the tribe as *Apaches de Navajo*, meaning "*Apaches of Navajo*." The term "*Navajo*" itself was derived from the *Tewa "navahu"*, meaning "fields adjoining a ravine." The *Zuni* name for "enemy" is "*Apachu*."

Although the traditional *Navajo* homelands are sometimes referred to as "*Dinétah*", this term generally pertains to their homeland before the "Long Walk." It refers to the lands between the Four Sacred Mountains: Mount Taylor, *Blanca*

("White") Peak, Hesperus Mountains and the *San Francisco* ("Saint Francis") Peaks. Officially, the *Navajo* refer to their current reservation lands, or the *Navajo* Nation as "*Naabeehó Bináhásdzo.*"

The *Navajo* are a matrilineal and matrilocal society,[26] with the nuclear family, descent, inheritance and identity associated with the mother's extended family.

Navajo business and government is centered in Window Rock, Arizona just a few miles west of Gallup, New Mexico. The entire *Navajo* Nation lands span approximately 16 million acres between Arizona, Utah and New Mexico. The *Navajo* are the single largest Native American group in the U.S. One-third of the *Navajo* population lives in the State of New Mexico. Many who stay on the reservation in traditional style live in octagonal shaped dwellings called hogans. The portion of the reservation that lies in New Mexico extends from the northwestern part of McKinley County, just north of Gallup into the entire western half of *San Juan* County.

The reservation even touches the Four Corners region of the American Southwest, where it butts up to the Mountain *Ute* Indian Reservation. The *San Juan* River and the Chaco River run through this northwestern region of the state and the reservation. This region also contains the Chuska Mountain Range. The famous landmark and natural wonder, Shiprock Pinnacle, lies 12 miles southwest of the city of the same name. See Figure 11-14.

Shiprock Pinnacle[27] is a volcanic peak that dominates the surrounding landscape and towers over the reservation lands. This natural outcrop features in many *Navajo* legends and it has been part of the *Navajo* homeland for eons. Shiprock Pinnacle is a solidified lava and igneous rock formation that rises 1,700 feet above the surrounding lands. It is called *Tse be dahi* in the *Navajo* tongue, which means "rock with wings." *Navajo* legend says that this mighty rock formation was once a great bird that transported the *Navajo* to their current lands from the North.

The *Navajo* were driven from their lands in January 1864 and forced to march 300 to 450 miles to an encampment at Fort Sumner called *Bosque Redondo*, or "Round Wood", in the *Pecos* River Valley. Many *Navajo,* young and old died on this harsh trek that came to be known as the "Long Walk." After a failed experiment to "domesticate" the *Navajo* and turn them into farmers, they were returned to their homeland in June 1868.

It is a testament to their inner strength, tenacity and courage that the *Navajo* people today have not only survived but that they have preserved their culture, while adopting the American capitalist approach to develop timber, mining and other business enterprises that ultimately benefit the lives of all the people of the *Navajo* Nation. The original treaty granted the *Navajo* Nation 3.5 million acres of their original homeland. One and one half centuries later the *Navajo* Nation comprises 16 million acres, more than quadruple the original reservation size. Numerous Presidential Executive Orders and confirmations by Congress granted additional lands between 1868 and 1934. The tribe also purchased other lands to expand their domain. It is a true success story.

The *Navajo* have more natives speaking their language (just under 200,000) than any other tribe in the U.S. *Navajo* is classified as a Southern *Athabascan* language, which is linguistically related to northwestern Canadian and Alaskan forms. The U.S. Armed Services in World War Two, enlisted native *Navajo* speakers as Code Talkers. The Japanese were never successful in decoding their coded messages, transmitted in the *Navajo* language. See the discussion in Chapter Three, on the patriotic contribution of the *Navajo* Code Talkers during World War Two.

The *Navajo* have shown themselves to be a very enterprising people. Besides their many commercial businesses, farming and herding, there is still a very strong artistic element that thrives in today's world. The *Navajo* people are known for their exquisitely beautiful silver and turquoise jewelry, that is world-renowned. In addition, their sand paintings originally constructed on the bare sand for healing and religious ceremonial purposes, but since produced on wooden backings for hanging and commercial display, are appreciated throughout the world for their primitive but colorful imagery and beauty. The paintings are made with different colored sand and they portray native religious and other symbols such as the Thunderbird, Yei, rain pools, lightning bolts, maidens, rainbows, etc. *Navajo* rugs with similar motifs and others with unique patterns, are also sought the world over. Figure 11-15 shows a *Navajo* weaver, photographed by Edward S. Curtis around 1904.

Whereas the rest of Arizona does not observe Daylight Savings Time (DST), the *Navajo* Nation does observe this time change, mainly because the reservation extends into two other states, Utah and New Mexico, which do observe DST. Most *Navajo* ceremonials are closed to the public, except for the single annual public celebration held at Shiprock in September or October each year, called the *Navajo* Nation Fair. It is held at the Shiprock Fairgrounds. *Navajo Yei bei chi* dancers usually perform at this annual event.

Figure 11-15: *Blanket Weaver-Navajo.*** (Photo by Edward S. Curtis, c. 1904. (Library of Congress, Rare Books Division, Edward S. Curtis Collection.)

Initially opposed to developing gaming resorts and casinos on *Navajo* lands, agreements were eventually reached among the various tribal organizations and governing bodies. A referendum was presented to the tribal people proposing to allow gaming in six *Navajo* locations, four in Arizona and two in New Mexico. This original agreement was reached in June 2006.

Because of recent casino[28] successes the plans were extended and modified somewhat. Since the initial agreement, the *Navajo* Nation opened its first casino in November 2008 just east of Gallup, NM and it is called Fire Rock Casino. It has been very well received. Building on their initial success with the Fire Rock Casino, the tribe has opened a second casino called the Flowing Waters Casino. This location is in Hogback, NM and the casino is built near a sandstone rock formation called the Hogback. The *Navajo* name *Tse Daa K'aan* of the location translates as "rock ground into water." The Flowing Waters Casino has more limited gaming options than at Fire Rock Casino. For example, there are no card games, and slot machines play against each other, instead of against the house. A third casino was built near Farmington and it is called the Northern Edge *Navajo* Casino. Additional plans call for three more casinos to be built in Arizona: at Twin Arrows, Arizona, 20 miles east of Flagstaff, another in *Navajo*, Arizona on Pinta Rd off I-40 and yet another in Chinle, Arizona. These casinos will hopefully bring an economic boost and employment to the locals in these areas, and provide fine entertainment to visitors.

The *Navajo* Nation owns and controls three other reservations within the *Navajo* Nation. The *Ramah, Alamo* and *Tojahiilee Navajo* Indian Reservations are not physically contiguous with the main reservation, but are part of the extensive *Navajo* Nation.

Ramah Navajo Indian Reservation – This *Navajo* Reservation is a non-contiguous part of the *Navajo* Nation, and comes under its jurisdiction. It is located in *Cibola* County, between the towns of *Zuni* and Grants, New Mexico. It lies just a few miles east of the *Zuni* Reservation.

Alamo ("Cottonwood") Navajo Indian Reservation – This site is located in northwestern *Socorro* County, adjacent to the southeastern part of the *Acoma* Reservation. The reservation has about 2,000 native residents. This *Navajo* reservation is also a non-contiguous part of the *Navajo* Nation, and comes under its jurisdiction.

Tojahiilee Indian Reservation – This reservation is the third remaining non-contiguous part of the *Navajo* Nation within New Mexico, and it comes under the jurisdiction of the *Navajo* Nation. It lies in *Bernalillo* County, just north of I-40, a few miles west of Albuquerque. It was formerly known as *Cañoncita* or "little canyon."

Jicarilla Apache[29, 30, 31, 32] Reservation – This *Apache* Reservation is located in west of north central New Mexico. It extends down from the Colorado border, to the region around Cuba, New Mexico. It is found primarily in *Rio Arriba* County, and northwestern Sandoval County. Headquartered at *Dulce* ("Sweet"), it is 90 miles east of Farmington, on Hwy 64. It is one of two *Apache* reservations in the state.

The term, *Apache*, was assigned to various "*Apache*" tribes by their enemies, the *Zuni*. The *Zuni* name for "enemy" is *"Apachu."* It may also have its roots in the *Yuma* Language meaning "fighting men." The *Jicarilla Apache* language is an Eastern Southern *Athabascan* language. This indicates that at one time, in the 1300's to 1500's, they came south from Canada.

Before the coming of the *Comanche*, the *Jicarilla Apache* were ascendant in the territory that stretched across western Kansas, Oklahoma, Texas and southeastern Nebraska. They were semi-nomadic, meaning they engaged in seasonal agriculture along the river valleys that crossed their territory. Mainly, they were quite mobile, moving from place to place. They also hunted antelope, deer and buffalo on the Great Plains. They were very successful raiders, even though they only used dogs as pack animals. Their raiding success increased with the coming of the Spaniards and the introduction of the horse. However, the *Comanche* and the *Ute* came in the 1700's and eventually drove the *Jicarilla Apache* off the Great Plains.

During their decline in the late 18th century they started to encroach into the *Sangre de Cristo* Mountains area of New Mexico. They became allied with the *Pueblo* Peoples, the Spanish settlers and their former enemies, the *Ute*. Their territory shrank to the region bounded by the Four Sacred Rivers: Arkansas River, Canadian River, *Rio Grande* and the *Pecos* River.

After they were driven off the Plains, the *Jicarilla Apache* were split into two large clans: the *Olleros* (Sp. "potters", pronounced "oh-yer'-ohs") and the *Llaneros* (Sp. "plains people", pronounced "yah-nehr'-ohs").[33] The *Olleros* settled in the mountainous regions of northern New Mexico and southern *Colorado* as farmers. They became potters and lived in villages that were similar to their neighbors, the *Pueblo* Peoples. They also came to be called *Hoyeros* meaning "mountain-valley people." Among other *Apache*, they were known as the *Sai T'inde* or "Sand people or Mountain people." They planted and harvested corn, squash, beans, pumpkin, peas, wheat, tobacco and cantaloupe using irrigation methods, learned from the *Pueblo* Peoples.

The *Llaneros* continued to live on the plains of eastern New Mexico, eastern *Colorado* and Texas as nomads, living in *tipis*, or *"kozhan"*, in the *Jicarilla Apache* language. Here they hunted bison like the Plains Indians. The *Llaneros* were called the *Kolkhahin* or *Gulgahen*, in their native language. The *Jicarilla Apache* refused to aid the U.S. military in their attempts to locate *Geronimo*, the notorious *Chiricahua Apache* from southern Arizona.

Jicarilla in Mexican means "little basket" or "little gourd." They are known for their fine basket making. To the other nearby *Apache* tribes, such as the *Mescalero* and the *Lipan* (Texas), the *Jicarilla* were referred to as the *Kinya Inde* or "people who live in fixed houses." All the *Jicarilla Apache* call themselves *N'de* or *Inde*, or *Tinde*, meaning "the People." The *Jicarilla Apache* are a matrilineal and matrilocal society.[34]

The present day *Jicarilla Apache* Reservation occupies about 1.5 million acres with a population of about 3,000. Almost all (95%) of the *Jicarilla Apache* population lives in *Dulce*, the tribal center near the border with *Colorado*. The reservation spans the Continental Divide in the northern regions of New Mexico.

The reservation hosts a Visitor Center with exhibits of local native beadwork and basketry. It also hosts demonstrations of artisans at work.

The reservation makes available "trophy hunts"[35] on their lands, with *Jicarilla*

Apache guides, working out of *Dulce*. Mule deer and bull elk hunts are the most popular, but hunts for turkey, black bear and mountain lion are also available. Turkey is usually best in the southwestern regions of the reservation. Black bear can be hunted in spring or fall, using either bait or hunting dogs. Mountain lion hunts usually occur in the winter, using hunting dogs for tracking in the snow. Fishing for rainbow trout with purchased permit is also permitted out of seven different lakes within the *Jicarilla* Lake System: *Dulce* Lake, Enbom Lake, Hayden Lake, *La Jara* ("The Potato" or "Rockrose shrub") Lake, Stone Lake, *Mundo* ("World") Lake and Horse Lake. Stone Lake also carries cuttroat trout and largemouth bass, when open. Check with *Jicarilla* Game & Fish at 575-759-3255 for current conditions and to see if any lakes are dry. Camping is available, but facilities are limited and vary among sites.

The tribe owns the *Apache* Nugget Casino, located on the reservation, north of Cuba, New Mexico. It also owns the Best Western *Jicarilla* Inn and Casino, which is located in *Dulce*, in *Rio Arriba* County, New Mexico.

Further visitor information can be obtained at:
Jicarilla Apache Tribe- (575) 759-3242
P.O. Box 507,
Dulce, NM 87528
Farmington information: (800) 448-1240
Casino information: (575) 759-3777

Mescalero Apache Reservation[36, 37, 38] – The *Mescalero Apache* Reservation is the one other *Apache* Reservation in New Mexico. It is located in Lincoln County, in south central New Mexico. Lincoln National Forest surrounds it on the north and south. It is centered in the town of *Mescalero*, next to the tourist town of *Ruidoso* ("Noisy"), New Mexico.

The name *Mescalero* derives from the Spanish, meaning "users of *mescal.*" The Mexican term *mescal* or *mezcal* comes from the *Nahuatl* word, *mexcalli*, meaning "oven-cooked *agave.*" The *Mescalero* collected *mescal* and used it as a fast food. See Figure 11-16. It was eaten while traversing large distances on horseback. They ground the *mescal* into a meal that was easily consumed on the move. They also used the *mescal* as a beverage and for its fiber. The *mescal* stalks were once used for *tipi* poles, until the *Mescalero* were confined to the mountainous reservation lands. They then used branches from surrounding trees instead.

The *Mescalero Apache* speak a form of the Southern *Athabascan* language. They too migrated south from Canada in the 1300s to 1500's. *Shis-Inday*, is what they call themselves, meaning "people of the mountain forests." An alternate name is *Inday* or *Indee*, meaning "the People." However, to other *Apache* tribes they became known as *Nadahéndé*, meaning "people of the *mescal*" because of their reliance on *mescal* as a food source. The *mescal agave* food source was stored and used in times of privation. It is clear how the Spaniards later called them the "*Mescaleros.*" There are ten bands within the *Mescalero Apache* tribe.

The *Mescalero Apache* have always been a matrilineal society. More recently the *Mescalero* society is becoming more patrilineal or bilateral, meaning from either the father's or the mother's side.[39] However, the mother's side is still more heavily favored.

Figure 11-16: *Cutting Mescal-Apache.*** (Photo by Edward S. Curtis, c. 1906. Library of Congress, Rare Books Division, Edward S. Curtis Collection.)

The *Mescalero Apache* were raiders and a semi-nomadic people. About five hundred *Mescalero Apache* were rounded up in 1864 by Carlton and brought to the *Bosque Redondo*, next to Fort Sumner. They were corralled together with about 8,500 of their enemy, the *Navajo*. After several years of failed crops, disease, starvation and infighting between the two tribes, the *Mescalero Apache* began to leave in small groups and returned to their homeland around *Sierra Blanca*. Santana, the great *Mescalero Apache* War Chief, secured the mountainous part of their homelands in an agreement with the U.S. Government that became the core of today's reservation.

The present day reservation occupies about 400,000 acres and consumes most of *Otero* ("Hillock") County, although reservation lands are also in Lincoln County. The reservation has a population of about 4,000. These lands enclose the sacred *Sierra Blanca* ("White Mountain") Mountain and the sacred *Sacramento* Mountains. The *Mescalero* opened their arms to the *Chiricahua Apache* who had been exiled to Fort Sill, Oklahoma after the *Apache* Wars ended, and to the *Lipan Apache* of western Texas. Many now live on the *Mescalero Apache* Reservation.

The *Sierra Blanca*, at 12,000 feet offers excellent skiing and snowboarding at the *Mescalero*-owned and operated Ski *Apache* Resort. The small Cultural Museum, located on Hwy 70 in *Mescalero*, describes the culture and history of the *Apache* people.

Rainbow trout, brook trout and brown trout fishing are available at any of several lakes and streams that run through the reservation lands. Big game deer and elk hunting with *Mescalero* hunting guides are also available. Camping is permitted.

The *Mescalero* tribe owns and operates the Inn of the Mountain Gods Resort/ Casino, in *Mescalero*, just outside *Ruidoso* in Lincoln County, New Mexico. The site is truly beautiful, overlooking the man-made *Mescalero* Lake that is dominated by the towering and majestic *Sierra Blanca*, and surrounded by imposing and beautiful tall pines and spruce, of various kinds. The resort is a four diamond rated facility with spacious lodging, world-class entertainers, first-rate dining which includes Wendell's Restaurant, skeet shooting, and miles of walking trails and riding trails. The grounds also sport an 18-hole golf course alongside *Mescalero* Lake. Pedal boating on the lake is available.

The interior lobby of the resort has fine displays of original paintings and sculpture works by native artists. The displays are beautiful and informative, if one takes the time to view them and learn about them. Alongside the stairway that takes the visitor downstairs to a bar and lounge area, there is giant replica of a *Mescalero* Medicine Basket, with a placard explaining it. The view across the Medicine Basket, out the huge set of glass windows, is a spectacular scene showing the towering *Sierra Blanca*, the surrounding pines below it and the *Mescalero* Lake. Out in front of the resort entry stands a beautiful bronze statue set of *Mescalero Apache* Crown Dancers to welcome the visitor to the Inn of the Mountain Gods Resort/Casino.

Inside there is a modern casino, with slot machines, gaming tables and a bar. The *Mescalero Apache* tribe also runs and operates the older Casino *Apache* on Highway 70, located in *Mescalero*, near *Ruidoso*.

At certain times of the year, images of Mountain Spirit or Crown Dancers can be seen on the altar cloth covering the altar of St. Joseph's Catholic Church in *Mescalero*. This shows how both native and Christian traditions have managed to become merged over time among the native *Mescalero Apache*.

Apache Tribes of the Past in Southwestern New Mexico

There were several *Apache* tribes that roamed or, in some cases, settled in the southwestern regions of New Mexico. These included the White Mountain, *Gila*,[40] Warm Springs[41] and the *Chiricahua*[42] *Apache*. The White Mountain *Apache* once lived in New Mexico. However, they were transported to the *San Carlos* Reservation and the Fort *Apache* Reservation in Arizona in the mid 19th century. The *Gila Apache* occupied the area west of *Socorro* and around the *Gila* River in southwestern New Mexico, even extending into Arizona. In 1853, they were then rounded up and transported to Fort Webster in Arizona.

The Warm Springs *Apache*[43] were actively engaged in the *Victorio* Wars and later in the continuing *Apache* Wars under the leadership of Nana. They belonged to the *Chihene* ("Red Paint") Branch of the *Chiricahua Apache*. Many were transferred to the *San Carlos* Reservation in Arizona. Others were killed with *Victorio* in 1880 at *Tres Castillos* ("Three Castles") in Mexico. The *Chiricahua Apache* also continued to fight the U.S. during the *Apache* Wars. Both *Chiricahua* and Warm Springs *Apache* were killed in the continuing *Apache* Wars, until *Geronimo's* surrender in 1886. Those few remaining Warm Springs *Apache* and *Chiricahua Apache* were exiled first to Florida and later to Fort Sill, Oklahoma. There is no *Apache* Reservation assigned for the Warm Springs *Apache* or the *Chiricahua Apache*, presumably because of their prolonged opposition to U.S. subjugation. In later years, the *Mescalero Apaches* opened their arms to welcome these *Apache* to live on the *Mescalero Apache* Reservation.

PART C: *Uto-Aztecan* Tribe & Reservation (Mountain *Ute*[44, 45])

The Mountain *Ute* Reservation extends down from *Colorado* in the north and it touches the northern end of the *Navajo* Nation in the northwestern part of New Mexico. It is located in *San Juan* County, New Mexico and of course, it extends down from counties within *Colorado* and Utah. The Mountain *Ute* Reservation is the smallest of the three *Ute* Indian Reservations. It is centered in *Towaoc, Colorado*. This *Ute* Reservation is populated by the historic *Weeminuche* Band. *Ute* is a *Uto-Aztecan* language. The state of Utah takes its name from this great tribe.

The name *Ute*[46] comes from the Spanish *Yuta*, which may in turn have been a corruption of "*Nuutsiu*" or "*Nunt'zi*", meaning "the People" or "the people of the mountains." It may alternately have come from the Western *Apache* word *Yudah*[47], meaning "high up."

PART D: Eastern Raiders & Traders of the Past (*Comanche, Kiowa* and *Lipan Apache*)

Comanche[48]

The *Comanche* migrated into the northeastern part of New Mexico in the early 1700's. They obtained breeding stocks of horses from the *Pueblo* tribes, after the *Pueblo* Revolt of 1680. The horse became a central and crucial factor in the subsequent development of *Comanche* trade and culture. They gained a reputation as the best horsemen in the U.S. and were known as formidable fighters on horseback.

They both traded and raided the northernmost *pueblos* such as *Taos* and *Pecos,* and other settlements along the *Rio Grande* Valley, for horses, corn and slaves. *Gran Quivera,* in central New Mexico was also a big trading center. After a strong show of Spanish force against the *Comanche* in 1779, by Governor Juan Bautista de Anza, raiding stopped and relative tranquility gradually came. A peace treaty was agreed upon at the *Pecos Pueblo* in 1786, between the *Comanche* and the Spanish in New Mexico. Subsequent to this peace treaty, the *Comanchero* trade began to flourish.

The name *Comanche* has been attributed to the *Ute*, who called these nomadic people "enemy" or "*kimmantsi*" or "*kohmahts*" meaning "enemy"[49] or "those who are against us", in the *Ute* language. The *Comanche* referred to themselves as "*Nemene*"[50] or "*Numinu*" meaning "our people" or "the People." The *Comanche* were a patrilineal and patrilocal tribe.[51]

Comanche natives served in World War II in the Atlantic Theater, as Code Talkers against the Germans in Europe. Charles Chibbity[52, 53] was the last *Comanche* Code Talker. He died on July 20, 2005 at the age of 83 years.

The *Comanche* never really settled in New Mexico, in any significant numbers. Being a nomadic tribe, they were frequently on the move. They were only raiders and traders in New Mexico. No reservation was assigned to the *Comanche* in New Mexico.

Kiowa[54]

As a nomadic people, the *Kiowa* shared common enemies and hunting grounds with the *Comanche*, including areas of northeastern New Mexico.

The name, *Kiowa,* is derived from the Spanish name for the tribe, *Caygua* (Kai'-wah). The *Kiowa* people call themselves *Kaui-gen* or *Kaui-gu,* or possibly even "*Gaigwu.*"[55] The sign language hand-gesture used by other tribes to describe the *Kiowa* is two adjacent fingers held together and drawn from the eyes alongside the head, to just behind the ears. This was a representation of how the *Kiowa* at one time cut the hair at the side of the head, so as not to interfere or get tangled when drawing a bow. Very practical indeed!! George Catlin portrays this *Kiowa* style in a few of his paintings.

The *Kiowa* were a patrilineal tribe but the men lived with their wive's extended families.[56]

The *Kiowa* National Grasslands of New Mexico is the only indication that the *Kiowa* were present in New Mexico. These protected grasslands include 12 miles of the Canadian River Canyon. The region from Roy to Mills along Highway 39, and the Canadian River Canyon both are within the *Kiowa* National Grasslands.

The American Indian Head nickel, minted between 1913 and 1938, was partially modeled after a *Kiowa* chief and warrior, *Adoeette,* or Chief Big Tree. There is no *Kiowa* reservation in New Mexico.

Lipan Apache[57, 58] - Enemies of the *Mescalero* and the *Comanche*

The *Lipan Apache* spoke a Southern *Athabascan* language. At one time they were spread throughout Texas, New Mexico, *Colorado,* as well as the northern states of Mexico. The name *Lipan* comes from the *Lipan Apache* language. It may mean "light gray people."[59] It may come from a combination of two terms, "*kleh pai*" meaning "light grey color" and the word meaning people, "*indeh*" or "*n'dé*." This seems rather cryptic until one realizes how the *Apache* viewed the world, in a cosmological sense. They viewed the earth as a circle suspended in the cosmos at the cardinal points of direction. Each cardinal direction has an associated color: East is black, west is yellow, north is white and south is blue. In ancient times, the *Lipan Apache* migrated from the north in Canada to the east in Texas, from the white region to the black region. When white and black are mixed on the color chart, the resulting color is gray. That may be the symbolic meaning behind their otherwise cryptic name "the light gray people"!

Some sources[60, 61] claim the *Lipan Apache* called themselves "*Nizhan*" or "*Nà-izhan,*" meaning "our" or "our kind" or that the name is derived from a personal name of a great chief or warrior named, *Ipa-n'de,* where "*n'dé*" means "the People." Others claim that *Lipan Apache* really means "warriors of the mountains."[62] Lots of possibilities.

Their traditional enemies were the *Mescalero Apache* and the *Comanche.* In the 1700's, the *Lipan Apache* territory extended from Texas, west to the *Colorado* River, which included the modern state of New Mexico. Today, *Lipan Apache* natives live throughout North America, and on the *Mescalero Apache* Reservation.

Chapter Twelve:
Native American Celebrations in New Mexico

This chapter discusses *Pueblo* Feast Day and non-Feast Day celebrations, as well as the notable celebrations of the *Apachean* tribes, including those of the *Navajo* Nation, *Jicarilla Apache, Mescalero Apache*, and the Red Paint *Apache*.

Selected native dances and celebrations are described including: Basket, Bow & Arrow, Butterfly, Buffalo, Cloud, Corn, Deer, Eagle and Turtle dances, *Zuni Shalako* and Rain dances, *Navajo Yei bei chi dance*, and the *Apache* Crown or Mountain Spirit dances. An explanation is also given of the *Pueblo* Transfer of Canes, Kings' Day and Governors' Feast celebrations.

In addition, overviews are given of various non-*Pueblo* native events such as the *Navajo* Nation Fair, *Jicarilla Apache Go-Jii-Ya, Jicarilla Apache* Little Beaver Roundup, *Mescalero Apache* Puberty /Mountain Spirit Dance celebration, and the Red Paint *Apache* Pow-Wow and Indian Trade Show.

The discussions within this chapter are organized into the following three parts:
PART A: Typical *Pueblo* Celebration Schedules
PART B: Explanation of Ancient *Pueblo* Dance Cycles, *Pueblo* Dances
       Performed Today, and *Pueblo* Celebrations of New Tribal Authorities
PART C: Celebrations of the *Apachean* Peoples

PART A: Typical *Pueblo* Celebration Schedules

***Pueblo* Feast Days** – Feast Days celebrate the patron saints that were assigned to each *pueblo* by the Spanish conquerors or their missionaries. Of late, some *pueblos* are changing their *pueblo* names back to their native names. Two examples of this are *Ohkay Owingeh Pueblo*, which was formerly named *San Juan Pueblo*, and the *Kewa Pueblo*, formerly the *Santo Domingo Pueblo*. Although the Feast Days of the various *pueblos* in New Mexico occur throughout the year, most occur between June and September. The specific patron saint for each *pueblo* and the associated Feast Day are listed below in Table 12-1.[1, 2] These festivities are generally open to the public and they are very popular.

The Feast Days celebrations follow a fairly general model. Feast Day celebrations are always held on the specified date, even if it occurs mid-week. However, the events and dances performed may be subject to change from year to year. Sometimes the celebration starts the evening before the actual Feast day, with a Mass or a benediction. This may be followed the next morning by a procession from the church to the *pueblo plaza,* carrying a small statue of the patron saint. At other times, the celebration starts on the Feast Day with prayer and a Mass at the *pueblo* church. A procession bearing an image of the *santo* (patron saint) around the village *plaza* then follows, with the *santo* placed in a bower, or tented flowered shrine at the edge of the *plaza*. Celebration dances are then held shortly after this procession, and continue throughout the day into the late afternoon or evening. When dancing ends, another procession returns the *santo* to the church.

During the celebration, artists, artisans and craftspeople from various *pueblos*

Southern *Pueblo*	Patron Saint & Typical dances	Feast Day		Northern *Pueblo*	Patron Saint & Typical dances	Feast Day
Cochiti	St. Bonaventure (*San Buenaventura*) (Corn Dance)	Jul. 14		Taos	St. Jerome (*San Geronimo*) (Trade show, ceremonial foot races and pole-climb)	Sep. 30
Santo Domingo (Kewa)	St. Dominic (*Santo Domingo*) (Corn Dance)	Aug. 4		Picurís	St. Lawrence (*San Lorenzo*) (Ceremonial foot races, pole-climb & traditional dances)	Aug. 10
San Felipe	St. Philip (*San Felipe*) (Corn Dance)	May 1		San Juan (Ohkay Owingeh)	St. John the Baptist (*San Juan Bautista*) (Corn Dance)	Jun. 24
Santa Ana	St. Ann (*Santa Ana*) (Various Dances)	Jul. 26		San Ildefonso	St. Ildefonse (*San Ildefonso*) (Buffalo, Deer and *Comanche* Dances)	Jan. 23
Zia	Our Lady of the Assumption (*Nuestra Señora de la Asunción*) (Corn Dance)	Aug. 15		Santa Clara	St. Clare (*Santa Clara*) (Buffalo, Harvest or Corn Dance)	Aug. 12
Jemez	St. James (*San Diego*) (Various Dances)	Nov. 12		Nambé	St. Francis of Assisi (*San Francisco de Asís*) (Buffalo and Deer Dances)	Oct. 4
Sandia	St. Anthony (*San Antonio*) (Corn Dance))	Jun. 13		Pojoaque	Our Lady of Guadalupe (*Nuestra Señora de Guadalupe*) (*Los Matachines* Dance Drama)	Dec. 12
Isleta	St. Augustine (*San Augustin*) (Harvest Dance)	Sep.4		Tesuque	St. James (San Diego) (Various Dances)	Nov. 12
Laguna	St. Joseph (*San José*) (Various Dances)	Sep. 19				
Acoma	St. Stephen (*San Estéban*) (Harvest Dance)	Sep. 2				
Zuni[3]	Our Lady of Guadalupe (*Nuestra Señora de Guadalupe*)	N/A				

Table 12-1:[4, 5] Patron Saints and Feast Days of the 19 New Mexican *Pueblos*.
Note: Specific dances performed are subject to change.

display their wares for sale. Food and beverage booths are also available throughout the celebration. Some *pueblos* hold additional dances that are not open to the general public. Any schedule of native dances or other events that are declared open to the public may change or may even be withdrawn, without notice. Specific dances may also change, from year to year, or from *pueblo* to *pueblo*. Please confirm with each *pueblo* shortly before a scheduled event. Consult Appendix A (Contact Information for the various *pueblos* and reservations in New Mexico) to obtain contact phone numbers and current schedules of events at each *pueblo*.

Pueblos Celebrating Patron Saints' Feast Days of Other *Pueblos*

Besides celebrating their own Patron Saint Feast Day, some *pueblos* also celebrate the Feast Days associated with other *pueblos*. These additional celebrations may also vary from year to year or from *pueblo* to *pueblo*.

The most common additional Feast Days celebrated among the various *pueblos*, beyond their own Patron Saint Feast Days, are indicated in Table 12-2.

Saint's Name (Sp.)	Saint's Celebration Date	Dances
San Paolo	January 22	Various
San Antonio	June 13	Various
San Juan Bautista	June 24	Various
San Pedro	June 29	Various
Santiago	July 25	Various
Santa Ana	July 26	Various
San Lorenzo	August 10	Various
San Diego	November 12	Various

Table 12-2:[6] Additional Feast Day Celebrations

The short list in Table 12-2 is subject to change. It is presented here only as a rough guide. It is best to call a particular *pueblo*.

Other Major *Pueblo* non-Feast Day Ceremonies[7]

Pueblo dances and ceremonies are not restricted to the Feast Day celebrations. Other celebrations occur throughout the year in various *pueblo* communities. However, not all ceremonies are open to the public.

There are many *pueblo* celebrations and events throughout the year. Only the most significant events are described here.[8]

There are three occasions early in each year when the *pueblos* celebrate the new *pueblo* governorships. These celebrations are usually accompanied with dance performances at numerous *pueblos*. The three celebrations include the Transfer of Canes (of tribal governing authority) on January 1, Kings' Day on January 6, and the Governor's Feast, which occurs on the first or second weekend of February. In addition, there are other dance celebrations for Easter, Thanksgiving and Christmas.

Other dances are sprinkled throughout the year to seek good harvests or to celebrate a successful harvest. *Nambé* Falls usually holds its own unique celebration during the Fourth of July weekend each year, with the performance of various native dances.

The following dates and occasions are most often celebrated with *pueblo* dances, except for the Arts and Crafts Fairs. These dates represent the 2011 schedule, and they may change from year to year. They are presented here as a guide. Consult the Indian *Pueblo* Cultural Center in Albuquerque or see Appendix A for contact information.

Easter Celebrations:
Easter weekend: Celebrated each year with various dances held among the *pueblos*. Most *pueblos* perform the Basket and Corn Dances. However, *Nambé Pueblo* usually performs the Bow & Arrow Dance.

Summer Celebrations:
Memorial Day weekend: Annual *Jemez Pueblo* Red Rocks Arts & Crafts Show and Pow-Wow. This event kicks off the summer season.

First Saturday of June: Blessings of the Fields is celebrated at *Tesuque Pueblo* with a Corn Dance.

July 4th Celebration at the *Nambé* Waterfall: Various dances are performed on the July 4th weekend. This event can be cancelled without notice.

First weekend in July (usually). *Taos Pueblo* Annual Inter-tribal Pow-Wow: Please consult *Taos Pueblo* or the following website: www.Taospueblopowwow.com.

Third weekend of July (usually). *Ohkay Owingeh Pueblo* holds its Annual Eight Northern Indian *Pueblos* Arts & Crafts Fair.

Labor Day Weekend: *Santo Domingo Pueblo* holds its Annual Arts & Crafts Market. This event denotes the end of summer.

Thanksgiving Celebrations:
Thanksgiving weekend: *Acoma* Sky City holds its Annual Indian Arts & Crafts Show and Auction.

Thanksgiving Day: *Zuni Pueblo* conducts its Christmas Light Parade.

Christmas Eve Celebrations:
Christmas Celebrations are held at various *pueblos*. Many hold events on Christmas Eve, Christmas Day and the day after Christmas as follows:

Laguna:	24th – After 10 pm Mass. Various dances.
Nambé:	24th – Buffalo Dances after Mass.
Ohkay Owingeh:	24th - *Los Matachines* drama/dances and Pine Torch Procession.
Old *Acoma*:	24th – *Luminarias* are lit beginning at the Scenic Viewpoint and continuing as far as Sky City.
Picurís:	24th – Sundown Torchlight Procession of the Virgin Vespers Mass. Procession followed by *Los Matachines* drama and dances.
Santa Ana:	24th – Dances after Midnight Mass.
Taos:	24th – Sundown Procession with bonfires.

Tesuque: 24th – Dances after Midnight Mass.

Christmas Day Celebrations:

Ohkay Owingeh: 25th – Various tribal dances.
Picuris: 25th – Christmas celebration. *Los Matachines* dances.
San Ildefonso: 25th – *Los Matachines* dance drama.
Santo Domingo: 25th – Special Dances
Taos: 25th - Deer Dances or *Los Matachines* drama, dances.
Tesuque: 25th – Various dances.
Zia: 25th – Various Dances

Post-Christmas Day Celebrations:

Laguna Village: 25th through 27th, Mass followed by a Harvest Dance.
Ohkay Owingeh: 26th, Turtle Dance.
Picuris: 28th, Holy Innocents' Day, Childrens' dances.
Most *pueblos:*   26th through 28th, Christmas Dances. *Santo Domingo* holds a Corn Dance.

As can be seen above, the northern *pueblos* have the most active Christmas season, including Torchlight Processions at Sundown on Christmas Eve, *Los Matachines* Dances on Christmas Day, and Dances of the Holy Innocents on December 28, and other various dances in the holiday period. Southern *pueblos* hold fewer celebrations and are more limited in scope.

Zuni Celebrations

Although the *Zuni Pueblo* is within the Southern *Pueblo* Group, this *pueblo* holds its own schedule of traditional events. *Zuni* celebrations occur throughout the year but the public celebrations are much more limited in number. The patron saint of *Zuni* is Our Lady of Guadalupe, and the Feast Day is celebrated non-publicly on 12 December each year. Several other events are made available to the public. A selected number of public and non-public *Zuni* events are summarized in Table 12-3. The celebrations listed in this table may not be complete or totally comprehensive. However, they do give an idea of the full range of events celebrated by the *Zuni* throughout the year. Some celebrations may not occur as listed in Table 12-3, but may occur in an adjacent month, instead. Please consult with *Zuni Pueblo* or use the contact information in Appendix A.

See also:

www.zunitourism.com/events_calendar.htm

Fourteen key events and celebrations are listed in Table 12-3 below. Of these, eight are opened to the public, while the remaining six are not accessible to the general public. This includes, the Feast Day celebration of Our Lady of Guadalupe. Although all other *pueblos* are opened to the public during their Feast Day celebrations, *Zuni* is unique in disallowing public viewing or participation.

Event	Location	Date	Access?	Comments
Soyal' New Year Feast	*Zuni Pueblo*	Dec. 21 thru Jan. 9	No	Time of renewal and purification. Winter Solstice celebration.
Earth Day Celebration	*Zuni Pueblo* grounds	April 20	Yes	Honoring the deities' manifestation as Earth Mother, one of 3 powerful *Zuni* deities:[10] Sun Father, Earth Mother and Moonlight-giving Mother.
Green Corn Dance	*Zuni Pueblo*	May 1-4	No	Welcomes the return of the Corn Maidens,[11] after a long cold winter.
Ancient Ways Arts Festival & Market	*Zuni Pueblo*	May 6-7	Yes	Arts, crafts and vendors.
Corn Dance	*Zuni Pueblo*	June 24-27	No	Prayers for fertility and rain. Prayer sticks planted in the ground.[12]
Rain Dance	*Zuni Pueblo*	Consult *Zuni Pueblo*. See Appendix A.	Yes	Solicitation for rains to water the crops and to provide a good harvest.[13] (Some sources claim this dance occurs in June. Others claim it occurs every August 15th. Please consult *Zuni Pueblo* as the final authority.
Harvest or Corn Dance	*Zuni Pueblo*	August 5-7	No	Thanksgiving for a successful maize harvest,[14] in which the *Zuni's* bid farewell to the Corn Maidens for another year, and to the *Kokos* (nature spirits).
Zuni Annual Arts & Cultural Expo	*Zuni Pueblo*	August 13-14	Yes	Arts & crafts, and cultural activities.
Zuni Fair	*Zuni Pueblo*	Between the 3rd and 4th weekend in August until the Labor Day weekend in September.	Yes	*Zuni Pueblo* hosts the McKinley County Fair (Rodeo, Pow-Wow and contests).
Ancient Ways Fall Festival & Arts Market	*Zuni Pueblo*	October 8	Yes	Arts, crafts and vendors.
Ancestors' Day	*Zuni Pueblo*	November 2	No	Honors *Zuni* Ancestors. Food offerings to ancestors are given into the rivers & lakes.[15, 16]
Zuni Christmas Lights Parade	*Zuni Pueblo*	Thanksgiving	Yes	Christmas Lights parade.
Shalako Ceremony[17, 18]	*Zuni Pueblo*	Nov 23 thru Dec 6	Yes	*Shalako* home blessings normally performed after the harvest. The *Shalako* are messengers of the deities, but they also carry Zuni solicitations for rainfall to the deities.
Our Lady of Guadalupe Feast Day	*Zuni Pueblo*	December 12	No	Annual Feast Day - closed to the Public.

Table 12-3: Summary of Selected *Zuni* Events and Celebrations
(Approximate Dates only and subject to change.)

PART B: Explanation of Ancient *Pueblo* Dance Cycles & *Pueblo* Dances Performed Today, and *Pueblo* Ceremonies Honoring New Tribal Officials

Ancient Native *Pueblo* Dance Cycles[19]

Much of the information gathered here in this section is derived from the various descriptive signposts along the walking tour path at *Pecos* National Historical Park and other written sources. Today, the *pueblos* perform various dances throughout the ceremonial year. These dances are indigenous, and most are religious or spiritual in nature. Many are actually dynamic prayers that are tied to the annual Natural Cycle of life, and to the seasons. They may also be tied to the old Subsistence Cycle that related seeding, harvesting, wild food gathering, hunting and trading activities of the *Pueblo* Peoples. A rough look at how these various cycles related to one another and to some of the associated ceremonial dances in ancient times is shown in Figure 12-1. The cycles rotate clockwise, starting with the Winter Solstice at the top of the page. Then comes the Spring or Vernal Equinox, followed by the Summer Solstice. This is followed by the Autumnal Equinox. The cycle moves on again to the Winter Solstice of the following year, completing the Natural Cycle.

The concept shown in Figure 12-1 is somewhat hypothetical (based on various sources), but it does give some framework for how the *Pueblo* Peoples may have viewed their relationship to nature and their associated rituals.

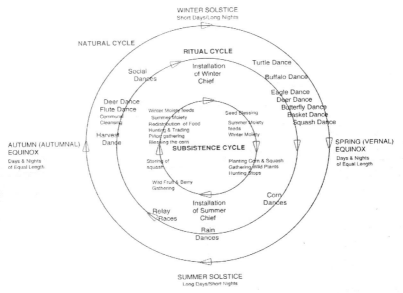

Figure 12-1: Ancient *Pueblo* Ritual & Subsistence Cycles vs Natural Cycles. (Concept courtesy of *Pecos* National Historical Park, from a wayside interpretive plaque. In addition, see Chapter 12, Note 19. Drawing by the author.)

(The description and representation that follow may not be exactly reflective of the practices or beliefs at all *pueblos*. The discussion below is based upon descriptive placards at *Pecos* National Historical Park and upon a second source: *The Tewa World: Space, Time, Being and Becoming in a Pueblo Society*, by Alfonso Ortiz. As such, the description may be more reflective of the *Kiowa-Tanoan Pueblo* Groups, especially the *Tewa* and possibly, the ancient *Towa*. The *Pecos Pueblo* was once occupied by *Towa*-speaking *pueblo* natives. No source was available, to the author, regarding *Keres* practices and beliefs, or the relationships between the Natural, Subsistence and Ritual Cycles, as viewed by the *Keres*-speaking peoples.)

(However, it should be noted that the *Keres*-speaking *Santo Domingo [Kewa]*

Pueblo does observe two moieties, Winter and Summer, which they call the Pumpkin and Turquoise groups, respectively. The *Keres*-speaking *Cochiti Pueblo* also, observes, these two moieties.)

However, even with this clear shortcoming, the discussion is still worthwhile, as it demonstrates that there is an underlying general structure to the various cycles and to the ritual observances among *Pueblo* Peoples, even if there are variations in the exact structure. The overarching conclusion is simply that the various cycles are related to nature, and the dances are religious in nature. They are tied to the natural cycles. They are by no means random.

In Figure 12-1, the Ritual Cycle is shown following the patterns of nature with dances and ceremonials suitable for each season. For example, Corn Dances were performed between spring and summer as prayers for a successful planting. The Summer (moiety) Chief was installed around the Summer Solstice. Rain Dances were held at the beginning of summer in prayer for rainfall for the new plantings

Sacred relay footraces were held just after the Summer Solstice. The Harvest Dance celebrated a successful crop harvest at the time of the Autumn Equinox. Deer Dances occurred about this same time as the natives prepared for the approaching hunting season. Social dances occurred in the few months just before the Winter Solstice, after the harvest was collected. Installation of the Winter (moiety) Chief occurred around the Winter Solstice. Following the Winter Solstice, the Turtle Dance appears in January. Buffalo, Eagle, Deer, Butterfly, Basket and Squash dances occurred near the end of winter and anticipated the spring. So the Ritual Cycle repeated itself again.

The Subsistence Cycle related the planting, gathering and hunting activities of the people to the other two cycles just discussed. For example, the seed blessing was done in spring, just before planting. Feeding of the people of the Winter Moiety by the people of the Summer Moiety occurred before the Spring Equinox. Gathering of wild foods and berries occurred from the spring through the summer. Hunting ceased in the spring. The blessing of the harvested corn, initiation of trading and hunting expeditions, gathering of salt and the harvesting of *piñon* nuts all occurred right after the Autumnal Equinox. Squash may have been stored just before or shortly after the Autumnal Equinox. Before the onset of winter, the Winter Moiety fed the Summer Moiety, in reciprocation. Redistribution of food to others also occurred at this time. As winter approached, the Subsistence Cycle repeated itself. It is clear from this discussion that the native peoples lived in a natural harmony with the cycles of life, and they gave thanks and celebrated their harvests and good fortune. Their prayers of gratitude, supplication and celebration were manifested in many of the colorful native *pueblo* dances we see today!

Overview of the *Pueblo* Traditional Dance Experience

The earlier sections of this chapter have already highlighted the approximate Feast Day celebration schedules associated with each *pueblo's* Catholic patron saint. The following sections give brief descriptions of a selected number of currently practiced traditional dances. Some of these dances are performed on these Feast Day Celebrations. Many of these dances developed in ancient times. However, others such as the *Comanche* Dance, the Kings' Day celebration and the Transfer of Canes Day ceremonials, evolved in the last four centuries. An Overview is first given here of selected *pueblo* dance celebrations, to highlight and to communicate a sense of the overall *pueblo* traditional dance experience. This brief discussion is followed by a section entitled, *Brief Descriptions of Pueblo Dances*, where fuller descriptions of a selected number of *pueblo* dances will be given.

Pueblo dances are widely recognized as the high point of the Feast Day and other *pueblo* celebrations. They are repetitive and almost hypnotic in nature, but they represent a spiritual reverence for nature. One cannot help but get caught up in the primal pulsating rhythms, and share the sense of closeness to the natural world. Tens and scores of natives may participate as they move together slowly in a large circle or in long lines, thumping their feet, and dancing to the deep and mesmerizing drumbeat. The participants are usually dressed in traditional tribal costumes, with elaborate headdresses. Men and women, old and young, participate in many of the dances. In some dances the men may appear with bare chests, arms and legs painted in various colors, with native religious and tribal symbols. In other dances, the men may wear some coverings representative of the particular dance. In dances that include women, the women usually wear black or white *mantas,* that are beautifully embroidered. It is truly heartwarming to see the very young and the elderly alike partake in these ceremonies.

In these *pueblo* dances, usually, three to ten Native Americans gather in one or more small groups to share in the tribal drumming. Often, drummers will sing native chants and songs to the rhythm of the drumbeat. Large or small chorus groups sometimes sing to accompany the dances.

When witnessing these dances, close your eyes, and take in the primitive chants. Allow yourself to follow the hypnotic rhythms, and the ancient chants. It can carry you to a more primal, elemental time and space, that is both rewarding and liberating to the spirit. After a short while, open your eyes to see the native dancers all around you wearing their traditional costumes. The experience will then be complete and you will later leave the ceremony, feeling a sense of connectedness with nature, with the primitive world and with a distant past. It is an unforgettable and colorful experience!

One large-scale and spectacular dance, that is fairly common, is the Corn Dance. It is very popular with tourists, and various Corn Dances can be seen at numerous *pueblos,* on Feast Days, throughout the warm months of May through September. The Green Corn Dance is performed early in the planting season. Sometimes, the Corn Dances are performed seeking rain and fertility for the seedling crops. Later, it can be performed more as a celebration in gratitude for the harvest. It pays homage to the corn, for the sustenance it has brought to the *Pueblo* Peoples. As an example, the *Zuni* perform the Corn Dance three times throughout the growing and harvest season, each time for a different purpose. See the discussion later in this chapter, under *Zuni* dances. The Corn Dance is quite spectacular and usually involves many, many dancers. One can sense the power and the sacred nature of this dynamic prayer.

In contrast to the Corn Dance, the Buffalo Dance celebrates the buffalo as a sacred source of game meat. It is a prayer soliciting good luck in the hunt. It may also be a prayer of thankfulness for the buffalo's life sacrifice as a source of food for the tribe. It is usually performed at several *pueblo* Feast Day dances in the winter months. Buffalo meat helped to provide protein and nutrition through the cold winter months, long after the fall crop harvest.

The Buffalo Dance sometimes begins the night before the formal celebration with the lighting of log bonfires. In some cases, the celebration continues at dawn on the day of the ceremony, with animal dancers coming down from the neighboring hills under the leadership of the Game Priest Dancer. Corn meal may be spread on the ground forming a path. The corn and the buffalo are actually seen in harmony and unity, each providing a separate, but necessary element of nutrition and sustenance to the *Pueblo* Peoples. This helped ensure their survival. The dances are held in reverence and thanksgiving to these elements of nature.

Koshare[20] appear in some but not all Feast Day celebrations of the *Keres*-speaking *pueblos*. They may appear in a serious ritualistic role or they may act in a "comic" role. Some call them "clowns" but this terminology belies their sacred role. However, clowns as an ancient element of *pueblo* religious tradition are very different from the *Anglo*-American concept of clowns. The two major "clowns" in *pueblo* dances are the *koshare* and the Mudheads.[21] In their "clown" roles, these two ritualistic groups may represent the unexpected, the chaotic, the disruptive, and maybe even the ironic elements of nature and society. The *koshare* may even represent the "ancient ones", the spirits of the ancestors. They often play a very serious oversight and ritualistic role in many *Keres*-speaking southern *pueblo* celebrations.

The *koshare* of the *Santo Domingans* appear to be very solemn and serious during the Corn Dances, as they maintain order among the dancers and coordinate their movements. To Western eyes, they seem to represent the spirits of the withered and darkened corn and corn husks from the previous harvest. This is inferred from the color of their outfits (black and white, or gray) and the stalks made of corn husks atop their heads, or protruding vertically from above their ears. They seem to flow in synchronization with the music, the drum and the dance rhythms. They clearly play a sacred and essential role in the Corn Dance. Their outfits are not dissimilar to the *chiffonetes* of the northern *Tiwa* (*Taos* and *Picuris*).

The "*chiffonetes*", are a form of northern *koshare*.[22] At *Taos*, on *San Geronimo* Feast Day, September 30, a ritual relay foot race to a group of sacred stones, is held. This is later followed by a ritual pole-climb.[23]

At *Taos*, festivities actually begin the night on the evening before the 29th. Catholic vespers are first completed, followed by an evening or sundown dance. Foot races commence early the next day with runners running east and west, to symbolically give power to the sun and the moon. Then native dancers fill the village *plaza* with their rhythmic dances, while vendors sell their wares or refreshments in the perimeter area. Later the *chiffonete* ceremonial "clowns" arrive to lighten the atmosphere. They poke fun at themselves, at others and at the human condition generally. Later, the *chiffonetes* try to climb a very tall pole, in excess of 40 feet, to reach treats at the top. The pole is erected in the middle of the village *plaza*. Their antics bring laughter and delight to all. However, climbing the pole requires extraordinary strength, stamina, courage and a big dose of athleticism.

Chiffonetes also perform annually at the *San Lorenzo* Feast Day celebration, in *Picuris Pueblo*, held on August 10. The *chiffonetes* usually paint their bodies with alternating stripes of gray and black, or white and black, and wear breechcloths and skullcaps with horns made from corn husks. They may also wear necklaces made from donuts or plastic representations of fruit. They may lead certain dances or they may mix with the crowds and tease the tourists. However, once the ceremony gets started the *chiffonetes* assume a more subdued and serious aspect. At *Picurís* there is an event, like the *Taos* pole-climb, wherein the main objective is to climb a 40-foot tall pole in order to retrieve the carcass of a sheep.

Centuries ago, survivors from the now extinct *Pecos Pueblo* moved onto the *Towa*-speaking *Jemez Pueblo*.[24] Here, the descendants of these survivors celebrate the *santo* of the extinct *Pecos Pueblo*. They hold their annual Feast Day celebration of St. Persíngula, on August 2, and they celebrate the *Pecos* Bull.[25] A man dresses up as a bull wearing a large wooden frame covered with black cloth. A sheepskin covers his face. He charges about the village, while young boys with blackened faces chase him.

The Feast Day celebration at the *Santa Clara Pueblo* occurs on August 12th. The patron saint is of course *Santa Clara* (St. Claire). The dances at this *pueblo* are representative of the *Tewa* tradition. The dances are smaller in scale than the *Santo Domingo* Corn Dance celebration (August 4th) but the scene is still beautiful and stunning, with male and female dancers in very colorful outfits. In some dances, the men are bare-chested and barelegged. In others, the male dancers wear white embroidered cotton shirts and leggings. The women may wear black or white *mantas*. They may or may not wear beautiful silk shawls over one shoulder. The shawls are often different colors depending upon the dance. Evergreen is used profusely on their bodies to denote everlasting life and abundance.

Oftentimes, the women wear beautifully decorated *tablitas* on their heads with groups of feathers on the back. The men's headdresses can also be quite stunning, with turkey and long multi-colored parrot feathers protruding sideways from the head. The other side of the headdress may show a small wreath of evergreen gathered around a paper or cardboard form made to represent what appears to be a squash blossom. The rhythms of the music may at first seem unvaried, but if one cares to listen carefully, the rhythms vary quite a bit and the dancers alter their movements, with short hesitations and varied dance tempos, matching the changing drum rhythms. It is a real delight to observe these colorful and beautiful sacred dances!!

As can be seen from this short discussion, there is a wide variation among the dances and ceremonies celebrated among the various *pueblos*. Each one is unique, but interesting and colorful in its own way. The following section, describes some of the more popular or "better known" native dances.

Brief Descriptions of *Pueblo* Dances Performed Today

The dance descriptions included here are: Basket Dance, Bow & Arrow Dance, Buffalo Dance, Cloud Dance, *Comanche* Dance, Corn or Harvest Dance, Deer/ Antelope Dance, Eagle Dance, Turtle Dance, *Zuni* Rain Dance and *Zuni Shalako* Dance. The meaning behind the Kings' Day, Transfer of Canes Day and the Governors' Feast Day celebrations is also briefly described.

Many of these dance descriptions are gathered from several informative sources and publications, referenced in the rear Bibliography. Among the most significant are: *Southwestern Indian Ceremonials* by Tom Bahty; *The Pueblo Children of the Earth Mother, Volume II*, by Thomas Mails; *Masked Gods, Navajo and Pueblo Ceremonialism* by Frank Waters; *Pueblo Gods and Myths* by Hamilton A. Tyler; and *Dances of the Tewa Pueblo Indians: Expressions of New Life* by Jill D. Sweet. Others are based on observation of some of these dances. It should be noted that there are significant differences among the various *pueblos* as to how these dances are performed. Therefore, the following descriptions may not exactly match the dances as performed at any given *pueblo*. These descriptions are merely meant to convey a sense of these dances. The key is to expect variation.

There are a few points to be observed while viewing any of these (mostly religious) native dances. First, generally speaking, photography, videography, audio recording, sketching, note taking, and recording of any kind, are prohibited during many of these ceremonies. If in doubt, ask first! Second, applause is frowned upon, as these dances, even races, are viewed as religious in nature. Also, do not approach any of the dancers, especially while they are dancing. It is considered impolite to cross a *pueblo plaza*, where dances are currently being performed, or where they are scheduled to be performed. Instead, please walk around the *plaza* perimeter. Lastly, talking during dances is also frowned upon and is considered disrespectful. Beyond these basic rules of respect and courtesy, the viewer is generally welcomed to observe these beautiful, sacred and primal dances.

Basket Dance[26]

This dance takes its name from the use of the food basket in the ceremony. The dancers can be male or female, and the dance is usually conducted in the early spring or early summer. However, among the northern *Tewa* tribes, the dance usually requires an equal number of male and female dancers. There are various stages to the Basket Dance with each stage representing the stage of the food carried within it. The food of course is symbolic of the life and sustenance it brings to the tribal people. The basket may carry the seed that is yet to be planted in the ground, or it may contain the harvested fruit or grain. The basket may simply be empty, so that the dancer can interpret the doings of Mother Earth in producing and nourishing the crops through various dance gestures. Or, ground meal may fill the basket. Instead, the basket may bear loaves of bread, reinforcing the earth's bounty and female labors in producing the re-formed sustenance of life.

Whatever variation the dance assumes, the Basket Dance acknowledges the gift of plant life for survival, with its demonstration of the various stages of growth and development. It is a dance of gratefulness and gratitude for the earth's bounty. It is a message about the earth's fertility and fecundity. Some see parallels with the path of young womanhood.[27]

At *San Juan*[28] or *Ohkay Owingeh*, the Basket Dance celebrates the crops, fertility and the essential role of the female. At this *pueblo*, there are two phases to the dance. The first stage requires the dancers to stand with slow movements. The second stage is more rapid, wherein the female performers form a line kneeling facing a group of male performers who dance in front of them. While the males dance, the women scrape notched sticks over baskets. There is no drum accompaniment nor is there a male chorus, as in some other dances. The headdress of the men includes yucca stalks in an arc crown around the front and three upright feathers in the rear. They wear the standard white kilts with jingle bells just below their knees. Their exposed chest, back, arms and legs are daubed in clay. They wear moccasins with skunk fur over them. They also carry evergreen sprigs and a gourd rattle. Their bodies are usually draped in evergreen.

The female dancers wear wrapped moccasins and a black *manta*. They wear a white shawl over their shoulders. The shawl is beautifully embroidered along the edges. They carry an evergreen sprig in one hand and a woven basket in the other, as they perform this dance.

A similar dance is performed at *Santa Clara Pueblo,*[29] only instead the men wear fashioned squash blossom headdresses.

The Basket Dance is often performed in January in celebration of the Transfer of Canes, or at most *pueblos* on Easter weekend. Non-*pueblo Navajo* dancers performed a Basket Dance at the 2011 New Mexico State Fair.

Bow & Arrow Dance

There are several different variants of this popular dance. In some cases, the entire village participates in the Bow & Arrow Dance.[30] The dance is meant to signify and dramatize the close relationship between the villagers and the local prey. The movement of the hunters and the hunted are mimicked by representative gestures. The dance formations are symbolic. The dancers may arrange themselves alternately as the hunting parties and then as large symbolic bows and arrows. Oftentimes, the dancers are all male, carry bows and sometimes arrows, and they are brightly painted.

The Bow & Arrow Dance is often performed on Easter weekend at *Nambé Pueblo.* A different version is often performed at *Tesuque.*[31] Male dancers wear large white animal capes over their right shoulders, and carry a bow in their left hand, without any arrows. The dancers form a row and usually dance in place. Occasionally, they pivot to change direction. They sing as they dance and periodically move the unarmed bow from its initial horizontal passive position to the upright vertical active position

Buffalo Dance[32]

Another dance that is commonly performed among the various *pueblos* is the Buffalo Dance. Like so many of the animal dances, the Buffalo Dance is a prayer of thanksgiving. The dancer is thought to assume the spirit and physical resemblance of the buffalo during the dance. As always, the spirit of the buffalo is thanked for his gift of life. The dance is also a prayer for future good fortune in the hunt. The famous 19th century western photographer, Edward S. Curtis, took the photograph of two *Tesuque Buffalo Dancers*, shown in Figure 12-2. It is common for the dancers to wear the native *pueblo* kilt with a buffalo head and horns to represent the ritual animal. The dancers may also carry rattles that they shake to the rhythm of the drums and the music.

Among the various *pueblos*, the number of dancers, their costumes and the dances themselves may vary. In each case, the dance is a dynamic prayer for snow and success in hunting, while recognizing the sacrifice of the buffalo's life. There is a majestic statue of a Buffalo Hunter that stands outside the entrance to the Buffalo Thunder Resort in *Pojoaque*. See Figure 12-3. George Rivera, the famous artist and the current Governor of *Pojoaque Pueblo*, sculpted this statue. Although the Buffalo Dance is performed mostly in the winter and early spring months, it is sometimes performed at other times of the year because of its popularity.

There are up to five different variations of *Tewa* Buffalo Dances![33] *San Ildefonso* is famous for its variation of the dance, which is really more of a "game animal" dance as

Figure 12-2: *Tesuque Buffalo Dancers.*** (Photo by Edward S. Curtis, c. 1925. Courtesy Palace of the Governors Photo Archives (NMHM. DCA) neg. # 144657.)

Figure 12-3: *Buffalo Dancer* statue at Buffalo Thunder Resort entrance. (Sculptor George Rivera, courtesy of Buffalo Thunder Resort, and by permission of the sculptor and the *Pojoaque Pueblo.*)

the bison, the deer and antelope are all celebrated. The ceremony begins in the early morning (dawn) hours of the *San Ildefonso* Feast Day, January 23rd. There are usually an equal number of male and female dancers, wearing black face paint. The game mother is usually identified by a brightly colored fringed shawl over a black *manta*. There are various headdresses corresponding to the various game types being represented. Several drummers and a male chorus accompany the dancers.

Butterfly Dance

The Butterfly Dance[34] is a beautiful, graceful and complex dance that hails the beginning of summer. It involves two dancers, a male and a female. These two dancers flutter and follow each other through symbolic fields of corn, wheat, squash and alfalfa. The chorus and drummers sing in an appeal for moisture, fertility, abundance and prosperity. Although the dance varies among *pueblos*, the male dancers often dress in conventional traditional dress. The female costume, however, is quite spectacular. The female wears a basic framework or plaque on her back, which serves as a platform for an array of white and red down feathers. Eagle wing feathers are attached horizontally to the framework to form wings that, in some cases, can move as she dances. This is the most beautiful and dramatic part of her costume!

Spiking up vertically, on top of her head, she wears orange and blue macaw feathers. Various smaller feathers are clustered around the base of the headpiece.

Figure 12-4: *Butterfly Dancer* statue at Buffalo Thunder Resort. Sculpted by George Rivera. (Courtesy of the Buffalo Thunder Resort, and by permission of the sculptor and the *Pojoaque Pueblo*.)

Another cluster of eagle body feathers hangs down from these to cover the rear of the head. A white embroidered *manta* is worn on the body. The Butterfly Dancer also wears high wrapped moccasins covered with skunk fur protect the dancer from evil. She carries wooden wands in her hands. These wands have eagle tail feathers attached to them.

San Juan or *Ohkay Owingeh, Santa Clara*

and *Nambé* each perform a different version[35] of this dance that celebrates the spring, fertility and the female role. At *Ohkay Owingeh*, each male dancer wears the traditional white kilt, with a rain sash. He also wears crocheted leggings and a white shirt. However, an otter fur bib is worn over the shirt. He also wears a headband with three large feathers. In his right hand, he carries a tomahawk, that is actively swung around as he dances.

At *Ohkay Owingeh*, the dance performance starts with a *"wasa"*[36] or weaving motion of the dancers. At *Santa Clara,* there is a different variation, in which the dance starts with a counterclockwise circular motion. In either case, there are a number of dance movements where the male and female dancers move together and then apart again.

The Butterfly Dance is a solicitation for fertility and productivity. As such, it is symbolic of fructification and abundance, and of the promise of summer. Figure 12-4 shows a fine statue of a Butterfly Dancer as conceived by George Rivera, as it appears at the Buffalo Thunder Resort/Casino, second floor.

Cloud Dance[37]

This late winter or early spring dance can often be seen at *Santa Clara, San Juan* (*Ohkay Owingeh*) and *San Ildefonso*. The dance dramatizes the tension between the seasons. It represents the rising of one season as the preceding season retreats. It shows the tension between the clouds of summer and the clouds of winter as they struggle for supremacy. It is a dance relating to the desired control of the weather, fertility and the planting of seeds and hoped for growth. Hence, it is often performed before spring planting begins.

Mails[38] describes the *Ohkay Owingeh* form of the dance. In this form, performers include eight girls who together symbolize the four cardinal directions. Four girls represent summer and four symbolize winter. Two girls dance at given time. The male dancers wear the traditional embroidered white cotton kilt and a collar of spruce. At the back of the head and in their hair, they may wear upright golden eagle tail feathers. Male performers sing as they dance. Two women dance with each single male dancer.

According to Sweet,[39] the women wear black *mantas* with white blouses underneath and brightly colored shawls on top. They also wear elaborate fan-shaped headpieces consisting of a dozen or so eagle feathers, carrying an ear of corn or a sprig of evergreen in each hand. The dance usually begins with a *"wasa"* movement (mentioned earlier), and then moves on to a series of single line dances. The men are shirtless and may wear white or back body paint on the bare parts of their bodies. They often carry a gourd rattle and evergreen sprigs. Instead of a spruce collar they may wear a kerchief around the neck. Sometimes races attend the dance.[40] The races trace the course of the combating seasonal clouds.

At times, this dance may be performed in celebration of the Transfer of Canes on January 1st of each year.

Comanche Dance

This dance[41] was performed in earlier times, when the *pueblos* lived in fear of deadly raids by *Comanche* raiders and warriors. This ritual was meant to gain power to deal with these enemies. In modern times, these dances have been adapted to give thanks for freedom from any and all enemies, sickness, drought, or any other threatening "enemy." The dancers generally wear Plains-type war bonnets. They whoop and howl as they dance in imitation of the *Comanche* raiders.

At *San Ildefonso,*[42] the male *Comanche* Dancers often wear brightly feathered war bonnets, fringed buckskin pants or breechclouts, war paint on their faces and body, bone breast plates, etc. Each male warrior usually carries a banner with one or more feathers on it in his right hand, while he carries a rattle in his other hand. The women may wear *mantas* or a colorful dress with lace shawls. They usually wear a headband with several upright feathers. Drummers and singers accompany the dancers. The movement of the female dancers is more subdued, dancing with small short steps. The dance movements of the male warrior dancers is much more active and pronounced, as they weave among the female dancers.

As in all native "dances", they are not truly dances in the modern sense, but are instead sacred prayers that are performed to give thanks or to make supplications for some tribal need. In this case, the need is protection of the people. The dance usually begins with the dancers emerging from the *kiva*. They also return to the *kiva* at the dance's end. However, the *Comanche* Dance seems more secular in its feel compared with other *pueblo* dances, such as the sacred Corn Dance.

Corn, Harvest or *Tablita*[43] Dance

The Harvest Dance, the Corn Dance[44, 45, 46] and the *Tablita* Dance are all "*tablita*" dances, because the female dancers wear *tablitas* on their heads. These dances are all basically the same in form, costume and in meaning. The *Keresans* (Southern *Pueblo* Group) typically describe these dances as Corn Dances whereas the *Tewa* (most *pueblos* in the Northern *Pueblo* Group) sometimes call them Harvest Dances. This rule is not rigid however. The dances used to be performed in the midsummer or just preceding the fall. However, since the dances are so popular they are now performed at other times of the year. These dances are a prayer of supplication. They are also a prayer of thankfulness and gratitude to the Earth Mother, for the life-giving land and for the moisture that ensures a bountiful crop. In Figure 12-5, a *Tablita* Dance performance, by a small group of native *pueblo* dancers, is captured at *San Ildefonso*.

Figure 12-5: *San Ildefonso Tablita Dancers.*** (Photo by Edward S. Curtis,
c. 1925, Courtesy Palace of the Governors Photo Archives
(NMHM.DCA) neg. # 143732.)

This photo was taken by the famous photographer, Edward S. Curtis. The dance may involve a hundred or sometimes even more people. One can see the parrot feathers on top of the heads of the male dancers, the *tablitas* on the female dancers, the sprigs of evergreen in the mens' armbands, the corded rain sashes, white kilts, etc. The male dancers can be seen holding a gourd rattle in the right hand and a sprig of evergreen in the left hand. This photograph shows how conservative these dance traditions are. They have changed very little since the time this photo was taken, over one hundred years ago!

(The Indian *Pueblo* Cultural Center in Albuquerque, has a beautiful mural painted on one of the courtyard walls, portraying what appears to be a *Jemez Pueblo* Corn Dance or Harvest Dance. José Rey Toledo is the artist.)

At *Santo Domingo*,[47, 48] during their Feast Day celebration on August 4, the Corn Dance may involve up to one thousand dancers. In addition, there are large male choruses that accompany the dancers. The description that follows gives the broad outlines of the *Santo Domingo* Corn Dance.

The day begins with the processional of the *santo*, *Santo Domingo*, from the mission church to the bower at the nearest end of the long *plaza*. Soon after, the tribal ceremony begins.

There is commotion around one of the two *kivas* involving the *koshare*. Soon after the dancing begins.

The *koshare* are the first group to be noticed. They are usually smeared with white or gray clay on their bodies. They may either have broad black horizontal stripes across their bodies or they may be dotted with black spots. They wear a black gauzy breechclout with a turtle shell attached just below their waist in the back. The turtle shell has pigs hooves attached by leather thongs to the outer surface to create a rattling sound with movement. Their faces are similarly painted with black spots around their eyes and mouth. Their hair is tied up towards the crown of the head and caked with a gray-white mud or clay. On top of their heads, at the crown, several corn husks are gathered together to stand vertically. At other times, corn husks may rise vertically or from just above either ear. Some *koshare* are painted in ochre or reddish brown clay instead and may reverse the colors from black on white to white on black, or they may color the left side of their bodies in one pattern or color, and paint the opposite side in a different color or scheme.

The various movements of the *koshare* are not random but symbolize some deep native meaning. Some say the *koshare* represent the "ancient ones", or that they represent the dead corn stalks and husks from the prior year. The *koshare* dance solemnly while supervising the structure and decorum of the dance. They help to maintain the dress of the dancers. They are clearly in control, but in an unobtrusive, attentive and caring manner, while maintaining the dignity and the spiritual nature of the sacred dance.

Five dance cycles last from 10 am until about 7 pm. Although the Corn Dance is beautiful to behold, it must be a grueling event for the dancers. It is clearly an act of community sacrifice, soliciting the spirits to bring the needed rain and fertility, and the sun's blessing to ensure successful harvests. Dancers volunteer to participate in the day-long Corn Dance.

There are an equal number of male and female dancers in costume. These are divided into two divisions: the Summer Group and the Winter Group. Each division dances alternately for about 45 to 50 minutes. They assemble in their respective separate *kivas* just prior to each dance cycle. The Turquoise Group represents the summer, while the Pumpkin Group represents the winter. The Summer or Turquoise people are the first to emerge from their *kiva* as each dance cycle begins to the accompanying chants from their chorus. After about 50 minutes of constant dancing, this first group leaves the *plaza*, while the Winter or Pumpkin Group appears from their own *kiva*. In this way, winter follows summer as it does in the natural cycle. Some say the Winter Group represents the masculine principal while the Summer Group represents the feminine principal. Each group follows the same basic dance routine, dancing back and forth four or five times throughout the day, to the increasing tempo and volume of the chants.

Each dance group is accompanied by its chorus, which is led by a Rain Priest, who wields a 10-foot long wand or standard to purify the people. The standard bears symbols of the sun and the rain, and of corn. As the dance progresses the Rain Priest waves the wand over the dance group. In this way, the Corn Dancers are blessed and purified, as the wand movement represents a simultaneous request to the *Shiwana*, or rain cloud people, to bless the *pueblo* with rain for the crops.

The *koshare*, painted in black and gray (or white), or red-brown, weave elegantly and gracefully around the dancing groups. Their manner is serious and solemn, unlike their joking selves before the ceremonies begin.

The women dress in a simple ceremonial costume consisting of a black dress, which hangs on one shoulder. This is called a *manta*. They usually wear a red embroidered belt and are bedecked with turquoise or beaded necklaces and bracelets. Their hair is usually long and black, and flows freely, although some women have short hair too. They wear a *tablita*, on top of their heads. They dance barefooted, until the sand gets too hot. They then change over to wearing moccasins. By dancing barefoot, the women are able to absorb the natural fertility of Mother Earth.

The men's costumes are more colorful. Each man wears a broad or corded (rain) sash draped over the right side of his white cotton kilt. The kilt is richly and beautifully embroidered with ritualistic symbols. A fox skin usually hangs from his belt behind. Some dancers allow their long black hair to hang freely down their backs, while others have short hair. The men wear a girdle of shells over the left (right) shoulder that crosses to the right (left) hip. There are tufts of parrot and woodpecker feathers tied into the top of the head. Their arms sport painted rawhide armbands and on each ankle they wear a skunk fur covering over the moccasins. The skunk fur is said to protect the dancer from evil. Around the waist or on the knees they may wear sleigh bells. The men are usually bare-chested with ochre, red or dark clay smeared on the upper body, but with white clay on the thighs and around the waist, i.e. wherever the body comes in contact with the white kirtle. While the men carry a gourd rain rattle in the right hand and a sprig of evergreen in the left hand, the women carry a spray of evergreen in each hand, representing life. Both the men and the women wear evergreen in abundance.

The on-going rhythm of the dance throughout the day's ceremony and the intensity of the sacrifice in terms of the dancers' endurance is a measure of the intensity and power of this dynamic and dramatic prayer of gratitude and of supplication. The constant drumbeat is the heartbeat of this religious drama. The sense of community, acting in concert, is unmistakable. After a full day of dancing, one walks away having felt the real presence of that power!!

In summary, the Corn Dance appears to be a community prayer of supplication and gratitude to the spirits for the gift of corn, and a plea for fertilizing rain and the sun's gentle warmth, as well as for divine help in nurturing and maturing the corn. The scale of the *Santo Domingo* or *Kewa* Corn Dance suggests it is a dynamic prayer by the entire community.

One has to admit the power of the sacred Corn Dance, as the thunderclouds gather towards the closing of the ceremony and the rain follows shortly afterwards!

Although the Corn Dance and the Harvest Dance appear to be very similar, the Corn Dance was usually performed to solicit rain and fertility for the planted corn, while the Harvest Dance celebrated the successful harvesting of the corn and other crops, near the end of the growing season.

This description may not be totally reflective of every Corn or Harvest Dance, for variations occur between *pueblos* and at different times of the year. Nonetheless, this short discussion does give a sense of the ceremony.

Deer[49] or Antelope Dance/Ceremony

The annual Deer Dance is performed by most New Mexico *pueblo* Indians. The meaning of the Deer Dance varies slightly from *pueblo* to *pueblo*. Among the *Laguna Pueblo* people there is a double significance to the dance: first, it is a supplication to the hunting spirit to enable the hunters to be successful in killing a deer for an essential food, and for its hide to be used for clothing; second, it is also a plea for forgiveness in the taking of the deer's life in order to provide for the welfare and survival of the tribe.

Figure 12-6: *Deer Dancer* statue at Buffalo Thunder Resort. Sculpted by George Rivera. (Courtesy of Buffalo Thunder Resort, and by permission of the sculptor and the *Pojoaque Pueblo*.)

Jemez natives pay tribute to several different game animals in a single ceremony. These game animals include the deer, buffalo, ram and antelope. *San Ildefonso's* celebration also pertains to several game animals, including the deer.

The men of the tribe usually perform the ritual dance. The Deer Dancer wears a costume simulating the appearance of the deer. The dancers' heads are usually adorned with antlers. They hold a pair of wooden sticks covered in fur to simulate the deer's two front legs. Deer pelts may drape down their backs. Clattering seashells are usually wrapped around the dancer's legs, emanating rhythmic sounds as the performers dance to the tribal chants and drumbeats during the ritual. A large statue of a Deer Dancer, is displayed at Buffalo Thunder Resort/Casino. See Figure 12-6.

At *Taos*,[50] the Deer Dancers are flanked by two deer watchmen in front, and two deer watchmen in the rear. These dressmen are costumed as hunters. Two deerchiefs follow the deer watchmen, wearing traditional white kilts, crocheted leggings and white beaded moccasins. They also wear white-painted antlers on their heads. Deer mothers too participate in the dance, wearing white dresses that are embroidered, woven belts and ribbons. They also wear high wrapped moccasins. The women wear vertical parrot feathers and a single eagle feather at the backs of their heads. They also wear short parrot feathers on top of their heads. A wild duck skin hangs below the feathers at the rear of the head. On occasion they may try to seize a deer and carry it off. If a deer watchman catches the deer, it is returned to the dance.

In addition to the deer pelts that cover the head and back, the male dancers wear black or dark-brown kilts, a leather belt, and high-topped moccasins. During the *Taos* version of the Deer Dance, clowns take aim and shoot straw arrows at the deer prey.

The dancers perform graceful movements simulating the movement of the deer, as it senses that it is under pursuit. The first movements are small rapid tentative steps, becoming more pronounced as the dancers' motions become more rapid. He becomes more deliberate as he sprints, jumps and leaps, in a vain attempt to avoid the pursuing hunter. Each dancer's movements are accompanied by the intonations and chants of native singers, and by the increased tempo of the drumbeats.

Tesuque, Santa Clara and *Ohkay Owingeh* all celebrate their own version of the Deer Dance with expected variations. The male dancers at *Ohkay Owingeh*[51] wear yucca stalks with their antlers. In addition, the dance starts with an evening prelude the night before. Early the next morning, at dawn, the Deer Dancers enter the village from the east. A chorus of male singers and drummers accompany the Deer Dancers.

These dances are exhilarating and colorful. Another different depiction of a Deer Dancer is presented at the entrance to *Sandia* Resort & Casino. Estella Loretto sculpted the *Sandia* statue. Here the headdress is much simpler, but the antlers and the wooden forelegs are still essential elements of the costume.

Eagle Dance[52]

Although the Eagle Dance is primarily a winter dance, it is so popular that it is also performed in the early spring and on occasion, it is even performed, in the summer, at the *Santa Fe* Indian Market®. The eagle plays a significant symbolic role among many Native American tribes throughout the nation. Because this noble and majestic bird soars through the sky, it is thought to be able to communicate with the powers of the sky. When a tribal member wears the eagle feathers as part of his costume, he is said to assume some of the special powers of the eagle. The eagle may be venerated because of his freedom to fly anywhere, without restriction. It may also be because he is a hunter who hunts his prey. The eagle is strong with keen vision and strong talons. He lives in high places. All these attributes probably contribute to the cause for his veneration. See Figure 12-7 for a modern image of an Eagle Dancer.

Figure 12-7: Eagle Dancer (With permission of YTC Summit International, Summit Collection.)

The Eagle Dance is also thought to be a curing dance as the eagle symbolizes strength. In addition, the eagle is most likely revered because the bird represents thunder, lightning and rain.[53] The dance simulates the relationship between the Spirit Powers, man, and the eagle. The dancer's costume and dance movements stress this symbiotic relationship. Typically, the dance includes two male dancers. One impersonates the male eagle, while the other impersonates the female eagle. However, this too is not always the case among the various *pueblos.* Sometimes the dance is performed only by a handful of male dancers.

Because the dance requires the performers to bend, squat, stoop, swoop and other strenuous motions it is usually performed by healthy, athletically fit young men.

Oftentimes, Eagle Dancers wear costumes of cotton-covered head caps with wooden or artificial eyes and beak. Their wings are made of long strips of cloth with eagle feathers attached to the arms. Each of the dancers wears a tail of eagle feathers, a breechclout or kilt, and sometimes moccasins. In the dance, the Eagle Dancers imitate the great bird in flight, mating, perching and diving gracefully to the ground to receive the prayers of the humans, which they then transport to the Spirit Powers on high. The Eagle Dance is popular for its color and its grace.

Turtle Dance[54, 55]

The Turtle Dance marks the end of one year, and the beginning of a new year, especially among the *Tewa*-speaking *pueblos.* This dance celebrates the first creation, when Sky Father coupled with Earth Mother to conceive all life. As such it is a celebration of life, of fertility of the soil, youth, new beginnings and rain. The turtle is believed to be the first hibernating life form that becomes active again after the year turns, and so the turtle has come to represent the beginning of each new annual cycle.

The dance begins at dawn with the dancers emerging from a *kiva.* The dancers are most often unclothed except for breechcloths and moccasins. At *Taos*, the dancers wear face paint to represent the mouths of turtles. On the other hand, no face paint is worn at *Ohkay Owingeh*, and the male dancers wear kilts. The *Ohkay Owingeh* male dancers also wear body paint and headdresses consisting of a yarn squash blossom and two feathers.

In each case, the dancers are all male and they line up in a long horizontal line, each man extending a gourd shell rattle and some evergreen branches in front of him. Each man usually wears a turtle shell on or at the back of his right knee. Pigs' hooves are attached to the tops of these shells using leather thongs. This makes a rattling sound with the dancers' movements. There is no separate chorus, as in the Corn Dance. Instead, the dancers form a chorus of their own, with the best singers among them. These are placed at the center of the line. The men sing their ceremonial songs. New songs are composed each year for each new celebration. The dance is performed with the expected tribal variations at the *Isleta, Taos* and *Ohkay Owingeh (San Juan) Pueblos*. The *Ohkay Owingeh Pueblo* considers the Turtle Dance to be of special significance.

The songs sing of a renewable dawn, the re-emergence of life, of life's beauty and joy, and of the four cardinal directions, honored in the prescribed ritualistic order of north, west, south and then east. The Turtle Dance and the singing bring forth the joy and hope of a new year. It is often performed during the Transfer of Canes celebration on January 1st of the New Year.

Zuni Rain Dance

Once the summer reaches its solstice, the days begin to shorten as the year marches towards the short days of winter. Yet the crops still need rain to grow and flourish in the warmth of the sun, so they can be harvested in the fall and bring nourishment to the people. The need for rain is clear and yet its coming is far from certain. This brings about the need, among the *Zuni*, to supplicate the gods to bring forth the much-needed rain, by means of the *Zuni* Rain Dance.

Descriptions of this sacred dance vary among sources. One version now follows.[56]

Sacred mud is gathered from the Sacred Lake, through which the *Zunis* are said to have emerged from the underworld, many ages ago. The male dancers impersonate both males and females, by dressing accordingly. They smear the sacred yellow mud on their bodies. Eight of the men impersonate women by wearing the female dress and mantle, while their long black hair is tied up in the *Hopi* Squash Blossom style that is representative of fertility. The "women" are completely covered except for their heads and bare feet. Their dresses and hands are covered by shawls.

The "male" dancers also wear spruce anklets, typifying life, and carry cattails, symbolic of moisture. They may also wear a necklace of beads and a fox skin hanging from their waists in the back. They wear an embroidered white kirtle or kilt and leather or silver bracelets around their wrists. The male dancers wear moccasins on their feet. The men distinguish themselves as male representatives by wearing topknots of macaw feathers on the crown of the head with three fluffy white eagle plumes hanging down the back, suspended by a string. Their saffron-yellow torsos highlight the white kirtles they wear around their waists. Spruce is tied around their ankles and they carry either live tortoises or gourd rattles. The dancing continues all night.

Early the next morning, the dancers are escorted to a ceremonial room. Soon after, the dancers emerge. Now the dancers are dressed differently. They wear masks that are a turquoise blue in color and flat-faced with long black beards, carrying long cattails. The color combination is remarkable. They appear with yellow upper bodies and legs, bright blue faces, black hair and beards, and waving green cattails. The "men" and "women" dancers repeatedly meet, then pass and turn, performing a complicated pattern. They dance in the morning four times, in a different place each time. This is repeated in the afternoon. The hope is that the dance-prayer has been executed properly to obtain the needed rain. If rain does not follow, the dance will try to be executed more properly another time.

A slightly different description[57] of the *Zuni* Rain Dance can be found at the following website: www.inquiry.net/outdoor/native/dance/rain_zuni.htm

In the late nineteenth century, the U.S. Government forbade all Native Americans to perform the sacred but feared Sun Dance. Other sacred dances were also forbidden. Natives circumvented this restriction, by telling the U.S. authorities that some of the sacred dances they were performing were only the "safe" Rain Dance. Clever!

Zuni Shalako Dance[58, 59, 60, 61, 62]

This dance is performed among the *Zuni* in early December, on or about December 1st. The *Zuni* Bow priests determine the exact date of the ceremony. Traditionally it was always the 49th day past the tenth full moon. That formula has been modified in modern times to be the weekend nearest the date set by the traditional method.

The *Shalako* Dance is usually performed following the harvest. Unlike other *Zuni* dances, visitors are invited to observe this sacred ceremony. The coming of the *Shalako* signifies the time for house blessings and the time to give thanks and to show gratitude for the blessings of the harvest. It is a ceremony that lasts through the night.

The *Shalako* are the couriers of the divine rainmakers who are stationed at each of the four cardinal points and also at the zenith and the nadir. When it is announced that the *Shalako* are coming there is feverish activity in the homes of the village. Food is prepared and the homes are cleaned and decorated in anticipation of the *Shalakos'* arrival, in the next week or so. The harvest of corn and beans is gathered. New mud is applied to the *adobe* home exteriors and the roofs are reinforced. *Piñon* and cedar wood branches are gathered and stacked as fuel to feed the hearth. The women work away grinding the newly harvested corn to make corn meal.

The *Shalako* Dancers[63] wear colorful costumes and masks, and stand ten feet tall. They represent the giant gods in effigy. They have painted still eyes, horns for ears and a big, horizontal snout made of wood. The wooden snout is made so that it can open and close with a loud snapping sound. Each figure wears a huge headdress of eagle or turkey feathers. A hoopskirt hangs around the figure's waist. It is made of white cotton and it may show a colored inverted pyramid pattern around the bottom edges, to represent rain clouds. The figure hangs on a frame that is supported underneath by a concealed *Zuni* native with a tall pole. A belt around his waist supports the pole above. As the figure moves, it utters a shrill whistle and the snout opens and closes with a sharp snapping noise. Artist Mac Schweitzer created a painting that portrays the action of the *Zuni Shalako*[64] figures carrying prayer sticks[65] to be planted, and showing their blessing of the shrines and households during the *Shalako* ceremony.

The dancers just seem to appear suddenly out of the dark of night. The ceremony starts with a ritual crossing of the small river that traverses the *pueblo* grounds. The ritual ceremony then proceeds to the selected and prepared houses in the village. The giant figures approach the open doors of each house to the chanting of a chorus and the continual sprinkling of some sacred meal. The local priest or shaman lays a small bunch of sacred feathers at the doorstep. These feathers carry the prayers of the priests to the powers above. Stooping during this process, the great effigy moves on to the doorstep of the next household. This festive and colorful ceremony is very popular with both residents and visitors. Feasting, singing and dancing begins in each blessed house until the dawn of the next day.

Usually a wide ditch has been specially prepared in the selected houses to allow the very tall *Shalako* to enter and to dance within. Six houses are traditionally selected to receive each of the six *Shalako*, although there are usually two impersonators per *Shalako*. In addition, two other houses are selected to receive and entertain the Council of the Gods[66] and the *koyemsi* or *koyemshi*.[67] Although these houses are supposed to be new, they are mostly replastered existing homes. Also, in modern times, the *Shalako* will sometimes double up on some of the selected homes. The *Shalakos* participate in some of the interior celebrations, but as the morning approaches they quietly leave and vanish back into the young rising sun, and into the deep gully from which they first emerged.

Pueblo Celebrations of New Tribal Authorities. Meaning of the Transfer of Canes Day, Kings' Day & Dances, and the Governors' Feast

These three events are celebrated according to the following schedule, at the beginning of each new year, by various *pueblos*:

...Transfer of Canes

January 1st. The transfer of tribal authority at the beginning of the New Year is celebrated with various dances at most *pueblos*. *Taos Pueblo* typically performs a Turtle Dance on this occasion. *Ohkay Owingeh* typically performs a Cloud or Basket Dance. *Santo Domingo* may perform a Corn Dance.

Among the *pueblos of New Mexico*, the transfer of authority between the past year's Tribal Governors and the new year's officials takes place on the Transfer of Canes Day,[68] which is usually on the first day of January in the New Year. The canes represents the sovereignty of the *pueblos* and the Transfer of Canes Day represents the day upon which this transfer occurs. It is the transfer of power from one group of *Pueblo* Governors to the succeeding group. It is usually celebrated with accompanying tribal ceremonies and dances.

Taos Pueblo usually celebrates the Transfer of Canes, and the dawning of a new year and a new administration, with the very appropriate Turtle Dance (please refer to the Turtle Dance section earlier in this chapter). However, it should be noted that new tribal officials are not necessarily installed each year for each and every *pueblo*. Some *pueblos* replace their officials on a multi-year basis (every two or three years).

The meaning behind the Tribal Canes themselves is also worthy of some brief explanation. When New Mexico was still a royal province of New Spain, after the *Santa Fe ReConquista*, the indigenous natives were ordered, under the authority of the crown, to elect a governor for each *pueblo*. These *Pueblo* Governors were intended to aid the Spanish Province Governor in settling local affairs and to represent each *pueblo's* native concerns and needs. Each elected *Pueblo* Governor was awarded a cane as a symbol of office from the Spanish officials. The Spanish cane was topped with metal in which was carved a Spanish cross. The cross represents the blessing of the Catholic Church and the support of the Spanish Crown.

Over time, as government of the region was transferred from the Spanish to the Mexicans to the Americans, two additional canes were awarded. The Mexican cane had a silver top. In modern times, the Lieutenant Governor usually receives the Mexican cane. Unfortunately, several *pueblos* have lost their Mexican canes.

The American cane[69] from the United States also had a silver top with "A. Lincoln" engraved into it. The cane itself was made of ebony wood. It was presented in 1863.

More recently, in 1980, New Mexico Governor Bruce King awarded a fourth cane to each *Pueblo* Governor to reaffirm each *pueblo's* sovereignty.

Again, in modern times, King Juan Carlos of Spain presented a fifth cane to each of the *pueblos*. This second Spanish cane was awarded in September 1987, during the king's travel to the state of New Mexico.

Generally speaking, four of the five canes are usually transferred to the incoming Tribal Governor. The incoming Tribal Lieutenant Governor usually receives the Mexican cane, if it exists. However, there may be significant variations among the *pueblos*.

During the yearly Transfer of Canes[70] ceremony held on January 1st, held by each participating *pueblo,* new tribal officials are installed and tribal authority is transferred to the new officials.

However, some Tribal Governors and other tribal officials may continue their term from one year into another. A particular *pueblo* may choose their tribal officials for longer than a one-year term. In this case, the canes are blessed in morning masses on Kings' Day and celebration of the event may or may not be recognized with tribal dances, at that particular *pueblo*, on Kings' Day.

The canes themselves are representative of each *pueblo* tribe's continuing sovereignty and the concept of tribal self-governance. They are also symbols of justice and leadership, and of tribal authority.

...Kings' Day Celebration

Dance celebrations are held at various *pueblos* in honor of the new Tribal Officials each January 6. The celebration usually includes a blessing of the tribal canes of authority for the new year.

The first honoring of the new officials takes place on Kings' Day[71] or Reyes Day. It is celebrated five days following the Transfer of Canes Day, on January 6th. This date celebrates the blessing of the tribal canes. It also recognizes and honors any new Tribal Governors and officials. Some *pueblos* perform native dances in recognition of the general event, even when the particular *pueblo* has continuing tribal officials from the year before. Others only perform native dances when the *pueblo* has chosen its own new tribal officials.

It is called Kings' Day because it falls on the traditional Christian holy day (January 6th) associated with the recognition of Jesus' divinity, by the visiting Three

Kings in Bethlehem. (It was once known as Twelfth Night or Twelfth Day, since the celebration takes place twelve days after Christmas. It is also known among Christians as the Day of the Epiphany, meaning "manifestation." The Three Kings are said to have arrived late after the birth of the Christ-child. Hence it is celebrated after Christmas). This celebration takes place throughout the world, where it is called Three Kings' Day. It is especially celebrated in Hispanic communities.

This same date has been chosen, at many of the *pueblos*, to recognize and honor new Tribal Governors and officials, and to bless the retained or the newly transferred canes of authority. The blessings usually take place during morning mass on Kings' Day. During the day's remainder, native dances are performed publicly, and later, privately, for the officials themselves. In 1980, the state of New Mexico presented its own additional cane to each of the *pueblos*. Spain also reaffirmed *pueblo* sovereignty with presentation of its second set of tribal canes in 1987.

...Governors' Feast Day

This third related event is held in the first or second weekend of February to celebrate the installation of the new Tribal Governors. Various dances are held at selected *pueblos.*

This event is the second honoring of the newly installed Tribal Governors. On this day, the newly installed *Pueblo* Tribal Governors gather at a designated *pueblo*, where they are collectively acknowledged, honored and celebrated. Various native dances are also performed. In 2013, the Governors' Feast was held at Sky City, also known as Old *Acoma.*

The significant feature of all these *pueblo* celebrations, as far as the viewing public is concerned, is the performance of various fascinating traditional native tribal dances. These dances may include deer or antelope dances, buffalo dances or eagle dances. Sometimes elk dances are performed instead. These celebrations are local to each participating *pueblo.*

As with all native events and celebrations, please consult the tribal offices for each pueblo, or the Indian *Pueblo* Cultural Center to determine events and schedules. See Appendix A.

More Information on Pueblo Celebrations

Information on a number of events can be found at the *Santa Fe* Convention and Visitor Bureau, at 505-955-6200. Alternately, contact the Eight Northern Indian *Pueblos* Council, at 505-747-1593, or the Five Sandoval Indian *Pueblos,* at 505-867-3351. The Governor's office of the individual *pueblo* can also be contacted for information. The contact information for each of the nineteen *pueblos* is given in Appendix A.

The Eight Northern *Pueblos* Group is headquartered in *Ohkay Owingeh* (aka *San Juan) Pueblo.* Each year they publish a booklet that describes each of the eight northern *pueblos,* and a schedule of *pueblo* events.

The Five Sandoval *Pueblos* Group consists of *Cochiti, Jemez, Zia, Santa Ana* and *Sandia.* For more information, contact NM Dept. of Indian Tourism, (1-800-545-2070). The Five Sandoval Indian *Pueblos* can be found at: 1043 Hwy 313, *Bernalillo*, NM 87004. Take I-25, Exit 550. Feast Day schedules for this sub-group of *pueblos* are decided upon in advance, but they are not published, as they are for the Eight Northern

Indian *Pueblos.*

All native event dates may vary slightly from those discussed here. The listed dates above serve as an approximate guide and schedule of events.

PART C: Celebrations of the *Apachean* Peoples

Apachean Festivities and Celebrations

Although much less numerous than the many *pueblo* celebrations, there are several public events and festivities sponsored by the *Navajo, Jicarilla Apache, Mescalero Apache* and the Red Paint *Apache* of southwestern New Mexico. Please see the summary shown in Table 12-4.

Events often include a Pow-Wow and some form of traditional native dance. Annual events discussed include the *Navajo* Nation Fair, *Jicarilla Apache Go-Jii-Ya* Feast, *Jicarilla Apache* Little Beaver Roundup, *Mescalero Apache* Maiden & Crown Dancers Ceremony, and the Red Paint *Apache* Pow-Wow and Indian Trade Show.

Tribe	Event	Date (approx.)	Dances & Celebrations (Potentially)	Event Duration	Location
Navajo	Northern *Navajo* Fair (aka *Navajo* Nation Fair)	Annual, Early September or October	Various, incldg *Yei bei chi* Dances. Wild horse races, Pow-Wow, Rodeo, etc.	7 days, M-Su	Shiprock Fairgrounds, Shiprock, NM
Jicarilla Apache	*Jicarilla Apache Go-Jii-Ya* Feast	Annual, mid-September	Various	2 days, on a weekend	Stone Lake (18 mi. south of *Dulce*), NM
Jicarilla Apache	*Apache* Little Beaver Roundup	Annual, mid-July	Various	7 days, M-Su	*Dulce*, NM
Mescalero Apache	*Apache* Maiden Ceremony & Mountain Spirits Dances	Annual, July 4th weekend	Crown Dance of the Mountain Spirits, Maiden Puberty Ceremony	4 days long, holiday week-end	*Mescalero*, NM
Warm Springs (*Chihene* or Red Paint) *Apache*	Red Paint *Apache* Pow-Wow and Indian Trade Show	Next to last weekend in January	Gourd Dance, Hoop Dance, Mountain Spirits Dance & various others	3 days	Silver City, NM

Table 12-4: *Apachean* (includes *Navajo*) Public Events in New Mexico.

Navajo Nation Fair or Northern *Navajo* Shiprock Fair[72, 73, 74]

This yearly event is also called the *Navajo* Nation Fair or even the Shiprock *Navajo* Fair, because it is held at the Shiprock Fairgrounds in the fall, either in early September or early October. It is a seven-day week long series of events. Events include marching bands, a Miss Central *Navajo* Pre-Teen Contest, a musical, fine arts & crafts exhibitions and contests, butchering and frybread competitions, a rodeo, a parade, Miss *Navajo* Queen Contest, a wild horse race, a Pow-Wow, native song, drumming and dance contests, a horse show, a horticulture exhibit, a public speaking/ talent show, a baby contest, a comedy show, golf events and contests, 4-H cookout & awards, livestock judging, a carnival, social dancing, BBQ, poultry, waterfowl & rabbit judging, poetry slam contests, hip-hop dancing and country singing. Wow!! Typically, there is also *Yei bei chi* dancing. There really is something here for everyone!

Note however, that there are separate admission fees for some of the major events such as the comedy show, the concerts and several rodeos. There is a nominal parking fee of several dollars. Children are considered to be between the ages of 6 -12, adults from 13 – 59, seniors are 60+. A three-day pass is also available. Accommodations can be found in Gallup, New Mexico, or in Window Rock or St. Michaels, Arizona. Camping permits are available on a "first come, first serve" basis.

To sample what the schedule was like for the 65th Annual *Navajo* Nation Fair, held in 2011, visit the following website: www.northernnavajonationfair.org

Navajo Nightway and the Y*ei bei chi* Dance[75, 76]

The *Navajo* perform an annual multi-night ceremony called *Yei bei chi*, Night Chant or even Nightway. The ceremony lasts for nine days and nights. It culminates in the *Yei Bei Chi* Dance. In this dance,[77] masked *Yei bei chi* dancers personify up to nine

Figure 12-8: *Yebichai Dancers - Navaho.*** (Photo by Edward S. Curtis, c. 1906, Library of Congress, Rare Books Division, Edward S. Curtis Collection.)

Yei, including Talking God. Water Sprinkler is often portrayed as a clown, and may even be an alternative representation of the *kokopelli*. The purpose of the ceremony is to restore balance and tranquility to the universe caused by any inadvertent or inappropriate human behavior, that may be especially offensive to the *Yei*, or that may have created an imbalance in the universal order.

This is the central concept behind *Navajo* beliefs: cosmic balance. It is the lack of balance that creates man's ills and misfortune or disease. It is not about preparation for death. The Nightway Chant ceremony entails many smaller ceremonies. The nine-day ceremony includes the initiation of young people (boys and girls) into the mysteries of the *Navajo* belief system, its spirituality and its rituals. Other rites and ceremonies occur over this same nine-day period. The highlight for many, however, is the *Yei bei chi* dance.

A *Yei Bei Chi* dance is also often performed at the annual *Navajo* Nation Fair in early September or October, in Shiprock, NM. See Figure 12-8.

Jicarilla Apache Annual *Go-Jii-Ya* (Feast)

Every year in mid September, the *Go-Jii-Ya* Feast is held at Stone Lake, 18 miles south of *Dulce*. This event initially started hundreds of years ago, when the two clans of the *Jicarilla Apache*, the Red Clan and the White Clan, were still nomadic, and were hunter-gatherers and raiders. When the two clans met up again they celebrated their reunion with a feast, the *Go-Jii-Ya*. Once the *Jicarilla Apache* moved onto the reservation in the 1800's, the event took place on a scheduled date. *Tipis* were set up and cooking took place outdoors. Hospitality is the main theme of this event. This feast and the associated events celebrate the tribal harvest.

The *Go-Jii-Ya* includes a trading bazaar, a Pow-Wow, ceremonial dances and rituals, and the traditional sacred relay foot races of the Red (*Llanero*) and White (*Ollero*) Clans. The footrace takes place at Stone Lake, and the runners are usually young boys of the two competing *Jicarilla Apache* Clans (Red and Black). The race developed from a *Jicarilla Apache* legend that speaks of a race that once occurred among all the animals and birds of the world. The losing clan gives gifts of fruit and vegetables, which are to be accepted gracefully. (Please note that during the race, clapping is NOT considered appropriate encouragement, whereas yelling is looked upon as the appropriate means of showing support for competitors.)

The *Go-Jii-Ya* is classified as a "give-away" festival to demonstrate sharing and giving, as examples of noble achievement, generosity and hospitality. These qualities are highly regarded among the *Jicarilla Apache* people.

Photography is NOT allowed at the annual *Go-Jii-Ya* celebration.

Jicarilla Apache Little Beaver Roundup[78]

Each year in mid-July, the *Jicarilla Apache* host a seven-day, week-long roundup that includes a stunning number of events and activities. Early in the week, on weekdays, there is a career expo, a pageant, a youth art show, a dog show, an amusement carnival, a kiddies parade, a youth basketball tournament, a spam carving contest, and a few other activities.

Some bigger events occur on Friday through Sunday. These include an annual Pony Express Race, a *Jicarilla* Veterans Memorial Ceremony, a Battle of the Bands, a Miss *Jicarilla Apache* Pageantry crowning, a Men's and a Women's Open Softball Tournament, a Pow-Wow Contest, a Rodeo, a five-mile run and a two mile run/walk, a live-music Concert, an Archery Shoot-out, Food Sales and Arts & Crafts Sales. No lack of things to do here!

The Pony Express Race is 70 miles long and crosses the *Jicarilla Apache* Nation lands. The 2010 event required an entry fee of $600 or $700. The race includes six horses and two riders on each Pony Express team. The fee allows substantial gifts to be awarded to the winners, typically including saddles, cash prizes, trophies, and jackets.

The Pow-Wow event includes twenty traditional dance contest categories, such as drumming, singing, and all kinds of native dances. Substantial cash prizes are awarded to the winners, from $500 to $1,500. Limited camping is available without hookups.

Photography is permitted at these various events in the *Jicarilla Apache* Little Beaver Roundup. For more information please visit the following website:

www.jicarillaonline.com

Mountain Spirits: *Mescalero Apache* Maiden & Crown Dancers Ceremony

Each year the *Mescalero Apache* conduct what is perhaps their most sacred ritual, the Puberty Rite Ceremony. It is sometimes referred to as the Sunrise Ceremony. It may also be called the *Apache Maiden* Ceremony and it is often combined with the Dance of the Mountain Spirits Ceremony. The four-day dance ceremony is open to the public, and it usually is held over the July 4th Independence Day weekend, in *Mescalero*, near *Ruidoso*.

In their native language the puberty ceremony is called *Nah-ih-es,* or *Na-ii-ees*. It means "preparing her" or "getting her ready".[79] It is a celebration of the sanctity of the newfound ability of young maidens to create life. The ceremony also encourages young maidens to be chaste in order to participate. Additionally, it encourages fidelity after marriage. It is thought that the Mountain Gods speak through the minds of the male dancers, who then communicate their knowledge to the minds of the young maidens. The maidens in turn, reveal the godly thoughts to the medicine man, for the benefit of all the tribal people. The ceremony lasts for four days and nights, because the number four is sacred and represents the four cardinal directions.

Each *Mescalero* Maiden may appear in a long pale yellow (to represent pollen) or white buckskin dress from shoulder to ankles. Her dress may be beautifully beaded and jeweled with silver medallions, studs, tin cone-tinklers and leather thongs, or with colored vertical strips of leather. Leather thongs may drape over the arms and fringes of the dress. The fringes may represent sunbeams. The dress may also be painted with symbols associated with White Painted Woman[80] or Changing Woman, a potent female *Apache* deity. These may be the crescent moon, morning star, rainbows, and/or sunbeams. Many hours of intensive and personal family labor goes into the making of these maiden dresses for this special and significant ceremony. Sacred corn pollen coats the young maidens' faces.

Through this ceremony, a young maiden is transformed in the eyes of her tribal community from a young maiden into a fully recognized fertile woman, ready to perform her role alongside the other women of the tribe.

The ceremony[81] begins when the tribal holy man gives the signal. It is usually considerably later than sunrise, however, in spite of the alternate name for the ceremony. The holy man blesses a few 30-foot long pine or spruce logs that have been stripped of their leaves and branches. Chanting continues by tribal women enwrapped in blankets and shawls. Meanwhile, a group of male tribal members pick up the logs, putting them on end, to form the framework for a *tipi*. The tops of the logs are lashed together to form the open conical structure. In this way, the ceremonial *tipi* is built for the ensuing ceremonies. When completed, the *tipi* opening faces the rising sun in the east. Inside reeds are placed on the floor. Buckskin may also be placed on the floor. The young female initiates often dance on this buckskin, inside the *tipi*, during the lengthy chants of the holy man.

The ceremony then proceeds to follow. Three women arrive wearing doeskin dresses colorfully decorated with quills and beadwork. They wear colorful ribbons to adorn their hair.

During the ceremony, the young female candidates run eastward from the ceremonial *tipi* towards a basket, multiple times. Each time the basket is moved closer to the *tipi*. The young girls are then made to lie on their backs on the ground. This ceremony re-enacts the myth of White Painted Woman or Changing Woman. At the end of this sacred ceremony, the young women can receive gifts from the guests. Each young woman's family then gives small gifts to the ceremony's participants. Finally, all are invited to share a meal with the participants. For the day's remainder and for the following three days, additional rituals, prayers and dances ensue as each new young woman is introduced into the ways and expectations of *Mescalero Apache* womanhood.

Each maiden is given a "Medicine Basket"[82] as part of the ceremony. The woven basket contains various natural items that represent the *Mescalero Apache* universe. These items represent the spiritual elements that the maiden will need on her journey to becoming a woman, and on her journey through life. The pollen of the cattail plant or corn pollen is usually placed upon the brow of those who enter into the sacred *tipi* during the Puberty Ceremonials. The power of White Painted Woman is thereby bestowed upon the maidens participating in the Maiden Ceremonies. Those who pray for healing or other blessings, and who have faith are thought to have their prayers answered.

When the four-day ceremony draws to an end,[83] the ceremonial *tipi* is dismantled, and the visitors leave. However, the young woman and her family remain at the campground until the ninth day. On that day, the young woman is given a sacred bath in yucca suds. This is her final purification ritual. After that point she is recognized as a marriageable young woman.

The *Mescalero Apache* Maiden's Coming of Age Ceremony represents the importance of *Apache* women, indeed of all women, because of their strength, wisdom and tenacity. It also symbolizes the young initiate's life journey as she matures. Women are so honored because they are the bearers of life and the insurers of cultural continuity.

Mountain Spirit Dancers[84] are significant participants in these ceremonies. There are usually four different Crown Dancers, representing the benevolent Mountain Spirits, each of which has a unique function. Each represents the spirit of a place or person.

Some say that each *Gahn* may represent a cardinal direction. In addition, there may appear one or more clowns. The most powerful and main spirit is the clown. The dancers are meant to impersonate the Mountain Spirits, or *Gahns* (*Gaans*). These dancers are touched by the power of the *Gahn* or *Gaan* as they dance, and they therefore assist the tribal medicine man in healing and puberty ceremonies. See Figure 12-9 for an image of a modern Crown Dancer.

The modern attire of the male dancers is roughly as follows. They usually wear a black mask about their heads and face, and wear a decorated wooden crown atop their heads. This is why they are also known as Crown Dancers. They wear a red *bandana* or kerchief covering the lower part of their faces and head. Other Crown Dancers wear a red *bandana* that covers the area below the eyes but above the mouth area, while still covering their heads and faces with a black material to the neck.

Their upper bodies are naked but are painted black, with white markings. However, some Crown Dancers reverse this paint order, instead painting their bodies gray or white, with black markings. A red thong might be tied around their biceps, with the excess length of the thongs dangling down their arms. These red thongs are said to represent the blood of the *Apache* people.

Figure 12-9: Modern *Apache* Crown Dancer. (With permission of YTC Summit International, Summit Collections.)

They wear a fringed buckskin kilt, with multiple spherical jingle bells tied all around their waists, and calf-high moccasin boots. It is said that Mountain Spirit Dancers may sometimes wear a small piece of abalone beneath their masks, to provide good luck.

In each hand they carry a wooden wand in the shape of a cross or perhaps a trident. This wand is used to touch the sick, and thereby transfer their sickness to the wand, which can then be dispersed into the air and the universe. It is not unusual to see a Crown Dancer approach the old and infirmed during a ceremony, and touch them with the wand to take away their ailments. The wand is then raised high to allow the negative energy to dissipate into the sky. These dancers usually appear after nightfall on each of the four nights of the celebration. The Mountain Spirit (Crown) Dancers are dramatic looking figures. Other *Apache* tribes observe a similar ceremony, with variations. The dance is quite

Figure 12-10: Close-up of one of the Dancers in the Crowned Dancer statue set, in front of the Inn of the Mountain Gods Resort/Casino, *Mescalero*. Sculpted by Freddie Peso. (By permission of Mrs. Sophia Peso and the *Mescalero Apache* Tribe.)

different from *pueblo*-style dances. The motions are more dramatic and somewhat jerky. They crouch a great deal and often pose moving their heads from side to side to emphasize the crown.

They also make motions towards the sky with their wands. Their dance steps are also more pronounced and exaggerated. They are dramatic figures and active dancers, and they are extremely interesting to watch! The visitor has to wonder how they manage all of their athletic movements, and yet still manage to breathe and see adequately beneath their black masks.

Several Crown Dancers are grouped in a majestic, modernistic statue set that greets the visitor, outside the entry to the Inn of the Mountain Gods Resort/Casino, in *Mescalero*. Figures 12-10 shows a close-up view of one of the several dancers shown in the statue group.

During the four-day celebration, the *Mescalero Apache* Reservation is opened to the public. It provides a parade, various rodeos, daily and nightly traditional dancing, and of course the aforementioned Coming of Age Ceremony. For more information, call (575) 464-4494, or contact:

> *Mescalero Apache* Reservation
> P.O. Box 227
> *Mescalero*, NM 88340

Red Paint *Apache* Pow-Wow[85] and Indian Trade Show

The Red Paint *Apache* Pow-Wow is held near the end of January each year in Silver City. This event is held in memory and recognition of the *Chihene* Band (of the *Chiricauhua Apache*) or Red Paint *Apache* people, otherwise known as the Warm Springs *Apache*. *Victorio* and later *Nana* were famous leaders of the Warm

Springs *Apache* in the late 1800's. Many of the warriors, who remained alive after the *Apache* Wars ended, were exiled and imprisoned in prison camps, in Florida and later in Oklahoma. They never saw their homeland again. No reservation was ever established for the Warm Springs *Apache*! These *Apache* people occupied the lands of southwestern New Mexico, around Truth or Consequences, Silver City, etc.

The first Red Paint *Apache* Pow-Wow was held in January 2003. Today, the tradition continues in honor of these brave and displaced people. This annual event is a Pow-Wow, an Indian Market and a Native Arts Concert, all combined into a single weekend event. The event usually includes Drum Contests, Gourd Dances, Hoop Dances and Mountain Spirit Dancers. A Pow-Wow is held, and there is also a Fashion Show! There are arts and craft vendors. Food vendors are also available for food and refreshment. The event extends from Friday through Sunday evening of the celebration weekend.

More Information on Native American Culture

The Indian *Pueblo* Cultural Center or IPCC presents a full schedule of artist workshops (weaving, watercolors, basket weaving, gourd art, micaceous clay pottery, etc), dance exhibits by various native tribal dance groups, lectures and summer day camps. The dances that are presented change each week. Personal photography is allowed at these dances. To check the current schedule of activities go online to:

www.indianpueblo.org

Downstairs in the IPCC there is a very interesting museum of *pueblo* pottery artifacts in one section and a review of *pueblo* history in the other section. What makes this museum so fascinating and informative is that the history narrative is from the *pueblo* natives' perspective.

However, don't let the center's (*pueblo*) name fool you. Non-*pueblo* as well as *pueblo* native dance groups perform here through the summer months.

Two major activities occur in Gallup, New Mexico each year: the Inter-Tribal Indian Ceremonial (ITIC) and the Gallup Summer Indian Dance Program (GSIDP). The ITIC takes place at Red Rock State Park, 7 miles east of Gallup, early in the month of August. In 2012, the event was held from August 8 through August 12. This all-Indian ceremonial includes a Pow-Wow, Rodeo, Indian crafts and arts, a parade, food booths and performance arts. Tribes from the U.S., Mexico and Canada are featured at this event. For more information call: 1-800-233-4528 or visit the following website:

http://theceremonial.com

The GSIDP is presented at the same Red Rock State Park location. However, the program lasts through the entire summer season, Memorial Day through Labor Day. Each evening, traditional tribal dances are performed by one of seven dance groups from the *Zuni, Navajo* and *Acoma* tribes. A discussion period follows the dances with topics on tribal and regional histories, native foods, arts and crafts, and traditions.

Each year, since 1984, the city of Albuquerque has sponsored what is called the Gathering of Nations Pow-Wow. It is usually held at the very end of April and it includes over 3,000 participants. There is Native American singing, drumming and dancing, an Indian Traders Market with many shopping booths, native foods and music, and the selection and crowning of the Miss Indian World. For more information contact:

www.gatheringofnations.com

or

www.itsatrip.org/events/spring/PowWow

Chapter Thirteen: National Monuments, Parks and Historic Trails

Numerous natural and cultural national treasures in New Mexico are designated as National Monuments, National Historical Parks, National Parks or as National Historic Trails. These unique sites are protected for future generations, as a common heritage for all Americans. They include, in alphabetical order, the *Aztec* Ruins, Bandelier, *Capulin* Volcano, *Carlsbad* Caverns, Chaco (Canyon) Culture, *El Camino Real de Tierra Adentro* Trail, *El Malpais*, *El Morro* (Inscription Rock), Fort Union, *Gila* Cliff Dwellings, *Kasha Katuwe* Tent Rocks, Old Spanish Trail, *Pecos*, Petroglyph Park, *Salinas Pueblo Missions*, *Santa Fe* Trail and White Sands National Monuments. These sites are discussed in this chapter but they are organized according to their basic categories, as listed immediately below.

PART A: National Monuments (11) (*Aztec* Ruins, Bandelier, *Capulin* Volcano, *El Malpais*, *El Morro*, Fort Union, *Gila* Cliff Dwellings, *Kasha Katuwe* Tent Rocks, Petroglyph, *Salinas Pueblo* Missions and White Sands)
PART B: National Historical Parks (2) (Chaco Culture, *Pecos*)
PART C: National Parks (1) (*Carlsbad* Caverns)
PART D: National Historic Trails (3) (*El Camino Real de Tierra Adentro* Trail, Old Spanish Trail, *Santa Fe* Trail)

Many of the sites in chapters 13 and 14 require some hiking. Please dress appropriately and wear hiking boots for proper traction and support, head cover to protect from the sun and bottled water to prevent dehydration. Also, hikers should be aware that Western Diamondback Rattlesnakes can be found in many of these areas, especially off-trail. So be aware of your surroundings and where you step! In chapters 13 and 14, key points of interest are highlighted in **bold** text.

PART A: National Monuments (11)

Aztec Ruins National Monument[1, 2, 3, 4, 5]

This monument is located in the town of *Aztec* in *San Juan* County, in the northwestern part of New Mexico, near the *Colorado* border. The site and its buildings date back to 11th and 13th centuries A.D. Ancient *pueblo* structures are preserved here from the *Anasazi* peoples. The name, *Aztec,* is incorrectly applied. Early (19th century) American settlers falsely attributed the site to the *Aztec* civilization. Other *pueblo* structures, the **Salmon Ruins** and **Heritage Park**, lie shortly to the south of the *Aztec* Ruins National Monument site, near the *San Juan* River and Bloomfield, New Mexico. (Although the monument contains the contemporary term "ruins" in its name, Native Americans do not apply this terminology in referring to this or other ancient *pueblos. A pueblo* is seen as having its own life cycle. Its current state is the state it is meant to be in, according to its own life cycle.)

The *Aztec* Ruins National Monument preserves a large walled settlement, dating from the 12th century. It contained close to 400 rooms.

Contained in the same community are a dozen *kivas* used for religious, spiritual and ceremonial purposes. A large reconstructed *kiva* is a popular attraction. At the **Row of Doors**, one can see what appears to be a corridor of stoned doorways that are horizontally aligned with one another. A view from the end allows one to see the other doorways in line in a telescoping fashion.

The original inhabitants were related, or were in some manner associated, with either the *Mesa Verde* ("Green Mesa") culture of the Four Corners area or the Chaco Culture, 55 miles further south, or possibly with both cultures.

The monument has a small Visitor Center and hosts a short video on the site, local *flora* and *fauna*. The "**East Ruins**" have not been fully excavated and they are closed to the public. However, the "**West Ruins**" have been excavated and are available for viewing. A short walking tour takes the visitor around and through the "**West Ruins**." It requires about 30 to 45 minutes to complete.

The walking trail leads to a high point, allowing the visitor to get a good view of the ancient *pueblo* village. The trail then leads along the outside wall to the small **Hubbard Tri-Wall** site. Here one finds the remains of small former buildings that are partially buried, with three concentric walls. It reminds one of a curiously built *kiva*. See Figure 13-1. The trail leads back to the main village area, where one finds

Figure 13-1:
Hubbard Tri-Wall,
at the *Aztec* Ruins
National Monument.

a number of ground floor rooms, which still have roofs on them. Continuing, one enters the main *plaza* of the **West Ruins**, surrounded by numerous building remains and *kivas*. See Figure 13-2.

There is a magnificent, large 50-foot wide **reconstructed kiva** in this *plaza*. It was rebuilt in 1934, under some archeological assumptions, to give visitors a sense of what it was like in the 12th century. This **reconstructed *kiva*** is very large and very impressive! Eventually, the short trail returns to the Visitor Center. The *Aztec* Ruins National Monument is not as massive in scope as the Chaco Culture National Historical Park, to be discussed later, nor is its location as scenic or isolated. It is much more intimate. However, this small compact site is well worth seeing!!

There are three other archeological sites at this location, further to the east. However, these eastern sites have not yet been excavated.

It is thought that the *pueblo* was abandoned either due to drought or exhaustion

Figure 13-2: West Ruins, at the *Aztec* Ruins National Monument.

of the soil, and that the residents moved on to other neighboring sites. Many tribes still consider this area sacred.

To get there, drive to *Bernalillo* via Interstate 25. Then take Hwy 550 northwest towards *Nageezi*. Continue on Hwy 550 northeast through Bloomfield, towards the town of *Aztec*.

This national monument is located just two miles from the center of downtown *Aztec*, near Farmington, New Mexico. Once in *Aztec*, follow the signs to the monument. The *pueblo* remains lie within the 27 acres reserved for the monument. It preserves the cultural continuity and legacy of native peoples. However, these archeological remains are also a legacy for all Americans.

Bandelier National Monument[6, 7, 8]

This famous monument is located near the towns of *Los Alamos* and White Rock. It spreads across both *Los Alamos* County and Sandoval County, New Mexico. The national monument preserves the homes, living sites, and agricultural areas of the Ancestral *Pueblo* people in this region. The site name was designated in 1916, in honor of the Swiss anthropologist Adolph Bandelier, who researched much of the ancient native *pueblo* and contemporary cultures of the area.

In Bandelier National Monument, one can see ancestral *pueblo* homes, sacred ceremonial underground structures known as *kivas,* rock paintings and petroglyphs. Small caves were carved into the volcanic (tuff) cliff walls, which have a thin hard exterior but a very soft interior. Some dwellings were built against these caves in the cliff walls, known as "*cavates*", while other dwellings were built on the canyon floor. Bandelier is a very fascinating and interesting national monument, with the added attraction that it is less than a one hour drive from *Santa Fe* (48 miles) and less than two hours from Albuquerque (98 miles). Bandelier protects approximately 30,000 acres of natural lands and the dependent wildlife.

Bandelier National Monument allows for various options depending on the time available to you for your visit. The Visitor Center provides a short 15-minute orientation and touring video that is worth watching. If the visitor has only about one hour to spare then walking the **Main Loop Trail** will take the visitor through the first part of the *Frijoles* ("Beans") **Canyon**. This trail passes the ***Tyuonyi Pueblo***

Figure 13-3: *Tyuonyi Pueblo* at Bandelier National Monument. (Note the circular chamber, which was once a *kiva*, just left of the central *plaza* area.)

and the big underground *kiva* on the canyon floor.

Tyuonyi Pueblo shows a nearly circular layout with three underground *kivas,* within the central *plaza* of the village. See Figure 13-3. (**Tyuonyi** is pronounced "Qu'-whe-nee"). The *pueblo* buildings probably rose to two or three stories in height. Native peoples occupied this region between 1150 AD and 1500 AD. Hunter-gatherers once sporadically inhabited this region, for about 10,000 years prior to this time period. Descendants of the original **Tyuonyi Pueblo** still inhabit some of the neighboring present-day *pueblos*. One can imagine the smell of *piñon* or envision the crop fields surrounding the *pueblo*, or the native people going about their daily tasks. One can almost hear the sounds of the villagers, adults and children, and domesticated dogs barking, in this once thriving community on the **Frijoles Canyon** floor. The *Pueblo* Peoples from some of the surrounding areas claim that they are descendants of those who once lived in the Bandelier area. Other *pueblos* also have a connection to Bandelier and they all work together with park officials to ensure their ancestral legacy is properly preserved and maintained.

Figure 13-4: Surrounding tuff cliff faces, at Bandelier National Monument.

Figure 13-5:
Reconstructed Talus
House, at Bandelier
National Monument

Figure 13-6: Ladder access to the
cavates, at Bandelier National
Monument.

As one looks around, one can see the pock-marked tuff cliff faces. It is currently thought that the holes in the cliff walls were caused by erosion, working over a long time period. See Figure 13-4.

The **Main Loop Trail** climbs up gradually alongside the talus (loose rock) houses, and cliff dwellings. See Figure 13-5. Access to these small cliff caves or *cavates* is available via wooden ladders. See Figure 13-6. Houses made of stone once stood in front of these *cavates*. One can see a reconstructed **Talus House** with the exposed roof beams, projecting out from the cliff face along this same path. This house is a modern reconstruction.

If the visitor has about two hours to spare, then continue the hike along the **Main Loop Trail** for another half mile or so, to the **Alcove House**. On the way, one will pass the **Long House** cliff dwellings, an 800-foot long expanse of connected multi-storied stone houses. Here cave rooms in the rear were used as back rooms or perhaps for storage. The **Alcove House** is reached by an arduous climb of over 140 feet, reached via four tall wooden ladders.

An alternate moderate length trail can take the visitor, in the other direction, to the opposite end of the *Frijoles* **Canyon**, to the **Upper Falls**. This **Upper Falls Trail** is approximately 1.5 miles in length, one way, with an elevation change of about 400 feet. The uphill return hike is more tiring than the gradual downhill hike to the falls. Currently, the **Lower Falls Trail**, which extends beyond the **Upper Falls**, is closed due to safety concerns. In 2011, a flashflood washed away part of the **Lower Falls Trail,** making the trail and this approach to the *Rio Grande* inaccessible. The *Rio Grande* is located about 2.5 miles from the Visitor Center.

Yet another option for those with time to spare, and for those in good physical condition, is to view the *Tsankawi* (San' kuh wee) section of the monument, along the *Tsankawi* **Trail**. This area is found near the monument front gate. *Tsankawi* is located along NM4, about 2.5 miles distant from the town of White Rock. Upon entry to the monument, ask the park ranger for specific directions. It offers a 1.5-mile primitive trail loop, wherein one can see petroglyphs, cave dwellings and an unexcavated village.

There are additional hiking trails within the monument. Ask for further information at the Visitor Center.

To reach Bandelier National Monument from Albuquerque, take I-25 to the NM 550 North exit. Follow this road to *San Ysidro,* where NM 4 East can be picked up. NM 4 East will lead through the *Jemez* Mountains.

It will pass through the *Valles Calderas* ("Crater Valleys") National Preserve. Then proceed towards *Los Alamos.* This road reaches an elevation of 9,000 feet in places. Please inquire about road conditions before taking this route during or directly after winter storms. Ignore the northward turnoff towards NM 501 and towards *Los Alamos.* Stay on NM 4 East to the Bandelier National Monument. The monument entrance eventually appears on the right side of the road.

Alternately, one can take the less scenic I-25 north from Albuquerque to *Santa Fe,* and proceed from there. To get to Bandelier National Monument from *Santa Fe,* take Route 85/285 north to NM502 in *Pojoaque.* Follow NM502 west to NM 4 West. Follow the signs to the Bandelier National Monument entrance, which will appear on the left on NM4 West.

Bandelier National Monument is open every day of the year except for Christmas Day and New Year's Day. The park may also close for fires, snowy weather or other hazardous conditions.

Capulin Volcano National Monument[9, 10, 11]

Capulin Volcano National Monument is located near the High Plains area of northeastern New Mexico, within and near the eastern border of Union County. It is near the town of *Capulin*, meaning "wild cherries or choke cherries" (Spanish). *Capulin* Volcano appears like a mountain with a sawed-off top. See Figure 13-7. A spiral road carries visitors to the parking lot at the base of the volcano rim.

Figure 13-7: *Capulin* Volcano National Monument.

The volcano featured at *Capulin* Volcano National Monument is an extinct symmetrical cinder cone volcano. It lies within the *Raton*-Clayton Volcanic Field. *Capulin* Volcano National Monument preserves a volcanic cone that is approximately 60,000 years old. Crater Rim is about a mile in circumference with a depth of about 400 feet. The top elevation of the volcano rim is 8,182 feet, which is higher than the mean or average elevation of 5,700 feet, throughout New Mexico.

A small Visitor Center (VC) and bookstore is located at ground level to purchase books, maps and other materials. The monument park has nearly five miles of hiking trails. One can explore the lave flows around the volcano's base. Alternately, one can drive uphill to the parking lot at the base of the crater's rim, explore the volcano rim or take hikes down into the inactive volcano.

There is no camping within the park. Camping facilities can be found within a reasonable driving distance of the park. There are also no gasoline facilities within a ten-mile radius of the national monument. Make sure you arrive with a full gas tank!

Several trails originate near the base of the *Capulin* Volcano National Monument. These include:

Lava Flow Trail: This unimproved trail at the base of the volcano is one mile long. It is a loop that takes the visitor across volcano lava flows. The Visitor Center has a Trail Guide that discusses the lava flows.

Nature Trail: This trail is located just outside the Visitor Center and it forms a figure eight. It is wheelchair accessible. Descriptions are given of the various *flora* and *fauna* that can be found along the way, as well as the local geology.

Boca Trail: This unimproved trail is roughly 2-miles long. It takes the visitor through the *Boca* or "Mouth" area. This is where the lava flows vented out from the volcano base, or from the "mouth" of the volcano base. A self-guiding trail brochure is available from the Visitor Center. One can obtain close-up views of some of the local geological features along this trail.

Separate from the base trails, access to the top of the cinder cone is made by car via a two-mile paved road that spirals around the cone, as it climbs towards the rim on top. The ascent to the top is along the outer edge of the spiral road. There are guardrails only at selected points. Most of the roadway does not have an outer rail or wall. Caution is required! Do NOT get distracted by the scenery. It may be very dangerous to do so! There will be ample opportunities to view the surrounding scenery at the summit. The road is windy, and subject to short tight turns and twists near the summit. If the visitor suffers from acrophobia, it may not be the best choice to make this ascent.

Visitors can drive this road up to the parking lot at the base of Crater Rim. Hikers can follow trails on top that circle the rim, or that lead down into the mouth of the volcano. The warmer months are probably best for accessing the volcano top, without fear of snow, ice and cold weather. Because of the high altitude, the top area is somewhat cooler than other parts of New Mexico. Highs in the summer rarely exceed 85 degrees Fahrenheit. At the volcano rim top, one has unobstructed, panoramic views of the volcanic field surrounding the volcano below, distant snow-capped mountains, great expanses and landmarks of northern New Mexico, as well as distant views, with some luck on very clear days, towards several neighboring states (Oklahoma, Texas and Colorado).

The surrounding views of northern New Mexico, are also quite stunning in their beauty. One can see *Sierra Grande* ("Great Mountain", at 8,720 feet) to the southeast, **Laughlin Peak** (8,820 feet) to the southwest, and the *Sangre de Cristo* **Mountains** far to the west. North of **Laughlin Peak,** but still in the southwest quadrant, one can see a long flat *mesa*. It is called *Mesa Larga* ("Long Mesa"), appropriately enough. *Palo Blanco* ("White high timber") **Mountain** and **Horseshoe Crater** can also be seen in the southwestern direction. The very distinctive *José Butte* (8,185 feet), with its sloping flat top, lies relatively close by, just south of the northwestern direction. See Figure 13-8. **Emery Peak** and **Purvine** *Mesa* can be seen in the northeast quadrant. To get the best view looking directly northward one has to climb to the very top of the volcano rim. Here one can look towards *Colorado*. The 360-degree view from the top rim allows visual access to the horizon in every direction. The views are simply stunning! Figure 13-9 shows *Sierra Grande* from the Crater Rim.

Figure 13-8: Looking just south of northwest, towards *José Butte*, from the Crater Rim, at *Capulin* Volcano National Monument.

Of course, the visitor can also look below into the bottom of the volcanic crater, or take a hike into it. See Figure 13-10. ***Capulin* Volcano** is an outstanding and stunning landmark.

Two major trails are available from the small parking lot located near the volcano summit. These are:

Crater Rim Trail: a one-mile paved loop around the volcano rimtop. It features wayside exhibits that explain the various features of the ***Raton*-Clayton Volcanic Field**. Some parts of this hike are quite steep and arduous. It is not recommended for the timid or for those with health or fitness limitations. Hiking boots or shoes are recommended. The starting altitude of the trail is 7,877 feet. The peak altitude at the top of the crater rim is 8,182 feet. (For reference the Visitor Center is located at an altitude of 7,242 feet.) Crater Rim experiences an elevation change of 400 or 500 feet, from the depths of the crater to the crater rim peak. Therefore, it is not amenable to wheelchairs, strollers, segways or bicycles.

Figure 13-9: Looking towards the southeast and *Sierra Grande*, from the Crater Rim at *Capulin* Volcano National Monument.

Figure 13-10: Volcano Crater (depression on the lower right), as seen from the Crater Rim, at *Capulin* Volcano National Monument.

Crater Vent Trail: This paved trail into the bottom of *Capulin's* crater is roughly 0.2 mile one-way. The elevation change is only 100 feet.

To get to *Capulin* Volcano National Monument take I-25 north towards *Raton.* Take NM 64/87 for 33 miles east, to the town of *Capulin.* Take NM 325 from *Capulin* north three miles to the monument entrance. If your approach is from the east, the monument lies 58 miles west of Clayton via NM 64/87.

Capulin Volcano National Monument is just one more fascinating and scenic place to visit in New Mexico. It is a natural wonder that is awesome to behold!

El Malpais National Monument[12, 13, 14]

El Malpais National Monument is found in western New Mexico near *San Rafael* and Grants, just south of I-40, in *Cibola* County. It lies on federal lands between the *Ramah Navajo* Reservation in the west, and the *Acoma Pueblo* Reservation on the east. The Spaniards named the area *El Malpais,* meaning "the badlands." The local landscape is barren with rugged volcanic fields. Ancient *Pueblo* Peoples, Spanish Colonials, and *Anglo*-American pioneers and explorers have frequented *El Malpais.* National Monument. There are numerous archeological sites within the park.

This national monument is the second largest volcanic field located in the Basin and Range Region of New Mexico. *El Malpais* lies within a basin formed by the surrounding higher elevation sandstone bluffs. These are visible in the distance and are recognized by their lighter color, which contrasts with the dark grayish volcanic rock of the *El Malpais* area. Many inactive volcanoes abound in this area, that is known for its geothermal activity.

El Malpais National Monument contains numerous lava tube caves, that are closed to the public.

One prominent natural feature is **La Ventana Natural Arch,** a huge natural sandstone arch, located near the eastern edge of the *Malpais* Lava Fields. It is located within the **El Malpais National Conservation Area** that is managed by the Bureau of Land Management (BLM). (*El Malpais* National Monument is managed separately by the National Park Service (NPS)). **La Ventana** means "window" in Spanish.

The elevation at *El Malpais* ranges from 6,500 feet to 8,300 feet. Early fall may be the most comfortable time of year to visit this site, avoiding the weather extremes of summer and winter, and the unpredictability of spring.

There are numerous trails available at *El Malpais:*

El Calderon ("Large kettle") Area Trail: This 3-mile trail is open to hikers, mountain bike and four-wheel drive vehicles. The trail takes the traveler to the following stops on the loop trail: Junction Cave, Double Sinks, Bat Cave, Lava Trench, *El Calderon* Cinder Cone, Fire Ecology and Life on the Edge. *El Calderon* area is located 20 miles south of Grants on NM53.

Lava Falls Area Trail: This one-mile loop trail is marked by stone cairns. It leads to the lava of the **McCarty's Flow.** It is located 36 miles south of I-40 on NM 117.

Zuni-Acoma Trail: This ancient trail connects the *Zuni* and *Acoma Pueblos.* The trail uses many of the lava bridges and rock cairns built by the ancient native inhabitants of this area. This trail is rugged and about 7.5 miles in each direction. It could consume an entire day to complete. Most of the trail follows along a portion of the Continental Divide. If one is traveling from the east, this trail may be found on NM 117, 15 miles south of I-40. Traveling from the west it may be found at NM 53, 16 miles south of I-40.

Sandstone Bluffs: The top of the bluffs provides a breath-taking view of the surrounding lava flows and the scenic landscape. Caution must be exercised however, not only for reasons of safety, but also to preserve the micro-ecosystems in the soil. Avoid areas where there appears a knobby black crust on the earth below where you are hiking. This crust is called **cryobiotic** soil. It is a living micro-ecosystem of **cyanobacteria**, better known as blue-green algae, soil lichens, mosses, microfungi, green algae and various bacteria. The crust preserves the loose soil, by preventing its erosion. The loss of this cryobiotic crust can result in the loss of hundreds of years of cyanobacterial growth and allows the wind and the rain to carry away the underlying sand and micro-ecosystem.

Garrett Homestead: The remains of this mid-1930's era homestead are preserved here. Homesteaders from the Dust Bowl and the Great Depression came to areas such as this to start life anew. The homestead can be found on the gravel trail to the Sandstone Bluff Overlook.

Big Tubes Loop Trail: This loop trail is marked by stone cairns and it is roughly 2-miles long. Various volcanic formations can be seen along this trail including a lava collapse at Caterpillar Collapse, a lava wall, a lava bridge at Seven Bridges, along with two lava tube caves at Big Skylight Cave and Four Winds Cave. However, all caves have been ordered closed to visitors. Please check with the Visitor Center before planning on taking this or any other trail mentioned above.

All of these hikes should be undertaken with caution in mind. Consult with the park rangers about open/closed condions, weather conditions and the like. Wear sturdy hiking boots. Carry bottled water. Pack a snack and a first aid kit. Wear clothing appropriate to the weather conditions. Inform some other person of your specific plans. Finally, consult park rangers about any further needs for specific trails.

During World War Two, the *Malpais* **Lava Fields** were one of eight sites that the Manhattan Project considered for detonation of the first atomic bomb. This became known as the Trinity Test. The final site selected for the Trinity Test was the northern part of the White Sands Missile Range. See Chapters Three and Four.

El Morro (Inscription Rock) National Monument[15, 16, 17]

Known also as **Inscription Rock**, *El Morro* is located very near the *Ramah Navajo* Reservation, in *Cibola* County, New Mexico, along NM 53. The Spaniards called it *El Morro*, meaning the "Headland." *Anglo*-Americans called it **Inscription Rock**. The native *Zuni* called it "*A'ts'ina*", meaning "place of writings on the wall."

The most significant feature of the park is the great sandstone promontory that is *El Morro*. It dominates the surrounding landscape. Below the sandstone bluff there is a small pool of water. This location with its cooling shade and its available water supply became a favorite resting place for weary travelers in the 17th through the 19th century.

The national monument provides a Visitor Center. In addition, there is a short half-mile loop trail that leads the visitor past the small pool mentioned above, and past rocks with petroglyphs. It also takes the traveler past **Inscription Rock** itself, where one can view ancient inscriptions as well as the inscriptions left by the Spanish explorers, Don Juan de Oñate and Don Diego de Vargas. A longer, two-mile trail takes the visitor to the top of *El Morro*, where the *pueblo* remains can be seen.

The top of *El Morro* bluff provides a spectacular view of the surrounding landscape. Don't miss the chance to partake of this wonderful experience!

Figure 13-11: *El Morro (Inscription Rock).*** (Photo by Edward S. Curtis, c. 1925, Courtesy Palace of the Governors Photo Archives (NMHM. DCA) neg. # 144700)

Between 1275 and 1350 A.D., *Pueblo* Peoples inhabited the top of the *mesa*. **Two ancient *pueblos*** lie at the top of the promontory. Archeologists have identified 875 rooms, which may have housed up to 1,500 people. These ancient *pueblos* can be seen on the longer two-mile loop trail.

The shorter half-mile loop trail allows viewing the various inscriptions that have given *El Morro* its English name, **Inscription Rock**. There are numerous inscriptions on the sandstone rock. In pre-Columbian times, the *Anasazi* made carvings and incised petroglyphs on the rocks. Travelers made yet other inscriptions, from as far back as the 17th century up through modern times. Here, these voyagers documented their names, dates, signatures and tales of their travels. See Figure 13-11.

In April 1605, the Spanish explorer and Governor, Don Juan de Oñate, left his own inscription on *El Morro*, on his return from his exploration of the *Colorado* basin. This old and famous inscription was made fifteen years before the Pilgrims landed at Plymouth Rock.

Oñate left the new settlement of *San Gabriel Pueblo* in 1604 to seek out "the South Sea", known to us as the Pacific Ocean. He took thirty men with him on this expedition. What he and his men found was the Gulf of California. On his return trip, Don Juan de Oñate left the following Spanish inscription:

"Paso por aq[u]i el adelantado Don Ju[an] de Oñate del descubrimyento de la mar del sur a 16 de Abril de 1605."

Oñate's inscription reads: "Governor Don Juan de Oñate passed through here, from the discovery of the South Sea on 16th of April, 1605." See Figure 13-12.

Figure 13-12: *Don Juan de Oñate's Inscription on El Morro, 1605.*** (Photo by Edward S. Curtis, c. 1925, Courtesy Palace of the Governors Photo Archives (NMHM.DCA) neg. # 006197)

Another famous Spaniard passed this way centuries ago, and he too left an inscription. This was Don Diego de Vargas, the reconqueror of *Santa Fe* in 1692-93, following the *Pueblo* Revolt of 1680. He traveled the area of *El Morro* in 1692, on his way to subdue the *Zuni Pueblo*. Don Diego de Vargas left his own inscription in Spanish, which reads (with some abbreviations):

"Aqui estuvo de General Don Diego de Vargas, quien conquisto a nuestra Santa Fe y a la Real Corona todo el Nuevo México a su costa, Ano de 1692."

The De Vargas inscription is easier to read than Oñate's. It reads as follows: "Here was General Don Diego de Vargas, who conquered for our Holy Faith and for the Royal Crown, all of New Mexico at his own expense, year of 1692."

Note De Vargas' reference to the expense of these expeditions, "at his own cost"!

Other famous Spaniards left inscriptions here too. Today, carving on any of the ruins is forbidden and illegal.

El Morro National Monument can be reached from the east or from the west via I-40, between the Grants and Gallup areas. For specific directions, see:

www.nps.gov/elmo/planyourvisit/directions.htm

El Morro National Monument is fascinating for its ancient and historical inscriptions, for the **ancient *pueblos*** and for its natural beauty and majesty!

Fort Union National Monument[18, 19, 20, 21]

Located near **Watrous** in *Mora* County, New Mexico, the ruins of **Fort Union** are preserved here as a national monument. The **Fort Union National Monument** was founded on April 5, 1956.

The Fort Union National Monument is situated near the confluence of the *Cimarron* and Mountain Routes of the **Santa Fe** Trail. It was positioned here to protect wagon trains, and new settlers and traders, from Indian raids and attacks, or from marauders and *desperados*. The fort acted as a military base and supply depot for other forts in the American Southwest. Over time it also grew the local economies, engaging traders, mercantilists, blacksmiths, animal handlers, etc. It helped to convert the local economy from a barter-based system to a cash-based system.

The fort is located on a barren open plain with very few trees, with mountains in the far distance, and with a bluff a few miles from the fort. Being so open and exposed, it is subject to strong winds, duststorms, thunderstorms and lightning. It experiences cold weather in the winter and burning heat in the summer. Even tornados pass through on occasion in the summer months. Please wear appropriate clothing for any trip to Fort Union. The site has its own special beauty, but it is very open, exposed and windy.

The first fort at the site was built close to nearby hills. It was hastily constructed of timber and *adobe* starting in August 1851. There was a post sutler's store where trail wagons could reload much needed supplies for the remainder of the journey to *Santa Fe*. The fort also acted as a military supply depot. The initial fort was part of a consolidation plan by the military under Lt. Col. Edwin V. Sumner, commanding the Ninth Military District, which included the New Mexico Territory. (Sumner later became a Military Governor of the Territory.) This plan called for the closure of various widely distributed forts along the *Rio Grande,* and for forts, instead, to be located nearer hostile Indian sites. It also called for Fort Union to become one of the largest forts in the American Southwest and to serve as a supply depot for other smaller forts. This fort lasted less than 10 years because of shoddy planning, deterioration and erosion due to weather, and poor workmanship. Virtually nothing remains today of this first fort or site.

In 1856, the second fort was built to replace the initial fort. It was located between the first and third fort locations. The fort site was moved one mile further east and away from the bluffs nearest the first fort site. Here a star-fort was built. This fort never saw any of the action for which it was built. In 1862, the Confederate forces were defeated at *Glorieta* and the invading Texans subsequently retreated back to Texas, removing any threat to the star fort at Fort Union.

Today, all that can be seen of the star fort are the earthworks or earthen embankments that surrounded the internal fortifications and buildings. The outline

Figure 13-13: Vestiges of the Mechanics Corral, among the Third Fort Ruins, at Fort Union National Monument, Watrous, New Mexico.

of the star fort can best be seen from aerial photography. Such a photo hangs in the Visitor Center, behind the front desk, showing the star fort outline.

During the American Civil War in 1862, Fort Union (star-fort) was the interim destination for the southbound *Colorado* Volunteers, where they joined up with the New Mexico Volunteers and the regular Union forces, to meet the oncoming Confederate forces. General Sibley's Texans, representing the Confederate forces, also saw Fort Union as their destination, as it was a strategic fort and supply depot for the American Southwest. Capturing Fort Union almost ensured a subsequent conquest of *Colorado,* with its newly-found gold deposits, which could help fund the Confederate war effort. Both forces raced to this juncture for strategic reasons.

Figure 13-14: A well-preserved, grim, damp, dark and claustrophobic Territorial/Post Jail, at the Third Fort Ruins, Fort Union National Monument.

Only, the *Colorado* Volunteers arrived there first, thwarting Sibley's subsequent plans to invade *Colorado.* The two enemies met a little further west at *Glorieta* Pass on March 26th through 28th, 1862. There the Confederates lost their wagon supply train and they were forced to abandon the New Mexico Campaign. See Chapter Three for more details.

Construction of the third fort, whose ruins are the most visible today at Fort Union, was started in 1863. It took 6 years to complete the project. It was initiated under the command of Brigadier General James H. Carleton. It was the most extensive military installation built in the New Mexico Territory, which then included the current states of New Mexico, Arizona and the most southern part of Colorado.

This last fort was built far enough away from the nearby bluffs to prevent enemy artillery of that period, from reaching it. The fort served multiple functions. It was first and foremost a military post with all the usual attendant military structures. It included a separate quartermaster depot with associated warehouses, corrals (for hundreds of horses), shops, offices and and quarters for the soldiers. Figure 13-13 shows ruins of the third fort's **Mechanics Corral**, at Fort Union National Monument

The site includes a small **Territorial/Post Jail** or military prison for traitors, deserters, murderers, miscreants, law-breakers or those who were caught selling firearms to the native Indians. It incarcerated both civilian and military miscreants. The jail building was very small, with several prisoners in each cell, who slept on straw mats on the floor. Each cell was without windows or light. It had no privy. Entry was via a wooden door. The jail cells were dark, damp, rough and uncomfortable. The interior and exterior of this grim, cold territorial jail were built of stone and mortar. The ceiling was made of arched stone and mortar. The military prison building was located near the guardhouse. It was surrounded by other buildings, and by post corrals. See Figure 13-14.

Fort Union also had a post hospital that included six wards, with 36 beds. It had a maximum capacity of 60 beds. The medical staff included a surgeon and his assistant, and additional staff of eight. The soldiers and their families received medical care, at no cost. However, the facility also provided medical care to local civilians at a cost of 50 cents per day for board.

The fort's function as a supply depot caused the local economy to flourish, as it employed many civilians in various trades. In its heyday, the fort had its own band and its own baseball team. It also had its own chapel and sutler store, and held its own dances. There were separate quarters for laundresses. Wives and families of some of the soldiers lived at the post, even though the life was harsh and difficult, and often very boring.

Figure 13-15: Wagon Wheel Ruts on the *Santa Fe* Trail, at the Fort Union National Monument.

The fort was originally conceived to support four military companies, but it was later expanded to support six companies.

With the coming of the railroad in the 1870's and 1880's, use of the *Santa Fe Trail* declined. In addition, the *Apache* Wars ended in the late-1880's. Fort Union started to decline in usefulness. It was eventually abandoned in 1891.

As mentioned earlier, the earthworks of the second fort or star fort, can still be seen today at this site. However, the main attraction includes the ruins of the third fort site, which are preserved as part of this national monument. Wagon wheel ruts from the *Santa Fe* Trail are also visible. See Figure 13-15. The fort ruins are accessed by means of a 1.2-mile trail. The site also has a Visitor Center with fort-related exhibits, and a 14-minute film about the famous *Santa Fe* Trail, and the various forts built at Fort Union.

The third fort ruins show the remains of the company quarters and headquarters, depot officers' quarters, quartermaster's office and quarters, commissary office, mechanics corral, post corral, transportation corral and military prison. Removed a small distance and close to the Visitor Center are the better-preserved ruins of the post hospital.

To reach Fort Union National Monument, take I-25 north from either *Santa Fe* or Albuquerque past *Glorieta* and later *Las Vegas*. Take Exit 366 to NM 161. Cross over the highway (left) and continue on NM 161 for 8 miles to the park entrance.

Gila Cliff Dwellings National Monument[22, 23]

These cliff dwellings are located in the *Gila* **Wilderness**, within Catron County in southwestern New Mexico. On November 16, 1907, the 533-acre *Gila* **Wilderness** was declared the Nation's First Wilderness Area by executive proclamation under President Theodore Roosevelt. From Silver City, the site can be accessed traveling from US 180 to NM 15.

The *Gila* **National Forest** surrounds the *Gila* Cliff Dwellings National Monument. Both of these are included within the *Gila* **Wilderness**. There is a Visitor Center in the park, where park information can be obtained. Books and other reading material can also be purchased. A museum is also available which gives exhibits of archeological finds from the *Mogollón* period.

The 553-acre site terrain is quite rugged. It has steep-walled canyons that have been cut by rivers. It is forested with oak, Douglas fir, ponderosa pine, *piñon* pine and New Mexico juniper.

Volcanic activity created the cliffs. Within the cliffs, the *Mogollón* People built dwellings that were linked together. However, only the remains of these *pueblos* can be seen today. The cliffs contain the remains of interlinked cave dwellings. Five cliff alcoves accommodate these dwellings. These cave alcoves contained up to 46 rooms, enough to house about a dozen families. They were built by the *Mogollón* People. The site was occupied between 1275 and 1300 A.D. According to *Hopi* oral tradition, the site was abandoned due to changing climate and modified belief systems.

These dwelling sites were very suitable for human habitation. Caves provided needed shelter and security, and the forested area kept the homes hidden from sight. Areas in close proximity to the caves allowed for some agriculture, gathering of wild foods and hunting.

Close examination of the cliff dwellings requires completing a one-mile hike along a trail loop that includes several footbridges, which cross over a stream. The loop takes about one hour to complete.

Elevations at the monument park vary from 5,700 feet to 7,300 feet. However, the *Gila* **Cliff Dwellings** vicinity itself is no greater than 6,000 feet.

As of this writing, the *Gila* Cliff Dwellings National Monument is closed. For availability and access, please check with the following website:

www.nps.gov/gicl/index.htm

There are also several hot springs in the area. **Lightfeather** is the closest hot spring, located via a short twenty-minute walk from the Visitor Center. **Jordan Hot Spring** is a five to eight mile hike from the Visitor Center, depending upon the trail selected.

As always, make sure that appropriate clothing, footwear, headwear ar worn. Also, be sure to carry bottled water and carry a snack. If you have any questions or are in doubt about anything, please ask the nearest park ranger.

Kasha Katuwe **Tent Rock National Monument**[24, 25, 26]

In 2001, *Kasha Katuwe* Tent Rock National Monument was created and located on federal grounds west of the **Cochiti Pueblo** lands. Among the local *Cochiti* People the site is known as *Kasha Katuwe*. In *Keres,* this means "White Cliffs." The site is located 40 miles southwest of *Santa Fe.*

This monument protects a formation of *tipi*-shaped rocks carved into mountains of volcanic tuff.[27] Volcanic explosions eons ago caused layers of volcanic rock and ash to be deposited. Over time, weathering and erosion created small canyons and tent rocks. The tent rocks themselves are cones of soft pumice and volcanic tuff, covered by harder cap rocks.

Figure 13-16: Slot Canyon at *Kasha Katuwe* Tent Rocks National Monument, *Cochiti.*

There are two main hiking trails available: the **Canyon Trail** and the **Cave Loop Trail.** The first trail is a bit more difficult than the second. It leads to the summit allowing one to overlook the **Tent Rocks.** The second trail is easier and it avoids the ascent, leading around the base of the mountains.

A lookout point above the canyon provides a stunning view of the tent rocks. To reach this point, follow the 1.2-mile **Canyon Trail**, which winds through a slot canyon and eventually leads to a path that takes one to the summit above. See Figure 13-16 for a view of the **Slot Canyon**. Initially, this trail consists of ash and sand, but it progresses towards sand and rock further on, as the grade increases. This trail could be considered a bit difficult by some, especially as one approaches the summit. However, the view and the surrounding scenery are quite beautiful, and well worth the effort. At the summit, there is another 1.3-mile loop that allows for a closer examination of the tent rocks. See Figure 13-17. The foothills along the cliff face below are dotted with Ponderosa pine, juniper and *piñon.*

For those who wish to avoid the **Slot Canyon** and the ascent to the upper heights, there is an alternate 1.2-mile **Cave Loop Trail** available. It is a flatter hike. This trail is at the base of the mountains.

Lastly, one can avoid all the hiking by bypassing the first parking lot, and continuing straight ahead for about four miles to the **Veterans Memorial Scenic Overlook**. Most of the road is unpaved but manageable for most vehicles. From this overlook one can see for many miles around. Incidently, the Bureau of Land Management (BLM) just recently added a one-mile wheel chair accessible (ADA) loop trail at this site.

Figure 13-17: *Kasha Katuwe* Tent Rocks National Monument, *Cochiti.*

To reach this national monument, see the discussion and the directions to reach *Cochiti* Reservation in Chapter Eleven. Follow those directions on NM 22 towards *Cochiti Pueblo* and the monument. Follow the signs to the monument. The *Kasha Katuwe* Tent Rock National Monument lies just beyond the left side turnoff towards the *Cochiti Pueblo.* Pass this *pueblo* turnoff, staying on NM 22. Signs for the monument will appear shortly beyond. A right turn, off NM 22, takes the visitor to the monument entry.

The parking lot is about 3.5 miles further down the asphalt road on the right hand side. Dogs are not allowed in the monument. The site is co-managed by the *Cochiti Pueblo* and the Bureau of Land Management. The site is generally open during daytime hours. However, the *Cochiti* Tribal Governor can order the monument closed at any time. Please check open/close status when planning a trip to this monument. Call 505-761-8700 or visit the following website:

www.blm.gov/nm/st/en/prog/recreation/Rio_Puerco/kasha_katuwe_tent_rocks.html

Petroglyph National Monument[28, 29, 30]

These **ancient petroglyphs**, located in Albuquerque, *Bernalillo* County, preserve numerous cultural and natural features from the past. The park also includes five dormant volcanoes.

The monument extends along 17 miles of **Albuquerque's West Mesa.** It is found off I-40 Exit 154, Unser Boulevard. The natural items of interest include a number of volcanic cones. In addition, there are hundreds of archeological sites and approximately 25,000 petroglyphs, carved by Ancestral *Pueblo* Peoples, preserving the cultural heritage of an ancient people. There are also images carved by early Spanish settlers. The images include animals, people, crosses, brands, native symbols and geometric designs. The petroglyphs were formed eons ago by etching or picking at the volcanic basalt rock to expose the grayish white that lies beneath the black surface. This national monument has been established to protect these petroglyphs, the adjacent open space lands and the archeological sites.

The Visitor Center is separated from the four major non-contiguous sites within the monument. Here one can gather information on the various sites. They also sell books and compact discs of interest. Restrooms are available. Three sites provide access to petroglyphs. These are ***Boca Negra*[31] Canyon** and ***Piedras Mercadas*[32] Canyon** both of which lie north of the Visitor Center, and ***Rinconada*[33] Canyon**, which is one mile south of the center. These three sites are located within a few miles of the Visitor Center. The fourth site, called the **Volcanoes Day Use Area**, has five inactive volcanoes (from north to south): **Butte, Bond, Vulcan, Black** and **JA Volcano**. Trails within the **Volcanoes Day Use Area** lead to the last three volcanoes listed.

At all four park sites, the area is open and there is very little shade. There is much desert vegetation around. Small access gates need to be passed through to gain entry. Be sure to wear head covering, hiking boots, and to carry bottled water. It can get very hot and dry in the summer heat, and it is important to remain covered and properly hydrated! Be sure to adhere to the indicated trails. Also, please watch where you step and be on the lookout for rattlesnakes. Do not attempt any of these hikes in sandals, sneakers, tennis shoes, flat-soled shoes, or open-toe shoes!!

Treaded covered footwear is best for both safety and traction reasons.

The most popular site is ***Boca Negra***, which charges a $1 parking during the week and $2 on weekends. (It is open 8am to 5pm.) There are three trails at this site: **McCaw Trail, Cliff Base Trail** and ***Mesa* Point Trail**. The first two trails are relatively flat and easy to hike. *Mesa* **Point Trail** requires a climb of 113 feet above the parking lot. This trail requires an arduous hike up a steep boulder-laden hillside. It is not for the faint of heart, especially the descent from the summit area once reached. However, the view from the summit is worth the climb. See Figure 13-18 for an example of the petroglyphs to be found along the *Mesa* **Point Trail** at *Boca Negra.*

The ***Piedras Mercadas*** site lies near Paradise Blvd. It is a desert area with black volcanic boulders on the hillsides, adjacent to a modern suburban area. The contrast between nearby civilization and the raw wild natural desert environment is quite remarkable. One has to pass through a small gate to access the trail. The trail initially bears to the left and it meanders for about a half mile. It is poorly and sparsely marked but it is fairly level and does not require a hike up a hillside. There are six numbered markers along the trail that identify significant petroglyph concentrations. Again, please stay on the indicated trails. The hike requires walking in loose silty sand that makes the hike tiring, but the site is naturally quite beautiful!

Figure 13-18: Petroglyphs at the Petroglyph National Monument, Albuquerque.

The third site, *Rinconada* **Canyon** is located one mile south of the Visitor Center. It is similar in terrain and structure to *Piedras Mercadas*, but larger. Here one also has to pass through a small gateway to enter the trail. The hike trail to the rear of the canyon is 1.2 miles long. The hike through silty sand takes about 1.5 hours to complete. The trail itself is better marked than at *Piedras Mercadas*. Unfortunately, however, no signposts are visible to point out the petroglyphs.

The final or fourth site is the **Volcanoes Day Use Area**. To reach this last site, I-40 must be taken to Exit 149. Then proceed north on *Atrisco Vista* for 4.8 miles. The access road is not clearly marked, but there is a gateway there. The access road is asphalt. About 0.5 miles from the entry there are a small parking area, restrooms and a covered outdoor sitting area. There is no Visitor Center here, and there are no park attendants. Two of the inactive volcanoes lie further to the north: *Butte* Volcano and Bond Volcano. However, a dirt, sand, and gravel footpath, located within walking distance of the parking lot, leads up to and around three of the five volcanic cones: **Vulcan, Black** and **JA Volcano**. See Figure 13-19. The hikes to the summits are very manageable but steep in some places.

Figure 13-19: Volcano site in Petroglyph National Monument, Albuquerque.

The view of the surrounding landscape and of Albuquerque looking far to the east is quite remarkable. All five extinct volcanoes lie in the **Rio Grande Rift Valley**, a geological area between two dynamic fault lines or cracks in the earth's crust. The *Sandia* Mountain Range to the east is one fault. The other fault lies near the *Rio Puerco* far to the west. Gradual rock movements along the *Sandia* fault still occur, causing the *Sandia* Mountains to continue to rise and the *Rio Grande* Valley to broaden and sink. There are no petroglyphs at the **Volcanoes Day Use Area** site.

Salinas Pueblo Missions National Monument[34, 35, 36]

The main Visitor Center of this national monument is located in Mountainair. The *Salinas Pueblo* Missions National Monument is actually comprised of three physically separate sites: **Gran Quivira, Quarai** and **Abó.** These various sites are located within the central grasslands of the *Estancia* Basin, south of Albuquerque. **Gran Quivira** is located within the northern end of *Socorro* County. The other two sites are located within Torrance County. Annual visitation to these remote locations is quite low.

Salinas means "salt pits" or "salt mines" in Spanish. This national monument is important because it reveals the cultural and economic interaction between the native *Pueblo* Peoples and the Spaniards. The location of these sites in the near center of New Mexico enabled the region to evolve into a central trade and distribution hub. These sites are roughly 30 to 60 miles east of the *Rio Grande*.

The *Salinas* District, as named by the Spaniards, was once a flourishing trading community inhabited by *Pueblo* Peoples, who spoke *Tiwa* or *Tompiro*. Early in the 17th century the Spanish Franciscans were very active with missionary efforts. In the late 17th century, the native *Puebloans* and the Spaniards abandoned the area. However, both left reminders of the contact between their two peoples.

Included in this widespread national monument park are the partially excavated *pueblo* at **Gran Quivira**, and three mission church ruins at **Gran Quivira, Quarai** and **Abó.** See Figures 13-20, 13-21 and 13-22.

The **Pueblo** of **Las Humanas**, known today as the **Gran Quivira Pueblo**, occupies the same site as the **Gran Quivira** mission church, 26 miles south of the park headquarters, in Mountainair. This ancient *pueblo* is only partially excavated.

Fig.13-20: *Gran Quivira* (*Salinas Pueblo* Missions National Monument)

Figure 13-21: *Quarai* (*Salinas Pueblo* Missions National Monument)

Figure 13-22: *Abó* (*Salinas Pueblo* Missions National Monument)

Quarai is located at *Manzano*, New Mexico, about 8 miles north of Mountainair, in Torrance County. *Abó* is located about 9 miles west of Mountainair, in Torrance County. Abó is located about 9 miles west of Mountainair, in Torrance County. No *pueblos* have yet been excavated at either *Quarai* or *Abó.*

For more information contact the following website:

www.nps.gov/sapu/planyourvisit/directions.htm

White Sands National Monument[37, 38, 39, 40]

This famous landmark is located 25 miles southwest of the city of *Alamogordo.*[41] It stretches from the southwestern part of *Otero* County into the southeastern part of the neighboring county, *Doña Ana*[42] County. The national monument is surrounded by the **White Sands Missile Range**, which is used by the U.S. Army to test missiles. The missile range and testing grounds run north and south of the monument, on either side of the *San Andrés* Mountains. The range also includes the ***Tularosa Valley***, which is located between the *Sacramento* and *San Andrés* Mountains.

To reach this monument site, drive into *Alamogordo* on US 70 and follow it across the bridge as you leave *Alamogordo*. Continue on US 70 south and west just past the 199-mile marker to the monument entrance.

A small Visitor Center just near the entrance shows a 17-minute video describing the white sands phenomenon, the unique animal and plant life, and other features of the monument. A paved auto tour has signboards at key locations. This short 8-miles long (one-way) loop folds back on itself at the end. There are also several walking trails at various points within the main drive if you wish to examine the dunes and dune-life more closely. Although vehicles are not allowed on the sand, visitors are permitted to walk. Two popular trails are the **Dune Life Nature Trail**, and the **Alkali Loop Trail**. There is also a very interesting but short **Nature Boardwalk** that allows one to get out into some of the dunes without walking in the sand. See Figure 13-23.

There are no overnight campsites. However, backpacking campsites for day use are made available. Although some sheltered areas are available, there is no water source within the monument. So bring your own bottled water to prevent dehydration! Leashed pets are allowed.

The scenery is spectacular! Be sure to bring your camera. Also, be sure to dress appropriately for high day temperatures in the summer. If you wish to hike, wear shorts and hiking boots, head cover and sunglasses. Carry plenty of bottled water too. Try to plan your trip to complete before noon or 1 pm at the latest, to avoid the worst heat of the day!

Two words can describe **White Sands**: Awesome!! Ethereal!! It is unlike any other place you have ever been! The sands look like snow and it remains cool, even on hot summer days! There is an amazing amount of plant life! It is simply beautiful and unforgettable! It seems unreal!

White Sands National Monument is aptly named. It is comprised of white sands that contain gypsum crystals, giving the sands and the dunes their world-renowned, spectacular, stunning, pristine-white appearance. Gypsum is washed down from the *Sacramento* Mountains in the east and the *San Andrés* Mountains in the west. This gypsum ends up in the ***Tularosa*** **Basin**, which is part of the *Chihuahuan* Desert. No river drains this basin.

Gypsum is water-soluble, so it is very rare to see gypsum sands, as the crystals can dissolve and be washed away by creeks, rivers, lakes etc. However, the area that the monument resides within is a land-locked basin, so that even if the crystals dissolve, the water containing the dissolved crystals eventually evaporates, leaving the crystals behind once again. There is one other interesting feature of the gypsum sands. Unlike quartz crystal sands, which retain the sun's heat, gypsum crystals do not easily convert the sun's energy into heat, making the sands safe to

Figure 13-23: White Sands National Monument.

walk upon, even on hot days! Scientists claim that the planet Mars has gypsum sand dunes in its north-pole region!

Visitors will be surprised to see that life does find a way to survive even in this most barren and hostile environment. Unseen, there is water a few feet underground, enough to support the unique plant and animal life here. There are 240 species of plants, insects and animals in the **White Sands** region! Some plants have evolved to grow only in the gypsum sand and in no other soil. Because the sands shift with time, many plants cannot survive in this environment. They become buried eventually. Some plants are uniquely suited to survive here. Examples are the yucca that grows upward fast enough to avoid being buried. Yuccas that appear to be only a few feet tall may actually be tens of feet high, with the biggest part of the plant buried in the surrounding sands. The cottonwood tree is the only deciduous tree that can survive in this environment. There is a species of the rosemary bush that also survives here because it sends out a vast network of roots that keep it alive

The Kangaroo Rat has evolved so that it never needs to ever drink water in its lifetime! The Bleached Earless Lizard has differentiated itself from its darker version that lives outside White Sands. It is lighter in color to ensure it camouflage and survival. It is longer and faster. It digs holes more easily than its darker counterpart. Its mouth is wider and it can eat a wider variety of insects. These adaptations allow it to better survive in **White Sands**. Most life in the monument region is nocturnal, to retreat from the daytime sun and heat. Kitfoxes, snakes, lizards, Kangaroo Rats, weasels, insects, the *Apache* pocket mouse, and others make White Sands their home.

About twice weekly, for about 2 hours duration, missile tests are periodically conducted within the surrounding **White Sands Missile Range**, and access to the White Sands National Monument is disallowed for safety reasons. The missile range itself is not accessible to the public. The **Trinity Test Site**, where the world's first atomic bomb was detonated on July 16, 1945, is located in the northernmost part of the **White Sands Missile Range**. It is opened only twice yearly to tourists.

In 2010, the White Sands National Monument held **Special Events** that are both unique and enjoyable. Available to visitors were Sunset Strolls, Patio Talks by the Rangers, a Balloon Invitational, a Christmas Season Holiday Open House at the historic *adobe* Visitor Center with *luminarias* and interpretive programs, Full Moon Bike Rides, and Lake *Lucero* Tours. Of course, these activities vary from year to year, but this presents some idea of the kind of activities available at **White Sands**. Please consult:

www.nps.gov/whsa/index

PART B: National Historical Parks (2)

Chaco Culture National Historical Park[43, 44, 45, 46, 47]

This site is located near *Nageezi* (*Navajo*, "squash") in northwestern New Mexico, between Albuquerque and Farmington in a remote canyon that has been cut over millennia by the Chaco Wash. This park contains the densest and most extraordinary concentration of ancient **pre-Columbian *pueblos*** in the American Southwest and north of Mexico. The site is located within Chaco Canyon. It is a huge, magnificent and astounding site located in a stunning setting. Be sure to visit this park if you have the chance. The site is remote but very much worth the effort to get there!! The scenery alone is awesome! The visitor is sure to come away with a much greater appreciation of the advanced native culture that once thrived here and of its astounding capabilities!!

One will also be impressed by the ubiquitous presence of *kivas* and of the spiritual world in the daily lives of the inhabitants here. There is a small Visitor Center (VC) and bookshop at the park. Here, a 26-minute video describes the site and the Chaco Culture. The Chaco Museum features artifacts from archeological digs in the area. The museum displays fine examples of Chacoan pottery, arrowheads, *atlatls*, beaded jewelry, awls and needles, bowls, cordage, drilling sticks, drills, *manos* and *metates*, fetishes, pendants, pipes, pitchers, sandals, etc.

Chaco Canyon was a major cultural center for the Ancient *Pueblo* Peoples, between 850 and 1250 A.D. This area appears to have served as a commercial, religious and trade hub for the Four Corners region. The Chacoans were adept at astronomy, geometry, landscaping and engineering. They excelled in the development of pre-planned architectural designs. They were able to create and build spectacular urban centers with exceptional public buildings. Many of these public buildings were multi-storied.

Archeologists term these people as Chaco *Anasazi*. They built structures including rooms, *kivas*, terraces and *plazas*, as well as four and possibly five-storied public buildings. They built roadways that spread out from **Chaco Canyon** to distant villages in the Four Corners region. The Chacoan culture was an advanced culture in the American Southwest, long before the arrival of the Spaniards.

Chacoans quarried sandstone blocks and hauled timber over great distances, in order to build up to 15 major complexes in North America. There is some evidence that the Chacoans practiced an ancient form of astronomy.

Figure 13-24: *Fajada Butte* at Chaco Culture National Historical Park.

The **Sun Dagger petroglyph** at the top of *Fajada Butte* is a popular example. (*Fajada Butte* can be seen, on the left, just before one turns into the VC parking lot.) See Figure 13-24. Selected **Chacoan buildings** appear to have been aligned to observe and identify solar and lunar cycles. These celestial building alignments must have required many generations of detailed astronomical observations, together with centuries of very skilled construction, in coordination with the religious leaders. A fifty-year drought, which started in 1130 A.D., may have led to the gradual abandonment of the **Chaco Canyon** site.

Most sites at the park are opened year round and most are accessed by self-guided tours. The **Canyon Loop Drive** is 9-miles long, but it takes the visitor to six attractions in sequence: *Una Vida* ("One Life"), next to the VC, *Hungo Pavi, Chetro Ketl, Pueblo Bonito* ("Beautiful Village"), *Pueblo del Arroyo* ("Town of the Wash"), and *Casa Rinconada* ("Cornered House"). Self-guided tour books can be purchased at either the Visitor Center or borrowed at the individual trailheads. From May to October, Ranger-guided tours are made available. Both daytime and evening programs are provided to allow observations of the sun, or of constellations, etc.

A fascinating site in this park is the great house of *"Hungo Pavi."* It is believed that this name is a corruption of the *Tewa "Shungopovi"* the name of a *Hopi* village. Lieutenant James Simpson and his Mexican guide Carravahil named the site *"Hungo Pavi"* during an 1849 military expedition into the Southwest. This 1,000 year-old structure is a multi-storied building made of sandstone bricks. This great house is believed to contain 150 rooms with a raised two-storied *kiva* near the center of the structure. This site also features a large great *kiva* situated in the central plaza. The *Hungo Pavi* site is located nearest the VC on the **Canyon Loop Drive**, at the entrance to **Mockingbird Canyon**.

Another interesting site, next on the loop, is *Chetro Ketl*. See Figure 13-25. It is the second largest Chacoan Great House. Only *Pueblo Bonito* is larger. It features a great *kiva* and several elevated *kivas*. The central *plaza* is elevated 12 feet above the valley floor. **Chacoan buildings** here were built 2 or 3 stories high.

The **Great *Kiva*** in the *plaza* cannot be missed. See Figure 13-26. This ancient

Figure 13-25: *Chetro Ketl* at Chaco Culture National Historical Park.

Figure 13-26: Great *Kiva* at *Chetro Ketl,* in Chaco Culture National Historical Park.

site is extraordinary and the scale of the *kiva* is massive. The outline of the *kiva*, with the attached stonework, looks like a giant keyhole dug into the center of the *plaza*. One can easily see where the giant stone columns supported the roof overhead. The *kiva* is built of sandstone quarried from the local area. A stone bench is built into the circular walls. Numerous square niches are built into the enclosing walls of the *kiva*.

The very notable **Pueblo Bonito** or "Great House" is located at the next stop on the loop. Strictly speaking, **Pueblo Bonito**, means "Beautiful Town" (or "Village"). It is one of the main features at Chaco Culture National Historical Park.[48] This ancient *pueblo* is laid out in a D-shape on an open plain. A nearby Overlook provides a splendid panoramic view of **Pueblo Bonito** below. This **"Great House"** has roughly 700 rooms! The buildings were up to 4 or 5 stories high. This set of buildings most probably served multiple purposes, including ceremonial, administrative, trading, storage, hospitality, astronomical and others. Very little appears to have been used as actual living quarters. See Figure 13-27.

Besides the massive scale of this enterprise, there is another interesting feature associated with it. The layout is oriented according to the cardinal directions. A line drawn through the half circle portion of the "D", or perpendicular to the diameter (vertical side of the letter "D"), aligns perfectly with a north-south axis. If one looks to the southern wall, along the diameter, one will find that its eastern portion aligns itself perfectly with the east-west axis. In other words, the very top of the vertical part of the "D" corresponds to the west, and the very bottom of the vertical part of the "D" corresponds to the east. During the Spring and Fall Equinoxes the sunrises and sunsets line up with this wall!! These celestial observations by the Chacoans allowed them to set the proper time for planting, harvesting and hunting. They also most likely established the timing for related ceremonial events.

The three-acre **Pueblo Bonito** site shows two *plazas*, numerous public buildings, and numerous *kivas* that were central to the Chacoans religious and spiritual belief system. **Pueblo Bonito** is a very impressive site!

The next site on the loop is **Pueblo del Arroyo** ("Town of the Wash"). Although interesting in its own right, it pales compared to **Pueblo Bonito**.

The last major fascinating site at this park is **Casa Rinconada**[49] ("cornered house" or "house where the canyons meet", or even "box canyon house"), a very large *kiva*. The *kivas* preserved in the park are round, and they are partially above and partially below ground. Most great houses in the area have their own *kiva*. However, **Casa Rinconada** is unique in that it is not associated with any great house, but must have been used for communal ceremonial and religious purposes. No one knows for certain but there is a small window opening near the top rim of this great *kiva*, through which the sun enters during the Summer Solstice, but at no other time in the year. The uncertainty arises because there appear to be ruins of outer rooms that may have blocked this window. So, the mystery remains.

There are also four backcountry-hiking trails provided for the more adventurous. These hikes lead to more remote sites where petroglyphs, ancient roads, and overlooks can be accessed. Check with the Visitor Center for more information and for opened/closed status and weather conditions. A permit purchase will be required to access these trails.

Figure 13-27: *Pueblo Bonito* at Chaco Culture National Historical Park.

The park also sponsors lectures and presentations by knowledgeable guest speakers on related topics, which are usually conducted during the summer months. Guests may include archeologists, artists, musicians or Native Americans, each bringing their own unique perspective to Chaco Culture National Historical Park.

The many sites at the park are still considered sacred by the *Hopi* and other *Pueblo* Peoples of today. The tribal peoples have maintained oral accounts of their historical migration from Chaco centuries ago, as well as their continuing spiritual relationship with the land.

The National Park Service works closely with tribal representatives to maintain knowledge and understanding of the Chacoan culture, and to maintain the appropriate respect for this rich heritage, while being cognizant and respectful of current native religious beliefs.

The historical park is home to a herd of about 50 to 60 elk, which have adopted the parklands as their home, since the year 2000.

To get to this fascinating national monument, drive to *Bernalillo* via Interstate 25, from either Albuqueruque (I-25 north) or from *Santa Fe* (I-25 south). Then take Hwy 550 northwest towards *Nageezi*. Follow the signs just southeast of *Nageezi* that indicate the turnoff towards **Chaco Canyon**. The remainder of the drive is about 26 miles. The first few miles are on an asphalt road. The remaining 20 miles or so is via a dirt road to **Chaco Canyon**. This road may be difficult to travel in rainy or winter weather.

Driving directions can also be obtained from the NPS website as follows:

www.nps.gov/chcu/planyourvisit/directions.htm

Pecos National Historical Park[50, 51, 52]

This national park is located in *Pecos,* about 25 miles east of *Santa Fe*, New Mexico. It includes the *Pecos Pueblo*, a National Historical Landmark. Between 1965 and 1990, it was designated *Pecos* National Historical Monument. After additional lands were added in 1990, the park was redesignated the *Pecos* National Historical Park. The park is comprised of several distinct and noncontiguous sections. The primary section of the park preserves the remains of the *Mission Nuestra Señora de los Angeles de Porciúncula de los Pecos* (Our Lady of the Angels of *Porciúncula* of *Pecos*), which was built in the early 17th century just outside the walls of the *pueblo.* The remains of the **old Spanish Mission** can be seen in the background of Figure 13-28.

Underground *kivas* and the remains of old *pueblo* room-blocks are easily accessible. At one time the village supported up to 2,000 inhabitants and the *pueblo* reached as high as five stories. The *pueblo* was continuously inhabited from the 15th century through the early 19th century. The original *Tanoan* name of the **Pecos Pueblo** was *Cucuye*. The more commonly recognized name, *Pecos*, derives from the *Keresan* version of the *Tanoan* name *Cucuye*[53] [(48)], which is "*P'e'-a-ku'*." *Pecos Pueblo* was a prominent *pueblo* in the native pre-Columbian era, among the *pueblos* of central New Mexico, and in the early years of the Spanish Conquest. The *pueblo* was located at a trade nexus that allowed the natives to actively participate in and coordinate trade between the *Pueblo* Peoples of the *Rio Grande* Valley and the

Figure 13-28: Overlooking a *kiva,* towards the Mission remains, at *Pecos* National Historical Park.

nomadic tribes of the eastern Plains. ***Pecos Pueblo*** inhabitants acted as middlemen and traders between these two trading groups. They also engaged actively in agriculture, growing and storing corn, squash, beans and cotton. The Plains Indians traded animal skins and hides, flint shells, tallow and other goods for crops, turquoise, textiles and pottery produced by the *Pueblo* Peoples of the *Rio Grande* Valley. ***Pecos Pueblo*** had a surrounding wall to protect its inhabitants. ***Pecos Pueblo*** dwellers built tall impressive *pueblo* buildings. They were experienced in war and defense, and they were culturally sophisticated. They had an active religious life with sacred ceremonials and *kivas.*

However, the ***Pecos Pueblo*** was abandoned in the 19th Century, and its remaining inhabitants moved onto and joined their *Towa*-speaking relatives at *Jemez Pueblo*. See Figure 13-29 for the remains of the ***Pecos Pueblo***. ***Pecos Pueblo*** was excavated between 1915 and 1929 by archeologist A. V. Kidder. His work was sponsored by the Phillips Academy.

Other sections of the park protect the historical American Civil War site of the **Glorieta Pass Battlefield**, fought March 26th through March 28th, 1862. These sections of the park are accessible via a 2.25 mile hiking trail. Interpretive van tours

Figure 13-29: Remains of the *Pecos Pueblo,* at *Pecos* National Historical Park.

provide an additional option. These are also available throughout the year. Interpretive van tours last about 2.2 hours and require payment of a small additional fee. A final option is available on or near the anniversary date (March 26-28) of the **Glorieta** Battle. Around that time, the park sponsors a special event, usually with living history demonstrations and lectures.

Please visit the park website for details at: www.nps.gov/peco/index.htm

or, more specifically at:

www.nps.gov/peco/planyourvisit/upload/NEWGlorieta-battlefield-2.pdf

or, call by telephone at:
(505) 757-7241

Another area of the park includes a small section of wagon ruts along what was once the old **Santa Fe Trail**. This trail wound through **Apache Canyon** over a sixty-year period.

Lastly, the park also includes the **Forked Lightning Ranch** home designed by John Gaw Meem for Tex Austin, and later occupied by actress Greer Garson. (John Gaw Meem was an American architect who was a key developer and promoter of the *Pueblo* Revival architectural style that became popular in and around *Santa Fe*, New Mexico, in the late 1920's through 1956.) Tours of the home are offered by the *Pecos* National Historic Park, throughout the year. Please visit the park website for details:

www.nps.gov/peco

PART C: National Parks (1)

Carlsbad Caverns National Park[54, 55, 56]

New Mexico is blessed with having many natural and man-made wonders above ground: rivers, mountains, *mesas, buttes,* pre-Columbian ruins, forests, lakes, *pueblos,* and many more. However, there is also a great natural wonder that is underground! Who hasn't heard of *Carlsbad* Caverns? It is world famous for its massive underground caverns.

It is located in southeastern New Mexico in the Guadalupe Mountains, near the city of *Carlsbad*, in Eddy County. The main attraction in the park is the show cave, called the **Big Room**. The park entrance is approximately 18 miles southwest of the town of *Carlsbad,* New Mexico, on Highway 62/180.

An additional seven miles beyond this entrance, there is a Visitor Center that is open from 8 am to 5 pm with hours extended to 7 pm in the summer months. The park is opened every day except Christmas Day. Included within the *Carlsbad* Caverns portion of the park is the third largest natural limestone chamber in the U.S. This is one feature that all visitors should plan to visit. This portion is viewed by self-guided tour. The large cave chamber is called the **Big Room**, which is almost 4,000 feet long, 625 feet wide, and approximately 350 feet high.

Figure 13-30: Stalagmites at *Carlsbad* Caverns National Park.

It is breathe-taking in scope, magnitude and variety. The large cave also shows spectacular formations of stalagmites, stalactites, columns and other speleothems throughout the huge cave. See Figure 13-30 for an example of stalagmites seen in the **Big Room**.

This self-guided tour is about a one and a half to two hour-long stroll covering 1.3 miles in distance, through a huge chamber. Most visitors enter and exit the chamber via elevator. However, some visitors may choose to descend from the surface to the **Big Room** via the **Natural Entrance** (self-guided) **Tour**. The trail is mostly on level ground and is wheelchair accessible. See Figures 13-31 and 13-32, for examples of the stunning sights to be found within the **Big Room**.

The **Natural Entrance Tour** is also self-guided, but it is much more arduous. It is very steep and narrow in places, with paved switchback pathways. This tour takes the visitor to the **Big Room** below, by means of a natural pathway, which gradually descends some 750 feet below the surface. If you have health problems or acrophobia this tour may not be advisable. This self-guided trail is about one hour in duration and covers about one mile in length, as it descends to the **Big Room** below. The visitor can opt to descend to the **Big Room** using this trail or just take the elevator down. If one takes this **Natural Entrance Tour**, one can continue onto the **Big Room Trail** (see above) at the trail's end, or return to the surface via the elevator.

The cave maintains its cool temperature of roughly 56 degrees Fahrenheit throughout the year with little variation. Please dress with a light jacket or sweater and with rubber-soled footwear for adequate traction. Baby strollers are not permitted in the cave. If you are bringing a small child make sure that you bring a backpack to accommodate the child. Because of the environment of the caves, there are restrictions regarding children and minors, especially on guided tours. See the following website:

www.nps.gov/cave/planyourvisit/cave_tours.htm

Figure 13-31: Draperies in the Big Room, at *Carlsbad* Caverns National Park.

Figure 13-32: Chinese Theater Group in the Big Room, at Carlsbad Caverns National Park.

Here one can obtain updated information on rules and restrictions, and schedules. Guided tours are also available. However, reservations are highly recommended. Guided tours are available for: **Left Hand Tunnel, King's Palace, Slaughter Canyon Cave, Lower Cave, Spider Cave** and **Hall of the White Giant**. An entrance fee, in addition to the guided tour fee, is required for these tours. There are various age restrictions for these guided tours. Some will require the use of a tour-provided cave helmet and headlamp. The **Left Hand Tunnel Tour** is the easiest of all the guided tours. It covers a half-mile in distance. **King's Palace Tour** is also fairly easy. The more difficult tours require that the visitor provide his or her own gloves, kneepads and AA batteries for the headlamp. Crawling along cave crawlways is required for the last two guided tours (**Spider Cave** and **Hall of the White Giant**). So, if you are at all claustrophic, these special underground guided tours may not be suitable. Reservations for these guided tours can be made, by calling (877) 444-6777.

One free outdoor feature is the **Bat Flight**. Visitors gather in the evening at the outdoor **Bat Flight Amphitheater** before dusk to observe the emergence of thousands of bats as they exit their bat caves, in search of insect food. Bats fly south in the winter months, so if you plan to see the bats, please plan and time your visit accordingly.

Several outdoor nature hike trails expose the hiker to the desert terrain, xeric plant life and animal life. These include the **Rattlesnake Canyon Trail** and the **Yucca Canyon Trail**. Hikers are sure to see yuccas, sotol, prickly-pear cactus, *chollas, lechuguilla, ocotillo,* and many other desert plants along the trail. Animal life is less likely to be seen during the hot daylight hours. (Once, about 250 million years ago, during the Permian Age, much of the region in the Delaware Basin formed a seabed and the *Carlsbad* Cavern National Park lay on a gigantic undersea reef.)

A 9.5-mile (one-way) **Walnut Canyon Desert Drive** allows motorists to explore the area from their cars. The road does get narrow and twisty, so the trail is not recommended for trailers or motor homes.

The name given to the national park and the caverns is clearly taken from the name of nearby *Carlsbad* City. The name *Carlsbad* can be translated from the German (*Karlsbad*) to mean "Carl's Bath." It was named after a Czechoslovakian town of the same name (*Karlsbad*).

The majority of the park is designated as wilderness to ensure its protection. *Carlsbad* Caverns National Park is part of the northern *Chihuahuan* Desert ecosytem.

This site is a natural wonder! The underground mineral formations are truly beautiful and stunning! If the visitor is driving down from Albuquerque, *Santa Fe* or *Taos* areas, the drive is certainly worth the experience, as are any of the tours described above at *Carlsbad* Caverns National Park.

PART D: National Historic Trails (3)

El Camino Real de Tierra Adentro National Historic Trail[57, 58, 59]

This trail was designated as a national historic trail in October 2000. The name means "the Royal Road to the Interior Lands" in Spanish. It follows the main route north and south between the former colonial Spanish capital of Mexico City, Mexico and its Spanish provincial capitals in northern Mexico, in what is now the state of New Mexico. The trail was actively used between the 1600's and the 1800's for both administrative and trade purposes. It allowed direct contact between the Spaniards and the indigenous *Pueblo* Peoples, *Apache, Ute, Navajo* and other non-*Pueblo* tribes. It fostered cultural and economic intercourse between the European and native peoples.

The 1,600-mile trail extends from Mexico City, Mexico, through northern Mexican cities such as Durango, *Lagos* ("Lakes"), Zacatecas, *Chihuahua,*[60] Juarez, and others. It then crossed the *Rio Grande* at the border into *El Paso*, Texas and then proceeded north into New Mexico, through Albuquerque, *Santa Fe* and finally, it terminated at *Ohkay Owingeh (San Juan) Pueblo*, New Mexico. Only the 404-mile U.S. segment running almost the full length of the state of New Mexico (north-south) was designated a national historic trail.

Don Juan de Oñate used this trail on his march northwards from Mexico across the *Rio Grande*, paralleling the great river north to the native village of *Ohkay Owingeh (San Juan)*. The trip northwards normally took about 5 or 6 months to complete. Early Spanish colonists brought oxen-drawn wagons filled with belongings and foodstuffs for the long dangerous trip. They complemented their food with game that they managed to capture along the route. The route was used by new colonialists and settlers, and by traders who exchanged goods between the northern Spanish provinces and Mexico.

Portions of the trade route are available today. In the south, **Fort Seldon** and **Fort Craig** lie along the trail. The current ***Paseo del Bosque*** **(Wood Boulevard) Trail** in Albuquerque, and portions of the proposed ***Rio Grande*** **Trail** follow what was once the ***El Camino Real***. *El Rancho de las Golondrinas* was once a stop over or rest stop, called a *paraje*, along the famous trail. A drivable route follows the general direction of the ***El Camino Real*** from the ***El Paso*** area, just across the Texan border with New Mexico, north to ***San Juan*** or ***Ohkey Owingeh Pueblo***. This motorway, ***El Camino Real,*** has been designated a **National Scenic Byway**.

Interesting places to visit while traveling along the trail include:

> ***Mesilla Plaza***, *Mesilla*
> **New Mexico Farm and Ranch Heritage Museum**, *Las Cruces*
> **Antonio Store**, *Doña Ana* County
> **John M. and John D. Barncastle House**, *Doña Ana* County
> **Fort Selden State Monument**, Radium Springs
> ***El Camino Real*** **International Heritage Center**, outside *Socorro*
> ***Tomé*** **Hill**, outside *Los Lunes*
> **Gutiérrez-Hubbell House**, Albuquerque
> **Albuquerque Museum of Art and History**, Albuquerque
> ***Casa San Ysidro***: **The Gutiérrez-Minge House**, *Corrales*
> ***Coronado*** **State Monument**, *Bernalillo*
> ***Camino Real*** **Site**, near *La Cienega*
> ***El Rancho de las Golondrinas***, *La Cienega*
> **Museum of Spanish Colonial Art**, *Santa Fe*
> **Palace of the Governors**, *Santa Fe*

Several of these attractions are discussed elsewhere in this book. More information on these sites can be found at the following website:

www.nps.gov/elca/planyourvisit/places-to-go-in-new-mexico.htm

Note: If you would like to take a virtual tour, rather than a real tour, of *El Camino Real de Tierra Adentro* National Historic Trail go to the following site, and click on the Virtual Tour near the bottom of the page:

www.blm.gov/heritage/adventures/menu/featured_site_nm.html

This National Historic Trail was incorporated in 2005 into the **El Camino Real** International Heritage Center, in a joint effort with the Bureau of Land Management. See **El Camino Real International Heritage Center** discussed in Chapter Fourteen: State Monuments of New Mexico.

A map of the trail can be downloaded at the following website:

www.nps.gov/olsp/planyourvisit/directions.htm

Old Spanish National Historic Trail[61, 62]

The **Old Spanish Trail** was designated a National Historic Trail because of its rich history and its cultural significance to the American Southwest. Trade between *Santa Fe*, New Mexico and *Los Angeles*, California was set up by means of this 1,200-mile long trail. It was an arduous trade route that weaved through dry deserts, steep canyons and over high mountains. However, it allowed exchange of goods between settlers in both regions, and with neighboring Native American tribes. The trail followed some ancient pathways used by Native Americans, Spanish explorers and *Anglo*-American traders and trappers. The **Old Spanish Trail** extended from *Santa Fe,* New Mexico through the southwestern corner of *Colorado*, across Utah, through the southeastern corner of *Nevada* and across California's *Mojave*[63] Desert to *Los Angeles*, California. It also touched the extreme northwestern corner of Arizona.

Large mule pack trains, numbering in the tens to hundreds, were used on the Old Spanish Trail to carry trade goods in both directions. The muleteers were often Hispanics who were called *arrieros*. The trail was used from about 1840 to the mid 1850's.

Traders from New Mexico brought finished goods such as woven blankets, in exchange for California's horses or mules. Horses were also stolen from local ranches that lay close to the trail. This same route was used in support of an active slave trade. Mexicans, ex-trappers, miscreants and various tribes raided local homesteads for horses, women and children. They were usually sold as domestic servants to Californian or Mexican households.

The best time to leave New Mexico, for California, was in November. This allowed arrival in California by early February. Traders could then cross the otherwise hot and dry deserts, using the winter rains to keep them cool and to provide available drinking water. However, this approach also carried with it the risk of winter snowstorms and blizzards. Whether a trader travelled in winter or in summer it was equally treacherous, risky and dangerous! In addition, the travel was arduous and difficult.

Although the **Old Spanish Trail** was used for at least fifteen years prior to John Fremont's expedition to California in 1844, it became better known after his report, as the **Old Spanish Trail**. It was Kit Carson who led Fremont's expedition west to California, using this old trail. However, it was gradually abandoned after the United States gained the territories of the Southwest, following the end of the Mexican-American War in 1848. The terrain of the Spanish Trail was too difficult for wagons. Other trade routes were developed and the **Old Spanish Trail** fell into disuse, as wagons and wagon trains were introduced and became popular. These wagon trains eventually replaced the mule trains as the more effective means of trade.

A map of the trail can be downloaded at the following website:

www.nps.gov/olsp/planyourvisit/directions.htm

Santa Fe National Historic Trail[64, 65, 66]

In the 19th century, the 1,000-mile *Santa Fe* Trail provided a transportation route for settlers through central North America, that connected western Missouri with *Santa Fe*, New Mexico. In 1821, after Mexican Independence from Spain, a trader named William Becknell opened up the *Santa Fe* Trail. He was nicknamed the "Father of the *Santa Fe* Trail." Later, the same trail was used by American troops to attack the Mexicans in the Mexican-American War of 1846 - 1848. In both cases, the **Mountain Route** was taken to *Santa Fe*, New Mexico. In the 1860's, up to 5,000 wagons a year traversed the trail. Usage of the trail declined with the advent of a railroad track to *Santa Fe.* See the short discussion of the *Santa Fe* Trail and its significance in the development and settlement of the American Southwest, in Chapter Three.

Today, the *Santa Fe* Trail is commemorated as the *Santa Fe* National Historic Trail. Two modern highway routes roughly follow the two branches of the **Old *Santa Fe* Trail** northward from *Santa Fe* through central and northern New Mexico. These highway routes have been designated the ***Santa Fe* Trail National Scenic Byway**. The New Mexico state portion of the **Old *Santa Fe* Trail** includes the northern portion of **Interstate 25** and all of **Route 56**. Other roadways connect in neighboring states to complete the *Santa Fe* National Historic Trail.

From Independence, Missouri, the **Old *Santa Fe* Trail** started out on a single westward trail that split over time into two basic trails: the original, longer **Mountain Trail** (through *Colorado* and the **Raton** Pass into New Mexico), and the shorter but more dangerous ***Cimarron* Cutoff Trail** (through northeastern New Mexico, bypassing *Colorado* and the **Raton** Pass).

Both trails started at Independence, Missouri, split just outside of Dodge City, Kansas, and rejoined at **Watrous** (then called *La Junta)* New Mexico, before proceeding along a common trail to their final destination: ***Santa Fe***, New Mexico.

The **Mountain Route** started from Independence, Missouri. In modern times, Highway 56 proceeds westward from Independence, Missouri, towards Dodge City, Kansas. Here, Highway 50 is picked up and it roughly follows the

Mountain Route westward towards *La Junta, Colorado.* In *Colorado,* Highway 350 then carries the traveler to Trinidad, *Colorado.* **Interstate 25** proceeds south from Trinidad across the famous *Raton* **Pass** into New Mexico. **I-25** does proceed south from *Raton* to Springer, but in this region it does not strictly follow either the *Cimarron* **Branch** or the **Mountain Branch** of the *Santa Fe* Trail. The interstate highway does however cross over the *Raton* **Pass,** as the **Mountain Route** once did from *Colorado* into northern New Mexico.

Of the two branches, modern highways most closely follow the old **Mountain Route** from Missouri, through Kansas and *Colorado,* into northern New Mexico. Present-day highways also roughly follow the old *Cimarron* **Cutoff Route** (west of Dodge City, Kansas), but less closely through Kansas and Oklahoma into New Mexico.

Strictly speaking, south of Springer, New Mexico, Interstate 25 roughly follows the *Cimarron* **Cutoff Route** of the *Santa Fe* Trail southward towards **Wagon Mound,** and then on to **Watrous** (formerly *La Junta*). At **Watrous,** the *Cimarron* **Cutoff Route** and the **Mountain Route** joined onto a common path towards *Santa Fe,* through *Las Vegas.* **Interstate 25** roughly follows this final portion of the common routes of the *Santa Fe* Trail.

The *Cimarron* **Cutoff Route** also started in Independence, Missouri. It was discovered years after the **Mountain Trail**. It was used because it shortened the distance of the trip by 100 or 200 miles and the duration of the trip by up to a week. However, it was a more dangerous trip because of the need to traverse the 200-mile Waterscape region, in Kansas, before reaching the waters of the *Cimarron* River. In addition, the voyage was open to Indian attacks and a hostile open and barren landscape, void of shelter.

Today, from Independence, Missouri, Highway 56 travels westward, following the *Santa Fe* Trail to Dodge City, Kansas…the same path taken along the initial stages of the **Mountain** or *Raton* **Route**. Then Highway 56 proceeds southwesterly and diagonally across Kansas, through the extreme northwestern corner of Oklahoma, through Clayton, New Mexico towards Springer, New Mexico. This highway route approximately follows the *Cimarron* **Cutoff Route** of the *Santa Fe* Trail. At Springer, **Highway 56** meets up with **Interstate 25**, which proceeds southward towards **Watrous,** the original juncture point of the two *Santa Fe* Trail Routes. **Interstate 25** proceeds south and then west from **Watrous,** through *Las Vegas* and *Glorieta* towards *Santa Fe*, New Mexico, along a path that parallels the joint routes of the *Santa Fe* Trail towards the final destination: *Santa Fe.*

In the mid-1800's, the **Watrous Cutoff** was utilized to allow a shorter route between **Wagon Mound** and **Watrous**. From **Wagon Mound,** the trail proceeded directly westward and then directly southward, around the Turkey Mountains in *Mora* County. This allowed the *Cimarron* **Cutoff Route** to join the **Mountain Route** just north of **Fort Union**, instead of south of the fort at **Watrous** *(La Junta)*, the original juncture point.

Today **wagon train ruts** on the **Old** *Santa Fe* **Trail** can be seen at *Pecos* **National Historical Park** and at **Fort Union National Monument**. See also the discussion of these two national monuments in this chapter. In addition, see the discussion of the *Santa Fe* Trail in Chapter Three.

In *Santa Fe,* along the Old *Santa Fe* Trail, next to the **Museum of Spanish Colonial Art**, there is an impressive statue set called ***Journey's End.***These statues capture the final moments of the 1,000 mile wagon trip, as the travelers approach their final destination: *Santa Fe,* New Mexico. The sculptor was Reynaldo "Sonny" Rivera. The landscape architect was Richard Borkovetz. If you get the chance, please see this exciting sculpture set, as a reminder of the courage and stamina of these brave souls that ventured on the **Old *Santa Fe* Trail.**

The terminal point of the famous *Santa Fe* Trail is marked by a **small stone monument** on the ***Santa Fe Plaza,*** near the corner of East *San Franciso* Street and **Old *Santa Fe* Trail**. See the discussion about the *Santa Fe* Trail and a photograph of the small stone monument in Chapter Three.

Late breaking Addendum: As of March 25, 2013, President Barack Obama designated the *Rio Grande* Region, as the *Rio Grande del Norte* National Monument. Discussion of the *Rio Grande* Gorge Bridge and the *Rio Grande* Gorge is discussed briefly in Chapter Ten.

Chapter Fourteen: New Mexico State Monuments

There are seven significant monuments managed by the state of New Mexico. These are the *Coronado* State Monument, *El Camino Real* International Heritage Center (jointly managed with the Bureau of Land Management), Fort Selden State Monument, Fort Stanton State Monument, Fort Sumner State Monument & *Bosque Redondo* Memorial, *Jemez* State Monument, and the Lincoln State Monument. Each of these state monuments is discussed in this chapter. Information about any of these sites can be obtained at the following web site: www.nmmonuments.org

In this chapter, key points of interest are highlighted in **bold** text.

Coronado State Monument[1, 2, 3]

The site of this state monument is located just north of Albuquerque (Exit 242, I-25) in *Bernalillo*, Sandoval County. This monument commemorates the location where Francisco Vasquez *de Coronado* embarked on his expedition in search of the fabled Seven Cities of Gold. His expedition was large in scope and number. *Coronado* brought with him, 300 Spanish soldiers and 800 Indian allies from New Spain. After his initial disappointment near *Zuni,* he turned eastward and decided to start an expanded search for the fabled cities at this site. What he found here were many prosperous but modest native villages. *Coronado* and his expedition party camped near the *Tiwa* village of **Kuaua**. *Coronado* called the villages "*pueblos*."

The *pueblo* name, **Kuaua**, means "evergreen" in the *Tiwa* language. It was first settled around 1300 AD, taking advantage of the fertile river valleys of the *Rio Grande.* The *pueblo* flourished and expanded over time as the natives enjoyed success with agriculture in that area. The **Kuaua** site is thought to have been part of the *pueblo* community identified as **Tiguex** (pronounced "Tee-weh") by *Coronado* and the Spaniards. The *Pueblo* Peoples of *Sandia* and *Santa Clara* claim to have come originally from **Kuaua**. See Figure 14-1.

In the 1930's, the **Kuaua** earthen *pueblo* was excavated by archeologists Edgar Lee Hewitt and Marjorie F. Tichy (Lambert). They found a *pueblo* that was built on an axis that ran from north to south. The archeologists also uncovered six *kiva's* in round, square and rectangular configurations. In the south *plaza* of the **Kuaua**

Figure 14-1: Reconstructed *Kuaua Pueblo* remains, at *Coronado* State Monument, with *Sandia* Mountains in the background.

Pueblo community, a square *kiva* was excavated containing many layers of mural paintings, some of the finest examples of pre-Columbian mural art in the nation. These original murals were removed and they are available for viewing in the **Mural Room** in the Visitor Center.

To help preserve the underlying original *pueblo* remains from erosion, new *pueblo*-style wall "ruins" were reconstructed, by archeologists, over the re-buried excavated *pueblo*. Both the *kiva* and one of the mural layers have been reconstructed at the site in modern times.

Viewing the inside of the **reconstructed *kiva*** requires descending into the structure by means of the wooden ladder that projects up from the *kiva* floor to the roof. Although most *kivas* are round in shape, this *kiva* is square in form. The walls are partially covered by murals reproduced by the notable native artist **Ma Pe Wi** or **Velino Shije Herrera**. The artist died in 1973 and so now even this artist's modern mural reproductions are prized. Seeing the inside of this **reconstructed *kiva*** is highly recommended!

The Visitor Center contains both pre-historic and historic native *pueblo* Indian, and Spanish Colonial artifacts on exhibit. One can hold an old heavy Spanish harquebus, and see first-hand why it needed a support below the barrel to enable accurate shooting. The Visitor Center also shows a large altar screen (reredo or *retablo mayor*) and the hub of an old Spanish *carreta* (cart). Just outside the Visitor Center on the covered patio, there is a reconstruction of a medium-sized Spanish *carreta*. In the **Mural Room** in the Visitor Center, several preserved original mural segments excavated from the original *kiva* can be viewed. These murals are stunning to behold, with a wide range of colors and religious/spiritual themes and figures.

There is a short trail that one can take around the monument grounds. There is even an offshoot of the trail that one can take down to the nearby *Rio Grande,* with the beautiful *Sandia* Mountains as a stunning backdrop.

The site also has a **picnic area** for casual enjoyment and rest. For additional information about this site call: (505) 867-5351.

El Camino Real International Heritage Center[4, 5, 6]

The **Heritage Center** opened in November 2005. It relates the story behind the *El Camino Real de Tierra Adentro*, the "Royal Road to the Interior." This trade route extended for 1,500 miles from Mexico City to *San Juan Pueblo* in northern New Mexico. See the discussion of the Royal Road and trail in Chapter Thirteen: National Monuments, Parks and Historic Trails. The trail itself extends from the southern border of New Mexico, northward to *Santa Fe* in north central New Mexico. The **Heritage Center** relates the story of this historic trail in New Mexican history. It also features discussions and displays of the regional culture and its people.

The **Heritage Center** was developed in concert with the Bureau of Land Management. The development of the road from pre-historic times through to today's modern highway is traced and described. Special emphasis is given to its use by the Spaniards. Don Juan de Oñate designated this road as a "royal" road linking the two capitals, Mexico City and *Santa Fe.*

The site can be found between the towns of *Socorro* and Truth or Consequences,[7] lying just east of I-25. Visitors should take Exit 115 to the Highway 1 Frontage Road, and then follow the signs to the site. The **Heritage Center** is situated in the northern *Chihuahuan* Desert. It overlooks the *Rio Grande* at the northern end of ***La Jornada del Muerto***. The building has a large exhibit area, an auditorium and an outdoor amphitheater. The **Heritage Center** building is shown in Figure 14-2. It provides an overview and description of the Royal Road, its people, its culture and its history. For additional information call (575) 854-3600.

Figure 14-2: Entrance to the *El Camino Real* International Heritage Center.

On the short drive (less than three miles), to the Visitor Center, one can see a beautiful modern-style monument on the right hand side, a little less than two miles before reaching the center. It stands alone on a small hilltop, with reddish colored sides representing the local mountain ranges between which the *Rio Grande* flows. The *Rio Grande* is represented in a turquoise color in the center top of the monument. This monument is called "***Camino de Sueños***", meaning "Road of Dreams." It was created by Greg E. Reiche and funded by the Cultural Corridors Arts Program of the State of New Mexico.

Fort Selden State Monument[8, 9]

This state monument is located about 13 miles north of *Las Cruces,* off I-25, Exit 19, in *Doña Ana* County. The monument is closed on Tuesdays. Fort Selden was established in 1865, to bring peace to this region of New Mexico. It was an *adobe* fort built along the banks of the *Rio Grande*, to house both infantry and cavalry troops, and to protect the settlers of the ***Mesilla*** **Valley** from *Apache* raiders and *desperados,* that roamed and raided the area. Buffalo Soldiers were among those stationed here. Fort Seldon housed one company of infantry and one company of cavalry.

The **125th US Colored Infantry Regiment** comprised the first troops to occupy the fort. Following the end of the American Civil War, many African-American men could not obtain employment. Many enlisted in the U.S. Army, which was in need of fresh recruits at the time. A large number of these "colored regiments" obtained their recruits from Kentucky. As recruitments gained in size, other "colored regiments" were created, such as the **9th** and **10th U.S. Cavalry.** These black troopers came to be called **Buffalo Soldiers.**

Fort Selden was decommissioned in 1891. There was no longer any need for settler or traveler protection in the region after the surrender of *Geronimo* and his

Chiricahua Apache band. Most *desperados* had been subdued, and the land was reasonably tamed and safe for settlers. There was no longer any dire need for the *adobe* fort...and so it was abandoned. In this period, numerous forts were abandoned by command of General William T. Sherman, in an effort to concentrate military power and to introduce operational efficiencies. The forces and resources in these regions were combined into southwesterly larger forts such as Fort Bliss, Texas.

Figure 14-3: Ruins at Fort Selden State Monument, Radium Springs.

Figure 14-4: Frontier wagon at Fort Selden State Monument, Radium Springs.

There is an impressive statue dedicated to the bravery of the Buffalo Soldier at the monument site. This statue shows a Buffalo infantryman leaning against a rock, holding his rifle in his left hand, ready to use, and holding binoculars in his right hand. There is also a frontier wagon on the grounds, together with the ruins of the old fort. See Figures 14-3 and 14-4.

The Visitor Center at Fort Selden, in Radium Springs, occasionally gives living history demonstrations during the summer months, between May 1 and September 15. An overview of frontier life can be obtained at the Visitor Center. For additional information on this site call: (575) 526-8911.

Fort Stanton State Monument[10, 11, 12, 13]

Fort Stanton is located near *Capitán*, in Lincoln County. It was built as a military fort, in 1855, in the New Mexico Territory, to protect frontier settlements along the *Rio Bonito* (Beautiful River) from marauding *Mescalero Apache* and other raiding tribes. At the time, the *Mescalero Apache* claimed the region as tribal lands. The fort was named for Captain Henry W. Stanton. "Black" cavalry regiments were once stationed here. These regiments (and other black regiments) were termed "Buffalo Soldiers" because of their short curly hair being similar to buffalo hair, and also because of their fierce fighting prowess and spirit.

Kit Carson once was stationed at this fort. Also, John "Black Jack" Pershing is known to have been stationed here on two occasions. The fort operated as a military installation until 1896. See Figure 14-5.

In the first part of the 20th century, it operated as the first Federal tuberculosis hospital in the U.S. Later, during World War II, it served as an internment camp for German and Japanese prisoners of war (POW's).

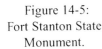

Figure 14-5:
Fort Stanton State
Monument.

There are numerous buildings that surround a central grassy quadrangle. These buildings include a museum, former military barracks, officers' quarters, hospital and other facilities. The fort is situated near the **Rio Bonito**, surrounded by the nearby **Capitán** and the **Sacramento Mountains**. The famous and prominent *Sierra Blanca* ("White Mountain"), sacred to the *Mescalero Apache*, can be seen in the distance. The surrounding landscape is beautiful! Thousands of acres surrounding Fort Stanton are part of the **Smokey Bear Ranger District** of the **Lincoln National Forest**. The Bureau of Land Management (BLM) manages these lands. The BLM manages hundreds of miles of trails, a camping area and horseback riding through these lands. The BLM also runs a large caving program that includes **Fort Stanton Cave and Snowy River**. Plans include opening these areas to the public, eventually.

This state monument is located at 104 Kit Carson Road, Fort Stanton, NM 88323. From nearby *Ruidoso*, follow NM 48 North for 7 miles to NM 220. Turn right onto NM 220 and stay on this roadway for about 12.5 miles. The Fort Stanton State Monument will appear on the left. It can also be reached by taking U.S. 380 through *Capitán* until it reaches NM 220. At this point, take a right turn onto NM 220, which leads to Fort Stanton.

In the winter months of December through March, Fort Stanton is opened on weekend days only, until 4 pm. Visiting hours in the warmer months of April through November are as follows:

Closed Tuesday and Wednesday
Sunday- 12 Noon – 4 pm
Remaining days of the week: 10 am – 4 pm.

Fort Stanton Live is an annual summer event, in July or August, in coordination with **Old Lincoln Days**. This event features re-enactments of **Buffalo Soldiers** and American Civil War battles. It also features *Apache* dancers, storytelling, candlelight tours, historical presentations, live music and concessions. To arrange tours please call: (575) 336-1436. For further information visit the following website:

http://www.discoverruidoso.com:80/Fort-Stanton-State-Monument

Fort Sumner State Monument & *Bosque Redondo* Memorial[14, 15, 16, 17]

To visit this site, take I-40 to U.S. Highway 60-84. This site is located off U.S. Highway 60-84, just three miles east of the Village of Fort Sumner, then south on Billy the Kid Road.

The **Old Fort Sumner Museum & Gift Shop**, the **Old Fort Sumner Post Cemetery** and the *Bosque Redondo* **Memorial** are all located on Billy the Kid Road, within one mile of each other. The **Old Fort Sumner Museum & Gift Shop** is the first spot encountered on the road to the memorial. This museum requires a small entry fee, but is well worth visiting. It shows copies and transcriptions of letters written by Billy the Kid to the likes of Lew Wallace, the Territorial Governor at the time. It also has other related artifacts of the period. The gift shop sells Billy the Kid and western memorabilia.

The Fort Sumner "post" cemetery is just outside the museum/giftshop, less than one hundred yards to the right, as one leaves the shop. Surrounded by a wrought iron fence, one can see the gravesites and headstones for Billy the Kid, and two of his comrades, Charlie Bowdrie and Tom O'Folliard. See Figure 14-6. The gravesites of Pete Maxwell and his father Lucien Maxwell are located within this same cemetery. (Billy the Kid was killed in Pete Maxwell's house).

The *Bosque Redondo* **Memorial** is located less than one half a mile further down the road. This Memorial stands as a testimony to the tragic events that occurred here to two Native American tribes in the 1860's. About 8,500 *Navajo* and several hundred *Mescalero Apache* natives were incarcerated at *Bosque Redondo*. Thousands of *Navajo* prisoners died here from disease and starvation, after their infamous forced "**Long Walk**" from Arizona and western New Mexico. The march covered more than 450 miles and it was conducted in the dead of winter! The suffering was a traumatic,

Figure 14-6: Gravesite of Billy the Kid, and his sidekicks, Tom O'Folliard and Charlie Bowdrie, at the Old Fort Sumner Post Cemetery, just outside the Fort Sumner/*Bosque Redondo* State Monument.

unforgettable experience in the *Navajo* psyche. The *Navajo* call **Bosque Redondo** *H'wééldi* or *H'wéélde*, "place of suffering." The **Mescalero Apache** also suffered here but in smaller numbers. The **Mescalero Apache** fled the *bosque* in November 1865 and slowly returned to their homeland in small numbers. The *Navajo*, much greater in number, had to wait three more years to be released, until the Treaty of 1868 established their sovereignty as a people, laying the groundwork for the recognition of the *Navajo* **Nation** by the United States.

Fort Sumner was abandoned in 1869. The fort was named a New Mexico State Monument in 1968. A *Navajo* architect, David N. Sloan, was selected to develop a memorial museum at the site. It is called the **Bosque Redondo** **Memorial**.

Eventually, the U.S. set aside lands as reservations for these two tribes. It is unfortunate that the peoples of these two tribes suffered so harshly, but, ironically, it saved their people from extinction, in the end.

The memorial monument dedicated to this site of suffering is beautiful and the Visitor Center is very modern. See Figure 14-7. The **Monument Building** has a small room with native artifacts and a small but fine gift shop with native crafts. It also provides a 30 minute-video that is informative and very moving. It reveals the real suffering these native peoples endured. On the site, there is a short river walk by the shores of the nearby **Pecos River**. There is also a small and simple **Navajo Memorial** that was dedicated in 1971 by visiting *Navajo* natives. They brought items from their *Navajo* homeland, which they left in place and dedicated to the memory of their people who suffered and died on this site in the 1860's. To the *Dineh*, these victims will never be forgotten. Their suffering is part of the tribal memory!

Figure 14-7: *Bosque Redondo* Memorial Building, at the Fort Sumner/*Bosque Redondo* State Monument.

A plaque in the **Memorial Park** eloquently captures the longing of the *Navajo* to return to their homeland. A *Navajo* presented this plaque in 1865. It simply states,

"Cage the badger and he will try to break from his prison and regain his native hole. Chain the eagle to the ground – he will strive to gain his freedom, and though he fails, he will lift his head and look up at the sky which is his home – and we want to return to our mountains and plains, where we used to plant corn, wheat and beans." (Courtesy of the *Bosque Redondo* Memorial Monument Park).

Simple and powerful eloquence! Three years later (June 18, 1868), the *Navajo* survivors began their long trip home.

The **Monument** recognizes another significant event in New Mexico history. A **granite marker** identifies the spot where the Billy the Kid was shot dead by Sheriff Pat Garrett in 1881, at the site of the old **Maxwell House**. Unfortunately, past *Pecos* River floods washed away most of the remains of the old fort, the **Maxwell House** and other points of interest.

The ***Bosque Redondo*** video and the memorial leave a lasting impression of the great suffering endured here! For additional information, call (575) 355-2573.

Jemez State Monument[18, 19]

The *Jemez* State Monument is located in the village of *Jemez* Springs, in Sandoval County, New Mexico. In *Bernalillo*, take the I-25 exit that leads to US 550 North and West. Take US 550 North for 23 miles, and just at the White *Mesa*, take a right, heading north on NM 4 through *Jemez Pueblo*. Continue north on NM 4 to about the 18-mile marker in *Jemez* Springs. The state monument site is on the right by the roadside.

Here one can see the site of the 14th century **Gisewa** (Gees-eh-wa) or **Giusewa Pueblo**, as well as remains of the 17th century **San José de los Jemez** **Mission Church. Gisewa** means "place of the boiling waters" in *Towa*, referring to the hot springs in the area, which still attract tourists today. The *Jemez* People occupied the ***Gisewa Pueblo*** and other neighboring *pueblos*. During the 1680 *Pueblo* Revolt, local natives burned down the church and killed the Spanish priest, to protest their overbearing subjugation by the Spaniards.

There is a modern **reconstruction of a** *kiva* on site, together with some small former *pueblo* building remains. See Figure 14-8. The tour trail is only about 700 feet long. One can also see the mission church ruins and the supporting missionary buildings. See Figure 14-9. The surrounding mountains and forests provide a breathtaking setting. The small museum attached to the Visitor Center is well worth

Figure 14-8: Reconstructed *Guisewa kiva* at *Jemez* State Monument.

Figure 14-9: *San José de los Jemez* Church remains at *Jemez* State Monument.

seeing. It has some very interesting and informative displays about *Jemez* life and traditions. No photography is permitted in the museum. For more information on this state monument call: (505) 829-3530.

Lincoln State Monument[20, 21, 22]

This site preserves the historic **Old Town** section of Lincoln, where so many notables in the Lincoln County War were active in the late 1800's. Seventeen of Lincoln's two score building structures are preserved as part of this monument. Among these are: **Dr. Wood's Office, Watson House, Wright House, Wortley Hotel, Curry Saloon, Penfield Shop and Home, Tunstall Store, Old Mill, Ellis Store, Old Lincoln County Courthouse** and **Montano Store.** An additional six

Figure 14-10: Old Lincoln County Courthouse. Lincoln State Monument.

Figure 14-11: The site where Billy the Kid shot and killed Sheriff Bob Olinger, is indicated by the small white stone ground marker, near the outside corner of the Courthouse. The Kid shot Sheriff Olinger from the upstairs side window, nearest the building front. Lincoln State Monument.

structures are part of the state monument. The Lincoln State Monument is considered to be the best-preserved "cow town" in the U.S.

Lincoln looks much as it did in the time of the **Lincoln County War** (1878 to 1881). Today, unless there is some notable event occurring, the **Old Town** is sleepy and relatively inactive. One can almost see characters such as **Billy the Kid** or **Lawrence Murphy** stalking down the main street of Lincoln.

Lincoln is the site where **Billy the Kid** was brought after his conviction at the *Mesilla* trial. He was jailed upstairs in the **Old Lincoln County Courthouse & Jail.** Here he made his bold escape from the temporary jail in April 1881. See Figure 14-10. This location appears almost as it did back then. There is a bullet hole in the wall of the staircase leading to the courtroom upstairs. Supposedly, **Billy the Kid** left this mark during his escape from the temporary second floor jail.

Before escaping, **Billy the Kid** shot two sheriffs: **James Bell** and **Bob Olinger**. **James Bell** was shot inside at the top of the stairwell leading to the jail. **Sheriff Bob Olinger** was shot outside from one of the second floor windows, near the "makeshift" upstairs jail, as he rushed over from the **Wortley Hotel** across the street. A white marker near the front left outside corner of the courthouse/jail marks the spot where he was shot. See Figure 14-11.

The most popular main attractions in the **Old Town of Lincoln** are as follows:

Old Lincoln County Courthouse – This building, built in 1874, was once the **L. G. Murphy and Co. Store** and residence of **Lawrence G. Murphy**. Later, it became the **Murphy & Dolan Mercantile Store**. Some short time later still, but before the end of the **Lincoln County War** (1878 – 1881), it was converted to a courthouse and upstairs jail. Here, **Billy the Kid** was jailed after his conviction in the town of *Mesilla*. He was sentenced to be hanged until dead, in the town of Lincoln. He made his escape from the upstairs jail in April 1881. There are exhibits, photographs, storyboards, and artifacts to show the building's use as a country mercantile store, a residence, a **Masonic Lodge** and eventually a courthouse and jail. See Figure 14-10. This building was the headquarters of the **Murphy-Dolan-Riley faction** during the **Lincoln County War.**

Tunstall Store – Across, and down the street from the **Old Lincoln County Courthouse** stands the **Tunstall Store**. Original 19th century merchandise is on display in the store. See Figure 14-12. This mercantile store was set up to compete (fairly) with the monopolistic **L.G. Murphy** (and later **Dolan**) **Mercantile Store** across the street and up the road. It was Tunstall's murder by the Murphy-Dolan-Riley faction that started the infamous **Lincoln County War**.

Torreón **Tower**- Originally built in the 1860's near the center of town, the 20-foot-high round stone fort, that is called the *Torreón* **Tower**, stood as a refuge for settlers during *Mescalero Apache* attacks. It played a central role in the **Battle of Lincoln**. See Figure 14-13.

Montano Store - Features exhibits on the Hispanic culture and *adobe* construction as it was during the **Lincoln County War**. Most of the buildings in the Lincoln community are built according to the Territorial Style of architecture.

La Iglesia de San Juan Bautista[23] - Originally built in 1887, the *San Juan Bautista* ("Saint John the Baptist") Mission Church is open to the public. Services are still held here to this day.

Anderson-Freeman Visitors Center - The Visitor Center is a non-historical building. It contains exhibits of the town's history from American Indian pre-historic times through the **Lincoln County War** era. A short video outlines the events of the

Figure 14-12: Tunstall's Store and Museum – Still standing today! Lincoln State Monument.

Figure 14-13: *Torreón* Tower (back view), showing the rear door entry to the tower. Lincoln State Monument.

notorious **Lincoln County War.**

The *adobe*- and stone-built *Torreón* **Tower** is just down the road from the **Tunstall Store** on the same side of the road. Access to the tower was via a small rear wooden doorway. The **Murphy-Dolan-Riley** faction used this tower to fire on the **Regulators** and on the **McSween faction**, during the **Battle of Lincoln**. See Figure 14-13. During this battle, **McSween's house** was burned down and he was killed. The home was never rebuilt. Today, all that remains is an empty lot to the immediate left of the buildings that house the **Tunstall Store**.

The Lincoln State Monument can be found on U.S. Route 380 about 12 miles east of *Capitán* and 57 miles west of Roswell. For additional information on this site call: (575) 653-4372.

Chapter Fifteen: New Mexico State Fairs & County Fairs

Not to be overlooked for entertainment and sheer Americana are the state and county fairs. These events reflect the rural life of America. Fairs in New Mexico add a special twist that reflects our special Hispanic and Native American culture and heritage, as well as the *Anglo*-American heritage. These annual events are lively, fun-filled and "must see, must do" events. A brief overview of the state, regional and county fairs here.

New Mexico State Fair

The very first New Mexico State Fair[1] was held in 1881 and lasted for five days. This was held while New Mexico was still a Territory and before it officially became the 47th state on January 6, 1912. Today, the New Mexico State Fair is open for several weeks. It is very popular with both business owners and with the huge crowds that attend each year. See Figure 15-1.

Figure 15-1: 2011 New Mexico State Fair.

Entertainment is a big part of the attraction of these state fairs. Included in the fair are many artisans and performers. Of course, there are also food and gift vendors who emphasize New Mexico's rich Hispanic and Native American culture and heritage. The state fair also features traditional livestock exhibits, competitions, auctions and shows, as well as gardening and cooking competitions. Live music from well-known headliners is another feature of these fairs. *Mariachi* bands, Andean music, *Navajo* singers and others can be seen playing at the fair. Additional attractions can include games, carnivals, and rodeo events. Each year, a New Mexico State Fair Queen is selected and crowned during the fair.

The New Mexico State Fair is an attraction and activity well worth seeing and enjoying. The 2011 state fair had *Navajo* native dancers and singers, *Mariachi* bands, Andean musicians, blacksmithing, antique car exhibitions, Chinese acrobats, vendors of all kinds, photo booths, ferris wheels, a large (caged bucket) bungy "Sling-Shot", Bungy Trampoline and Walk-on-Water bubbles for the kids, FFA farm animal exhibits, sheep shearing exhibitions, horseback riding competitions, pitching cages and a whole lot more. There was also a Pee-Wee Rodeo for youngsters, a Flying Canine Show and a Lion Show. Youngsters and teens alike enjoyed the gyro rides too. Thousands attend to see the exhibits, to enjoy the shows and to participate in the rides and the fun!

Like to eat fast food goodies? There's an abundance of regular and crazy fast foods available such as: *nachos*, turkey legs, sausage on a stick, *kielbasa* or Polish sausage, Italian sausage, pizza, *chile relleno* dogs, *chile* dogs, taters on a stick, *taco in a bag*, *chile* cheese dogs, corndogs, *chile* cheese fries, *chile* burgers, hamburgers and hot dogs. Do you care for Greek food? You can choose from *dolmas, falafel, gyros, hummus* or *spanakopita*. How about *bakalava* for dessert? Or, how about frozen bananas, root beer floats, cinnamon rolls, hot apple dumplings, snow cones or *churros* (cinnamon sticks)? Wilder yet, you could go for chocolate dipped bacon or a fried Snickers bar! The fast food options seem almost limitless! So, throw caution to the wind (if you dare) and indulge. You'll really love it as you eat it…but you may regret it later! In any case, it's all part of the enjoyment of the state fair. Be sure to get out there and enjoy it. It's great fun!

Do you like antique cars? There was even an exhibit of fine looking top condition antique cars at the 2011 New Mexico State Fair! See Figure 15-2.

Figure 15-2:
Antique Cars
on exhibit,
2011 New
Mexico State
Fair

For 2011, the New Mexico State Fair took place in Albuquerque between September 9 - 25, 2011. The fair was held at the Expo Racetrack (The Downs), where it is usually held each year in mid-September. To obtain more information about the New Mexico State Fair, the following website can be accessed:

www.exponm.com/fair

In addition, a virtual video tour is provided at the following website:

Figure 15-3: Goin' fer a Walk at the End of the Day.
2011 New Mexico State Fair.

www.virtualalbuquerque.com/VirtualABQ/StateFair

This last site gives one a "feel" for the events and the sights at the state fair. You never know what you are going to see there! See Figure 15-3.

Regional State Fairs
Various regions of the state also hold state fairs, such as the Southern New Mexico and the Eastern New Mexico State Fairs. These fairs make it easier for folks local to that region to attend and participate in a state fair. These regional state fairs contain many of the same features and events that are held at the main state fair. Consult the web for locations and schedules.

County Fairs
Many counties in New Mexico hold their own County Fairs. These too are usually held in the months of September or October. These county fairs are scaled down versions of the regional and state fairs. They also feature livestock shows, competitions and auctions, games, entertainment and home craft competitions, similar to what you might expect at state fairs. Rodeos and carnivals may or may not be included in county fairs.

There are usually quilting, crocheting, baking, photography, sketching, woodcraft, beadwork, fruit and vegetable canning, clay modeling, gardening and other home craft competitions and awards. 4-H, FFA and other youth development organizations usually sponsor these events. Check the web for local county fairs.

Afterward: A Peek Into the Future in the Land of Enchantment

New Mexico is not just a land with strong and colorful ties to the traditional past. The state is looking forward to the future with excitement and daring. Through partnership between the state and private enterprise, New Mexico is stepping boldly into the future with the development of Spaceport America. Although New Mexico is also active in the development of wind power and solar technologies, and it is expanding the film industry within the state, the most exciting future technology development is by far the visionary Spaceport America. This promises not only to launch a new era in space technology development, but also to transform space travel into a commercially viable enterprise! Only the future awaits us!

Let's take a brief look at the future of New Mexico in this newly developing Second Space Age.

The Sky Is <u>Not</u> the Limit: Spaceport America [1,2,3,4]…Here we Come!

The shuttle program has just completed its final flight, signaling the demise of the NASA-sponsored U.S. Space Program. From this point forward, the federal government's intention is to rent space on Russian launchers to put our astronauts into space!

Fortunately some forward thinking entrepreneurs and New Mexico state officials see this as an opportunity to explore the possibilities of commercial space flight.

The initial plan launched in December 2005, called for a $225 million spaceport to be built in New Mexico, with the New Mexico Legislature contributing $100 million to the project over the following three years. The deal was sealed during Governor Bill Richardson's term in office. The primary entrepreneur on the private industry side is Virgin Group Chairman and billionaire Sir Richard Branson. The project plan called for the spaceport to be built on a 27 square mile site on state-owned lands near the White Sands Missile Range, 45 miles north of *Las Cruces*, New Mexico. The spaceport construction has been completed. Only further flight-testing and liability issues remain to be resolved.

Virgin Galactic intends to eventually pay off all its initial expenses as the commercial business grows. Virgin Galactic will lease the spaceport facilities for some number of years until that time. The spaceport not only creates jobs, but it also adds to the prestige of the state. This enterprise opens the Second Space Age as it transforms from government to commercial endeavors. It is expected to open opportunities in point-to-point cargo delivery, as well as private and business travel.

Initially, Virgin Galactic plans to offer suborbital spaceflights. It will also be the primary initial tenant of the completed spaceport. Virgin Galactic expects to have a fleet of five craft, using technology pioneered with the SpaceShipOne rocket plane. This plane is the first commercially developed craft to reach the fringe of outer space. This endeavor will open up an entirely new and exciting space industry.

Most of the facility has already been built underground to preserve the natural beauty of the surrounding desert terrain, and to save water and energy. The SpaceShipOne (or SpaceShipTwo) rocket is carried to a high altitude using the White Knight One (or White Knight Two) carrier plane or mother craft. SpaceShipOne (or Two) is then dropped from the carrier plane. At this point, the SpaceShipOne (or

Two) engines are ignited and the sub-orbital spacecraft is launched. It then eventually follows a sub-orbital trajectory that carries the vehicle to heights greater than 70 miles. Passengers experience weightlessness for a few minutes, see the curvature of the Earth against a dark cosmic backdrop, and feel the effects of several G's of acceleration on their trip. Tens of thousands of people from over 126 countries have already signed up for an experience that will deplete their savings accounts by a couple of hundred thousand dollars.

As of March 2012, 500 well-to-do individuals have fully paid for a future sub-orbital space flight. Many others have paid down payments towards future flights, preserving their place in the queue. In addition, other states including Texas and Florida are developing their own spaceports and are seeking to develop commercial space travel. A Middle Eastern investment group is even considering the construction of a spaceport in the emirate of *Abu Dhabi*!! So, Branson and New Mexico seem to be "onto something big!" However, New Mexico is currently far ahead in the space race!

It is expected that as many as two thousand jobs may be created over the next five years. In addition, Spaceport America expects to attract 200,000 visitors per year starting in 2014. Of course, most of these visitors will be tourists, curious about this great venture. Spaceport America has the potential of becoming an architectural landmark or space-travel landmark that will be associated with the state of New Mexico, just as the Statue of Liberty has long been associated with the state of New York.

New Mexico was chosen for the site because of the region's climate and sunshine, its low population density and its open airspace. Virgin Galactic expects to be able to launch about 340 days out of the year. The other site, the *Mojave* Desert in California, was used only for initial developments and initial flights while the New Mexico site was being developed. The *Mojave's* winds and the airspace needs of the neighboring Edwards Air Force Base excluded it as the final spaceport site.

With the completion of Spaceport America, the Land of Enchantment is leading the globe in the world's Second Space Age. The spaceport was officially opened on October 18, 2011. New Mexico Governor Susana Martinez attended the dedication of the 120,000 square-foot Terminal with Sir Richard Branson.

The spaceport is located in *La Jornada del Muerto,* 90 miles north of *El Paso,* Texas, 45 miles north of *Las Cruces*, New Mexico, and 30 miles east of Truth or Consequences (T or C). A Visitor Center is to be set up in T or C. A shuttle bus service is also planned to carry passengers to and from T or C, and the spaceport. The site occupies about 670,000 square feet. This spaceport houses support and administrative buildings to accommodate Virgin Galactic and the New Mexico Spaceport Authority, in the western zone. The eastern zone of the spaceport consists of the main training area, departure lounge, spacesuit dressing areas, and celebration areas. The central zone contains the extra-high hangar that houses the latest two space vehicles, the White Night Two and the SpaceShipTwo. Visitors and mission controllers can view the eastern part of the spaceport from the restaurant or the Mission Control Room, respectively, and see the apron, the runway and the natural landscape in the background.

The spaceport was designed with environmental considerations in mind. It includes solar thermal panels, underfloor radiant cooling and heating, and it incorporates "earth tubes" to help cool the building in this otherwise hot location. It also includes natural ventilation at selected times of the year.

Virgin Galactic is the anchor tenant of the spaceport. Hence, it has primary access to the 10,000-foot long runway. The round-trip suborbital flight time is about two and one half hours. Flights are suborbital, as described above. The suborbital trajectory reaches an apex of more than 70 miles above the earth, for those who are wealthy enough to afford the trip....and fearless enough to venture that far above the earth!! During the flight the craft reaches speeds of 2,000 miles per hour. However, to share this experience the traveler needs to participate in three days of pre-flight preparation, bonding and training onsite at the spaceport.

As of this writing, the spaceport has obtained its first tenant, UP Aerospace, which has already utilized some of the vertical launch facilities, for several successful vertical takeoff launches. Also, Virgin Galactic has obtained a new suborbital trajectory apex height of 73 miles, and ten test missions have been completed.

When the test flights are all completed, sometime in 2013 or 2014, Sir Richard Branson, and his two adult children, expect to be the first passengers to fly aboard a commercial spacecraft. Full operation awaits completion of certain test milestones and approval by the New Mexico State Legislature of certain liability exclusions for parts suppliers. Exemption of spacecraft operators has already been granted. The original planned start of flights has been pushed back from 2011 to 2014.

The spaceport has set up its own website. For more information and for current views of the construction and other information go to:

www.spaceportamerica.com

Appendix A: Contact Information (NM): Native Tribes & Other Sources

The first group of of phone numbers listed is for the nineteen (19) individual *pueblos*. The second group of phone numbers lists other contact numbers for various *pueblo* groups and for non-*pueblo* tribes and reservations:

Pueblo	Phone Number
Acoma (Sky City Cultural Center)	800-747-0181
Cochiti	505-465-2244
Isleta	505-869-3111
Jemez (*Walatowa* Visitor Center)	505-834-7235
Laguna	505-552-6654
Nambé	505-455-2036
Picurís	575-587-2519
Pojoaque (Visitor Center)	505-455-3460
San Felipe	505-867-3381
San Ildefonso (Visitor Center)	505-455-3549
Ohkay Owingeh (formerly *San Juan*)	505-852-4400
Sandia	505-867-3317
Santa Ana	505-867-3301
Santa Clara (Tourism Dept.)	505-753-7326
Santo Domingo (Kewa)	505-465-2214
Taos (Tourism Dept.)	575-758-1028
Tesuque	505-983-2667
Zia	505-867-3304
Zuni (Tourism Office)	505-782-7238

Other Sources	Phone Number
Santa Fe Convention & Visitor Bureau	505-955-6200
NM Dept. of Indian Tourism	800-545-2070
Eight Northern *Pueblos*	505-747-1593
Five Sandoval Indian *Pueblos*	505-867-3351
Indian *Pueblo* Cultural Center	505-843-7270
Mescalero Apache Tribe	575-464-4494
Jicarilla Apache Tribe[1]	575-759-3242
Navajo Nation	928-871-6436

Chapter Notes

Welcome!
1. *Norte Americanos* – Sp., lit. North Americans, referring to U.S. Americans or *Anglo*-Americans.

Chapter One
1. en.wikipedia.org/wiki/New_Mexico
and en.wikipedia.org/wiki/History_of_New_Mexico
2. *Athabascan* – Named after Lake *Athabasca* in Canada, where these indigenous people came from. They also settled in large parts of Alaska. The term *Athabascan* comes from the anglicized version of a *Cree* Indian word meaning "where there are plants one after another." It defines the second largest indigenous language group in North America. (*Uto-Aztecan* is the largest). It is also referred to as the *Na-Dene* language group. The *Navajo* and *Apache* languages are both *Athabascan*.
3. *Pueblos* - In Spanish, *pueblo* means town, in reference to their structured communities or towns, that had buildings of several stories in height, built from simple *adobe* bricks of mud and straw.
4. *Navajos* – The name of this great semi-nomadic tribe comes from the Spanish allusion to them as the *"Apachu de Navabo"* in the 1620's.
5. *Chiricahua* - *Apache* meaning "great mountain." Refers to the *Apache* people who roamed mostly Arizona, New Mexico and old Mexico. *Geronimo* was their war chief during the *Apache* Wars.
6. *Mescalero* – Sp. meaning "those who deal with mescal", as the *Mescalero Apache* harvested *mescal (mezcal)* for food and drink.
7. *Jicarilla* – Sp. meaning "little basket" because this *Apache* tribe of northeastern New Mexico, often wove little baskets, hence the name associated with that tribe.
8. *Coronado* - Famous Spanish explorer and *Conquistador*; Sp. meaning "crowned."
9. en.wikipedia.org/wiki/List_of_New_Mexico_state_symbols
10. Ibid.
11. en.wikipedia.org/wiki/Flag_of_New_Mexico
12. en.wikipedia.org/wiki/Zia_people
13. en.wikipedia.org/wiki/List_of_New_Mexico_state_symbols
14. en.wikipedia.org/wiki/Seal_of_New_Mexico
15. en.wikipedia.org/wiki/List_of_New_Mexico_state_symbols
16. en.wikipedia.org/wiki/Greater_roadrunner
17. en.wikipedia.org/wiki/Geococcyx
18. en.wikipedia.org/wiki/List_of_New_Mexico_state_symbols
19. www.defenders.org/wildlife_and_habitat/wildlife/black_bear.php
20. en.wikipedia.org/wiki/List_of_New_Mexico_state_symbols
21. www.treenm.com/education/pinon.shtml
22. en.wikipedia.org/wiki/Colorado_Pinyon
23. en.wikipedia.org/wiki/List_of_New_Mexico_state_symbols
24. Turquoise Trail: National Scenic Byway brochure, P.O. Box303, *Sandia* Park, NM 87047.
25. *Muy sabrosa* – Sp. meaning "very tasty".
26. en.wikipedia.org/wiki/List_of_New_Mexico_state_symbols
27. www.proflowers.com/flowerguide/new-mexico
28. www.statesymbolsusa.org/New_Mexico/flower_yucca.html
29. aster – a colorful star-shaped hardy flower.
30. www.e-referencedesk.com/resources/state-flower/new-mexico.html
31. www.livestrong.com/article/228317-yucca-flower-facts
32. en.wikipedia.org/wiki/New_Mexico_(state)
33. Ibid.
34. Ibid.
35. Ibid.
36. en.wikipedia.org/wiki/List_of_counties_in_New_Mexico
37. *Cibola* - *Zuni*, meaning "buffalo."
38. en.wikipedia.org/wiki/New_Mexico_(state)
39. *AAA Arizona & New Mexico Tour Book,* 2011 Edition.
40. en.wikipedia.org/wiki/Albuquerque,_New_Mexico
41. *ReConquista* – Sp. meaning "Reconquest." A period of approximately 750 years over which the

lands of Spain and Portugal were slowly but eventually re-conquered and returned to Christian control from the Moors or Arabs. The Muslims invaded the Iberian Peninsula in 722 AD and the last Moorish stronghold, Granada, fell in 1492, to the Christians, completing the long *ReConquista.*

42. *AAA Arizona & New Mexico Tour Book,* 2011 Edition.

43. *en.wikipedia.org/wiki/Santa_Fe,_New_Mexico*

44. *Santa Fe de Nuevo México* - Sp. meaning "Holy Faith of New Mexico", or *"Santa Fe* of New Mexico".

45. According to the article, *Down at the Shell Bead Water* by David H. Snow, in *All Trails Lead to Santa Fe* (Anthology), Published by Sunstone Press, Santa Fe, p. 40.

46. Georgia O'Keefe Museum – See Chapter Nine, Fascinating Things To Do & Places To See.

47. *Zia* – Refer to: *Where the Sun Shines- The Zia Flag*, earlier in this chapter.

48. See Chapter Ten.

49. *El Rancho de las Golondrinas* – Sp. meaning "The Ranch of the Swallows."

50. *AAA Arizona & New Mexico Tour Book,* 2011 Edition.

51. en.wikipedia.org/wiki/Taos,_New_Mexico

Chapter Two

1. en.wikipedia.org/wiki/New_Mexico

2. *Llano Estacado* – Sp.meaning "Staked plains."

3. *La Jornada del Muerto* – Sp. *meaning, "The* Day's Journey of Death or of the Dead Man", referring to a deadly stretch of desert in southern New Mexico.

4. en.wikipedia.org/wiki/List_of_rivers_of_New_Mexico

5. *Butte* – Derived from French meaning "small hill"; a small, short (in length) *mesa.*
Common in plains or mountain areas, it is an isolated hill that stands out from its surroundings, with steep almost vertical sides and a relatively flat top, much like a small *mesa.*

6. *Caballo* - Sp. meaning "horse."

7. *Chama* - Spanish approximation of the *Tewa* word *Tsama,* meaning, "here they wrestled." However, it may instead be a Spanish corruption of the *Tewa* word *tzama,* which is said to mean the color "red", referring to the color of the River *Chama's* water.

8. *Gila* - Pronounced Hee'la.

9. *New Mexico Easy Finder Map,* Rand McNally, 1999.

10. *New Mexico SealMap,* by Eureka Cartography, 2005.

11. *Topographic Map of New Mexico,* GTR Mapping, 1993, 2010 Edition.

12. *Fra Cristóbal* – Brother Christopher; *fra* is a Latin abbreviation for *Frater* or "Brother."

13. en.wikipedia.org/wiki/Mesa

14. www.anglerguide.com/NewMexico/fishing.html

15. www.goingoutside.com/lakestates/nm.html

16. www.fishingworks.com/lakes/new-mexico/

17. www.wildernet.com/pages/area.cfm?areaID=NMLR&CU_ID=1

18. www.emnrd.state.nm.us/PRD/BOATINGWeb/boatingmainpagewaters.htm

19. *Abiquiu* – A scenic location in north central New Mexico, often associated with Georgia O'Keefe. The Spanish named the location *Santa Rosa de Lima de Abiquiu.* In 1300 AD, it was inhabited by *Tewa* pueblo Indians. Some claim *Abiquiu,* in *Tewa,* could mean "ruins", "timber end place", "hooting of an owl" or even "chokecherry." Who knows?

20. en.wikipedia.org/wiki/Carson_National_Forest

21. en.wikipedia.org/wiki/Cibola_National_Forest

22. en.wikipedia.org/wiki/Gila _National_Forest

23. en.wikipedia.org/wiki/Lincoln_National_Forest

24. en.wikipedia.org/wiki/Santa_Fe_National_Forest

Chapter Three

1. *Anasazi* - The name *Anaasázi,* is a *Navajo* word meaning "the ancient ones." It may even mean "ancient enemy." According to Wikipedia*, the term is used to represent the ancient, prehistoric Native American culture that thrived in the Four Corners area of the Southwest starting around 1 AD.

2. Ancestral: www.desertusa.com/ind1/du_peo_ancient.html

3. See article entitled, *Ancient Cultures of the Southwest*, pages 178-180, by Martin Link at: nmgs.nmt.edu/publications/guidebooks/downloads/24/24_p0177_p0180.pdf

4. *Anasazi:* It may even mean "ancient enemy." According to Wikipedia*, this term is not preferred among *Pueblo* Indians. See: en.wikipedia.org/wiki/Ancient_Pueblo_Peoples

5. *Mogollón* - The *Mogollón* Culture, named after the mountain region in which the culture developed, were the first of the two great ancient New Mexican cultures to develop advanced ways of living. The other New Mexican culture was the *Anasazi* culture.

6. *Hohokam* - A pre-Columbian desert culture that thrived in southern Arizona, between 300 AD and 1450 AD, in the area where the *Gila* and Salt Rivers drain.

7. *Pima*: A Native American tribe that may be culturally descended from the Hohokam. Also, a county located in southern and central Arizona.

8. Four Corners region – This is the region near and around the juncture of four present day states: New Mexico, Arizona, *Colorado* and Utah.

9. See article entitled, *Ancient Cultures of the Southwest*, page 178, by Martin Link at: nmgs.nmt.edu/publications/guidebooks/downloads/24/24_p0177_p0180.pdf

10. *Atlatl* – A throwing stick used to hold a spear or lance that extended the throwing arc of the hunter, thereby increasing the speed and range of the weapon. In scientific terms, the *atlatl* increases the "moment", defined as the product of the force and the fulcrum distance. The *atlatl* increases the fulcrum distance.

11. *Metate* – Mealing or milling stone used to crush and grind grains. The *metate* is the stationary part of the *metate* & *mano* hand milling system. The grain is placed in the *metate* and hand ground using the *mano* in a horizontal motion. It is similar to the European pestle and mortar hand grinding system that uses a vertical motion instead. The mortar is the equivalent of the *metate*, and the pestle is the handheld equivalent of the *mano*. The mortar is more like a stone bowl and the pestle is a small bat shaped stone tool that does the grinding or crushing of the grain in the mortar.

12. *Mano* – The second hand-held part of the *metate* & *mano* hand milling system. See note above.

13. See article entitled, *Ancient Cultures of the Southwest*, page 178, by Martin Link at: nmgs.nmt.edu/publications/guidebooks/downloads/24/24_p0177_p0180.pdf

14. See article entitled, *Ancient Cultures of the Southwest*, page 179, by Martin Link at: nmgs.nmt.edu/publications/guidebooks/downloads/24/24_p0177_p0180.pdf

15. Windmills - Don Quixote, the delusional knight-errant chased after and charged at windmills with his joust, only to find that they were not what he thought they were (dark knights).

16. en.wikipedia.org/wiki/Francisco_Vázquez_de_Coronado

17. en.wikipedia.org/wiki/Pueblo_Revolt

18. *encomienda* – Sp. This term is derived from the Spanish verb, *encomendar,* meaning, "to entrust." This was a Spanish system of tribute, enforced on the indigenous peoples of the Southwest. It empowered soldiers to collect tribute in the form of labor, gold, wheat, corn, poultry, etc, in return for their military service, but in lieu of pay from the king! "In return", the indigenous peoples would "benefit" from instruction in a foreign language (Spanish) and a foreign religious faith (Catholicism)!! What was there for the natives not to like or embrace? Over time, this became an annual tribute from each family of one bushel of corn in the fall, and a blanket or animal skin each spring. In times of scarcity this was a great hardship.

19. *Ohkay Owingeh Pueblo* – This *pueblo* was once called the *San Juan Pueblo*. In recent times the *pueblo* has renamed itself according to its pre-Columbian name.

20. *Isleta Pueblo* – Sp. meaning "Island Town."

21. *El Paso del Norte* – Sp. meaning "Northern Pass."

22. www.neh.gov/news/humanities/2002-11/pueblorevolt.html, article by Pedro Ponce, entitled *Trouble for the Spanish, the Pueblo Revolt of 1680.*

23. en.wikipedia.org/wiki/Diego_de_Vargas

24. *El Ciudad Juarez* – Sp. meaning "the City of Juarez."

25. De Vargas – He had quite a "handle." His full name and title was Don Diego de Vargas Zapata Luján Ponce de León, El Marques de la Nava de Barcinas. Try to say that several times, in an extreme hurry!

26. *ReConquista* – Sp. meaning "Reconquest." In this context it refers to the Spanish reconquest of *Santa Fe*, New Mexico, not to the reconquest of Spain by the Christians, from the Moors.

27. en.wikipedia.org/wiki/Penitentes_(New_Mexico)

28. www.sangres.com/history/penitente01.htm

29. Archbishop Lamy – See Chapter Ten, *Fascinating Things To Do & Places To See*. Specifically see the section entitled: *Archbishop Lamy's Legacy: Cathedral Basilica of St. Frances of Assisi, Santa Fe.*

30. en.wikipedia.org/wiki/Santa_Fe_Trail

31. *Santa Fe Trail National Historic Trail* brochure by the National Park Service

32. www.lsjunction.com/events/santafe.htm

33. en.wikipedia.org/wiki/Texas_Santa_Fe_Expedition

34. Texas – Takes its name from the Caddo word *"tejas"* meaning "friends" or "allies." The Spanish later applied the term to the *Caddo* people of eastern Texas.

35. en.wikipedia.org/wiki/Mormon_Battalion

36. eom.byu.edu/index.php/Mormon_Battalion

37. Ibid.

38. Ibid.

39. en.wikipedia.org/wiki/Mexican-American_War

40. www.newworldencyclopedia.org/entry/Mexican-American_War

41. *Nueces* – Sp. meaning "Nuts."

42. References: The Mexican War 1846 – 1848, by K. Jack Bauer. McMillan Publishing Co., 1974; *Eagles and Empire, The United States, Mexico, and The Struggle for a Continent*, by David A. Clary. Bantam Books, 2009; *Invading Mexico, America's Continental Dream and the Mexican War, 1846 – 1848*, by Joseph Wheelan. Carroll & Graf Publishers, 2007.

43. Arizona and New Mexico – The final current outlines of the states only took complete shape after the Gadsden Purchase of 1853, which added the southernmost border areas to these states, and after the award of the northeasternmost part of the New Mexico Territory to the new state of Colorado in 1862.

44. en.wikipedia.org/wiki/Compromise_of_1850

45. en.wikipedia.org/wiki/Gadsden_Purchase

46. gadsdenpurchase.com

47. *La Venta* – Sp. meaning "The Sale."

48. Ibid.

49. Ibid.

50. *Glorieta* – Sp. meaning "A round-about, an arbor or a bower." See the discussion of the *Pecos* National Historical Park in Chapter Thirteen, National Monuments, Trails and Parks.

51. en.wikipedia.org/wiki/New_Mexico_Campaign

52. *Baja California* – Sp. meaning "Lower California."

53. Fort Union – A National Monument. See Chapter Thirteen, National Monuments, Parks and Trails.

54. Fort Craig – Listed on the National Register of Historic Places, it is located 105 miles north of *Las Cruces*, and 32 miles south of *Socorro*. It can be reached off Interstate 25 between exits 1-15 and 1-24. Fort Craig was a U.S. Army fort located along *El Camino Real de Tierra Adentro*, near Elephant *Butte* Lake and *Rio Grande*, in *Socorro* County.

55. *Valverde* – Sp. meaning "Green valley", an American Civil War battle site in southern New Mexico.

56. militaryhistory.about.com/od/civilwar/p/glorietapass.htm

57. americancivilwar.com/statepic/nm/nm002.html

58. en.wikipedia.org/wiki/Battle_of_Glorieta_Pass

59. *3 Days in March*, Article by Scott Karlson in The Mew Mexico Free Press, p.12-14, March 25, 2009.

60. *Cañoncita* – Sp. meaning "Little canyon", a region that lies east of *Santa Fe*, near *Glorieta*.

61. Chivington – John M. Chivington, a Methodist preacher and a commander in the 1ˢᵗ *Colorado* Volunteers. He became famous for his daring feats in the Battle of *Glorieta* Pass. However, he had a dark side that became more obvious later in his career. When he overran the Confederate supply train at Johnson's Ranch, near *Glorieta*, he first threatened to kill all the prisoners, but afterwards reneged. Later, in 1864, his fame was replaced with odium and notoriety for his role in leading the Sand Creek Massacre of about 150 peacefully encamped *Arapaho* and *Cheyenne*, mostly women and children.

62. *Mesa* – Sp. meaning "table (flat top)." See *Mesas* in Chapter Two, *Lay of the Land*

63. en.wikipedia.org/wiki/Kit_Carson

64. en.wikipedia.org/wiki/Long_Walk_of_the_Navajo

65. southernnewmexico.com/Articles/Southeast/De_Baca/FortSumner/BosqueRedondo-destination.html

66. *Bosque Redondo* – Sp.meaning " Round Wood(s)."

67. southernnewmexico.com/Articles/Southeast/De_Baca/FortSumner/BosqueRedondo-destination.html

68. en.wikipedia.org/wiki/Buffalo_soldier

69. *The Buffalo Soldiers: A Narrative of the Black Cavalry in the West,* by Williams H. Leckie, with Shirley A Leckie. University of Oklahoma Press. P. 211-233.

70. See *Black Warriors of the West: A Visual History of the Buffalo Soldier*. Article by John Langellier, True West Magazine, November/December 2010. p. 34-43.

71. *Ojo Caliente* – Sp. Literally meaning "hot eye" or "natural hot spring", but most often, interpreted as "Warm Springs" or "Hot Springs."

72. *Tres Castillos* - Sp. meaning "Three Castles."

73. *Chihuahua* – *Nahuatl*, meaning, "place where the waters of the river meet"; a state in northern Mexico.

74. en.wikipedia.org/wiki/Lincoln_County_War

75. www.legendsofamerica.com/nm-lincolncountywar.html

76. *The Real Billy the Kid with New Light on the Lincoln County War*, by Miguel Antonio Otero. Sunstone Press, 2007, pp. 27-109.

77. Murphy-Dolan-Riley: One side in the Lincoln County War. Lawrence Murphy sold his business interest to his partners in 1875. In October 1878, he died of cancer while living in the *Santa Fe* area. Most of the violence occurred in the first eight months of 1878 in Lincoln. However, Murphy was involved in business and hiring decisions until the last several months of his life. He exerted his influence from *Santa Fe*. James Dolan partnered with Murphy in 1874. John Henry Riley, a clerk in the company, joined as Dolan's partner in 1876. All three were Catholic Irish immigrants. Their business monopoly, in the Lincoln area, was threatened by the newcomers. See Note 78 next, below.

78. Tunstall-McSween: The other side in the Lincoln County War. John Tunstall was an upper-class English Protestant, while Alexander McSween was a Scotsman. They set up a competing mercantile business in Lincoln, along with a bank. They were also ranchers. They were seen as competition against the Murphy-Dolan-Riley faction's businesses. The fact that they were not Irish and that they were Protestant, while the other faction was Irish Catholic, probably only helped to fan the flames of hatred and animosity between the two factions.

79. John Chisum – A wealthy rancher and cattleman who partnered with Tunstall and McSween. Although he was initially sympathetic towards Billy the Kid, as one of Tunstall's men, he later turned against The Kid, once his murdering spree continued unabated.

80. en.wikipedia.org/wiki/Apache_Wars

81. See *Victorio & Nana*: Freedom Fighters in Chapter Four.

82. See *Life Long Vengeance: Geronimo* in Chapter Four.

83. Lozen – Female *Apache* warrior. See *Womens' Liberation: Apache Style* in Chapter Four.

84. en.wikipedia.org/wiki/Rough_Riders

85. www.newmexicohistory.org/filedetails.php?fileID=21636

86. *The Legend of the Child's Grave.* Article by Cindy Bellinger, Enchantment Newsmagazine, October 2011, p.11.

87. en.wikipedia.org/wiki/Pancho_Villa

88. *Villistas* – Sp. meaning "Followers of Pancho Villa."

89. en.wikipedia.org/wiki/Code_talker

90. *Code Talker: The First and Only Memoir by One of the Original Navajo Code Talkers of WWII*, by Chester Nez with Judith Schiess Avila. Berkley Caliber, 2011, pp. 104-105.

91. Ibid. p. 108.

92. Ibid. p. 110.

93. Ibid. p. 114.

94. See the following U.S. Mint website to view the Congressional Medal of Honor:
www.usmint.gov/kids/campCoin/medalMania/veteransMedals.cfm

95. See note 94 directly above.

96. en.wikipedia.org/wiki/Trinity_test

97. *La Jornada del Muerto* – Sp. meaning "Day's Journey of the Deadman", or "Route of the Deadman." See *La Jornada del Muerto*, in Chapter Nine.

98. Trinity Test Site, National Historic Landmark – See Chapter Thirteen.

99. See Father of the Bomb: J. Robert Oppenheimer, Chapter Four.

100. *Hymn to God, my God, in My Sickness* by John Donne, English poet.

101. *Bhagavad Gita* – Ancient *Sanskrit* religious & philosophical text that is part of the great *Sanskrit* religious epic, the *Mahabharata.*

Chapter Four

1. *El Explorador y El Gobernador*; Sp. The Explorer and the Governor.

2. en.wikipedia.org/wiki/Juan_de_Oñate

3. Colonial Governor – although Don Juan de Oñate was the first Colonial Governor, he was succeeded by Don Pedro de Peralta in 1609, who was appointed the first Royal Governor.

4. New Spain - The original name given by the Spaniards to what would later become known as Mexico, and even regions of Central and South America.

5. *El Adelantado* – Sp. meaning "one who goes forward or leads", used as a title for a Governor of a Spanish Colonial Province, or for any of the early explorers or conquerors of Spanish America.. This is the same title, *El Adelantado,* mentioned in the inscription left at Inscription Rock by Oñate. See Chapter

Thirteen. This title also gave the holder the right to develop and engage in commercial enterprises, and to develop the new colony. In some ways, he would be much like a modern venture capitalist, hoping to gain the fruits of his investment and management. In other ways, he possessed much more authority and much more responsibility!

6. *Acoma* – A *pueblo*, also called Sky City lies atop a massive *mesa* in western New Mexico.

7. *Oñate's Foot Cut Off.* Article by Nancy Plevin and Ben Neary, The New Mexican newspaper, p. A1 &A6, January 8, 1998.

8. Ibid.

9. Ibid.

10. en.wikipedia.org/wiki/Juan_de_Oñate

11. en.wikipedia.org/wiki/Popay

12. *Casi Hermanos* – Sp. meaning "Almost Brothers."

13. en.wikipedia.org/wiki/Popay

14. Ibid.

15. Ibid.

16. en.wikipedia.org/wiki/Comanchero

17. www.tshaonline.org/handbook/online/articles/dfc02

18. tallow - animal fat used for making candles.

19. *Cañon del Rescate* – Sp. meaning "Ransom Canyon."

20. *Ciboleros* – Sp. meaning "Buffalo hunters", taken from the *Zuni* word *cibola*, which means "buffalo."

21. www.tshaonline.org/handbook/online/articles/poc02

22. See the following website for more information on the fandango dance: www.streetswing.com/histmain/z3fndgo1.htm

23. en.wikipedia.org/wiki/Charles_Bent

24. www.absoluteastronomy.com/topics/Charles_BentChapter

25. See Notes at the rear of this book: Chapter Ten, notes 47, 48 and 49.

26. en.wikipedia.org/wiki/Kit_Carson

27. www.absoluteastronomy.com/topics/kit_carson

28. Ibid.

29. *Blood and Thunder* by Hampton Sides. Published by Doubleday, 2006.

30. *Santana: War Chief of the Mescalero Apache*, Almer N. Blazer.

31. www.answers.com/topic/victorio

32. en.wikipedia.org/wiki/Victorio

33. en.wikipedia.org/wiki/Nana_(Apache)

34. en.wikipedia.org/wiki/Santa_Fe_Ring

35. www.legendsofamerica.com/nm-maxwell4.html

36. Lucien Maxwell was an adventurer and explorer who married Luz Beaubien, the heiress to a huge Spanish land grant. After her father, Carlos Beaubien, died in 1860, Lucien Maxwell bought out all the other interests in the grant. By 1865 Lucien and his wife Luz, were in sole possession of the land grant, which was then renamed the Maxwell Land Grant. Lucien Maxwell decided to sell the land in 1870. He then left the *Cimarron* area of New Mexico, moved south to *Santa Fe* and finally retired to the Fort Sumner area. He died there in 1875. The land grant passed through different hands, until it finally came into the hands of the Maxwell Land Grant Company. Subsequent actions, to remove squatters from the land, resulted in 200 deaths. The *Santa Fe* Ring was very much involved in the legal actions surrounding the Maxwell Land Grant. All of the controversy regarding the so-called Maxwell Land Grant occurred after Lucien Maxwell sold the property and after his death. Although his name is forever associated with this black mark in New Mexico history, Lucien Maxwell actually had absolutely nothing to do with it!

37. en.wikipedia.org/wiki/Maxwell_Land_Grant

38. en.wikipedia.org/wiki/Lew_Wallace

39. en.wikipedia.org/wiki/Billy_the_Kid

40. Mrs. Barber: quote from *The Real Billy the Kid, with New Light on the Lincoln County War*, by Miguel Antonio Otero. Published by Sunstone Press, 2007. See pages 113 and 114. Mrs. Susan McSween Barber was the widow of the Lincoln Lawyer and businessman, Alexander McSween, who was slain in the Lincoln County War.

41. Mrs. Barber: quote from *The Real Billy the Kid, with New Light on the Lincoln County War*, by Miguel Antonio Otero. Published by Sunstone Press, 2007. See page 57.

42. Mrs. Barber: quote from *The Real Billy the Kid, with New Light on the Lincoln County War*, by Miguel Antonio Otero. Published by Sunstone Press, 2007. See page 111.

43. Big Casino & Little Casino – Reference from *The Real Billy the Kid, with New Light on the Lincoln County War*, by Miguel Antonio Otero, former Governor of the Territory of New Mexico, from 1897 to 1906. See page 92.

44. According to author Mark Lee Gardner in his Wild West Magazine article (p. 30) of August 2011, entitled: *Pat Garrett, The Life and Death of a Great Sheriff*, p.29-37.

45. Ibid.

46. Ibid, p. 32-37.

47. Even today, sheriffs in Lincoln County wear a patch on the upper left arm, which shows an image of Sheriff Pat Garrett and the Old Lincoln County Courthouse. However, on this patch, Sheriff Pat Garrett is shown wearing the sheriff's badge on his right pectoral, whereas it is supposed to be worn on the left pectoral.

48. en.wikipedia.org/wiki/Lozen

49. *In the Days of Victorio: Reflections of a Warm Springs Apache*, by Eve Ball, p. 9.

50. *In the Days of Victorio: Reflections of a Warm Springs Apache*, by Eve Ball, p.15.

51. *Gouyen* or *Goyan* was a *Mescalero Apache* woman also known for her bravery and heroism. She avenged her husband's death by a *Comanche* warrior, by tracking his killer down and killing him with his own knife.

52. www.meyna.com/lozen.html

53. Ibid.

54. www.bellaonline.com/articles/art22654.asp

55. *Nana* - War Chief of the Warm Spring *Apache* following *Victorio*'s death at *Tres Castillos* in Mexico. *Nana* was a wily and capable Warm Springs *Apache* warrior. The text quote is from *In the Days of Victorio: Recollections of a Warm Springs Apache*, by Eve Ball, 1970, p. 15.

56. en.wikipedia.org/wiki/Geronimo

57. en.wikipedia.org/wiki/J._Robert_Oppenheimer

58. Trinity Test - See Chapter Two: Unholy Trinity.

Chapter Five

1. *American Indian Trickster Tales*, Selected and Edited by Richard Erdoes and Alfonso Ortiz. Penguin Books 1998. P. xiii and xiv. pp. 4- 89.

2. en.wikipedia.org/wiki/Yeii

3. *Southwestern Indian Ceremonials* by Mark Bahti. KC Publications, 1970 & 1982, pp. 10, 11 and 13.

4. en.wikipedia.org/wiki/Kachina

5. *A Guide to Hopi Katsina Dolls*, Kent McManus. Published by Rio Nuevo, 2000, p.26.

6. *The Making of an Icon, Kokopelli*, by Ekkehart Malotki. University of Nebraska Press, 2000.

7. *Kokopelli Ceremonies*, by Stephen W. Hill. *Kiva* Publishing, 1995.

8. en.wikipedia.org/wiki/Kokopelli

9. *Mimbres* – These peoples inhabited the *Mimbres* River valley in southwestern New Mexico. The *Mimbres* were an eastern (Desert) cultural subdivision of the prehistoric *Mogollón* Culture, which occupied both the southern part of New Mexico and the southeastern part of Arizona. The Western or Mountain *Mogollón* Culture thrived from about 150 BC to 1350 AD, while the Eastern or Desert *Mogollón* flourished between 800 AD and 1400 AD. See Note 5 in Chapter Three Notes above.

10. *Hohokam* – See Note 6 in Chapter Three Notes above.

11. As observed at the *Santo Domingo* and the *Picurís Pueblos* mentioned in the text.

12. *Southwestern Indian Ceremonials*, by Mark Bahti. KC Publications, Inc., 1982, 1992, p. 19 and p. 25.

13. *Dancing Gods: Indian Ceremonials of New Mexico and Arizona*, by Erna Fergusson. Published by University of New Mexico press, 1931, 2001, pp. 31-33 and 57-58.

14. Mudheads – See the discussion on Mudheads later in this chapter.

15. Information gathered from the plaque installed at the base of the Medicine Bowl in the lobby of the Inn of the Mountain Gods Resort/Casino in *Mescalero*, New Mexico.

16. www.firstpeople.us/FP-Html-Legends/Teaching-The Mudheads-How to Copulate-Zuni.html

17. www.unique-design.net/library/nature/dance/mudhead.html

18. mudhead.kachina.us/index.htm

19. www.inquiry.net/outdoor/native/dance/mudheads_zuni.htm

20. *Southwestern Indian Ceremonials* by Mark Bahti. Published by KC Publications, Inc.1982, 1992, p. 8-10.

21. en.wikipedia.org/wiki/Sandpainting

22. *Hogan* – traditional *Navajo* dwelling place. A *hogan* may be round-shaped, or shaped as an octagon, a

cone, or it may even be square-shaped. The entrance usually faces the rising sun in the east. See Glossary.

23. Harmony – Many native peoples believe that lack of harmony is the root cause of much disease, as modern Westerners are only now beginning to appreciate.

24. Sit on the sand painting - The *Navajo* word for sand painting, *"iikaah"*, reflects their religious beliefs. This word is interpreted as the "place where the gods come and go." In other words, the *Navajo* believe that the sacred sand painting acts as a portal through which the *Yei bei chi* may enter or leave the physical world.

25. Native American potter Reyes Madalena from *Jemez Pueblo*, New Mexico: Traditional, genuine, hand-coiled, natural clay pottery. Contact information: Phone: (435) 259-8419; e-mail: reymadalena@ hiddenpots.com; website: www.hiddenpots.com

26. Clay slip – According to Wikipedia*, the Free Encyclopedia, a clay slip is " a suspension in water of clay and/or other materials used in the production of ceramic ware."

27. en.wikipedia.org/wiki/Prayer_stick

28. *Legends of the Hopi Indians: Spider Woman Stories* by G. M. Mullett. Published by The University of Arizona Press, 1979.

29. en.wikipedia.org/wiki/Spider_Grandmother

30. en.wikipedia.org/wiki/Storyteller_doll

31. en.wikipedia.org/wiki/Three_Sisters_(agriculture)

32. See the following website: www.usmint.gov/about_the_mint/coinLibrary/#2009NativeAmerican

Chapter Six

1. *El Santuario de Chimayo; The Shrine of Our Lord of Esquipulas.* Published by *Santuario de Chimayo,* pp. 5-13. This source also provides an excellent illustrated discussion of the *retablos* and reredos within *El Santuario.* See pp. 21-27.

2. *Retablos* and reredos - See discussion later in this chapter. See also the Glossary at the end of the book.

3. Esquipulas- A town in Guatemala. *El Señor de Esquipulas*, or the Lord of Esquipulas refers to a statue created in 1594 by a Portuguese sculptor, named Quirio Cataño, at the behest of the local natives of Esquipulas, Guatemala. The hue of the Christ was intentionally made dark to represent the complexion of the indigenous peoples. Over time however, the image darkened even further.

4. *Penitente* – Penitent. See discussion in Chapter 4.

5. *El portrero* – Sp. meaning "Pasture."

6. Lord of Esquipulas statue in *Chimayó* - The body of Christ portrayed in the *Chimayó* statue is said to be of darker hue than in most other representations of Christ.

7. Child of Atocha - The legend of the Child of Atocha comes from Spain. Sometime after 711 AD, Atocha, Spain was conquered by the invading Moors, as they swept across the Iberian Peninsula. The Christian men were imprisoned. They were denied food and were forbidden visitors, except for children under the age of twelve. The women of Atocha prayed to the Virgin Mary to ask Jesus Christ for help, knowing that without divine help, their men-folk would surely die of starvation. A miraculous child dressed as a Spanish pilgrim, made entry into prison and brought food for them to eat. This child became known as *Santo Niño* of Atocha and is believed to be the Christ child.
See: en.wikipedia.org/wiki/Santo_Niño_de_Atocha

8. *Bultos* – See discussion later in this chapter. See the Glossary at the end of the book. See also, *El Santuario de Chimayo; The Shrine of Our Lord of Esquipulas.* Published by *El Santuario de Chimayo,* pp.24-25, which discusses the *santero* art, including *bultos.*

9. en.wikipedia.org/wiki/Cinco_de_Mayo

10. Artificial electric *farolitos* are, of course, strung together, much like Christmas lights. The bag is usually made of plastic, and contains no earth, dirt or sand. The "bag" is usually inverted with the bag open at the bottom and closed along as seam at the top. A small light bulb resides near the bag opening at the bottom.

11. en.wikipedia.org/wiki/Los_Matachines

12. *The Matachines Dance,* Silvia Rodriguez. Published by Sunstone Press, 2009.

13. The description of the dance as performed by *Los Matachines de Bernalillo* was obtained verbally from the group leader.

14. *A Dictionary of New Mexico and Southern Colorado Spanish* by Rubén Cobos, Museum of New Mexico Press, *Santa Fe,* (July 2003), p. 147.

15. *The Richness of the Pastorela Play.* Article by Marjorie Lilly. Enchantment Newsmagazine, December 2007, pp. 12-14.

16. *Las Posadas y Las Pastorelas.* Article by Paul Harden, El Defensor Chieftain Newspaper, Dec. 6,

2008.

17. *Las Posadas* – Sp. meaning "Inns or lodging places."

18. *Los Peregrinos* – Sp. meaning "Pilgrims'.

19. *La Pastorela* – Sp. A Christmas play about the Nativity from the shepherds viewpoint.

20. *Los Pastores* – Sp. meaning "The shepherds."

21. *Santo Niño* – Sp. meaning "Holy child, baby Jesus."

22. en.wikipedia.org/wiki/Retablo

23. Ibid.

24. Ibid.

25. gesso – Mixture of gypsum and glue used to prepare a board for painting as in a *retablo*.

26. According to helpful comments from the Curator, Robin Farwell Gavin, of the Museum of Spanish Colonial Art, *Santa Fe*, New Mexico.

27. Ibid

28. www.zianet.com/focus/chile.htm

29. en.wikipedia.org/wiki/Ristra

30. en.wikipedia.org/wiki/Descanso_(memorial)

31. santafefiesta.org/History%20of%20Fiesta.htm

32. www.santafefiesta.org/Schedule%20of%20Events.htm

33. *La Conquistadora* – A religious statue of the Virgin Mary in her role as "Conqueror of Love", "Our Lady of the Rosary" or "Queen of Solace", from Spanish Colonial times in New Mexico. She is also known as "Our Lady of the Assumption."

34. *La Reina de Santa Fe* – Sp. meaning "The Queen of *Santa Fe* (Sp. Holy Faith)"; another name for *La Conquisitadora*.

35. *El Pregon de la Fiesta* – Sp.*meaning* " Public announcement or proclamation" of the *fiesta*.

36. *cuadrilla* – Sp. meaning "military staff."

37. *La Merienda* – Sp. meaning "The Snack."

38. The *Mariachi Nuevo Sonido* Band consists of seven *Mariachi* musicians from *Chihuahua*. According to their website: "Music ranges from traditional *Mariachi* to jazzy Tijuana brass and catchy NM *Rancheras*." Contact information: Band leader: Mr. Marvin Teitelbaum. Phone: (505) 899-3075; Address: 6232 Prairie Sage Dr. NW, Albuquerque, NM; E-mail address: mariachinuevosonido@msn.com; Website: mariachinuevosonido.com.

39. *Baile Folklorico de Santa Fe* has been in existence since the 1970's. *Baile Folklorico* performs at a variety of festivities in New Mexico throughout the year. Please contact Angela Clayton for more information at (505) 660-0476.

40. en.wikipedia.org/wiki/Santo_(art)

41. Carving "in the round" – a form of carving that results in a three dimensional sculpture. When completed the observer may view every side or dimension of the sculpted object, and even walk around it. Called a "*bulto*", in Spanish.

42. www.spanishcolonialblog.org/?page_id=340

43. en.wikipedia.org/wiki/Straw_marquetry

44. Mr. Mel Rivera specializes in straw *appliqué* artwork. This includes straw *appliqué* designs on crucifixes, jewelry boxes, candlesticks and other wooden objects. Contact information: Studio at *Nambé* Trading Post, Phone: (505) 455-2819; e-mail: melvin.rivera@q.com.

45. en.wikipedia.org/wiki/Our_Lady_of_Guadalupe

46. *Nuestra Virgen de Guadalupe* – Sp. meaning "Our Virgin of Guadalupe."

47. According to the *Saint Juan Diego Cuauhtlatoatzin: The History* brochure available at *El Santuario de Guadalupe* the source of the Mexican Legend is derived mostly from the indigenous *Nahuatl* document *El Nican Mopohua*, written in 1556 by the *Nahuatl* writer, Antonio Valeriano. Valeriano wrote using Latin characters to represent the unwritten *Nahuatl* language. He recorded the events of Juan Diego's vision of Guadalupe and other events of his life. The brochure mentioned shows that the information was part of a homily presented by Pope John Paul II.

48. Juan Diego- born in 1474 in Cuautlitlán, Mexico, which is now part of Mexico City. His *Nahuatl* birth name was *"Cuauhtlatoatzin"*, meaning "the talking eagle." He was born as one of the *Chichimeca* people, a group living in the Anáhuac Valley. He was baptized 50 years after his birth. He had his vision in 1531, on his way to morning Mass, approximately seven (7) years after his baptism. He died in 1548. His beatification took place on May 6th, 1990, by Pope John Paul II in the Basilica of *Santa Maria de Guadalupe*, in Mexico City. Juan Diego was canonized or declared a saint in 2002. He is now recognized as *San Juan Diego*, among Hispanic peoples, especially those from Mexico and the American Southwest.

See the brochure handout available from *El Santuario de Guadalupe*, entitled *Saint Juan Diego Cuauhtlatoatzin, The History.*

49. thequeenofheaven.wordpress.com/2011/01/13/virgin-of-guadalupe-spain/

50. *Christianity in America, a History*, by Ondina E. González, and Justo L. González. Cambridge University Press, 2008, *p.* 59.

51. *Our Lady of Guadalupe: Mother of the Civilization of Love*, by Anderson Carl and Chavez Eduardo. Doubleday, New York, 2009.

52. en.wikipedia.org/wiki/Our_Lady_of_Guadalupe

53. A very informative discussion of the Virgin of Guadalupe and the associated symbolism is given at the following website:
www.scribd.com/doc/10274441/Virgin-of-Guadalupe-Symbolism-of-the-Image
This site is maintained by Catholic Online. Also worthy of note is the brochure that can be obtained from *El Santuario de Guadalupe*, entitled *Welcome to the Shrine of Our Lady of Guadalupe.*

54. *The Bible with the Apocrypha,* New Revised Standard Version, *Book of Revelations,* Chapter 12, Verses 1 through 5. Collins Publishers, 1989.

55. *Huizilopochtli - Aztec* god of war, a sun god. His name translates as "left-handed Hummingbird." See: en.wikipedia.org/wiki/Huitzilopochtli

56. *Tezcatlipoca- Aztec* god of night and the wind, discord, war and strife. His name translates as "Smoking Mirror." See: en.wikipedia.org/wiki/Tezcatlipoca

57. en.wikipedia.org/wiki/La_Llorona

58. *Cuentos From My Childhood- Legends and Folktales of Northern New Mexico*, by Paulette Atencio. Published by Museum of New Mexico, 1991. pp. 3-6.

59. *Santa Fe Nativa a Collection of Nuevomexicano*, by Rosalie Otero, A. Gabriel Melendez and Enrique R. Lamadrid. Published by University of New Mexico Press, 2009.

60. *La Malinche* – Sp., often used as a derogatory reference to *Malinali, Malinaltzin* or *Malintzin*, a *Nahua* slave-woman among the coastal tribe of *Tabascans* (*Chontal Maya* of Potonchan), previously conquered by the *Aztecs*. She was given as a gift to Cortés by the *Tabascans*, along with nineteen other women. Knowing how to speak *Nahuatl* and *Mayan*, she soon became Cortés' guide and translator. Also, she eventually learned Spanish.

Malinali, received her *Nahuatl* name in honor of the Goddess of Grass. Later, she was given another name, *Tenepal*, meaning " one who speaks with liveliness." In her youth, *Malinali's* father died. Some time later, her widowed mother re-married and had a son. Subsequently, the mother sold *Malinali* to *Mayan* slave-traders. Upon her Christian baptism, the Spaniards referred to her as *Doña Marina.*

She has been held in contempt by later generations for her perceived betrayal of the indigenous Mexican people. However, at that time, there was no such concept as "Mexican" people, unless one is referring to the brutal *Aztecs* of the *Mexica* tribe, who savaged every other "Mexican" (in the modern sense) tribe around them. The *Aztecs* were generally hated and feared by the surrounding tribes in the land we now call Mexico.

The name *La Malinche* may derive as a corruption of *Malinali's Nahuatl* name, *Malintzin*. On the other hand, Bernal Diaz, the author of *The Conquest of New Spain*, and an eye-witness to many of the events that transpired during the Conquest, claimed that Cortés was often addressed as *Malinche*, and hence because of *Malinali's* constant presence near him, she was called *La Malinche*. Diaz claimed that *Malinche* meant "Marina's Captain", whereas Prescott, the later author of the great work, *The Conquest of Mexico*, claimed it was applied in the sense of "Captain." Whatever the original meaning, and regardless of how one judges *Malinali's* actions, the name *La Malinche* or *Malinche* today it is a term of derision, disdain and betrayal in Mexico. This name is incorporated into the term "*malinchista*" meaning one (a Mexican) who is disloyal or traitorous.

Oddly enough, *La Malinche* is also used as the name for the young innocent in the dances of *Los Matachines.*

61. Mr. Joe Morales, artist and *santero*, specializes in unpainted *bultos*, *santos*, crosses and innovations within the woodcarving tradition. Contact information: Phone: (505) 424-8313; e-mail: joemrls3@gmail.com.

Chapter Seven

1. www.museumofhoaxes.com/photos/jackalope.html

2. www.jackalope.com/legend_of_jackalope.html

3. en.wikipedia.org/wiki/jackalope

4. ww2.lafayette.edu/~hollidac/jacksforreal.html

5. ww2.lafayette.edu/~hollidac/jackalope.html
6. ww2.lafayette.edu/~hollidac/jacknews.html
7. en.wikipedia.org/wiki/Pecos_Bill
8. en.wikipedia.org/wiki/Roswell_UFO_Incident
9. www.angelfire.com/indie/anna_jones1/roswell.html
10. Occam's Razor – Alternatively, Ockham's Razor; originally attributed to the logician and Franciscan friar, William of Ockham of the 14th Century, who stated, " entities should not be multiplied unnecessarily." This is interpreted in modern terms to mean, "...of two theories or explanations, the simpler of the two is the most likely." The razor analogy is appropriate because the razor shaves away the obfuscation and clutter that obscures the essential and central principle of simplicity. See: en.wikipedia.org/wiki/Occam%27s_razor
11. See the following website: www.smokeybear.com/vault/history_main.asp
12. en.wikipedia.org/wiki/Smokey_Bear
13. www.emnrd.state.nm.us/FD/SmokeyBear/SmokeyBearPark.htm
14. en.wikipedia.org/wiki/Truth_or_Consequences,_New_Mexico

Chapter Eight

1. Bricks – They may have made mud balls rather than "bricks" to build *pueblos*.
2. *The Journey of Coronado* , by Pedro de Casteñada. Published by Dover Publications, Inc., 1990.
3. Roberts, Calvin A. and Susan A. *New Mexico*. Published by University of New Mexico Press, 2006.
4. Ibid.
5. *Canales* – Sp. meaning "channels."
6. *Horno* – See discussion in the next section.
7. *Kiva* fireplaces – See discussion in the next section below.
8. en.wikipedia.org/wiki/Horno
9. en.wikipedia.org/wiki/Tumbleweed
10. Ibid..
11. Ibid
12. en.wikipedia.org/wiki/Windmill
13. Ibid.
14. Ibid.
15. Ibid.

Chapter Nine

1. en.wikipedia.org/wiki/New_Mexican_Food
2. *Muy sabrosa* – Sp. meaning "Very tasty!"
3. en.wikipedia.org/wiki/New_Mexican_Food
4. Hominy - Dried maize or corn that has been treated with an alkali, such as lye. The lye kills the seed's germ, keeping it from sprouting in storage. It also converts some of the niacin into more absorbable forms for the body, and it improves the availability of the amino acids.
5. The Spanish word "*tamale*" is actually taken from the *Nahuatl* word "*tamalli*" meaning "steamed cornmeal dough."

Chapter Ten

1. en.wikipedia.org/wiki/Albuquerque_International_Balloon_Fiesta
2. *Placitas* – Sp. meaning "little *plazas*."
3. *en.wikipedia.org/wiki/San_Felipe_de_Neri_Church*
4. *River of Lights* - Although not currently copyrighted, as of December 14, 2011, the Albuquerque BioPark is seeking copyright protection for the name *River of Lights*.
5. *en.wikipedia.org/wiki/Sandia_Peak_Tramway*
6. Tony Duncan: Hoop Dancer, 2011 World Hoop Dance Champion, dancing at the 2011 *Santa Fe* Indian Market*.
7. www.lorettochapel.com/staircase.html
8. en.wikipedia.org/wiki/Loretto_Chapel
9. *Novena* – In the Catholic Church, a series of devotions of prayer, over a period of nine successive days and nights, reserved for special supplications.
10. en.wikipedia.org/wiki/Loretto_Chapel
11. Ibid.

12. en.wikipedia.org/wiki/Palace_of_the_Governors
13. www.palaceofthegovernors.org/index.php
14. en.wikipedia.org/wiki/Cathedral_Basilica_of_St._Francis_of_Assisi
15. *Parroquia* – Sp. meaning "Parish church."
16. *Tekawkitha* – *Mohawk* or *Algonquin* meaning "she moves things," and pronounced *"dega'gwit-ha."* Pope Benedict XVI pronounced *Kateri Tekakwitha* a saint, on October 21, 2012. This canonization makes her the first Native American Catholic saint, north of Mexico. She had been orphaned at the age of four. Smallpox killed her brother and her parents, and left her with visible scars and severe visual impairment. *Kateri*, meaning Katherine, was baptized into the Catholic faith when she was 18 years of age. She was known for her chastity, her piety and for her practice of corporal mortification, using established methods usually reserved for *Mohawk* warriors. She died at the very young age of 24. Upon her death, her smallpox scars reportedly disappeared.
       Three post-death miracles are attributed to her…a requirement for sainthood. Most recently, a Washington boy, Jake Finkbonner, made a miraculous recovery from a deadly, flesh-eating bacterial infection, after praying to *Kateri Tekakwitha*. His miraculous recovery was attributed to *Kateri Tekakwitha*. The newly declared saint's remains reside in a shrine in Kahnawake, near Montreal, Canada, where she lived after her Catholic conversion, until her early death.
Sources: *Kateri's Canonization Stirs Feelings of Pride, Skepticism* by Mary Esch, Article in the Santa Fe New Mexican, pages A-1 and A-4, October 29, 2012. Also: *Kateri Tekakwitha Becomes First American Indian Saint* by Alyssa Newcomb, ABC News, Article on AT&T Yahoo News, October 22, 2012, obtained at the following web-site: http://news.yahoo.com/kateri-tekakwitha-becomes-first-american-indian-saint-184421489--abc-news-topstories.html.
See also Note 17 below.
17. en.wikipedia.org/wiki/Kateri_Tekakwitha
18. These doors, the handles and the inset panels were all crafted or sculpted by Donna Quasthoff, the same sculptress who crafted the small statue of De Vargas, in the adjacent Cathedral Park. See the discussion further on in this same sub-section.
19. *"Dios da y Dios quita"* – Sp. meaning "God gives and God takes away."
20. *Historia de la Nueva Mexico* – Sp. meaning History of New Mexico.
21. travel.yahoo.com/p-travelguide-2735097-santuario_de_guadalupe_santa_fe-i
22. See *Welcome to the Shrine of Our Lady of Guadalupe* brochure, available at the *El Santuario de Guadalupe*. According to the brochure, the statue was made in Mexico City, brought to *Tepeyac*, the site of *San Juan Diego's* vision and to Don Juan de Oñate's home town of Zacatecas, Mexico. It eventually followed *El Camino Real* in Mexico and went to *Chihuahua*. After some travail and a temporary loss, it crossed the border, proceeded to *Rio Rancho* and finally to its resting place in the small courtyard at *El Santuario de Guadalupe* in *Santa Fe*. The statue was sculpted by the famous Mexican sculptress, Doña Georgina Farias, or "Gogy". She is known for her reverence towards Our Lady of Guadalupe.
23. Mark Garcia, *santero* and artist. Painted *bultos* and *retablos*. Winner of numerous awards. Contact information: Phone: (505) 453-7742, e-mail address: zorba118@comcast.net, website: southvalleyart.com.
24. *Retablos*, Tinwork, Oil and Acrylic Paintings by Carmelita Laura Valdes Damron. Contact information: Phone: (505) 983-4033.
25. *Retablos* and Tin Art by *santera* Christine Montaño Carey, *Santa Fe*, New Mexico.
26. "Will Shuster's *Zozobra*©® is a *Santa Fe* tradition presented by The Kiwanis Club of *Santa Fe* the first Thursday after Labor Day. Funds raised provide college scholarships to *Santa Feans*, grants to non-profits who focus on the children and youth of *Santa Fe*, and an Endowment whose goal is to fund the college scholarships allowing even more funds to be given to the community." (Quote from *Zozobra*©® official tag line. Italics added by the author.)
The website can be found at: www.zozobra.com
Zozobra TM (c), Will Shuster's *Zozobra*©®, Old Man Gloom®, and the *Zozobra*©® image TM (R) (c) 2011 The Kiwanis Club of *Santa Fe* are Registered Trademarks of the Kiwanis Club of *Santa Fe*.
All Rights Reserved. Used by permission. (Italics added by the author).
27. en.wikipedia.org/wiki/Zozobra
28. en.wikipedia.org/wiki/Wicker_Man
29. en.wikipedia.org/wiki/Zozobra
30. en.wikipedia.org/wiki/Wicker_Man
31. Ibid.
32. Ibid.

33. www.burningman.com/
34. Ibid.
35. See *El Rancho de las Golondrinas* handout obtained upon paid entry to the *rancho*.
36. en.wikipedia.org/wiki/Santa_Fe_Opera
37. www.santafeopera.org/yourvisit/generalinformation/index.aspx
38. Ibid.
39. en.wikipedia.org/wiki/Santa_Fe_Opera
40. www.puyecliffs.com/history.htm
41. en.wikipedia.org/wiki/Puye_Cliff_Dwellings
42. Talus rock – It is a collection or accumulation of broken rock that gathers at the base of mountain cliffs, forming an unstable sloping surface. "Talus" comes from the French word meaning "slope or embankment." It is also termed *"scree"*, from the Norse, meaning "landslide."
43. www.nmrailrunner.com
44. See en.wikipedia.org/wiki/New_Mexico_Rail_Runner_Express
45. See *Turquoise Trail: National Scenic Byway* brochure produced by the New Mexico Department of Tourism, or visit the website at: www.turquoisetrail.org.
46. See also: *Sightseeing Information: Turquoise Trail, Scenic and Historic Area*, brochure, produced by the Turquoise Trail Association.
47. *Governor Bent,* article by Ted E. Metzger, in The New Mexican, March 2, 1974. Reprint obtained at the Bent House/Museum.
48. *The Story of Gov. Bent's Massacre, as Told by his Daughter, Teresina Bent Scheurich, Who Was a Witness.* Reprint obtained at the Bent House/Museum. Source and Date unknown.
49. *Life Story of Teresina Bent Scheurich, Daughter of Governor Charles Bent,* Article in The *Taos* Review and The *Taos* Valley News, date not indicated. Reprint obtained at the Bent House/Museum.
50. en.wikipedia.org/wiki/Rio_Grande_Gorge_Bridge
51. Ibid
52. Molleno – This is the same artist who painted *retablos* in *El Santuario de Chimayó.*
53. www.fws.gov/refuges/profiles/index.cfm?id=22520
54. en.wikipedia.org/wiki/Bosque_del_Apache_National_Wildlife_Refuge
55. www.cumbrestoltec.com
56. Ibid.
57. en.wikipedia.org/wiki/Cumbres_and_Toltec_Scenic_Railroad
58. *Cumbres & Toltec Scenic Railroad, Chama, New Mexico: Narrow Gauge Railroad.* For contact and fare information see Note 59 below.
59. cumbrestoltec.com/schedule-rates/
60. See the David McGary Studio in *Ruidoso*, where he displays his outstanding statues of Native American warriors.
61. en.wikipedia.org/wiki/Jornada_del_Muerto
62. *El Paso del Norte* – Sp. meaning "The Northern Pass."
63. *Malpais* – Sp. meaning "Badlands."
64. en.wikipedia.org/wiki/Rodeo
65. Ibid.
66. en.wikipedia.org/wiki/Very_Large_Array

Chapter Eleven
1. In Table 11-1, P = patrilineal, M = matrilineal, E = exogamous, N = non-exogamous.
2. www.indianpueblo.org/19pueblos/language.html
3. Exogamous – This is the custom of marrying outside of the family, clan, tribe or other social unit.
4. Matrilineal – This is the custom of tracing lineage and inheritance through the mother's family.
5. Non-exogamous – The term means the opposite of exogamous. This social custom permits marriage within a given social unit.
6. Patrilineal – This is the practice of tracing lineage and inheritance through the father's family.
7. www.indianpueblo.org/19pueblos/language.html
8. North, south – The Visitor Center and the entry to the *pueblo* is on the north or "cold elevated" side of the *pueblo.*
9. *The North American Indian: The Complete Portfolios, Edward S. Curtis.* Published by Taschen 1997, p. 598.

10. *Peñasco* – Sp. meaning "Rocky."

11. micaceous – clay containing mica flakes, that give the finished pottery a natural and subtle glaze effect to the copper brown hue.

12. *San Juan de los Caballeros* – Sp. meaning "Saint John of the Gentlemen (lit. Horsemen)."

13. *Rio Arriba* – Sp. meaning "Upper River."

14. *El Paragua* – Sp. meaning "The umbrella."

15. *Puyé* Cliff Dwellings – A National Historic Landmark.

16. *sgraffiti* – Plural of *sgraffito*. Per Wikipedia*, this is …" in ceramics, by applying to an unfired ceramic body two successive layers of contrasting slip, and then in either case scratching so as to produce an outline drawing." See the following website: en.wikipedia.org/wiki/Sgraffito.
According to Webster's New World Dictionary, p. 1340," slip" is "…ceramics clay thinned to the consistency of cream for use in decorating or casting, or as a cement or coating."

17. www.indianpueblo.org/19pueblos/language.html

18. Volcanic tuff – According to Wikipedia*, "Tuff (from the Italian *tufo*) is a type of rock consisting of consolidated volcanic ash ejected from vents during a volcanic eruption. Tuff is sometimes called *tufa*, particularly when used as construction material, although *tufa* also refers to a quite different rock. Rock that contains greater than 50% tuff is considered tuffaceous."
See the following website: en.wikipedia.org/wiki/Tuff

19. Storyteller – See Chapter Five: Native American Customs and Traditions.

20. *Nuestra Señora de la Asunción* – Sp. meaning " Our Lady of the Ascension."

21. *The Art Collection of Tamaya* brochure, available from Hyatt Regency *Tamaya*. Sharon Fullingim sculpted the entry statue set.

22. *Sandia* – Sp. meaning "Watermelon."

23. *Isleta* – Sp. meaning "Island."

24. *Nuestra Señora de Guadalupe* – Sp. meaning "Our Lady of Guadalupe."

25. en.wikipedia.org/wiki/Navajo_(tribe)

26. Matrilocal: living near or with the wife's parents. *Navajo* matrilineal: navajo-arts.com/clans-navajo.html

27. *Enchanted Lifeways*, Compiled by the New Mexico Office of Cultural Affairs, New Mexico Magazine. p. 22.

28. There are numerous websites that discuss the various casinos and plans for casinos to be built in Arizona and New Mexico. Just do a search on Yahoo or Google under "*Navajo* Casinos", and multiple relevant sites will be identified.

29. en.wikipedia.org/wiki/Jicarilla_Apache

30. www.jicarillaonline.com

31. *The People Called Apache* by Thomas E. Mails. Published by BDD Illustrated Books, 1974, 1993, pp. 411-485.

32. www.ausbcomp.com/redman/jicarilla.htm

33. The *Llanero* and *Ollero* groups correspond to the Red and White Clans, respectively.

34. *Jicarilla* matrilineal: en.wikipedia.org/wiki/Jicarilla

35. www.jicarillahunt.com

36. en.wikipedia.org/wiki/Mescalero

37. www.mescaleroapache.com

38. *The People Called Apache* by Thomas E. Mails. Published by BDD Illustrated Books, 1974, 1993, pp. 341-410.

39. *Mescalero*, matrilineal: www.encyclopedia.com/doc/1G2-3458000142.html

40. *Gila* – Lived in the area around the *Gila* River, aka Xila River, but pronounced "Hee' la."

41. Warm Springs *Apache* – aka *Ojo Caliente Apache*, *Chihene* or Red Paint *Apache* branch of the *Chiricahua Apache*.

42. *Chiricahua* – *Apache* for "great mountain."

43. See Chapter Three, *Victorio Wars, and Relentless Pursuit: Buffalo Soldiers in New Mexico.*

44. en.wikipedia.org/wiki/Ute_Mountain_Ute_Tribe

45. www.utemountainute.com

46. www.native-languages.org/utah.htm

47.en.wikipedia.org/wiki/List_of_place_names_in_the_United_States_of_Native_American_origin

48. *Comanche*: en.wikipedia.org/wiki/Comanche

49. *Comanche*:"enemy" or "stranger": www.bigorrin.org/comanche_kids.htm

50. digital.library.okstate.edu/encyclopedia/entries/C/CO033.html

51. Patrilocal: living near or with the husband's parents. *Kohmahts*: www.tolatsga.org/ComancheOne.html
52. Chibitty: en.wikipedia.org/wiki/Charles_Chibitty
53. www.aaanativearts.com/article1145.html
54. en.wikipedia.org/wiki/Kiowa_Indian_Tribe_of_Oklahoma
55. www.bigorrin.org/kiowa_kids.htm
56. See note 54.
57. *Lipan*: www.manataka.org/page1432.html
58. www.absoluteastronomy.com/topics/Lipan_Apache
59. www.lipanapache.org/Museum/museum_lipanname.html
60. www.accessgenealogy.com/native/tribes/apache/lipan.htm
61. *The Lipan Apaches: People of the Wind and Lightning*, Thomas A Britten. Published by University of New Mexico Press, 2005. p. xiv.
62. Ibid

Chapter Twelve

1. Table 12-1 concerning the final *pueblo* entry, *Zuni*: Although *Zuni* celebrates its own patron saint Feast Day (Our Lady of Guadalupe, or *Nuestra Señora de Guadalupe*) these celebrations are closed to the public, unlike all the other 18 *pueblos*. Dates – Please consult the *Zuni Pueblo* for the exact celebration dates for the listed public events. See Appendix A for contact information.
2. *Calendar of Pueblo Feast Days & Other Events at the Pueblos* brochure from the Indian *Pueblo* Cultural Center. Please consult their website at: www.indianpueblo.org.
3. Ibid.
4. See note 1 above.
5. See note 2 above.
6. Ibid.
7. Ibid.
8. For a more complete listing of typical *pueblo* events see: *Native New Mexico Land of Enchantment* brochure, aka *The Native New Mexico Guide*, produced by the New Mexico Tourism Department, or visit their website at: www.newmexico.org/nativeamerica. Their phone number is: 1-800-545-2070.
9. en.wikipedia.org/wiki/Soyal
10. www.newworldencyclopedia.org/entry/Zuni
11. www.wheeloftheyear.com/2011/native&mesoamerican.htm
12. www.gratefulness.org/calendar/detail.cfm?id=56&d=all
13. www.indianpueblo.org/19pueblos/zuni.html
14. www.wheeloftheyear.com/2011/native&mesoamerican.htm
15. www. ic.arizona.edu/~anth4206/206/module_04pr.htm
16. www.wheeloftheyear.com/2011/native&mesoamerican.htm
17. southwest.library.arizona.edu/inte/body.1_div.16.html
18. *Southwestern Indian Ceremonials*, Mark Bahti. KC Publications, 1982, 1992, pp. 28-35.
19. Information gathered from interpretive placards and informational posts at *Pecos* National Historical Park. Also, from *The Tewa World: Space, Time, Being and Becoming in a Pueblo Society*, Alfonso Ortiz, pp. 98 through 119. Published by University of Chicago Press, 1969 and from *The Pueblo Children of the Earth Mother, Vol. II*, Thomas E. Mails. Published by Doubleday & Co., 1983. pp. 441-443.
20. *Koshare*: See discussion in Chapter Five.
21. Mudheads: See discussion in Chapter Five.
22. *Chiffonetes*: See *Southwestern Indian Ceremonials*, Mark Bahti. KC Publications, 1982, 1992, pp. 25.
23. *San Geronimo* Feast Day: See *The Insider's Guide to Santa Fe*, Bill Jameson, p. 99.
24. Enchanted Lifeways, Compiled by the New Mexico Office of Cultural Affairs, New Mexico Magazine, p.125.
25. *The Insider's Guide to Santa Fe*, Bill Jameson, Harvard Common Press, 1987. p.99.
26. *The Pueblo Children of the Earth Mother, Vol. II*, Thomas E. Mails. Published by Doubleday & Co., 1983, p. 449.
27. *The Pueblo Children of the Earth Mother, Vol. II*, Thomas E. Mails. Published by Doubleday & Co., 1983, p. 449.
28. *Dances of the Tewa Pueblo Indians: Expressions of New Life*, Jill D. Sweet. Published by School of American Research Press, 1985, 2004. p. 54 (Figure 26) and p. 78.
29. Ibid. p. 78.
30. *The Pueblo Children of the Earth Mother, Vol. II*, Thomas E. Mails. Published by Doubleday & Co.,

1983, pp. 447-448.

31. *Dances of the Tewa Pueblo Indians: Expressions of New Life,* Jill D. Sweet. Published by School of American Research Press, 1985, 2004, pp. 78-79.

32. *The Pueblo Children of the Earth Mother, Vol. II,* Thomas E. Mails. Published by Doubleday & Co., 1983. pp. 445-447.

33. *Dances of the Tewa Pueblo Indians: Expressions of New Life,* Jill D. Sweet. Published by School of American Research Press, 1985, 2004. p. 79.

34. *The Pueblo Children of the Earth Mother, Vol. II,* Thomas E. Mails. Published by Doubleday & Co., 1983. p. 454.

35. *Dances of the Tewa Pueblo Indians: Expressions of New Life,* Jill D. Sweet. Published by School of American Research Press, 1985, 2004. p. 80.

36. Ibid. A "*wasa*" movement is a wavelike or weaving motion created by the movement of the dancers.

37. *The Pueblo Children of the Earth Mother, Vol. II,* Thomas E. Mails. Published by Doubleday & Co., 1983. p. 449.

38. Ibid.

39. *Dances of the Tewa Pueblo Indians: Expressions of New Life,* Jill D. Sweet. Published by School of American Research Press, 1985, 2004. p. 26 (Figure 18) and p.80.

40. *The Pueblo Children of the Earth Mother, Vol. II,* Thomas E. Mails. Published by Doubleday & Co., 1983. p. 449.

41. Ibid. p. 455.

42. *Dances of the Tewa Pueblo Indians: Expressions of New Life,* Jill D. Sweet. Published by School of American Research Press, 1985, 2004. p. 80 and p.81.

43. *Tablita* – a headpiece shaped from thin wood and painted with symbols of the sun, moon and clouds.

44. *Dancing Gods: Indian Ceremonials of New Mexico and Arizona* by Erna Fergusson. University of New Mexico Press, 1931, 2001, pp. 55, 56.

45. *Masked Gods: Navajo and Pueblo Ceremonialism,* Frank Waters. Swallow Press, 1950, 1984, 1987, pp. 261-263.

46. *The Pueblo Children of the Earth Mother, Vol. II,* Thomas E. Mails. Published by Doubleday & Co., 1983, pp.451-454.

47. *Dancing Gods: Indian Ceremonials of New Mexico and Arizona* by Erna Fergusson. University of New Mexico Press, 1931, 2001, pp 56-60.

48. *Masked Gods: Navajo and Pueblo Ceremonialism,* Frank Waters. Swallow Press, 1950, 1984, 1987, pp. 263-268.

49. *The Pueblo Children of the Earth Mother, Vol. II,* Thomas E. Mails. Published by Doubleday & Co., 1983. p.447.

50. Ibid.

51. *Dances of the Tewa Pueblo Indians: Expressions of New Life,* Jill D. Sweet. Published by School of American Research Press, 1985, 2004. p.81.

52. *The Pueblo Children of the Earth Mother, Vol. II,* Thomas E. Mails. Published by Doubleday & Co., 1983. p.449.

53. *Dances of the Tewa Pueblo Indians: Expressions of New Life,* Jill D. Sweet. Published by School of American Research Press, 1985, 2004. p.82.

54. Ibid. pp. 85-86.

55. *Masked Gods: Navajo and Pueblo Ceremonialism,* Frank Waters. Swallow Press, 1950, 1984, 1987, pp. 268-269.

56. *Dancing Gods: Indian Ceremonials of New Mexico and Arizona* by Erna Fergusson. University of New Mexico Press, 1931, 2001, pp. 86-89.

57. www.inquiry.net/outdoor/native/dance/rain_zuni.htm

58. For various discussions of the *Shalako* Dance see the following notes (59 through 62).

59. *The Pueblo Children of the Earth Mother,* Vol. II by Thomas E. Mails, p.235-256.

60. *Southwestern Indian Ceremonials,* Mark Bahti, pp. 28-35.

61. *Dancing Gods: Indian Ceremonials of New Mexico and Arizona,* Erna Fergusson. pp. 91-101.

62. nativeamericanencyclopedia.com/the-shalako-ceremony

63. *Shalako* dancing usually begins sometime after midnight.

64. *Southwestern Indian Ceremonials,* Mark Bahti. KC Publications, 1982, 1992, pp. 34-35.

65. Prayer sticks: see discussion in Chapter Five.

66. Council of the Gods: *Sayatasha* (Rain God of the North, aka Long Horn, *Hututu* (Rain God of the

South), *Sholawitsi* (Fire God, representing the Sun) and two *Yamuhaktu* (Warriors of the East and West, representing oversight over the forests and trees).

67. *Koyemshi or koyemsi*: Mudheads- See the discussion in Chapter Five.
68. www.newmexico.org/nativeamerica/enjoy/feast_days.php
69. Lincoln Canes: www.newmexicohistory.org/featured_projects/nmlincoln200/canes.html
70. Tribal Canes: www.visitsantafe.com/businesspage.cfm?businessid=1641
71. www.newmexico.org/nativeamerica/enjoy/feast_days.php
72. newmexico.org/western/play/shiprock_fair.php
73. northernnavajonationfair.org/
74. Visit the following site to see the scope and scale of the 2011 Northern *Navajo* Shiprock Fair held between September 28 and October 9, 2011:
northernnavajonationfair.org/northern-navajo-nation-fair-2011-events-calender
75. en.wikipedia.org/wiki/Yeii
76. *Southwestern Indian Ceremonials*, Mark Bahti. KC Publications, 1982, 1992, p. 10-13.
77. See the following reference: *Masked Gods: Navajo and Pueblo Ceremonialism*, Frank Waters. Swallow Press, 1950, 1984, 1987, pp. 228-240.
78. www.jicarillaonline.com/
79. 140.247.102.177/maria/sunrisedance.html
80. White Painted Woman – According to *Apache* beliefs, White Painted Woman bore a son who killed the personification of evil in the world, and so allowed the *Apache* people to survive.
81. explorenm.blogspot.com/2010/06/mescalero-maidens-puberty-ceremony.html
82. Medicine Basket: See the discussion of the sacred Medicine Basket in Chapter Five.
83. *Southwestern Indian Ceremonials*, Mark Bahti, pp. 46-48
84. Ibid.
85. redpaintpowwow.net

Chapter Thirteen

1. www.nps.gov/azru/index.htm
2. en.wikipedia.org/wiki/Aztec_Ruins_National_Monument
3. *Aztec Ruins, A Trail Guide to*, Published by Western National Parks Association, 2008.
4. *Aztec Ruins National Monument*, Published by Southwest Parks and Monument Association, 1992.
5. *Aztec Ruins*, Published by the National Park Service.
6. www.nps.gov/band/index.htm
7. *Bandelier National Monument* brochure by the National Park Service.
8. en.wikipedia.org/wiki/Bandelier
9. www.nps.gov/cavo/index.htm
10. en.wikipedia.org/wiki/Capulin_Volcano_National_Monument
11. *Capulin Volcano*, Published by the National Park Service.
12. www.nps.gov/elma/index.htm
13. en.wikipedia.org/wiki/El_Malpais_National_Monument
14. *El Malpais*, Published by the National Park Service.
15. www.nps.gov/elmo/index.htm
16. en.wikipedia.org/wiki/El_Morro_National_Monument
17. *El Morro*, Published by the National Park Service.
18. www.nps.gov/foun/index.htm
19. en.wikipedia.org/wiki/Fort_Union
20. *Fort Union National Monument* brochure by the National Park Service.
21. *Fort Union, National Monument (Robert M. Utley)*. Published by the National Park Service.
22. www.nps.gov/gicl/index.htm
23. en.wikipedia.org/wiki/Gila_Cliff_Dwellings_National_Monument
24. en.wikipedia.org/wiki/Kasha-Katuwe_Tent_Rocks_National_Monument
25. www.blm.gov/nm/st/en/prog/recreation/rio_puerco/kasha_katuwe_tent_rocks.htm
26. *Kasha Katuwe Tent Rocks National Monument* brochure, by the Bureau of Land Management.
27. Volcanic tuff – According to Wikipedia®, "Tuff (from the Italian *tufo*) is a type of rock consisting of consolidated volcanic ash ejected from vents during a volcanic eruption."
28. en.wikipedia.org/wiki/Petroglyph_National_Monument
29. www.nps.gov/petr/index.htm

30. *Petroglyph National Monument* brochure by the National Park Service.

31. *Boca negra* – Sp. meaning "Black mouth."

32. *Piedras Mercadas* – Sp. meaning "Marked Stones."

33. *Rinconada* – Sp. meaning "Cornered (inside corner vs outside corner)." May refer to "boxed", as in *Casa Rinconada* ("Cornered House"), or in this case, as in *Rinconada* Canyon, meaning "Boxed" or "Cornered" Canyon.

34. en.wikipedia.org/wiki/Salinas_Pueblo_Missions_National_Monument

35. www.nps.gov/sapu/index.htm

36. *Salinas Pueblo Missions*, Published by the National Park Service.

37. en.wikipedia.org/wiki/White_Sands_National_Monument

38. www.nps.gov/whsa/index.htm

39. *White Sands* brochure by the National Park Service.

40. *White Sands National Monument* by Western National Parks Association.

41. *Alamogordo* – Sp. meaning "Fat poplar" or, more likely, "Fat cottonwood" tree.

42. *Doña Ana* – Sp. meaning "Lady Ann."

43. www.nps.gov/chcu/index.htm

44. en.wikipedia.org/wiki/Chaco_Canyon_National_Monument

45. *Chaco Culture*, Published by the National Park Service.

46. *Chaco Culture: Chaco Canyon Place Names*, Article, Published by the National Park Service.

47. *A Kid's Guide to Exploring Chaco Culture National Historical Park*, Written by Mary Maruca. Published by Western National Parks Association.

48. *Pueblo Bonito*, Published by Western National Parks Association.

49. *Casa Rinconada*, Published by Western National Parks Association.

50. en.wikipedia.org/wiki/Pecos_National_Monument

51. www.nps.gov/peco/index.htm

52. *Pecos National Historical Park* brochure by the National Park Service.

53. www.accessgenealogy.com/native/tribes/pecos/pecoshist.htm

54. www.nps.gov/cave/index.htm

55. en.wikipedia.org/wiki/Carlsbad_Caverns_National_Park

56. *Carlsbad Caverns*, Published by the National Park Service.

57. newmexico.org/explore/monuments/camino_real_adentro.php

58. elcaminoreal.org

59. en.wikipedia.org/wiki/El_Camino_Real_de_Tierra_Adentro_National_Historic_Trail

60. See Chapter Note 73 in Chapter 3.

61. www.nps.gov/olsp/index.htm

62. en.wikipedia.org/wiki/Old_Spanish_National_Historic_Trail

63. *Mojave* – Alternatively, written as *Mohave*. Either way, it is a corruption of the name of a California Native American tribe, who call themselves, "*aha mocave*", meaning "along or beside the water." ("*Aha*" means "water" and "*mocave*" means "along or beside"). Information obtained from the following website: http://wiki.answers.com/Q/What_does_the_place_name_Mohave_mean

64. en.wikipedia.org/wiki/Santa_Fe_Trail

65. newmexico.org/explore/monuments/sf_trail.php

66. *Santa Fe Trail National Historic Trail* brochure by the National Park Service.

Chapter Fourteen

1. en.wikipedia.org/wiki/Coronado_State_Monument

2. nmmonuments.org/coronado-state-monument

3. *Coronado State Monument* brochure by the Museum of New Mexico Office of Cultural Affairs.

4. nmmonuments.org/el-camino-real

5. elcaminoreal.org/

6. en.wikipedia.org/wiki/El_Camino_Real_de_Tierra_Adentro_National_Historic_Trail

7. Truth or Consequences – Formerly called Hot Springs, New Mexico.

8. nmmonuments.org/fort-selden

9. en.wikipedia.org/wiki/Fort_Selden

10. www.discoverruidoso.com:80/Fort-Stanton-State-Monument

11. www.billybyway.com/fortstanton.html

12. en.wikipedia.org/wiki/Fort_Stanton

13. fortstanton.org

14. nmmonuments.org/bosque-redondo
15. en.wikipedia.org/wiki/Bosque_Redondo
16. *Bosque Redondo Memorial At Fort Sumner State Monument* brochure.
17. *Billy the Kid's Old Fort Sumner* brochure by Michael E. Pitel, 2007.
18. en.wikipedia.org/wiki/Jemez_State_Monument
19. nmmonuments.org/jemez
20. en.wikipedia.org/wiki/Lincoln_State_Monument
21. nmmonuments.org/Lincoln
22. *Billy the Kid's Lincoln* brochure by by Michael E. Pitel, 2007
23. *La Iglesia de San Juan Bautista* – Sp. meaning "The Church of Saint John the Baptist."

Chapter Fifteen
1. exponm.com/state-fair

Afterward
1. http://en.wikipedia.org/wiki/Spaceport_America
2. http://spaceportamerica.com
3. *Spaceport, Prepare for Liftoff; Destination, The Next Frontier.* Article written by Betsy Model and published by New Mexico Magazine, May 2012.
4. *Out-Of-This-World-Ripoff?* Article written by Jeri Clausing and published by the *Santa Fe* New Mexican newspaper (pages A-1 and A-4), Thursday, December 13, 2012.

Appendix A
1. See additional contact info. in Chapter Eleven. See the section on the *Jicarilla Apache*.

Glossary of Terms (Primarily Spanish)

(Helpful hint: For the sake of simplicity and brevity, gender is not indicated. In general, in Spanish, for nouns, the masculine singular indefinite article is indicated by "un", the feminine singular indefinite article by "una", the masculine singular and plural definite article (s) by "el" and "los", respectively. Likewise, the feminine singular and plural definite article (s) are shown by "la" and "las", respectively. These articles precede the noun.

Also, the noun in the plural case usually ends in "s" or "es". Masculine adjectives usually, but not always end in "n" or "o" in the singular case, or in "es" or "os" in the plural case. Feminine adjectives usually, but not always, end in "a" in the singular case, or "as" in the plural case. Nouns are listed here, without articles. Adjectives are shown, close to how they appear in the text, to avoid confusion. In addition, adjectives, with some exceptions, usually follow the noun. Examples: *agua fresca* [adjective follows the feminine noun *agua*] and an exception, *Baja California*, [adjective precedes the feminine noun *California*]).

Generally, when spoken, the accent is on the penultimate (second last) syllable. When this rule is violated, the accented syllable is usually written with an accent mark above it. Example: *bandito* (ban-di'-to), places the stressed accent on the second last syllable, as usual, whereas, *ladrón* (*lad-ron'*) places the stressed accent on the final syllable. Note however, that New Mexican Spanish is sometimes lax in the proper use of accent markings.

Just a few helpful pronunciations hints: 'll' is pronounced like 'y' in English; 'qu' is pronounced like 'k' in English, while 'cu' is pronounced like 'kw'; 'h' at the beginning of a word is silent; 'j' and 'g' are pronounced like an aspirated 'h'; 'z' is pronounced like 's'; finally, 'ñ' is pronounced like 'ny' in English.

Acequia – Sp. Water ditch used for irrigation of field.
Adelantado – Sp. This was a medieval term or office that was eventually re-established in New Spain, in which a rich or well-to-do individual entered into a legally binding contract with the Spanish Crown to conquer, colonize and defend the conquered territory in the name of Spain. It often required significant personal initial investment on the part of the *Adelantado* to fund and supply the expedition and the endeavor, in the risky expectation of administrative and military power, privelege, title and financial reward. The expected reward did not always materialize to the utter dismay and sometimes to the financial ruin of the

Adelantado. These individuals were essentially a form of government-advocated entrepreneurs and developers, with military, governing and administrative powers.
Adentro – Sp. Inside or internal.
Adovado – Sp. Marinated with *chiles*.
Afuera – Sp. Outside or external.
Agua – Sp. Water.
Agua fresca – Sp. Cold bottled water.
Alabados – Sp. Sacred songs of worship of the *Penitentes*.
Alameda – Sp. From the poplar (Spain) or cottonwood (New Mexico) tree; a wide public walkway or roadway, lined with trees.
Alamo – Sp. In Spain, a poplar tree; in New Mexico, a cottonwood tree.
Alamogordo – Sp. Fat poplar (Spain) or cottonwood (New Mexico) tree.
Alamosa – Sp. Of cottonwood (New Mexico).
Alma – Sp. Soul.
Alta - Sp. High, upper, as in *Alta* California.
Amarillo – Sp. Yellow.
Angeles – Sp. Angels.
Animos – Sp. Spirits.
Animas – Sp. Lively, spirited.
Animas River – Sp. Lively River.
Antonito – Sp. Little Anthony.
Arriba – Sp. Up, upwards, overhead, above or (upper).
Arrieros - Sp. Teamsters or muleskinners, possibly derived from *arreos*, meaning harness, or from *arre*, meaning "get up" or giddap."
Arroyo – Sp. Intermittent stream, dry-bed or wash, that occasionally fills and flows… usually, in a canyon or gully.
Arroyo Chico – Sp. Little Wash.
Arroyo, Cienega del Macho – Sp. Tough wash or marsh.
Arroz – Sp. Rice

Baca – Sp. Roof or carrier rack, in Spain. In New Mexico, it is probably a corruption of *vaca*, meaning beef or cow, since a 'v' and a 'b' are very similar sounds in Spanish. At one time, it was most likely an occupational name, signifying a cowherd, or someone involved in the cattle business, as in the last name de Baca.
Baja California – Sp. Lower California.
Banderas – Sp. Banners or flags.
Bandito – Sp. Bandit.
Belen – Sp. Bethlehem.
Bernalillo - Sp. Little or young Bernal (family name).
Berrendo – Sp. Mottled, speckled, brindle, two-colored; pronghorn antelope.
Bievenidos – Sp. Welcome (s).
Blanco, a – Sp. White.
Bonito, a – Sp. Pretty, beautiful.

Bosque – Sp. Wood, clump or group of trees.
Bosque del Apache – Sp. *Apache* Wood.
Bosque Redondo – Sp. Round Wood.
Brazos – Sp. Arms (part of the body).
Buen provecho: Good eating!
Buenaventura – Sp. Good fortune.
Bulto – Sp. A three-dimensional carved, wooden image or statue of a saint.
Burro – Sp. Small donkey, used as a pack animal.
Butte – Derived from French meaning "small hill"; a small, short (in length) *mesa*; Common in plains or mountain areas, it is an isolated hill that stands out from its surroundings, with steep almost vertical sides and a relatively flat top, much like a small *mesa*.

Caballo – Sp. Horse.
Caballero – Sp. Horseman, knight.
Cabeza – Sp. Head.
Café - Sp. Coffee.
Caldo - Sp. Thin soup or broth.
California Alta – Sp. Upper (High) California.
Caldera – Sp. In Spain, a kind of potato; in New Mexico, it usually means, a crater or depression caused by a collapsed volcanic cone, or by volcanic explosions.
Calderon – Sp. Large kettle.
Caliente –Sp. Hot.
Calvario – Sp. Cavalry (hill).
Camino – Sp. Road.
Camino de la Placita – Sp. Road of the Little *Plaza*, Little *Plaza* Road.
Camino Real – Sp. Royal Road.
Canjilo – Sp. Deer antler (s.) (in New Mexico).
Canjilon – Sp. Deer antlers (pl.) (in New Mexico).
Cañon de Rescate – Sp. Ransom Canyon.
Cañon Largo – Sp. Long Canyon.
Cañoncita – Sp. Little canyon.
Capilla –Sp. Chapel.
Capitán – Sp. Captain.
Capulin – Sp. Wild cherries or chokecherry tree and fruit.
Carne - Sp. Meat
Casa – Sp. House.
Carretas – Sp. Carts.
Cavates – Sp. Cavities.
Cebolla – Sp. Onion.
Cebolleta – Sp. Little onion.
Cerveza – Sp. Beer.
Cerro - Sp. Hill.
Cerrillo - Sp. Small hill.
Chama - Spanish approximation of the *Tewa* word *Tsama*, meaning "here they wrestled."
Champurado – Sp. Hot chocolate with cinnamon and *maseca* (corn flour).
Cibola – *Zuni* term for a buffalo or bison.
Ciboleros – Sp. Those who hunt the buffalo (bison), buffalo hunters

Cienega – Sp. Marsh, swamp or bog.
Cieneguilla – Sp. Small marsh or swamp.
Cimarron – Sp. wild or unruly; may also refer to the bighorn sheep of the Rockies, i.e. *carneros cimarrones* ("wild sheep"); it can also mean "wild animal" or "runaway slave", or even "wild, rowdy place."
Cinta – Sp. Band.
Ciudad - Sp. City.
Ciudad de Juarez – Sp. City of Juarez.
Coca – Sp. Coca-cola.
Colatoral – Sp. Side or secondary.
Colorado – Sp. Colored.
Comedor – Sp. Dining room.
Comancheros – Sp. Those who deal or trade with the *Comanche*.
Conchas – Sp. Shells.
Conquista – Sp. Conquest.
Conquistador - Sp. Conqueror, Spanish soldier of the Conquest era.
Conquistadora – Sp.(female) Conqueror, refers to Our Lady of the Rosary, or Our Lady of the Assumption, statue in the Cathedral Basilica of St Francis of Assisi in *Santa Fe*, NM.
Corona – Sp. Crown.
Coronado – Sp. Crowned.
Crucificio – Sp. Crucifix.
Cuadrilla – Sp. Staff (military).
Cristóbal – Sp. Proper name, meaning Christopher or " a follower of Christ". Pronounced "krees-stoh'- bal".
Cruces – Crosses.
Cruz – Sp. Cross.
Cuchara – Sp. Spoon.
Cuchillo – Sp. Knife.
Cuento – Sp. Tale, story.
Cuesta – Sp. Cost (pronounced qwesta).
Cumbre – Sp. Crest or summit.
Cupa – Sp. Cup.

Datil – Sp. Palm date.
Descanso – Sp. Rest (stop).
Desfile - Sp. Parade or procession.
Desperado – Sp. A "desperate" man, usually referring to a bold, reckless or dangerous outlaw, criminal or renegade.
Dolores – Sp. Sorrows.
Doña Ana – Sp. Lady Ann.
Dulce – Sp. Sweet, soft, gentle.

Embudo – Sp. Funnel.
Encarnación – Sp. Incarnation.
Encina – Sp. Evergreen oak.
Encinal – Sp. Oak grove.
Encomienda – Sp. Grant of Native American taxes in the form of labor or tribute, in goods or food, such as corn, livestock, blankets, etc. in return for providing the natives with Spanish military

protection, and exposure to the Spanish language and the salvation of the soul via conversion to Roman Catholicism. This tribute was in lieu of direct payment of the Spanish military and officials by the Spanish Crown. In times of hardship, such as drought, this tribute placed a heavy burden and great hardship on the *Pueblo* Peoples who worked on the *encomiendas*.

Encomendero – Sp. A holder of an *encomiendo*, who, in return for this grant, was bound to provide military services when called upon.

Enfermeria – Sp. Infirmary.

Entrada – Sp. Entrance; Spanish expedition.

España – Sp. Spain.

Española – Sp. "Spanish."

Estancia – Sp. Stay, or a large estate or cattle ranch.

Estrellar – Sp. To star, or sprinkle with stars; to fry eggs, sunny side up as in "*huevos estrellados*."

Explorador – Sp. Explorer.

Fajada – Sp. Girdled, banded, stripped.

Farol – Sp. Lantern.

Farolitos – Sp. "small lanterns." Small illuminated decorations used in northern New Mexico during the Christmas Season. They are small paper bags filled with sand on the bottom to anchor a small candle within it. The candle is lit and these illuminated bags are placed around the top edges of roofs and building outlines. In southern New Mexico, the term *luminaries* is often used to describe the same thing.

Fauna – L. Animals of a given region or time.

Felix – Sp. Happy, lucky.

Fiesta – Sp. Festival.

Flora – L. Plants of a given region or time.

Fra Cristóbal – Brother Christopher; *fra* is a Latin abbreviation for "frater" or brother.

Frijole – Sp. Bean.

Frito – Sp. Fried.

Gallinas – Sp. Hens

Gallo – Sp. Rooster.

Gallo Arroyo – Sp. Rooster Wash.

Gente – Sp. People.

Gila – (Pronounced Hee'Lah) Sp. Idiot, twit.

Glorieta – Sp. A roundabout, bower or arbor.

Gobernador – Sp. Governor.

Gordo – Sp. Fat.

Grande – Sp. Big, great.

Guerra – Sp. War.

Guerrilla - Sp. Little war; in modern usage: "hit and run" warfare, with limited goals, forces and resources.

Helado – Sp. Ice cream.

(Los) Hermanos – Sp. (The) brothers or brotherhood; another name for *(Los) Penitentes*,

the Penitents.

Hidalgo – Sp. Gentleman or Lady, lit., "son of something or someone"; someone belonging to the lowest rank of Spanish nobility. The title allowed the "*hidalgo*" to be addressed as "*Don*" or "*Doña*." An "*hidalgo*" owned inherited land.

Hielo – Sp. Ice.

Hija – Sp. Daughter.

Hijo – Sp. Son.

Hogan – Navajo. It usually refers to an eight-sided family dwelling place. See Note 22, Chapter 5.

Hogar – Sp. Home.

Hondo - Sp. Deep.

Horchata – Sp. Rice milk drink.

Hoyeros – Sp. Mountain valley people.

Huevos: Sp. Eggs.

(Las) Humanas – Sp. lit. (The) Humans; also refers to a *pueblo* tribe that occupied one (known today as *Gran Quivira*) of the three *Salinas Pueblos*. See the *Salinas Pueblo* Missions National Monument.

Jara – Sp. In Spain, a cultivated form of potato; in New Mexico, it more likely means a rockrose, or a flowery shrub of the Cistaceae family; small branch of a shrub or tree.

Jicarilla – Sp. meaning "little basket", because this *Apache* tribe of northeastern New Mexico, often wove little baskets, hence the name.

Jornada – Sp. Day's journey.

Jornada del Muerto – Sp. Day's Journey of Death, or of the Deadman, referring to a deadly stretch of desert in southern New Mexico. Or, "Route of the Deadman.'

Joya – Sp. Jewel.

Joyeria – Sp. Jewelry shop.

Ladrón – Sp. Thief.

Lagos – Sp. Lakes

Latir – Sp. To beat or throb.

Llaneros – Sp. Plains people.

Llano Estacado – Sp. Staked plains.

Llorona – Sp. Weeping woman.

Loma: Sp. Hillock, slope.

Leche: Sp. Milk.

Lucero- Sp. Translucent.

Luna – Sp. Moon.

Lunas – Sp. Moons.

Luminarias – Sp. lit. Luminaries. Log bonfires in northern New Mexico. The term is also used in southern New Mexico to represent the small paper bag Christmas illuminations, which are called *farolitos ("little lanterns")* in northern New Mexico.

Lunes – Sp. Monday or Mondays.

Machucar - Sp. To pound, crush or mash.

Madre – Sp. Mother.

Magdalena – Sp. Magdalene, referring to Mary of Magdalene.

Maiz – Sp. Corn.

Malpais – Sp. Badlands; lit. bad country.

Mangas - Sp. sleeves. The name of the famous *Apache* leader, *Mangas Coloradas*, means "colorful sleeves"

Mantequilla – Sp. Butter.

Manzana – Sp. Apple (fruit).

Manzanita – Sp. Little apple (fruit).

Manzano –Sp. Apple tree.

Masa – Sp. Dough; *Masa de maiz*- dough made from dried corn.

Maseca – Sp. Corn flour.

Manta – Sp. A mantle, cloak, blanket or coarse cotton fabric; among *pueblo* native females, it usually means a single-colored (black or white) cotton type of skirt or simple dress that extends from the shoulder to the lower calf, covering the chest, torso, legs and upper arms. It usually is embroidered on the lower edges and on the short sleeve edges, and hangs on only one shoulder. It is often worn at tribal ceremonials.

Mayor – Sp. Major or older.

Merienda – Sp. Snack or light dinner.

Mesa – Sp. Table or flat-topped geological formation with steep slopes, commonly found in the American Southwest.

Mesa Encantada – Sp. Enchanted table, or in New Mexico, Enchanted *Mesa*.

Mesilla – Sp. Little *mesa*.

Mesita – Sp. Little table or little *mesa*

Minor – Sp. Minor or younger.

Mora - Sp. Blackberry or mulberry.

Moradas –Sp. Meeting houses of the *Penitentes*.

Morro - Sp. Headland or bluff.

Morar – *Sp.* To dwell.

Muerte – Sp. Death.

Muerto – Sp. Dead one.

Mundo – Sp. World.

Nacho(s) – Sp. Triangular-shaped *tortilla* chips covered with melted cheese (or spiced cheese), and possibly spices. Usually provided as an appetizer. *Nacho* is also used as a shortened form of the boy's name Ignacio.

Nacimiento – Sp. Birth.

Nativo, nativa – Sp. native (male, female).

Nevada – Sp. Snowy, or snow-capped.

Niños- Sp. Children, sons

Norte – Sp. North.

Norte Americanos – Sp. North Americans or "Americans."

Nueces – Sp. Nuts (food).

Nuevo, (a) – Sp. New.

Nuevomexicano – Sp. New Mexican.

Nutria – Sp. Otter.

Ojito – Sp. Little eye or small natural spring.

Ojo – Sp. Eye or natural spring.

Ojo Caliente – Sp. Hot eye; frequently, hot spring.

Ollero – Sp. Potter.

Oscura, o – Sp. Dark or obscure.

Otero – Sp. Hill or hillock.

Padre – Sp. Father or priest.

Pajarito – Sp. Little bird (*Pajaro*).

Palmilla - Sp. Small palm.

Palo – Sp. Stick or high timber.

Pan - Sp. Bread.

Pancho – Sp. Nickname for Francisco, as in "*Pancho*" Villa aka Francisco Villa (his pseudonym), the nickname of José Doroteo Arango Arámbula, the famous Mexican Revolutionary; as an adjective, it can also mean peaceful or calm.

Paraje – Sp. A stop or resting place.

Paroquia – Sp. Parish church.

Paseo de Peralta – Sp. Peralta's Promenade, Drive, Boulevard.

Paseo del Pueblo Norte – Sp. North *Pueblo* Promenade, Drive, Boulevard.

Paseo del Norte – Sp. North Promenade, Drive, Boulevard.

Pasión – Sp. Passion.

Paso – Sp. Pass.

Pastorela – Sp. A Christmas play about the Nativity, from the shepherds' viewpoint.

Pastores – Sp. Shepherds.

Peregrinos –Sp. Pilgrims.

Pescado – Sp. Fish.

Peñasco – Sp. Large rock, crag or cliff; rocky.

Penitentes – Sp. Penitents, a religious brotherhood in New Mexico and *Colorado*, that arose after many priests were withdrawn from New Mexico, due to financial difficulties in Mexico.

Pia – Sp. Pious.

Piadosa – Sp. Pious.

Picante - Sp. Piquant or spicy.

Pico de Gallo – Sp. lit., Beak of the Rooster, or Rooster's Beak; a Mexican or New Mexican side dish consisting of tomato, *cilantro*, onions and *chile*. Often eaten with corn chips.

Piedra – Sp. Stone or rock.

Piñon – Sp. Pine tree.

Piños – Sp. Pines

Pinta – Sp. Sight, look.

Pintada Arroyo – Sp. Painted Wash.

Plata – Sp. Silver.

Plato – Sp. Plate.

Plaza - Sp. A square, *plaza* or open area.

Plaza Mercado – Sp. Market *Plaza*.

Pocito – Sp. A small well; the diminutive of *pozo* meaning a "well."

Potrillo - Sp. A young, male horse, or colt.

Portrero – Sp. Pasture.

Posadas – Sp. Inns or lodging places.

Pregón – Sp. Proclamation or announcement.

Pueblo - In Spanish, *pueblo* means town, in

reference to their structured communities, or towns that had buildings of several stories in height. They were built from simple *adobe* bricks of mud and straw.

Puerco – Sp. pork; filthy, dirty.

Quemado – Sp. Burnt or burned.

Queso - Sp. Cheese.

Questa – Ital. This; or perhaps a corrupted spelling of the Spanish "*cuesta*"

Rancho de las Golondrinas – Sp. Ranch of the Swallows.

Raton – Sp. Mouse.

Real – Sp. Royal.

Redentor –Sp. Redeemer.

Refresco – Sp. Soft drink.

Reina – Sp. Queen.

Reredo – An English term for an altar screen; Hispanic peoples may call this a *retablo mayor,* instead.

Retablo – Sp. A painting of a saint, Jesus Christ, the Virgin Mary or the Virgin of Guadalupe. In Mexico, *retablos* were painted on canvas, copper, tin-plated sheets and wood. However, in New Mexico, *retablos* were usually painted only on wood panels, by native artists. The Spanish term, *retablo,* is often used interchangeably with the English term reredo for alter screens.

Rey – Sp. King.

Reyes - Sp. Kings

Rinconada, o – Sp. Cornered.

Rio Arriba – Sp. Upper River.

Rio Bonito – Sp. Pretty or Beautiful River.

Rio Brazos – Sp. Arms River.

Rio Cebolla – Sp. Onion River.

Rio Chamita – Sp. Little Chama River.

Rio Chupadero – Sp. Sucker River.

Rio del Oso – Sp. Bear River.

Rio Felix – Sp. Happy or Lucky River.

Rio Grande – Sp. Great (Big) River.

Rio Hondo – Sp. Deep River.

Rio Nutrias – Sp. Otter River.

Rio Peñasco – Sp. Rocky River.

Rio Ojo Caliente – Sp. Hot Eye River, but more commonly, Hot Springs River.

Rio Puerco – Sp. Hog or Dirty River.

Rio Ruidoso – Sp. Noisy River.

Rio Salado – Sp. Salty River.

Rio San José – Sp. Saint Joseph River.

Rio Tusas – Sp. Horses' Manes River.

Rio Vallecitos – Sp. River of the valleyfolk.

Ristra – Sp. String; also, used to refer to a string of red *chiles* hung to dry, or used as decoration.

Rita Blanca – Sp. White Rite or White Ceremony; in New Mexico; more likely, it means White Creek or Small White River.

Rito – Sp. Rite or Ceremony; but, in New Mexico, it can mean "little river" or "creek" instead, as in *El Rito de los Frijoles,* meaning *Frijoles* or Bean Creek.

Rosario – Sp. Rosary.

Rosca, roscón – Sp. Ring.

Ruidoso – Sp. Noisy.

Sabroso, sabrosa: Sp. Tasty.

Sacramento – Sp. Sacrament.

Sagrado, a – Sp. sacred.

Salinas – Sp. Salt Pits, or salt mines

Salsa - Sp. Sauce.

San Acacia – Sp. Saint Acacia.

San Andrés – Sp. Saint Andrew.

San Antonio – Sp. Saint Anthony.

San Augustín – Sp. Saint Augustine.

San Buenaventura – Sp. Saint Bonaventure.

San Carlos - Sp. Saint Charles.

San Diego – Sp. Saint James.

San Estéban – Sp. Saint Stephen.

San Felipe – Sp. Saint Philip.

San Francisco – Sp. Saint Francis.

San Francisco de Asís – Sp. Saint Francis of Assisi.

San Gabriel – Sp. Saint Gabriel.

San Geronimo – Sp. Saint Jerome.

San Ildefonso – Sp. Saint Ildefonse.

San José – Sp. Saint Joseph.

San Juan – Sp. Saint John.

San Juan Bautista – Sp. Saint John the Baptist.

San Juan Diego – Sp. Saint Juan (John) Diego (James).

San Lorenzo – Sp. Saint Lawrence.

San Mateo – Sp. Saint Matthew.

San Miguel – Sp. Saint Michael.

San Paolo – Sp. Saint Paul.

San Pedro – Sp. Saint Peter.

San Rafael – Sp. Saint Rafael.

San Ysidro – Sp. Saint Isidore.

Sandia – Sp. Watermelon.

Sangre – Sp. Blood.

Sangre de Cristo – Sp. Blood of Christ, or Christ's Blood.

Santa, o – Sp. Saint.

Santa Ana – Sp. Saint Ann(e).

Santa Clara – Sp. Saint Claire.

Santa Cruz – Sp. Holy Cross.

Santa Fe - Sp. Holy Faith.

Santa Fe de Nuevo México - Sp. Holy Faith of New Mexico, *Santa Fe* of New Mexico.

Santa Maria – Sp. Saint Mary.

Santa Rosa – Sp. Saint Rose or holy rose

Santera (o) – Sp. A maker of images of saints. *(santero* – male, *santera* – female).

Santiago – Sp. Saint James.

Santo Domingo – Sp. Saint Dominic.

Santo Niño – Sp. Holy Boychild, or the Christchild, associated with the Child of Atocha, Spain.

Santuario – Sp. Sanctuary.

Señor - Sp. Lord, gentleman, mister, sir, master (Mr.).

Señora - Sp. Lady, madame, (Mrs.).
Señorita – Sp. Diminutive of *Señora*; "Young" lady, (Miss).
Sevillita – Sp. Little Seville.
Sierra – Sp. Mountain or mountain range.
Socorro – Sp. Succor, help, aid.
Sombrero- Sp. An extra wide-brimmed hat, with a conical high-pointed crown, particularly associated with Mexico. It usually casts a wide shadow over the head, neck, and shoulders, having slightly upturned brim edges. Derived from the Spanish word, *sombra*, meaning "shade" or "shadow."
Sonido- Sp. Sound.
Sonoro, a – Sp. Loud or resounding.
Sopa - Sp. Soup.
Sur – Sp. South.

Tan, tanto (a) - So, so much.
Taoseños – Sp. *Taos* residents.
Taza – Sp. Cup.
Tenador – Sp. Fork.
Tetilla – Sp. Small breast, nipple or teat. Also refers to the form of a popular Galician cheese, which reflects that of a small breast. In New Mexico, *Las Tetillas* refers to a group of breast-shaped hills, just south of *Santa Fe*.
Tienda – Sp. Shop.
Tierra – Sp. Earth or land.
Tijeras – Sp. Scissors.
Tilma – Sp. Peasant cloak.
Torre- Sp. Tower.
Torreón – Sp. Tower.
Tres - Sp. Three.
Tres Castillos – Sp. Three castles.
Tres Piedras – Sp. Three Stones.
Tularosa – Sp. Derived from the Spanish word *tule* meaning reed or cattails.
Tule – Sp. Reed or cattails.
Tusas – Sp. Corn husks, corncobs, rubbish.
Té - Sp. Tea.

Vaca – Sp. Cow.
Vado – Sp. Ford (river crossing).
Valle – Sp. Valley.
Valverde – Sp. Green valley.
Vaso – Sp. Drinking glass.
Vegas – Sp. Fields.
Venta – Sp. Sale.
Ventana – Sp. Window.
Vermejo – Sp. A bright, reddish color.
Villista (s) – Sp. Armed Mexican Revolutionary follower (s) of Pancho Villa or Francisco Villa, whose birth name was José Doroteo Arango Arámbula.
Vino - Sp. Wine.
Virgen – Sp. Virgin.

Zozobra – Sp. Anxiety or worry.

Bibliography

Books (alphabetical by author):

Anaya, Rudolfo. *Billy the Kid and Other Plays*, University of Oklahoma Press, 2011.

Anderson, Carl and Chavez, Eduardo. *Our Lady of Guadalupe: Mother of the Civilization of Love*, Doubleday, New York, 2009.

Atencio, Paulette. *Cuentos¹ From My Childhood - Legends and Folktales of Northern New Mexico*. Museum of New Mexico, 1991.

Bahty, Tom. *Southwestern Indian Ceremonials*. KC Publications, Inc., 1972.

Ball, Eve with Nora Henn and Lynda A. Sanchez. *An Apache Odyssey*. University of Oklahoma Press, 1988.

Ball, Eve. *In the Days of Victorio, Recollections of a Warm Springs Apache*. University of Arizona Press, 2000.

Blazer, Almer N. *Santana: War Chief of the Mescalero Apache*. Dog Soldier Press, 1999.

Bordewich, Fergus M. *America's Great Debate*. Simon & Schuster, 2012.

Britton, Thomas A. *The Lipan Apaches: People of the Wind and Lightning*. University of New Mexico Press, 2005.

Buchanan, Kimberly Moore. *Apache Women Warriors*. Texas Western Press, 2000.

Casteñeda, Pedro de. *The Journey of Coronado*. Dover Publications, Inc., 1990.

Cobos, Rubén. *A Dictionary of New Mexico & Southern Colorado Spanish*. Museum of New Mexico Press, *Santa Fe*, 2003.

Colton, Ray C. *The Civil War in the Western Territories*, Arizona, *Colorado*, New Mexico, Utah. University of Oklahoma Press, 1959.

Edrington, Thomas S. and John Taylor. *The Battle of Glorieta Pass: A Gettysburg in the West, March 26 – 28, 1862*. University of New Mexico Press, 1998.

Erdoes, Richard and Ortiz, Alfonso, Selected and Edited by. *American Indian Trickster Tales*. Penguin Books, 1998.

Ferguson, Erna. *Dancing Gods: Indian Ceremonials of New Mexico*. University of New Mexico Press, 2001.

Garrett, Pat. *The Authentic Life of Billy the Kid*. Skyhorse Publishing, 2011.

Geronimo, Taken Down & Edited by S.M. Barrett. *Geronimo: the True Story of America's Most Ferocious Warrior*. Skyhorse Publishing, 2011.

Gibson, Daniel. *Pueblos of the Rio Grande, A Visitor's Guide*. Published by *Rio Nuevo* Publishers, 2001.

González, Ondina E. and Justo L. González. *Christianity in America, a History*. Cambridge University Press, 2008.

Haile, Father Berard. *Navajo Coyote Tales: The Curly Tó Aheedliinii Version*. University of Nebraska Press, 1984.

Haley, James L. *Apaches, A History and Cultural Portrait*. University of Oklahoma Press, 1981.

Hill, Stephen W. Illustrations by Robert B. Montoy. *Kokopelli Ceremonies*. Kiva Publishing, 1995.

Jamison, Bill. *The Insiders Guide to Santa Fe*. The Harvard Common Press, 1987.

Lavash, Donald S., PhD. *A Journey Through New Mexico History*. Sunstone Press, 2006.

Leckie, William H. with Shirley A. *The Buffalo Soldiers, A Narrative of the Black Cavalry in the West*. University of Oklahoma Press, 2003.

Mails, Thomas E. *The Pueblo Children of the Earth Mother, Volume II*. Doubleday & Company, Inc., 1983.

Mails, Thomas E. *The People Called Apache*. BDD Illustrated Books, 1974, 1993.

Malotki, Ekkehart. *The Making of an Icon: Kokopelli*. University of Nebraska Press, 2000.

McManus, Kent. *A Guide to Hopi Katsina Dolls*. Rio Nuevo Publishers, *2000*.

Mullett, G. M. *Legends of the Hopi Indians: Spider Woman Stories*. The University of Arizona Press, 1979.

Nez, Chester with Judith Schiess Avila. *Code Talker: The First and Only Memoir by One of the Original Navajo Code Talkers of WWII*, Published by Berkley Caliber, 2011, pp. 104-105.

Otero, Miguel Antonio. *My Life on the Frontier:1864-1882. Facsimile of Original 1935 Edition*. Sunstone Press, 2007.

Otero, Miguel Antonio. *The Real Billy the Kid, with New Light on the Lincoln County War*. Sunstone Press, 2007.

Otero, Rosalie, A. Gabriel Melendez and Enrique R. Lamadrid, writing and edited by. *Santa Fe Nativa² a Collection of Nuevomexicano¹*. University of New Mexico Press, 2009.

Ortiz, Alfonso. *The Tewa World: Space, Time, Being and Becoming in a Pueblo Society.* University of Chicago Press, 1972.

Reed, Evelyn Dahl. *Coyote Tales*, Sunstone Press, 1988.

Riley, Carroll L. *Rio del Norte, People of the Upper Rio Grande From Earliest Times to the Pueblo Revolt.* University of Utah Press, 1995.

Roberts, Calvin A. and Susan A. *New Mexico.* University of New Mexico Press, 2006.

Roberts, David. *The Pueblo Revolt: The Secret Rebellion That Drove the Spaniards Out of the Southwest.* Simon & Schuster, 2004.

Rodriguez, Sylvia. *The Matachines Dances.* Sunstone Press, *Santa Fe,* 2009.

Sando, S. and Herman Agoya, Editors. *Po'Pay: Leader of the First American Revolution.* Clear Light Publishing, 2005.

Sides, Hampton. *Blood and Thunder.* Doubleday, 2006.

Silverberg, Robert. *The Pueblo Revolt.* University of Nebraska Press, 1994

Simmons, Marc. *The Last Conquistador: Juan Onate and the Settling of the Far Southwest.* University of Oklahoma Press, 1991.

Simmons, Marc, Edited by. *On the Santa Fe Trail.* University of Kansas Press, 1986.

Sliffer, Dennis and James Duffield. *Flute Player Images in Rock Art: Kokopelli.* Ancient City Press, 1994.

Sonnichsen, C. L. *The Mescalero Apaches.* University of Oklahoma Press, 1973.

Swartley, Ron. *The Billy the Kid Travel Guide.* Frontier Image Press, 1999.

Sweet, Jill D. *Dances of the Tewa Pueblo Indians: Expressions of New Life.* School of American Research Press, 1985, 2004

Thompson, Jerry, Edited and with an Introduction by. *Civil War in the Southwest: Recollections of the Sibley Brigade.* Texas A & M University Press College Station, 2001.

Tyler, Hamilton A. *Pueblo Gods and Myths.* University of Oklahoma Press, 1964.

Waters, Frank. *Masked Gods, Navaho and Pueblo Ceremonialism.* Swallow Press, 1950

Whitlock, Flint, *Distant Bugles, Distant Drums; the Union Response to the Confederate Invasion of New Mexico.* University Press of *Colorado,* 2006.

Young, John V. *Kokopelli: Casanova of the Cliff Dwellers.* Filter Press, 1990

Eight Northern Indian Pueblos Visitor's Guide Magazine, 1998.

All Trails Lead to Santa Fe : An Anthology Commemorating the 400th Anniversary of the Founding of Santa Fe, New Mexico in 1610. Sunstone Press, *Santa Fe,* 2010.

Articles (alphabetical by author):

Bellinger, Cindy. *The Legend of the Child's Grave.* Article, in *Enchantment News Magazine,* October 2011, p.11.

Clausing, Jeri. *Out-Of-This-World-Ripoff?* Article, in *Santa Fe New Mexican* newspaper (pages A-1 and A-4), Thursday, December 13, 2012.

Gardner, Mark Lee. *Pat Garrett, The Life and Death of a Great Sheriff.* Article, in *Wild West, The American Frontier Magazine,* August 2011.

Greenwood, Phaedra. *Riding with the Buffalo Soldiers.* Article, in *Enchantment News Magazine,* December 2008.

Harden, Paul, *Las Posadas y Las Pastorelas.* Article, in *El Defensor Chieftain Newspaper,* December 6, 2008.

Karlson, Scott. *3 Days in March.* Article, in *New Mexico Free Press News Magazine,* March 25, 2009.

Langellier, John. *Black Warriors of the West: A Visual History of the Buffalo Soldier.* Article in *True West Magazine,* November/December 2010. p.34-43.

Lilly, Majorie. *The Richness of the Pastorela Play.* Article, in *Enchantment News Magazine,* December 2007.

Model, Betsy. *Spaceport, Prepare for Liftoff; Destination, The Next Frontier.* Article, in *New Mexico Magazine,* May 2012.

Plevin, Nancy and Neary, Ben. *Oñate's Foot Cut Off.* Article, in *The New Mexican* newspaper, January 8, 1998.

Vigil, Maurilio E. *Why Santa Fe?* Article, in *La Herencia Magazine, Volume 58,* Summer 2008.

Other:

AAA Arizona & New Mexico Tour Book, 2011 Edition.

The Bible with the Apocrypha, New Revised Standard Version, Book of Revelations. Collins Publishers, 1989.

Life Story of Teresina Bent Scheurich, Daughter of Governor Charles Bent. Article, in *The Taos Review*
and *The Taos Valley News*, date not indicated. Reprint obtained at the Bent House/Museum.
New Mexico Office of Cultural Affairs. *Enchanted Lifeways*. Published by *New Mexico Magazine*.

Official Maps, Brochures & Guides: (alphabetical by title)

Maps: (alphabetical by title)
New Mexico Easy Finder Map. Rand McNally, 1999.
New Mexico Road & Recreation Atlas, Benchmark Maps, 2012
New Mexico SealMap. Eureka Cartography, 2005
Topographic Map of New Mexico. GTR Mapping, 1993, 2010 Edition
Turquoise Trail: National Scenic Byway brochure. P.O. Box 303, *Sandia* Park,
NM 87047

Brochures & Guides: (alphabetical by title)
Aztec Ruins, A Trail Guide to. Western National Parks Association, 2008.
Aztec Ruins National Monument. Southwest Parks and Monument Association, 1992.
Aztec Ruins. National Park Service.
Bandelier. National Park Service.
Billy the Kid's Lincoln brochure. Michael E. Pitel, 2007.
Billy the Kid's Old Fort Sumner. Michael E. Pitel, 2007.
Bosque Redondo Memorial At Fort Sumner State Monument brochure.
Calendar of Pueblo Feast Days & Other Events at the Pueblos brochure. Indian *Pueblo* Cultural Center.
Capulin Volcano. National Park Service.
Carlsbad Caverns. National Park Service.
Casa Rinconada. Western National Parks Association.
Chaco Culture. National Park Service.
Chaco Culture: Chaco Canyon Place Names. Article, National Park Service.
Chetro Ketl. Western National Parks Association.
Coronado State Monument brochure. Museum of New Mexico Office of Cultural Affairs.
Fort Union. National Park Service.
Fort Union, National Monument (Robert M. Utley). National Park Service.
Kasha Katuwe. National Park Service.
A Kid's Guide to Exploring Chaco Culture National Historical Park, Written by Mary Maruca. Western
National Parks Association
El Malpais. National Park Service
El Morro. National Park Service
Native New Mexico Land of Enchantment brochure, aka *The Native New Mexico Guide*. New Mexico
Tourism Department.
Pecos. National Park Service
Petroglyphs. National Park Service.
Pueblo Bonito. Western National Parks Association
Pueblo del Arroyo. Western National Parks Association
Salinas Pueblo Missions. National Park Service.
El Rancho de las Golondrinas, handout obtained upon paid entry to the *rancho*.
Santa Fe Trail. National Park Service
El Santuario de Chimayo: The Shrine of Our Lord of Esquipulas. Published by *El Santuario de Chimayo*.
Saint Juan Diego Cuauhtlatoatzin, The History. Published by *El Santuario de Guadalupe*.
Welcome to the Shrine of Our Lady of Guadalupe. Published by *El Santuario de Guadalupe*.
The Art Collection of Tamaya brochure. Available from Hyatt Regency *Tamaya*.
A Trip Map to the Cumbres & Toltec Scenic Railroad. 2010 Friends of the *Cumbres & Toltec* Scenic
Railroad, Inc.
Sightseeing Information: Turquoise Trail, Scenic and Historic Area, brochure. Turquoise Trail Association.
Turquoise Trail: National Scenic Byway brochure. New Mexico Department of Tourism.
Visit, Relocate, Retire: Carlsbad, New Mexico. Carlsbad Chamber of Commerce.
White Sands. National Park Service.
White Sands National Monument. Western National Parks Association.

Index

Note: Meaning of acronyms within parentheses following a topic name mean as follows: ABQ = Albuquerque; SF = Santa Fe.

Author: John P. McWilliams